Oracle7 SQL Commands

SQL Command	Description
ANALYZE	Generates optimizer statistics or lists chained rows for a table, an index, or a cluster. Can also validate the structure of an index
AUDIT	Sets audit options for the system and database objects
COMMENT	Creates in the data dictionary a comment for a table, view, snapshot, or column
COMMIT	Commits a transaction to make transaction changes permanent in the database
CREATE CLUSTER	Creates an indexed or a hash cluster
CREATE CONTROLFILE	Creates a new database control file to replace a damaged or badly sized control file
CREATE DATABASE	Creates a database
CREATE DATABASE LINK‡	Defines a named path to a remote database. Database links are available without the Distributed Database option, but for read operations only
CREATE FUNCTION†	Creates a stored function
CREATE INDEX	Creates an index for a table
CREATE PACKAGE†	Creates a stored package specification
CREATE PACKAGE BODY†	Creates a stored package body
CREATE PROCEDURE†	Creates a stored procedure
CREATE PROFILE	Creates a named profile of resource limits
CREATE ROLE	Creates a role to group related privileges
CREATE ROLLBACK SEGMENT	Creates a rollback segment
CREATE SCHEMA	Creates a number of tables and views, all in one statement, in a current database account
CREATE SEQUENCE	Creates a named sequence of numbers

D1400930

†Available only with the Oracle7 Procedural option

‡Available only with the Oracle7 Distributed Database option

MASTERING

ORACLE7® & CLIENT/SERVER
COMPUTING

Steven M. Bobrowski

SYBEX®

San Francisco • Paris • Düsseldorf • Soest

Acquisitions Editor: Dianne King
Developmental Editor: David Peal
Editor: Dusty Bernard
Project Editor: Valerie Potter
Technical Editor: Walter Lindsay of Compuware EcoSystems Business Group
Book Series Designer and Production Artist: Suzanne Albertson
Screen Graphics Specialist: Cuong Le
Technical Artists: Cuong Le and Rick Van Genderen
Typesetters: Deborah Maizels and Alissa Feinberg
Proofreader/Production Assistant: Lisa Haden
Indexer: Matthew Spence
Cover Designer: DesignSite
Cover Photo Art Direction: Ingalls + Associates
Cover Photographer: David Bishop

To my Kathleen,
who unselfishly supports me in the
wonderful adventure of life

ACKNOWLEDGMENTS

I'd like to thank the many people who helped produce this book.

First of all, writing this book would not have been possible without endless contributions of time, effort, and software from my many friends at Oracle Corporation. I'd especially like to thank Ken Jacobs, Vice President of Product Planning, Oracle Corporation, for his foreword to the book. I'd also like to thank my friends at Oracle for their significant contributions to this book: Gary Hallmark, Gordon Larimer, Dennis Moore, David Markowitz, Ellen Brout, Linda Vetter, Merrill Holt, Mike Hartstein, John Frazzini, Tim Smith, Bhushan Fotedar, Gordon Smith, and Stuart Read.

While Oracle software is the primary focus of this book, you can't take advantage of Oracle software without a great operating system to support it. For this I'd like to extend my gratitude to the folks at The Santa Cruz Operation for their SCO UNIX software and support, especially Sal Bruno, Barbara LoFranco, and Bob Walsh.

Many of my esteemed colleagues and friends in the industry helped me with specific areas of this book. Thanks to Robert Bolt, President of Database Server Systems, who helped point me in the right direction concerning the endless list of independent client tools available for Oracle7; Beth Marcum, who helped me get SQL*Net just right; and David Kalman, editor-in-chief of *DBMS Magazine*, for his opinions concerning the database industry.

Editing a book this large, and one that covers such diverse topics, is no small task. I can't begin to express my gratitude to the two primary editors for this book: Dusty Bernard for her patience and extreme attention to detail while combing the manuscript for my goofs, and Walter Lindsay, for his outstanding technical review and invaluable input, which contributed significantly to the technical value of this book.

Last but not least, I'd like to thank the many folks at Sybex for extending me the opportunity to write this book, especially David Peal, for getting the book started in the right direction, and Val Potter, for her calmness and patience while coordinating the book's production. I'd also like to thank Rick Van Genderen of Van Genderen Studios for his fine work in translating my pencil-scribbled drawings into meaningful graphics that help illustrate the tough concepts of Oracle7 and client/server computing. Thanks also to Cuong Le, technical artist and screen graphics specialist; Deborah Maizels and Alissa Feinberg, typesetters; Lisa Haden, proofreader; and Suzanne Albertson, book series designer and production artist.

CONTENTS AT A GLANCE

TABLE OF CONTENTS

3 The Client in Client/Server   73

PART II Database Administration in an Oracle7 Client/Server System **151**

6 Understanding Oracle7 Database Administration and Administrative Utilities 153

15   Designing an Application's Schema   475

FOREWORD

Occasionally, computer technology makes a dramatic break with the past. The relational model of database management, with its simple, tabular data structures and powerful data manipulation operations, is one such revolution. The year 1994 marks the 25th anniversary of the introduction of the relational model by Dr. E.F. Codd, then of IBM Research. The relational model has helped focus computer science research on the problems of data management, and relational database management system products have resulted in tremendous improvements in accessing data and developing applications. Although object databases have recently received much attention, the industry consensus is that leading relational database management systems will successfully incorporate object database ideas as an extension of the basic relational model; the extended relational model of database management will survive and thrive for years to come.

Another revolution in computing technology, client/server computing, took place in the last decade with the spread of minicomputers and microcomputers. These highly cost-effective and flexible open systems have made client/server computing possible. In the early 1980s the introduction of minicomputers made it economically feasible to dedicate computing resources to departmental applications. Before, computer resources were dedicated to centralized mainframes running corporate applications. Then, microcomputers lowered the cost of computing so much that desktop computers became attractive for personal productivity applications. Along with these advances in computing platforms came improvements in networking technology, permitting widely dispersed computers to communicate reliably and efficiently with each other.

These hardware changes were accompanied by significant changes in software technology. Modern graphical user interfaces increasingly are replacing traditional character-mode screens, providing dramatic gains in ease of use and flexibility. New application development tools reduce and may one day eliminate altogether the need for traditional programming. Today, most companies are designing and using applications that employ a client/server architecture, in which the application runs on the user's PC or workstation and accesses a centrally maintained and managed file or database server. This approach exploits the client machine's ability to provide highly responsive and intuitive presentation services while using a powerful server to manage shared data securely and efficiently.

In 1979 a tiny Silicon Valley company introduced Oracle, the first commercial relational database incorporating the SQL data access language. Today, Oracle Corporation is the world's largest supplier of database management systems and associated products. Oracle version 5, released in 1985, was the very first client/server database system. Oracle7 is the latest version of the Oracle database server. This product, introduced in 1992, represents the industry's most advanced product implementing both the extended relational model and the client/server architecture.

Oracle7 includes a full-featured and government-certified implementation of the ANSI/ISO standard SQL language. The Oracle7 server can be an active part of applications, enforcing data integrity and business rules through "declarative means" (that is, without programming), as well as through the industry's most complete and robust set of programming features, such as stored procedures and triggers. Oracle7 also includes industrial-strength distributed database facilities, enabling enterprise-wide access to data, no matter where it is stored or on what kinds of platforms. Last but not least, Oracle7 maximizes the performance and reliability of online transaction processing applications through a range of architectural features, such as row-level locking, online backup and recovery, and support for a wide variety of platforms.

Oracle Corporation is also a leader in another revolution taking place in computer technology: the emerging use of parallel computing platforms, which can deliver unprecedented levels of performance with significant cost effectiveness. These platforms are constructed of low-cost components, with tens, hundreds, or even thousands of highly interconnected, independent CPUs, each with its own memory. Historically, such massively parallel platforms were considered applicable only to scientific computing problems, such as weather simulation or other highly computer-intensive operations. As Oracle Corporation has shown, data management is also an application well suited for these machines.

For transaction-processing applications, the Oracle parallel server allows multiple CPUs to access a single database. The parallel server and appropriate hardware can provide extraordinary levels of transaction processing throughput.

The newest update of Oracle7, Release 7.1, exploits the power of parallel platforms for processing sets of records, a common requirement in relational databases. On either shared-memory symmetric multiprocessors or massively parallel platforms, Oracle Release 7.1 greatly speeds creating and querying large databases by decomposing bulk data operations and executing them in parallel on multiple CPUs. With open systems and parallel technology, Oracle Corporation is lowering the cost of decision support applications, just as it has for transaction-processing applications.

Oracle Corporation's experience in building portable data management software for massively parallel computers has enabled it to take a leadership role in the most recent and exciting computing technology revolution: the construction of the so-called "information highway." The information highway will bring to our daily lives vast quantities of multimedia data—for home shopping, video conferencing, video-on-demand, personalized electronic newspapers, and other applications. These changes may well affect society as significantly as did the telephone and the automobile. The Oracle relational database management system, as well as specialized massively parallel software produced by Oracle Corporation, will be critical components of the information highway.

Steve Bobrowski has written *Mastering Oracle7 & Client/Server Computing* to give you an in-depth understanding of the Oracle7 relational database server and its use in a client/server environment, without burdening you with esoteric information you might never need. You will quickly learn just what you need to know to design, build, and employ applications using the Oracle7 server and Oracle's Cooperative Development Environment (CDE) tools.

If you are designing a new application to run on Oracle7, you will appreciate the thorough treatment of Oracle7's SQL language and extensive facilities for enforcing data integrity through declarative referential integrity and procedurally, through PL/SQL stored procedures and triggers. This book also provides an excellent overview of database administration, including the vital issues of database security, backup and recovery, and performance tuning.

Steve Bobrowski is especially qualified to explain how to use the Oracle7 server and application development tools in a client/server environment. Steve worked closely with the developers, product managers, and technical writers associated with the development of Oracle7 and was the principal author of the extensive Oracle7 server documentation published by Oracle Corporation. Few people understand Oracle7 better than he does, and no one can do a better job of making the technology understandable to others. It's been a particular pleasure for me to have known and worked with Steve for over five years.

Part of the excitement in working with database management as a technology, and Oracle in particular, comes from participating in a revolution, contributing to the development of products that empower people, and from imparting to others our enthusiasm for these products. Steve shares with many people at Oracle this special passion for the technology. It is his fond hope, as it is mine, that you will also share this feeling as you come to know and use the technology we call Oracle7.

Ken Jacobs
VP Product Planning, Server Technologies
Oracle Corporation

February, 1994

INTRODUCTION

All businesses, small and large, must manage the company data in a fashion that allows the business to run smoothly. Some businesses might use file cabinets to manage their data, but most companies choose to use computerized database management systems that efficiently store, retrieve, and manage large amounts of data. Oracle7 is a multi-user database management system—a software product that specializes in managing a single, shared set of information among many concurrent users. This book explains how to configure and use Oracle7 in an information management system, with a special focus on using Oracle7 in a client/server system—one that operates among a number of computers that work together and communicate using a network.

Is This Book for You?

Oracle7 & Client/Server Computing is of interest to a broad audience. If you fall into one or more of the following categories, this book is for you:

- You would like to learn about the world of client/server computing, its advantages and disadvantages, and whether or not it's right for you and your company.
- You want to find out the basics on relational and multi-user database management systems, with a special focus on the features of the Oracle7 relational database management system.
- You want to master the many jobs necessary to administer an Oracle7 client/server system, from basic tasks like using SQL*DBA (Oracle7's administrative utility), controlling database availability, and database backup to more advanced operations, such as configuring, monitoring, and tuning Oracle7, SQL*Net V2 (Oracle's networking product), and the Oracle7 Parallel Query option.
- You would like to learn what end-user database applications are and how you can develop custom applications for an Oracle7 system.

- You want a quick introduction to the most important application development tools in Oracle's Cooperative Development Environment (CDE) set of application development tools, including Oracle's CASE*Dictionary, CASE*Designer, CASE*Generator, and Oracle Forms for Microsoft Windows.
- You are an application developer who wants a clear understanding of the key Oracle7 features to take advantage of when developing applications specifically for a client/server system—such as integrity constraints, procedures, triggers, database alerts, and SQL functions.
- You are an end user who wants more insight into how database management systems, especially client/server systems, and Oracle7 work to serve your processing needs.

The Technology

The pace at which new technology is being introduced in the computing industry is nothing less than astonishing. As companies compete for market share and profits, they quickly deliver new innovations in hardware, software, and computing paradigms that drive forward the overall state of information management technology. But the real winner in this race is you, the consumer. That's because if you can grasp new technology as it becomes available and then use it to your benefit, your business gains a significant advantage over those competitors of yours who do not follow suit.

The evolution of database management system (DBMS) software is a perfect example of how pervasive the new technology is. Whether or not you realize it, every segment of society benefits from electronic database management systems that allow for the quick storage and retrieval of various types of information. For example, airline companies use databases to track flight reservations; banks use databases to accurately manage bank transactions; and video stores and their customers benefit from database systems that allow for quick, easy check-in and check-out of video tape rentals. In all these examples, database management systems benefit both the companies and their consumers.

Client/Server Computing

What is client/server database computing, and how can it benefit those who choose to take advantage of it? Client/server computing, a relatively new computing model, is nothing more than the distribution of a multi-user database application's processing requirements across a number of networked computers, such as PCs and workstations. What does client/server offer that the traditional mainframe (single-computer) computing environment does not? If you correctly implement a client/server system, the result is an information management system that delivers a much better price/performance ratio and one that can grow and adapt easily to ever-changing business needs. And these are just a couple of the reasons you can benefit from understanding client/server and implementing it in an information management system.

How Does Oracle7 Fit In?

Oracle7 is one of the many servers that you can plug into a client/server database system. And because a client/server system depends heavily on the features of its server, it's important for you to understand how it works and what it can do.

This book provides an in-depth discussion of client/server systems, with a special focus on the features available when you use Oracle7 as the server in the system.

What You Need to Use
This Book

This book's primary focus is the central component of an Oracle client/server system: the Oracle7 database server. However, the book also examines the other Oracle products useful for assembling a complete Oracle7 client/server database system. If you want to follow along with all the examples in the book, you'll need the following:

- Oracle7 database server (includes SQL*DBA and SQL*Loader)
- Oracle7 Procedural option

- Oracle7 Parallel Query option
- SQL*Net (version 2)
- CASE*Dictionary
- CASE*Designer
- CASE*Generator
- Oracle Forms
- SQL*Forms
- SQL*Menu
- SQL*Plus

NOTE To install the Oracle CASE products, you will probably need to install other Oracle products, including SQL*Report, SQL*ReportWriter, and Oracle Terminal.

About the Examples in This Book

Learning by example is perhaps one of the fastest ways to understand new things. This book includes literally hundreds of code examples and screen shots to illustrate the workings of Oracle7. Many of the examples are based on table definitions listed in the book or standard system tables that come with Oracle7. Therefore, if you have Oracle7 and want to try out the examples yourself, you can create the example tables in your database and then try the examples that use the example database tables.

Not all the examples in this book build upon example table definitions, but don't let this discourage you from getting your feet wet by trying the examples anyway. Once you develop an understanding of the examples in the earlier chapters, you'll have no problem creating the necessary tables and data to make later examples work well. Don't be afraid to apply the knowledge presented in this book. It's a good test of how well you have learned what this book teaches.

Conventions Used in This Book

The following sections explain the conventions used in this book.

Margin Icons In certain sections of this book you will see a margin icon like this:

This icon indicates features new to Release 7.1 of the Oracle7 database server.

Terms Defined When a new term is introduced and defined in this book, it appears in italics. Look for italicized terms to build your vocabulary in client/server computing and Oracle7.

Key Names This book refers to the different keys of the Oracle products by their functions, enclosed in square brackets, rather than their exact keyboard names. For example, you might see "the [List] key" rather than "the F10 key." The reason for this convention is that Oracle products run on many types of computers, operating systems, and terminals. Consequently, Oracle binds product function keys to different keyboard keys depending on the system you are using. Using the help facility of each Oracle product, you can quickly display the key bindings for the different product functions. On most types of terminals, Ctrl+K gives a listing of the specific key mappings for your terminal.

Example Statements Many of the examples in this book appear in the form of code examples—specifically, SQL and PL/SQL statements. (If you aren't familiar with SQL or PL/SQL, don't worry; you'll learn about them in the book.) SQL and PL/SQL are not case sensitive; that is, you can enter command words in uppercase, lowercase, or a mix of both. However, the example statements in this book, such as the following SQL statement, contain a mix of uppercase and lowercase words:

```
SELECT id FROM customer;
```

To help you distinguish between keywords of the SQL and PL/SQL languages and user-inserted words, all language *keywords* (words key to the language) appear in uppercase letters (for example, "SELECT" and "FROM"). User-inserted words usually appear in lowercase letters (for example, "id" and "customer"). The only exception occurs when a user-inserted word is case sensitive (for example, if it is an operating system filename).

The preceding example also includes a *statement terminator*—a character or set of characters that indicates the end of a statement. The terminator for Oracle SQL statements is the semicolon. Depending on the environment in which you issue statements, SQL statements may or may not require terminators. As a matter of convention, this book uses terminators only where absolutely necessary for technical accuracy in all situations.

PART I

Introduction to Client/Server Computing and Oracle7

Chapters 1 through 6 constitute the introductory part of this book. In reading these chapters you'll get a clear understanding of the "big picture" of an Oracle7 client/server system. This part of the book introduces client/server computing, describes how the Oracle7 server fits into a client/server computing system, and provides an overview of Oracle7's features. You'll also learn about the role of clients in an Oracle7 client/server system and networking issues, and you'll get an introduction to the Oracle SQL and PL/SQL languages.

CHAPTER

ONE

What Are Client/Server and Oracle7 Anyway?

- The evolution of corporate models from centralized to distributed computing

- The client/server computing model

- Advantages and disadvantages of client/server computing

- How Oracle7 fits into a client/server system

If you or your company works with computers, you have no doubt heard terms such as "database," "database server," and "client/server." Do you really know what they mean and why they are so important in management information systems circles? If you don't know, don't worry; this chapter introduces each of these terms and explains how Oracle7 fits into the same picture.

Evolution of Corporate Computing Models

Why is client/server computing so important in the information systems industry? One way to answer this question is to study the evolution of corporate computing models. The next few sections introduce the evolution from the host-based computing model to the client/server computing model.

The Mainframe/Minicomputer Computing Model

First, let's go back to the days of corporate computing when a centralized *host computer* (that is, a corporate mainframe or minicomputer) was boss. In this setting, any company employee could use an application on the corporate mainframe by pulling up a chair to a *dumb terminal* that was physically connected to the mainframe. It's called a "dumb" terminal because that's what it is—a terminal has no processing capability, only the ability to send information to and display information given to it by the central mainframe. Figure 1.1 illustrates two host-based computing models.

First, notice that the mainframe application is a single component responsible for both the interaction with the user and the management of data in a multi-user environment. It quickly became apparent that this application development strategy was inefficient because developers had to reinvent the same data management component with each new application. Therefore, mainframe and minicomputer applications evolved so that the application's processing was split into two parts: a *front end*, responsible for interaction with the user, and a *back end*, responsible for management of data. The back end, a database management system (DBMS), is a central component that can be used with each new front-end application. The split of the front and back ends of an application also allows more system flexibility because multiple front ends can access the database managed by a single back-end DBMS.

Like anything else, the host-based computing models have both advantages and disadvantages. On the positive side, a mainframe computer is centralized. Therefore, dedicated system administrators can reliably manage the single computer to make sure that data is available when users need it and that valuable corporate data is being backed up for protection. Centralized systems also allow users to share expensive hardware peripherals such as disk drives, printers, and modems. However, there are also many negatives to the mainframe model. For example, the greater the number of company workers who need to access the mainframe, the more horsepower the mainframe needs to adequately serve the company's ongoing business. Traditionally, a few companies control the mainframe and minicomputer industries, meaning that they can charge large amounts of money for the proprietary operating systems, processors, applications, memory, and disk storage necessary to make the mainframe or minicomputer work for a company. The more you need, the more you pay.

The Disconnected, Personal Computing Model

Something happened in the 1980s that forever changed the corporate computing model: the introduction of personal computers and workstations. With IBM's introduction of the PC and its operating system (DOS), Apple's introduction of the Macintosh, and, later, the introduction of UNIX workstations from companies like Hewlett-Packard and Sun Microsystems, independent computing workstations quickly became prevalent throughout a corporation, ending the centralized control that mainframes once had on all corporate data.

Independent personal workstations are popular because they have several advantages over a mainframe system:

- Personal workstations are very inexpensive and easy-to-use computers that deliver the processing power and performance once available only with expensive mainframes.

FIGURE 1.1:

Centralized host-based computing models allow many users to share a single computer's applications, databases, and peripherals.

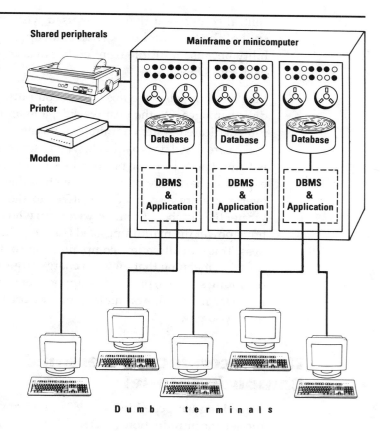

- A user can make a computer workstation "personal" by picking the type of workstation, operating system, and application that best fits the user's needs.

- PC applications (such as word processors, spreadsheets, graphics, and database management systems) are abundant and typically very inexpensive to purchase. A user who cannot find a prebuilt application that meets a requirement can use an easy-to-use development tool to create a custom application.

- A workstation's data is an autonomous set of information that is personal. Each workstation user is responsible for managing it and backing up the data to protect it. Individual users, not a high-priced data center engineer, administer their own PCs.

FIGURE 1.1:
This figure is continued from previous page.

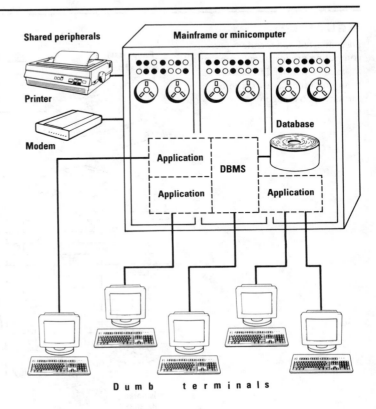

Unfortunately, the move toward independent personal computing and away from centralized mainframe computing introduces problems as well as advantages. Most notably, corporate information, once centralized and available to all employees on a mainframe, is now distributed among the mainframe and personal workstations throughout a company. The data on PCs is not readily available to all users who may need it. Therefore, the gains in the price/performance ratio and ease of use from personal computing can easily be nullified by the loss in productivity of workgroups that need access to information dispersed throughout a corporation. Figure 1.2 shows the problems of a disconnected personal computing model.

FIGURE 1.2:

Disconnected, independent personal computing models allow processing loads to be removed from a central computer but isolate data sources throughout a company.

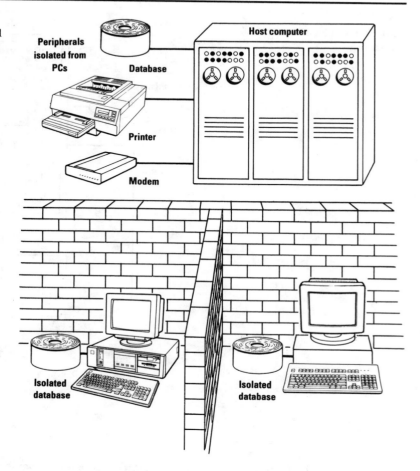

Besides not being able to share data, disconnected personal workstation users cannot share other expensive resources that mainframe system users can share: disk drives, printers, modems, and other peripheral computing devices.

The Network/File Server Computing Model

The data- and peripheral-sharing problems of independent personal PCs and workstations quickly led to the birth of the *network/file server computing model*. In fact, if you use a personal computer or workstation at work today, chances are that your computer is connected to a *local area network* (*LAN*). A LAN lets a workgroup continue to reap the benefits of easy-to-use PCs but also permits the workgroup to share data and peripherals like a mainframe system. Figure 1.3 shows the network/file server computing model.

To share data in a LAN, users store files on a *file server*. A file server is a central *node* (computer in the network) that stores data files where all users can access them. Typically, the file server in a LAN is also the central hub for sharing peripherals like printers, print queues, and modems. Because the file server is an independent computer in the network, it's best to specialize it for its job by giving it lots of disk storage area.

In a LAN, an application running on a workstation reads and writes files on the LAN's file server. In many cases entire files are pumped across the network on behalf of the operations taking place on LAN PCs. A file server plays no part in the processing of an application. The file server does nothing more than store files for applications that run on LAN PCs. For example, you might have a personal database manager on your LAN PC. First, you start your personal database manager and then request information in a file on the file server. The LAN's file server sends all or part of the data file across the network to your workstation. As you work with your personal database manager and the database on your workstation, the file server doesn't participate at all. When you save the file, you copy the data file back to the file server across the network.

Unfortunately, the inherent design of the LAN/file server computing model prevents it from adequately servicing demanding multi-user, shared-data applications that mainframes can easily support. Two flaws limit a file server system for multi-user applications. First, the file server model does not deliver the *data concurrency*

FIGURE 1.3:

Network/file server computing models link PCs together so they can share data and peripherals.

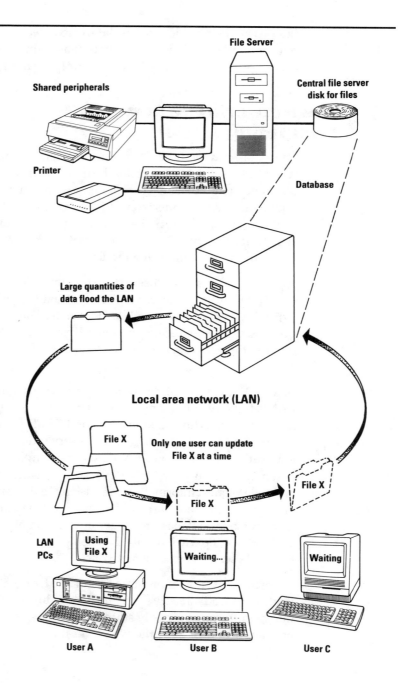

(simultaneous access to a single data set by multiple users) that is required by multi-user applications. That's because the file server operates in files, which are very large data sets, and prevent a user from sharing a file when another user has it locked out. In short, users that operate on the same data usually bump into each other and are forced to wait in line to access a file. Second, if many workstations request and send many files in a LAN, the network can quickly become saturated with traffic, creating a bottleneck that degrades overall system performance.

The Client/Server Computing Model

The problems of the LAN have led to the genesis of the *client/server computing model*. Client/server computing (also called *distributed application processing* and *cooperative application processing*) delivers the benefits of the network computing model along with the shared data access and high performance characteristics of the host-based computing model.

A client/server system has three distinct components, each focusing on a specific job: a database server, a client application, and a network. Figure 1.4 shows the components of the client/server computing model.

A *server* (or "back end") focuses on efficiently managing a resource such as a database of information. The server's primary job is to manage its resource optimally among multiple clients that concurrently request the server for the same resource. Database servers concentrate on tasks such as

- Managing a single database of information among many concurrent users
- Controlling database access and other security requirements
- Protecting database information with backup and recovery features
- Centrally enforcing global data integrity rules across all client applications

FIGURE 1.4:

Client/server database systems share data in small sets (rows), which allows for a high degree of data concurrency and system performance.

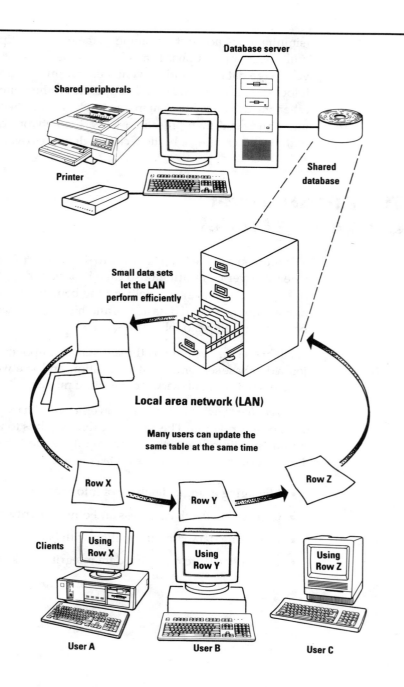

A *client application* (the "front end") is the part of the system that users employ to interact with data. The client applications in a client/server database system focus on jobs such as

- Presenting an interface a user can interact with to accomplish work
- Managing presentation logic such as popup lists on a data entry form or bar graphs in a graphical data presentation tool
- Performing application logic, such as calculating fields in a data entry form
- Validating data entry
- Requesting and receiving information from a database server

Last but not least, a *network* and *communication software* are the vehicles that transmit data between the clients and the server in a system. Both the clients and the server run communication software that allows them to talk across a network.

A client/server system can deliver better performance than a file server system because a client application and a database server work together to split the processing load of an application (thus the term "distributed application processing"). The server manages the database among a number of clients, while the clients send, request, and analyze the data they receive from the server. In a client/server application, the client application works with small specific data sets, such as rows in a table—not files, as in the file server system. A database server is intelligent, locking and returning only the rows a client requests, which ensures concurrency, minimizes network traffic, and improves system performance.

Benefits and Pitfalls of Client/Server Computing

Now that you understand what the client/server computing model is and how it came about, let's learn the benefits and problems of the client/server computing model so you understand the model well and use it appropriately in an information system design.

Distributing an Application's Processing for Flexibility and Scalability

Several benefits of the client/server model stem from the fact that the client and server portions of a system usually run on separate computers. First, each computer in the system can be selected to best meet the requirements of each component. For example, it's best to use a computer with powerful processors and lots of disk space and memory to run the database server. This way, the server can store large amounts of data and adequately handle many simultaneous client requests. In contrast, it's best to use a less expensive computer with minimal disk storage and memory, a mouse, and excellent graphics capabilities to run the client application. This way, a company can inexpensively equip scores of users with a productive, easy-to-use tool to enter and analyze data.

Second, the system is very responsive and flexible to all the inevitable types of hardware and software changes. For example, suppose a new type of computer becomes available that delivers twice the computing performance of a system's current server at half the price. In a client/server system, it is easy to take out the old server and plug in the new one without disturbing the functionality of client applications or the productivity of users.

Third, it is easy to scale the system to accommodate changes in a workgroup. For example, when a department hires several new workers, they can immediately plug into the network system with new client workstations.

Using Client/Server to Focus on Areas of System Development

Another benefit of client/server is that each functional component in the system can specialize to do something the best way it can. For example, to develop a client application a programmer concentrates on the presentation and analysis of data. Meanwhile, the database server concentrates on the management of data. In short, developers do not have to design and code a database management system every time they create a new application.

Using Client/Server to Deliver Cost Savings

A widely believed benefit of client/server computing is cost savings versus the cost of mainframe or minicomputer systems. In the past, the only choice for running a demanding multi-user database application was to use an expensive, powerful mainframe or minicomputer. This meant using nonintuitive character-based end-user terminals, hiring a team of well-paid programmers to get an application up and running, and then maintaining the complicated system around the clock with a team of specialized and pricey administrators. Initial and ongoing expenses for such a system can be astronomical. In many cases, a client/server system can support a mainframe application with greatly reduced cost. That's because a client/server system distributes the processing load of a large application across many inexpensive computers connected by a network. Even the application is easier to develop and use because of user-friendly workstation graphical user interfaces (GUIs) and object-oriented application development tools.

Some Disadvantages

Now, a dose of reality. Client/server computing does have its disadvantages. First, anticipated cost savings of a client/server may not actually appear in real-world situations. When projecting the cost of a computer system, system designers must include many factors, not just hardware expenditures. For example, the productivity of users, including application users, developers, and administrators, is an important consideration in measuring cost. Developers may well notice improved productivity by using the GUIs and *computer-aided software engineering* (*CASE*) development tools available for client/server database computing. However, application users and administrators may actually notice a drop in productivity. Why? The reliability of a client/server system, a mix of independently developed, manufactured, and managed hardware and software components, is inherently less than that of a homogenous, centrally managed mainframe or minicomputer. And whom do you call for technical support when something goes wrong? Downtime due to an unreliable system takes away from end-user and administrator productivity. And as the old saying goes, time is money. Figure 1.5 illustrates the heterogeneity of client/server systems.

FIGURE 1.5:

The inherent heterogeneity of client/server systems makes system integration, administration, and maintenance a formidable challenge.

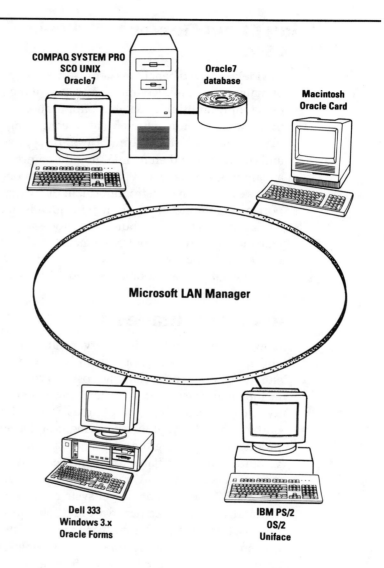

The key factor in realizing a cost saving is choosing the correct type of application to run on a client/server system. For example, it might be unrealistic to run and manage a massive mission-critical airline reservation system completely on a client/server database system, considering the hundreds of thousands of reservation terminals and dial-in hookups that stretch out across the world. However, it is perfectly reasonable to run a company's or department's localized accounting and manufacturing applications on a client/server database system.

Client/server computing is a very important part of an overall corporate information strategy, but it isn't the right choice for every application. As you learn more about client/server database systems in this book, use your understanding to correctly apply client/server where you think it will work and when it will save your company money.

Oracle7 and Client/Server

What about Oracle7—how does it figure into the client/server model? Oracle7 is one of many database servers that you can plug into a client/server equation. Oracle7 works to efficiently manage its resource, a database of information, among the multiple clients requesting and sending data in the network. As this book explains, Oracle7 has many important features that make it not only an exceptional database management system but also an excellent database server choice for client/server database computing.

- Oracle7 supports all major operating systems for both clients and servers, including MS DOS, NetWare, UnixWare, OS/2, and most of the UNIX flavors. Oracle networking software, SQL*Net, also supports all major network communication protocols, including TCP/IP, SPX/IPX, Named Pipes, and DECNet. Therefore, Oracle7 can be the link that joins the many data stores and networks throughout the heterogeneous computing systems prevalent in most corporations.

- Oracle7 has client/server features developers can use to minimize network I/O between clients and servers. Therefore, applications based on Oracle7 can deliver the performance that users require to be productive in their jobs.

- Oracle7 has features that make it easy to administer a complicated client/server system. Therefore, Oracle7 can deliver the advantages of client/server and keep the administration cost in a large, complicated system within reason.

There aren't many specifics about Oracle7 in the preceding list, but don't worry—you'll learn all you need to know about Oracle7 and client/server database computing as you continue to read this book.

This chapter has given you a very quick overview of client/server computing and has shown how Oracle7 fits into the client/server model. The remaining chapters in Part I are a broad overview of each of the three components in an Oracle7 client/server database system: the database server, the client, and the communication between the server and its clients.

CHAPTER

TWO

The Server in Client/Server

- Structure of an Oracle7 database

- Data integrity

- Security features

- Controlling data availability

- Protecting an Oracle7 database

Now that you understand the term "client/server," let's learn some specifics about each of the components that make up a client/server system. This chapter focuses on the database server part of the client/server equation. After reading this chapter, you'll have a broad understanding of the most important issues that surround the database server:

- Databases, relational databases, and Oracle7 databases
- The structure of an Oracle7 database, including tables, views, tablespaces, and data files
- Data integrity and how to enforce it in an Oracle7 database using integrity constraints, stored procedures, and triggers
- Oracle7's concurrency mechanisms, which allow multi-user access to a single database
- Oracle7's security features, such as database users and passwords, privileges, and roles
- Control of data availability with database startup and shutdown, and online and offline tablespaces
- Protection of an Oracle7 database with a transaction log and backups, and use of these features to recover from damaging circumstances
- Database administration in an Oracle7 client/server database system

Databases and Relational Database Management Systems

We've all been exposed to a countless number of databases. For example, every time you pick up the phone book to find a number, you're using a database. And every time you get a piece of junk mail, it is the result of someone using a mailing list, which is a database of names.

In simple terms, a *database* is a set of related information. Using our previous examples, a phone book is a database of names and phone numbers, and a mailing list is a database of prospective customer names and addresses.

One of the most common ways to manage a database is the filing cabinet. Neatly organized with hanging file folders and name tags, a filing cabinet is an example of a paper database. While the filing cabinet does a fine job of organizing data, it has many limitations. For example, what if you need to use a file someone else is already using? In this case you have two options: You can wait until the other person finishes with the file or you can make your own copy of the file. If you are the patient type and decide to wait for the file, with luck the other person is a fast worker and promptly returns the file so you don't have to wait too long. If you can't wait and decide to make a copy of the file, you must gamble that your work won't depend on the other person's work.

The paper database in a filing cabinet has other important disadvantages. Think about all the office space a series of full-size filing cabinets can consume. And what if a fire destroys your building? Do you have a set of filing cabinets at home to keep up-to-date copies of important files such as employee lists, customer names, product orders, and billing information? Your answer is probably no, especially if your business is larger than a lemonade stand.

Database Servers

You probably already know that computers can do a much better job than a filing cabinet of managing databases. Using a network of computers or a multi-user computer, many users can concurrently share the same set of data much more easily than with a file cabinet. Computers can store billions of characters of information on a single magnetic or optical disk, which makes it easy to protect valuable data from unforeseen catastrophes. And the affordability and power of the personal computer allows even the household bill payer to manage a database by computer.

What you might not realize is that you need the correct piece of computer software to actually manage data. This software is the database management system (DBMS), or database server. And just as filing cabinets come in many different colors and sizes, each type of database server has its own characteristics. If you understand the characteristics of your database server, you'll no doubt make better use of it, no matter what type of user you are.

Relational Database Servers

The Oracle7 database server is based on the relational database model. The *relational database model* is a well-defined theoretical model of working with and managing a set of data (a database) that attends to three specific things: data structure, data integrity, and data manipulation. Let's learn about Oracle7's presentation of the relational database model by studying the components of Oracle7 that address the four fundamental areas of the relational model: tables, integrity constraints, data access, and transactions.

Data Structure: Tables

The fundamental rule of the relational model is that data is seen as *tables*, and nothing but tables. Because the concept of a table is simple and intuitive, the relational model is easy to understand.

There are several specific rules for tables in the relational model. For example, a table, formally called a *relation*, has a finite number of *columns* (also called *fields* or *attributes*) and can have a variable number of *rows* (also called *records* or *tuples*). Figure 2.1 shows examples of typical tables in a relational database.

Data Integrity: Integrity Constraints

The relational model also concerns itself with data integrity. If a relational database has *data integrity*, it means that all of the data in the database is valid according to a set of rules. For example, all customers in the CUSTOMER table must have a unique customer ID; otherwise, you would not be able to distinguish between two customers with the same name and same address. This standard data integrity rule of the relational model is called *entity integrity*, which implies that you can uniquely identify each row in a table from all others.

You can define standard data integrity rules of the relational model within an Oracle7 relationship using *integrity constraints*. When you create a table in an Oracle7 relational database, you *declare* (specify) integrity rules with simple command options. Once declared, integrity constraints are a statement about the integrity of the data in an Oracle7 relational database because they automatically prohibit invalid data from existing.

FIGURE 2.1:

The CUSTOMER, STOCK, ORDERS and ITEM tables are all examples of tables in a relational database.

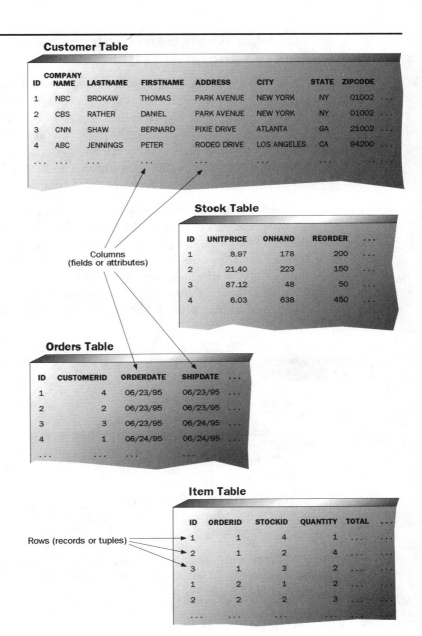

Customer Table

ID	COMPANY NAME	LASTNAME	FIRSTNAME	ADDRESS	CITY	STATE	ZIPCODE	
1	NBC	BROKAW	THOMAS	PARK AVENUE	NEW YORK	NY	01002	...
2	CBS	RATHER	DANIEL	PARK AVENUE	NEW YORK	NY	01002	...
3	CNN	SHAW	BERNARD	PIXIE DRIVE	ATLANTA	GA	21002	...
4	ABC	JENNINGS	PETER	RODEO DRIVE	LOS ANGELES	CA	94200	...
...	...	...	...	...	...	...	...	

Stock Table

ID	UNITPRICE	ONHAND	REORDER	
1	8.97	178	200	...
2	21.40	223	150	...
3	87.12	48	50	...
4	6.03	638	450	...

Columns
(fields or attributes)

Orders Table

ID	CUSTOMERID	ORDERDATE	SHIPDATE	
1	4	06/23/95	06/23/95	...
2	2	06/23/95	06/23/95	...
3	3	06/23/95	06/24/95	...
4	1	06/24/95	06/24/95	...
...	...	...	...	

Item Table

ID	ORDERID	STOCKID	QUANTITY	TOTAL	
1	1	4	1	...	...
2	1	2	4	...	...
3	1	3	2	...	...
1	2	1	2	...	...
2	2	2	3	...	...
...	...	...	...		

Rows (records or tuples)

Data Manipulation: Structured Query Language (SQL)

The relational model also describes how users can manipulate data within tables using relational algebra. *Relational algebra* is a finite set of operators that are used on tables to manipulate database data. For example, the *restrict relational operator* collects specific rows from a table, the *project relational operator* collects specific columns from a table, and the *join relational operator* creates a new table by joining related data from two or more tables. In summary, relational algebra is a set of mathematical principles that precisely control how to manipulate data in a relational database.

To interact with a relational database, you must use an access language that embodies the principles of relational algebra. Although not part of the relational model, the industry-standard data access language for relational databases is called *SQL* (pronounced "es-que-el" or "sequel"). SQL is an easy-to-use, English-like language that has all the commands necessary to work with a relational database server like Oracle7. Following are some quick examples of SQL commands that retrieve table data using restrict, project, and join relational operators.

> **NOTE** Comments in a SQL statement begin with the characters "- -" and proceed to the end of the line.

```
-- example of restrict relational operator in SQL
SELECT *
  FROM customer
  WHERE ID = 3

-- example of project relational operator in SQL
SELECT id, lastname, firstname
  FROM customer

-- example of join relational operator in SQL
SELECT item.orderid, item.id, stock.description
  FROM item, stock
  WHERE item.stockid = stock.id
```

SQL also has other types of commands that permit users to create and drop data structures, manipulate table data, and control access to specific database data. Here are a few quick examples:

```
CREATE TABLE orders ...
DROP TABLE item ...
INSERT INTO orders VALUES (...)
UPDATE item SET quantity = 2 WHERE orderid = 2345 AND id = 2
DELETE FROM orders WHERE id = 597
GRANT SELECT ON customer TO rnixon
REVOKE SELECT ON orders FROM gbush
```

NOTE   The word "query" is a common term used when discussing relational databases and SQL. Some use "query" to mean any type of SQL statement that manipulates data (for example, insert, update, delete, or retrieve). Others use the term specifically to mean a SELECT statement that retrieves data from a database. In this book, we'll use the term "query" to mean a SELECT statement.

Data Manipulation: Transactions

Before the age of the automated teller machine and phone banking systems, you would go to the bank and talk to a human being when you needed to transfer money between your savings and checking accounts. A transfer of money between accounts is a banking transaction that has several different but related operations. For example, first you go up to the teller and say, "Hi, I'd like to transfer some savings into my checking account." Then you hand the teller your bank book and the transaction slip. After the teller increments your checking account and decrements your savings account, the teller records the transfer in a log or journal. Finally, you get a receipt of the transfer for your records.

Each operation of the transfer banking transaction is important in the grand scheme of things. Think what would happen if some steps were completed but others left undone. In your favor but at the expense of the bank, you might get extra funds in your checking account if the teller forgets to record the savings funds withdrawal.

Even worse, you may come out behind if the teller withdraws the savings funds but forgets to credit your checking account. Therefore, the banking transfer transaction is not complete unless the teller carries out all the steps.

Banking and other operations are no different with SQL because the language incorporates the important concept of a transaction. A database *transaction* is a unit of work made up of the work done by one or more SQL statements. For example, to complete the several related steps of the transfer action using a relational database and SQL, you perform the following steps:

1. Update the ACCOUNT table to reflect the new savings account balance after the transfer.

2. Update the ACCOUNT table to reflect the new checking account balance after the transfer.

3. Insert a new entry into the JOURNAL table, recording your ID, the account numbers, the transaction type, the transfer data, and the transfer amount.

4. Commit the transaction as complete.

Before step 4 takes place, the changes of steps 1, 2, and 3 are considered temporary because the transaction has not yet been committed. Step 4 is the critical step. You *commit* a transaction using the SQL command COMMIT, which marks the end of the current transaction. At this point the database server makes all changes of the current transaction permanent.

SQL even gives you another choice for transaction control. If in step 4 you decide that you don't want to commit the transaction, you can *roll back* the transaction using the SQL command ROLLBACK. This command undoes any effects caused by the SQL statements in the current transaction as if they had never happened.

The previous three sections have given you a basic understanding of the foundations of the Oracle7 relational database server: tables, SQL, and transactions. The following sections provide you with the specifics of an Oracle7 relational database management system.

Oracle7 Relational Databases

Just as a company organizes a warehouse of goods, Oracle7 structures a database both logically and physically. An Oracle7 database's *logical structure* is the set of tables in the database. A database's *physical structure* is the set of operating system files that store the bits and bytes of database information on disk.

> **NOTE**
>
> One of the characteristics of a relational database system is *data independence*. An Oracle7 relational database's physical structure is independent of and hidden from an end user's logical view of the data. The benefit is that users can easily access data in logical structures like tables by using simple SQL commands, without having to know anything about the physical organization of the data. Oracle7 takes care of mapping columns and rows of table data to files and physical bytes on disk. In contrast, pre-relational database systems require users to program applications to access data by using complicated physical addressing mechanisms. The major drawback of such *data-dependent* database systems is that database applications have compiled access paths to data. Therefore, when someone changes the physical location or organization of the data, it's likely that all applications need major modifications to account for such changes. Because relational database systems like Oracle7 have data independence, they don't fall prey to similar problems.

To take complete advantage of Oracle7's data-independence qualities, it's important to understand the logical and physical components in an Oracle7 database. The next few sections describe these components, including tables, views, tablespaces, and data files.

Tables: Oracle7's Logical Storage Building Blocks

The Oracle7 relational database system stores and presents all data in tables like those in Figure 2.1. A table, sometimes called an *entity,* is a focused collection of related information—a set of data records that all have the same attributes. The attributes of a table are the table's columns, and the data records are the table's rows. For example, all the records in the CUSTOMER table in Figure 2.1 have the same attributes: ID number, company name, last name, first name, address, city, state, country, zip code, phone number, and fax number. The CUSTOMER table can have any number of customer records, but each customer must have the same set of fixed attributes.

Column Datatypes

Each table column, or attribute, contains a specific type of data. For example, the ID column in the CUSTOMER table stores numbers, and the remainder of the columns store text strings. (The zip code field is a text string to allow for leading zeros, and the phone and fax number columns are text strings to allow for hyphens and other delimiting characters.) When a user creates a table, the user specifies the table's columns and the *datatype* for each column.

Oracle7 supports many different datatypes. Table 2.1 describes some of them.

TABLE 2.1: Some Oracle7 Datatypes

Datatype	Description
CHAR(size)	Stores fixed-length character strings
VARCHAR2(size)	Stores variable-length character strings
NUMBER (precision, scale)	Stores numbers of all types, including integer, floating-point, and so on
DATE	Stores time-related information, including dates and times
LONG	Stores large, variable-length character strings, up to 2 gigabytes
RAW(size)	Stores small binary strings, less than 2000 bytes
LONG RAW	Stores long binary strings, up to 2 gigabytes

Administrators need to pay particular attention when specifying the datatypes for columns. The datatype an administrator specifies for a column can significantly affect the amount of space Oracle7 uses to store the column's data. Chapter 10 explains how to choose the correct datatypes for the columns of a table.

Tablespaces and Data Files: Oracle7's Physical Storage Building Blocks

When a user creates a new table, the user tells Oracle7 where to physically store the table's data. The user does this by specifying a tablespace for the new table. A *tablespace* is a partition or logical area of storage in a database that directly corresponds to one or more physical *data files*. After an administrator creates a tablespace in a database, users can create one or more tables in the tablespace. Figure 2.2 illustrates the relationship among tables, tablespaces, and data files.

FIGURE 2.2:

A tablespace is a logical database division that maps to one or more physical data files. Table data in each tablespace therefore maps to the tablespace's data files.

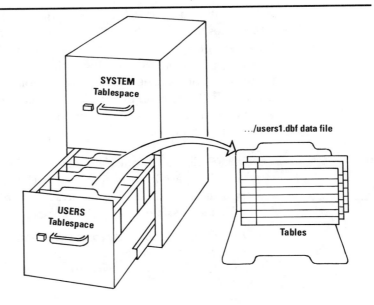

29

Notice that the table-tablespace-data file chain is what gives Oracle7 the inherent relational database characteristic of data independence. After a user creates a table, other users can insert, update, and delete rows in the table just by naming the table in a SQL statement. Oracle7 takes care of mapping a SQL request to the correct physical data on disk.

The SYSTEM Tablespace: The Tablespace of All Tablespaces

Every Oracle7 database has at least one tablespace, the SYSTEM tablespace. When creating a database, the administrator specifies the names and sizes of the initial data files for the database. These files are the physical storage for the SYSTEM tablespace. Oracle7 uses the SYSTEM tablespace to hold the data dictionary. The *data dictionary* is a set of internal system tables that holds all sorts of information about the database. For example, there are data dictionary tables that provide information about the tables, tablespaces, and data files in the database.

Why Use Multiple Tablespaces?

After creating an Oracle7 database, the administrator will want to create other tablespaces to physically partition the data planned for the database. For example, there will likely be many client applications that access a database in your client/server system. When adding each new client application to the system, it's best to create one or more new tablespaces to hold each application's data separate from the data dictionary and the data of other applications. Why should an administrator bother to use tablespaces to organize data storage? There are many good reasons. Here are a few:

- Oracle7 allows administrators to control the availability of a database's data on a tablespace-by-tablespace basis. Therefore, they can effectively take an application offline by taking the application's tablespace offline, making its tables inaccessible.

- Oracle7 allows administrators to back up a database at the tablespace level. When administrators want to back up just a specific application's data, not the entire database, it's easy; they can back up just the application's tablespace.

- Administrators can improve the performance of client applications if they use tablespaces wisely. For example, if the administrator places the data files of each application's tablespace on different disks of a database server, applications won't contend with each other for disk access and space.

If you are going to administer your Oracle7 client/server system, you'll want to learn more about designing and managing your database's tablespaces and data files. Chapter 7 thoroughly explains how to configure these components of a database.

Now let's take a look at some of the other components in an Oracle7 database system.

Views: Looking at Table Data in Different Ways

When you look into the night sky, you see stars. When you look into a telescope at night, you also see stars. As you know, the stars aren't actually in the telescope; you're just looking at the stars in the sky with a different perspective—a much closer view.

A *view* and tables in a relational database are analogous to the telescope and the stars. When users use a view, they see the same data that's in database tables, but with perhaps a different perspective. And just as the telescope doesn't contain any stars, a view doesn't contain any data. Instead, a view is a *virtual table*, deriving its data from *base tables*. Figure 2.3 illustrates the concept of a view.

You can think of a view as a *stored query*. That's because you define a view with a query. Here is the SQL definition of the REORDER view in Figure 2.3:

```
CREATE VIEW reorder AS
   SELECT id, onhand, reorder FROM stock
   WHERE onhand < reorder
```

The CREATE VIEW statement defines the REORDER view. Its query corresponds only to those rows in the STOCK table where the part's current inventory quantity is lower than its reorder point.

One of the primary rules of a relational model is that all data must be seen as tables. Therefore, a view maintains the characteristics of a table. For example, the defining query names the columns of the view. And users can employ data manipulation

FIGURE 2.3:

A view is a virtual table: You see information derived from one or more tables, but the view itself doesn't store any information.

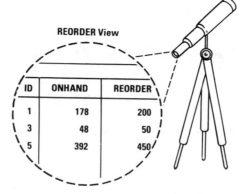

		STOCK Table		
ID	UNITPRICE	ONHAND	REORDER	DESCRIPTION
1	8.97	178	200	
2	21.40	223	150	
3	87.12	48	50	
4	6.03	638	450	
5	6.97	392	450	

REORDER View

ID	ONHAND	REORDER
1	178	200
3	48	50
5	392	450

SQL statements against a view just as they can a table (with some restrictions). Of course, because a view derives its data from a base table, Oracle7 manipulates the data of the base table when a user queries, inserts into, updates, or deletes from a view. But unless you specifically know you're using a view, it's hard to distinguish a view from a table.

Views are a powerful tool in a relational database such as Oracle7. The next few sections discuss some of the ways administrators and developers can use views in a database.

Using Views to Increase Security

If an administrator allows an ordering clerk to query the STOCK table, the clerk can see all the information about all the parts in inventory. However, if the security administrator allows the clerk to query only the REORDER view, the clerk can see only the part numbers, quantity, and reorder point for the parts that need reordering. Therefore, the REORDER view increases the security of the STOCK table.

Developers can limit access to specific table columns using a view and create value-based security by defining a view for specific rows. The REORDER view is an example of both options.

Using Views to Present Additional Information

A developer can use a view to derive other columns not present in any table—for example, to create calculated fields using a view. Here is the SQL definition of a view that calculates the total for all the line items in each order:

```
CREATE VIEW ordertotal AS
   SELECT orderid, SUM(total) "ORDER TOTAL"
   FROM item
   GROUP BY orderid
```

If a user queries the ORDERTOTAL view, Oracle7 calculates the totals for the requested orders. Here is a typical output when querying the ORDERTOTAL view:

```
SELECT * FROM ordertotal WHERE orderid = 1

ORDERID     ORDER TOTAL
----------- ----------------
1           265.87
```

Using Views to Hide Complex Queries

Developers can hide complicated queries from users by using a view. The benefit is that users issue simple queries against the view and the view takes care of all the complicated work. For instance, a developer might create a view to hide a *join* query—a query that pulls together related information. A developer might create a view to join order and corresponding line item information from the ORDERS and ITEM tables. Here is a view with a join and a typical output when a user queries the view:

```
CREATE VIEW orderreport AS
   SELECT orders.id "ORDER ID", orders.orderdate, item.id "LINE ID", stockid
   FROM orders, item
   WHERE item.orderid = orders.id

SELECT * FROM orderreport WHERE "ORDER ID" = 2
```

ORDER ID	ORDERDATE	LINE ID	STOCKID
2	06/23/95	1	1
2	06/23/95	2	2

The previous sections explain just three examples of how to use views in an Oracle7 database.

Limitations When Using Views

There are certain limitations when using views. For example, users can't insert, update, or delete records using the ORDERTOTAL and ORDERREPORT views. Oracle7 doesn't allow you to manipulate data using views that have a defining query with a group operator (for example, the GROUP BY operator in the ORDER-TOTAL view) or a join (for example, the ORDERREPORT view). In these cases, it's not clear to the database server how to map a data manipulation operation back to the underlying base table(s) of a view.

Other limitations apply to views. If you are an administrator or application developer, you'll want to learn more about the powers and limitations of views. Chapter 15 explains how to use views effectively in an Oracle7 database.

Ensuring Data Integrity

It's important to make sure the data in a database has integrity or that the data is valid according to a set of rules. The relational model describes several intrinsic rules that must be enforced to guarantee data integrity in a relational database: domain integrity, entity integrity, and referential integrity. Figure 2.4 and the following sections explain the integrity rules in our example database.

FIGURE 2.4:

Diagram showing several related tables and their associated data integrity rules

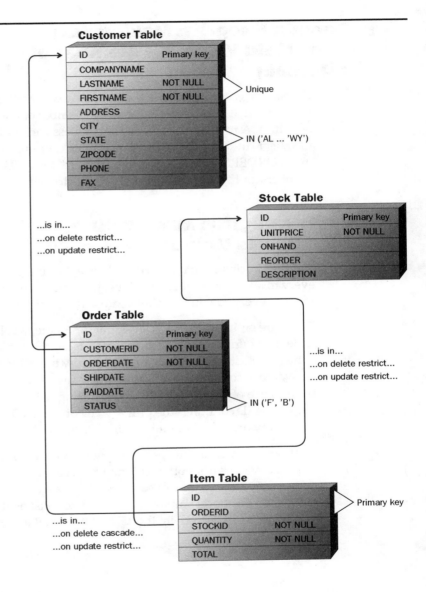

Customer Table

ID	Primary key
COMPANYNAME	
LASTNAME	NOT NULL
FIRSTNAME	NOT NULL
ADDRESS	
CITY	
STATE	
ZIPCODE	
PHONE	
FAX	

Unique

IN ('AL ... 'WY')

Stock Table

ID	Primary key
UNITPRICE	NOT NULL
ONHAND	
REORDER	
DESCRIPTION	

...is in...
...on delete restrict...
...on update restrict...

Order Table

ID	Primary key
CUSTOMERID	NOT NULL
ORDERDATE	NOT NULL
SHIPDATE	
PAIDDATE	
STATUS	

IN ('F', 'B')

...is in...
...on delete restrict...
...on update restrict...

Item Table

ID	
ORDERID	
STOCKID	NOT NULL
QUANTITY	NOT NULL
TOTAL	

Primary key

...is in...
...on delete cascade...
...on update restrict...

Domain Integrity: Making Sure Every Field Value Is a Member of a Domain

Domain integrity makes sure that a database doesn't contain any nonsense values. It ensures that a value in a column is a member of the column's *domain*, or legal set of values. A row cannot be in a table unless each of the row's column values is a member in the domain of the corresponding column. For example, there can't be a row in the ORDERS table with the character "A" for an ID because the ID column holds numbers and "A" is not a member of the domain of numbers.

Entity Integrity: Making Sure Each Row Is Unique

Another intrinsic data integrity rule is entity integrity. *Entity integrity* means that every row in a table must be unique. If a table has entity integrity, you can uniquely identify every row in the table because there are no duplicate rows.

To ensure entity integrity, a developer designates a column or a set of columns in a table as its *primary key*. Each row in a table must contain a unique primary key value. Implicitly, this means that every row in a table must indeed have a primary key value (a complete set of values in the case of a composite primary key) because the absence of value, a *NULL*, is not distinguishable from another NULL. For example, the ID column is the primary key of the ORDERS table in Figure 2.4. Therefore, every order has a unique order ID.

A table can have only one primary key. In many cases developers need to eliminate duplicate values from other columns as well. For this a developer can designate a non-primary key column or set of columns as an *alternate key* or a *unique key*. A table can't have duplicate values in a unique key, just as it can't in a primary key. For example, every record in the CUSTOMER table has a unique last-first name combination.

Referential Integrity: Making Sure Related Tables Stay in Sync

Referential integrity, or relation integrity, is another elemental data integrity rule of the relational model. *Referential integrity* defines the relationships among different columns and tables in a relational database. It's called referential integrity because the values in one column or set of columns refer to or must match the values in a related column or set of columns.

For example, the CUSTOMER and ORDERS tables in Figure 2.4 track different, but related, information. The CUSTOMER table keeps track of customer names, addresses, and phone numbers. Each customer record has a unique customer ID. The ORDERS table keeps track of orders that customers place. ORDERS has a column to indicate the customer, by customer ID, that places each order. As you can see, the customer ID column in ORDERS refers to the customer ID column in CUSTOMER. Referential integrity simply makes sure that at all times, each order has a customer ID that matches a customer ID in the CUSTOMER table.

There are several terms you can use when discussing referential integrity. The dependent column or set of columns is a *foreign key*. The referenced column or set of columns is a *parent key*, which must be a primary key or unique key. The foreign key is in the *child*, or *detail*, table, and the parent key is in the *parent*, or *master*, table. If the parent and foreign keys are in the same table, it is called *self-referential* integrity. For example, Figure 2.5 shows how the MANAGER column of the EMPLOYEE table refers to the primary key of the same table.

FIGURE 2.5:

Self-referential integrity occurs when one column of a table refers to the values in another column of the same table.

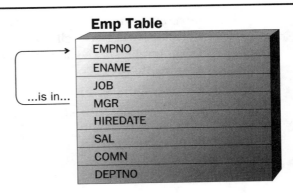

Emp Table

...is in...

EMPNO
ENAME
JOB
MGR
HIREDATE
SAL
COMN
DEPTNO

NOTE

The ability to relate values in different tables and maintain referential integrity is an important characteristic of relational databases. Relational database servers are very efficient at storing data and because of their ability to link different tables. For example, think about the redundant customer data a database would have to track if it couldn't relate the ORDERS and CUSTOMER tables. Without a relational database, every order would have to have a full set of customer information, including customer name, address, and phone number. Additionally, if a customer's phone number changed, someone would have to go back and update every one of the customer's orders to indicate the new phone number. Fortunately, no one will have to do this with an Oracle7 relational database if you lay it out correctly because it is very flexible and efficient at storing data.

Business Rules: Custom Data Integrity Rules

So far we've learned about the standard data integrity rules that are built into the relational database model. However, every company's database has its own unique set of *business rules* that are just as important as the standard set of data integrity rules. For example, a security administrator might want to disallow changes to a table during abnormal business hours or derive a value for a column when a user inserts or updates a record.

To ensure complete database integrity, there must be a way for the system to enforce custom business rules as well. The following sections explain the features of Oracle7 that developers and administrators can use to enforce standard and complex data integrity rules.

Enforcing Data Integrity with Oracle7

One way to enforce data integrity rules is to code every integrity rule inside each application that accesses your database. Although this approach works, two significant problems arise:

- Developers have to code, test, and debug the same integrity rules in each database application. If a rule changes, developers need to modify all applications. As you can imagine, this is a time-consuming and unproductive development process.

- An application must request a great deal of data from the database to enforce data integrity rules inside the application. If a client application and database server operate on different machines joined by a network, the server ships lots of data across the network so that each application can enforce integrity rules; consequently, this generates excessive traffic that can saturate the network and diminish system performance.

For these two reasons alone, it's very important to enforce data integrity rules inside the server instead of in the application when you use a client/server database system. Oracle7 is a very powerful database server for client/server computing because it has several features to enforce data integrity rules at the database server: datatypes, integrity constraints, and triggers.

Using Column Datatypes to Enforce Domain Integrity

Oracle7 automatically enforces domain integrity using the datatypes for the columns in a table. A record can't be in a table unless the data for each column is the correct type. For example, a record can't be in the ORDERS table with an alphabetic character in the ID column because the ID column holds numbers, and an alphabetic character isn't in the domain of valid numbers.

All Oracle7 datatypes allow developers to declare the datatype or domain for a column. Table 2.1 shows that some datatypes allow further limitation of the domain of a column. For example, the NUMBER datatype can define the *precision* (total number of significant digits) and *scale* (total number of digits to the right or left of the decimal place) of acceptable numbers in the column. Oracle7 doesn't allow a row in a table if the row has a number in a column that exceeds the column's precision. Oracle7 automatically manipulates all acceptable numbers to match the scale you specify for the column. The character datatypes also allow additional domain integrity control by specifying the maximum length of acceptable text strings for the column. Oracle7 doesn't allow a row in a table if the row has a text string in a column that is longer than the column's length.

Using Integrity Constraints to Enforce Standard Data Integrity Rules

Integrity constraints allow relational database systems to easily enforce the standard data integrity rules that are part of the relational model. Integrity constraints are simple to use because developers declare standard data integrity rules as part of a table's definition. Here are some Oracle7 CREATE TABLE statements that include the declaration of several integrity constraints:

```
CREATE TABLE customer
( id NUMBER(5,0) PRIMARY KEY,
  companyname VARCHAR2(50),
  lastname VARCHAR2(50) NOT NULL,
  firstname VARCHAR2(50) NOT NULL,
  address VARCHAR2(100),
  city VARCHAR2(50),
  state CHAR(2),
  zipcode VARCHAR2(10),
  phone VARCHAR2(20),
  fax VARCHAR2(20),
  UNIQUE (lastname, firstname),
  CHECK (state IN
    ('AL','AK','AZ','AR','CA','CO','CT','DE','DC','FL','GA','HI','ID',
     'IL','IN','IA','KS','KY','LA','ME','MD','MA','MI','MN','MS','MO',
     'MT','NE','NV','NH','NJ','NM','NY','NC','ND','OH','OK','OR','PA',
     'PR','RI','SC','SD','TN','TX','UT','VT','VA','WA','WV','WI','WY') ) )
```

```
CREATE TABLE stock
( id NUMBER(5,0) PRIMARY KEY,
  unitprice NUMBER(10,2) NOT NULL,
  onhand NUMBER(5,0),
  reorder NUMBER(5,0),
  description VARCHAR2(2000))

CREATE TABLE orders
( id NUMBER(5,0) PRIMARY KEY,
  customerid NUMBER(5,0) NOT NULL,
  orderdate DATE NOT NULL,
  shipdate DATE,
  paiddate DATE,
  status CHAR(1),
  CHECK (status IN ('F','B')),      -- F is filled, B is backlogged
  FOREIGN KEY (customerid) REFERENCES customer )

CREATE TABLE item
( id NUMBER(5,0),
  orderid NUMBER(5,0),
  stockid NUMBER(5,0) NOT NULL,
  quantity NUMBER(5,0) NOT NULL,
  total NUMBER(10,2),
  PRIMARY KEY (id, orderid),
  FOREIGN KEY (orderid) REFERENCES orders ON DELETE CASCADE,
  FOREIGN KEY (stockid) REFERENCES stock )
```

NOTE Remember the definitions above of the CUSTOMER, ORDERS, ITEM, and STOCK tables. We'll be using them throughout the remainder of the book.

Let's learn a little about the different integrity constraints in the preceding statements that create the CUSTOMER, ORDERS, ITEM, and STOCK tables.

In many cases, it's necessary to narrow the acceptable domain of a column's values further than datatyping permits. Most commonly, a developer might want to eliminate absent values, or NULLs, from the domain of a column. This way, every row in a table has a value for the column. The developer can eliminate NULLs from the

THE SERVER IN CLIENT/SERVER

domain of a column by declaring a NOT NULL integrity constraint with the column's definition. For example, the preceding CUSTOMER table definition declares NOT NULL integrity constraints for both the LASTNAME and FIRSTNAME columns to make sure every customer record has a complete customer name. If someone tries to insert or update a row with a NULL in a column designated as NOT NULL, Oracle7 doesn't accept the row.

After datatyping and NULLs, a developer might find it necessary to narrow a column's domain even more. For example, only valid state code abbreviations—'AL', 'AK', 'AZ', ... 'WY'—should be in the STATE column of the CUSTOMER table. This example of domain integrity is an expression that specifically defines the domain of a column. A developer can express a custom domain integrity rule easily using a CHECK integrity constraint. For example, the preceding CUSTOMER table declares a CHECK constraint to enforce the custom domain integrity expression for valid state codes.

A developer can declare a PRIMARY KEY integrity constraint to define a table's primary key and enforce entity integrity. Every table definition above declares a PRIMARY KEY integrity constraint to enforce entity integrity. The CUSTOMER table also declares a UNIQUE integrity constraint to enforce uniqueness of customer names.

A developer can establish referential integrity by declaring a referential or FOREIGN KEY integrity constraint to define a foreign key in a table. The column(s) of a foreign key must match the datatypes of the column(s) in the parent key.

Remember that referential integrity makes sure that each foreign key value always matches a parent key value. Therefore, a referential integrity constraint not only determines acceptable data in the foreign key of the child table, it defines the *referential action* when operating on the parent key. For example, there are two referential integrity constraints in the ITEM table in the previous example. The first referential integrity constraint references the ORDERS table; the *delete cascade referential action* of this constraint is to cascade the delete of a parent row to all dependent child rows. Therefore, when a user deletes an order from the ORDERS table, Oracle7 automatically deletes the line items for the order. It's not apparent, but by the absence of the ON DELETE CASCADE option, the second referential integrity constraint restricts all operations on a parent key that has dependent child rows. Therefore, Oracle7 prohibits a user from updating a part number or deleting a part from the STOCK table if the part has dependent order line items. This rule is called the *restrict referential action.*

Using Stored Procedures and Triggers to Enforce Custom Business Rules

Integrity constraints can enforce a large percentage of the data integrity rules in a database. However, there will always be business rules that developers cannot enforce with integrity constraints. Developers need to enforce these custom integrity rules as well to ensure complete database integrity. And as we've already learned, it's best to be able to centralize the enforcement of all integrity rules inside the database server of a client/server system.

To enforce a complex business rule, Oracle7 offers stored procedures. A *stored procedure* is a compiled collection of SQL statements, flow-of-control statements, variable declarations, assignment operators, and so on that a developer creates and stores in a database. Developers can use procedures to enforce complex data integrity because when a user performs an operation using a procedure, Oracle7 forces the user to touch data in a prescribed or predefined manner.

For example, let's assume you need to enforce the following business rule: When a user deletes a customer record from the CUSTOMER table, the user should log the customer ID and name in a history table. Here is the definition of a stored procedure that enforces this business rule:

```
CREATE PROCEDURE deletecustomer (custid IN INTEGER) AS
   last VARCHAR2(50);
   first VARCHAR2(50);
BEGIN
   SELECT lastname, firstname INTO last, first
     FROM customer WHERE id = custid;
   INSERT INTO customerhistory VALUES (custid, last, first);
   DELETE FROM customer WHERE id = custid;
EXCEPTION
   WHEN NO_DATA_FOUND THEN
     raise_application_error (-20123, 'Invalid Customer ID');
END deletecustomer;
```

NOTE   The preceding example introduces statement terminators for SQL statements. A *statement terminator* is a character or set of characters that indicates the end of a statement. For example, the terminator used to indicate the end of Oracle SQL statements is the semicolon. Depending on the environment in which you issue statements, SQL statements may or may not require terminators. As a matter of convention, this book uses terminators only where absolutely necessary for technical accuracy in all situations.

To enforce your business rule, users and applications shouldn't be able to issue DELETE statements against the CUSTOMER table. Instead, only give users the privilege to execute the DELETECUSTOMER procedure; this way, when someone executes this procedure, it automatically logs the removal of a customer record before deleting the specified customer.

If you want to allow users to delete rows from the CUSTOMER table but still automatically enforce your business rule, you can use a trigger instead. A *trigger* is a stored procedure that Oracle7 automatically *fires* (executes) under the appropriate conditions. The following example is a trigger that automatically enforces the same business rule as the DELETECUSTOMER procedure:

```
CREATE TRIGGER deletecustomer
BEFORE DELETE ON customer
FOR EACH ROW
BEGIN
  INSERT INTO customerhistory
    VALUES (:old.id, :old.lastname, :old.firstname);
END deletecustomer;
```

This code creates a trigger. The *trigger condition* for the DELETECUSTOMER trigger is a DELETE statement that targets the CUSTOMER table. Oracle7 fires the trigger body of the DELETECUSTOMER trigger just before someone issues a statement to delete a row from the CUSTOMER table. A *trigger body* is the procedure in a trigger that includes the logic for a business rule. Note that if a user deletes multiple rows with one SQL statement, the DELETECUSTOMER trigger fires once before the deletion of each customer record.

By enforcing custom data integrity rules using stored procedures and triggers, developers centralize the enforcement of complex business rules at the database server instead of inside individual applications. Therefore, applications keep the amount of network traffic to a minimum so that network performance isn't a bottleneck in a client/server system. Figure 2.6 demonstrates this benefit of stored procedures and triggers.

FIGURE 2.6:

By centralizing complex data integrity rules inside the database using triggers and stored procedures, you can eliminate network traffic generated from otherwise necessary SQL statements.

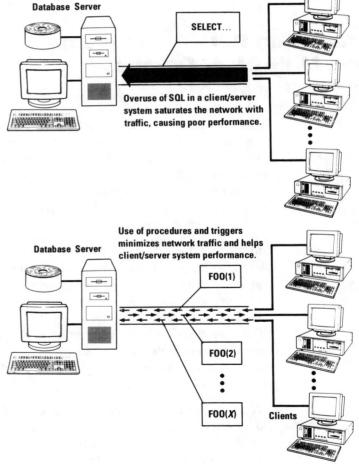

Procedures and triggers can also increase development productivity. That's because a single developer codes, tests, and debugs each integrity rule once in the server instead of once for each application that accesses the server.

You now have a solid introduction to data integrity and how to enforce it in your Oracle7 client/server database system. To learn more about integrity constraints, stored procedures, and triggers, be sure to read Chapters 15 and 18. Now let's learn about one of the most important functions of the database server in a client/server database system: data concurrency.

Managing Data Concurrency in a Multi-User Database System

So far, our discussions of data integrity, SQL statements, and transactions consider database operation in *isolation* only, as though a user executes the statements of a transaction operating in a single-user database system. The only requirement mentioned so far is that all statements in a transaction must leave the database in an acceptable state of data integrity. If a statement violates an integrity constraint or an integrity rule in a trigger, Oracle7 automatically rolls back the statement to preserve database integrity. Simple, right?

Unfortunately, single-user databases don't cut it for workgroups, even when you use a file cabinet. Consider the problem of interference with a filing cabinet. You want to use the same file someone else is already using. If you want to see all the work done by the other person, you have to wait. If you want to gamble that the work the other user is doing won't affect your work, you can make a copy of the file. In either case, there is a penalty—waiting for the other user to finish work or incurring the risk of inaccurate work because you can't see what the other person does. The filing cabinet illustrates the concurrency problems involved when many users attempt to use the same database.

A computerized multi-user database system, like a file cabinet, must solve the problem of *contention*, or concurrent attempts by many users to use the same data. In fact, the job of data concurrency (managing concurrent access to the same set of data) is one of the most important and perhaps the most apparent job of a database server. A database server must manage data so that contending users wait the least amount of time for each other to complete work without sacrificing data integrity. If a database server fails at either objective, users surely notice the repercussions, especially during times of heavy system use; as many transactions contend for the same data, users observe poor application performance or get inaccurate results from their work.

Now that I've scared you with all of these data concurrency problems, here's some good news. Oracle7 has an automatic concurrency control system, so developers don't have to worry about the problems just described. Let's take a quick look at how Oracle7 solves the problems of data concurrency in a multi-user client/server database system.

Using Data Locks to Prevent Destructive Interference

Consider what can happen if you and your spouse want to withdraw the remaining balance of your checking account at the same time from different ATMs. If the database server permits you both to update your checking balance in an ACCOUNT table at exactly the same time, one of two very bad things can happen. Either one of the updates is lost or the account has a final checking balance that is negative. The former result translates to the bank giving you and your spouse a bonus every time you pull this trick. The latter result violates a cardinal business rule of the bank database: Don't carry credit for checking accounts.

This scenario illustrates *destructive interference*, when two operations contending for the same data interfere with each other to produce inaccurate results or sacrifice data integrity. Most database systems use locks to prevent destructive interference when different users concurrently access the same data. Just as the lock on an airport locker prevents two people from using the same locker at the same time, *data locks* prevent destructive interference in a multi-user database system. The following sections explain the different types of locks Oracle7 uses to control data concurrency.

Exclusive and Share Locks

When you get the key to an airport locker, you have the exclusive right to use it. No one else can store stuff in your locker until you return the key. Alternatively, it's likely that there is more than one key to the lock on the front door of your house or apartment because you share the use of your house with a spouse, relative, or roommate. This notion of exclusive and shared locks is similar to how Oracle7 locks data.

When a user attempts to operate on some data, Oracle7 automatically acquires a lock on the data to prevent the possibility of destructive interference. Oracle7 always acquires a *share lock* on the data if doing so leaves no possibility of destructive interference. A share lock allows other transactions to acquire share locks as well on the same data, thereby maximizing the level of concurrency in the database. However, if a share lock leaves open the possibility of destructive interference, Oracle7 must acquire an exclusive lock on the data that your transaction requests. An *exclusive lock* prevents other locks of any type on the same data to preserve data integrity at the expense of eliminating concurrent access to the same data. The following examples demonstrate when Oracle7 uses share locks and exclusive locks.

Let's assume you want to update the balance for account 65 in the ACCOUNT table. When you update the row for account 65, Oracle7 gives your transaction a share lock on the ACCOUNT table. If another user tries to update account 71 at the same time you're updating account 65, the other transaction also gets a share lock on the ACCOUNT table. Therefore, Oracle7 allows you both concurrent shared access to the same table because you are not interfering with each other. So far, so good.

Now let's assume another user wants to update account 65 at the same time you're updating it. If you try to update the account first, Oracle7 gives your transaction an exclusive lock on the row for account 65. Until you decide to commit or roll back your transaction, you hold the exclusive lock on the row for account 65. Now the other user's transaction tries to update account 65. However, Oracle7 won't let this user update the account right now. That's because your transaction holds the exclusive lock on the row that the other user's transaction requests.

This example illustrates how Oracle7 creates *serializability* in a multi-transaction environment. Oracle7 processes concurrent transactions that contend for the same resource on a first-come-first-serve basis in a serial fashion. In the example, you attempted to update account 65 first, so Oracle7 prevents the other user from updating the row until you're finished with it.

Hidden in the previous example is one of Oracle7's nicest concurrency features, *row-level locking*. To maximize concurrency by minimizing data conflicts, Oracle7 always locks data row by row, which is great for data concurrency. Unless two users attempt to update the same row in the same table at the same time, they'll be able to go about their business without interfering with each other's work.

NOTE Many database servers don't offer the row-level locking that Oracle7 provides. Instead, other systems use *page-level locking*. If a server uses page-level locking and a user updates a row, the server exclusively locks the entire page (or data block) that stores the row that the user's transaction updates. Unfortunately, this means all of the rows in the page are exclusively locked from other transactions, resulting in less data concurrency because of the increased potential that two transactions will interfere with each other's work.

Queries, Read Consistency, and Multi-Versioning: Reporting Accurate Data with Excellent Data Concurrency

The previous examples show how Oracle7 handles two different updates that contend for the same set of data. But what about queries, which are read-only statements? How does Oracle7 address contending queries and queries that contend with updates and still return accurate results?

Oracle7 uses an interesting approach to address these situations. First, a transaction doesn't acquire row locks of any type for queries. This means that two transactions can issue exactly the same query at the same time without any contention for the same set of rows. No read locks also means that a query can never block an update, and vice versa. But how can Oracle7 return accurate results if it doesn't take locks on behalf of queries? You would think that without row locks for queries, an update that contends with a query could create an inaccurate set of results for the query, as in the example in Figure 2.7.

Oracle7 can do without row locks for queries and still return accurate results because Oracle7 has a *multi-versioning mechanism*. For every query, Oracle7 returns a timepoint-based version of the data that the query requests. Oracle7 ensures that every row in a query's result set is consistent at the time you issue the query.

FIGURE 2.7:

Inconsistent query data can result
from a contending update in a
multi-transaction system that does
not use multi-versioning.

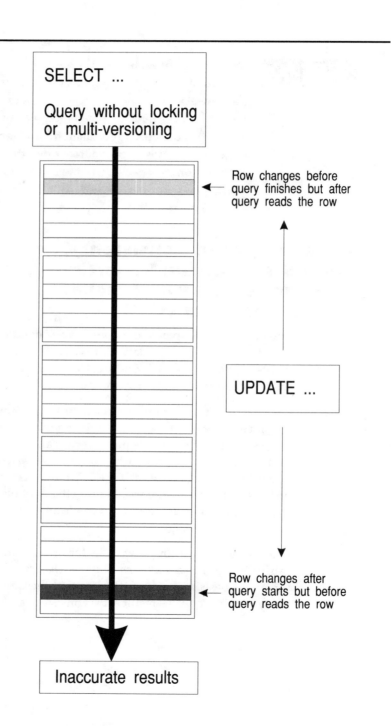

SELECT ...

Query without locking
or multi-versioning

Row changes before
query finishes but after
query reads the row

UPDATE ...

Row changes after
query starts but before
query reads the row

Inaccurate results

Rollback Segments

Oracle7 can create *read-consistent snapshots* (result sets) of data for queries using the data it stores in rollback segments. A *rollback segment* is a storage area Oracle7 uses to temporarily store old data values of rows that a transaction updates or deletes. If a user rolls back a transaction, Oracle7 reads the rollback segment assigned to the transaction and changes the affected rows to their previous state. Oracle7 also uses rollback segments for its multi-versioning mechanism. If a query requests data that changes during the execution of the query, Oracle7 generates a timepoint-based, read-consistent snapshot using data in the rollback segments. Figure 2.8 illustrates how Oracle7 uses the data in rollback segments to generate a read-consistent snapshot for a query.

Relax, It's All Automatic!

If you've used another relational database system that requires you to consider complicated locking strategies, I'm sure you'll agree that one of the nicest things about Oracle7's locking and multi-versioning mechanisms is that they are all automatic. Developers don't ever have to worry about complex locking mechanisms and multi-versioning to make sure that multiple applications and users concurrently access the same database with both adequate system performance and complete accuracy. However, if developers want to squeeze out every last drop of application performance, Oracle7 does provide the controls to override the default locking mechanisms. To learn more about Oracle7's manual concurrency controls, you'll want to read Chapter 17.

Ensuring Data Security

Can anyone get into an Oracle7 database and start using the data, reading table data and modifying it at a whim? Of course not! If this were the case, users would be able to see data not intended for their eyes (such as the boss's salary), and malicious users could erase or change data to their liking (such as giving themselves salary raises). Part of the job of a database server is making sure that all the data in a database is secure. Whether you want to protect your data from the eyes of unauthorized users or from malicious intent, security is an important function of a database server.

FIGURE 2.8:
Oracle7 rollback segments are the key component that delivers multi-versioning.

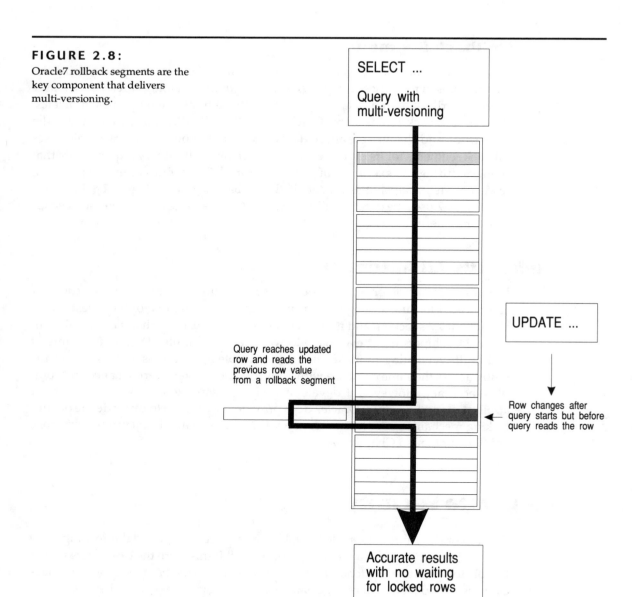

SELECT ...

Query with multi-versioning

UPDATE ...

Query reaches updated row and reads the previous row value from a rollback segment

Row changes after query starts but before query reads the row

Accurate results with no waiting for locked rows

Oracle7 maintains database security using a system of *discretionary access controls*. This simply means that at an administrator's discretion, the administrator creates registered database users and then grants them the privileges to perform specific database operations and use specific data. The next few sections introduce the different security controls of Oracle7.

Granting Access to Database Users

Have you ever used your bank's 24-hour phone banking system? To access your account, you first call the system's phone number. However, you can't do anything until you actually get inside the system by indicating your account number and a password using the keypad on your touch-tone phone. Once you pass these system access controls, you can do such things as check the balance of your accounts and transfer money among your accounts.

Accessing an Oracle7 database is very similar to accessing your phone banking system. First, a user needs to get general access to the database. To give someone access to an Oracle7 database, an administrator registers the person by creating a new *username* in the database. To maintain database access security, the new username has a corresponding password. A user must give both a username and password to connect to the database. This SQL statement creates a new user:

```
CREATE USER gwashington IDENTIFIED BY P1ew2w
```

As the example demonstrates, administrators should choose meaningful usernames, perhaps the concatenated string of everyone's first initial and last name. Users should choose complicated, meaningless passwords so malicious users cannot easily determine their passwords. For example, don't give George Washington the password "cherrytree" or "president."

After a user gains access to an Oracle7 database, other security controls limit what the user can do inside the database. The next section discusses these controls.

Extending and Restricting Privileges

Once you are in the 24-hour phone system for your bank, you can do only a limited number of things. For example, you can request the balance of your checking and savings accounts, but you can't get the balance of other users' accounts. You are privileged to look at the information regarding your accounts only.

Again, Oracle7's security system is very much like the phone banking system. The administrator can control all database operations and data access—among them, which users can create tables and views, which users can create and modify tablespaces, and which users can read and modify the various tables and views in the database. Administrators do this by granting and revoking different *privileges*, or rights of access. Here are examples of the SQL GRANT and REVOKE commands:

```
GRANT CREATE SESSION, CREATE TABLE TO gwashington
```

```
REVOKE CREATE TABLE FROM alincoln
```

The GRANT statement gives the user GWASHINGTON the privilege to connect to the database (that is, start a database session) and create tables. The REVOKE statement takes away ALINCOLN's ability to create tables.

Oracle7 has two broad classifications of privileges, which we'll learn about in the next two sections: system privileges and object privileges.

System Privileges: Controlling Powerful System Operations

A *system privilege* is a broad, powerful privilege that gives a user the right to perform an operation on a database-wide basis. For example:

- A user with the ALTER DATABASE system privilege can alter the physical structure of the database by adding new files to it.
- A user with the DROP TABLESPACE system privilege can drop any tablespace in the database (not including the SYSTEM tablespace).
- A user with the SELECT ANY TABLE system privilege can query any table in the database.

These are just a few of the many Oracle7 system privileges. Chapter 9 further discusses system privileges, and Appendix A has a complete list of them.

Because system privileges are very powerful, administrators should consider granting system privileges to other administrators and application developers only.

Database Object Privileges: Controlling Access to Data

A *database object privilege* controls a database operation on a specific database object. (An *object* is something inside a database, such as a table, view, role, procedure, or user.) For example, an administrator can control who can query the CUSTOMER table by granting only specific users the SELECT privilege for the CUSTOMER table. Similarly, there is an INSERT, UPDATE, and DELETE object privilege for each table, just to mention a few. (See Chapter 19 for a complete list of the object privileges available for each type of database object.) The important thing to remember is that database object privileges give the administrator the ability to precisely control data access within a database.

Using Roles to Manage Security

Managing the job of database security in a large client/server database is a challenge, to say the least. The many users and applications in the system are all going to require specific sets of privileges to do their jobs. Without some type of administrative tool, security management can become a nightmare.

Fortunately, Oracle7 has just the answer for privilege management in a large, complicated client/server system. A *role* is a collection of related privileges that an administrator can grant collectively to database users and other roles. For example, let's say that there is an accounting application, and the 100 users of the accounting application will need the privileges to query and modify the data in the ACCOUNTSRECEIVABLE and ACCOUNTSPAYABLE tables. Without roles, the administrator would have to grant four object privileges (SELECT, INSERT, UPDATE, and DELETE) on two tables to 100 users. That's up to 800 individual grants:

$$4 \times 2 \times 100 = 800$$

(You could make it two very large GRANT statements because you can grant multiple object privileges for a single object to multiple users in the same GRANT statement. However, these would be huge GRANT statements!)

With roles, an administrator can dramatically simplify privilege management. For example, these statements show how to manage the security for the accounting application using a role:

```
CREATE ROLE accounting

GRANT SELECT, INSERT, UPDATE, DELETE
  ON accountspayable
  TO accounting
GRANT SELECT, INSERT, UPDATE, DELETE
  ON accountsreceivable
  TO accounting

GRANT accounting TO user1, user2, user3 ...
```

When your company hires a new accounting clerk, just grant the new person the accounting role. If the privileges for the accounting application change, just modify the privilege set of the role. All users who have the role automatically see the changes in the role's privilege set. These are just a few examples of how roles can simplify privilege management in a large client/server database system.

Simplified privilege management is not the only benefit of using roles. Perhaps even more significant, developers can use roles to dynamically change the *privilege domain* (the current privilege set) of users as they use different applications. An application can ensure that all of its users have the correct privilege domain when using the application simply by enabling the appropriate role at application startup:

```
SET ROLE accounting
```

The accounting application includes this SET ROLE statement. When a user starts the accounting application, it enables the ACCOUNTING role and disables all other roles granted to the user. This way, the user has all the privileges needed to work with the ACCOUNTSRECEIVABLE and ACCOUNTSPAYABLE tables but can't use privileges that aren't intended for use with the accounting application.

To learn more about system and application security issues, see Chapters 9 and 19.

Understanding Schemas in Oracle7

When working with Oracle7, you'll often come across the term "schema." This word has a very distinct meaning. Just as administrators can physically organize the tables in an Oracle7 database using tablespaces, they can logically organize tables and views in a relational database using schemas. A *schema* is a logical collection of related tables and views (as well as other database objects, as we'll see later in the book). For example, when adding a new application to a client/server database system, the administrator should create a new schema to organize the tables and views that the application will use. Figure 2.9 shows the schema for a sales application.

Oracle7 doesn't really have a true implementation of database schemas. With Oracle7, an administrator creates a new database user, which effectively creates a default database schema for the user. When a database user creates a new table or view, by default the object becomes part of the user's schema. In fact, with Oracle7 schemas you can say that a user *owns* all the objects in his or her default schema.

FIGURE 2.9:

Related collections of objects can be logically organized into schemas within an Oracle7 database.

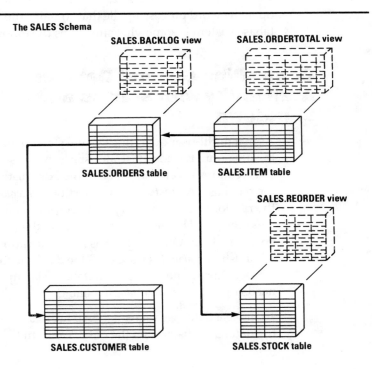

The SALES Schema

SALES.BACKLOG view

SALES.ORDERTOTAL view

SALES.ORDERS table

SALES.ITEM table

SALES.REORDER view

SALES.CUSTOMER table

SALES.STOCK table

Relational database systems with a more advanced schema implementation would allow users to switch their default schema among the different schemas in a database and perform various operations that correspond to their current schema. Perhaps future versions of Oracle will allow such features.

Data Availability: Making Sure Data Is Available When Users Need It

With any computer program, a user cannot access a file unless the user starts an instance of the application and then opens the file. For example, to open a report created with a word processor, a user first has to start the word processor and then open the word processing file that contains the report. Working with an Oracle7 database system is somewhat similar, as the following sections explain.

Controlling General Database Availability with Startup and Shutdown

As in a multi-user operating system startup, in an Oracle7 database no one can use the data until the administrator starts up the server to make the database available. This requires several steps. First, the administrator needs to start up an instance of the database. An *instance* is a collection of *memory buffers* (temporary data caches in the random access memory of a computer) and *operating system processes* (tasks or jobs scheduled by the operating system) that work together to provide multiple users access to an Oracle7 database. After an administrator starts a new instance, the administrator *mounts* (associates) the database to the instance and then opens the database. During the phases of database startup, Oracle7 opens the different files it needs to make the database available.

To make a database unavailable to normal database users, an administrator closes the database, dismounts the database from the instance, and then shuts down the instance. During database shutdown, Oracle7 closes the operating system files that make up the database. Figure 2.10 illustrates the cycle of database availability.

Once an administrator starts a database instance and opens the database, privileged users can connect to the database instance and create a new *session.* You can think of a database session as the time that elapses between a user's connecting to and disconnecting from a database instance. A session in a database is just like a session at a doctor's office—when you enter the office the session begins, and when you leave the office the session ends.

Parameter Files and Instance Startup

Each time an administrator starts a new instance, Oracle7 reads an initialization parameter file to configure the new instance. For example, an administrator can set different parameters to control the size of an instance's various memory buffers.

FIGURE 2.10:
An Oracle7 database server undergoes database startup to make the system available for use and database shutdown to take the system offline.

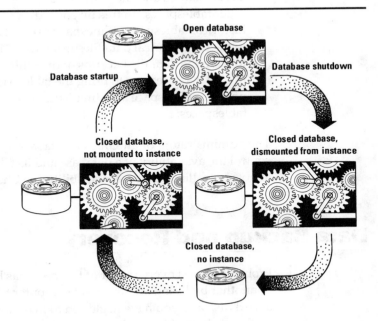

Controlling Partial Database Availability with Online and Offline Tablespaces

An administrator can also control the availability of the data in an open database on a tablespace-by-tablespace basis. If a tablespace is *online*, privileged users can query and modify the tables in the tablespace. However, if a tablespace is *offline*, no one can use the data in the tablespace.

Oracle7's tablespace availability feature can be quite useful for many administrative operations.

- If all of an application's tables are in a tablespace, an administrator can effectively take down the application by taking the application's tablespace offline.

- Suppose a tablespace contains historical data that is useful only in very rare circumstances and the administrator needs extra disk space to store data for other tablespaces. To free up some disk space, the administrator can take the historical tablespace offline, back up the tablespace's data files, and then remove the historical data files from disk. The administrator must make sure to store the data file backups of the offline historical tablespace in a safe place in case it's necessary to bring the tablespace back online. Meanwhile, there is now free disk space an administrator can use to store information for other tablespaces.

The administrators of an Oracle7 database system should be the only users who control the availability of a database and its tablespaces. For complete information about controlling database availability, see Chapter 7.

Data Backup and Recovery

Probably almost every reader of this book has lost some data and work at one time or another by losing an important computer file. If your boss accidentally formats a hard disk and you have neglected to make a backup copy of an important report on that disk, you've lost that report, along with the hard work it took to produce it. And in this case, the fault is as much yours as your boss's.

Accidents and problems are inevitable, so an administrator needs to prepare to be able to recover from them. The next few sections introduce the different protective mechanisms built into the Oracle7 database server.

Protecting Transaction Work: The Transaction Log

The flight log of a commercial airliner records what goes on in the cockpit during a flight. An almost indestructible box houses the flight log recorder to protect the log if the airplane crashes. After a crash, investigators can use the flight log to reconstruct the incidents leading up to the crash and discover what went wrong.

Oracle7 keeps a log, similar to a flight log, of the changes that occur in a database. Each time a user issues a SQL statement that makes a change to the database, Oracle7 records the change in its *transaction log* (also called the *redo log*). When a user commits a transaction, Oracle7 immediately writes a record to the log stating that the transaction and its changes are now permanent.

Oracle7 uses the transaction log to recover from different failures that might occur. For example, if a power failure suddenly crashes the current database instance, there might be some committed data that Oracle7 hasn't yet written to the data files. Not to worry. During the next instance startup, Oracle7 automatically performs crash recovery to recover the database as it was just after the very last transaction that committed before the power failure. Oracle7 applies the committed changes in the transaction log to the data files to reconstruct the lost transactions.

The section "Database Backups" a little later in this chapter describes how Oracle7 uses the transaction log along with data file backups and rollback segments to recover from more serious problems like disk crashes. However, first let's learn a little about the transaction log.

Structure of the Transaction Log

A database's transaction log contains two or more *groups* of fixed-size *log files*, or *members*, that Oracle7 uses to physically record changes to the database. Figure 2.11 illustrates the physical structure of a typical database's transaction log.

FIGURE 2.11:

A database's transaction log contains two or more log groups, and each group contains one or more members (files) that are exactly the same but are stored on different disks.

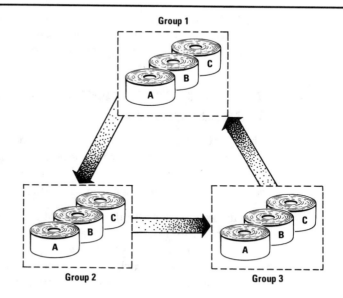

A transaction log has one or more groups. After transactions fill up the log space in one group, Oracle7 switches to the next available group to continue logging ongoing changes to the database. Meanwhile, Oracle7 automatically *archives* (backs up) the filled group in parallel (at the same time), without interfering with ongoing transaction logging. As Oracle7 switches groups to continue logging, it increments the database's *log sequence number* to keep track of current and archived log groups. After Oracle7 backs up a filled log group, the group will be available the next time Oracle7 needs a group to log ongoing transactions. The cyclical reuse of the log groups allows Oracle7 to continually log transactions using a very small, fixed amount of disk space. And the archiving of filled log groups builds a permanent, offline, sequential transaction log for the database.

Because it is a vital component in the Oracle7 database recovery mechanism, the transaction log itself has protective features. To protect against a single point of failure like a disk crash, an administrator can *mirror* a database's log groups. An administrator mirrors a log group by creating the group with multiple members, physically placing the members on different disks. As Oracle7 logs transactions to a mirrored group, it writes the changes in parallel to all members of the group. If a disk crashes, the group member on the damaged disk becomes unavailable. However, this won't stop Oracle7; it can continue logging changes to the other, intact, members of the current log group.

Database Backups

For serious problems like a disk crash or an accidental file drop or disk format, an administrator needs more than just the transaction log to recover an Oracle7 database. An administrator needs physical backups of all the files that make up the database.

Data File Backups

The data files of an Oracle7 database hold all the table data for that database. As users modify the data in tables or add new objects to the database, Oracle7 updates the data files to record the changes. An administrator will want to back up data files on a regular basis to make sure there are always relatively fresh data file backups.

Oracle7 gives an administrator several options to back up a database's data files. The simplest option is to back up all the data files after closing a database. However, many systems need continuous availability and can't afford to shut down the database to perform regular backups. For such high-availability systems, Oracle7's online tablespace backup feature permits the backup of data files while the system is online and in use.

Transaction Log Backups

As the previous section mentions, an administrator can configure Oracle7 to automatically archive or back up transaction log groups as they fill.

Other File Backups

Besides data files and log files, there should always be a copy of the parameter files for a database. Another file you will want to back up is the database's *control file*. This is a very small file that Oracle7 uses to keep track of the physical structure of the database, storing the names of all data and log files of the database and the current log sequence of the transaction log. Oracle7 uses the control file during database startup to identify the database's data and log files and during recovery operations to guide the application of the transaction log groups. Much as with log groups, Oracle7 allows an administrator to configure a database to mirror the control file to protect against single points of failure. However, an administrator will also want to make a backup of a database's control file every time there is a change to the database's physical structure (such as adding a new data or log file) just in case a catastrophe damages all copies of the control file.

Recovering from Disk Failures

With luck, no one will format a hard disk by accident or damage the disk, causing an Oracle7 database to be damaged. But just in case trouble does strike, an administrator can recover an Oracle7 database without losing any work at all. Here's how it's done:

1. The administrator fixes the hardware problem, if necessary. This might mean replacing a damaged disk with a new one.

2. The administrator restores any damaged data files with the most current backup copies and restores archived transaction log groups to any available disk, if necessary.

3. The administrator starts the recovery process, which includes roll forward and rollback recovery. *Roll forward recovery* is the application of the necessary transaction log groups to the backup copies of the damaged data files. *Rollback recovery* is the rolling back of any uncommitted transactions that are left after roll forward recovery.

Figure 2.12 illustrates these steps.

Once the administrator finishes the recovery process, Oracle7 leaves the database in a transaction-consistent state, as it once appeared just after the last committed transaction, right before the disk was damaged.

If you want to learn more about Oracle7's backup and recovery features, see Chapter 11.

FIGURE 2.12:
Oracle7 database recovery is the process of restoring a damaged data file and then applying information in the transaction log to redo lost work.

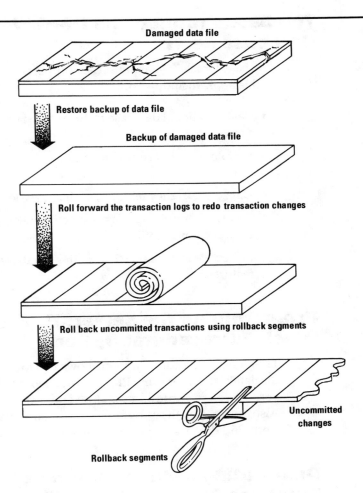

The Oracle7 Product Options

The Oracle7 relational database management system ships as a base product that comes with several options to enhance the functionality of the base database server. The following sections briefly explain the features in the base Oracle7 database server and each of the available options.

The Base Product: The Oracle7 Database Server

The base Oracle7 database server supports most of the features you'll read about in this book, including

- Basic relational database features, like SQL, tables, integrity constraints, and views

- Supplemental performance features, such as sequences, indexes, and hash data clusters

- Data concurrency features, such as row-level locking and multi-versioning

- Security controls, such as system privileges, object privileges, roles, and resource limit profiles

- Protective features, such as online database backups and database recovery features.

Programming the Server: The Oracle7 Procedural Option

The Oracle7 Procedural option allows you to store blocks of application logic inside the database server using PL/SQL extensions to Oracle SQL. The Procedural option permits you to create and use stored procedures, functions, packages, and triggers. Also, several of the programmer and administration utilities, such as database alerts and database pipes, require the Procedural option.

Distributing Data on Different Database Servers: The Oracle7 Distributed Database Option

The Oracle7 Distributed Database option supports distributed database functionality. A *distributed database* is a collection of related but physically independent databases.

To give you a better idea of what a distributed database is, let's take another look at our paper database example, the file cabinet. First, assume that a small, one-office company uses a single set of file cabinets to track its information. If an employee needs some information, there's no problem because the information is right there at the company's office. Now consider a larger company with branch offices. Each branch office has its own set of file cabinets to keep track of information specific to the branch office. Therefore, as a whole, the large company's database is distributed among the file cabinets in the branch offices. When you need information stored in a file at another branch office, you must somehow get a copy of that file.

Large companies that use computer databases experience the same problem. For example, each department in a company might have its own Oracle7 database to manage information that is relevant to its work. But an employee in one department might occasionally need some information in another department's database.

Oracle7 supports such distributed databases with the Oracle7 Distributed Database option. If the different databases are on different computers, you must connect the database servers using a network. With the Distributed Database option, you can access and change the information in any Oracle7 database, including the data your local database server manages and the data remote database servers manage. Figure 2.13 shows an Oracle7 distributed database.

The features of the Oracle7 Distributed Database option address the needs of a somewhat select audience—those who need to link disparate Oracle7 databases. Since distributed database technology is an advanced topic and it is not the focus of this book, the book does not spend much time discussing distributed databases and the features available using the Oracle7 Distributed Database option.

Providing Parallel Access to an Oracle7 Database: The Oracle7 Parallel Server Option

In a typical Oracle7 database server configuration, a single Oracle7 database server or instance accesses a single database. Users connect to the database server to perform any work with the Oracle7 database. With the Oracle7 Parallel Server option, more than one instance can access a single database in parallel (at the same time). This makes multiple access points available to a single Oracle7 database.

What are the benefits of using the Oracle7 Parallel Server option? One advantage is availability. If one instance of the database crashes unexpectedly because of a

FIGURE 2.13:

A distributed database is two or more physically disparate databases that logically make up one database. Users of any server can access information throughout the distributed database.

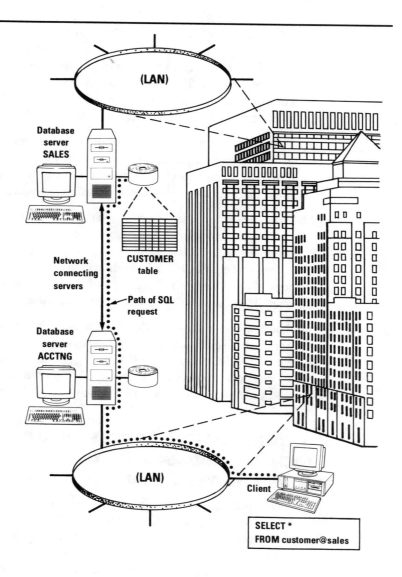

software or memory failure, other instances are available to provide access to the Oracle7 database. If an administrator correctly configures an Oracle7 Parallel Server system and applications, another possible benefit is increased performance.

You can't take advantage of the Oracle7 Parallel Server option unless the system you use (or plan to use) to run Oracle7 is a loosely coupled *multiprocessor computer*— one that has multiple processors to perform work. A *loosely coupled computer system* is a type of multiprocessor computer that gives each processor its own private area of memory but allows all processors to share files on all disks. In terms of the Oracle7 Parallel Server option, the memory used by each Oracle7 instance is private to a specific processor, while all instances can share a single database—that is, the files that make up the database on disk.

As with the Distributed Database option, the features of the Parallel Server option pertain to a select audience seeking its specific features for loosely coupled hardware systems.

The Ultimate Data Security Fortress: Trusted Oracle7

Many users require more security features than those present in the base version of Oracle7. Some organizations require access controls based on the sensitivity or classification of data. For example, government agencies often classify information in levels such as "top secret." To satisfy particular security requirements of a select group of users, Oracle offers a special release of Oracle7 called Trusted Oracle7.

Parallelizing Database Operations for Speedup: The Oracle7 Parallel Query Option

Oracle7 release 7.1 offers the Oracle7 Parallel Query option. This option allows Oracle7 to take full advantage of all types of multiprocessor computer systems to dramatically increase the performance of many types of database operations. Here's how it works.

Without the Parallel Query option, Oracle7 uses a single processor to perform all steps necessary to complete a database operation, such as a query or a database recovery operation. If a database operation is complicated or touches large amounts of data, completion time can be long; Oracle7 is limited by the speed with which a single processor can accomplish work. With the Parallel Query operation, Oracle7 automatically breaks down complicated database operations into smaller subtasks that it then hands off to multiple processors, which complete each task in parallel. Because Oracle7 uses multiple processors to reduce the overall time needed to process individual database requests, application performance is dramatically improved, especially for complicated operations or those operations that touch large amounts of data.

The Oracle Parallel Query option is available for all types of multiprocessor computer systems, so many users can gain significant benefits from using this option. Appendix B focuses on configuring and using the Oracle7 Parallel Query option.

Database Administrators

At this point, you can see that Oracle7 is a very powerful and complex database management system. That's why there needs to be a *database administrator,* someone responsible for managing an Oracle7 client/server database system. The administrator of a client/server database system can be responsible for some or all of the following jobs:

- Planning the database and making sure the database server has enough memory and disk storage to accommodate the proposed system
- Configuring or aiding in the configuration of the computer network
- Installing Oracle7 and other software on the database server
- Creating Oracle7 databases
- Managing the space requirements for a database
- Working with application developers to create database objects such as tables and views
- Creating new users and privilege management

- Backing up all databases on a regular basis and performing recovery operations when necessary

- Controlling access to the database using operating system, network operating system, and Oracle7 security features

- Monitoring and tuning Oracle7 databases

There may be other jobs the administrator can handle as well.

In large systems, administration is typically split among a team of administrators. For example, one administrator might be responsible only for the operating system, another for the network, another for database backups, and still another for system security.

For More Information about Database Administration...

Administrators of Oracle7 need to concentrate on managing the database server. Part II of this book describes all facets of the tasks necessary to manage an Oracle7 client/server database system.

Part of the job of database administration is daily interaction with application developers and end users. Therefore, in addition to knowing Oracle7 thoroughly, an administrator needs a good understanding of other users' requirements. Part III of this book describes many different topics regarding client application development.

This chapter has provided an introduction to many of the important concepts of a relational database management system and the components of the Oracle7 relational database server, including

- How users interact with an Oracle7 database using SQL and transactions

- What tables are (the primary storage structures in a database) and what the Oracle7 column datatypes are

- How to physically organize Oracle7 table data using tablespaces and data files

- How to use views to present table data with a different look and increase security

- How to ensure complete data integrity inside an Oracle7 database using integrity constraints, stored procedures, and database triggers

- How the Oracle7 server automatically delivers a high level of data concurrency within a multi-user database system using row-level locking and multi-versioning mechanisms

- How to manage database security using usernames, passwords, privileges, and roles

- How to control the availability of an Oracle7 database using startup and shutdown procedures as well as online and offline tablespaces

- How to protect all the work and data in an Oracle7 database with the transaction log, database backups, and database recovery

- What an Oracle7 distributed database is

- Who an Oracle7 database administrator is and what that person does

Now that we know a little about the "server" in client/server, let's learn more about the "client."

CHAPTER

THREE

The Client in Client/Server

- Different categories of client applications

- Client applications in the Oracle Cooperative Development Environment (CDE)

- Client application user interfaces

- Who develops client applications

- Who uses client applications

A database server is just one part of the picture in a client/server system. Another significant component is the clients—the applications that interface with the database server to input, modify, and retrieve database data. This chapter provides a broad introduction to the issues that surround the clients in a client/server system.

Your Window to Database Access: Client Applications

A client application is the front-end component of a database system that users work with to input, retrieve, and analyze business data. Client applications come in all shapes and sizes. For example, the primary client application in a sales department would be an order entry application that sales people use to record customer orders. In the product warehouse, the primary work tool would be an inventory management and tracking application. In short, whatever data a workgroup must track, there is usually a client application to suit the job at hand.

Chapter 2 showed how a back-end database server focuses on managing a database and the data requests of many front-end client applications. A client application uses SQL statements to send information to and request information from the database server (usually across a network). It is the job of the client to present or analyze information. A client application includes no data management component; the database server is responsible for such operations.

The division of responsibilities between client and server is what makes a client/server system so effective. For example, a company's order entry application and inventory application both need to work with the same set of product inventory data. Instead of requiring each application to have its own database manager and database of inventory information, they both work with a single database server—such as Oracle7—to manage a single inventory database. Custom application development is straightforward and productive because the most complicated part of the system—a multi-user database management system—is a predeveloped software package that someone can install right out of a box.

Because client applications are the front ends to a database system, all types of users must use client database applications to get work done. Administrators use utilities to manage a database server, end users run applications to get work done, and developers make custom client database applications. The two types of users most involved with client applications are developers and end users. Look for the sections later in this chapter that discuss more about these two types of application users.

There are many categories of client applications for a database system. For example, end users run form applications for data entry and reporting applications for generating database reports. The next few sections describe forms, reporting, and other types of client applications. You'll also find an overview of *Oracle's Cooperative Development Environment* (*CDE*), a set of integrated tools you can use in an Oracle7 client/server system.

Data Entry and Online Transaction Processing Using Form Applications

Forms are all around us—forms to order a product, forms to apply for a loan, forms to pay taxes, even forms to get more forms. When you fill out the fields of a paper form, you are entering data that eventually ends up in some sort of database.

In a computer database system, users can use a *form application* to enter, view, and print reports of database data. Figure 3.1 is an example of a form in which an end user enters customer orders.

A form application in a computer system is relatively simple to learn and use because, for the most part, it appears on a computer screen the same way it would on a piece of paper. However, form applications have several important advantages over standard paper forms. Aside from the advantages of using a computer database, form applications are vastly more versatile and powerful than paper forms.

- A form can read a database server's data dictionary to learn about data integrity rules. As a user enters data in the fields of a form, the application automatically validates data according to the integrity rules.

- An entry field in a form can present a list of valid values from which users can pick to fill out the field easily.

- An area on a form can display a picture that is associated with the current record(s) displayed on the form.

FIGURE 3.1:

Form applications, such as this order entry application, permit users to input and display using a database system.

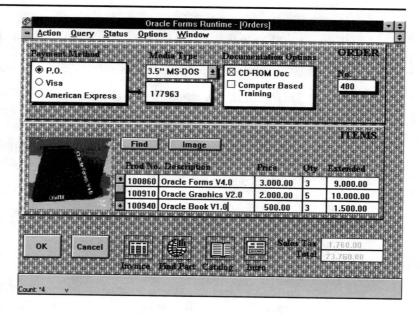

- A button on the form can play a sound file that is associated with the current record(s) displayed on the form.

- A form can display context-sensitive instructions, reducing training time.

- A form can adjust its input fields based on data the user enters.

Form applications are often *online transaction processing* (OLTP) applications. OLTP applications are characterized by short, simple transactions to input or update data in a database. A bank's automated teller machine is a perfect example of an OLTP form application. Thousands of ATM users can simultaneously withdraw money from bank accounts. Each user simply enters an identification number and a withdrawal amount. The ATM application then sends data manipulation requests to a database server to update the account balance and record the user's transaction in two very simple operations.

Oracle Forms and Oracle Card are tools you can use to create and run form applications in an Oracle7 client/server database system.

Oracle Forms

Oracle Forms is an Oracle tool that both end users and application developers use for form applications. A developer uses the Oracle Forms development system to create visually appealing client data entry applications that can integrate text and graphics and deliver high-transaction throughput in a demanding OLTP environment. Using Oracle Forms on a client workstation, an end user can run a form application for data entry and on-screen reporting with an Oracle7 database. Figure 3.1 shows an Oracle Forms application. Chapter 14 introduces you to developing and using form applications using Oracle Forms.

Oracle Card

Oracle Card is a graphical application generator for simple applications. You use Oracle Card's tools and easy-to-use scripting language to create simple or throwaway applications for small numbers of users in an Oracle7 system.

Support for Analysis and Decision Making Using Query Tools and Reporting Applications

Analyzing and presenting data is just as important as entering and storing it. Computer systems use reporting, query, and decision-support applications to retrieve database data and present it in a way that provides useful information, drives decision making, and supports business projects. For example, monthly account statements help bank customers balance their checkbooks; quarterly sales and financial reports of publicly owned businesses drive the stock markets of the world; and mailing labels make it easy for a company to conduct a direct-mail advertising campaign.

Different reporting applications present data in different ways. Custom text reports with a multiple-column listing of some records in a database table are probably the most common type of report. For example, printed bank statements typically have columns that list the date, description, amount, and resulting account balance corresponding to monthly bank transactions. To generate a bank statement for a customer, a reporting application pulls a customer's transaction records from a database and then calculates a running account balance for each new transaction. Other types of text reports list only a single table record per printed page. For example, a mailing label is a record of a person's name, company, address, city, state, and zip code.

Graphical reports are another type of report. In many cases, graphs and charts present database data more effectively than text. For example, a company's financial report might include a pie chart to indicate graphically the percentage of total revenues in different countries. A bar or line graph can better show trends in sales revenues, profits, and expenses from quarter to quarter.

In many cases, reports may not show the exact piece of information that someone needs to help make an important decision—no compiled reporting application can anticipate every possible question you might want to ask a database server. In these cases, query reporting tools come in handy. For example, a giant corporation may have to make a sudden decision to renew the contract of its advertising firm and the CEO says, "I need sales trend information regarding the new series of commercials that our company has been printing in the trade rags. And I need the report in five minutes." There's no time to make a fancy report. But by using a query tool to issue an ad hoc query, the person under the gun can get the information quickly and help the CEO make the correct decision.

The next sections give an overview of the query and reporting tools available in Oracle's CDE: Oracle Reports, Oracle Graphics, SQL*Plus, and Oracle Data Browser.

Oracle Reports

Oracle Reports is a tool that both application developers and end users can use for reporting applications. Like Oracle Forms, a developer uses the complete Oracle Reports development system to design custom reports of data in an Oracle7 database. An end user uses a runtime version of Oracle Reports and a pre-built report application to actually generate and print out reports. Figure 3.2 shows an Oracle Reports application.

FIGURE 3.2:

Example Oracle Reports application

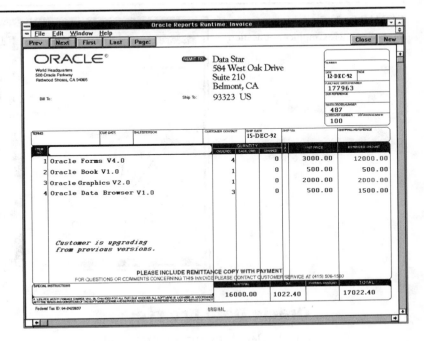

Oracle Graphics

Oracle Graphics is a tool developers and end users use for visual reporting applications. Developers can use Oracle Graphics to design graphical reports that present Oracle7 database information using text, charts, drawings, and images. End users can then use Oracle Graphics applications to make intelligent decisions using database data. Figure 3.3 shows an Oracle Graphics application.

SQL*Plus SQL*Plus is an interactive query tool. Using SQL*Plus, you can issue ad hoc queries and other SQL statements to a database as you think of them. SQL*Plus has a very simple command-line interface. At the command prompt, you can type a SQL or SQL*Plus command and then execute it. Therefore, you must know the syntax of SQL to use SQL*Plus effectively. (See Chapter 5 for a primer on SQL.)

FIGURE 3.3:

Example Oracle Graphics application

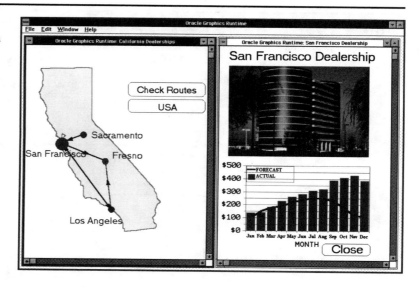

Oracle Data Browser

Oracle Data Browser is a graphical, interactive data access tool. You can use Data Browser's graphical user interface to build and send ad hoc queries to Oracle7 while insulating yourself from the complexity of SQL. Figure 3.4 is an example screen of Oracle Data Browser.

Developing Custom Applications with Application Development Tools

An *application development tool* is an application that developers use to create custom client applications that end users can then use to access a database system. The next section explains the different types of application development tools.

3GL and 4GL Development Tools

Application development tools come in two varieties: 3GLs and 4GLs. A developer can create a client application with procedural programming techniques by using a third-generation language (3GL) development tool along with a third-generation

FIGURE 3.4:

Oracle Data Browser is an ad hoc query tool that uses a graphical user interface to hide the complexity of SQL commands.

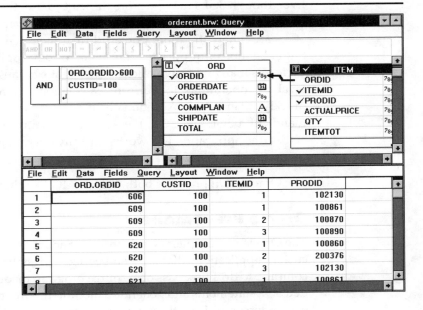

programming language such as C, Ada, or COBOL. To develop a 3GL client database application, the developer programs the source code of the application using the procedural commands of a 3GL compiler along with embedded SQL statements that make calls to a database server. Alternatively, a developer can use a fourth-generation language (4GL) application development tool to develop a client application with nonprocedural programming techniques such as visual form layout and screen painting.

So what are the primary differences between a 3GL and 4GL client application development environment? The first major difference is in ease of use and productivity of application developers. 3GL development environments require the developers to know how to program in a 3GL and to know the functional extensions provided by the 3GL development tool. For example, to display a box on a form, a developer must be able to call library functions inside the form application to make the box appear. On the other hand, 4GLs use nonprocedural techniques to make most areas of application design much easier and more productive. For example, to draw a box on a form, the developer simply needs to know how to use a line-drawing tool in the 4GL application development tool.

Even though 3GLs may be more difficult to use, they do have certain advantages. Because 3GLs like C are flexible and developers can program anything imaginable, 3GLs are inherently more powerful than their 4GL counterparts. For example, C might be more appropriate than a 4GL for developing a scientific application that performs many intensive calculations. That's because developers can use C's low-level bit operations to perform calculations more efficiently (and thus more quickly) than a 4GL. Additionally, if a client application uses the standard commands of a 3GL and SQL, the application source code is automatically portable across (the application will work with) any operating system that supports the programming language.

The Oracle CDE provides both 3GL and 4GL application development tools.

Oracle Precompilers

The Oracle precompilers work with a standard 3GL language compiler to develop custom applications that have embedded SQL statements. A developer uses a precompiler to do a first pass on a source program to identify and translate all embedded SQL statements and generate a modified source program that the 3GL compiler can understand. Then the developer uses a standard language compiler to compile and link the program to its finished and executable form. To aid in the development of portable client database applications, each Oracle precompiler includes a flagger to detect and mark source code statements that do not conform to ANSI-standard SQL syntax.

Oracle Call Interfaces (OCIs)

The Oracle Call Interfaces (OCI) also let you use a 3GL language and embedded SQL statements to create custom applications that access data in an Oracle7 database. However, the OCIs also provide low-level, proprietary procedure and function calls that can give you more power and flexibility than the precompilers when developing Oracle7 applications. For example, an OCI program can control the actual steps of SQL statement processing (parse, bind, execute, rebind, reexecute, and so on) to achieve absolute optimal application performance and minimal network traffic between the client application and the database server.

Oracle 4GL Application Development Tools

Oracle Forms, Oracle Card, Oracle Reports, and Oracle Graphics are all examples of 4GL application development tools in Oracle's CDE tool set. As explained earlier in this chapter, developers use these 4GL tools to develop custom forms or reporting applications that allow end users to enter and access data in an Oracle7 client/server database system.

Computer-Aided Systems Engineering (CASE) Tools

As you might have already gathered from this book, a business's computer database and application system is a very complex thing to plan, develop, validate, and manage. Computer-aided systems engineering (CASE) tools can dramatically simplify all stages of the business system life cycle, including system analysis, design, implementation, and maintenance.

CASE tools are based upon many different modeling techniques that make it easy to develop a business's computer system. Using different diagrammers that work in a graphical user interface, CASE tools usually allow you to model the different processes and data that make up the system. For example, Figure 3.5 shows the Entity Relationship Diagrammer of Oracle's CASE*Designer.

FIGURE 3.5:
Entity Relationship Diagrammer of Oracle CASE*Designer

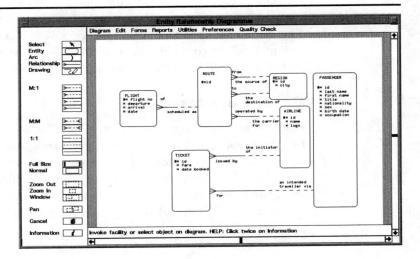

To keep track of the data they generate, CASE tools have a special component called a repository. A *repository* is a dictionary of *metadata*—information about the processes, data, and relationships in a business system. A repository is the fundamental component of a CASE tool set because it provides the information necessary to automatically create the system's underlying database and generate front-end client applications.

The following sections explain the functions of the different Oracle CASE tools and how they work together, including CASE*Designer, CASE*Dictionary, CASE*Generator, and CASE*Exchange.

CASE*Dictionary

CASE*Dictionary is the central product in the Oracle CASE tool set because it manages the repository of information that the other CASE tools create and use. System developers can use CASE*Dictionary's form-based user interface to create, modify, and document all stages of system development. CASE*Dictionary also includes the critical features necessary to manage complicated system development in large workgroups, such as user access and system version control.

CASE*Designer

CASE*Designer is the graphical modeling tool that system developers use to design the processes and data of a business system. For example, Figure 3.5 shows the Entity Relationship Diagrammer of CASE*Designer that developers use to model the data (tables and relationships) that a system will require. CASE*Designer also has other diagrammers that permit the modeling of the business processes and data flow in the system. As developers work with CASE*Designer, CASE*Dictionary automatically records all information so that system development information is stored in the central system repository.

CASE*Generator

Once the system design is complete, CASE*Generator is the product that makes the design into a real system. Using system design information stored in CASE*Dictionary, CASE*Generator can automatically generate the system's back-end database and front-end form and reporting applications. Consequently, system implementation time is dramatically reduced because developers avoid lots of programming with 3GL and 4GL application development tools.

CASE*Exchange

CASE*Exchange allows third-party CASE tools to work in an Oracle CASE development environment. With CASE*Exchange, Oracle CASE tools can use the models from non-Oracle CASE tools, and third-party tools can access the data models in CASE*Dictionary.

Managing Databases Using Administrative Utilities

An *administrative utility* is an application a database administrator uses to manage a database system. Oracle Corporation ships a number of utilities with the Oracle7 database server, including SQL*DBA, SQL*Loader, Import, and Export.

SQL*DBA

SQL*DBA is the Oracle7 utility administrators use for most administrative operations. Figure 3.6 is an example screen of SQL*DBA.

SQL*DBA has a graphical user interface to make database administration somewhat intuitive. (It's still a very complex job.) Among many operations, administrators can use SQL*DBA to start up and shut down databases and to create, modify,

FIGURE 3.6:

Using SQL*DBA, Oracle administrators can easily perform all basic administrative operations, such as database startup and shutdown, tablespace management, transaction log configuration, and system security.

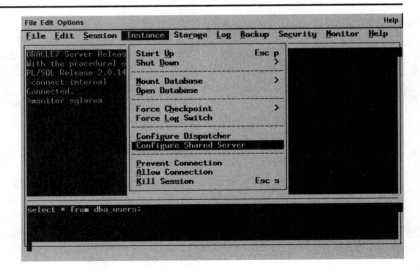

and drop tablespaces, rollback segments, users, and roles. SQL*DBA also has an interactive query window so administrators can issue ad hoc queries. Integrated into SQL*DBA are a number of *monitors* that let the administrator look at database performance and system usage statistics. Figure 3.7 is an example screen of a SQL*DBA monitor.

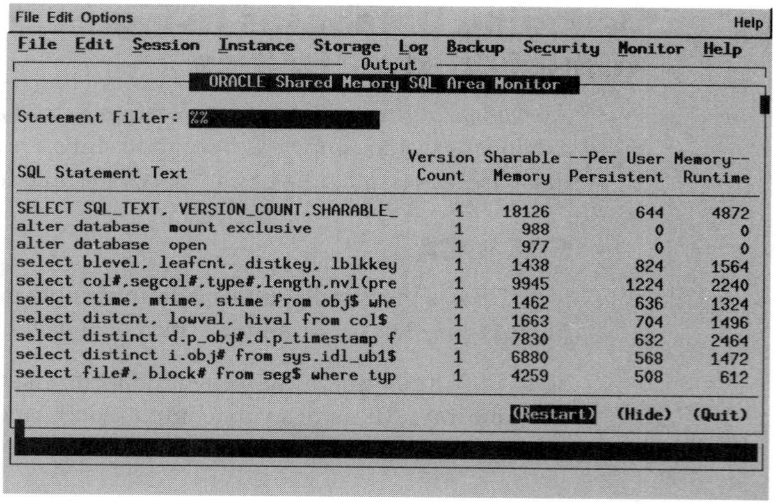

FIGURE 3.7:

The SQL*DBA monitors let Oracle administrators take a look at real-time database server status.

SQL*Loader
=========

SQL*Loader

SQL*Loader is a utility that administrators use to load data from external files into tables in an Oracle7 database. For example, SQL*Loader can load data from an ASCII fixed-format or delimited file into an Oracle7 table.

Utilities for Importing and Exporting Data

Administrators use Oracle's Import and Export utilities to move data into and out of Oracle7 databases not connected by a network. Export writes data from an Oracle7 database to operating system files. Import reads the data from Export files back into an Oracle7 database. The Export utility is also useful to create supplemental database backups for added recovery flexibility.

To learn more about the utilities discussed in the previous sections, see Part II of this book—it discusses many of the different operations performed by a database administrator using the Oracle7 utilities, especially SQL*DBA and SQL*Loader.

Vertical Client Applications

Vertical client applications are pre-built applications that work right out of the box. Oracle Corporation offers many vertical client applications for different tasks. For example, Oracle offers these tools in the area of financial and human resources applications:

- Oracle General Ledger
- Oracle Order Entry
- Oracle Inventory
- Oracle Personnel
- Oracle Payables
- Oracle Receivables
- Oracle Purchasing
- Oracle Assets
- Oracle Alert

Oracle also offers the following vertical applications in the area of manufacturing:

- Oracle Work in Process
- Oracle Bills of Material
- Oracle Engineering
- Oracle Master Scheduling/MRP
- Oracle Capacity

Third-Party Application Development Tools, CASE Tools, and Utilities

Oracle7 has an "open" architecture, which means that other companies can create development tools, utilities, and applications for Oracle7. Third-party companies offer all types of client applications that work in an Oracle7 client/server system. Appendix C provides information about the most important third-party applications that interface with Oracle7.

Client Application User Interfaces

The presentation and interaction method of a client application is perhaps its most important feature—that's what defines the way a user works with the application. The next few paragraphs explain the different types of user interfaces.

Character-Based User Interfaces (CUIs)

Character-based user interfaces (CUIs) use lines of simple alphanumeric characters to present an application to a user. For example, in mainframe and minicomputer environments, typical dumb terminal screen applications use CUIs.

In general, there are several reasons CUIs do not maximize an application user's productivity:

- CUIs are not necessarily easy to use because the interface is made up of screens with nonintuitive text and numbers. Therefore, a user has a significant learning curve with each new application.

- CUIs lack flexibility, forcing an application to be process driven and to rigidly control the flow of the program. For example, an application that uses a CUI might ask a question, wait for a response, ask another question, wait for a response, and so on. It is the program that determines what questions to ask and in which order to ask them.

In many cases, an application uses a CUI that is nothing more than a command-line interface with a prompt that waits for a user to enter a command. For example, operating systems such as MS-DOS, UNIX, and VAX VMS all use command-line interfaces. Figure 3.8 shows Oracle's SQL*Plus as an example of a client database application that uses a command-line interface.

The obvious drawback of an application that uses a simple command-line interface is that it is not very easy to use. The user needs to know the available commands and corresponding syntax (language) rules for a client application that employs a command-line interface. For example, to use SQL*Plus, a user needs to know how to use SQL commands. You'll get an introduction to SQL in Chapter 5.

FIGURE 3.8:

The command-line interface of SQL*Plus requires that users know the syntax of SQL statements.

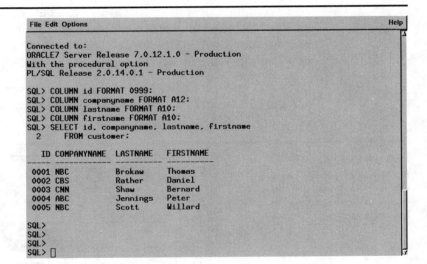

Graphical User Interfaces (GUIs)

Just as computing models have evolved, so have user interfaces. Apple Computer is widely recognized as the first company to offer a commercial *graphical user interface (GUI)*. GUIs make users more productive for several reasons:

- Instead of requiring a user to know application commands, a GUI uses an intuitive, easy-to-use shell with a pointing device (such as a mouse), as well as application windows, menus, dialog boxes, buttons, and so on, that hide the complexity of commands from the user. This enables the user to become more productive.

- GUIs can typically display multiple applications in different windows at the same time. This way, users can see what is happening in one application while working with another, or transfer information between different applications with cut-and-paste operations.

- Well-defined GUIs have specifications with which all applications must conform to make the look and feel of every application consistent. This way, users can easily learn new applications because they recognize certain functions from application to application.

The power and ease-of-use of a graphical user interface is available with almost every computer operating system you can buy. Popular graphical user interfaces include Macintosh on Apple computers, Microsoft Windows on IBM PCs and compatibles, and Motif on UNIX machines. Figure 3.9 shows an example of a graphical user interface—the Motif GUI used in SCO UNIX's Open Desktop (ODT).

Each ODT application has its own window, and every application window has corner and side border handles to size the window, as well as a menu bar across the

FIGURE 3.9:
SCO UNIX's Open Desktop is an example of a powerful graphical user interface that is intuitive to learn and use.

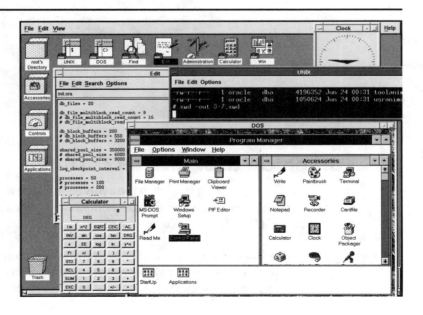

top border. The first items in every application's menu bar are "File" and "Edit," and the last item is "Help." These are all examples of conformance specifications that add to the ease-of-use in a GUI. SCO's ODT is a particularly powerful GUI because it can display another GUI within Motif—Microsoft Windows applications can run in a Motif window at the same time other Motif applications are running.

Many mainframe and minicomputer terminal applications now use pseudo-GUIs for applications, but these GUIs are constrained by the hardware limitations of the terminal. Specifically, the older variety of dumb terminals can display hardware-encoded characters only. More expensive bitmapped display terminals—monitors that can display bitmapped graphics—are much better suited for GUIs because they can display text in several different fonts, line art, and images in a WYSIWYG (what you see is what you get) format. WYSIWYG is obviously a big advantage for applications like desktop publishing and graphic arts that require you to see the layout of printed material as you work with it on a display screen.

Object-Oriented Programming

In most business environments, there is a requirement for several related applications to help run the business. Consequently, programmers have to spend time coding each application to the specifications of different parts of the system. However, while each application may have its own unique, high-level purpose, it is more than likely that individual parts of each application will perform the exact same or similar functions, functions that can be reused so as not to duplicate coding and testing throughout the business's application development process.

To address the opportunities for improving programmer productivity and more, today's programming environments now embrace what is called *object-oriented programming*. To supplement your existing knowledge about the application development process, let's learn a little about the principles of object-oriented programming so you can better understand how it can help you when you create applications for a database system.

Data Abstraction, Classes, and Objects

From what you already know about database systems (tables, rows, columns, datatypes, and so on), it's safe to say that the associated terms and concepts can get rather abstract when compared to everyday business terms. One principle of object-oriented programming is to raise the level of data abstraction so it more closely matches human terminology (for example, business terminology). Data abstraction in an object-oriented system centers around the definition of classes and objects.

A *class* is an abstract datatype that closely matches something in the real world. For example, you might have a class PERSON, which encapsulates common attributes, such as LASTNAME, FIRSTNAME, ADDRESS, and so on. An *object* is a specific instance of a class. For example, just as you would declare a variable of a specific datatype in a traditional programming language, you can declare an object of a specific class in an object-oriented language. BILL and SAMANTHA might be examples of objects of class PERSON.

Methods and Messages

Once you define a class in an object-oriented system, you also have to define the *methods* (functions) that will act upon objects of that class. For example, in a traditional programming language, you can add, subtract, multiply, and divide variables declared using a simple NUMBER datatype. Likewise, for an object-oriented programming system, you might define a method CHANGE_ADDRESS that can act upon objects of class PERSON. When you want to change a person's address, the program sends a *message* (calls a specific method) to the object for the specific person to get the job done.

Inheritance and Class Hierarchy

When you declare classes in an object-oriented system, you can create a *class hierarchy* by declaring classes as subclasses of others. Consequently, a subclass *inherits* the properties of its parent class. For example, the classes EMPLOYEE and CUSTOMER are both subclasses of PERSON. In this case, the EMPLOYEE and CUSTOMER classes are both PERSONs (people) and can inherit the structure of the base

PERSON class (LASTNAME, FIRSTNAME, ADDRESS, and so on), as well as the methods of the base PERSON class (CHANGE_ADDRESS and others).

A powerful characteristic of inheritance in the class hierarchy is that the inheritance only descends down the class tree and cannot ascend up it; this is important because a subclass typically extends the structure and/or functionality of its base class with additional attributes and methods, which would not necessarily have meaning if the class hierarchy allowed inheritance to extend upward. For example, in addition to using the attributes of the base class PERSON, the EMPLOYEE subclass might also have some unique attributes such as SALARY, DEPARTMENT, and so on. Another subclass of PERSON might not necessarily have a use for these attributes that are specific to EMPLOYEE. Additionally, the EMPLOYEE subclass can have some unique methods (CHANGE_SALARY, CHANGE_DEPARTMENT, and so on) of its own that would not make sense for all subclasses of PERSON. A new subclass method can even override the functionality of an inherited base class method of the same name if the need is warranted. In this case, the subclass version of the method affects only the behavior of the subclass, not the base class or any of its other descendants. For example, there may be some special requirement to consider that justifies a special version of the CHANGE_ADDRESS method for objects of class CUSTOMER, but all other subclasses of PERSON can use the standard CHANGE_ADDRESS method.

Other than the obvious benefit of reducing the complexity of class definition and minimizing the number of methods in the system, inheritance can also make the system easier to maintain. For example, if you decide that you need an attribute to record the middle names of all people in the system, you don't have to modify the PERSON class as well as all of its subclasses. Simply add the MIDDLENAME attribute to the PERSON class, and all subclasses including EMPLOYEE and CUSTOMER can automatically inherit the new attribute from the parent.

Polymorphism

As the previous section states, behavioral inheritance allows subclasses in the hierarchy to inherit the methods of their parents. Therefore, an object-oriented system's methods must be *polymorphic*, or act appropriately upon objects that traverse down the target class hierarchy. For example, the CHANGE_ADDRESS method is said to be polymorphic because it performs the correct behavior (changes a person's address) when a program sends a change address message to objects of class PERSON, or any of its subclasses, including EMPLOYEE and CUSTOMER.

How Does Object-Oriented Programming Help Application Development Productivity?

The benefits of object-oriented programming quickly become apparent when a business requires many related application systems. For example, related applications should all have the same look and feel and, in many cases, might overlap in function. Therefore, there are potentially many situations where an object-oriented programming environment can save time for programmers; the generation of windows, dialog boxes, menus, and business functions provides just a few examples of code segments that can all be reused throughout the business's different applications. As a result, all applications have standard appearance and behavior, and the overall amount of code needed to generate the system's applications can be kept to a minimum.

Due to its inheritance qualities, object-oriented programming also reduces the costs associated with application maintenance. For example, if you need to change a standard menu that all applications use, a single code update modifies all applications at once.

Most application development tool vendors have or will have object-oriented programming features in their products to help you be more productive in developing your system. Be sure to look for these features and make good use of them so your application systems are the best they can be, as fast as they can be.

For More Information about Application Development...

If you are a developer, there's a good chance you will not find a pre-built Oracle7 application that does what your business needs to accomplish. In this case, you can use one of the development tools listed in the previous sections to create a custom client application. Your responsibilities will include designing the data structures (such as tables and views) for the application; programming the application using a development tool; coordinating storage, security, and design issues with the database administrator; and tuning the application after implementation. To develop good client applications, you need to take advantage of the features in Oracle7 that are designed specifically for client/server systems. Part II of this book provides a sound overview of Oracle7, and Part III presents the information you need to develop client applications for Oracle7.

For More Information about Using Applications...

If you are an end user, you don't really need to know anything about how Oracle7 manages data, how the network relays data between a client and a server, or how to develop efficient client applications. You need only know how to use an application to get a job done. If the application has a GUI, you probably can use the application with very little instruction. If the application has a command-line interface (such as the one SQL*Plus offers), you must know a language (like SQL) to get work done. Refer to the user documentation for the application you are using or to other commercial books that explain your application.

This chapter has given you the basics of the client portion of a client/server system:

- You use client applications to input, modify, retrieve, or report information that the database server manages.

- Client applications come in all varieties, including form applications for data input, retrieval, and display and reporting applications for textual and graphical reports of database information.

- You can use the different Oracle CDE tools to develop custom client applications, including Oracle Forms, Oracle Reports, Oracle Graphics, and the Oracle CASE tools.

CHAPTER
FOUR

Between Client and Server 1: Networking Issues

- Star, bus, and ring network topologies

- Network configurations—LANs and WANs

- Hardware and software for a networked client/server system

- Middleware, including Oracle's SQL*Net

- Oracle7's distributed processing software architectures

As you learned in the previous chapters, a client/server system is a distributed application processing system where the processing load of a single application is split between a client component and a server component. Implicit in the design of a distributed application processing system is the ability of the client and the server components to communicate with one another so they can work together to perform the overall function of the business application. While communication between clients and servers is an implicit requirement of a distributed application processing system, it is not something you can forget about when you design your client/server system. This chapter examines the critical communication issues for an Oracle7 client/server system, including

- Network hardware, topologies, and communication software
- Middleware, including Oracle's SQL*Net and the standard middleware application programming interface
- Client and server processes in the Oracle7 client/server software architecture

First, let's learn more about the network hardware and software you need for an Oracle7 client/server system.

The Network in a Client/Server System

The client and server components of an Oracle7 client/server database system operate on physically different computers. Because of this, there must be a *network* to connect clients and servers so they can communicate and work together.

If you use a personal computer in a workgroup, chances are your workstation is connected to other computers in a local area network. A *local area network* (*LAN*) is one in which all the computers are close together and physically connected by wiring of some sort. For example, if all of a department's employees work together in the same building, they might use a LAN to connect their personal computers so they can share files and a printer, communicate using an electronic mail system, and have access to a central Oracle7 database server.

LANs can have many different *topologies,* or configurations, themselves. Figure 4.1 shows the star, bus, and ring network topologies.

FIGURE 4.1:

Different types of LAN topologies, including the bus, star, and ring topologies

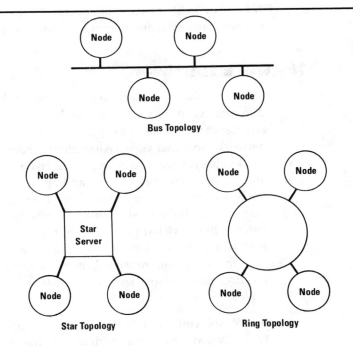

In the *star topology,* there is a central node that serves as a common connection point for all other nodes. All nodes in a star network can communicate *synchronously* (at the same time) through the central network node—that is, as long as the central node is available. The *bus topology* does not have a dependence on a central node for network availability and permits only *asynchronous* (one-at-a-time) network communication among the nodes in the network. A *ring network* offers the advantages of both the star and bus networks—*synchronous* communication without reliance on a central network node.

When a network includes remote computers that go beyond a small geographic area, the network becomes a *wide area network* (*WAN*). For example, if a company's departments are physically dispersed across the country, the company might use leased phone lines to connect department LANs so the entire company can communicate using an electronic mail system and have access to each other's local Oracle7 database servers.

A LAN or WAN consists of several different parts, including network hardware, network software, and communication software.

Network Hardware

The first thing necessary to form a network is some special *network hardware* so different computers can communicate. In a LAN, each computer has a network adapter card. A *network adapter card* has one or more outlets to plug in some sort of network cable that joins a computer to the network. There are several types of network cable you can use in a network: coaxial (coax) cable, twisted-pair cable (for example, a standard phone line), and optical fiber. Although it is the most expensive, the best of the bunch is optical fiber in terms of supporting the fastest communication rates with the least amount of noise interference. Coax cable is a bit more expensive than twisted-pair cable, but coax can support faster communication rates with less noise interference. And really fancy networks use *wireless network adapter cards* that allow different computers to communicate with each other using communication mechanisms such as high-frequency radio signals instead of physical cables.

In a WAN, computers are too far apart to use network cables. Therefore, WANs typically have to use a modem and the phone lines. To support long-distance communication, a computer might use an internal modem card or an external modem that you attach to a computer through a communications (COM) port. A modem has phone connections where you can plug in standard twisted-pair phone lines to gain access to the outside world.

Network Software

Every network has special *network software* that controls the operations specific to the network. For example, most networked environments include software to control things like user security, print queues, space allocation for user files, and mail messaging. If a network server uses an operating system not designed for networking (such as DOS), it typically uses a special network operating system like Novell's NetWare. If a network server uses an operating system designed for networking (such as UNIX), it can use the built-in networking capabilities without the need for a special network operating system.

Communications Software

In addition to network software, computers in a network need communications software. *Communications software* allows different computers connected in a network to send and receive packets of information on the network. The language the computers speak across a network is called the network *communications protocol*. For example, *TCP/IP* (short for Transmission Control Program/Internet Program) is the most common communications protocol in UNIX networks, while *SPX/IPX* (short for Sequenced Packet Exchange/Internet Package Exchange) is the protocol for Novell NetWare LANs. If a client and a server must be able to talk directly to each other, both computers need to use the same communications protocol. If the clients and the servers cannot use the same protocol, special equipment, such as a *communications bridge* or a *router*, may allow the clients and servers to communicate.

Middleware for Client/Server Database Systems

Imagine the complexity if a developer has to consider all the different network layers—hardware, topology, operating system, communication system—when writing an application for a database system. Luckily, developers don't have to think about network considerations and can be productive because client/server systems use *application middleware*, a software layer that makes it easy for different components of a distributed processing system to communicate. Middleware sits on both the clients and servers in a client/server system and translates the messages sent between them.

NOTE In distributed database systems, middleware allows different servers to communicate with one another. For example, a *database gateway* is middleware that heterogeneous distributed database systems use so one vendor's database server can talk to another vendor's database server (for example, Oracle7 and IBM's DB2). This book focuses on the role of middleware in client/server systems.

Types of Application Middleware

The system can use several different types of middleware to pass messages between clients and servers:

- With *conversational middleware,* a client and server connect and then pass a series of messages to complete a communication. Both components remain active during a conversation, which is usually asynchronous (messages go only one way at a time). Conversational middleware is typically not very efficient because of its back-and-forth message-passing scheme and its asynchronous communication method.

- With *remote procedure call (RPC) middleware,* one component communicates with a remote component using simple procedure calls. For example, a client requests information from a server by connecting to the server, making the request by calling a low-level procedure native to the database server, and then disconnecting. To respond to a request, the server connects to the application and calls a low-level procedure in the application. RPC middleware is typically transparent to a user, making it very easy to use.

Figure 4.2 illustrates these two types of middleware.

SQL*Net: Oracle's Own Middleware Product

If a client/server system includes only Oracle products (for example, the Oracle7 database server and Oracle CDE tools), the system uses Oracle's own middleware product, SQL*Net. The most common middleware product in an Oracle7 client/server database system, SQL*Net runs on both the clients and the server in a system to hide the complexity of the network.

Like Oracle7, SQL*Net works with almost every operating system and communications protocol and does not care which network topology is in use. In fact, SQL*Net's *multiprotocol interchange* even allows client/server connections to span multiple communication protocols without the need for expensive bridges and routers. Systems engineers can design a client/server system without ever considering which computers, operating systems, and protocols to use; SQL*Net will work in any configuration design. Given the heterogeneous nature of client/server

FIGURE 4.2:

Conversational and RPC middleware communication methods

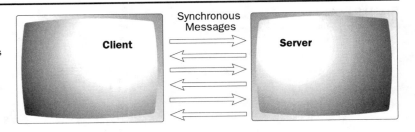

Conversational Middleware

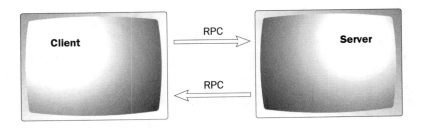

Remote Procedure Call Middleware

systems, this is an especially important feature of SQL*Net. Figure 4.3 demonstrates SQL*Net's function in a client/server system.

Other Examples of Middleware

If you use non-Oracle software in a client/server system, you might use another company's middleware product rather than Oracle's SQL*Net. For example, if you choose Gupta Corporation's SQLWindows instead of Oracle Forms to develop and run client form applications, client PCs must use Gupta's own middleware product, SQLRouter/Oracle, so SQLWindows can connect to Oracle7 across the network.

In addition, there are other types of middleware that attempt to standardize the *application programming interface (API)* between client application development tools

FIGURE 4.3:

SQL*Net in a client/server system

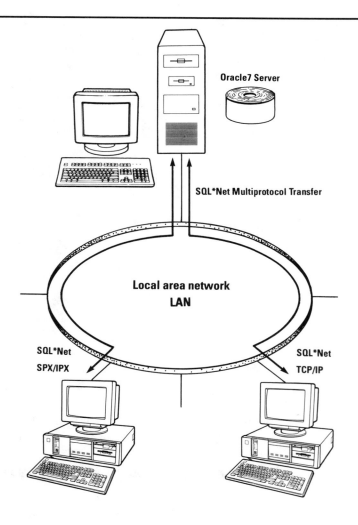

and many different types of database servers (Oracle7, Sybase SQL Server, Informix, and so on). In the client/server context, an API is simply a specification of a set of functions that allow client and server processes to communicate. Examples of standard APIs include Open Database Connectivity (ODBC) and the Integrated Database Application Programming Interface (IDAPI). Using tools and database servers that support standard API middleware when developing applications for a client/server system has both advantages and disadvantages.

The primary advantage of developing a client application using a standard API is that the resulting application can then use any back-end database server rather than just a specific server. Therefore, you have the advantage of choice when considering your database server—if you decide to buy or switch to/from Oracle7, Sybase SQL Server, Informix, and so on, your application continues to function without modification because all of these database servers support the standard API.

The primary disadvantage of standard APIs is that they generally include the "least common denominators" of all tools and database servers that support the standard. Therefore, when you develop a client application, you might not be able to take advantage of all the unique and special features that any one database server offers. This can result in poorly performing applications that are unusable.

In conclusion, consider the use of standard API middleware only if your client/server has or will include two or more different database servers. Even if your client/server environment falls into this category, do not commit to the use of a standard API for all of your applications until you perform serious testing to validate that the standard API will deliver the performance your applications require to make them useful.

Network hardware, communication software, and middleware enable clients and servers to distribute application processing. The next few sections explain more about the actual processing components that communicate using the network.

Client/Server Processing

Processing in a computer system is done by one or more operating system processes. A *process* is a task that a computer's operating system schedules and executes. A *multitasking operating system* can simultaneously process different tasks. Multitasking operating system technology makes it possible for Oracle7 to serve multiple users concurrently. As you might guess, the database server in a client/server system uses a multitasking operating system, such as UNIX, OS/2, or VMS.

A client/server system splits processing between two different components—client processes and server processes—and the network funnels the data between the two. Figure 4.4 illustrates the different types of processes and related components

FIGURE 4.4:

Processes in an Oracle7 client/server
system

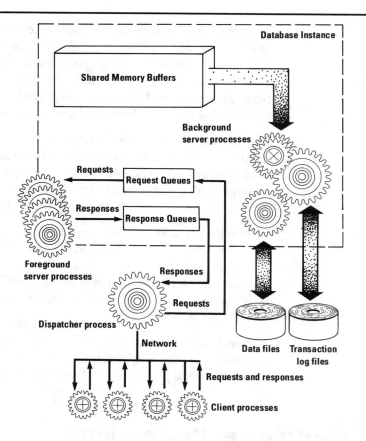

in an Oracle7 client/server system. Let's learn more about each of these different
types of processes.

Client Processes

A *client process* is responsible for executing a client application on a workstation. For
example, when you start Oracle Data Browser, your workstation's operating system creates a process in which to run Data Browser. This client process executes the
compiled application program that sends and receives data to and from the server
across the network, redraws the application display when necessary, and so on.

You cannot do any work with a client database application like Data Browser unless you first connect to the database server across the network. Therefore, one of the first things a client process does is to send an initial *connect request* across the network to the address of the database server. The initial connect request includes your Oracle username and password, which the application typically requests when you start the application. If the database server is available and you provide a valid username/password combination, Oracle7 connects you to the database. Now you can use your application and the corresponding client process to run the application.

Server Processes

Server processes work to handle the requests sent by client processes and operate the many functions of an Oracle7 database server. As you can see in Figure 4.4, Oracle7 makes a distinction between foreground server processes and background server processes. *Foreground server processes* directly handle requests from client processes, while *background server processes* handle other specific jobs of the database server, like writing data to data and transaction log files.

Processing in an Oracle7 client/server system works like this:

1. When a client process sends a request to the database server, the *dispatcher* background process receives the request and puts it into a *request queue*. The dispatcher places requests in the queue on a first-in/first-out basis.

2. The next available foreground server process picks up the oldest request in the queue and processes it. Once the foreground server process finishes processing the request, it places the results in the response queue.

3. The dispatcher monitors the response queue and sends back any request results to the client process that made the request.

During transaction processing, Oracle7 automatically adjusts the number of foreground server processes to match the processing load on the system. When requests build up in the request queue, Oracle7 starts more foreground processes so no user has to wait to accomplish work. When foreground processes sit idle because of a lack of requests in the queue, Oracle7 terminates some foreground processes to eliminate unnecessary and unused system process overhead.

NOTE   A single process can have multiple *threads* of execution. This simply means that a single multithreaded process can do the work of multiple single-threaded processes. The advantage of a multithreaded process is that it can do the work of many single-threaded processes but requires far less system overhead.

If a database server uses multithreaded server processes, it can support large numbers of clients with minimal system overhead. In your Oracle7 documentation, you will notice that the process architecture just described is classified as a multithreaded server. Technically, this is correct because, overall, a small number of foreground server processes can process the requests that come from many client processes. But don't take this to mean that the foreground server processes in Oracle7 are multithreaded themselves, because they are not—they execute only one thread per process.

As dispatchers and foreground server processes handle client requests, other background server processes work on other important database server operations. Here's an overview of the operations of the important Oracle7 background processes.

Database Writer (DBWR)   When a user transaction modifies some database data, a foreground server reads the data into the database server's shared memory buffer and makes the modification. The *database writer* (*DBWR*) writes data blocks that transactions modify in memory back to the appropriate data files. DBWR does not write modified blocks from memory to disk as transactions commit. To eliminate unnecessary I/O and boost server performance, DBWR writes a block in memory back to disk only when DBWR sits idle for a few seconds, a foreground server wants to read a new block into memory but there is no free space available, or Oracle7 performs a database or tablespace checkpoint (discussed shortly).

Log Writer (LGWR)   The *log writer* (*LGWR*) logs all Oracle7 database transaction activity to the database's transaction log. As transactions generate log information in the database's *transaction log buffer* (a shared memory area that temporarily buffers log information), LGWR reads the log buffer and physically writes the log entries to the current transaction log group. Like DBWR, LGWR writes information from the log buffer to disk only at certain times to keep disk I/O to a minimum. LGWR protects the commit of a transaction by immediately writing a commit record to the transaction log.

Archiver (ARCH)   The *archiver* (*ARCH*) is an optional process that automatically backs up transaction log groups when they become full. An administrator who uses ARCH doesn't have to worry about backing up a filled log group so it will be available the next time LGWR needs the log group for transaction logging. Once Oracle7 switches from a filled log group to the next log group, ARCH notices that there is a group for archiving and makes a copy of the group in a configurable destination.

System Monitor (SMON)   The *system monitor* (*SMON*) carries out many internal operations as Oracle7 processes transactions. For example, SMON performs different space management operations as transactions free up and request more space for database data. SMON accomplishes its job with minimal impact on system performance because it requests processing time only when it is needed; otherwise, it sleeps.

Process Monitor (PMON)   The *process monitor* (*PMON*) is a wake-and-sleep process responsible for cleaning up after a front-end server process abnormally dies. For example, if a user's connection to the database crashes, PMON wakes up to roll back the user's dead transaction and release the transaction's locks so they won't prevent other transactions from accessing the same data.

Checkpoint (CKPT)   As you just learned, DBWR does not necessarily write modified data blocks to disk when transactions commit. However, DBWR periodically performs a *checkpoint* (*CKPT*), or *consistency point*, to make sure all modified information in memory is physically stored on disk. The main purpose of a checkpoint is to serve as a post that indicates how much of the transaction log Oracle7 needs to apply should the system require crash recovery. Because Oracle7 knows that all data blocks before the last recorded checkpoint are present on disk, it needs to apply only the transaction changes since the last checkpoint.

During a checkpoint, LGWR stamps the headers in all the data files in the database with the most recent checkpoint's internal information. Normally, LGWR updates data file headers during a checkpoint. However, if your database has a large number of data files, you can improve the performance of transaction logging during checkpoints by configuring the instance with the optional checkpoint (CKPT) background server process to update data file headers during checkpoints.

Dispatcher   The *dispatcher* routes client process requests to the request queue and then returns the results from the response queue back to the appropriate clients. If the system load is heavy, you can start additional dispatchers dynamically without bringing down the current instance.

> **NOTE**   This section has given you a very quick overview of the Oracle7 process architecture. For more information about configuring and tuning the different Oracle7 server processes, see Chapter 8.

This chapter has presented a broad introduction to the communication issues present in a client/server system, including

- An explanation of the different types of network topologies, including star, bus, and ring topologies

- A discussion of the different types of networks, specifically local area networks (LANs) and wide area networks (WANs)

- The types of hardware and software necessary for networks to function

- The role of middleware in a client/server system, and an introduction to Oracle's middleware product, SQL*Net, as well as the standard API middleware specifications ODBC and IDAPI

- An explanation of the processes that cooperate to form a distributed application processing system, including client processes, foreground server processes, and the Oracle7 background server processes

At this point you have a basic understanding of all the primary components in an Oracle7 client/server database system, including the database server, the client, and the communication that occurs between clients and the server. The remaining chapter in Part I of the book provides a quick introduction to the languages that you will be seeing throughout the examples in this book: SQL and PL/SQL.

CHAPTER

FIVE

Between Client and Server 2: SQL and PL/SQL

- Common SQL commands

- The block structure approach of PL/SQL

- PL/SQL variables, constants, and datatypes

- PL/SQL flow control statements

- Different types of PL/SQL programs

Oracle7 is like a person who speaks only one language because users can interact with it using only one language: the structured query language (SQL). Other than using SQL, there is no way for a user or application to enter or retrieve data from an Oracle7 database. That's why most database users—and especially developers and administrators—need to know SQL commands to get work done with Oracle7. For those readers who have no understanding of SQL, this chapter provides a broad overview, including

- Data manipulation language (DML) commands, including SELECT, INSERT, UPDATE, and DELETE
- Transaction control language commands, including COMMIT, ROLLBACK, and SAVEPOINT
- Data definition language (DDL) commands
- Data control language (DCL) commands, including GRANT, REVOKE, and SET ROLE

This chapter also provides a solid foundation if you need to understand and use PL/SQL, Oracle's procedural language extensions to the SQL standard. You'll learn about

- The block structure approach of PL/SQL
- PL/SQL variables, constants, and datatypes
- Flow control statements
- Different types of PL/SQL programs, including anonymous PL/SQL blocks, database procedures, functions, packages, and triggers

NOTE   This chapter is by no means intended to be a complete SQL reference. For a complete syntax description of all SQL commands, see Martin Gruber's two books, *Understanding SQL* (1990) and the *SQL Instant Reference* (1993), both from Sybex.

A Quick Note about ANSI/ISO Standard SQL

Many, but not all, commercially available relational database servers support some version and level of the ANSI/ISO SQL standard. (ANSI is short for American National Standards Institute, and ISO is short for International Organization of Standards.) Support of industry-standard SQL allows users and SQL database applications to work identically with many different relational database servers.

NOTE Oracle7 Release 7.1 is 100-percent compliant with the entry-level ANSI/ISO SQL-92 standard, including the integrity enhancement feature, which outlines specifications for integrity constraint syntax and behavior.

To enhance the capabilities of the standard SQL language, each commercial relational database server has extensions to the ANSI/ISO SQL standard. Oracle7 is no different. Extensions to SQL can be in the form of nonstandard commands or nonstandard options to standard SQL commands. You are free to use the extensions of any commercial relational database server's SQL implementation, but understand that SQL extensions may not be the same or even present when you use another database server.

Data Manipulation Using SQL

Data manipulation or *data modification SQL commands* are the SQL commands almost everyone uses when working with an Oracle7 database. Data manipulation language (DML) commands let users move data into and out of a database. DML commands include SELECT, INSERT, UPDATE, and DELETE.

The SELECT Command

To query data from tables in a database, use the SQL command SELECT. The SELECT command has many different options you can use to generate a report of data. You can use the SELECT command in its simplest form to retrieve all data from a table. For example, this query requests the data in all columns of all rows in the CUSTOMER table:

```
SELECT * FROM customer
```

The wildcard character * indicates that you want to retrieve all columns in the table. If you want to narrow a query's *result set* (set of data that the server returns for a query) to specific columns of a table, you can include a column list:

```
SELECT id, lastname, firstname FROM customer
```

You can further narrow a query's result set to specific rows using a WHERE clause and a condition that limits the rows in the return or result set:

```
SELECT id, lastname, firstname FROM customer WHERE id = 32
```

A condition in a WHERE clause can take many forms. In the preceding example, the condition is a simple comparison expression. The following are all examples of a query with different types of expressions in the WHERE clause:

```
SELECT lastname, firstname, address, state, zipcode FROM customer
  WHERE state IN ('CA', 'FL', 'AZ')

SELECT id FROM orders
  WHERE orderdate BETWEEN '01-JUN-93' AND '30-JUN-93'

SELECT id, lastname FROM customer
  WHERE (address IS NULL) OR (city IS NULL)

SELECT id, lastname, firstname FROM customer
  WHERE id NOT IN (SELECT customerid FROM orders)
```

The last two examples are of particular interest. The next-to-last example includes a compound expression that is joined with the OR conjunction. As you might guess, Oracle7 includes a row in the query's result set if the row satisfies either of the conditions separated by the OR conjunction in the WHERE clause. If you use the AND condition (not shown in the examples), Oracle7 includes a row in a query's result set only if the row satisfies both conditions in the WHERE clause.

The last example of WHERE conditions includes a *subquery*—a query nested in an outer statement. The example is a query to return the IDs and names of all customers who have never placed an order.

You've probably guessed that the FROM clause indicates the target table, which in all of the examples is the CUSTOMER or ORDERS table. If the database has two different tables with the same name that are owned by different users, you can prefix the table name in the FROM clause with the name of the user who owns the table, as shown here:

```
SELECT id, lastname, firstname FROM gwashington.customer

SELECT id, lastname, firstname FROM wclinton.customer
```

The SELECT command also has options for formatting the output of the return set. For example, the ORDER BY clause allows you to order the rows in a query's return set:

```
SELECT id, lastname, firstname FROM customer
  ORDER BY lastname, firstname
```

You can even concatenate the output of two columns and give the concatenated column an alias column name:

```
SELECT CONCAT(CONCAT(firstname,' '),lastname) "NAME" FROM customer
```

The SQL function CONCAT concatenates the first name and last name, separating them with a space.

Now let's learn more about the other DML commands you'll be using frequently.

The INSERT Command

To insert new rows into a database, use the SQL command INSERT:

```
INSERT INTO orders
  VALUES (239, 2, '06-JUN-93', '06-JUN-93','23-JUN-93','F')

INSERT INTO orders (id, customerid, orderdate, status)
  VALUES (240, 7, '06-JUN-93', 'B')
```

The INTO clause specifies the target table and an optional list of column values, and the VALUES clause specifies the different column values for the new row. If you don't explicitly specify a list of the column values you will supply when inserting a new row, you must supply a value for every column in the table (as in the first example above).

You can also use a subquery instead of the VALUES clause to copy multiple rows from one table to another:

```
INSERT INTO orderhistory
  (SELECT * FROM orders WHERE orderdate < '31-MAY-93')
```

The UPDATE Command

To update rows in a table, use the SQL command UPDATE:

```
UPDATE customer SET fax = NULL
```

The example statement updates every customer's fax number to NULL. The SET clause includes an expression to update the target table. If you want to target specific rows, you can include a WHERE clause:

```
UPDATE customer SET address = '134 Rodeo Drive' WHERE id = 87
```

You can also use a subquery in the expression of the SET clause of an UPDATE statement:

```
UPDATE orders
  SET customerid = (SELECT id FROM customer
                    WHERE lastname = 'King' AND firstname = 'Martin')
  WHERE id = 562
```

This statement updates the customer ID of order 562 to the customer ID of Martin King.

The DELETE Command

To delete rows from a table, use the SQL command DELETE:

```
DELETE FROM orderhistory
```

Be careful—the example statement deletes all the rows in the ORDERHISTORY table. If you want to delete specific rows from a table, you must include a WHERE clause:

```
DELETE FROM item WHERE orderid = 739
```

That's your quick introduction to the DML commands in SQL. You should now be able to understand most of the examples in this book.

Transaction Control Using SQL

Transaction control commands let you determine the outcome of a transaction. Transaction control commands include COMMIT, ROLLBACK, and SAVEPOINT.

The COMMIT Command

To *commit* the changes made by your current transaction (to make the changes permanent and irreversible) and release any locks the transaction is holding, use this SQL command:

```
COMMIT
```

Once you commit a transaction, you implicitly end the transaction and begin a new transaction.

The ROLLBACK Command

To *roll back* the changes made by your current transaction (to undo the changes as if they had never happened) and release any locks the transaction is holding, use this SQL command:

```
ROLLBACK
```

Once you roll back a transaction, you implicitly begin a new transaction. In the next section you'll see another option of the ROLLBACK command.

The SAVEPOINT Command

Within a long transaction, you can declare intermediate *savepoints* to divide the work in the transaction:

```
INSERT ...
UPDATE ...
DELETE ...
SAVEPOINT one
INSERT ...
UPDATE ...
DELETE ...
SAVEPOINT two
```

```
INSERT ...
UPDATE ...
DELETE ...
    .
    .
    .
```

Using the savepoints you declare, you can roll back parts of a transaction and leave other parts intact:

```
ROLLBACK TO SAVEPOINT two
```

This statement rolls back the effects of all statements after savepoint TWO. Your transaction also releases any locks that rolled-back statements acquired so other transactions can modify the data. After a rollback to a savepoint, the transaction is still active.

> **NOTE**   It's important to understand how to design good transactions in an Oracle7 database application. See Chapter 17 for more information.

Data Definition Using SQL

Data definition language (DDL) commands are the SQL commands you use to create, alter, and drop (delete) different database objects in an Oracle7 database. Most types of database objects (tables, views, procedures, triggers, tablespaces, users, and so on) have CREATE, ALTER, and DROP commands; in other words, there are many DDL commands. In earlier chapters you saw example statements of the CREATE TABLE, CREATE VIEW, CREATE PROCEDURE, CREATE TRIGGER, CREATE USER, and CREATE ROLE commands.

Data Control Using SQL

Use the SQL *data control language (DCL) commands* to control which users can access an Oracle7 database and specific data (tables, views, and so on) within it. Data control statements include the GRANT and REVOKE commands, which you use to grant and revoke privileges, as well as the SET ROLE command, which enables or disables roles in your current session.

The GRANT Command

To grant a privilege or a role to a user or a role, use the SQL command GRANT:

```
GRANT CREATE TABLE, CREATE VIEW TO gwashington, alincoln
```

```
GRANT placeorders, updateorders, deleteorders TO orderentry
```

```
GRANT SELECT ON customer TO tjefferson
```

As these examples show, you use the GRANT clause to specify what you want to grant: a privilege, a role, or a comma-separated list of privileges or roles. Use the TO clause to specify a target or a list of the targets; valid targets include roles and users. The first example grants the system privileges CREATE TABLE and CREATE VIEW to the users GWASHINGTON and ALINCOLN. The second statement grants the roles PLACEORDERS, UPDATEORDERS, and DELETEORDERS to another role, ORDERENTRY. The third statement grants the SELECT privilege for the CUSTOMER table to the user TJEFFERSON. If you want to grant all object privileges for a particular object, use the keyword ALL:

```
GRANT ALL ON customer TO tjefferson
```

If you are granting system privileges or roles, you can grant them with the ADMIN option to allow the grantee the ability to pass the privilege or role grant to other users and roles:

```
GRANT CREATE TABLE TO rreagan WITH ADMIN OPTION
```

Now RREAGAN can grant the CREATE TABLE privilege to other users and roles. For example, RREAGAN might use this statement:

```
GRANT CREATE TABLE TO gbush
```

Similarly, if you are granting object privileges, you can grant them with the GRANT option to allow the grantee the ability to pass the privilege grant to other users and roles:

```
GRANT SELECT, INSERT, UPDATE, DELETE ON customer
  TO jkennedy WITH GRANT OPTION
```

The REVOKE Command

To revoke a privilege or role from a user or role, use the SQL command REVOKE:

```
REVOKE CREATE TABLE FROM alincoln
```

```
REVOKE placeorders FROM orderentry
```

```
REVOKE SELECT ON customer FROM tjefferson
```

With the REVOKE command, you can specify the privilege or role you want to revoke in the REVOKE clause. Use the FROM clause to indicate what should no longer have the privilege or role. If you want to revoke all object privileges from a user or a role, use the ALL keyword:

```
REVOKE ALL ON customer FROM rnixon
```

The SET ROLE Command

To enable or disable roles in your current session, use the SQL command SET ROLE:

```
SET ROLE orderentry
```

If a role is protected by a password, you must indicate the password in an IDENTI-FIED BY clause to enable the role:

```
SET ROLE orderentry IDENTIFIED BY Y10wer
```

You can enable more than one role using the ALL option:

```
SET ROLE ALL
```

```
SET ROLE ALL EXCEPT orderentry
```

If you use the EXCEPT clause with the ALL option, Oracle7 enables all roles except those listed. For the ALL option to work successfully, with or without the EXCEPT clause, roles must have no passwords.

When you enable a specific role or number of roles, you implicitly disable all other roles granted to you. You can disable all roles using the NONE option of the SET ROLE command:

```
SET ROLE NONE
```

> **NOTE**
>
> Application developers typically use the SET ROLE command as one of the first SQL statements in a client application. If you use the SET ROLE command, an application can set the correct privilege domain for application users when they start the application and connect to Oracle7.

For more information about security and DCL commands, see Chapters 9 and 19 of this book.

SQL Functions

Oracle7 SQL includes an extensive set of built-in *SQL functions* you can use to operate on data. Here are some examples of the many SQL functions you can use:

```
-- returns square root of 120

SELECT SQRT(120) FROM dual;

-- returns total order amount of line items for order 32

SELECT SUM(quantity * unitprice)
  FROM item, stock
  WHERE orderid = 32 AND item.stockid = stock.id

-- returns total number of customers in CUSTOMER table

SELECT COUNT(*) FROM customer

-- inserts your username into a table

INSERT INTO ... VALUES (USER, ...)

-- returns 'NONE AVAILABLE' if customer address is NULL

SELECT lastname, NVL(address,'NONE AVAILABLE') "ADDRESS"
  FROM customer
```

```
-- insert today's date with new order

INSERT INTO orders (id, customerid, orderdate)
  VALUES (34, 534, SYSDATE)
```

NOTE SQL functions are especially beneficial in a client/server database system because they allow you to perform more of the data processing at the server instead of in a client application. Consequently, you can improve overall system performance because less data is sent between the client and the server.

These are just a few examples of the SQL functions available with Oracle7. Look for more SQL functions in the examples throughout this book. For tables that provide a complete list of Oracle7 SQL functions, see Appendix A.

NOTE Every Oracle7 database has a publicly accessible data dictionary table named *DUAL*. The DUAL table has a single column, DUMMY, and a single row, with a value of X. You can think of the DUAL table as a scratch pad you can use to return the result of a SQL function. The first example above shows a query that uses DUAL to return the value of the square root of 120.

SQL and PL/SQL: What's the Difference?

SQL is a *nonprocedural language*—you simply tell the database server to do something, not how to do it. The database server translates SQL commands into internal procedures to process the request. SQL is easy to use because it hides all the details of data processing.

C, Ada, and Pascal are all examples of procedural languages. *Procedural languages* require you to know how to access data and create programs using a very structured design. Although a procedural language is more complex to use than a nonprocedural language, it can offer more flexibility and power.

To merge the advantages of both procedural and nonprocedural languages, Oracle7 offers *procedural language extensions* to SQL. The Oracle7 procedural language extensions are collectively called *PL/SQL*.

PL/SQL is an integrated component in many Oracle products. Oracle7 includes PL/SQL so you can create and use stored procedures and database triggers in the database server, and Oracle Forms includes PL/SQL so you can create form triggers as part of a client application. (These topics are covered later in the chapter.) PL/SQL programs in the different parts of an Oracle7 client/server system can work together. For example, a trigger in a form application can call a database procedure to accomplish some work.

If you are developing applications for a client/server database system, learning how to take advantage of PL/SQL is mandatory. Using PL/SQL, you can improve application and system performance because

- You use fast-executing compiled programs rather than uncompiled SQL statements.

- You significantly reduce network traffic between clients and servers.

The following sections provide a guide to the basics of PL/SQL.

NOTE If you already know how to use a procedural language such as C or Ada, the information in the following sections should be very familiar—especially familiar if you use Ada. That's because Oracle has modeled PL/SQL using the Ada programming language.

Blocking Code for Clarity

PL/SQL is a block-structured language. In a single PL/SQL program, you can group related sets of statements in *blocks* for easier programming and readability. Here is an example:

```
DECLARE
   ... set of statements ...
BEGIN
   ... set of statements ...
   BEGIN
     ... set of statements ...
   END
... set of statements ...
EXCEPTION
   ... set of statements ...
END
```

This PL/SQL program has four blocks. The DECLARE block is the section where you declare the variables, constants, and user-defined datatypes you want to use in the program body. The first BEGIN statement marks the beginning of the main program body. Nested within the main program body is another block that starts with another BEGIN statement and finishes with the END statement. Finally, the EXCEPTION block is where you write any exception handlers to handle error conditions in the program. (See the section "Error Handling" later in this chapter). Notice that a final END statement indicates the end of the main program body.

Using Variables, Constants, and Datatypes

As part of a PL/SQL program, you can declare *variables* and *constants*. Any variable or constant you declare must have a datatype.

```
DECLARE
  currentcustomer VARCHAR2(15);      -- variable for name of current user
  discount CONSTANT INTEGER := 0.1; -- constant for sales discount
```

NOTE You can include comments in a PL/SQL program. Comments start with the characters "--" and proceed to the end of the current line.

You can use any of the standard Oracle7 datatypes. The first of the preceding examples declares a variable using the VARCHAR2 datatype with a maximum length of 15 bytes. In addition to standard Oracle7 datatypes, PL/SQL supports other datatypes and subtypes. Table 5.1 lists all the PL/SQL datatypes, including the standard Oracle7 datatypes.

TABLE 5.1: Datatypes Available in PL/SQL

Datatype	Subtypes	Description
NUMBER (precision, scale)	DEC, DECIMAL, DOUBLE_ PRECISION, FLOAT, INT, INTEGER, NUMERIC, REAL, SMALLINT	Use the NUMBER datatype or any of its subtypes to create variables and constants that store fixed or floating-point numbers. Precision is 38 by default; valid values are 0..38. Scale is 0 by default; valid values are $-84..127$. If you specify a negative scale, Oracle7 rounds values to the left of the decimal point
BINARY_INTEGER	NATURAL, POSITIVE	Use the BINARY_INTEGER datatype or any of its subtypes to create variables and constants that store signed integers. Binary integers range from $-2^{31}-1$ to $2^{31}-1$. You can improve application performance if you use binary integer variables because Oracle7 avoids converting binary integers in calculations
CHAR (size)	CHARACTER, STRING	Use the CHAR datatype or any of its subtypes to create variables and constants that store fixed-length text strings. Maximum length is 32767 bytes
VARCHAR2 (size)	VARCHAR	Use the VARCHAR2 datatype or its subtype to create variables and constants that store variable-length text strings. Maximum length is 32767 bytes

TABLE 5.1: Datatypes Available in PL/SQL (continued)

Datatype	Subtypes	Description
DATE		Use the DATE datatype to create variables and constants that store time-related information such as dates, hours, minutes, and seconds
BOOLEAN		Use the BOOLEAN datatype to create variables and constants that store the logical values TRUE and FALSE
RECORD		Use the RECORD datatype to create your own record datatypes
TABLE		Use the TABLE datatype to create PL/SQL table datatypes

User-Defined RECORD and TABLE Datatypes

Of particular interest are the RECORD and TABLE PL/SQL datatypes because they allow you to create your own user-defined datatypes. Using the RECORD datatype, you can create a user-defined datatype as a record that matches the attributes of a table, as shown here:

```
DECLARE
  TYPE orderrecordtype IS RECORD
  ( id NUMBER(5,0) NOT NULL := 0,          -- field for order's ID
    customerid NUMBER(5,0) NOT NULL := 0,  -- field for order's customer
    orderdate DATE NOT NULL := SYSDATE);   -- field for order's date
```

This example declares a user-defined record datatype that matches the columns of the ORDERS table. Notice that you can include the NOT NULL constraint for a field declaration in a record to prevent the assignment of NULLs to the field. If you use the NOT NULL constraint for a field declaration, you must initialize the field.

Once you create a user-defined datatype, you can use it to declare *record variables,* or arguments for procedures and functions:

```
DECLARE
  currentorder ORDERRECORDTYPE;

PROCEDURE placeorder (currentorder ORDERRECORDTYPE) ...
```

The second example shows how easy it is to pass a number of related values in a row as a single-record argument in procedures and functions.

In a PL/SQL program you reference the fields in a record by indicating both the record and field names. This example assigns the current date and time to the ORDERDATE field of the CURRENTORDER record variable:

```
currentorder.orderdate := SYSDATE;
```

You can use the TABLE datatype to create a user-defined datatype as a single-column table. The following examples create a user-defined datatype for order numbers and a variable that stores a table of order numbers:

```
DECLARE
  TYPE ordernumbertype IS TABLE OF NUMBER(5,0)
    INDEX BY BINARY_INTEGER;

  ordernumbers ORDERNUMBERTYPE;
```

A variable that you declare with a table datatype is called a *PL/SQL table.*

Like database tables, PL/SQL tables can grow to an unlimited number of rows. You can reference a specific row in a PL/SQL table using its primary key number:

```
currentorderid := ordernumbers(1)
```

Like records, tables are especially useful for passing data sets as a single argument in procedures and functions.

PL/SQL offers two special attributes you can use to declare variables and user-defined datatypes that match table attributes. They are %TYPE and %ROWTYPE:

```
DECLARE
  TYPE orderrecordtype IS RECORD
  ( id orders.id%TYPE NOT NULL := 0,
    customerid orders.customerid%TYPE NOT NULL := 0,
    orderdate orders.orderdate%TYPE NOT NULL := SYSDATE);
```

```
DECLARE
   currentorder orders%ROWTYPE;
```

The preceding example declarations are alternatives to the explicit declaration of the same record datatype shown at the beginning of this section. The first example explicitly declares each field of ORDERRECORDTYPE depending on the datatypes of the matching columns in the ORDERS table. The second example declares a record variable CURRENTORDER to match the row structure of the ORDERS table without declaring even a record type.

Assigning Database Values to Variables

To allow a PL/SQL program to work with database data, you can assign database values in the return set of a query to PL/SQL variables. There are two different methods, depending on the number of rows the query returns.

SELECT... INTO...

To assign a single table value to a variable in a PL/SQL program, you can use a special clause of the SELECT command, the INTO clause. This example retrieves an order into a record variable:

```
DECLARE
   currentorder orders%ROWTYPE;
BEGIN
   SELECT id, customerid, orderdate
     INTO currentorder.id, currentorder.customerid, currentorder.orderdate
     FROM orders
     WHERE id = 453;
.
.
.
other statements
.
.
.
END
```

You can use the INTO clause to assign a table value to a variable only when the SE-LECT statement returns a single row. The next section explains how to assign values from queries that return multiple rows from the database.

Cursors

If a PL/SQL program includes a query that returns multiple rows from the database, you must declare a cursor for the statement. A *cursor* is essentially a name for a multi-row query. You use a cursor to process individual rows of the query's return set, one by one, as Oracle7 returns them from the database, as shown here:

```
DECLARE
  TYPE orderrecordtype IS RECORD
    ( id orders.id%TYPE NOT NULL := 0,
    customerid orders.customerid%TYPE NOT NULL := 0,
    orderdate orders.orderdate%TYPE NOT NULL := SYSDATE);
  currentorder ORDERRECORDTYPE;
  CURSOR ordercursor IS SELECT id, customerid, orderdate FROM orders;
```

The preceding statement declares a cursor for the rows in the ORDERS table. Once you declare a cursor, you use several different PL/SQL statements to process the rows in the cursor. The first step is to open the cursor:

```
OPEN ordercursor;
```

Once you open a cursor, you can *fetch* rows one by one into a variable that can receive the data from the cursor:

```
FETCH ordercursor INTO currentorder;
```

To narrow the return set of a cursor to a specific set of rows, you can declare *cursor parameters,* which you can then use in the WHERE clause of the cursor query:

```
DECLARE
  CURSOR ordercursor (ordernumber NUMBER) IS
    SELECT id, customerid, orderdate
      FROM orders
      WHERE id > ordernumber;
```

You set the value for a cursor parameter when you open the cursor:

```
OPEN ordercursor(3);
```

In the preceding examples, the return set of ORDERCURSOR includes all of the rows in the ORDERS table with an order ID greater than 3.

PL/SQL also provides methods for testing *cursor attributes*, including %ISOPEN, %ROWCOUNT, %NOTFOUND, and %FOUND.

- %ISOPEN simply tests a cursor to see if it is open. If the cursor is open, %ISOPEN evaluates to TRUE; if the cursor is closed, %ISOPEN evaluates to FALSE.

```
IF ordercursor%ISOPEN
  THEN CLOSE ordercursor;
  ELSE OPEN ordercursor;
END IF;
```

- %ROWCOUNT keeps a count of how many rows you fetch after you open a cursor. When you open a cursor, the cursor's %ROWCOUNT attribute is 0.

- %NOTFOUND and %FOUND are opposing attributes that reveal the state of the current cursor position. For example, %NOTFOUND always evaluates to FALSE (and %FOUND to TRUE) if the last fetch returned a row. %NOTFOUND evaluates to TRUE (and %FOUND to FALSE) only when the last fetch fails to return a row. %NOTFOUND eventually evaluates to TRUE, once you fetch the last row in the return set.

The following function is an integrated example of the different PL/SQL statements you can use to create and use a cursor. The ITEMTOTAL function returns the total price of all items for a specific order number.

```
CREATE FUNCTION itemtotal (ordernumber IN NUMBER)
RETURN NUMBER IS
  CURSOR ordercursor (ordernumber NUMBER) IS
    SELECT item.total
      FROM item
      WHERE item.orderid = ordernumber;
  ordertotal NUMBER (5,2) := 0;
  linetotal NUMBER (5,2) := 0;
BEGIN
  OPEN ordercursor (ordernumber);
  LOOP
    FETCH ordercursor INTO linetotal;
    EXIT WHEN ordercursor%NOTFOUND;       -- exit loop after last line item
    ordertotal := ordertotal + linetotal; -- add each linetotal to ordertotal
  END LOOP;
  CLOSE ordercursor;
  RETURN ordertotal;
END itemtotal;
```

Using Flow Control Statements

Procedural language programs are said to have flow—that is, they execute statements, one by one, in the order that the program issues them. Procedural languages usually have *flow control statements* that allow you to control the flow of statement execution within a program. For example, flow control statements typically allow a program to execute one or more statements based on a specific condition, repeatedly execute a number of statements in a loop, or skip a number of statements by moving to another part of the program. Oracle's PL/SQL has several flow control statements that allow you to control the flow of execution in a PL/SQL program, including IF...THEN, LOOP, WHILE, FOR, and GOTO. The next few sections explain the PL/SQL flow control statements.

The IF...THEN... Statement

The IF...THEN... statement lets you test for a condition and, depending on whether the condition is TRUE or FALSE, perform different blocks of statements.

```
IF quantity > 5 THEN ... END IF
```

You can extend conditional testing using the ELSE and ELSIF structures of the IF statement, as shown here:

```
IF quantity > 15
   THEN ... ; -- discount 15%
ELSIF quantity > 10
   THEN ... ; -- discount 10%
ELSIF quantity > 5
   THEN ... ; -- discount 5%
ELSE ... ; -- no discount
END IF;
```

The LOOP Statement

Use the LOOP statement to execute a sequence of statements a number of times. Loops are useful for processing multiple rows in a cursor, as shown by the excerpt from the ITEMTOTAL function in the earlier section "Using Cursors."

```
LOOP
  FETCH ordercursor INTO linetotal;
  EXIT WHEN ordercursor%NOTFOUND;
   ordertotal := ordertotal + linetotal;
END LOOP;
```

There are several ways to exit a loop. The preceding example shows the EXIT
WHEN construct. Alternatively, you can test for a condition with an IF statement
and use the EXIT statement. The next example is a rewrite of the previous loop, using IF and EXIT to exit the loop after you fetch the last row of ORDERCURSOR:

```
LOOP
  FETCH ordercursor INTO linetotal;
  IF ordercursor%NOTFOUND
    THEN EXIT;
  END IF;
  ordertotal := ordertotal + linetotal;
END LOOP;
```

WHILE Loops

WHILE loops are yet another option for iterative flow control. They allow you to
execute statements while a condition is TRUE. Here is another rewrite of the preceding loop:

```
WHILE ordercursor%FOUND LOOP
  FETCH ordercursor INTO linetotal;
  ordertotal := ordertotal + linetotal;
END LOOP;
```

You can use any of the preceding loop structures when you don't know how many
times you need to iterate the loop. You use a FOR loop when you know exactly how
many times you need to execute a loop:

```
FOR counter IN 1 .. 5 LOOP
  ... set of statements ...
END LOOP;
```

Loops are so useful for processing cursors that PL/SQL includes a special type of
FOR loop called a cursor FOR loop. A *cursor FOR loop* significantly simplifies coding
when processing the rows of a cursor because it implicitly declares a variable or record to receive the rows in the cursor, opens the cursor, fetches rows from the cursor

with each iteration of the loop, and closes the cursor after the last row has been fetched. Here is a rewrite of the ITEMTOTAL function using a cursor FOR loop:

```
CREATE FUNCTION itemtotal (ordernumber IN NUMBER)
RETURN NUMBER IS
  CURSOR ordercursor (ordernumber NUMBER) IS
    SELECT item.total
      FROM item
      WHERE orderid = ordernumber;
  ordertotal NUMBER (5,2) := 0;
BEGIN
  FOR line IN ordercursor(ordernumber) LOOP
    ordertotal := ordertotal + line.total;
  END LOOP;
  RETURN ordertotal;
END itemtotal;
```

Notice that cursor FOR loops also support cursor parameters.

The GOTO Statement

The GOTO statement allows you to continue program processing at a specific label in your program. You can label any part of a PL/SQL program using a unique identifier enclosed in double angle brackets. The following example shows how to label a loop and then go to the loop from another part of the program after checking for a condition.

```
<<orderitemloop>>
LOOP
  FETCH ordercursor INTO linetotal;
  IF ordercursor%NOTFOUND
    THEN EXIT;
  END IF;
  ordertotal := ordertotal + linetotal;
END LOOP orderitemloop;
.
.

.
other statements
.
.
.
```

```
IF ...
   THEN GOTO orderitemloop;
END IF;
```

Error Handling

Because we are all human, error conditions are inevitable in every type of data processing environment. For example, the user might mistakenly enter an incorrect spelling of a name when asking a database for a customer's address. To account for such errors when you develop programs such as PL/SQL blocks, you must pay specific attention to possible error conditions and plan programs so they react appropriately.

Good programming languages have specific mechanisms you can use to identify and handle error conditions separately from normal program processing. PL/SQL has an extensive error-handling mechanism called *exceptions,* which you can use to trap and process error conditions in a program. When a PL/SQL program encounters a defined error condition, PL/SQL *raises* the corresponding exception. You can specifically handle processing for an individual exception by defining an exception handler in the EXCEPTION block of a PL/SQL program. There are two types of PL/SQL exceptions: built-in and user-defined.

Built-In PL/SQL Exceptions

PL/SQL has *built-in exceptions* for common error conditions. For example, PL/SQL has a built-in exception that identifies when a program issues a SQL statement without first connecting to an Oracle7 database. Table 5.2 lists the built-in PL/SQL exceptions.

TABLE 5.2: Predefined PL/SQL Exceptions

Exception	Description
CURSOR_ALREADY_OPEN	You tried to open a cursor that is already open
DUP_VAL_ON_INDEX	You tried to insert a duplicate value into a unique column
INVALID_CURSOR	You referenced an invalid cursor or attempted an illegal cursor operation
INVALID_NUMBER	You tried to use something other than a number where one is called for
LOGIN_DENIED	Your connect request has been denied
NO_DATA_FOUND	No data matches the request of your SELECT INTO statement
NOT_LOGGED_ON	You are not connected to ORACLE7
PROGRAM_ERROR	You hit an PL/SQL internal error
STORAGE_ERROR	You hit a PL/SQL memory error
TIMEOUT_ON_RESOURCE	You've reached a timeout while waiting for an Oracle7 resource
TOO_MANY_ROWS	Your SELECT INTO statement returned more than one row
TRANSACTION_BACKED_OUT	A remote server has rolled back your transaction
VALUE_ERROR	You encountered an arithmetic, conversion, truncation, or constraint error
ZERO_DIVIDE	You tried to divide a number by 0

The following example program shows how you might use the NO_DATA _FOUND and TOO_MANY_ROWS built-in PL/SQL exceptions.

```
CREATE FUNCTION customerid (last IN VARCHAR2, first IN VARCHAR2)
RETURN INTEGER AS
-- This is a function to return the ID of a customer
-- given the customer's last and first names.
   customerid       INTEGER;
   errnum           INTEGER := -20000;
   errmess          VARCHAR2(2000) := 'Standard error';
BEGIN
   SELECT id INTO customerid FROM customer
     WHERE lastname = last AND firstname = first;
RETURN customerid;
```

```
EXCEPTION
  WHEN NO_DATA_FOUND THEN -- if no matching customer, return user error
    SELECT errornumber, errormessage INTO errnum, errmess
      FROM usererrors
      WHERE errormessage LIKE ('Invalid cust%');
    raise_application_error(errnum, errmess);
  WHEN TOO_MANY_ROWS THEN -- if there are multiple customers, then ...
    SELECT errornumber, errormessage INTO errnum, errmess
      FROM usererrors
      WHERE errormessage LIKE ('Multiple cust%');
    raise_application_error(errnum, errmess);
  WHEN OTHERS THEN    -- for undefined errors, return standard error message
    raise_application_error(errnum, errmess);
END customerid;
```

When a PL/SQL program encounters a built-in exception, PL/SQL automatically *raises* the exeception. This means that processing of the main program body stops and transfers to the corresponding *exception handler* in the EXCEPTION block, if present. The code in an exception's handler determines what happens from that point forward.

For example, in the previous example of the CUSTOMERID function, if the SELECT statement in the main program body fails to find a customer record with the given last and first names, the program automatically raises the NO_DATA_ FOUND exception—processing of the main program body terminates and transfers to the NO_DATA_FOUND exception handler in the EXCEPTION block of the program. The exception handler chooses to retrieve a user-defined error number and message from a table and then return them to the calling environment after rolling back the effects of the CUSTOMERID function.

Notice in the EXCEPTION block of the CUSTOMERID function that PL/SQL includes a special OTHERS exception handler. You use the OTHERS exception handler to generically handle any exceptions you don't otherwise explicitly handle in the EXCEPTION block. This is a very convenient way to trap unexpected errors and prevent unhandled exceptions.

User-Defined Exceptions

You can also name your own *user-defined exceptions* in the DECLARE block of a PL/SQL program. For example, you might declare a user-defined exception to handle a specific business rule in a PL/SQL program.

You declare user-defined exceptions in the DECLARE block of PL/SQL. For example, the following statement declares an exception AFTERHOURS:

```
afterhours EXCEPTION
```

When you declare a user-defined exception, you must also define a corresponding exception handler in the EXCEPTION block of a program. The exception handler for the AFTERHOURS exception might be similar to the following:

```
WHEN afterhours THEN
  SELECT errornumber, errormessage INTO errnum, errmess
    FROM usererrors
    WHERE errormessage
    LIKE ('Operation not allowed before 8 A.M. or after 6 P.M.');
  raise_application_error(errnum, errmess);
```

In the main program body, you typically check for user-defined errors at the appropriate time using conditional statements (IF...THEN). When detected, you raise a user-defined exception with the PL/SQL RAISE statement to transfer program processing to the corresponding exception handler.

```
IF (TO_CHAR(SYSDATE,'HH24')) < 8 OR (TO_CHAR(SYSTEDATE,'HH24')) > 28 THEN
RAISE afterhours;
END IF;
```

Unhandled Exceptions

If you don't explicitly handle an exception in a PL/SQL block and don't use the OTHERS exception handler to trap it, PL/SQL rolls back the operations performed by the block and returns the *unhandled exception* back to the calling environment. For example, procedure A calls procedure B, which calls procedure C. If procedure C encounters an unhandled exception, PL/SQL rolls back the effects of procedure C and returns the unhandled exception to procedure B. If procedure B doesn't handle the exception either, PL/SQL rolls back the effects of procedure B and returns the exception to procedure A, and so on.

An unhandled exception can eventually step all the way back to a client application. However, a well-designed PL/SQL program handles all exceptions the program might raise unless there is a specific reason for not doing so. Well-designed PL/SQL programs that correctly handle exceptions are especially important for an application in a client/server database system that calls database-stored procedures. To eliminate network traffic for unhandled exceptions that return back to a client, PL/SQL programs in the database should handle their own exceptions.

> **NOTE**
>
> If an application doesn't explicitly handle an unhandled exception returned from another program, the application typically rolls back the effects of the PL/SQL program call only, not the entire application.

The RAISE_APPLICATION_ERROR Procedure

Oracle7 includes a set of programming utilities you can use when designing client applications. (See Chapter 18 for a complete list.). You can use one utility—the RAISE_APPLICATION_ERROR procedure—to create your own application error numbers and messages. You can have up to 1000 valid user-defined error numbers that range between –20000 and –20999. If you decide to use the RAISE_APPLICA-TION_ERROR procedure extensively throughout your program designs, it's a good idea to centralize user-defined error numbers and corresponding error messages in a database table. This way, programmers won't make up unnecessary error messages and all user-defined error messages will be consistent across all applications. Here is an example:

```
CREATE TABLE usererrors
( errornumber    NUMBER(5,0) PRIMARY KEY,
  errormessage   VARCHAR2(2000));

INSERT INTO usererrors VALUES (-20000, 'Standard error');

INSERT INTO usererrors VALUES (-20001, 'Invalid customer ID');

CREATE PROCEDURE deletecustomer (customerid IN NUMBER) AS
  errnum    NUMBER := -20000;
  errmess   VARCHAR2(2000) := 'Standard error';
```

```
BEGIN
  DELETE FROM customer WHERE id = customerid;
  IF SQL%NOTFOUND THEN -- if no customer is found, return error message
    SELECT errornumber, errormessage INTO errnum, errmess
      FROM usererrors
      WHERE errormessage LIKE ('Invalid cust%');
    raise_application_error(errnum, errmess);
  END IF;
EXCEPTION
  WHEN NO_DATA_FOUND THEN   -- if no matching error message, use standard error
    raise_application_error(errnum, errmess);
END deletecustomer;
```

When you call the RAISE_APPLICATION_ERROR procedure in a program, you raise an exception (roll back the effects of the surrounding program) and return the error number and message to the calling environment (for example, the client application).

PL/SQL Programs

Now that you have a broad overview of the PL/SQL language components, the next few sections discuss different types of PL/SQL programs you can create.

Anonymous PL/SQL Blocks

An *anonymous PL/SQL block* is an unnamed PL/SQL program in an application. For example, you can send the DELETECUSTOMER procedure as an anonymous block of statements to the server when you use SQL*Plus, as shown here:

```
SQL>  DECLARE
SQL>    errnum    NUMBER := -20000;
SQL>    errmess   VARCHAR2(2000) := 'Standard error';
SQL>  BEGIN
SQL>    DELETE FROM customer WHERE id = 12;
SQL>    IF SQL%NOTFOUND THEN -- if no customer is found, return error message
SQL>      SELECT errornumber, errormessage INTO errnum, errmess
SQL>        FROM usererrors
SQL>        WHERE errormessage LIKE ('Invalid cust%');
SQL>      raise_application_error(errnum, errmess);
SQL>    END IF;
```

```
SQL>   EXCEPTION
SQL>     WHEN NO_DATA_FOUND THEN   -- use standard error if no matching error
SQL>        raise_application_error(errnum, errmess);
SQL>   END deletecustomer;
SQL>   /
```

> **NOTE**
> Notice in the example that when using SQL*Plus (or SQL*DBA) to send an anonymous block, you need to include a special program terminator (/) on a line by itself, immediately following the END statement that concludes the program. The program terminator signals SQL*Plus that you have finished typing the statements in the program, so SQL*Plus can process the program and send it to the database server as a single unit.

A client application sends an anonymous block to the database server as a single network I/O, greatly reducing network traffic that would otherwise be present if you send individual SQL statements one by one. However, each time the server receives a new anonymous block, it has to compile the block before it can execute it. This performance problem can be overcome if you store the PL/SQL program inside a database (see the next section). In summary, anonymous blocks are useful if you think of a new procedure that you want to issue just once and won't make use of in the future. If you will repeatedly use a PL/SQL program from a client application, it's better to store the PL/SQL program as a compiled stored procedure or function in the database server.

Procedures, Functions, and Packages

Oracle7 allows you to create and store compiled PL/SQL programs inside a database, including procedures, functions, and packages. *Functions* differ from *procedures* only in that a function returns a single value to the calling environment, while a procedure does not return anything to the calling environment. Your client/server application environment benefits tremendously from using procedures and functions:

- Developer productivity is better because you code, test, and debug common application logic once and store it centrally, where all client applications can use it.

- Application performance is better because an application calls and executes a compiled block of code stored in the database rather than sending an uncompiled block of statements across the network.

- Network overhead is reduced because client applications send a procedure call and a set of parameters rather than individual SQL statements or an entire anonymous PL/SQL block.

You create procedures and functions with the CREATE PROCEDURE or CREATE FUNCTION command, respectively. (See the examples of the CREATE PROCEDURE and CREATE FUNCTION commands earlier in this chapter.)

Defining Procedure and Function Parameters

When you create a procedurr function, you can give it values with which to work using *parameters.* Most CREATE PROCEDURE and CREATE FUNCTION statements in this book specify parameters. When you specify a parameter, you must indicate its datatype. You can use any valid PL/SQL datatype to declare a parameter.

When you specify a procedure or function parameter, you should indicate whether it is an IN, OUT, or IN OUT parameter. An *IN parameter* is one you want to assign a value to when you call the procedure but don't want to allow the procedure to change its value in the outside calling environment. As you might guess, an *OUT parameter* is the opposite of an IN parameter. You don't assign an OUT parameter a value when you call a procedure, but the procedure can assign the OUT parameter's value in the outside calling environment. An *IN OUT parameter* is one you can both assign a value to when you call the procedure and change inside the body of the procedure. Review the procedures in this book for examples of IN, OUT, and IN OUT parameters.

Executing Procedures and Functions

The way in which a client-side application calls a database procedure or function is specific to the development tool with which you create the application. You'll need to read the documentation for your client application development tool to learn the specifics. Here is a client-side PL/SQL block that calls the previously shown CUSTOMERID function and the DELETECUSTOMER procedure to find and delete a customer from the CUSTOMER table:

```
DECLARE
  custid NUMBER(5,0);
BEGIN
-- assign return value of CUSTOMERID function call to custid, and then
-- use the returned value to delete the customer.
  custid := customerid('Hamilton','Alexander');
  deletecustomer(custid);
END;
```

Using Packages

You can create and store related procedures, functions, and other PL/SQL constructs together in a *package*. Among other things, packages allow you to organize related PL/SQL programs for easier application development and for improved security and performance. Packages also allow you to create *global variables* that have persistent state. Here is a package for processing parts in a company's inventory:

```
CREATE PACKAGE partmanager AS
PROCEDURE newpart( price IN REAL, initnum IN INTEGER,
               reorderpt IN INTEGER, descr IN VARCHAR2);
PROCEDURE updatepart( fieldcode IN CHAR, partid IN INTEGER,
               numberupdate IN NUMBER, descupdate IN VARCHAR2);
FUNCTION checkpart(partid IN INTEGER) RETURN NUMBER;
PROCEDURE restockpart( partid IN INTEGER);
PROCEDURE deletepart(partid IN INTEGER);
END partmanager;

CREATE PACKAGE BODY partmanager AS
-------------------------DECLARE  BLOCK-------------------------
-- Private global variables to hold user-defined error numbers and messages
-- for all package procedures and functions.

  errnum    INTEGER;
  errmess   VARCHAR2(2000);
```

```
------------------------RETURNERROR FUNCTION----------------------------
-- This private procedure sets the error number and message for the error
-- asked for by a package procedure or function.

PROCEDURE returnerror (errorstring IN VARCHAR2) IS
BEGIN
  SELECT errornumber, errormessage INTO errnum, errmess
    FROM usererrors
    WHERE errormessage LIKE errorstring||'%';
  raise_application_error(errnum, errmess);
EXCEPTION
  WHEN NO_DATA_FOUND THEN -- if no matching error message, use standard error
  raise_application_error(-20000, 'Standard error');
END returnerror;
------------------------NEWPART PROCEDURE----------------------------
-- This public procedure creates a new part in the STOCK table, given the new
-- part's price, initial quantity, reorder point, and description.

PROCEDURE newpart  (price IN REAL, initnum IN INTEGER,
                     reorderpt IN INTEGER, descr IN VARCHAR2) IS
BEGIN
  INSERT INTO stock
    VALUES (stocksequence.NEXTVAL, price, initnum, reorderpt, descr);
END newpart;
------------------------UPDATEPART PROCEDURE----------------------------
-- This public procedure updates a part record given the part number and
-- either a number or a string for the update (one or the other is NULL),
-- and the code of the field to update (P = unitprice, O = onhand,
-- R = reorder, D = description).

PROCEDURE updatepart ( fieldcode IN CHAR, partid IN INTEGER,
                       numberupdate IN NUMBER, descupdate IN VARCHAR2) IS
  codetype CHAR := fieldcode;
BEGIN
  IF codetype IN ('P','p') THEN
    UPDATE stock SET unitprice = numberupdate WHERE id = partid;
  ELSIF codetype IN ('O','o') THEN
    UPDATE stock SET onhand = onhand + numberupdate WHERE id = partid;
  ELSIF codetype IN ('R','r') THEN
    UPDATE stock SET reorder = numberupdate WHERE id = partid;
  ELSIF codetype IN ('D', 'd') THEN
    UPDATE stock SET description = descupdate WHERE id = partid;
  ELSE
    returnerror('Invalid operation code');
```

```
END IF;
  IF SQL%NOTFOUND THEN
    returnerror('Invalid part');
  END IF;
END updatepart;
-------------------------CHECKPART FUNCTION-------------------------
-- This public function gets the difference between a given part's current
-- quantity and reorder point.

FUNCTION checkpart(partid IN INTEGER) RETURN NUMBER IS
  quantity INTEGER;
BEGIN
  SELECT (onhand - reorder) INTO quantity FROM stock WHERE id = partid;
  RETURN quantity;
EXCEPTION
  WHEN NO_DATA_FOUND THEN
    returnerror('Invalid part');
    quantity := NULL;
    RETURN quantity;
END checkpart;
-------------------------RESTOCKPART PROCEDURE-------------------------
-- This public procedure puts the given part's ID in the REORDER table along
-- with the current quantity and reorder point.

PROCEDURE restockpart (partid IN INTEGER) IS
  reorderstatus    INTEGER := 0;
  quantity         INTEGER := 0;
  reorderpt        INTEGER := 0;
BEGIN
-- First, check to see if part hasn't already been reordered.
  SELECT count(*) INTO reorderstatus FROM reorder WHERE id = partid;
-- If the part hasn't already been reordered, then reorder it now.
  IF reorderstatus = 0 THEN
    SELECT onhand, reorder INTO quantity, reorderpt
      FROM stock WHERE id = partid;
    INSERT INTO reorder VALUES (partid, quantity, reorderpt);
  END IF;
EXCEPTION
  WHEN NO_DATA_FOUND THEN
    returnerror('Invalid part');
END restockpart;
-------------------------DELETEPART PROCEDURE-------------------------
-- This public procedure deletes a part from the STOCK table. A foreign key
-- in the ITEM table prevents the deletion of a part if it is referenced in
-- a line item for an order.
```

```
PROCEDURE deletepart(partid IN INTEGER) IS
BEGIN
  DELETE FROM stock WHERE id = partid;
  IF SQL%NOTFOUND THEN
    returnerror('Invalid part');
  END IF;
END deletepart;

END partmanager;
```

Notice that you create a package in two parts: a package specification and a package body. In the *package specification*, you declare those procedures, functions, and global variables you want to make available to the outside world. Constructs that you declare in a package's specification are *public*. In the *package body*, you define all procedures, functions, and global variables, including others that you don't declare in the package specification. Constructs that you define in a package's body but do not declare in the package's specification are *private*. Applications cannot use private package constructs; only procedures and functions within the package can use them. In the PARTMANAGER package, all procedures and functions are public except the RETURNERROR procedure. The package body also declares two private global variables, ERRNUM and ERRMESS, that work with the RETURNERROR procedure.

Oracle7 has a useful feature called the *sequence generator* that an application can use to quickly generate unique numbers. You can use this facility to create primary keys whenever you insert a new row into a table. First, you must define and name a specific sequence of numbers:

```
CREATE SEQUENCE stocksequence
  START WITH 1
  INCREMENT BY 1
```

This statement creates a sequence of numbers an application can use to generate new part numbers for rows in the STOCK table. The INSERT statement in the definition of the PARTMANAGER.NEWPART procedure given earlier uses STOCKSEQUENCE to create a new part number when someone calls the procedure. Notice that to generate the next available sequence number, the procedure references the sequence using the NEXTVAL suffix.

To learn more about the sequence generator and using sequences, see Chapter 16.

Executing Package Procedures and Functions

To call a public procedure or function in a package, simply preface the call with the package name. The following examples call public procedures in the PARTMAN-AGER package.

```
partmanager.newpart(24.00, 100, 15, 'blue widget');

partmanager.updatepart('P', 304, 72.00, NULL);

partmanager.updatepart('D', 21, NULL, 'yellow-green widget');

partmanager.deletepart(31);
```

Using Database Triggers

A *database trigger* is a PL/SQL procedure that you associate with a table. When you issue a SQL statement for a table that meets a trigger condition, Oracle7 automatically fires (executes) the trigger's body (PL/SQL program body). As Chapter 2 mentions, you can use triggers to program the Oracle7 server to react to specific situations. For example, you can use triggers to enforce complex data integrity rules or to derive specific column values.

You can create a trigger using the CREATE TRIGGER command. The next example is a trigger that derives the total for each line item in the ITEM table.

```
CREATE TRIGGER linetotal
BEFORE INSERT OR UPDATE OF quantity ON item
FOR EACH ROW
DECLARE
  itemprice REAL;
BEGIN
  SELECT unitprice INTO itemprice
    FROM stock WHERE id = :new.stockid;
  :new.total := :new.quantity * itemprice;
END linetotal;
```

Defining Trigger Conditions

A *trigger condition* has a triggering statement and an optional trigger restriction. A *triggering statement* is an INSERT, UPDATE, or DELETE statement that references a specific table. The LINETOTAL trigger's statements are an INSERT statement or an UPDATE statement that references the QUANTITY column of the ITEM table. When you issue either of these statements, Oracle7 fires the LINETOTAL's trigger body to calculate the line item total for every row the statement touches.

You can further limit the firing of a trigger by using a trigger restriction. A *trigger restriction* is a simple Boolean condition that you specify in an optional WHEN clause of the CREATE TRIGGER command. A triggering statement also must satisfy the restriction for Oracle7 to fire the trigger's body. Here is an example:

```
CREATE TRIGGER reorder
AFTER UPDATE OF onhand, reorder ON stock
FOR EACH ROW
WHEN (new.onhand <= new.reorder)
BEGIN
   INSERT INTO reorder VALUES (:new.id, :new.onhand, :new.reorder);
END;
```

Firing Options

When you create a trigger, you can specify several options that determine how Oracle7 fires the trigger's body when the trigger's condition is met. First, you can indicate the number of times you want the trigger body to be executed for each triggering statement. For this, Oracle7 lets you create two different types of triggers: *statement triggers* and *row triggers*. Oracle7 fires a statement trigger's body once, no matter how many rows the triggering statement touches. Oracle7 fires a row trigger's body once for every row the triggering statement touches. When you create a trigger, you need to think about the behavior you want and decide which type of trigger is correct for your application.

The following STOCKCHANGES trigger creates a single, simple record of every statement issued against the STOCK table:

```
CREATE TRIGGER stockchanges
AFTER INSERT OR UPDATE OR DELETE ON stock
DECLARE
   dmltype VARCHAR2(6);
BEGIN
-- Set dmltype to the type of statement issued against the STOCK table.
  IF INSERTING THEN
     dmltype := 'INSERT';
  ELSIF UPDATING THEN
```

```
      dmltype := 'UPDATE';
   ELSE
      dmltype := 'DELETE';
   END IF;
-- Insert the statement user's name and the dmltype into the log table.
   INSERT INTO stockchangelog VALUES (USER, dmltype);
END stockchanges;
```

But what if you want more extensive logging of the changes to the STOCK table? Let's say you want to log every change to every part. In this case, you need to write the STOCKCHANGES trigger as a row trigger:

```
CREATE TRIGGER stockchanges
AFTER INSERT OR UPDATE OR DELETE ON stock
FOR EACH ROW
DECLARE
   dmltype VARCHAR2(6);
BEGIN
-- Set dmltype to the type of statement issued against the STOCK table.
   IF INSERTING THEN
      dmltype := 'INSERT';
   ELSIF UPDATING THEN
      dmltype := 'UPDATE';
   ELSE
      dmltype := 'DELETE';
   END IF;
-- For every row that's changed in the STOCK table, insert the old and new
-- column values for the row.
   INSERT INTO stockchangelog VALUES (dmltype,
      :old.id,:old.unitprice,:old.onhand,:old.reorder,:old.description,
      :new.id,:new.unitprice,:new.onhand,:new.reorder,:new.description);
END stockchanges;
```

You can also specify whether you want the trigger's body to fire before or after the execution of the triggering statement. Again, you need to consider the behavior you want and then create the appropriate type of trigger for your application. For example, the LINETOTAL trigger shown earlier is a BEFORE row trigger—Oracle7 fires the trigger's body once before inserting or updating each row in the ITEM table. A BEFORE row trigger is the correct trigger type for this application because you want to derive the line item total *before* inserting or updating a row in the trigger's table. Alternatively, the STOCKCHANGES trigger (either version) is an AFTER trigger. This is appropriate since Oracle7 doesn't have to roll back the changes to the STOCKCHANGELOG table if the triggering statement fails against the STOCK table.

Special PL/SQL Extensions for Trigger Bodies

To enhance the capabilities of triggers, there are several special PL/SQL extensions you can use in a trigger body: *conditional predicates* and *correlation values.*

The predicates INSERTING, UPDATING, and DELETING allow you to conditionally execute different blocks of statements depending on the type of triggering statement that fires a trigger. Naturally, you need to use conditional predicates only when a trigger's condition includes two or all three types of triggering statements. The previous examples of the STOCKCHANGES trigger (both versions) demonstrate the use of the conditional predicates.

Correlation values allow a row trigger to use the old and new column values of the row the trigger is currently positioned on when it is firing. For example, the second version of the STOCKCHANGES trigger logs the old and new column values when you issue a DML statement against the STOCK table. When the triggering statement is an INSERT statement, the old correlation values are NULLs (there is no old row from which to obtain values); when the triggering statement is a DELETE statement, the new correlation values are NULLs (there is no new version of the row from which to obtain values); and when the triggering statement is an UPDATE statement, both old and new correlation values are available.

NOTE You can reference correlation values in a row trigger's restriction. Correlation values are not available for statement triggers.

The last few sections have given you an overall sense of PL/SQL's capabilities to help you understand the remainder of this book, no matter what job you perform. See Chapter 18 for more information and examples of using PL/SQL in an Oracle7 client/server database system.

This chapter has given you a quick introduction to SQL and PL/SQL, including

- How to work with some of the most commonly used Oracle7 SQL commands: SELECT, INSERT, UPDATE, DELETE, COMMIT, ROLLBACK, SAVEPOINT, GRANT, REVOKE, and SET ROLE

- How to extend the functionality of Oracle7 SQL using the procedural language extensions provided through PL/SQL, such as program variables and constants, flow control statements (IF...THEN, LOOP, and so on), and the different types of PL/SQL programs you can create (procedures, packages, and triggers)

The discussions in this chapter should help you understand the SQL and PL/SQL examples seen throughout this book.

This chapter concludes the introductory portion of this book. You should now have a solid understanding of the big picture in an Oracle7 client/server database system—what the server, client, and network portions of the system do, and how clients can get work done using SQL and PL/SQL programs to communicate with the server. Parts II and III of this book focus on different jobs you might have in an Oracle7 client/server database system. To learn more about database administration, turn to Part II; to learn more about application development, turn to Part III.

PART II

Database Administration in an Oracle7 Client/Server System

Now that you have a foundation of knowledge about the scope of an Oracle7 client/server system, it's time to focus on the tasks of one of the key users of an Oracle7 system, the database administrator. Chapters 7 through 12 reveal detailed information about the job of managing an Oracle7 database, with a special emphasis on client/server database administration.

CHAPTER

SIX

Understanding Oracle7 Database Administration and Administrative Utilities

- Responsibilities of the database administrator

- Special security implications for Oracle7 database administrators

- Using Oracle's primary administrative utility, SQL*DBA

- Using Oracle's SQL*Loader utility

An Oracle7 database server is the central part of an Oracle7 client/server database system. If the database server has not been installed properly or configured correctly, or if it goes down because of a power failure or disk crash, or if it is not performing well, the productivity of many company workers will be hampered. Because the database server plays such an important role as the central manager of data in a client/server system, organizations typically designate one or more people as responsible for the administration of this special system component. This chapter introduces the task of database administration and the tools Oracle7 administrators can use to get their jobs accomplished:

- Responsibilities of the database administrator
- Database administrator security
- SQL*DBA, Oracle's primary database administration tool
- SQL*Loader, the utility for loading data into an Oracle7 database

What Does a Database Administrator Do?

To get you started and to begin this part of the book, this chapter explains the responsibilities of an administrator. These responsibilities include planning the database; configuring your system; creating the database; space management; application planning and installation; security administration; database backup, recovery, and performance monitoring; and dividing administrator responsibilities.

Planning a Database

One key to a successful client/server system design is planning. The more planning you do up front, the more you will know about your system requirements and the better prepared you will be when you have to make important decisions.

Always start the planning of a computer system by clearly identifying the goals and requirements of your application(s). Remember to include both current and future goals in your requirements list so you pick a system design that can grow with your business in the near future. In the planning phase of your system, answer the questions presented in the following sections.

Choosing Computer System Components

The first thing to do is to pick the correct hardware and software components for your system. These include client workstations (or dumb terminals), the database server, operating systems, network hardware, and the network operating system.

To decide which type of client workstations to buy, you'll need to examine the applications you are planning. For example, if your applications will use a bitmapped graphical user interface, make sure the workstations you buy have the correct type of display and a pointing device, such as a mouse. In this case you'll also need to outfit the workstations with an operating system that uses a GUI.

You'll also need to consider your applications to plan the memory and disk-space requirements for your client workstations. For example, make sure the client workstations have at least enough memory to run both the operating system and the proposed application(s). If you will install the application locally on each workstation, you'll need to determine how much disk space is necessary. If you don't want users to store any applications or work locally on the workstation, you may decide to buy inexpensive diskless workstations.

The type of computer and operating system you use for your database server is critical. You need to know, on average, how many transactions a second an application will need to process. Additionally, you must consider any background batch processing that might be necessary. Knowing these facts can help you decide how much processing power your database server will require. For example, if an application's transaction rate is relatively small, you may decide a single processor machine will suffice. If an application's transaction-processing rate is high and you need good performance, you may need to use more powerful computer configurations, such as a multiprocessor computer that can increase system throughput.

When choosing components, answer these questions to help you plan the amount of memory your database server needs:

- How many users will use the system?

- On the average, what number of users will be using the system at the same time?

- How much database data would you like to be able to cache in the memory of the database server to help reduce disk I/O and boost system performance?

Answering these questions will help you plan the amount of disk space your database server needs:

- On average, how much data do you expect the application(s) to generate?
- What are the characteristics of the application's data needs—will your database continue to grow and require more disk space or can you incrementally take older, historical data offline to free disk space?

To help you decide whether you want to purchase additional disks and/or tape storage devices for your database server, answer this question:

- How will you protect your system from possible failures?

Answer these questions to help you decide on the correct network and network operating system for your new applications:

- What type of operations do you want to be able to control on your computer network?
- Does your company's building already have network wiring and a computer network you can use for your new system?
- Is speed or ease-of-use more important to you?

All these questions will help you equip your database system properly. If you are going to use a computer system that you already have for a new application, you can still use the answers to these questions to help you make sure your current system will work for a new application. If you are building a new system, it might be best to plan and purchase a small development system first so you can test your planning before buying the full-blown production system for all system users.

Configuring Your System

Once you decide on and buy the components of your system, the next thing to do is to put them together. Installing the computer system, wiring the network, and integrating the components is a big job. If you work in a medium or large company that has specialists to do this or if you hire an independent consultant to help you, system integration may not be your responsibility. If you have to configure the system yourself, refer to other documentation that can assist you.

Installing Oracle7

Once you have the computer hardware, operating systems, network, network operating system, and communications software in place, you are ready to install the central software component of your system, Oracle7. Again, this job may not be your responsibility if there is a system administrator or consultant to do it for you.

If Oracle7 installation is your responsibility, follow the directions in the Oracle7 installation guide that comes with the software. As part of the Oracle7 installation procedure, you have the option of installing other Oracle software tools and utilities that you may have purchased. If you want to install this software at the same time, follow the directions; otherwise, you can always install additional software at a later time. For a client/server system, you'll definitely want to install your SQL*Net drivers for the communication protocol you'll be using.

Creating a Database

As the database administrator, you are responsible for planning and creating the databases for your Oracle7 system. The next few sections discuss some of the issues surrounding database creation. (Chapter 7 provides step-by-step procedures for database creation.)

The Initial Oracle7 Database

The Oracle7 installer offers you the choice of automatically creating an initial database on your database server. During installation, you can mold the initial database to meet the requirements for your application(s). If you choose the default database during installation and find later that it doesn't meet your needs, you can delete the initial database and start from scratch.

NOTE If you decide to delete the initial database and start from scratch, be aware that there is no "delete database" command to make this a simple operation. You have to identify the files that make up the initial database and delete them using the operating system commands.

Single or Multiple Databases?

When you plan your system and applications, you must decide whether all applications will use a single physical database or whether it is better to use multiple physical databases. If several applications need to use the same or related sets of data, it is much simpler to always organize your information in a single database. Even if applications use independent sets of tables, you can logically and physically separate the data for different applications in different tablespaces (that is, partitions) within a single Oracle7 database. In most cases it's best to use a single database for all applications because you have to configure only one Oracle7 instance and transaction log for all applications.

Use multiple databases when you want to insulate *production database* applications from *test database* application environments. It's a good idea to create a test database for application developers so they can have an unrestricted application development environment that won't affect the ongoing productivity of other workers who are using production applications. For example, if you create a test database for application developers, you can grant them the powerful system privileges to start up and shut down the test database but prevent them from controlling the availability of the production database.

Database Migration

If you want to upgrade to Oracle7 with a database you created with a previous version of Oracle, you'll need to follow the *database migration* steps listed in the database migration guide that comes with your Oracle7 software. If you want to use Oracle7 with data originating from a non-Oracle database, you'll have to load the data into an Oracle7 database using the SQL*Loader utility. For example, SQL*Loader allows you to load data from flat files (text files) into an Oracle7 database. For more information about data loading and SQL*Loader, see the section "Using SQL*Loader" later in this chapter.

Once you've configured your system, installed Oracle7, and created the database, it is time to turn your attention to other tasks, including

- Managing space
- Planning and installing the application
- Administering security

- Backing up and recovering the database
- Monitoring and tuning database performance
- Dividing administrator responsibilities

The following sections explain more about each of these administration tasks.

Space Management

An ongoing database administrator job is managing the space that is available to the database system. Space management encompasses many different but related tasks:

- Tablespace creation and growth: When you install a new application in your system, you typically create one or more new tablespaces in the Oracle7 database so you can physically separate the application's data from other application data. If the data in a tablespace approaches the boundary of the tablespace's preallocated space, you can create additional data files for the tablespace to increase its storage capacity.

- Tuning space usage: Application developers are typically responsible for designing the data structures of a database (tables, views, and so on). However, it is the database administrator who is responsible for implementing the production database design, including consideration of the space implications of the tables in the production database. Specifically, the administrator needs to understand and correctly set the storage parameters for tables and other database objects when creating them so the database will make the best use of space and deliver optimal performance regarding disk I/O.

- Monitoring of space usage: After you create a database, the job of space management is not finished. You need to consistently monitor storage structures for growth characteristics, anomalies, and so on. For example, if a table needs more space, Oracle7 will automatically extend it according to the table's space parameters; however, you might decide that you want to manually extend the table with specific storage parameters.

Planning and Installing an Application

As mentioned in the preceding section, a developer is typically responsible for designing an application's underlying tables, views, procedures, roles, and so on. After validating an application in a test environment, the developer can contact the production database's administrator and arrange to move the new application to the production environment.

As the database administrator, you are responsible for reviewing the *scripts* (batch command files) a developer provides to create the database objects for the new application. When reviewing an application script, consider things like the space parameters for the application objects (as the previous section mentions), object naming, schema design, and so on. After you edit the script, you can run it using SQL*DBA or SQL*Plus to create the application objects. After running the script, you must also consider the security operations necessary to get the application running and a backup strategy for the application's data, as described in the next two sections.

Deployment of an application on client workstations may or may not be your job, depending on your organization. If the client/server system is large, the database administrator typically focuses on managing the database server and lets special system administrators deploy client applications. However, if a system is small (for example, a departmental application), the administrator may be the only person capable of installing the new client application. For complete information about database administration on behalf of client applications, see Chapter 10.

Security Administration

Administrators are responsible for controlling access to a database using operating system, network operating system, and Oracle7 security features. Once you let someone inside an Oracle7 database, you have to control how that person can use the data within a database. If a system has many users and applications, the job of security administration can justify a full-time *security administrator.*

As the security administrator, you are responsible for creating new database users and controlling the privilege domain of each user. When you add a new application to the client/server system, you need to empower users to use the application by creating the application's role(s) and to grant the application role(s) to users and/or other roles, as necessary. (For more information, see Chapters 9 and 19.)

Database Backup and Recovery

Perhaps the most common administrator function is backing up a database's data to protect it from unforeseen problems. To adequately protect a database from damaging situations, you first must configure a database's transaction log and control files. Next you must devise, test, implement, and automate a backup strategy for your database.

If a failure damages your database at some time, it's your job as the database administrator to recover the database as quickly as possible so user productivity does not suffer. (For more information about database backup and recovery, see Chapter 11.)

Monitoring and Tuning Database Performance

Another primary job as database administrator is monitoring and tuning the performance of Oracle7 databases. This can include monitoring and adjusting instance settings, such as process and memory buffer configurations, as well as space management operations such as setting space parameters for database objects, regenerating object statistics for the Oracle7 optimizer, and rebuilding indexes when necessary. (See Chapter 12 for more information about database performance tuning.)

Dividing Administrator Responsibilities

In large systems with many databases, users, or applications, administration may be too big a job for one person. In these cases, it may be necessary to split database administration among a team of administrators. For example, one administrator might be responsible only for the operating system, another for the network, another for database backups, and still another for system security.

Database Administrator Security

If everyone who uses your client/server database system were database administrators, they would all be able to perform such powerful operations as starting up and shutting down Oracle7 databases, creating new tablespaces, creating new users, dropping users, killing user sessions, and so on. To maintain tight control over the power of a database administrator, Oracle7 has three different administrator accounts you can use: SYS, SYSTEM, and INTERNAL.

The SYSTEM Administrator Account

When you create a database, Oracle7 automatically creates the SYSTEM user for database administration connections. The Oracle7 installer prompts you to supply a password for this account in the initial database. When you create other databases, the initial password for this account is MANAGER.

If you don't create customized administration user accounts after installation and database creation, always connect to a database as SYSTEM to complete most database administration tasks. The next two sections describe specific exceptions to this rule.

The SYS Administrator Account

When you create a database, Oracle7 automatically creates the SYS user for special database administration connections. The Oracle7 installer prompts you to supply a password for this account in the initial database. When you create other databases, the initial password for this account is CHANGE_ON_INSTALL.

SYS is the "owner" of an Oracle7 database's data dictionary tables. This means that when you connect to an Oracle7 database as the SYS user, you have the potential of adversely affecting the database's data dictionary, thus preventing normal operation. Therefore, use the SYS account only in these situations:

- When you want to supplement or remove some data dictionary tables using scripts provided with the Oracle7 installation kit
- When you install a new Oracle application and must connect as SYS

The headers in all Oracle7 scripts specifically indicate when you must run a script as SYS, and the installation documentation for Oracle and non-Oracle applications also indicates when to use the SYS account.

NOTE Immediately after you create an Oracle7 database, change the default passwords for both the SYSTEM and SYS users to protect system security.

The INTERNAL Administrator Account

Oracle7 is designed so unauthorized users cannot affect database availability. The INTERNAL user is a special account you must use to start up and shut down a database. Using the INTERNAL user is really another way of connecting to Oracle7 as SYS, but with extra powers to start or stop a database. For this reason, connect as INTERNAL only to start or stop a database.

There are different ways to protect the use of the INTERNAL account, depending on your operating system. Some systems can use operating system security features (for example, UNIX groups) to protect the use of the INTERNAL account. For example, if you use Oracle7 on a UNIX platform, you can use the INTERNAL account only if you are a member of the operating system group called "dba." You can also assign a password for the INTERNAL account. Most client/server systems use a password to protect the INTERNAL account from security breaches.

Enhancing Security with Individual Administration Accounts

Once a database is operational, it's best to create individual administration accounts for all the administrators of the system and avoid giving group access to the standard administrative accounts SYSTEM and SYS. This policy has two primary justifications:

- Individual accounts are typically more secure than a group account because only one user knows the password for an individual account, while multiple users know the password for a group account.

- If access is given to multiple users for a single administrative account, it's hard to track which administrator does which operation.

Using SQL*DBA

Let's take a good look at the primary utility you use to administer an Oracle7 database system: SQL*DBA. When you, as the database administrator, install Oracle7 on your database server, you automatically install SQL*DBA, so it's important to know how it works. This section gives you an idea of the capabilities of SQL*DBA and how to use it in your Oracle7 system. The other chapters in this part of the book provide more specific examples of using SQL*DBA to manage an Oracle7 database system.

The SQL*DBA User Interface

The method for starting SQL*DBA depends on the operating system your database server or client workstation uses. When you start SQL*DBA, it presents you with a GUI that has a menu bar and different windows. Figure 6.1 shows the SQL*DBA user interface.

FIGURE 6.1:

SQL*DBA's user interface includes a main menu bar, from which you can perform most administrative operations. The input window allows you to enter ad hoc SQL statements, and the output window displays output from all menu operations and input window commands.

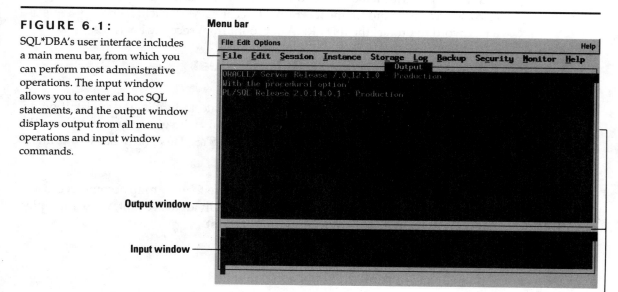

Let's look at the main windows of the SQL*DBA interface. At the bottom is the *input window*, where you can interactively enter any SQL or SQL*DBA command. At the top is the *output window*, where SQL*DBA displays the result when you execute a command in the input window or when you execute a menu option or dialog box. Both the input and the output windows have horizontal and vertical scroll bars that allow you to view text that has scrolled off the screen. The output window has a limited buffer to preserve the older lines of the output.

Across the top of the screen is a menu bar from which you can choose various options. Some options execute operations themselves, while others lead to hierarchical menus or dialog boxes. All in all, the menu options let you see the most common Oracle7 database administration operations and provide you with an easy way to execute them. To give you an idea of how to use SQL*DBA, the next few sections describe many of the most important menus and dialogs.

NOTE Throughout this book, different keys of Oracle products are mentioned by their function rather than their exact keyboard name. For example, you might see the "[List] key" rather than the "F10 key." That's because the Oracle products run on many different types of computers, operating systems, and terminals. As a result, Oracle binds product function keys to different keyboard keys depending on the system you are using. Using the help facility of each Oracle product, you can quickly display the key bindings for the different product functions. On most types of terminals, Ctrl-K will give a listing of the specific key mappings for your terminal.

Figure 6.2 shows an example of a SQL*DBA dialog. When you open a SQL*DBA dialog, the dialog may contain radio list buttons, check boxes, entry fields, list boxes, and so on. The bottom-right area of a dialog has an OK button to accept the current dialog and execute it and a Cancel button to terminate the dialog without performing any work. The bottom-left area of a dialog indicates when an entry field is mandatory and when there is a field builder to help fill the field—for example, the Members to Add field in the Add Online Redo Log Member dialog. To show the underlying field builder, position the cursor in the field and press the [List] key. A field builder appears, as shown in Figure 6.3.

FIGURE 6.2:

Each SQL*DBA dialog has control buttons and optional indicators that tell you when a list is available to help fill in a field or when a specific field is mandatory.

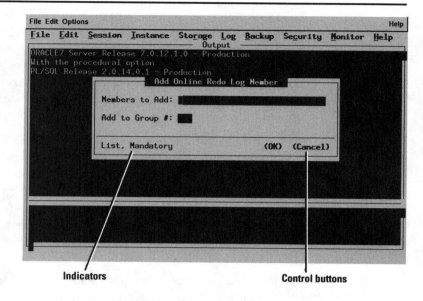

Indicators   **Control buttons**

FIGURE 6.3:

SQL*DBA has many field builder dialogs you can use to help fill in information about more complicated dialog box entry fields.

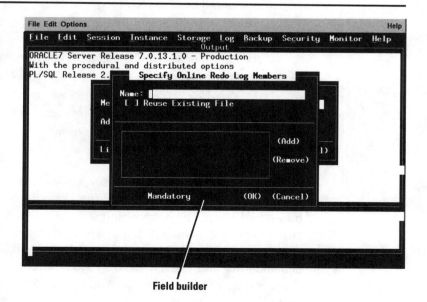

Field builder

Use the options in the field builder. Then select the OK button, and the field builder disappears and places an entry in the parent entry field of the dialog box from which you came.

Example SQL*DBA Dialogs and Menus

This section introduces SQL*DBA by showing you some of the most commonly used dialogs and menus, including

- The Connect dialog
- The Startup Instance dialog
- The Shut Down menu
- The Kill User Session dialog
- The Create Tablespace dialog
- The Begin Online Tablespace Backup/End Online Tablespace Backup dialogs
- The Create New User dialog

Connecting to a Database

Before you can do much with SQL*DBA, you have to connect to Oracle7 using the Connect dialog. To access the Connect dialog, select Session ➤ Connect. Figure 6.4 shows the Connect dialog.

NOTE   You can quickly display a dialog using the hot-key sequence shown in a menu next to the option. For example, on UNIX platforms, the hot-key sequence for the Connect dialog is Esc-O.

Enter your username or a predefined administrator username and a password, and then select the OK button.

FIGURE 6.4:

The Connect dialog allows you to connect to Oracle7 using your username and password.

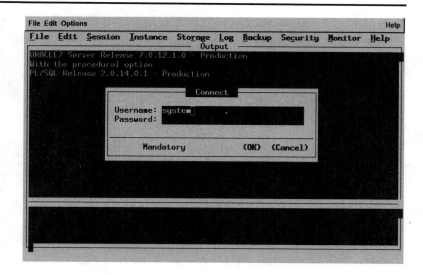

Starting a New Instance

After you connect as INTERNAL, you use the Startup Instance dialog box to start a new Oracle7 instance and optionally mount and open a database. To access this dialog, select Instance ➤ Start Up. Figure 6.5 shows the Startup Instance dialog.

The highest-level radio button list in the Startup Instance dialog, Open-Mount-No Mount, determines to what degree you start Oracle7. Normally you want to start a new instance and mount and open the database in one operation so the database is available to users. To perform a complete startup in one operation, select the Open radio button. Consider the other options, Mount and No Mount, only when you have specific administration operations in mind. For example, the only time you should use No Mount is in creating a new database.

The other options of the Startup Instance dialog allow you to customize your startup. In general, you won't use these other options unless you have special circumstances to address during startup. An exception, however, is the Parameter File entry field. This field allows you to specify the name of the parameter file to use when configuring the new instance. If you don't enter anything in the Parameter File entry field during startup, SQL*DBA uses the default parameter file for your

FIGURE 6.5:

SQL*DBA's Startup Instance dialog allows you to start up an Oracle7 database server so other users can connect to and use the database.

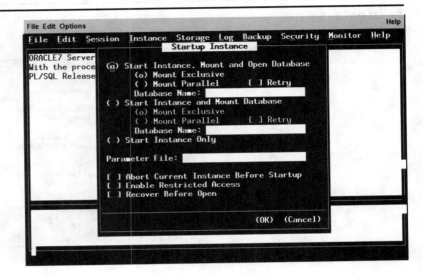

system to start up the database. In most cases you'll have a special parameter file for each database, and that is what you should enter in this field. You have to know the name of the file to enter in the entry field—unfortunately, SQL*DBA doesn't provide you with a list box option to browse and find the file you want.

NOTE The default parameter file varies, depending on your operating system. For example, if you run Oracle7 on a UNIX platform, the default parameter file is "*ORACLE_HOME*/dbs/init*ORACLE_SID*.ora," where *ORACLE_HOME* and *ORACLE_SID* correspond to specific UNIX environment variables. For more information about environment variables, ORACLE_HOME, ORACLE_SID, and default settings for your server's initialization parameter file, see Chapter 7.

Shutting Down the Database

After you connect as INTERNAL, you use the options of the Shut Down menu to stop an Oracle7 database. Figure 6.6 shows the Shut Down menu.

FIGURE 6.6:

The Shut Down menu permits you to stop an Oracle7 database server so it is not available for normal use.

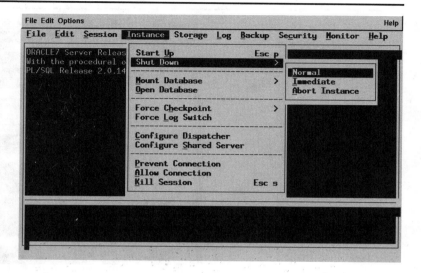

The Normal option of the Shut Down menu is the most user-friendly way of shutting down the database server; it waits for all database users to disconnect before shutting down the server. In situations in which you can't be patient when shutting down a database, you can use the Immediate option to disconnect all users, roll back their open transactions, and commence server shutdown. Use the Abort Instance option only when something has hung the system and the Immediate option doesn't work.

> **TIP**
>
> If your session hangs while you are trying to shut down a database (that is, because it is waiting for users to log off before commencing database shutdown), you can abort your last command using your terminal's normal interrupt key combination, such as Ctrl-C.

Killing a User Session

One of the more useful dialogs in SQL*DBA is the Kill User Session dialog. Many times in a client/server configuration, a client can abnormally disconnect from the

Oracle7 server and Oracle7 can't detect this event because the network does not indicate a disconnection. As a result, the user's remnant session wastes overhead on the server. You can use the Kill User Session dialog to kill such sessions and release the unused overhead. To access this dialog, select Instance ➤ Kill Session. Figure 6.7 shows the Kill User Session dialog.

FIGURE 6.7:
Using the Kill User Session dialog box, you can terminate remnant client user sessions that waste system resources on the server.

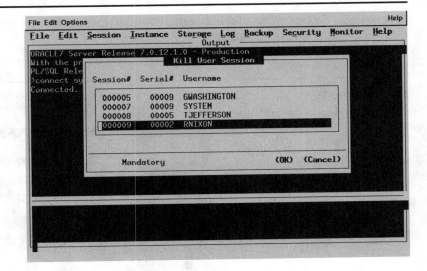

You might also want to kill a user session if you suspect that the session is causing some sort of problem. For example, a user session may be in an endless loop and wasting server processing time.

To use the Kill User Session dialog, look through the list of users and pick the session to terminate.

NOTE If a user has multiple sessions and you're not sure which one to kill, use the different monitors of SQL*DBA to determine the problem session.

Creating a New Tablespace

You can use the Create Tablespace dialog to create a new tablespace for your database. To access this dialog, select Storage ➤ Tablespace ➤ Create. Figure 6.8 shows this dialog.

To use the Create Tablespace dialog, enter a new tablespace name, build a list of data file specifications to store the tablespace's data, optionally set the tablespace's default storage options, and determine whether or not you want the tablespace to be online after creation. (For more information on using the Create Tablespace dialog, see Chapter 7.)

FIGURE 6.8:

The Create Tablespace dialog allows you to create a new tablespace and its storage settings.

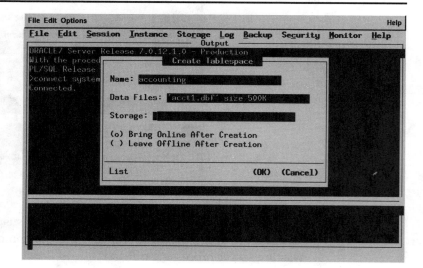

Backing Up the Database

Perhaps the database administrator's most frequently performed operation is database backup. SQL*DBA's Begin Online Tablespace Backup and End Online Tablespace Backup dialogs help you begin and end the process of backing up specific tablespaces while your database is online and in use by users.

The Begin Online Tablespace Backup dialog lists all the online tablespaces not currently in backup mode. To access this dialog, select Backup ➤ Begin Online Tablespace Backup. Figure 6.9 shows this dialog.

To begin the backup of an online tablespace, select the tablespace from the list box in the dialog and select the OK button. This simply tells Oracle7 to prepare the tablespace for backup—it doesn't actually back up the data files of the tablespace. To do the physical file backups, you have to use an operating system command or a backup utility. While this might seem like an inconvenience, it can actually be quite useful and make backup much faster. For example, you can back up different files in parallel to different disk drives or tape devices to speed up the tablespace backup operation. And by using the operating system or a utility that lets you compress the files during the backup, you can save lots of space on your backup media.

TIP You can automate your backups by creating scripts that you can run from SQL*DBA. You can use the options of the File menu to build and execute SQL scripts quickly. (Chapter 12 shows specific examples of how to build database backup scripts.)

FIGURE 6.9:
The Begin Online Tablespace Backup dialog lets you mark any online tablespace for a backup operation.

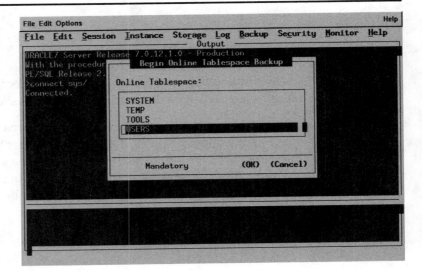

Once you finish backing up an online tablespace's data files, you must let Oracle7 know. You can do this using the End Online Tablespace Backup dialog, as shown in Figure 6.10. You access this dialog by selecting Backup ➤ End Online Tablespace Backup.

The dialog's list box lists only those online tablespaces in backup mode. Select the tablespace to take it out of backup mode and select OK.

FIGURE 6.10:

The End Online Tablespace Backup dialog box lets you unmark online tablespaces that are currently in backup mode.

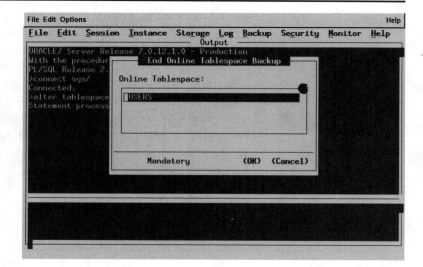

Creating a New User

You use the Create User dialog to create a new user for your database. To access the dialog, select Security ➤ Create User. Figure 6.11 shows the Create User dialog.

For every new user, you must specify a new username and then indicate how you want to authenticate the user. If you want the user to enter a password at connect time, select Use Password Authentication and then enter an initial password for the new user. Alternatively, you can let the operating system authenticate the new user when the user attempts a connection to the database. (See Chapter 9 for more information.)

FIGURE 6.11:

Using the Create User dialog, you can create new database users along with their security settings.

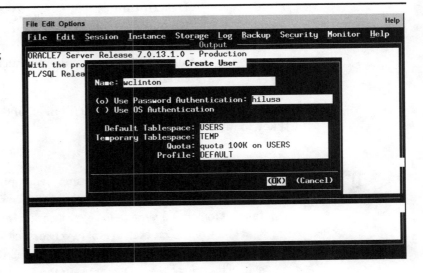

The remaining entry fields of the Create User dialog are optional and control security settings. Following is a quick reference to their meaning, but if you will be creating users, you must learn more about them (see Chapter 9).

Field	Description
Default Tablespace	Allows you to specify a new user's default tablespace, which Oracle7 uses, for example, if the user neglects to include a tablespace specification when creating a new table
Temporary Tablespace	Allows you to specify a new user's temporary tablespace, which Oracle7 uses for temporary work space—for example, when executing a complicated query
Quota	Allows you to indicate the tablespaces with which a new user can create objects and how much space in the corresponding tablespaces is available to the user

Field	Description
Profile	Allows you to assign a resource limit profile to a user. Resource limits control, for example, how many CPU cycles and how much disk I/O a user can use

Field builders are available to help you fill in all of these options. Simply press the [List] key to invoke the field builder.

TIP

As you execute SQL*DBA dialogs or menu options, notice that the output window echos the underlying SQL command. You can use this feature to your advantage in several cases. For example, assume that you want to create several new users, all with the same default tablespace, temporary tablespace, tablespace quotas, and profiles. For simplicity, create the first user using the Create User dialog box. To create the next user quickly, use the Previous Command option of the Edit menu (or even more quickly, use the hot key for this option) to place the previous CREATE USER command in the input window. Then just edit the command's username and password, and then execute the command. Repeat this procedure for the remaining users you need to create. If you want, you can also toggle to the output window to select some text, copy it, and then paste it into the input window.

An Example SQL*DBA Monitor

The Monitor menu of SQL*DBA reveals the different SQL*DBA monitors. Monitors are an administrative tool you can use to report information about ongoing database activity. For example, the System I/O monitor (displayed by selecting Monitor ➤ System I/O) shows the load split among current users of the system. Figure 6.12 shows the System I/O monitor.

Once you display a monitor, you can start it by selecting the Start button. Behind the scenes, the monitor you are using issues a query on one or more internal system tables to fill the monitor with useful information. For example, the System I/O monitor indicates the current system users (using process and session IDs) and the

FIGURE 6.12:

The System I/O monitor shows the processing loads currently in demand by different system users.

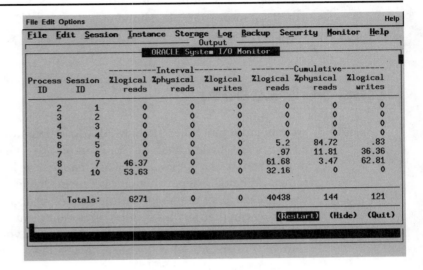

current and cumulative percentages of the load they are imposing on the database server.

TIP

You can have several monitors working at the same time and switch among them using the [Rotate Window] key.

WARNING

Once you start a monitor, it repeatedly issues its query at specific timed intervals to refresh the information in the monitor display. The default cycle is 5 seconds. If you have several monitors running at once and they all issue their queries frequently (say, every 5 seconds), the negative impact on the system performance can be significant. To avoid monitors hurting system performance, run only the monitors you need and terminate them when you are finished (using the Quit button). You can also adjust the monitor cycle interval using the SET CYCLE command of SQL*DBA.

The previous sections have simply introduced SQL*DBA. Throughout this book you'll see more examples showing how to use SQL*DBA to administer an Oracle7 database system.

Using SQL*Loader

At many different times you'll want to load data from a preexisting data source into a table in an Oracle7 database. For example, assume that each salesperson in a sales department uses a personal database manager on his or her PC to keep track of customers. When the department moves to an Oracle7 client/server database, it's best to centralize all of the customer information in a single table so every person in the company can then share a single source of information. SQL*Loader is a simple administrative utility you can use to load data that you output from non-Oracle data sources into an Oracle7 database. The next few sections give you the basics necessary to get started with SQL*Loader.

SQL*Loader Data Sources

To load data into an Oracle7 database using SQL*Loader, the data must be in a text file with the data records in a format that SQL*Loader can read—fixed-length or variable-length.

Fixed-Length Format

A text file containing data records in a *fixed-length format* is one in which each field of each data record is a fixed length. Fields in a fixed-length format are delimited by their position. Field values shorter than a field's maximum value are padded with blank spaces to adjust the field length of every record to exactly match the others. For example, customer records in a fixed-length format might look like the following:

```
1      NBC                  Brokaw                Thomas
2      CNN                  Shaw                  Bernard
```

Variable-Length Format

A text file containing data records in a *variable-length format* is one in which each field of each data record is its real length. To indicate the beginning and end of each field in a variable-length format, the fields must be delimited by special characters, such as commas and quotation marks. For example, customer records in a variable-length format might look like this:

```
1,"NBC","Brokaw","Thomas"
2,"CNN","Shaw","Bernard"
```

NOTE Most programs that store data in a tabular format—specifically, database managers and spreadsheet programs—allow you to output data into standard text files. Furthermore, such programs allow you to specify whether you want to dump data to a text file in a fixed- or variable-length format. If you have the option, choose to dump a file using a variable-length format; it is slightly easier to configure SQL*Loader to accept such data.

SQL*Loader Control Files

Once your data is in a text file, you need to create another text file, called a SQL*Loader control file. A *control file* is a very small text file containing a number of options and clauses that tell SQL*Loader how to load the data from a text file into an Oracle7 database. You can specify many, many clauses and options in a SQL*Loader control file to precisely control data loads. In this section we'll cover just a few of the more important options so you can get a quick start on using SQL*Loader.

LOAD/CONTINUE_LOAD Options The LOAD option is usually the first statement in a control file. It signals the beginning of a new data load. The CONTINUE_LOAD option signals the continuation of an interrupted data load so you can pick up a data load from the point at which it ended earlier (for example, because of an error).

INFILE Parameter Specifies the location of the data you want to load. After the INFILE parameter, specify a valid operating system filename. You can specify an asterisk (*) instead of a filename to indicate that the data to load is contained in the control file itself:

```
INFILE '/u/usr/oracle/rdbms/business.dat'
```

```
INFILE *
```

BEGINDATA Option Indicates the beginning of a block that contains data to load from within the control file itself. Specify the BEGINDATA option only if the INFILE parameter specifies an * to indicate that the data is within the control file and not in an external file. To include data in a control file, make sure the BEGIN-DATA option is the last control file keyword followed by the fixed- or variable-length data rows.

INTO TABLE Clause Specifies the target table for the data load. Specify the target table using standard SQL table name specifications (for example, owner.table):

```
INTO TABLE customer
```

INSERT/APPEND/REPLACE Options The INSERT option indicates that the target table is empty. Use this option if you just created a new table in preparation for a data load. If the table is not empty, SQL*Loader returns an error and cancels the load. The APPEND option indicates that the target table may or may not already have rows and that you want to load the data into the table without affecting any current table data. The REPLACE option indicates that you want to delete all rows in the table before inserting the data from the load. Use the REPLACE option if you periodically refresh a table in the database using data from an external source.

FIELDS Clause Use the FIELDS clause if you plan to load data from a variable-length format data source. In this clause, specify the character that delimits different fields using the TERMINATED BY parameter. Also, use the OPTIONALLY ENCLOSED BY parameter to indicate special characters that enclose different fields. Then specify an ordered list of the names of the columns in the target that correspond exactly to fields in the data to load. Enclose the column list within parentheses:

```
FIELDS TERMINATED BY ' , ' OPTIONALLY ENCLOSED BY ' " '
(id,companyname,lastname,firstname,address,city,state,zipcode,phone,fax)
```

SQL*Loader Command-Line Options

For most operating systems you execute SQL*Loader by invoking the program from the command line of the operating system. When you invoke SQL*Loader, you can specify several command-line options. Here are a few of the most important options to consider:

USERID= Specifies the name and password of the user to connect to Oracle7 when performing a data load. Be sure to specify a user who has the privilege to select and insert records into the target table. Additionally, if the control file specifies the REPLACE option, be sure the user you specify also has the privilege to delete records from the target table. If you don't specify a user account when you invoke SQL*Loader, the program prompts you for one.

CONTROL= Specifies the name of the control file to use to perform the data load. The filename you give must be a valid operating system filename. If you don't specify a control file when you invoke SQL*Loader, the program prompts you for one.

DATA= Specifies the name of the data file that contains the data to load into the target table. Specify the DATA option only if you don't include the INFILE parameter in the control file or if you want to override the INFILE setting in the control file.

LOG= Specifies the name of the file in which to log information about the data load. If you don't specify a log filename, SQL*Loader automatically creates a log file that has the same name as the control file, with the file extension .LOG.

BAD= Specifies the name of the file in which to store data records that are improperly formatted or records that SQL*Loader cannot insert because of errors during the data load. If you don't specify a "bad filename," SQL*Loader automatically creates a file that has the same name as the control file, with the file extension .BAD.

> **NOTE**
> The SQL*Loader command-line options CONTROL, DATA, LOG, and BAD are not case sensitive themselves; however, their inputs, file-names, may be case sensitive depending on your operating system. For example, DOS does not support case-sensitive filenames, but UNIX does.

This example shows how to use these command-line options of SQL*Loader:

```
sqlload USERID=gwashington/P1ew2w
   CONTROL=/u/usr/oracle/cust.ctl
   LOG=/u/usr/oracle/cust.log BAD=/u/usr/oracle/cust.bad
```

Example of Loading Variable-Length Data

The following example shows a control file—the CUST.CTL control file that also contains the data to load—that loads data from a set of customer records in variable-length format into the CUSTOMER table of an Oracle7 database:

```
LOAD DATA
INFILE *
INSERT
INTO TABLE gwashington.customer
FIELDS TERMINATED BY ',' OPTIONALLY ENCLOSED BY '"'
(id,companyname,lastname,firstname,address,city,state,zipcode,phone,fax)
BEGINDATA
1,"NBC","Brokaw","Thomas","Park Avenue","New York","NY","01002",
"1-800-NBC-NEWS","1-800-NBC-FAXS"
2,"CBS","Rather","Daniel","Park Avenue","New York","NY","01002",
"1-800-CBS-NEWS","1-800-CBS-FAXS"
3,"CNN","Shaw","Bernard","Dixie Drive","Atlanta","GA","21002",
"1-800-CNN-NEWS","1-800-CNN-FAXS"
4,"ABC","Jennings","Peter","Park Avenue","New York","NY","01002",
"1-800-ABC-NEWS","1-800-ABC-FAXS"
```

```
5,"NBC","Scott","Willard","Park Avenue","New York","NY","01002",
"1-800-NBC-NEWS","1-800-NBC-FAXS"
```

To load the data, execute SQL*Loader using this command:

```
sqlload USERID=gwashington/P1ew2w CONTROL=/u/usr/oracle/cust.ctl
```

This simple example shows just a few of the many options you can use to load data into an Oracle7 database using SQL*Loader. SQL*Loader has many other control file options that let you customize data loads. For example:

- You can specify a condition to selectively discard rows in the data source and store discarded rows in a separate file (for example, to load only the records with customer IDs > 25).
- You can specify multiple target tables for a single data load.
- You can set a column to NULL or 0 if it meets a condition.
- You can apply SQL functions to fields in a data load.
- You can specify indexes on which to sort data and then have SQL*Loader build the indexes in presorted order as a load proceeds.

Conventional and Direct Path Data Loads

SQL*Loader can load data into a database using two different paths: conventional path loads and direct path loads.

A *conventional path load* proceeds through the normal SQL processing layer of Oracle7. SQL*Loader creates arrays of records to insert and then ships the insert arrays to the database server using the SQL command INSERT.

A *direct path load* bypasses the SQL processing layer of Oracle7 to minimize the time necessary to complete a data load. When you use a direct load, SQL*Loader creates data blocks in the Oracle7 format and directly adds them to the data files in a database. Consequently, a direct path load is typically much faster than a comparable conventional data load.

The example in the previous section performs a conventional load. If you want to perform a direct path load, simply specify DIRECT=TRUE on the command line when invoking SQL*Loader:

```
sqlload USERID= ... CONTROL= ... DIRECT=TRUE
```

Choosing between the Different Types of Data Loads

When should you use a conventional load and when should you use a direct load? In most cases a direct path load is the right choice because it is faster than a conventional path load. However, there are certain restrictions or conditions that justify choosing a conventional path load over a direct path load. Use a conventional path load instead of a direct path load under the following conditions:

- You are loading data across a network in a client/server system.
- The target table must be available to DML transactions during the load.
- The target table has an index and the table must be available to queries during the load.
- The target table is stored in a cluster.
- The target table is being appended and it has frequent delete activity. A conventional load can reuse available space in existing data blocks.

Integrity Constraints, Database Triggers, and Data Loads

Integrity constraints and triggers, the mechanisms you use to maintain data integrity in an Oracle7 database, must be planned for when you use SQL*Loader. For example, if integrity constraints and INSERT triggers are enabled on the target table during a conventional path data load, the data load is slowed down; as SQL*Loader uses the INSERT statement to insert a new row, Oracle7 must check the row for integrity violations. Both conventional and direct path loads are subject to integrity constraints and triggers.

TIP   To speed a data load, it's best to disable constraints and INSERT triggers (UPDATE and DELETE triggers don't affect data loads) during the load and then reenable everything once the load is complete.

If you are going to perform a conventional path load, be sure to disable *all* of the target table's integrity constraints and INSERT triggers. You can do this using several forms of the ALTER TABLE command:

```
ALTER TABLE customer DISABLE CONSTRAINT sys_c00123
-- disables a constraint by its name
ALTER TABLE customer DISABLE PRIMARY KEY
-- disables a table's primary key
ALTER TABLE customer DISABLE UNIQUE (lastname, firstname)
-- disables a table's unique key
ALTER TABLE customer DISABLE ALL TRIGGERS
-- disables all of a table's triggers
```

If you try to disable a parent key before a data load and the dependent keys are enabled, you must either disable the dependent keys first or use the CASCADE option of the DISABLE clause to disable the parent key and all of its dependent keys:

```
ALTER TABLE customer DISABLE PRIMARY KEY CASCADE
```

SQL*Loader automatically disables check and referential integrity constraints and INSERT triggers before commencing a direct path data load. However, SQL*Loader does not automatically disable other types of constraints, including NOT NULL, PRIMARY KEY, and UNIQUE. You must use the ALTER TABLE statements above to disable any other integrity constraints before a data load.

Once a data load is complete, you can reenable any disabled constraints and triggers using the ALTER TABLE command. Remember to enable any related dependent keys not in the target table:

```
ALTER TABLE customer ENABLE CONSTRAINT sys_c00123
-- enables a constraint by its name
ALTER TABLE customer ENABLE PRIMARY KEY
-- enables a table's primary key
ALTER TABLE customer ENABLE UNIQUE (lastname, firstname)
-- enables a table's unique key
ALTER TABLE customer ENABLE ALL TRIGGERS
-- enables all of a table's triggers
```

If all rows in the table pass the integrity rule that you enable, Oracle7 enables the constraint without error. However, if the table contains *exceptions* to (rows in violation of) the integrity rule after a data load, Oracle7 cannot enable the constraint. When enabling an integrity constraint, you can generate a report of exceptions using the EXCEPTIONS INTO parameter of the ENABLE clause:

```
ALTER TABLE customer  ENABLE PRIMARY KEY EXCEPTIONS INTO exceptions
```

If no exceptions exist, Oracle7 enables the constraint. However, when exceptions exist for the constraint you specify, Oracle7 generates a report of exceptions as rows of information in a specially formatted table called EXCEPTIONS. You must run the UTLEXCPT.SQL script in your account to create the EXCEPTIONS table before trying to create an exceptions report. For example, assume that after a data load, there are two rows with the same primary key value. A query of the EXCEPTIONS table would provide information similar to the following to help you discover which rows violate the integrity constraint:

```
SELECT * FROM exceptions
```

ROW_ID	OWNER	TABLE_NAME	CONSTRAINT
00000005.0004.0005	GWASHINGTON	CUSTOMER	SYS_C00337
00000005.0005.0005	GWASHINGTON	CUSTOMER	SYS_C00337

You can automatically configure a SQL*Loader control file to reenable constraints after a data load by using the REENABLE control file keyword. You can even add an EXCEPTIONS parameter to specify an exceptions table to report constraint exceptions:

```
REENABLE EXCEPTIONS INTO exceptions
```

Checking data integrity after reenabling INSERT triggers is a different story. When you reenable a trigger, Oracle7 doesn't check the rule against all table rows before enabling the trigger. Therefore, it's up to you to check the integrity of your table with regard to triggers after a data load.

NOTE SQL*DBA and SQL*Loader are not the only administrative utilities you can use to administer and load data into an Oracle7 database. There are other administrative utilities you can purchase from independent software companies. Appendix C gives lists several different third-party database administration utilities.

This chapter has presented a clear picture of what an Oracle7 administrator does and has introduced the primary administration utility, SQL*DBA, that you use to accomplish administration tasks. The next chapter discusses basic Oracle7 database administration procedures, including how to create an Oracle7 database and control its availability.

CHAPTER
SEVEN

Basic Database Administration

- Operating system account settings for administration

- Initialization files and creating databases

- Controlling server and data availability

- Extending database storage capacity

- Reporting database structural and space information

As you read through the chapters in Part II of this book, you'll quickly learn that database administration is a big job. Given that you have to start somewhere, this chapter explains the most basic database administration tasks, including

- Working with operating system settings
- Creating and customizing initialization parameter files for databases
- Planning and creating a new Oracle7 database
- Starting and stopping an Oracle7 database server
- Controlling the availability of individual tablespaces within an Oracle7 database
- Extending the storage capacity of an Oracle7 database
- Reducing the size of an Oracle7 database

Establishing Operating System Settings for Database Administration

Before you perform any type of administrative function, it is important to configure several operating system session variables for your operating system session to make database administration easier. *Operating system session variables* serve as a kind of shorthand and provide file and device independence for files and directories.

Most operating systems have operating system session variables, although each operating system refers to them by a different name: UNIX calls them "environment variables," VAX VMS uses "logicals," and Novell NetWare and DOS refer to them as "CONFIG parameters." Whatever your operating system calls them, there are two important operating system session variables for you to set when working with Oracle7: ORACLE_HOME and ORACLE_SID.

- ORACLE_HOME specifies the home directory where Oracle7 is installed. During the installation procedure for Oracle7, ORACLE_HOME is configured, so it is likely that you will never have to adjust the setting for this operating system session variable on the server. However, each operating system has a different way of configuring ORACLE_HOME on the client, if necessary.

- ORACLE_SID (on UNIX) or ORACLE_SRVNAME (on Novell NetWare) identifies the database to work with in an operating system session. This operating system variable is especially important if one central server has more than one database. ORACLE_SID's value may change, depending on the database currently of interest. The ORACLE_SID for a particular database is typically the same as the database's name, although it can be different.

NOTE   Each operating system has its own method for setting operating system session variables. Use your operating system documentation to determine how to set these variables.

Creating and Editing Database Initialization Parameter Files

Before creating and starting up an Oracle7 database, you must create an initialization parameter file for the database. A database's initialization parameter file has many settings specific to the database, several of which must be configured before you actually create the database.

One way to create a parameter file for a new database is to make a copy of the example parameter file called INIT.ORA. You can find init.ora in the dbs directory of ORACLE_HOME on UNIX systems and in the RDBMS70 directory of ORACLE_HOME on Novell NetWare systems. Copy INIT.ORA to a filename that corresponds somehow to the name of the new database (for example, initsales.ora).

You can customize a parameter file for a database by using a text editor to change the settings for the parameters in the file. When you use a text editor to open a copy of the INIT.ORA initialization parameter file, you will see many initialization parameters. Oracle has conveniently included commented lines (lines that start with #) that suggest several parameter settings for small, medium, and large databases.

Choose the parameter settings that best work for your database and uncomment them (remove the #s at the beginning of the lines).

Creating an Oracle7 Database

Creating an Oracle7 database is a lot like building a new house. Both jobs have two major phases—the design phase and the creation phase. The database design phase includes planning file limits and file placements for the new database. The database creation phase is the execution of the plan using the SQL command CREATE DATABASE and some scripts. This section explains the design and creation phases for an Oracle7 database.

Planning an Oracle7 Database

Before constructing a new house, an architect must consider several things to create a quality design. Among other things, the lot and house foundation must account for water drainage, the house's infrastructure must meet local building electrical, plumbing, and earthquake codes, and the house's floor plan must suit the owner's taste. If the architect does not draft a good plan beforehand, it is difficult to go back and change the house after it is built.

Similarly, an Oracle7 administrator must plan several things about a database's foundation—its file structure—before creating the database because it is hard or impossible to change things later. As an administrator, your tasks include

- Determining appropriate values for the file limit parameters of the CREATE DATABASE command
- Planning the size and location of the initial data files of the new database's SYSTEM tablespace
- Planning the size and location of the new database's transaction log groups and members
- Determining the character set to store database data
- Creating an initialization parameter file for the new database and specifying the filenames of the database's control file

The following sections discuss each topic in planning a new Oracle7 database.

Determining Database File Limits

The SQL command CREATE DATABASE has several optional parameters that determine the maximum number of different types of files you will be able to create for a new database. These file limit parameters include the following:

Parameter	Description
MAXDATAFILES	Determines the maximum number of data files that can ever be allocated for the database
MAXLOGFILES	Determines the maximum number of log groups for the database
MAXLOGMEMBERS	Determines the maximum number of members for each log group

When planning a database, it is crucial to set the file limits for the new database correctly; it is very hard to go back and change them after you create the database.

All file limit parameters of the CREATE DATABASE command have default and maximum values. If you do not specify a particular file limit parameter, Oracle7 uses the default value when creating the database. The default and maximum values for file limits vary, depending on the operating system you use to run the Oracle7 server. For example, the default and maximum values for MAXDATAFILES on Oracle7 SCO UNIX are 30 and 1022, respectively. For Oracle7 on Novell NetWare, the values are 1 and 254.

TIP

All file limit parameters directly affect the size of the database's control file. Higher file limits allocate more space in the control file to make it slightly larger. Considering the minimal size effect on the control file and the difficulty of changing a database's file limits after database creation, it is much better to err on the high side when setting file-limit parameters.

Planning File Sizes and Placements

An architect has to determine the best placement for doors and windows in a house to make the house functional and aesthetically appealing. Similarly, a database administrator must plan the size and placement of a database's initial data files and log files to ensure maximum database performance and fault tolerance. Although Oracle7 allows you to correct poor choices for file sizes and placement after database creation, it is easier to plan and get it right during database creation.

The CREATE DATABASE command allows you to indicate the names, sizes, and locations for two different types of files for a new database:

File Type	Description
DATAFILE	Specifies the initial data file(s) for the database's SYSTEM tablespace
LOGFILE	Specifies the database's initial transaction log groups and members

File size is an important consideration when creating Oracle7 files because of the way Oracle7 allocates space to store database data. Oracle7 preallocates static, sized files to eliminate data fragmentation within a single file. *Preallocated files* are like empty buckets that a database server fills with data as users create tables and carry out transactions. This disk I/O optimization technique ensures that all of a file's data blocks are allocated at the same time and in a relatively contiguous location on disk. This reduces disk head movement during system operation, so the database server can deliver good disk I/O performance. However, because the files cannot grow, it's important to size database files correctly; they must be big enough to store the proposed data but not so large that they waste valuable disk space.

NOTE Some computer programs allocate data storage space using methods different from Oracle7's. For example, a word processor grabs disk space on an as-needed basis every time a user stores edits to a document. This means that a word processing file dynamically grows and shrinks and can become *fragmented* across the sectors of a disk; that is, different data blocks of a document file might be scattered in different sectors across a disk. Word processors can use this type of file space allocation scheme because it is unlikely that a user will notice any performance degradation as the disk head reads a single document's data from different sectors on a disk.

There are several important considerations when specifying the initial data file(s) of the SYSTEM tablespace. First of all, there is no advantage to specifying more than one initial data file for the SYSTEM tablespace. It is typically better to use fewer large data files than many small data files for a tablespace, to keep tablespace data fragmentation to a minimum. Regarding size, the SYSTEM tablespace's initial data file must have enough space to hold all data dictionary tables (about 5MB). Additionally, you might plan to install client tools and applications that create more data dictionary tables and require space in the SYSTEM tablespace. And if you have Oracle7 with the procedural option, Oracle7 automatically stores all database procedures and triggers in the SYSTEM tablespace. Therefore, you must make sure there is enough space for the procedures and triggers your system's applications will require. (See Chapter 10 for some help with planning space for procedures and triggers.)

The placement of Oracle7 database files is important for both performance and fault tolerance. For example, the different members of each mirrored transaction log group should be on different physical disks to protect the transaction log against isolated disk failures.

Determining the Database Character Set

When creating a new database, you can use the CHARACTER SET parameter of the CREATE DATABASE command to specify the character set Oracle7 will use to store database data. It is important to make the correct choice because after database creation you cannot change a database's character set. A database's character set is usually the character set most users employ when interacting with Oracle7. For example, those of you who live and work in the U.S. most likely will use the US7ASCII character set for Oracle7, a set of characters that corresponds to the English language as used in the U.S.

Creating the Database Initialization Parameter File

Before you can create a new database, you must create and customize an initialization parameter file for the database. (See the section "Creating and Editing Database Initialization Parameter Files" earlier in this chapter.) When you customize your new database's initialization parameter file, it is crucial that you properly set the CONTROL_FILES and DB_NAME parameters.

Parameter	Description
CONTROL_FILES	Determines the name and location of each copy of the database's control file. It is important to specify at least two control file names on different disks. This way, Oracle7 mirrors the database's control file to protect it against an isolated disk failure
DB_NAME	Sets the name of the database. A database's name is a literal, eight characters or less, made of alphabetic characters (case is insignificant), numbers, underscores (_), sharps (#), and dollar signs ($)

Here is an excerpt from an initialization parameter file, INITACCTING.ORA, that corresponds to a database named ACCTING (short for ACCOUNTING) on an Oracle7 for SCO UNIX database server:

```
.
.
.
DB_NAME = accting
CONTROL_FILES = /usr/oracle/dbs/controlaccting.ora,
/u2/usr/oracle/dbs/controlaccting.ora
.
.
.
```

In this case the two copies of the ACCOUNTING database's control file are on different disk drives—the first copy is in the root file system and the second copy is in the /u2 file system on a different disk drive.

Special Considerations

There are additional CREATE DATABASE command parameters and initialization parameters that apply to special circumstances. If your system supports the Oracle7 Parallel Server option, you will want to plan settings for the following CREATE DATABASE command parameters:

Parameter	Description
MAXLOGHISTORY	Specifies the amount of space to reserve in the control file for names of archived transaction log groups. These names are used by the Parallel Server option if certain recovery operations are necessary
MAXINSTANCES	Specifies the maximum number of instances to which the database can ever be simultaneously mounted

If you plan to make your new database part of a distributed database, it is also important to set the DB_DOMAIN initialization parameter to an appropriate *Internet network address*. A typical Internet network address for an Oracle7 database server is the Internet protocol (IP) address of the host computer. The DB_DOMAIN parameter takes a form similar to the following:

```
servername.companyname.com
```

An Example of Database Planning

Now that you have a good idea of what to plan before creating an Oracle7 database, let's look at a comprehensive, integrated example to demonstrate proper database planning.

Assume that a dentist's office is creating a database to track patient records and billing information. The database server will have two different client applications, one for tracking insurance billing and another for tracking medical information about patients. Both client applications use database procedures and triggers to centralize common application logic and business rules.

The database server has these characteristics:

- Oracle7 runs on a computer using UNIX.
- The server has two different disk drives, with the root file system on one disk drive and the /u2 file system on the other.
- The native user language is US English.
- The expected database growth rate is 12MB/year, approximately 50K/day.

Given this information, here's a good plan for the initialization parameter file settings:

```
CONTROL_FILES /usr/oracle/dbs/patient.ctl,
/u2/usr/oracle/dbs/patient.ctl
DB_NAME patients
```

And here's an acceptable CREATE DATABASE command for the new database:

```
CREATE DATABASE patients
LOGFILE
  GROUP 1 ('/usr/oracle/dbs/patient1.log',
  '/u2/usr/oracle/dbs/patient1.log') SIZE 50K,
  GROUP 2 ('/usr/oracle/dbs/patient2.log',
  '/u2/usr/oracle/dbs/patient2.log') SIZE 50K
```

```
MAXLOGFILES 10
MAXLOGMEMBERS 4
DATAFILE 'usr/oracle/dbs/patientsystem1.ora' SIZE 40M
MAXDATAFILES 100
CHARACTER SET us7ascii
```

MAXDATAFILES can be set to 100 because the dentist's database grows very slowly and predictably. It is a reasonable assumption that with proper planning, you can allocate space for one year's worth of records on a yearly basis to slowly extend the tablespace that stores patient records and insurance billing information. A setting of 100 for MAXDATAFILES is more than reasonable for the growth characteristics of this database.

DATAFILE specifies a single data file—'/usr/oracle/dbs/patientsystem1.dbf' SIZE 40M—for the SYSTEM tablespace. 40MB is ample space for data dictionary tables, as well as for many stored procedures and triggers.

Given the daily generation of data, the dentist's database probably needs only two or three log groups, with each file size being small; MAXLOGFILES is set to 10 just in case the future demand on the database grows and more log groups are necessary. Since the database server has only two disk drives, it makes sense that the maximum number of members per group will be two; however, MAXLOGMEMBERS is set to 4 in case additional disks are available in the future.

CHARACTER SET is set to US7ASCII because all users on the system will use US English as their language.

Planning Aid

Use Table 7.1 to help you plan a new Oracle7 database. This table includes the most important items of database planning, a short description of each item, and a blank space where you can make notes about the setting for a new database.

Using CREATE DATABASE to Create an Oracle7 Database

Once you have planned a new Oracle7 database, you can execute your plan using the SQL command CREATE DATABASE.

TABLE 7.1: Checklist for Database Creation Parameters

Parameter	Description	Your Setting
ORACLE_HOME—Operating system session variable	Points to the directory location where Oracle7 is installed	———— ————
ORACLE_SID (or ORACLE_SRVNAME)—Operating system session variables	Identifies the Oracle7 database of interest	———— ————
CONTROL_FILES—Initialization parameter	Determines the names of the database's control files. Specify at least two filenames, each on a different disk	———— ————
DB_NAME—Initialization parameter	Determines the name of the database	———— ————
MAXDATAFILES—CREATE DATABASE command parameter	Determines the maximum number of data files you can ever create for the database. Consider that every time you create a new tablespace or need to extend the storage space in a current tablespace, you create one or more datafiles	———— ————
DATAFILES—CREATE DATABASE command parameter	Identifies the names and sizes of the initial datafiles in the SYSTEM tablespace. It is better to create fewer large files than many small files, to reduce data fragmentation	———— ————
MAXLOGFILES—CREATE DATABASE command parameter	Determines the maximum number of log groups you can ever create for the database	———— ————
MAXLOGMEMBERS—CREATE DATABASE command parameter	Determines the maximum number of log members you can create for each log group. Therefore, MAXLOGMEMBERS determines how many levels of mirroring you can use to protect the transaction log	———— ————
CHARACTER SET—CREATE DATABASE command parameter	Determines the character set Oracle7 uses to store data in the new database	———— ————

To use the CREATE DATABASE command, first you must start SQL*DBA and connect to the Oracle7 database server using the INTERNAL account. Then, using the parameter file for the new database, start up a new instance only; do not mount or open the database, because it is not there! (If you are not familiar with database startup, see the section "Starting the Oracle7 Server" later in this chapter.)

Once you complete the prerequisite steps, you can issue a CREATE DATABASE statement. (See the preceding section for an example of the CREATE DATABASE command.)

A CREATE DATABASE statement takes a while to complete because Oracle7 must allocate disk space for several database files and create the internal data dictionary tables in the SYSTEM tablespace. After the statement completes, Oracle7 leaves the database mounted and open.

What to Do after Creating the Database

After you create a database, you'll probably want to run some scripts to build additional data dictionary tables and public views for the data dictionary. On UNIX systems, the following scripts can be found in the rdbms/admin directory underneath ORACLE_HOME. On Novell NetWare systems, the scripts can be found in the rdbms70\admin directory underneath ORACLE_HOME.

Script	Description
CATALOG.SQL	Creates data dictionary tables and views. Run this script as SYS for all databases
CATPROC.SQL	Creates additional data dictionary tables and views for the Oracle7 Procedural option. Run this script as SYS only if you install the Oracle7 Procedural option.

Both scripts build many data structures and will take some time to complete.

After you create a new database with the CREATE DATABASE command, the database has only one tablespace—the SYSTEM tablespace. To keep data dictionary information in the SYSTEM tablespace separate from application data, you'll want to create additional tablespaces for the new database. (See the section"Creating New Tablespaces" later in this chapter to learn how to do this.)

Another important step after database creation is to turn on media recovery. When Oracle7 creates a database, by default media recovery is disabled to avoid unnecessary logging of the database creation step and make database creation proceed more quickly. However, to fully protect a new database after creation, you need to enable media recovery. (For more information about this operation, see Chapter 11.)

Controlling Database Availability

Now that you have a database, the next step is to open it so people can use it. One of the most basic administrative operations for an Oracle7 administrator is controlling the availability of a database. Until an administrator opens a database, users cannot employ applications to interact with an Oracle7 database server. This section explains how to control the general availability of an Oracle7 database, as well as how to control the availability of individual tablespaces within a single database.

Starting the Oracle7 Server

There are three phases to database startup:

1. Start a new instance for the database.

2. Mount the database to the instance.

3. Open the mounted database.

You can start a database very easily using the Startup Instance dialog box of SQL*DBA. To access this dialog, use the hot-key sequence for your system (Esc-P for UNIX) or, from the SQL*DBA menu, select Instance ➤ Start Up. The Startup Instance dialog is shown in Figure 7.1.

FIGURE 7.1:

Use the Startup Instance dialog of SQL*DBA to start the Oracle7 database server and make the database available for use by applications and users.

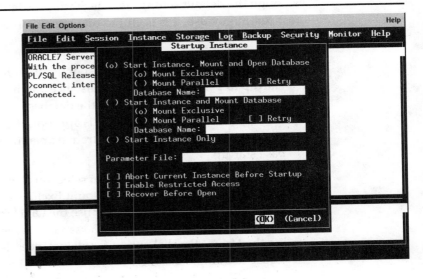

NOTE To use the Startup Instance dialog box of SQL*DBA, you must connect to Oracle7 as INTERNAL.

The default settings of the Startup Instance dialog start a new instance and mount and open the database, all in one step. In most cases this is just what you want to do, so you can simply select the OK button to start the database.

NOTE On UNIX systems, make sure that your operating system session variable ORACLE_SID is set for the target database and that the database's initialization file is $ORACLE_HOME/dbs/initORACLE_SID.ora. This way, the default settings of the Startup Instance dialog will automatically start, mount, and open a new database when you select OK.

Although the default settings for the Startup Instance dialog are the ones you will most commonly use, it is useful to understand all options in case there are special circumstances.

- The highest-level radio button list determines how many phases of database startup to perform: Start a new instance and mount and open the database, start a new instance and mount the database, or just start a new instance. In most cases, the default selection is appropriate; select one of the other choices when a specific administrative operation calls for an incomplete database startup.

- Each of the first two radio button selections has a second-level radio button list. For most sites, the default Mount Exclusive is appropriate; pay attention to the mount options only if you use the Oracle7 Parallel Server option. If this is the case, you can mount the same database to multiple instances by using the Mount Parallel option for all instances. Mount Exclusive limits the database to a single instance.

- Each of the first two radio button selections has a Database Name entry field where you can specify the name of the database to start up. You can usually leave this field blank because the DB_NAME parameter in the initialization parameter file specifies the name of the database to start. However, if you choose to specify the database's name, it must correspond exactly with the setting for the DB_NAME parameter in the initialization parameter file you use to start the instance.

- The Parameter File entry field specifies the name of the initialization parameter file to use to start the database. Again, in most cases you can leave this field blank because the default setting will specify the correct parameter file for database startup. However, you can override the default parameter filename by specifying a filename in this entry field.

- The Abort Current Instance Before Startup check box shuts down any current instance before starting the new instance. Use this option only if the previous instance is still present and operating in an abnormal state (that is, it is hung).

- The Enable Restricted Access check box limits database access to those users, typically administrators, who have the RESTRICTED ACCESS system privilege. Use this option only when you want to limit access to database administrators.

- The Recover Before Open check box performs database recovery, if necessary, before mounting and opening a database. Use this option only after you restore backups of data files because of a disk failure. (See Chapter 11 for more information about database recovery.)

After you start a new instance and mount and open the database, users can connect to the database using a client application and then perform work.

Special Considerations for Database Startup in Client/Server Environments

It is easiest to start up an Oracle7 database while directly connected to the database server itself, using a terminal or terminal emulator that creates a host session on the database server. However, there may be times when it is necessary to start up a database across a network using a remote client workstation.

When starting a database from a client workstation, the Oracle7 database server must allow remote connections using the INTERNAL account. When installing Oracle7, be sure to enable remote connections as INTERNAL. Additionally, be sure to allow INTERNAL connections using a password so administrators can connect as INTERNAL from a client workstation.

Because SQL*DBA is running on the client workstation, a copy of the database's initialization parameter file must be on the client workstation. When distributing a copy of a database's initialization file, make sure the file copy accounts for any operating system differences between the client workstation and the host database server. For example, if the client workstation uses MS-DOS and the database server uses UNIX, the initialization parameter file must be translated correctly between the two operating systems. SCO UNIX has the programs dos2unix and unix2dos to convert simple text files between the MS-DOS and UNIX operating systems.

Stopping the Oracle7 Server

Just as with database startup, there are three phases to database shutdown:

1. Close the database.

2. Dismount the database from the instance.

3. Terminate the instance.

You can shut down a database easily using the Shut Down menu of SQL*DBA. To access this menu from the SQL*DBA menu, select Instance ➤ Shut Down. The Shut Down menu is shown in Figure 7.2.

NOTE To use the Shut Down menu of SQL*DBA, you must connect to Oracle7 as INTERNAL.

The Shut Down menu has three options:

- The Normal option shuts down the database after all users disconnect from the database.

- As its name indicates, the Immediate option shuts down the database immediately after rolling back the effects of all current transactions.

- Use the Abort Instance option only in special circumstances—for example, when a previous instance is hung and will not terminate any other way. The

FIGURE 7.2:
Use the options of the SQL*DBA Shut Down menu to stop the Oracle7 server, thus making the database unavailable for normal use.

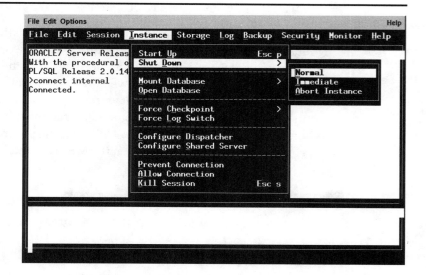

Abort Instance option does not roll back current transactions before aborting the instance. Therefore, it may take some additional time to start up the database after aborting an instance because Oracle7 must perform crash recovery.

In most cases, you will want to choose the first or second option.

Special Considerations for Database Shutdown in Client/Server Environments

As with the database startup, it is easiest to shut down an Oracle7 database while directly connected to the database server itself, using a terminal or terminal emulator. However, you can shut down a database from a client workstation running SQL*DBA if the Oracle7 database server allows remote connections to the INTERNAL account using a password.

Taking Individual Tablespaces Online and Offline

With a database open, Oracle7 lets you control the availability of individual tablespaces within the database. The data in a tablespace is available when it is *online* and not available when it is *offline*.

In certain circumstances, you may want to temporarily take a tablespace offline. For example, if all of an application's data is in a single tablespace, you can effectively take the application offline by taking the corresponding tablespace offline.

You can control the availability of a tablespace using the Set Tablespace Online and Set Tablespace Offline dialogs of SQL*DBA. To access either dialog, use the dialog hot-key combinations (Esc-N and Esc-F for UNIX) or, from the SQL*DBA menu, select Storage ➤ Tablespace and then choose either Set Online or Set Offline. Figure 7.3 shows the Set Tablespace Online dialog.

FIGURE 7.3:

Use the Set Tablespace Online dialog of SQL*DBA to bring an offline tablespace back online and make its data available for normal use.

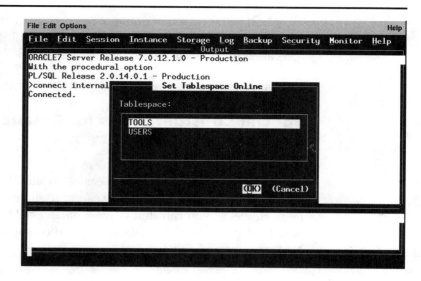

To use the Set Tablespace Online dialog of SQL*DBA, you must have the ALTER TABLESPACE or MANAGE TABLESPACE system privilege.

The Set Tablespace Online dialog list box shows only those tablespaces that are currently offline. Simply select the offline tablespace you want to bring online and select the OK button. Oracle7 brings the tablespace online. Figure 7.4 shows the Set Tablespace Offline dialog.

To use the Set Tablespace Offline dialog of SQL*DBA, you must have the ALTER TABLESPACE or MANAGE TABLESPACE system privilege. Furthermore, all rollback segments within the tablespace must currently be offline. (See Chapter 10 if you need more information about rollback segments.)

FIGURE 7.4:

Use the Set Tablespace Offline dialog of SQL*DBA to take an online tablespace offline and make its data unavailable for normal use.

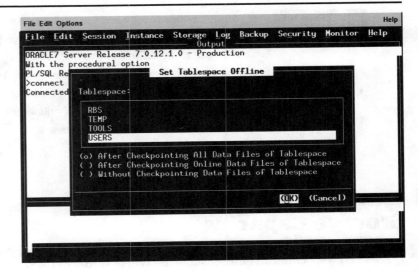

The Set Tablespace Offline dialog list box shows only those tablespaces that are currently online. Select the online tablespace you want to take offline. Next, select an offline option from the radio button list.

- When taking a tablespace offline, your first option is the default radio button, After Checkpointing All Data Files of Tablespace. When you use this option, Oracle7 writes all modified data in memory back to the data files of the tablespace before taking the tablespace offline. You can use this option only when all data files of the tablespace can be written (that is, when there are no disk I/O problems).

- If you encounter a disk I/O problem, use the next available radio button, After Checkpointing Online Data Files of Tablespace, to take the tablespace offline. When you use this option, Oracle7 writes modified data in memory to those files it can access and skips writing to files it cannot access.

- Use the last radio button, Without Checkpointing Data Files of Tablespace, only when the previous two buttons do not succeed.

Once you have made all selections, select the OK button to execute the dialog. Oracle7 takes the tablespace offline.

> **NOTE**
>
> If you use either the After Checkpointing Online Data Files of Table-space radio button or the Without Checkpointing Data Files of Tablespace radio button of the Set Tablespace Offline dialog to take a tablespace offline and Oracle7 can't write to all data files of the tablespace, you will have to perform tablespace recovery when you want to bring the tablespace back online. See Chapter 11 for more information about tablespace recovery.

Extending a Database's Storage Capacity

Often an Oracle7 database will outgrow its fixed storage capacity and require more space. For example, when you're installing a new client application to a database system, there might be new tables to create that will require more data storage space than is currently available to the database. This section explains how to extend the storage capacity for an Oracle7 database using two methods: creating new tablespaces and adding new data files to existing tablespaces.

Creating New Tablespaces

Several situations justify the creation of a new tablespace in an Oracle7 database:

- When you add a new client database application to your database system and the application uses data that is not already in your database, you will need to create the application's tables and indexes. In this case, it is best to logically and physically separate the new application's data into one or more of its own tablespaces. This way, you can manage all of the application's data very easily by managing the application's tablespace.

- You can use individual tablespaces to separate different types of data and spread disk I/O across different disks. For example, you can create one tablespace to store all of an application's table data on one disk and another tablespace to store all of an application's index data on another disk. This way, Oracle7 can read or write table and index data in parallel and improve application performance.

You can create a new tablespace using the Create Tablespace dialog of SQL*DBA. To access this dialog from the SQL*DBA menu, select Storage ➤ Tablespace ➤ Create. Figure 7.5 shows the Create Tablespace dialog.

NOTE To use the Create Tablespace dialog of SQL*DBA, you must have the CREATE TABLESPACE system privilege and there must be at least two online rollback segments in the SYSTEM tablespace. (See Chapter 10 for more information about rollback segments.)

The Create Tablespace dialog has three entry fields and a radio button list. First, enter the name for the new tablespace in the Name entry field. Next, enter one or more filenames and sizes in the Data Files entry field. If you are not familiar with specifying data files, press the [List] key to use the File Specification field builder attached to the Data Files entry field. The File Specification field builder asks for the

FIGURE 7.5:
Use the Create Tablespace dialog of SQL*DBA to create a new logical storage partition in an Oracle7 database, thus extending the database's storage capacity.

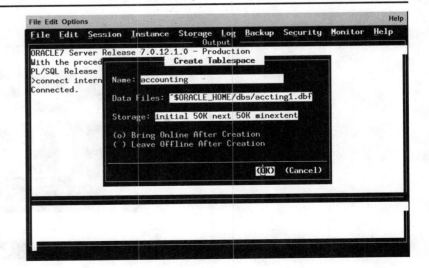

names and sizes of data files you want to create for the new tablespace. To reduce tablespace data fragmentation on disk, it is better to create fewer large data files than to create many small data files.

After you fill in the file specifications, use the Storage entry field to enter the default extent storage parameters for objects that users create in the tablespace. (To learn more about tuning data storage with storage parameters, see Chapter 10.)

Finally, select one of the radio buttons to indicate whether you want to bring the new tablespace online or leave it offline after creation. Then select the OK button to create the new tablespace. The operation may take some time because Oracle7 has to allocate space for the data files on disk.

Adding Data Files to Tablespaces

Because Oracle7 allocates fixed-size data files that cannot grow dynamically, you might need to extend the storage capacity for a tablespace. To add storage space in a tablespace, add a new data file to the tablespace.

You can add a new data file to a tablespace using the Add Data File to Tablespace dialog of SQL*DBA. To access this dialog from the SQL*DBA menu, select Storage ➤ Tablespace ➤ Add Data File. Figure 7.6 shows the Add Data File to Tablespace dialog.

FIGURE 7.6:
Use the Add Data File to Tablespace dialog of SQL*DBA to extend the storage capacity of a tablespace.

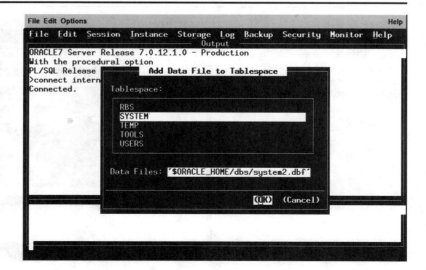

NOTE   To use the Add Data File to Tablespace dialog of SQL*DBA, you must
have the ALTER TABLESPACE system privilege.

The Add Data File to Tablespace dialog has a list box and an entry field. From the
list box, select the tablespace to extend with a new data file. Then enter one or more
filenames and sizes in the Data Files entry field. If you are not familiar with specifying data files, use the [List] key to display the File Specification field builder attached to the Data Files entry field. After completing the dialog, select OK. Oracle7
extends the storage capacity of the selected tablespace by allocating the new data
file(s). This operation can take a few minutes to complete.

Database Space Reduction

As an administrator, you can reduce the size of an Oracle7 database to reclaim valuable disk space for other uses. The next two sections discuss two different methods
for reducing the size of an Oracle7 database: archiving historical tablespaces and
dropping unwanted tablespaces.

Archiving Historical Tablespaces to Free Disk Space

Databases often contain historical data that is almost never used but is too important to discard. If you correctly plan the storage of historical data, you can take advantage of Oracle7 tablespaces to safely archive the historical data and then reclaim
the corresponding disk space. Follow these steps to make this plan work in your
system:

1. Isolate all of the historical data into a tablespace specifically created for the
   purpose of archiving this data.

2. Take the historical tablespace offline.

3. Back up the data files of the offline historical tablespace.

4. Delete the data files of the historical tablespace from disk to reclaim the corresponding disk space. (Do *not* drop the historical tablespace; you may need to restore it at a later time from the archives.)

Step 1 requires some application-specific design decisions. For example, consider an order entry application. Once an order is filled and the customer pays for the order, the order information is rarely used. To archive old orders from the main orders and line items tables, a management component of the order entry application can query those tables, copy the selected orders and line items to a historical copy of the table in another tablespace, and the historical tablespace can be archived on a regular basis. This example may not apply to your situation. No matter what your design, be sure to test the strategy before going to production with your application.

To be sure you can bring the tablespace online again in the future, you must be able to write all of a tablespace's data files before archiving the tablespace indefinitely. When performing step 2, then, be sure to take the tablespace offline using the After Checkpointing All Data Files of Tablespace option of the Set Tablespace Offline dialog.

To use the data in an archived historical tablespace at some point in the future, simply restore the tablespace's data files from the backup and bring the tablespace online.

NOTE If you cannot restore a historical tablespace's data files in their original location because no space is available, use the Rename Data File dialog of SQL*DBA to indicate the tablespace's new filenames before bringing the tablespace online.

Dropping Unwanted Tablespaces

Many times, data in a specific tablespace is no longer of use. To reclaim the disk space associated with a defunct tablespace, you can drop the tablespace.

You can drop a tablespace using the Drop Tablespace dialog of SQL*DBA. To access this dialog from the SQL*DBA menu, select Storage ➤ Tablespace ➤ Drop. Figure 7.7 shows the Drop Tablespace dialog.

FIGURE 7.7:

Use the Drop Tablespace dialog of SQL*DBA to drop a tablespace that is no longer needed.

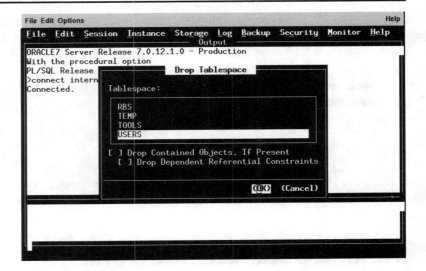

NOTE To use the Drop Tablespace dialog of SQL*DBA, you must have the DROP TABLESPACE system privilege. Furthermore, all rollback segments within the tablespace must currently be offline. (See Chapter 10 for more information about rollback segments.)

The Drop Tablespace dialog has a list box and two check boxes. First, select the tablespace to drop from the list box. If the tablespace to be dropped contains any tables or indexes, you must either drop them first or select the Drop Contained Objects, If Present check box to have the Drop Tablespace dialog automatically perform this operation. Make sure you are not dropping any required objects before selecting this check box—they are not recoverable after you drop the tablespace. If you select the Drop Contained Objects, If Present check box, you may also need to select the Drop Dependent Referential Constraints check box to drop the tablespace. This check box cascades the drop of referential integrity constraints if they depend on the primary or unique key of an object in the tablespace being dropped.

When dropping a tablespace, Oracle7 does not actually delete the dropped tablespace's data files from disk. Therefore, after dropping a tablespace, you also need to use operating system commands to delete the dropped tablespace's data files.

> **NOTE** On some operating systems (for example, UNIX), you have to shut down the database server before you can delete the data files corresponding to a dropped tablespace. That's because Oracle7 specifically opens all data files of online tablespaces during instance startup and closes data files only when you take the corresponding tablespace offline or shut down the database server.

Viewing Database Structural Information

The Oracle7 data dictionary contains numerous views you can use to reveal availability and structural information about a database. Listing 7.1 contains a stored procedure you can use to print out reports on all aspects of database structural information. Create the procedure in your database and use it whenever you want a quick report about your database's physical structure. The listing generates a report to show you information about the physical structure of a database, including tablespaces, data files, and the transaction log.

Listing 7.1: The DATABASEREPORT Procedure

```
CREATE or replace PROCEDURE databasereport AS
-- This procedure generates a report about the physical structure
-- of the database to which you are currently connected.
-- Run this script as an administrator such as SYSTEM that can
-- query the system-owned tables, and then grant the EXECUTE
-- privilege for the procedure to the desired users or roles.

-- variables to hold information returned by first query
var0 VARCHAR2(100);
var1 VARCHAR2(100);
var2 VARCHAR2(100);
```

```
-- cursor to display tablespace information
CURSOR tablespace IS
  SELECT tablespace_name, initial_extent, next_extent,
    min_extents, max_extents, pct_increase, status
    FROM sys.dba_tablespaces;

-- cursor to display data file information
CURSOR datafiles (tsname IN VARCHAR2) IS
  SELECT a.file_name, b.status
    FROM sys.dba_data_files a, v$datafile b
    WHERE a.tablespace_name = tsname
    AND a.file_name = b.name;

-- cursor to display transaction log group information
CURSOR loggroups IS
  SELECT group#, sequence#, bytes, members, archived
    FROM v$log;

-- cursor to display transaction log member information
CURSOR logmembers (groupnum IN NUMBER) IS
  SELECT member, DECODE(status,'INVALID','INACCESSIBLE',
    'STALE','INCOMPLETE','DELETED','DELETED','OK') memberstatus
    FROM v$logfile
    WHERE group# = groupnum;

BEGIN
-- print report header
  DBMS_OUTPUT.PUT_LINE('');
  DBMS_OUTPUT.PUT_LINE('Database Report '||SYSDATE);
  DBMS_OUTPUT.PUT_LINE('---------------------------------------------------');
  DBMS_OUTPUT.PUT_LINE('');

-- print general information about database
  SELECT name, created, DECODE(log_mode,'NOARCHIVELOG','NO','YES')
    INTO var0, var1, var2
    FROM v$database;
  DBMS_OUTPUT.PUT_LINE(' General Information');
  DBMS_OUTPUT.PUT_LINE(' ---------------------------------------------------');
  DBMS_OUTPUT.PUT_LINE('   Database Name:  '||var0);
  DBMS_OUTPUT.PUT_LINE('   Creation Date:  '||var1);
  DBMS_OUTPUT.PUT_LINE('');
```

```
-- print information about tablespaces and corresponding data files
  DBMS_OUTPUT.PUT_LINE(' Tablespace and Data File Information '
    ||'for Database '||var0);
  DBMS_OUTPUT.PUT_LINE(' -----------------------------------------------');
  DBMS_OUTPUT.PUT_LINE('');
  FOR dbtablespace IN tablespace LOOP
    DBMS_OUTPUT.PUT_LINE(' Tablespace Name: '||dbtablespace.tablespace_name);
    DBMS_OUTPUT.PUT_LINE(' Availability:    '||dbtablespace.status);
    DBMS_OUTPUT.PUT_LINE('');
    DBMS_OUTPUT.PUT_LINE(' Default Storage Parameter Settings in Tablespace '
      ||dbtablespace.tablespace_name);
    DBMS_OUTPUT.PUT_LINE('');
    DBMS_OUTPUT.PUT_LINE(' Default Initial Extent Size:    '
      ||dbtablespace.initial_extent);
    DBMS_OUTPUT.PUT_LINE(' Default Subsequent Extent Size: '
      ||dbtablespace.next_extent);
    DBMS_OUTPUT.PUT_LINE(' Default Minimum Object Extents: '
      ||dbtablespace.min_extents);
    DBMS_OUTPUT.PUT_LINE(' Default Maximum Object Extents: '
      ||dbtablespace.max_extents);
    DBMS_OUTPUT.PUT_LINE(' Default Extent Growth Size:     '
      ||dbtablespace.pct_increase||'%');
    DBMS_OUTPUT.PUT_LINE('');
    DBMS_OUTPUT.PUT_LINE(' Data Files for Tablespace '
      ||dbtablespace.tablespace_name);
    DBMS_OUTPUT.PUT_LINE('');
    FOR dbdatafile IN datafiles(dbtablespace.tablespace_name) LOOP
      DBMS_OUTPUT.PUT_LINE('   Data File Name:  '||dbdatafile.file_name);
      DBMS_OUTPUT.PUT_LINE('   Availability:    '||dbdatafile.status);
      DBMS_OUTPUT.PUT_LINE('');
    END LOOP;
  END LOOP;

-- print information about transaction log groups and corresponding members
  DBMS_OUTPUT.PUT_LINE('');
  DBMS_OUTPUT.PUT_LINE(' Transaction Log Information for Database '||var0);
  DBMS_OUTPUT.PUT_LINE(' -----------------------------------------------');
  DBMS_OUTPUT.PUT_LINE('');
  DBMS_OUTPUT.PUT_LINE(' Media Recovery Enabled?:  '||var2);
  DBMS_OUTPUT.PUT_LINE('');
  DBMS_OUTPUT.PUT_LINE(' Log Groups');
  DBMS_OUTPUT.PUT_LINE('');
  FOR dbloggroup IN loggroups LOOP
    DBMS_OUTPUT.PUT_LINE('   Group ID:                  '
      ||dbloggroup.group#);
```

```
    DBMS_OUTPUT.PUT_LINE('   Assigned Sequence Number:  '
      ||dbloggroup.sequence#);
    IF var2 = 'YES' THEN
      DBMS_OUTPUT.PUT_LINE('   Archived?:
        ||dbloggroup.archived);
    END IF;
    DBMS_OUTPUT.PUT_LINE('   Size (Bytes):
      ||dbloggroup.bytes);
    DBMS_OUTPUT.PUT_LINE('   Number of Members:
      ||dbloggroup.members);
    DBMS_OUTPUT.PUT_LINE('');
    DBMS_OUTPUT.PUT_LINE('   Member Information for Group '
      ||dbloggroup.group#);
    DBMS_OUTPUT.PUT_LINE('');
    FOR dblogmember IN logmembers(dbloggroup.group#) LOOP
      DBMS_OUTPUT.PUT_LINE('    Member File Name:  '||dblogmember.member);
      DBMS_OUTPUT.PUT_LINE('    Member Status:   '||dblogmember.memberstatus);
      DBMS_OUTPUT.PUT_LINE('');
    END LOOP;
  END LOOP;

END databasereport;
```

Use Listing 7.1 to create a copy of this procedure in your database. Then, using SQL*Plus or SQL*DBA, set server output on with a buffer size of 10,000 bytes and execute the procedure to get a detailed report of your database, as shown here:

```
SET SERVEROUTPUT ON SIZE 10000

EXECUTE databasereport;

Database Report 16-NOV-95
--------------------------------------------------------


General Information
--------------------------------------------------------
  Database Name:   SALES
  Creation Date:   10/06/95 08:40:47

Tablespace and Data File Information for Database SALES
--------------------------------------------------------


  Tablespace Name:   SYSTEM
  Availability:      ONLINE
```

Default Storage Parameter Settings for Tablespace SYSTEM

```
Default Initial Extent Size:      10240
Default Subsequent Extent Size:   10240
Default Minimum Object Extents:   1
Default Maximum Object Extents:   121
Default Extent Growth Size:       50%
```

Data Files for Tablespace SYSTEM

```
Data File Name:        /u/usr/oracle/dbs/systsales.dbf
Availability:          SYSTEM
```

```
Tablespace Name:  RBS
Availability:     ONLINE
```

Default Storage Parameter Settings for Tablespace RBS

```
Default Initial Extent Size:      131072
Default Subsequent Extent Size:   131072
Default Minimum Object Extents:   2
Default Maximum Object Extents:   121
Default Extent Growth Size:       0%
```

Data Files for Tablespace RBS

```
Data File Name:        /u/usr/oracle/dbs/rbssales.dbf
Availability:          ONLINE
```

```
Tablespace Name:  TEMP
Availability:     ONLINE
```

Default Storage Parameter Settings for Tablespace TEMP

```
Default Initial Extent Size:      262144
Default Subsequent Extent Size:   262144
Default Minimum Object Extents:   1
Default Maximum Object Extents:   121
Default Extent Growth Size:       0%
```

Data Files for Tablespace TEMP

```
Data File Name:        /u/usr/oracle/dbs/tempsales.dbf
Availability:          ONLINE
```

```
Tablespace Name:   TOOLS
Availability:      ONLINE

Default Storage Parameter Settings for Tablespace TOOLS

Default Initial Extent Size:      10240
Default Subsequent Extent Size:   10240
Default Minimum Object Extents:   1
Default Maximum Object Extents:   121
Default Extent Growth Size:       50%

Data Files for Tablespace TOOLS

Data File Name:        /u/usr/oracle/dbs/toolsales.dbf
Availability:          ONLINE

Tablespace Name:   USERS
Availability:      ONLINE

Default Storage Parameter Settings for Tablespace USERS

Default Initial Extent Size:      10240
Default Subsequent Extent Size:   10240
Default Minimum Object Extents:   1
Default Maximum Object Extents:   121
Default Extent Growth Size:       50%

Data Files for Tablespace USERS

Data File Name:        /u/usr/oracle/dbs/usrsales.dbf
Availability:          ONLINE


Transaction Log Information for Database SALES
-----------------------------------------------------------

Media Recovery Enabled?:   YES

Log Groups

Group ID:                   1
Assigned Sequence Number:   376
Size (Bytes):               512000
Number of Members:          2
```

```
Member Information for Group 1

  Member File Name:    /u/usr/oracle/dbs/log1sales.dbf
  Member Status:       INCOMPLETE

  Member File Name:    /u2/usr/oracle/dbs/log1sales.dbf
  Member Status:       INCOMPLETE

Group ID:                2
Assigned Sequence Number: 377
Size (Bytes):            512000
Number of Members:       2

Member Information for Group 2

  Member File Name:    /u/usr/oracle/dbs/log2sales.dbf
  Member Status:       OK

  Member File Name:    /u2/usr/oracle/dbs/log2sales.dbf
  Member Status:       OK

Group ID:                3
Assigned Sequence Number: 378
Size (Bytes):            512000
Number of Members:       2

Member Information for Group 3

  Member File Name:    /u/usr/oracle/dbs/log3sales.dbf
  Member Status:       INCOMPLETE

  Member File Name:    /u2/usr/oracle/dbs/log3sales.dbf
  Member Status:       INCOMPLETE
```

Whenever you want a report about a database's physical structure, simply execute the DATABASEREPORT procedure.

Sometimes it's useful to save the output of a SQL*DBA session to a text file so you have it to refer to or print out. For example, you might want to save the output of the report produced by the DATABASEREPORT procedure. To spool the output of a SQL*DBA session to a text file, select File ➤ Spool On to reveal the Spool Output to File dialog of SQL*DBA. Then enter a filename to hold the output. After you select the OK button, SQL*DBA begins spooling output to the file. When you want to turn off spooling, select File ➤ Spool Off.

Another useful administrative procedure is the SPACEREPORT procedure shown in Listing 7.2. This procedure prints a report that shows useful information about the space usage in each tablespace of the database.

Listing 7.2: The SPACEREPORT procedure

```
CREATE or replace PROCEDURE spacereport AS
-- This procedure reports the total and free space sizes of
-- each data file in the database, by tablespace.
-- Run this script as an administrator such as SYSTEM that can
-- query the system-owned tables, and then grant the EXECUTE
-- privilege for the procedure to the desired users or roles.

CURSOR datafile1 IS
  SELECT tablespace_name, file_id, max(bytes) largeextent,
    sum(bytes) totalfreespace
    FROM sys.dba_free_space
    GROUP BY tablespace_name, file_id
    ORDER BY tablespace_name, file_id;

CURSOR datafile2 (fileid INTEGER) IS
  SELECT name, bytes
    FROM v$datafile
    WHERE file# = fileid;

dbname VARCHAR2(8);

BEGIN

SELECT name INTO dbname
  FROM v$database;
```

```
DBMS_OUTPUT.PUT_LINE('');
DBMS_OUTPUT.PUT_LINE('Space Report for Database '||dbname);
DBMS_OUTPUT.PUT_LINE('----------------------------------');
DBMS_OUTPUT.PUT_LINE('');
FOR file IN datafile1 LOOP
  DBMS_OUTPUT.PUT_LINE('Tablespace Name:           '
    ||file.tablespace_name);
  DBMS output...Name:'|file...
  DBMS_OUTPUT.PUT_LINE('');
  FOR filedata IN datafile2 (file.file_id) LOOP
    DBMS_OUTPUT.PUT_LINE('Data File Name:           '
      ||filedata.name);
    DBMS_OUTPUT.PUT_LINE('Total File Size (KB):     '
      ||ROUND(filedata.bytes/1024,0));
    DBMS_OUTPUT.PUT_LINE('Free Space in File (KB):  '
      ||ROUND(file.totalfreespace/1024,0));
    DBMS_OUTPUT.PUT_LINE('% Free Space in File:     '
      ||ROUND(((file.totalfreespace/filedata.bytes)*100),0)||'%');
    DBMS_OUTPUT.PUT_LINE('Largest Extent (KB):      '
      ||ROUND(file.largeextent/1024,0));
    DBMS_OUTPUT.PUT_LINE('');
  END LOOP;
END LOOP;

END spacereport;
```

After you create the SPACEREPORT procedure as shown in Listing 7.2, execute it with server output on to show a printout of space information in the database's tablespaces, like the one shown here:

```
Space Report for Database SALES
----------------------------------

Tablespace Name:           RBS

Data File Name:            /u/usr/oracle/dbs/rbssales.dbf
Total File Size (KB):      6144
Free Space in File (KB):   32
% Free Space in File:      1%
Largest Extent (KB):       32

Tablespace Name:           SYSTEM

Data File Name:            /u/usr/oracle/dbs/systsales.dbf
Total File Size (KB):      25600
```

```
Free Space in File (KB):   6978
% Free Space in File:      27%
Largest Extent (KB):       5716

Tablespace Name:           TEMP

Data File Name:            /u/usr/oracle/dbs/tempsales.dbf
Total File Size (KB):      550
Free Space in File (KB):   548
% Free Space in File:      100%
Largest Extent (KB):       548

Tablespace Name:           TOOLS

Data File Name:            /u/usr/oracle/dbs/toolsales.dbf
Total File Size (KB):      15360
Free Space in File (KB):   10628
% Free Space in File:      69%
Largest Extent (KB):       8748

Tablespace Name:           USERS

Data File Name:            /u/usr/oracle/dbs/usrsales.dbf
Total File Size (KB):      1024
Free Space in File (KB):   738
% Free Space in File:      72%
Largest Extent (KB):       738
```

This chapter has introduced you to the most basic operations you'll have to perform as a database administrator, including

- Configuring your operating system account settings for Oracle7 database administration

- Planning and creating a new Oracle7 database

- Starting up and shutting down the Oracle7 database server to control database availability

- Taking tablespaces online and offline to control the availability of specific data within a database

- Extending the storage capacity of an Oracle7 database by creating new tablespaces and adding new data files to existing tablespaces

- Reducing the storage capacity of an Oracle7 database by dropping unwanted tablespaces

Now that you know how to create an Oracle7 database and get the server started, the next chapter explains how to configure the Oracle7 server for user connections.

CHAPTER

EIGHT

Configuring the Oracle7 Server for User Connections

- Oracle7 Server process architectures—the multi-threaded server, the dedicated server, and the single-task architectures

- Configuring the Oracle7 server as a multithreaded server for client/server systems

- Connecting to the Oracle7 server across a network

Once you as an administrator create and start up an Oracle7 database, users of the client/server system will need to connect to it to be able to start work. Before users can connect to a database, you must configure the database instance's front-end servers for user connections. This chapter discusses the following issues:

- Different types of front-end server process configurations
- Configuring the Oracle7 server in a client/server system
- Configuring the clients in an Oracle7 client/server system
- Connecting to Oracle7 from a remote client workstation

Types of Database Server Configurations

A highway architect in a populated metropolitan community has a tough job—the architect must design roadways that efficiently serve an ever-increasing number of people and cars on the road while keeping roadway construction projects within budgets and available land space. Like the highway architect, you must configure a database server so it efficiently serves all of the system's users without consuming an unnecessary amount of computer-system overhead.

Oracle7 can accommodate different types of computer systems and networks because it supports three different configurations for user connections and all types of network protocols:

- The multithreaded server, for most client/server connections
- The dedicated server, for administrative and batch operations in a client/server system
- The single-task server, for host-based system user connections

This section explains the different types of configurations and when it is appropriate to use each type.

The Multithreaded Server Architecture

Figure 8.1 shows the *multithreaded server architecture* used with client/server configurations. Notice that each client workstation uses a client process to run a client application. If the client is remote, it also uses SQL*Net to talk to Oracle7 across the network. Meanwhile, the RDBMS uses a multithreaded server architecture—a combination of dispatcher, listener, and front-end server processes—to serve the requests of many clients with minimal process overhead on the database server. The Oracle7 server also has SQL*Net to communicate across the network.

When a client application makes a network connection to Oracle7, the *listener process* gives the client the network address of a *dispatcher process*, to which the client then connects. Then, when the client makes a request of the database server, the dispatcher receives the request and places it on a *request queue*. As they become available, *shared front-end server processes* handle requests on the request queue on a first-in/first-out basis and return results to a *response queue*. From here, the dispatcher returns results to the proper client applications. Oracle7's multithreaded server architecture is a cooperative processing architecture that results in minimal server process overhead for each connected client. If you plan to use Oracle7 in a client/server system, take the time to read the section "Configuring Oracle7 for Client/Server Systems" later in this chapter. It explains how to configure the processes and queues in the multithreaded server architecture.

The Dedicated Server Architecture

Figure 8.1 also shows the *dedicated server architecture*, an alternative process configuration that has a special use in client/server systems. Dedicated client/server connections are necessary only for special database administrative operations, including database startup and shutdown as well as database recovery, or for batch mode operations, such as running long reports.

When a client application connects to Oracle7, the listener process starts a *dedicated front-end server process* and connects the client directly to the dedicated server, altogether bypassing the multithreaded server architecture. Because a dedicated server consumes a significant amount of database server memory for only a single user, dedicated servers should not be used for client application connections unless absolutely necessary.

FIGURE 8.1:

Oracle7 multithreaded server and dedicated server architectures are used by most client/server systems.

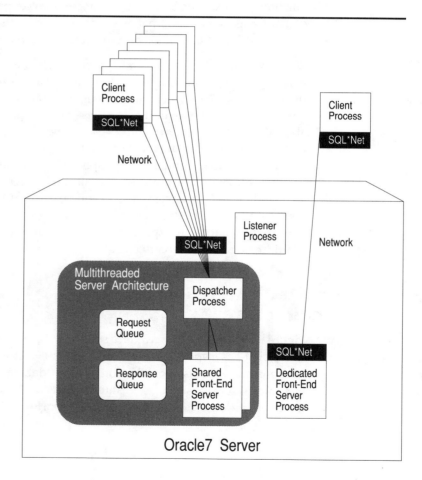

The Single-Task Server Architecture

Figure 8.2 shows the Oracle7 *single-task* process configuration used for certain non-networked, host-based database server systems. In host-based database server systems, a user employs a dumb terminal or terminal emulator to establish a session on the host computer and run the client database application. SQL*Net is not required in the single-task architecture. The host computer runs the processes of both the applications and database server.

The Oracle7 single-task configuration is very efficient because it requires only one process to run both the client application code and the front-end server process code for each connected user. However, only certain host operating systems support the Oracle7 single-task process configuration, including Digital's VAX VMS and IBM's MVS operating systems.

FIGURE 8.2:

The Oracle7 single-task server process configuration is used only by certain host-based systems.

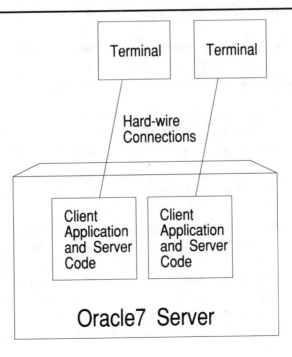

NOTE
Host-based UNIX systems, where users connect directly to a host UNIX computer with terminals, cannot reliably separate application code and RDBMS code. For this reason, host-based UNIX systems typically use the Oracle7 multithreaded server process architecture to separate application code and RDBMS code into different processes.

No matter which type of process architecture a database system uses, you must configure the system components so users can connect to the Oracle7 database. The next section explains how to configure Oracle7 instances for basic client/server systems.

Configuring Oracle7 for Client/Server Systems

Now that you understand the different types of process configurations that are available with Oracle7, let's concentrate on how to configure Oracle7 for client/server systems. Configuring Oracle7 for a client/server system includes several related steps:

1. Configure SQL*Net for use on all components of the client/server system. This includes configuration of the SQL*Net listener process on the Oracle7 server, as well as configuration of SQL*Net itself on both clients and the server for remote server connections.

2. Start the listener process to listen for client connection requests across a network.

3. Set up the server processes used in a multithreaded server configuration. As the previous sections explain, the multithreaded server architecture is without a doubt the server process configuration you want to utilize when using Oracle7 in a client/server system for client application connections. To configure Oracle7 as a multithreaded server, you must configure dispatcher and shared server processes before starting up the database server.

4. Tune the number of dispatcher and shared server processes after database startup to deliver maximum performance to clients without using too much overhead on the database server.

To illustrate these procedures, the following sections explain each step while configuring a simple UNIX Oracle7 client/server system that uses a single network protocol, TCP/IP. The system that these sections configure is similar to the one shown in Figure 8.3.

Notice that the files and processes in Figure 8.3 clearly show the different components you need to configure for Oracle7 in a simple UNIX client/server system. Even if you use Oracle7 on another platform, with a different network protocol, or

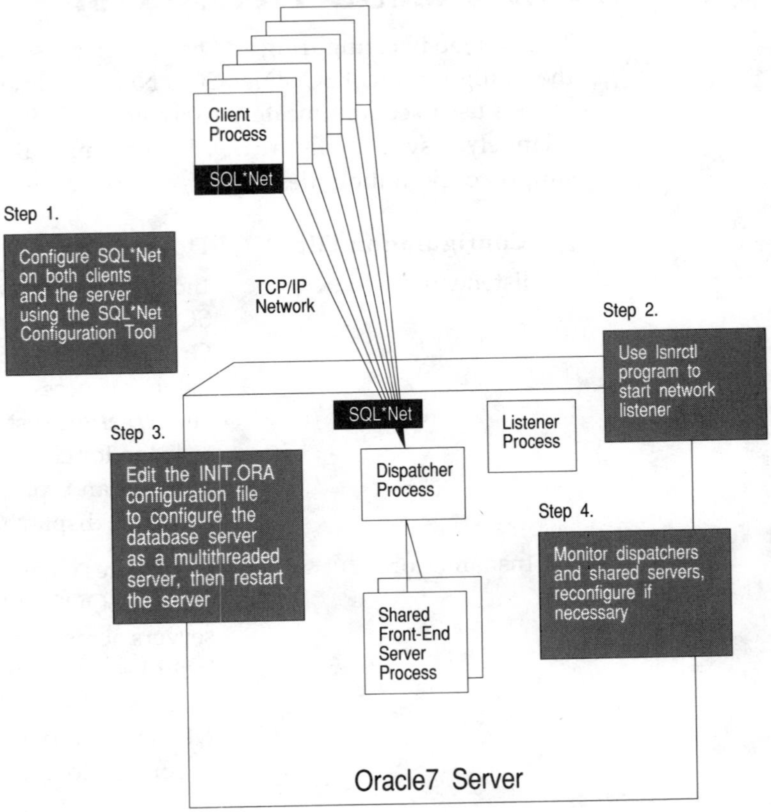

FIGURE 8.3:

A simple Oracle7 client/server system configuration running on UNIX that uses the TCP/IP network protocol

with several network protocols, the following sections are useful because they provide a solid foundation for understanding the SQL*Net configuration issues for all kinds of client/server systems.

> **NOTE**
>
> The following sections assume that you have already configured and tested the network hardware and software on your system. In addition, Oracle's SQL*Net V2 for the network's protocol must be installed correctly on both the clients and the database server in your system.

Configuring SQL*Net for an Oracle7 Client/Server System

The first job in configuring an Oracle7 client/server system for user connections is the configuration of SQL*Net. SQL*Net is middleware that both Oracle clients and servers use to communicate across a network. If you understand your network, it's relatively easy to configure SQL*Net because all you need to do is to create a few simple configuration files:

Configuration File	Description
listener.ora	Includes configuration parameters for the SQL*Net network listener process on the Oracle7 server. A SQL*Net network listener process is necessary in a client/server system to allow the server to listen for client application connection requests and route the connections to an available dispatcher process
tnsnames.ora	Configures clients and servers so they can use SQL*Net to connect to remote servers across a network. This file includes SQL*Net *aliases* (named database server addresses) you can use when you start an application and want to connect to a remote server

Configuration File	Description
sqlnet.ora	Includes configuration parameters for SQL*Net clients

Creating the different SQL*Net configuration files is painless if you have SQL*Forms 3.0 or Oracle Forms 4.0, because you can use the SQL*Net Configuration Tool. The SQL*Net Configuration Tool is a simple SQL*Forms application you can use to enter information about your network and then automatically generate the necessary SQL*Net configuration files for both the clients and servers in your system. If you don't have SQL*Forms or Oracle Forms, you must create the configuration files using a text editor.

The following sections provide instructions for using the SQL*Net Configuration Tool to create the different SQL*Net configuration files. However, even if you can't use the Configuration Tool and must create configuration files manually, you can learn how to create the necessary configuration files by closely examining the example files produced with the SQL*Net Configuration Tool.

Installing the SQL*Net Configuration Tool

Installation of the SQL*Net Configuration Tool requires two steps:

1. When you install a SQL*Net product, you have the option of installing the SQL*Net Configuration Tool. Be sure to do this. If you did not install the SQL*Net Configuration Tool when you installed SQL*Net, use the Oracle installer to reinstall SQL*Net along with the Configuration Tool.

2. After installing SQL*Net along with the Configuration Tool, you must run the script ncschema.sql. On UNIX platforms, this script can be found in the $ORACLE_HOME/network/config/sql directory. The ncschema.sql script sets up a schema for the SQL*Net Configuration Tool, including a new database username, NET_CONF, with the password NET_CONF, and some database tables to support the SQL*Net Configuration Tool form application. While connected as an administrator, run the ncshema.sql script from SQL*DBA or SQL*Plus.

Once you have successfully installed the SQL*Net Configuration Tool, you can start it to begin putting together your configuration.

Starting the SQL*Net Configuration Tool

After completing the installation steps for the SQL*Net Configuration Tool, you can start it by making your working directory the one that holds the tool's forms files. On UNIX platforms, this directory is $ORACLE_HOME/network/config/sql. From here, start the tool by entering

```
$ORACLE_HOME/bin/net_conf net_conf/net_conf
```

The first screen after the introductory screen is the Master screen. Figure 8.4 shows what the SQL*Net Configuration Tool's Master screen looks like before you perform any configuration steps.

The SQL*Net Configuration Tool's Master screen is a read-only screen that reports current SQL*Net configuration settings. To configure the parts of a Oracle7 client/server system, you simply move to the different areas on the Master screen and open up the different subforms that correspond to the different areas using the [Next Block] key. The following sections explain how to configure SQL*Net components for the simple example network described earlier.

FIGURE 8.4:

The SQL*Net Configuration Tool's Master screen reveals the current information about a SQL*Net network configuration. Before you configure a network, this screen is blank.

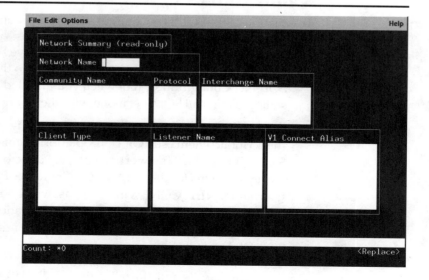

Naming a Network

The first step for configuring a network of Oracle clients and servers is naming the network. With the cursor positioned in the Network Name field of the Master screen, you can move to the Edit Networks screen using the [Next Block] key. Figure 8.5 shows the Edit Networks screen with the name and description of a network named SALES.

You can use the SQL*Net Configuration Tool's Edit Networks screen to list the names and descriptions of several different networks you want to configure. Once you are finished entering network names and descriptions, commit your changes and return to the Master screen using the [Previous Block] key. When you name a network and return to the SQL*Net Configuration Tool's Master screen, the screen is updated to show the name of the current network you are configuring. From this point forward, you will be configuring the listed network.

Configuring Network Communities

The first step in configuring a network for SQL*Net is identifying the network's communities. *Communities* are subnetworks of clients and servers that all use the same network protocol. A large client/server system might have many different communities that use different network protocols. For example, one community

FIGURE 8.5:
The Edit Networks screen allows you to enter a name and description for the different networks you want to configure.

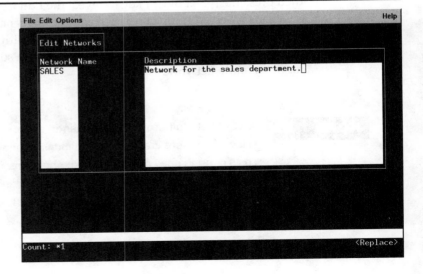

might be a LAN that uses the TCP/IP communications protocol, another community might be a different LAN that uses the SPX/IPX communications protocol, and so on. In the example shown in Figure 8.3, the network is made up of a single community that uses the TCP/IP communications protocol.

NOTE

Client/server systems are often made up of several different communities that join to form one large network of clients and servers. Bringing together heterogeneous network communities is one of SQL*Net's greatest features. Using a specific SQL*Net Multiprotocol Interchange adapter on a computer that is common to two different types of network communities, you can join the communities so they can work together and form one large distributed processing system. By using software—the SQL*Net Multiprotocol Interchange adapters— instead of expensive hardware like network routers and bridges, you create a client/server system that is more cost effective and more flexible to changes.

To configure a network community with the SQL*Net Configuration Tool, move to the Community Name block on the Master Screen using the [Next Field] key, and then press the [Next Block] key to reveal the Edit Communities screen. This screen has fields where you can enter each community's name, network protocol (a list of valid protocol abbreviation codes is available with the [List] key), and cost. Figure 8.6 shows the Edit Communities screen with some configuration information for our sample network.

NOTE

A SQL*Net Multiprotocol Interchange adapter uses a community's cost value when there are multiple communities and it needs to compare the costs of using one community or another to reach a destination in the network. Since the example network you are configuring here includes only one community, the default cost value is acceptable.

FIGURE 8.6:

The Edit Communities screen allows you to list the names and protocols for the different communities or subnetworks in an Oracle7 client/server system.

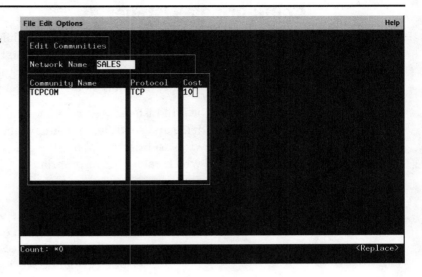

After you have entered your network's community information, press the [Previous Block] key to commit your changes and return to the Master screen of the SQL*Net Configuration Tool. You'll notice that the Master screen has been updated to show the community you configured, as well as a client type that corresponds to the community in your network.

Configuring an Interchange

By moving to the Interchange block on the Master screen, you can configure interchanges necessary to join different network communities in a heterogeneous client/server system. However, since the example network in this chapter doesn't include multiple network communities with different network protocols, there is no need to use a SQL*Net Multiprotocol Interchange adapter. Instead, let's move on to the task of configuring clients for the network.

Configuring a Client

Once you have configured a community for a network, the SQL*Net Configuration Tool automatically creates a client type that corresponds to the community. And if your network doesn't include any interchanges, no further configuration is necessary for clients. Instead, you can move on to configuring a listener for the network.

Configuring a Listener

Now let's configure a listener for the network. While in the Master screen, use the [Next Field] key to move into the Listener Name block, and then use the [Next Block] key to move to the Edit Listeners screen. Figure 8.7 shows how the Edit Listeners screen appears after the information for the example network has been filled in.

Once you reveal the Edit Listeners screen, you can use the [Next Field] key to move among the entry fields and set different configuration parameters for the network listener. The following list briefly explains the different entry fields in the Edit Listeners screen and which values are appropriate.

Entry Field	Description
Network Name	The name of the network that uses the listener. When you enter this screen, this field is already filled in with the name of the current network you are configuring

FIGURE 8.7:

The Edit Listeners screen lets you configure all the configuration parameters for a listener process.

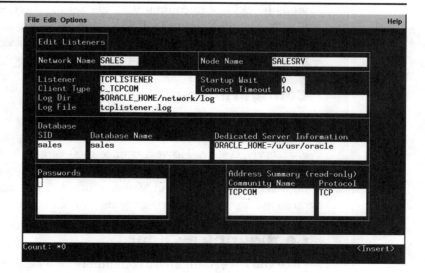

Entry Field	Description
Node Name	The name of the node on which the listener resides. Fill in this field with the name of the node on which the listener process will run. For example, if the server node's name is SALESRV, enter this name here
Listener	The name of the network listener process. The default name is LISTENER, but you can modify this to any name you like. In the example, TCPLISTENER is a good choice
Client Type	The type of clients for which the listener works. You can select a valid client type by pressing the [List] key. In the example, the only available client type is C_TCPCOM, which corresponds to the TCPCOM community
Log Dir	The directory where the listener process will write its log file. Enter a text string that points to any valid operating system location on the database server
Log File	The name of the log file that the listener process writes. The listener keeps track of status information in its log file, such as startup information and connection requests
Startup Wait	The amount of time in seconds to wait before starting up the listener when requested. The default of 0 starts the listener process immediately on request

Entry Field	Description
Connect Timeout	The amount of time to wait for a valid connection request after a connection has been started. The default of 10 seconds is adequate for most situations
Database SID	The system identifier that uniquely identifies a specific database instance
Service Name (Database Name)	The description of the service to connect to. In earlier versions of this tool, the field's name is Database Name
OS Oracle Environment (Dedicated Server Information)	Operating system information about the server's operating environment. For example, on UNIX systems you should enter **ORACLE_HOME=** followed by the location of $ORACLE_HOME. In earlier versions of this tool, the field's name is Dedicated Server Information
Passwords	The password that controls who can perform administrative tasks with the listener process, such as starting and stopping the listener. A password is optional but does permit more security regarding the listener

In the lower-right corner of the Edit Listeners screen is the Address Summary block. The information in the block is read-only. It reveals the communities and protocols for which the listener works. To edit this information, move the cursor inside the Address Summary block and press the [Next Block] key. This action reveals the Edit Addresses screen, as shown in Figure 8.8.

Most fields are already filled in for you when you enter the Edit Addresses screen. All that's really necessary is that you enter values for the HOST and PORT keywords. In this example, since the server is a UNIX system running TCP/IP, the HOST keyword specifies the server's Internet protocol (IP) address. The IP address can be given using either the numerical address or the domain-style name (as shown in Figure 8.8). The PORT keyword corresponds to the port number (connection to the outside world) that the listener process listens on. Oracle recommends using port number 1521 for all UNIX systems.

TIP

If you do not know the IP address of your UNIX server, you can easily find out by viewing the file /etc/hosts on the server.

When you are finished entering address information for a listener process, the Edit Address screen should look similar to the one in Figure 8.8. To commit your changes and return to the Edit Listeners screen, press the [Previous Block] key. The Address Summary block of the Edit Listeners screen now lists the new address information for the listener.

When you are satisfied with the configuration of the network listener, you can commit your changes and return to the Master screen by pressing the [Previous Block] key. The Master screen now lists the new listener. At this point SQL*Net configuration is complete for the example network. Now you are ready to generate the SQL*Net configuration files for your system using the information entered in the configuration tool.

FIGURE 8.8:

The Edit Addresses screen lets you configure the listener's address and port number

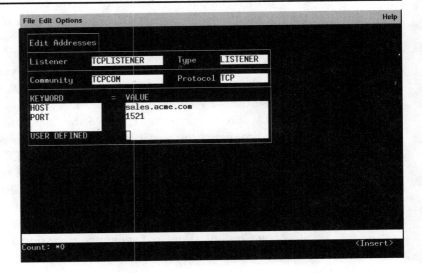

Generating the SQL*Net Configuration Files

After you finish using the SQL*Net Configuration Tool to configure the different components of an Oracle7 client/server system, you can automatically generate the necessary configuration files for SQL*Net. From the Master screen, simply position the cursor in the Network Name field, press the [Count Query Hits] key, and acknowledge any prompts that follow to begin the generation process. During the generation process, the SQL*Net Configuration Tool validates the proposed network configuration, checking it for any naming inconsistencies and so on. If you created a valid network configuration, the message line of the form application informs you that the generation process is done. If you attempt to generate configuration files using a configuration that has problems, the SQL*Net Configuration Tool informs you that an error occurred during file generation. You can find a log of errors encountered during the generation process in the file errors.log.

Examining and Editing the Generated SQL*Net Configuration Files

The SQL*Net Configuration Tool generates all the different types of configuration files necessary to configure SQL*Net on the different clients and servers in an Oracle7 client/server system. After you generate the configuration files, you can find them in a special directory structure that the Configuration Tool creates to organize the different files. The specific directory structure and location depend on where you start the Configuration Tool when you use it, the username you use when generating configuration files, and the names of the network, server node, and communities for which you generate files. For example, if you are using a UNIX computer; start the configuration tool in the $ORACLE_HOME/network/config/sql directory; use the NET_CONF username; and name the network SALES, the server SALESRV, and a community TCPCOM, the Configuration Tool generates the server's SQL*Net configuration files listener.ora, sqlnet.ora, and tnsnames.ora in the location $ORACLE_HOME/network/config/sql/NET_CONF/SALES/GEN1/SALESRV. It then places the client configuration files sqlnet.ora and tnsnames.ora in the location $ORACLE_HOME/network/config/sql/NET_CONF/SALES/GEN1/C_TCPCOM.

After you find the files, you can use a text editor to look at them and make minor modifications, if necessary. The following examples show three of the files the SQL*Net Configuration Tool generates according to the example information seen in earlier sections.

```
###########
# FILENAME: listener.ora (on the server)
# TIME....: 96-12-01 05:35:11
# NETWORK.: SALES
# NODE....: sales.acme.com
# SERVICE.: TCPLISTENER
###########
TCPLISTENER =
  (ADDRESS_LIST =
        (ADDRESS =
          (PROTOCOL = TCP)
          (HOST = sales.acme.com)
          (PORT = 1525)
        )
  )
STARTUP_WAIT_TIME_TCPLISTENER = O
CONNECT_TIMEOUT_TCPLISTENER = 10
LOG_DIRECTORY_TCPLISTENER = /usr/oracle/network/log
LOG_FILE_TCPLISTENER = tcplistener
SID_LIST_TCPLISTENER =
  (SID_LIST =
    (SID_DESC =
      (SID_NAME = sales)
      (ORACLE_HOME= /u/usr/oracle)
    )
  )
TRACE_LEVEL_TCPLISTENER = OFF


###########
# FILENAME: tnsnames.ora (on either the client or the server)
# TIME....: 96-12-01 05:35:11
# NETWORK.: SALES
# NODE....: C_TCPCOM
# SERVICE.: C_TCPCOM
###########
animalrn =
  (DESCRIPTION =
    (ADDRESS_LIST =
        (ADDRESS =
          (COMMUNITY = TCPCOM)
          (PROTOCOL = TCP)
          (HOST = sales.acme.com)
          (PORT = 1525)
        )
```

```
  )
  (CONNECT_DATA =
    (SID = sales)
  )
)


###########
# FILENAME: sqlnet.ora (on either the client or the server)
# TIME....: 96-12-01 05:35:11
# NETWORK.: SALES
# NODE....: C_TCPCOM
# SERVICE.: C_TCPCOM
###########
AUTOMATIC_IPC=OFF
TRACE_LEVEL_CLIENT = OFF
```

The commented lines (those beginning with the # symbol) in each file example clearly identify the name of each file and the type of machine (a client or a server) on which the file resides. Notice that each configuration file includes several parameters that allow you to configure the target component of SQL*Net on either a client or the server. Reviewing the different entry fields in the SQL*Net Configuration Tool's different screens makes it easy to determine the correspondence between the entry fields and the different configuration parameters in the preceding files. Many parameters can be parents to one or more child parameters to create hierarchical groups of parameters. When creating or editing any SQL*Net configuration file with a text editor, be careful with parentheses and indentation so that the parameter groupings are correct.

Distributing the SQL*Net Configuration Files

After creating and editing the various SQL*Net configuration files, it's time to distribute them to their proper location on the clients and servers in the network. If you need to copy the text files among different operating systems (for example, UNIX to DOS), be sure to convert the text files properly.

Each client should have a copy of the sqlnet.ora and tnsnames.ora configuration files. The server should also have the previous two files (although they might be slightly different from the client versions), as well as a listener.ora file. On each computer, locate the configuration files in the path pointed to by the operating system session variable named TNS_ADMIN. For example, on a UNIX system, it's common to create an environment variable TNS_ADMIN that points to the /etc directory and then locate the SQL*Net configuration files here. On a DOS system, it's common to create a CONFIG variable TNS_ADMIN that points to the \orawin\network\admin directory and then locate the proper SQL*Net configuration files here.

Setting the Port Address on the Server Computer for the Listener Process

The final step for configuring SQL*Net is to set up a port address on the server computer that corresponds to the port address specified for the SQL*Net network listener process during the configuration steps. Depending on the server's operating system, you do this in different ways. On UNIX systems, you configure a port by adding a line to the /etc/services file, which contains a service name, two spaces, and then a port address. Assuming that you are configuring a listener process for a TCP/IP communication protocol, the /etc/services file might contain a line such as

```
tcplistener  1525/tcp
```

In this example, notice that the tcplistener is the service name that matches the name of the listener process configured earlier. Additionally, this service uses the port address 1525/tcp, the same port specified earlier when configuring the listener process.

NOTE   When you look at the /etc/services file, you will notice many other names and corresponding port addresses. Make sure that the name you choose for each listener process is unique among service names and that the address you assign to each listener is unique among port addresses.

Starting the Network Listener

After you complete the SQL*Net configuration, start the listener on the server using the lsnrctl program. lsnrctl is a simple program with a command prompt that, among other things, allows you to start, stop, and check the status of the listener process(es) on your system. For example, the following commands start the lsnrctl program and the listener process named TCPLISTENER:

```
lsnrctl

Welcome to LSNRCTL, type 'help' for information.

LSNRCTL> start tcplistener
```

If you have configured everything correctly, the listener will start and lsnrctl will return a status report for the listener. Once the listener is running, you can exit LSNRCTL with the exit command:

```
LSNRCTL> exit
```

Configuring Dispatcher and Server Processes

The next step in setting up the multithreaded server is configuring the dispatcher and shared-server processes. You control the initial configuration of these processes with parameters in the initialization parameter file for the database. The parameters to adjust include

Parameter	Description
MTS_LISTENER_ADDRESS	Identifies the address of the listener process for the database instance. Configure this initialization parameter using the same listener address parameters set in listener.ora
MTS_SERVICE	Identifies the service name, or system identifier, of this database. Set the MTS_SERVICE parameter to match the value of SID_NAME in listener.ora

Parameter	Description
MTS_DISPATCHERS	Configures the initial dispatchers that start with database startup. To set this parameter, specify one or more protocols ("tcp" for TCP/IP, "decnet" for DECnet, "osi4" for OSI4, "spx" for SPX/IPX, and "soc" for UNIX domain sockets). For each protocol, specify the number of dispatchers to start
MTS_MAX_DISPATCHERS	Indicates the maximum number of dispatchers you can start for an instance. Initially, you might want to set this parameter high so you can experiment while tuning the server
MTS_SERVERS	Indicates the initial number of shared servers that start with database startup. Shared servers are protocol independent and can work with any available dispatcher. It is best to err on the low side when configuring the initial number of shared servers because Oracle7 automatically starts more servers if the system load is demanding

Parameter	Description
MTS_MAX_SERVERS	Indicates the maximum number of shared-server processes you can start for an instance. Initially, you might want to set this parameter high so you can experiment while tuning the server

An Example of Configuring the Initialization Parameters

Here is an example of configuring the initialization parameters for the multi-threaded server:

```
MTS_LISTENER_ADDRESS="(ADDRESS=(PROTOCOL=tcp)(PORT=1525)(HOST=sales.acme.com))"
MTS_SERVICES="sales"
MTS_DISPATCHERS="tcp,2","soc,1"
MTS_MAX_DISPATCHERS=5
MTS_SERVERS=5
MTS_MAX_SERVERS=20
```

When the Configuration Is Complete

Once you configure the multithreaded server initialization parameters, start the database. The instance will start with the dispatchers and shared servers that are configured in the parameter file. After startup, and once their client workstation is configured correctly, users can connect to the database using the multithreaded server. (See the section "Configuring Clients for Connections to the Multithreaded Server" later in this chapter.)

Monitoring and Tuning the Multithreaded Server

Once you start an instance with the multithreaded server, you should monitor the configuration to see if it is meeting the demands of the system. SQL*DBA has several monitors for the multithreaded server. However, SQL*DBA monitors cannot record system activity information that would let you see how your configuration responds over time to fluctuating demands. To supplement the SQL*DBA monitors for the multithreaded server monitoring, this section includes some listings of simple stored procedures that allow you to gather historical information about dispatcher and shared server loads. It also includes an explanation of how to use both to effectively monitor a multithreaded server configuration.

Accessing the SQL*DBA Monitor for Dispatchers

To access the SQL*DBA monitor for dispatchers, from the SQL*DBA menu select Monitor ➤ Multithreaded ➤ Dispatcher. Figure 8.9 shows an example of the Dispatcher monitor.

The key column on the Dispatcher monitor is Load. The load is expressed as a value from 0 to 1, with 1 being a 100 percent load. If the load on a dispatcher process of an instance is consistently high, it is likely that the dispatcher for that protocol is a bottleneck in serving the requests of system users.

To generate historical load information for dispatchers over time, use the table and administrative stored procedure in Listing 8.1.

FIGURE 8.9:
The Dispatcher monitor of SQL*DBA allows you to view cumulative information about the loads placed on dispatchers during their lives.

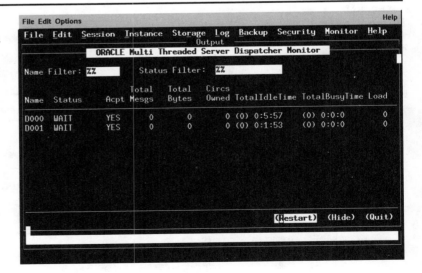

Listing 8.1: CAPTUREDISPATCHERLOADS Stored Procedure

```
CREATE TABLE dispatcherhistory (
  timepoint DATE,
  name VARCHAR2(10),
  network VARCHAR2(10),
  cumulativebusy REAL,
  cumulativeidle REAL,
  intervalload REAL)


CREATE PROCEDURE capturedispatcherloads
  (interval INTEGER, timepoints INTEGER) AS
-- This procedure wakes up at the given interval (specified in
-- minutes) and records the load placed on each dispatcher that
-- occurred during that interval.  Load information is placed
-- in the dispatcher history table.  You can then use the data
-- in the dispatcher history table to see the fluctuation in
-- dispatcher loads over time on the different dispatchers in your
-- system and make appropriate modifications in your multithreaded
-- server configuration.

counter INTEGER := 0;
previousbusy REAL;
previousidle REAL;
intervalbusy REAL;
intervalidle REAL;
load REAL;
CURSOR dispatch IS
  SELECT name, network, busy, idle
    FROM v$dispatcher;
BEGIN
  WHILE counter <= timepoints LOOP
    FOR status IN dispatch LOOP
-- special case the first datapoints in a session with a NULL load
      IF counter = 0 THEN
        INSERT INTO dispatcherhistory
        VALUES(SYSDATE,status.name,status.network,status.busy,status.idle,null);
      ELSE
        SELECT cumulativebusy, cumulativeidle INTO previousbusy, previousidle
          FROM dispatcherhistory
          WHERE name = status.name
          AND timepoint = (SELECT MAX(timepoint)
                             FROM dispatcherhistory
                             WHERE name = status.name);
```

```
         intervalbusy := status.busy-previousbusy;
         intervalidle := status.idle-previousidle;
-- special case when busy time is negative or zero to avoid divide-by-0 errors
         IF intervalbusy <= 0 THEN
            intervalbusy := 0.001;
         END IF;
         load := (intervalbusy/(intervalbusy+intervalidle))*100;
         INSERT INTO dispatcherhistory
         VALUES(SYSDATE,status.name,status.network,status.busy,status.idle,load);
      END IF;
   END LOOP;
   COMMIT;
   dbms_lock.sleep(interval*60);   -- convert interval from seconds to minutes
   counter := counter + 1;
  END LOOP;
END capturedispatcherloads;
```

Gathering Dispatcher Load Information

To start gathering dispatcher load information, establish a connection to the database server using SQL*DBA. Then create and execute the CAPTUREDISPATCHERLOADS procedure. For example, this statement gathers dispatcher information every 15 minutes for 8 hours (32 times):

```
EXECUTE capturedispatcherloads(15, 32);
```

The CAPTUREDISPATCHERLOADS procedure sleeps most of the time. It wakes at the specified interval to get dispatcher load information and then goes back to sleep. For this reason, you will have to dedicate a connection to gathering dispatcher load information and should use a dedicated server connection. (See the section "Connecting to Oracle7 Using a Dedicated Server Connection" later in this chapter.)

Once you have used the CAPTUREDISPATCHERLOADS procedure to get some history of the load on a multithreaded server configuration's dispatchers, you can query the DISPATCHERHISTORY table at any time. The output information will look something like this:

```
SELECT * FROM dispatcherhistory

TIMEPOINT NAME  NETWORK CUMULATIVEBUSY CUMULATIVEIDLE INTERVALLOAD
--------- ----- ------- -------------- -------------- ------------
02-DEC-96 D000  tcp              212344         507403
02-DEC-96 D001  soc               46754         672993
02-DEC-96 D000  tcp              487220         642911         67.0
02-DEC-96 D001  soc              105356        1024775         14.3
02-DEC-96 D000  tcp              667296         763882         59.8
02-DEC-96 D001  soc              148722        1263917         15.4
02-DEC-96 D000  tcp              893753         827610         78.0
02-DEC-96 D001  soc              190670        1548799         12.8
.
.
.
```

As you can see from this sample output, it might be wise to add another dispatcher for the TCP/IP protocol.

Modifying the Configuration

You can modify the configuration of the instance's multithreaded server by adding one or more dispatchers for any overloaded protocol. Alternatively, if the load on a dispatcher is consistently low and there is more than one dispatcher for a protocol, you can reduce process overhead on the server by terminating one or more of the dispatchers for that protocol.

If you find it necessary to modify the configuration of dispatchers for a database instance, you can do so without shutting down the instance. To modify the configuration of dispatchers, use the Configure Multi-Threaded Dispatchers dialog of SQL*DBA. To access this dialog from the SQL*DBA menu, select Instance ➤ Configure Dispatcher. Figure 8.10 shows the Configure Multi-Threaded Dispatcher dialog.

NOTE   To use the Configure Multi-Threaded Dispatcher dialog of SQL*DBA, you must have the ALTER SYSTEM system privilege.

FIGURE 8.10:

The Configure Multi-Threaded Dispatcher dialog of SQL*DBA allows you to start or stop dispatchers while the Oracle7 server remains online and in use.

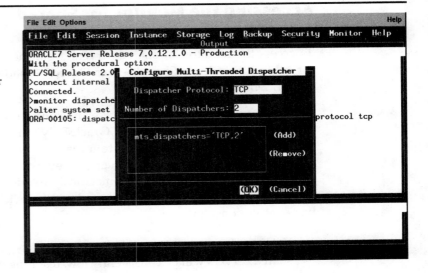

The Configure Multi-Threaded Dispatcher dialog allows you to build a list so you can adjust the configuration of the dispatchers for all network protocols in one dialog. Simply enter a protocol abbreviation code and the number of dispatchers for the protocol, and then add the entries to the list with the Add button. If you want to modify the dispatchers for another protocol, repeat the process. When the list is complete, select the OK button. Oracle7 then adjusts the configuration for the instance's dispatchers.

TIP

When you determine that the initial configuration for an instance's dispatcher processes is incorrect for normal system processing and then dynamically adjust the configuration, duplicate the configuration change in the MTS_DISPATCHERS initialization parameter so that the next time you start the database's instance, the configuration is correct.

Accessing the Monitor for Shared Servers

To access the monitor for shared servers, from the SQL*DBA menu select Monitor ➤ Multithreaded ➤ Shared Server. Figure 8.11 shows the Shared Server monitor of SQL*DBA.

Normally, you will not need to make any configuration modifications for an instance's shared servers because Oracle7 dynamically adjusts the number of shared servers based on the system load. However, as Oracle7 dynamically adjusts the number of shared servers, it never terminates shared servers below the current minimum set for the instance. Therefore, if you set MTS_SERVERS so that the minimum number of shared servers is too low or too high, there can be negative consequences.

- If the minimum number of shared servers is too high, the loads on the shared servers will be consistently low, resulting in wasted process overhead on the server.

- If the minimum number of shared servers is too low, Oracle7 will frequently start and stop shared servers during periods of fluctuating system load, resulting in spikes on system performance.

FIGURE 8.11:

The Shared Server monitor of SQL*DBA allows you to view cumulative information about the loads placed on servers during their lives.

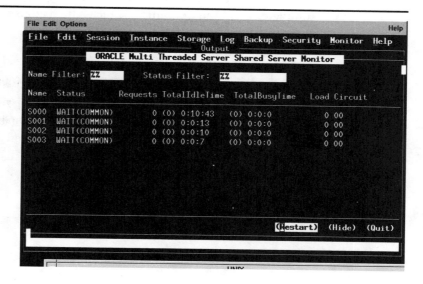

Recording Statistics for Shared Server Loads

To record statistics on how Oracle7 manages the shared servers of a multithreaded server configuration during a time period, you can use the table and administrative stored procedure in Listing 8.2.

Listing 8.2: CAPTURESERVERCOUNTS Stored Procedure

```
CREATE TABLE sharedserverhistory
(
  timepoint DATE,
  servercount INTEGER
)

CREATE PROCEDURE captureservercounts
  (interval INTEGER, timepoints INTEGER) AS
-- This procedure wakes up at the given intervals and records
-- how many servers are in use into a shared server history table.
-- You can then use the data in the server history table to
-- see how Oracle7 starts and stops servers over time in your
-- system and make appropriate modifications to MTS_SERVERS
-- in your multithreaded server configuration.

counter INTEGER := 0;
CURSOR server IS
  SELECT count(*) servers FROM v$shared_server;
BEGIN
  WHILE counter < timepoints LOOP
    FOR status IN server LOOP
      INSERT INTO sharedserverhistory
        VALUES (SYSDATE, status.servers);
    END LOOP;
    counter := counter + 1;
    dbms_lock.sleep(interval*60);
    COMMIT;
  END LOOP;
END captureservercounts;
```

Like the administrative stored procedure for recording dispatcher information, the CAPTURESERVERCOUNTS stored procedure sleeps most of the time, waking at the specified interval to get the server process count and then going back to sleep. For this reason, you will have to dedicate a connection to gathering shared server information and should use a dedicated server connection.

TIP
If you want to gather both dispatcher and shared server information at the same interval for the same amount of time, you can combine the logic of the previous two tables and example procedures. This way, you will have to dedicate only one session to gather all multithreaded server monitoring information.

Once you have used the CAPTURESERVERCOUNTS stored procedure to determine trends for shared server counts in a multithreaded server configuration, you can query the SHAREDSERVERHISTORY table at any time. The output information will look something like this:

```
SELECT * FROM sharedserverhistory

TIMEPOINT SERVERCOUNT
--------- -----------
15-JUL-96           2
15-JUL-96           8
15-JUL-96           9
15-JUL-96           7
15-JUL-96           3
15-JUL-96           8
15-JUL-96           9
15-JUL-96           8
    .
    .
    .
```

NOTE
If you haven't set the MTS_SERVERS and MTS_MAX_SERVERS parameters low and high enough, respectively, you won't see the true load fluctuation that normal processing places on the multithreaded server configuration. If results from the CAPTURESERVERCOUNTS procedure show server counts that either bottom out or top out according to the present limits, consider changing the limits to allow more fluctuation and then regather server information.

Adjusting the Number of Shared Servers

If you notice a trend in the number of servers typically used over a time period, you should adjust MTS_SERVERS to a number that matches this trend. You can adjust the minimum number of shared servers using the Configure Multi-Threaded Server dialog of SQL*DBA. To access the Configure Multi-Threaded Server dialog, from the SQL*DBA menu select Instance ➤ Configure ➤ Shared Server. Figure 8.12 shows the Configure Multi-Threaded Server dialog.

> **NOTE**
> To use the Configure Multi-Threaded Server dialog of SQL*DBA, you must have the ALTER SYSTEM system privilege.

To adjust the minimum number of shared servers, enter a number in the entry field. Oracle7 either terminates or starts shared servers to alter the minimum to the new number.

To summarize, configuring the dispatchers and servers for a multithreaded server configuration requires patience and some trial and error. However, with the help of

FIGURE 8.12:
The Configure Multi-Threaded Server dialog of SQL*DBA allows you to start and stop shared servers while the Oracle7 server remains online and in use.

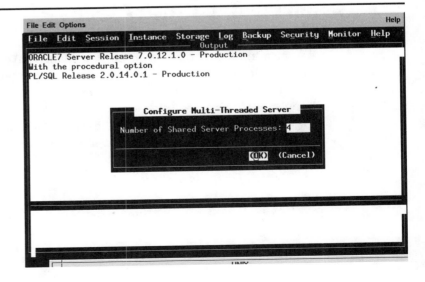

the stored procedures listed in this chapter, you can get a better feel for the requirements of a system over time and quickly get an Oracle7 server working at its best.

Connecting to Oracle7 from Remote Client Workstations

Once the multithreaded server is up and running and both clients and servers are configured with SQL*Net, a user can start a client application and establish a remote connection to the Oracle7 server. When starting the application, the user must specify a username and password, along with a database alias listed in the client's tnsnames.ora file. For example, the following operating system command starts SQL*Plus on the local workstation and establishes a remote connection to the SALES database:

```
sqlplus username/password@sales
```

Different tools use different methods for specifying the database alias, or *connection string*. However, in most cases a user's username/password combination is followed by the @ symbol to indicate a remote connection and then the alias name specified in the client's tnsnames.ora file.

Connecting to Oracle7 Using a Dedicated Server Connection

As an administrator, you will occasionally need to establish the remote connection using a dedicated server connection. For example, you need a dedicated server connection when you want to remotely start up or shut down an Oracle7 database, and you should use a dedicated server connection when using the procedures shown in Listings 8.1 and 8.2. To specifically establish a dedicated server connection to Oracle7 when the multithreaded server is present, modify your sqlnet.ora file to include the following parameter:

```
USE_DEDICATED_SERVER=ON
```

After modifying a client's sqlnet.ora to include this parameter, you can establish a connection similar to the preceding example. For instance, in the SQL*DBA Input window, you can enter

```
CONNECT internal/password@sales
```

This chapter has explained all aspects of configuring and using Oracle7 in a client/server system, including

- Using the SQL*Net Configuration Tool to configure SQL*Net for all clients and servers in an Oracle7 client/server system

- Starting the SQL*Net network listener process to accept and route remote client connections to the Oracle7 server

- Configuring and tuning the Oracle7 server as a multithreaded server to efficiently service remote client connections in a client/server system

- Connecting to Oracle7 from a remote client

Now that client workstations can create remote connections to the Oracle7 database server, it's time to learn how to create database users and make the database secure using Oracle7's security features, as described in the next chapter.

CHAPTER

NINE

Securing an Oracle7 Database

- Creating and managing Oracle7 database user accounts

- Managing database system security using Oracle7 system privileges and roles

- Controlling database system resource usage with tablespace quotas and resource limit profiles

Security is one of the most important jobs of a database administrator. Without adequate security controls, anyone would be able to access a database and query or change the data it contained. This chapter explains how you as an administrator can control access to a database and to a server's system resources using the security features provided by Oracle7. The chapter discusses these issues:

- Database users and user authentication
- Database access privileges and roles
- Resource limitation and user profiles

Controlling Database Access with User Accounts

Almost every business today has a voice-mail system, in which each employee has a mailbox to record incoming messages. To hear these messages, the employee must call the voice-mail system and then type his or her phone extension and password, using the phone's touch-tone keypad. After passing the system's security check, the employee can listen to the messages or administer his or her voice-mail box (change the greeting, change the password, and so on). Similarly, to control who can connect to a database, the database administrator registers users by creating database user accounts. The following sections explain how to manage user accounts in an Oracle7 database.

Creating Users

As with a voice-mail system, to connect to an Oracle7 database the user must have a database *username* and *password* or a *user account*. As the database administrator, you can create user accounts in a database system using the Create User dialog of SQL*DBA. To access the Create User dialog, use the Create User hot-key combination (Esc-U on UNIX) or, from the SQL*DBA menu, select Security ➤ Create User. Figure 9.1 shows the Create User dialog

FIGURE 9.1:

The Create User dialog of SQL*DBA allows you to quickly create a new database user and set the user's many account settings.

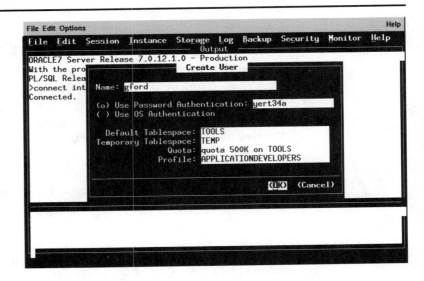

To use the Create User dialog of SQL*DBA, you must have the CREATE USER system privilege.

To create a new user account, first specify the new user's name in the Name entry field. The next step is to choose an authentication method from the radio button list.

Password Authentication versus Operating System Authentication

When a user attempts to connect to a database or to enable a role, Oracle7 ensures system security by *authenticating* the operation; that is, Oracle7 makes sure the user is a valid database user or has the right to enable the role. You can choose to handle authorization using either a password or the operating system. When a database uses passwords for authentication, Oracle7 asks users for a password when they want to create a new database session or enable a role. Alternatively, when a database uses operating system authentication, Oracle7 looks at who the user is according to the user's operating system session information and allows or disallows the user to connect or enable a role based on the information.

Each authentication method has advantages and disadvantages. The primary advantage of operating system authentication is that it centralizes all security in the operating system. Therefore, when using operating system authentication for database users and roles, the administrator does not have to manage passwords for operating system user accounts, database user accounts, and database privilege roles.

WARNING   Do not use operating system authentication when running Oracle7 in a client/server environment!

Using operating system authentication when running Oracle7 in a client/server environment opens up a large security hole. Any remote machine can try to establish a session with Oracle7 across a network, and many client workstations, such as personal UNIX workstations, are private machines that allow users to manage their own user accounts on the client. This makes it easy for a person on a client workstation to impersonate a real database user and break into an Oracle7 database system.

If you are using Oracle7 in a network client/server system, it is much more secure to use authentication by passwords.

Identifying Account Characteristics for the User

Once you choose an authentication method for a new user, the next step is to identify some important account characteristics for the user:

- The user's *default tablespace* is the tablespace where Oracle7 creates the user's objects (for example, tables and indexes) when no tablespace is explicitly specified in a CREATE statement. If you do not explicitly specify a default tablespace for the user, the default is the SYSTEM tablespace.

- The user's *temporary tablespace* is the tablespace where Oracle7 allocates temporary work space for completing complicated statements (for example, sorts and joins) on behalf of the user. If you do not explicitly specify a temporary tablespace for the user, the default is the SYSTEM tablespace.

- The user's *tablespace quotas* indicate how much space the user's objects can consume in specific tablespaces of the database. Tablespace quotas are a way to limit user access to disk space in a database. (For more information, see the section "Setting Space Quotas for Users" later in this chapter.)

- The user's *profile* is a set of system resource limits (for example, CPU processing time and idle time allowed). (For more information, see the section "Limiting Other System Resources Using Resource Limit Profiles" later in this chapter.)

TIP

If you need help, you can use the [List] key to access field builder dialogs for all of the entry fields in the Create User dialog.

To avoid problems, it is important to carefully plan out the account characteristics just described before creating each new user. For example, users with unlimited access to system resources can potentially run large, complicated queries that can adversely affect the performance of the system for all users. The remainder of this chapter will help you plan the characteristics for each new user in the system.

Before moving on, there's one important point to understand. After you create a new database user, no one can use the account to connect to Oracle7 until you grant the new user privileges to connect to the system. This ability is controlled by the CREATE SESSION Oracle7 system privilege. For more information about privilege management for Oracle7 database users, see the section "Privilege Management" later in this chapter.

TIP

If you need to create several user accounts, all with the same characteristics, take advantage of SQL*DBA's Input window command buffer to make repeated operations go more quickly. For example, create the first user using the Create User dialog box. To create the next user quickly, recall the previous command to place the previous CREATE USER command in the Input window. Then edit the command's username and password and execute the command. Repeat this procedure to quickly create the remaining users.

Changing Oracle7 Database Passwords

All Oracle7 users should regularly change their account's password to prevent security leaks. Without any special privileges, any user can change his or her password using the SQL command ALTER USER in any Oracle interactive query tool. For example, if a user is Abe Lincoln, the following statement changes Abe Lincoln's password to "yertqw":

```
ALTER USER alincoln IDENTIFIED BY yertqw
```

As the database administrator, it is your responsibility to determine how often users should change their passwords and then make sure they know how to change them using the ALTER USER command.

Altering Users

You may often want to change the characteristics for one or more users. For example, you may want to change a user's tablespace quotas to give the user more space or change a user's profile if the user changes jobs. After creating a user account, you can modify any of the account's characteristics using the Alter User dialog of SQL*DBA. To access the Alter User dialog, from the SQL*DBA menu select Security ➤ Alter User. Figure 9.2 shows the Alter User dialog of SQL*DBA.

NOTE To use the Alter User dialog box of SQL*DBA, you must have the ALTER USER system privilege.

From the list of user accounts, select the user to modify. You can then alter any of the selected account's characteristics using the authentication radio button list and entry fields as you did with the Create User dialog.

Setting a User's Default Roles

The Alter User dialog allows you to set an additional user account characteristic not available in the Create User dialog: a user's *default role*. When a user establishes a

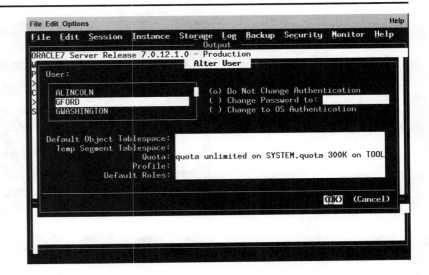

FIGURE 9.2:
The Alter User dialog of SQL*DBA allows you to quickly change the account settings of any Oracle7 database user.

new session in a database, Oracle7 automatically enables all of the user's default roles to establish the user's initial privilege domain. To set the default role list for a user, use the Default Roles entry field in the Alter User dialog. (To help you set a user's default role list correctly, see the section "Privilege Management" later in this chapter.)

Dropping Users

A user account often becomes unnecessary because a user transfers to a different division in a company or leaves the company altogether. In this case you will want to delete unnecessary user accounts to keep a database's user account table current.

You can delete a user account using the Drop User dialog of SQL*DBA. To access the Drop User dialog, use the hot-key sequence (Esc-D for UNIX) or, from the SQL*DBA menu, select Security ➤ Drop User. Figure 9.3 show the Drop User dialog of SQL*DBA.

FIGURE 9.3:

You can drop an Oracle7 database user with the Drop User dialog of SQL*DBA.

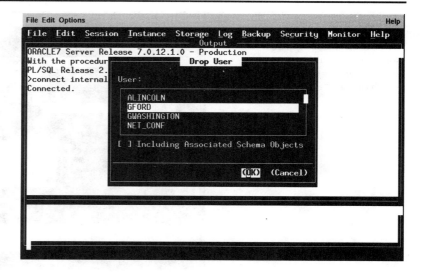

NOTE

To use the Drop User dialog box of SQL*DBA, you must have the DROP USER system privilege.

To drop a user, select the user from the list box. If the user owns any objects, you must also select the Including Associated Schema Objects check box; otherwise, Oracle7 will not drop the user.

NOTE

If you are not sure whether a user to be dropped owns any objects, do not select the Including Associated Schema Objects check box and execute the dialog. If the user owns any objects, Oracle7 returns an error and does not drop the user. You can then query the data dictionary to determine which objects the user owns and whether or not you want to copy them into another schema or drop them along with the user.

Using Encryption to Secure Remote Connections in a Client/Server Environment

 Many networks in the client/server world are not secure. In other words, it is easy for a malicious user to figure out database passwords in a network client/server database system by using some special software that can "sniff" the network for *unencrypted* packets of information. A persistent bandit can eventually get network packets containing users' connection requests, which include database usernames and passwords. At this point, access to the database system is as easy as walking through an unlocked door.

To prevent this security hole, you can configure an Oracle7 client to *encrypt* the username and password before sending it across the network. To do this, you set the ORA_ENCRYPT_LOGIN operating system session variable on the client to TRUE. (The name of this session variable may be different on different operating systems.)

Privilege Management

Once a person connects to a voice-mail system, the system restricts the person to working only within his or her own voice-mail box; for example, the system prevents anyone from hearing other people's voice-mail or changing someone else's greeting. Similarly, after a user connects to a database, Oracle7 controls the user's capabilities according to the user's database system privileges and database object privileges. To simplify privilege management in an Oracle7 database system, the administrator uses roles to control a user's privilege domain.

The privileges of a database user should always correspond to the application the user is currently running. The sections that follow provide general information about privilege management for different types of users in a database system. (For more information about application security, see Chapter 19.)

Managing Privileges for Database Administrators

Database administrators perform important system operations—including database startup and shutdown, database backup and recovery, security management, and instance configuration, just to name a few—that affect all users of the database. The ability to perform each different administrative operation is protected by a database system privilege. For example, to create users, an administrator must have the CREATE USER system privilege; to drop tables, an administrator must have the DROP ANY TABLE system privilege; and to alter triggers, an administrator must have the ALTER ANY TRIGGER system privilege. These are just a few examples of the many different powerful system privileges an administrator might require to complete the job.

> **WARNING** Avoid risking the security of a database system by granting a powerful system privilege to a database user other than a database administrator or, in certain cases, an application developer. (See the section "Managing Privileges for Application Developers" later in this chapter.)

Protecting Database Availability

Oracle7 allows an administrator to start up or shut down a database only when using the INTERNAL account. Since database startup and shutdown are extremely powerful operations, only a very few individuals should have access to the INTERNAL account.

In host-based systems, it is most common to protect the INTERNAL account using operating system authentication. For example, in a host-based UNIX system, only those users who are members of the "dba" group can connect to Oracle7 as INTERNAL. In client/server systems, it is highly recommended that you secure the INTERNAL account and remote connections using a password; you cannot reliably ensure security from a remote location using operating system authentication on the database server. (See the section "Password Authentication versus Operating System Authentication" earlier in this chapter.)

When you install Oracle7, the installer normally asks if you want to set a password for the INTERNAL account and if you want to permit remote connections as INTERNAL. On UNIX systems you can adjust the settings for INTERNAL on the Oracle7 server by using the command-line utility orapasswd. Of course, be careful to protect access to the orapasswd utility; a malicious user could use it to penetrate security for the INTERNAL account.

Using Roles to Manage Database Administration System Privileges

With over 70 different system privileges, it is important to use roles to simplify privilege management. With each Oracle7 database, there is a default database administration role named DBA. Initially, the DBA role has every system privilege, so a user with the DBA role can do anything within the database.

While the DBA role may be adequate for smaller systems where only one administrator is present, medium-sized and large Oracle7 systems will have multiple administrators, each with a specific job. To make sure no one administrator has more power than is necessary to accomplish that administrator's job, several specialized administrative roles are necessary. To create new roles, use the Create Role dialog of SQL*DBA. To access the Create Role dialog, from the SQL*DBA menu select Security ➤ Create Role. Figure 9.4 shows the Create Role dialog of SQL*DBA.

To use the Create Role dialog of SQL*DBA, you must have the CREATE ROLE system privilege.

To create a role, give it a new name in the Name entry field and then decide an authentication method for the role. As with user accounts, you can use either passwords or the operating system to protect the use of a role. For client/server systems, always choose to use passwords rather than the operating system to close network security holes.

FIGURE 9.4:

Using the Create Role dialog of SQL*DBA, you can create a new role and determine its authentication method.

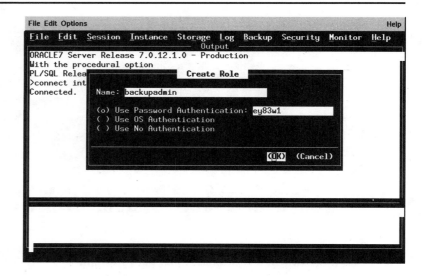

After creating a new administrative role, craft the role's privilege domain by granting system privileges and other roles to it. You can grant system privileges and roles to a role using the Grant dialog of SQL*DBA. To access the Grant dialog, from the SQL*DBA menu select Security ➤ Grant. Figure 9.5 shows the Grant dialog of SQL*DBA.

> **NOTE** To grant roles and system privileges successfully using the Grant dialog of SQL*DBA, you must have the role or system privilege with the ADMIN option, or you must have the GRANT ANY ROLE system privilege or the GRANT ANY PRIVILEGE system privilege.

Each entry field has a field builder dialog (use the [List] key to access it) that helps you choose which system privileges and/or roles to grant to what or whom.

FIGURE 9.5:

Use the Grant dialog of SQL*DBA to grant system privileges and/or roles to users and/or other roles.

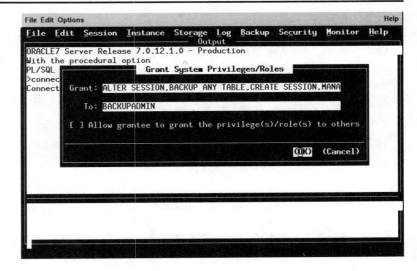

Example Database Administration Roles

Listing 9.1 shows several example statements that suggest how to create specialized administrative roles for the different administration duties in a system.

Listing 9.1: Custom Roles for Database Administrators

```
CREATE ROLE backupadmin IDENTIFIED BY password
GRANT CREATE SESSION, ALTER SESSION, RESTRICTED SESSION,
  MANAGE TABLESPACE, BACKUP ANY TABLE
  TO backupadmin

CREATE ROLE securityadmin IDENTIFIED BY password
GRANT CREATE SESSION, ALTER SESSION, RESTRICTED SESSION,
  CREATE USER, ALTER USER, DROP USER,
  CREATE ROLE, ALTER ANY ROLE, DROP ANY ROLE, GRANT ANY ROLE,
  GRANT ANY PRIVILEGE,
  AUDIT ANY, AUDIT SYSTEM,
  CREATE PROFILE, ALTER PROFILE, DROP PROFILE,
  ALTER RESOURCE COST,
```

```
CREATE PUBLIC SYNONYM, DROP PUBLIC SYNONYM,
CREATE ANY SYNONYM, DROP ANY SYNONYM
TO securityadmin WITH ADMIN OPTION

CREATE ROLE spaceadmin IDENTIFIED BY password
GRANT CREATE SESSION, ALTER SESSION, RESTRICTED SESSION,
  ALTER DATABASE,
  CREATE ROLLBACK SEGMENT, ALTER ROLLBACK SEGMENT,
  DROP ROLLBACK SEGMENT,
  CREATE TABLESPACE, ALTER TABLESPACE, DROP TABLESPACE
  TO spaceadmin

CREATE ROLE objectadmin IDENTIFIED BY password
GRANT CREATE SESSION, ALTER SESSION, RESTRICTED SESSION,
  ANALYZE ANY,
  CREATE ANY CLUSTER, ALTER ANY CLUSTER, DROP ANY CLUSTER,
  CREATE ANY INDEX, ALTER ANY INDEX, DROP ANY INDEX,
  CREATE ANY PROCEDURE, ALTER ANY PROCEDURE,
  DROP ANY PROCEDURE,
  CREATE ANY SEQUENCE, ALTER ANY SEQUENCE,
  DROP ANY SEQUENCE,
  CREATE ANY TABLE, ALTER ANY TABLE, DROP ANY TABLE,
  LOCK ANY TABLE, COMMENT ANY TABLE,
  CREATE ANY TRIGGER, ALTER ANY TRIGGER, DROP ANY TRIGGER,
  CREATE ANY VIEW, DROP ANY VIEW
  TO  objectadmin
          .
          .
          .
```

Notice how each of the preceding roles has only specific privileges that allow assigned users to perform a specific administration task—the BACKUPADMIN role has only the privileges necessary to connect to the server and perform database backup, the SECURITYADMIN role has only the privileges necessary to connect to the server and administer database security (such as creating users or roles), and so on.

NOTE Notice that every administrative role has the RESTRICTED SESSION privilege. This ensures that any type of administrator can connect to a database started in restricted mode.

As you can see, Oracle7's many system privileges offer very precise control over almost every system operation. (For a complete list of the different Oracle7 system privileges, see Appendix A.)

Managing Privileges for Application Developers

Application developers, like database administrators, need some powerful system privileges to complete their jobs. For example, an application developer needs to create database objects, such as tables, indexes, stored procedures, and triggers. It is important for the security administrator to carefully plan a security policy for application developers.

Privilege management techniques for an application developer vary, depending on the environment in which the application developer works:

- If the application developer works in a test database environment (as opposed to a production database environment), privilege management for the developer can be somewhat relaxed—because the data in a test database is not real, it is not important to real users of the system. To remove unnecessary barriers to productive application development, a developer in a test database is usually given many system privileges, including those normally reserved for database administrators.

- If the application developer works in a production database environment, privilege management should be very tight so the developer does not unnecessarily affect the productivity of other users. For example, an application developer should not be able to start up and shut down a production database system.

Using Roles to Manage Developer System Privileges

By default, every Oracle7 database has a role intended for application developers: the RESOURCE role. However, the RESOURCE role is present primarily for backward compatibility with previous versions of Oracle. Even smaller systems might find that the system privileges granted to RESOURCE are inadequate for productive application development. Consequently, you need to create custom application development roles for the application developers in an Oracle7 system. You can do this with the techniques presented in the previous section—using the Create Role and Grant dialogs of SQL*DBA.

To create database objects necessary for applications, developers are normally given space quotas for one or more tablespaces in a database. When developers work in a test database, you can give them unlimited quotas on all tablespaces in the database using the UNLIMITED TABLESPACE system privilege. However, when developers work in a production database, use specific tablespace quotas to restrict them to only the tablespaces they need to perform their job. (See the section "Resource Limitation" later in this chapter.)

> **NOTE** Strangely enough, even though Oracle7 stores all procedures, functions, packages, and triggers in the data blocks of the SYSTEM tablespace, no quota is necessary to create stored procedures. All an application developer needs is the necessary system privilege to create the PL/SQL program.

Example Accounts and Roles for Application Developers

Listing 9.2 shows several example statements that suggest how to create application development user accounts and a custom role for application developers in a production database system.

Listing 9.2: Custom Application Developer Accounts and Roles

```
CREATE USER applicationdeveloper IDENTIFIED BY password
  DEFAULT TABLESPACE testapplications
  TEMPORARY TABLESPACE testapplications
  QUOTA UNLIMITED ON testapplications
  PROFILE developerprofile

CREATE ROLE productiondbdeveloper IDENTIFIED BY password

GRANT CREATE SESSION, ALTER SESSION,
  CREATE TABLE, CREATE CLUSTER, CREATE VIEW,
```

```
CREATE SEQUENCE, CREATE PROCEDURE, CREATE TRIGGER,
CREATE ROLE, CREATE SYNONYM
TO productiondbdeveloper
```

Managing Privileges for Application End Users

In general, application users need object privileges only to access the objects associated with an application. Chapter 19 explains how application developers can plan and create roles for applications that dynamically manage the privilege domains of end users as they switch between different applications.

Application users should never have more than a select few system privileges. For example, every database user needs the CREATE SESSION system privilege to establish a connection to the Oracle7 database. The CONNECT role, present in every Oracle7 database, is intended for typical end users. However, this role includes some system privileges you might not want typical end users to have, such as the CREATE TABLE system privilege. Therefore, you might want to create your own default connection role for end users of your database system, including at least the CREATE SESSION privilege.

Resource Limitation

Once you have created users and given them access to a database, the next thing to consider when designing a good security policy is limiting their use of system resources within the database system. For example, if user sessions can remain idle for only 30 minutes before being terminated by Oracle7, unused sessions cannot stick around to forever waste valuable resources on the database server that active sessions could be using. This section explains how to limit the consumption of valuable system resources using the built-in resource limitation features of Oracle7: space quotas and resource limit profiles.

Setting Space Quotas for Users

One of the most valuable system resources to control in a database system is disk space for data storage. If you give a user the privilege to create database objects such as tables, the user's objects will consume disk space. If you allow the user un-limited access to any tablespace in the database, the user's objects can potentially hoard too much of the disk space allocated to the database.

To control the disk space consumption per user, Oracle7 uses *tablespace quotas*. You set space quotas to a user using the Create User or Alter User dialog of SQL*DBA. With each dialog, there is a field builder for the Quota entry field that allows you to build a list of tablespace quotas for the user. As Figure 9.6 shows, you can give a user a finite or an infinite quota for a tablespace.

FIGURE 9.6:
Both the Create User and Alter User dialogs of SQL*DBA permit you to control a user's access to disk space with tablespace quotas.

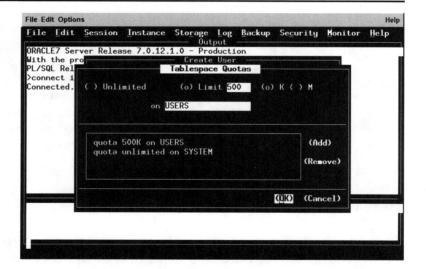

In most cases it is not necessary for a user to have any space quotas at all because typical users normally cannot create database objects that consume disk space (for example, tables and indexes). Even if you give a user the privilege to create objects such as views and synonyms, the user does not need any tablespace quotas because those types of database objects make simple entries in the data dictionary. End us-ers do not even need a tablespace quota for their temporary tablespace—Oracle7 does not consider tablespace quotas for temporary statement work space.

Application users and administrators are the users you should be concerned with when setting tablespace quotas. If an administrator or application developer is working in a test environment, it is relatively common to give the user unlimited access to every tablespace in the system, as described in the following section. Alternatively, if an application developer works in a production environment, the developer will likely need a quota for any tablespaces that hold application objects. Space and object administrators in a production environment are generally the only administrators who need access to tablespaces in a system.

Using the UNLIMITED TABLESPACE System Privilege

To grant unlimited access to all tablespaces in a database, use the UNLIMITED TABLESPACE system privilege instead of explicitly assigning quotas for all tablespaces in the system. Oracle7 ignores any explicitly specified tablespace quotas for a user when the user has the UNLIMITED TABLESPACE system privilege. Use this powerful system privilege only for application developers in a test database or for administrators who perform space and database object management.

NOTE The UNLIMITED TABLESPACE system privilege is unique because Oracle7 does not allow you to grant the system privilege to a role. The only way to grant a user this powerful system privilege is by directly granting the user the privilege.

Limiting Other System Resources Using Resource Limit Profiles

To control the consumption of other types of system resources, use Oracle7 system resource limits. *Resource limits* control

- A user's CPU usage and disk I/Os, both on per-statement and per-session intervals
- The number of sessions per user
- The maximum connect time and idle time per session
- The memory used by a multithreaded server session

You can manage all of these resource limits easily by first creating profiles that describe different types of user needs and then assigning the profiles to the appropriate users.

> **NOTE**
>
> Oracle7 resource limits wisely pay attention to logical disk I/Os, not physical disk I/Os. *Logical I/Os* occur when Oracle7 reads or write a data block in memory. *Physical I/Os* occur when Oracle7 reads or writes a block from disk into memory. Since Oracle7 caches large amounts of data in shared memory and must perform both a physical and logical I/O when reading new data from disk into shared memory, Oracle7 counts the number of logical I/Os to get an accurate account of a user's operation.

The DEFAULT Profile

Every Oracle7 database has a default profile, appropriately named DEFAULT. Oracle7 automatically limits the operations of all users not assigned to a specific profile in accordance with the limits specified in the DEFAULT profile. Other profiles can also defer to the settings in the DEFAULT profile for specific limits. Initially, all resource limits in the DEFAULT profile are set to unlimited; therefore, it is important that you alter the settings for the DEFAULT profile after you create a database.

Creating New Profiles for Users

When you want to create a new resource limit profile, you use the Create Profile dialog of SQL*DBA. To access the Create Profile dialog, from the SQL*DBA menu select Security ➤ Create Profile. Figure 9.7 shows the Create Profile dialog of SQL*DBA.

> **NOTE**
>
> To use the Create Profile dialog of SQL*DBA, you must have the CREATE PROFILE system privilege.

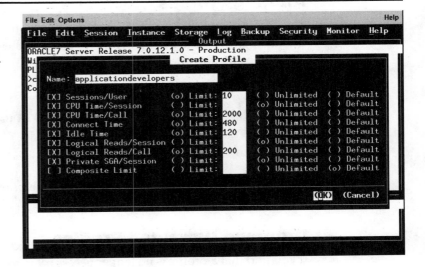

FIGURE 9.7:

Using the Create Profile dialog of SQL*DBA, you can create different resource limit profiles to control user consumption of server resources.

To create a new resource limit profile, specify a name for the new profile and then set the different resource limits for the profile. Notice that for each resource limit, you can specify a specific limit, specify an unlimited setting, or defer to the setting in the DEFAULT profile. The settings for CPU time limits are in hundredths of a second, connect and idle time limits are in elapsed minutes, and private memory per session is in bytes (although you can specify K for kilobytes and M for megabytes).

NOTE Oracle7 doesn't actually perform resource limit checking unless the server is started with the initialization parameter RESOURCE_LIMIT set to TRUE. This initialization parameter can be useful in tuning server performance because, as you might guess, the Oracle7 server incurs additional processing overhead to perform resource limit checking for all user sessions and requests.

Altering Profiles

To alter a resource limit profile, use the Alter Profile dialog of SQL*DBA. To access this dialog, from the SQL*DBA menu select Security ➤ Alter Profile. Figure 9.8 shows the Alter Profile dialog of SQL*DBA.

> **NOTE**   To use the Alter Profile dialog box of SQL*DBA, you must have the ALTER PROFILE system privilege.

To alter a profile, select the profile from the list box and then alter the setting for any of the limits in the profile.

Dropping Unwanted Profiles

If you find that a profile is no longer necessary in a database, you can drop the profile using the Drop Profile dialog of SQL*DBA. To access this dialog, from the SQL*DBA menu select Security ➤ Drop Profile. Figure 9.9 shows the Drop Profile dialog of SQL*DBA.

FIGURE 9.8:

You can change a resource limit profile's setting with the Alter Profile dialog of SQL*DBA.

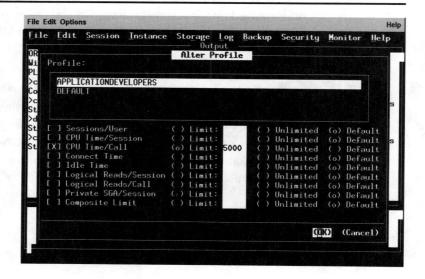

FIGURE 9.9:
Use the Drop Profile dialog of SQL*DBA when you need to drop a resource limit profile.

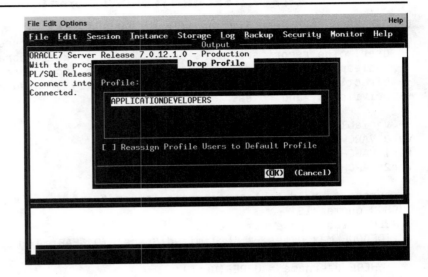

To use the Drop Profile dialog of SQL*DBA, you must have the DROP PROFILE system privilege.

Select the profile to drop from the list box and then select OK. When you drop a profile that is assigned to users of the database, Oracle7 automatically assigns those users to the DEFAULT profile. Be sure to review those users assigned to the DEFAULT profile and assign them to another profile if necessary.

Reporting Security Settings for Users

The data dictionary of every Oracle7 database has several views that reveal the security settings for all users in a database. Listing 9.3 shows a stored procedure you can use to generate a report of the security settings for a user in a database.

Listing 9.3: SECURITYREPORT Stored Procedure

```
CREATE PROCEDURE securityreport (user VARCHAR2) AS
-- This procedure generates a security report for the specified
-- user.  The report shows the user's default and temporary
-- tablespaces, resource limit profile, tablespace quotas,
-- directly granted system privileges, directly granted object
-- privileges, and roles.

-- variables to hold account information
var0 VARCHAR2(100);
var1 VARCHAR2(100);
var2 VARCHAR2(100);

-- cursor to hold tablespace quota information
CURSOR quotas IS
  SELECT tablespace_name, bytes,
    DECODE(max_bytes,-1,'Unlimited Space',TO_CHAR(max_bytes)) quota
    FROM sys.dba_ts_quotas
    WHERE username = UPPER(user);

-- cursor to hold system privilege information
CURSOR sysprivs IS
  SELECT privilege, admin_option
    FROM sys.dba_sys_privs
    WHERE grantee = UPPER(user);

-- cursor to hold object privilege information
CURSOR objprivs IS
  SELECT owner, table_name, privilege, grantable
    FROM sys.dba_tab_privs
    WHERE grantee = UPPER(user);

-- cursor to hold role information
CURSOR roles IS
  SELECT granted_role, admin_option, default_role
    FROM sys.dba_role_privs
    WHERE grantee = UPPER(user);

BEGIN
-- Gather account information about user for first part of report.
-- If the specified user does not exist, return an error message.

  SELECT default_tablespace, temporary_tablespace, profile
    INTO var0, var1, var2
```

```
      FROM sys.dba_users
      WHERE username = UPPER(user);

-- print report header
DBMS_OUTPUT.PUT_LINE('');
DBMS_OUTPUT.PUT_LINE('Security Report for User: '||UPPER(user));
DBMS_OUTPUT.PUT_LINE('----------------------------------------');

-- print user's account settings
DBMS_OUTPUT.PUT_LINE('');
DBMS_OUTPUT.PUT_LINE(' '||UPPER(user)||' Account Settings');
DBMS_OUTPUT.PUT_LINE(' ---------------------------------------');
DBMS_OUTPUT.PUT_LINE('   Default Tablespace:      '||var0);
DBMS_OUTPUT.PUT_LINE('   Temporary Tablespace:    '||var1);
DBMS_OUTPUT.PUT_LINE('   Resource Limit Profile:  '||var2);

-- print user's tablespace quotas, if any
DBMS_OUTPUT.PUT_LINE('');
DBMS_OUTPUT.PUT_LINE(' '||UPPER(user)||' Tablespace Quotas');
DBMS_OUTPUT.PUT_LINE(' ---------------------------------------');
FOR userquota IN quotas LOOP
  DBMS_OUTPUT.PUT_LINE('   Tablespace:    '||userquota.tablespace_name);
  DBMS_OUTPUT.PUT_LINE('   Bytes Used:    '||userquota.bytes);
  DBMS_OUTPUT.PUT_LINE('   Quota (Bytes): '||userquota.quota);
  DBMS_OUTPUT.PUT_LINE('');
END LOOP;

-- print user's system privileges, if any
DBMS_OUTPUT.PUT_LINE('');
DBMS_OUTPUT.PUT_LINE(' '||UPPER(user)||' Directly Granted System Privileges');
DBMS_OUTPUT.PUT_LINE(' ---------------------------------------');
FOR usersyspriv IN sysprivs LOOP
  DBMS_OUTPUT.PUT_LINE('   Privilege:     '||usersyspriv.privilege);
  DBMS_OUTPUT.PUT_LINE('   Admin Option?: '||usersyspriv.admin_option);
  DBMS_OUTPUT.PUT_LINE('');
END LOOP;

-- print user's object privileges, if any
DBMS_OUTPUT.PUT_LINE('');
DBMS_OUTPUT.PUT_LINE(' '||UPPER(user)||' Directly Granted Object Privileges');
DBMS_OUTPUT.PUT_LINE(' ---------------------------------------');
FOR userobjpriv IN objprivs LOOP
  DBMS_OUTPUT.PUT_LINE('   Object Name:   '||userobjpriv.owner||'.'
    ||userobjpriv.table_name);
```

```
  DBMS_OUTPUT.PUT_LINE('  Privilege:       '||userobjpriv.privilege);
  DBMS_OUTPUT.PUT_LINE('  Grant Option?:   '||userobjpriv.grantable);
  DBMS_OUTPUT.PUT_LINE('');
END LOOP;

-- print user's roles, if any, indicating which are default roles
DBMS_OUTPUT.PUT_LINE('');
DBMS_OUTPUT.PUT_LINE('  '||UPPER(user)||' Roles');
DBMS_OUTPUT.PUT_LINE('  ----------------------------------------');
FOR userroles IN roles LOOP
  IF userroles.default_role = 'YES' THEN
    DBMS_OUTPUT.PUT_LINE('  Default Role:   '||userroles.granted_role);
  ELSE
    DBMS_OUTPUT.PUT_LINE('  Role:           '||userroles.granted_role);
   END IF;
  DBMS_OUTPUT.PUT_LINE('  Admin Option?: '||userroles.admin_option);
  DBMS_OUTPUT.PUT_LINE('');  END LOOP;

EXCEPTION
-- if user does not exist, raise user-defined error message
  WHEN NO_DATA_FOUND THEN
    raise_application_error(-20000, UPPER(user)
     ||' is not a valid database user.');
END securityreport;
```

> After creating the SECURITYREPORT procedure, you can use it in SQL*DBA or
> SQL*Plus by setting server output on and then executing the procedure with a spe-
> cific user's name:

```
SET SERVEROUTPUT ON SIZE 10000

EXECUTE securityreport('alincoln')

Security Report for User: ALINCOLN
------------------------------------------------------------

ALINCOLN Account Settings
------------------------------------------------------------
  Default Tablespace:      TEST
  Temporary Tablespace:    TEST
  Resource Limit Profile:  DEVELOPERS
```

```
ALINCOLN Tablespace Quotas
--------------------------------------------------------------
  Tablespace:      TEST
  Bytes Used:      0
  Quota (Bytes):   Unlimited Space

  Tablespace:      SYSTEM
  Bytes Used:      10452
  Quota (Bytes):   204800

ALINCOLN Directly Granted System Privileges
--------------------------------------------------------------
  Privilege:       CREATE SESSION
  Admin Option?:   NO

ALINCOLN Directly Granted Object Privileges
--------------------------------------------------------------
  Object Name:     SALES.CUSTOMER
  Privilege:       SELECT
  Grant Option?:   NO

ALINCOLN Roles
--------------------------------------------------------------
  Default Role:    APPDEVELOPER
  Admin Option?:   NO

  Role:            MINIDBA
  Admin Option?:   NO
```

This chapter has explained the aspects of database system security that are important for an administrator to consider, including

- Enrolling new users for an Oracle7 database and configuring their account settings

- Altering user account settings, including changing a user password

- Managing the system privileges required by different types of Oracle7 users using roles

- Controlling the consumption of important system resources, such as disk space, processing time, and disk I/Os

After reading this chapter and the previous chapters in this part of the book, you should have a clear understanding of the many important tasks for which an Oracle7 administrator is responsible. The next chapter discusses the many administrative jobs related to supporting client applications.

CHAPTER

TEN

Database Administration on Behalf of Applications

- Fine-tuning application schema settings, such as object storage settings

- Checking application security settings

- Creating and managing rollback segments for applications

- Generating optimizer statistics for an application schema

As a client/server database system takes shape, part of your job as the administrator is to be closely involved with the application developers' efforts. This is important because when a new application is ready for use in the production database environment, you must perform a number of jobs to get the application installed and running. This chapter explains the tasks an administrator must perform on behalf of client database applications, including

- Reviewing, editing, and running an application's DDL script to create the application schema
- Creating and managing rollback segments to handle application transactions
- Generating and maintaining optimizer statistics for the objects in application schemas

Creating the Application Schema

Let's assume that a new application has passed all of the rigorous trials in a test database environment and everything is now ready to move to the production database. As the database administrator, some or all of a database application's installation will be your responsibility. This section explains the part of application installation that always falls into the database administrator's lap: running the application's DDL script to create the tables, views, and other database objects on behalf of the application.

What Is an Application's DDL Script?

When a developer creates a new database application, part of the job is to design the *application schema*—the tables, views, procedures, triggers, and other database objects that are part of the application. When the application is finished and ready for implementation, the developer must hand off the application's source code and executable to the database administrator, along with a script file that includes the DDL SQL statements for creating the application schema.

Developers can generate an application's DDL script using several approaches. If the developer has CASE or database design tools, such as Oracle's CASE products, the developer diagrams the entities and relationships in the database, and the CASE tool automatically creates much of the corresponding DDL script. Even when using a sophisticated CASE or database design tool, the developer must write at least part of an application's DDL script by hand, including the DDL statements that create database triggers, stored procedures and packages, and the application's privilege roles. In the absence of a CASE tool, the developer must write all of an application's DDL script by hand.

A developer who generates an application's DDL script does not pay much attention to low-level storage considerations for an application's database objects—considerations that can affect the performance of the application and storage requirements on the database server. Such storage considerations are the responsibility of the database administrator. The next two sections explain the different storage parameters for database objects and how to set these parameters appropriately within an application's DDL script.

Setting Object Tablespace Placement

The primary storage characteristic to consider for database objects is where to store them. You can manage the physical location of many database objects, including tables, indexes, and clusters, using tablespaces. For example, if you store the ACCOUNTSREC table in the ACCOUNTING tablespace, Oracle7 physically stores the table's data in one or more of the data files that make up the tablespace.

```
CREATE TABLE accountsrec
( ... column specifications ....)
TABLESPACE accounting
.
.
.
```

Note that Oracle7 stores other objects, such as procedures, functions, packages, and database triggers, all within the SYSTEM tablespace and offers no option to physically locate them elsewhere. Therefore, it is important to plan enough space for objects that Oracle7 stores in the SYSTEM tablespace. (See the section "Estimating Space Requirements for Application Database Objects" later in this chapter.)

Setting Object Storage Parameters

To control how Oracle7 uses the space with the data blocks of a table, index, or cluster, Oracle7 has several types of *storage parameters:*

- INITIAL, NEXT, MINEXTENTS, MAXEXTENTS, and PCTINCREASE
- PCTFREE and PCTUSED
- INITRANS and MAXTRANS

Different types of storage parameters have different purposes. The following sections describe each class of storage parameters, based on their functions.

NOTE As you read the following sections, keep in mind that all of the storage parameters in Oracle7 are options you can specify when you create a table, index, or cluster; Oracle7 does not require you to specify any storage parameters because there are default values for each. However, when you want to squeeze out every last bit of performance related to disk I/O while at the same time use every last byte of available disk space, you will need to learn how to set the Oracle7 storage parameters correctly.

Controlling Space Allocation with Extent Storage Parameters

Much as Oracle7 preallocates contiguous disk space for tablespaces using data files, Oracle7 preallocates contiguous space within the data files of a tablespace for tables, indexes, and clusters using extents. An *extent* is nothing more than a number of contiguous data blocks that Oracle7 allocates for an object when more space is necessary for the object's data. The group of all the extents for an object is called a *segment.*

The single preallocation of many data blocks as an extent delivers a tremendous performance advantage for applications; otherwise, Oracle7 would have to allocate blocks every time a user inserts new data into an object. Figure 10.1 shows how Oracle7 allocates data blocks for an object using extents.

When you create a table, index, or cluster, Oracle7 allocates one or more extents to hold the object's initial data. As users insert data into the object, Oracle7 automatically allocates additional extents, as needed, to hold data that does not fit the current set of extents for the object.

There are several storage parameters that allow you to control how Oracle7 allocates extents for tables, indexes, and clusters. In general, the Oracle7 extent storage parameters are available so you can force all of an object's data within a small number of extents, thereby reducing data fragmentation and increasing performance with respect to disk I/O. The following list explains each extent storage parameter and its purpose:

Parameter	Description
INITIAL	Determines the size, in bytes, of an object's initial extent. You can use INITIAL to preallocate all or a large majority of the space you ever expect an object to require. This way, all or most of the object's data resides in a contiguous set of data blocks. To set INITIAL accurately, you must estimate an object's size. (see the section "Estimating Space Requirements for Application Database Objects" later in this chapter)

FIGURE 10.1:

Oracle7 allocates data blocks for an object in clusters of data blocks called extents.

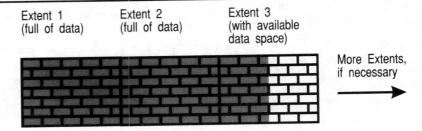

Extent 1 (full of data) Extent 2 (full of data) Extent 3 (with available data space)

More Extents, if necessary →

Object Segment (e.g., Table, Index)

Parameter	Description
NEXT	Determines the size, in bytes, of the next extent Oracle7 will allocate, if necessary, for the object. You can explicitly set the size for the second extent of an object using NEXT, but the value of NEXT may grow, depending on the value for PCTINCREASE (see below)
MINEXTENTS	Determines how many extents to preallocate when creating a table, index, or cluster. For example, if you create a table and specify MINEXTENTS as 2, Oracle7 immediately allocates two extents for the table
MAXEXTENTS	Determines the maximum number of extents Oracle7 can ever allocate for a table, index, or cluster. You use MAXEXTENTS to effectively control the maximum size of an object. There is an operating system–dependent upper bound when setting MAXEXTENTS
PCTINCREASE	Determines the growth factor as Oracle7 allocates new extents to a table, index, or cluster. For example, if you set a table's NEXT to 200K and PCTINCREASE to 50, the second extent will be 200K, the third extent will be 300K, the fourth extent will be 450K, and so on. You use PCTINCREASE to increase the size of subsequent extents and try to reduce data fragmentation within an object

Figure 10.2 demonstrates how Oracle7 uses the extent storage parameter settings for a table as the table grows.

When setting extent storage parameters for a table, index, or cluster, consider these issues:

- If you specify a size for INITIAL and NEXT that is not a multiple of the database's data block size, Oracle7 rounds the number up.

- You can change the value for NEXT to explicitly set the size of an object's next extent. If you change PCTINCREASE, the new value does not take effect until Oracle7 allocates the extent subsequent to the very next extent.

- Changing the setting for an object's INITIAL or MINEXTENTS parameter has no effect since the initial number of extents has already been allocated for the object.

- In general, concentrate on sizing object extents correctly so you can set PCTINCREASE to 0.

To set extent storage parameters for an object, use the STORAGE clause of the CREATE and ALTER commands. For example, this statement shows the STORAGE

FIGURE 10.2:

Storage parameters determine the size and growth characteristics of a segment's extents.

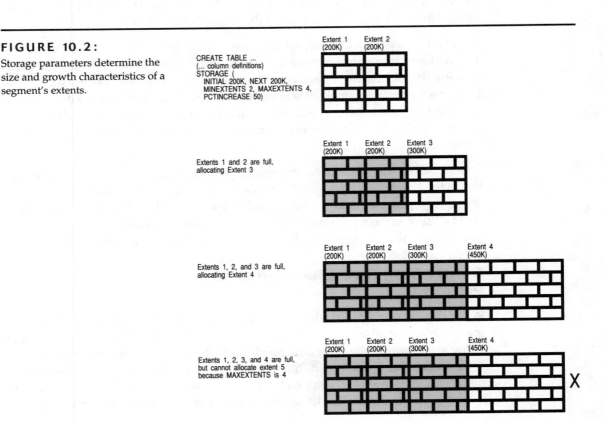

297

clause that sets the extent storage parameters for the ACCOUNTSREC table:

```
CREATE TABLE accountsrec
( ... column specifications ... )
STORAGE   (INITIAL 100K
           NEXT 100K
           MINEXTENTS 2
           MAXEXTENTS 10
           PCTINCREASE 0)
     .
     .
     .
```

The STORAGE clause is available for many commands, including ALTER TABLE, CREATE INDEX, ALTER INDEX, CREATE CLUSTER, ALTER CLUSTER, CREATE ROLLBACK SEGMENT, and ALTER ROLLBACK SEGMENT.

Each tablespace in an Oracle7 database has a set of *default extent storage parameters*. When a user creates an object in a tablespace and chooses not to set storage parameters for the object, the object's storage parameters take the values set for the tablespace's default extent storage parameters. Setting a tablespace's default storage parameters can make space administration easier when you have determined that many objects in a tablespace should have the same extent storage parameter settings.

To set a tablespace's default extent storage parameters, specify the storage parameters in the Create Tablespace or Alter Tablespace dialog of SQL*DBA. You can enter the storage parameters in the entry field or use the field list builder dialog to help build a list of storage parameters. Figure 10.3 shows the entry field list builder you can use with the Storage entry field of the Create Tablespace dialog of SQL*DBA.

Controlling Row Chaining Using PCTFREE

When you are managing the health of a database, it is important to avoid row chaining in tables if at all possible. A *row chain* occurs when Oracle7 does not store all of a row's data within the same data block but instead is forced to break the row into *row pieces* and store them in different data blocks. In other words, the row is fragmented among multiple data blocks. To return all of a row's data for a query, Oracle7 must piece the row back together by traversing the row's chain of data blocks.

FIGURE 10.3:

A child dialog of the Create
Tablespace dialog of SQL*DBA lets
you build a list of default extent
storage parameters for a tablespace.

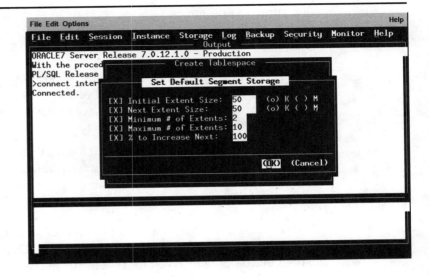

As with other types of data fragmentation on disk, significant amounts of row
chaining within a table can degrade disk I/O performance because Oracle7 must
read more data blocks to read rows in the table. Figure 10.4 shows a row chain in
an Oracle7 table.

FIGURE 10.4:

Row chaining can occur when an
Oracle7 table's rows are too large to
fit in a single data block.

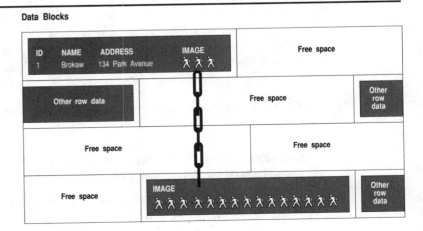

In most circumstances, Oracle7 chooses to store an entire row within the same block. However, there are two situations in which Oracle7 cannot avoid chaining rows:

- If a row has more data than can fit inside a single data block. For example, when you have a table with a LONG RAW column that stores large images, each row will probably require several data blocks. Unfortunately, there is nothing you can do to avoid this type of row chaining.

- If a user updates a row to make it longer than the original version. If the data block that holds the row does not have ample space for the additional bytes of information for the new version of the row, Oracle7 must fragment the row among multiple data blocks.

PCTFREE is a storage parameter you can use to minimize row chaining resulting from the second situation described above. PCTFREE controls how much of the space in a block is reserved for statements that update existing rows in the object. For example, if a table's PCTFREE is set to its default value of 10, Oracle7 will allow users to insert rows into a data block of the table until 10 percent of the free space remains in the block. Oracle7 reserves the remaining 10 percent of free space in the block for updates that might make the table's existing rows grow in size.

The guidelines for setting PCTFREE are relatively straightforward. If a table is one in which users will update original rows to make them grow, set the table's PCTFREE storage parameter to a higher number to reserve more space for updates to the table. For example, if a table's rows are much smaller than the database block size and they grow by a factor of x, you might set PCTFREE for the table to (1/x)*100 (plus a little bit extra). Alternatively, if the table rarely experiences updates or updates that make rows larger, set the table's PCTFREE storage parameter to a lower number to make more data block space available for row inserts.

The next section explains the procedure for setting an object's PCTFREE storage parameter.

Controlling Data Block Free Space Availability with PCTUSED

When you and a friend go to a restaurant for dinner, the first person you see is the maitre d'. The maitre d' has a list of available tables and takes you and your friend to a table when one is ready. Similarly, when a user inserts a row into a table, Oracle7 must choose a data block to store the new row. To make block selection for row inserts fast and easy, Oracle7 keeps one or more *free space lists* for each table—lists that state which data blocks have available free space for new rows.

Oracle7 decides which data blocks appear on free space lists using the PCTFREE and PCTUSED storage parameters. When users insert new rows into a data block that cause the PCTFREE threshold to be reached, as described in the preceding section, Oracle7 takes the data block off the table's free space lists. After reaching PCTFREE, Oracle7 does not return a data block to the table's free lists until another threshold, PCTUSED, is reached. PCTUSED is a percentage of used space in a data block that triggers the data block to return to the table's free space list. As users delete rows from a table, Oracle7 frees space in the table's data blocks. When there are enough deletes to cause PCTUSED to be reached, Oracle7 returns the data block to the table's free space lists. For example, when a table's PCTUSED is set to its default value of 40, Oracle7 will not return a block to the table's free space lists until users delete enough rows that only 39 percent of the space in the block is used. After returning the block to the table's free space lists, Oracle7 uses the block for new row inserts until the block again fills to PCTFREE. Figure 10.5 illustrates the cycle described above where PCTFREE and PCTUSED govern a data block's status in the free space lists of a table.

FIGURE 10.5:

A data block's movement on and off free space lists is determined by PCTFREE and PCTUSED.

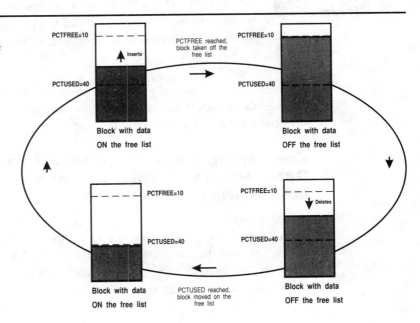

The guidelines for setting PCTUSED affect both storage utilization and system performance. Higher PCTUSED settings make sure that Oracle7 keeps data blocks relatively full, but these settings can also degrade system performance as Oracle7 constantly moves blocks on and off free space lists. Alternatively, lower PCTUSED settings can lead to pockets of wasted storage space when users often delete rows. You have to look at the characteristics of your application and set PCTUSED to obtain an acceptable compromise between performance and space usage.

To set an object's PCTFREE and PCTUSED storage parameters in a CREATE or ALTER statement, simply specify each option and an integer indicating the setting. For example, this statement creates the ACCOUNTSREC table with PCTFREE set to 15 and PCTUSED set to 60:

```
CREATE TABLE ACCOUNTSREC
( ... column specifications ... )
PCTFREE 15
PCTUSED 60
.
.
.
```

NOTE   The sum of PCTFREE and PCTUSED cannot be greater than 100. Additionally, avoid setting PCTFREE to 0, since this can create block space allocation problems for other internal operations.

After creating an object, you can always change the settings for PCTFREE and PCTUSED. However, the new settings will apply only to new data blocks added to the object as part of a subsequent extent allocation.

Controlling Transaction Access to Data Blocks with INITRANS and MAXTRANS

As a transaction touches data in an object, Oracle7 must allocate small amounts of space in the corresponding data blocks of the object to hold internal processing information until the transaction commits or rolls back. Oracle7 has two storage parameters, INITRANS and MAXTRANS, that allow you to tune performance with respect to this internal processing mechanism on behalf of transactions.

Parameter	Description
INITRANS	Preallocates space for a specified number of *transaction entries* in each data block of an object. This way, Oracle7 does not have to dynamically allocate space for transaction entries as they enter data blocks. The default value is 1
MAXTRANS	Limits the number of transactions that can concurrently enter a data block and thus the amount of space that transaction entries can consume in a block at any given time. If MAXTRANS number of transactions are using a block at the same time, the next transaction to request information in the block must wait until another transaction using the block either commits or rolls back

The guidelines for setting INITRANS and MAXTRANS correspond to table characteristics and application behavior. For example, if many application users concurrently need access to a small lookup table, set the table's INITRANS and MAXTRANS parameters to higher numbers for better performance and no waiting among application users. Alternatively, large tables reduce the likelihood of several users touching the same data blocks at the same time; therefore, you can make more data block space available to actual data by using a smaller setting for INITRANS.

To set an object's INITRANS and MAXTRANS storage parameters when creating or altering the object, simply specify each option and an integer indicating the setting. For example, this statement creates the ACCOUNTSREC table with INITRANS set to 4 and MAXTRANS set to 20:

```
CREATE TABLE ACCOUNTSREC
( ... column specifications ... )
INITRANS 4
MAXTRANS 20
 .
 .
 .
```

Estimating Space Requirements for Application Database Objects

To set certain extent storage parameters correctly for tables and indexes in an application's DDL script (as described in the section "Setting Object Storage Parameters" earlier in this chapter), it is useful to get an estimate of the space a table and associated indexes will require in the production database. Specifically, size estimates help you set the values for INITIAL and MINEXTENTS to preallocate all or much of a table's and index's storage space. Similarly, it is useful to estimate the sizes of other application objects, like packages and triggers, so you can make sure the SYSTEM tablespace contains enough free space to support the new application when you run the application's DDL script. The following sections show how to easily estimate the space requirements for all types of application objects.

Estimating Space for Tables and Indexes

Space estimates for tables and indexes are useful if you want to plan disk storage requirements and preallocate all of the space a table and its indexes will ever need. For example, after estimating a table's size, you can use this information to set the INITIAL and MINEXTENTS storage parameters in the table's CREATE TABLE statement.

Correctly estimating the size of a table and associated indexes is relatively simple if you perform the following steps:

1. Create a prototype of the table and indexes in either the production or test database. When creating the table and indexes, be sure to set PCTFREE as you plan to have it when the application is in production.

2. Insert approximately 1000 representative rows into the prototype table.

3. Gather statistics on the prototype table and its indexes.

4. Estimate the maximum number of rows you think the table will store.

5. Create and execute the ESTIMATETABLESIZE procedure given in Listing 10.1 a little later in this chapter.

Step 1, creating a prototype table and its indexes, is simple because the application's DDL script already has the CREATE statements for the table and its indexes. All you need to do is add the PCTFREE parameter and run these statements.

Step 2, inserting approximately 1000 representative rows into the table, is also easy to accomplish with a simple anonymous PL/SQL block:

```
DECLARE
x DATE := SYSDATE;
y NUMBER := 10000.12;
BEGIN
  FOR counter IN 1 .. 1000 LOOP
    INSERT INTO prototypetable
      VALUES ( ... x, y, other column values ... );
    x := x + 1;
    y := y + 4;
  END LOOP;
END;
```

Notice that this example block inserts a representative range of index key values into the table and its indexes by using variables in the anonymous PL/SQL block that change with each iteration through the insertion loop. This trick makes the rows in the prototype table and its indexes more representative of the production table and indexes.

For step 3, use the ANALYZE command to gather some statistics about the prototype table and its indexes:

```
ANALYZE TABLE prototypetable COMPUTE STATISTICS
```

The ESTIMATETABLESIZE procedure will need these statistics later. (If you are not familiar with the ANALYZE command, see the section "Generating Optimizer Statistics" later in this chapter.)

Step 4 is up to you; only you know your data and can reasonably estimate the maximum number of rows the table will ever hold.

Step 5 is the fun part. The ESTIMATETABLESIZE procedure in Listing 10.1 simplifies what would otherwise be the laborious process of estimating space requirements for a table and its indexes. Comments in the code explain the procedure's functionality.

Listing 10.1: ESTIMATETABLESIZE Procedure

```
CREATE PROCEDURE estimatetablesize (tableowner IN VARCHAR2,
  tablename IN VARCHAR2, rowestimate IN INTEGER) AS
-- This procedure estimates the size of a table and its indexes.
-- This procedure requires that you first create a prototype
-- table and any indexes, insert representative rows, and then
-- use the ANALYZE command to gather statistics about the table
-- and indexes.

-- variables to hold various numbers necessary for calculations
blocksize INTEGER;
reservedblockspace INTEGER;
averagerowlength INTEGER;
numberofrows INTEGER;
tablesizeestimate NUMBER;
indexsizeestimate NUMBER;

-- cursor to retrieve statistics for the table's indexes
CURSOR indexdata (own IN VARCHAR2, tab IN VARCHAR2) IS
  SELECT index_name, leaf_blocks
  FROM sys.dba_indexes
  WHERE table_owner = own AND table_name = tab;

BEGIN
-- query to capture statistics about the table
SELECT avg_space, avg_row_len, num_rows
  INTO reservedblockspace, averagerowlength, numberofrows
  FROM sys.dba_tables
  WHERE owner=UPPER(tableowner) AND table_name=UPPER(tablename);

-- query to get the database's block size
SELECT value INTO blocksize
  FROM v$parameter
  WHERE name='db_block_size';

-- calculation for table size estimate
tablesizeestimate := CEIL(rowestimate/FLOOR((blocksize-reservedblockspace)/
  averagerowlength)) ;

-- print report header
DBMS_OUTPUT.PUT_LINE('');
```

```
DBMS_OUTPUT.PUT_LINE('Size Estimates for Table:'||UPPER(tableowner)||'.'
  ||UPPER(tablename));
DBMS_OUTPUT.PUT_LINE('------------------------------------------');
DBMS_OUTPUT.PUT_LINE('');

-- print table size estimate in bytes
DBMS_OUTPUT.PUT_LINE('Size in KBytes:  '
  ||ROUND((tablesizeestimate*blocksize)/1000,0)||'K');
DBMS_OUTPUT.PUT_LINE('');

 -- header for index size estimates, if any
DBMS_OUTPUT.PUT_LINE('  Associated Index Size Estimates');
DBMS_OUTPUT.PUT_LINE('');
-- print index size estimates, if any
FOR tableindexes IN indexdata(UPPER(tableowner), UPPER(tablename)) LOOP
  DBMS_OUTPUT.PUT_LINE('  Index Name:        '||tableindexes.index_name);

-- calculation for index size estimate
  indexsizeestimate := tableindexes.leaf_blocks*(rowestimate/numberofrows);
  DBMS_OUTPUT.PUT_LINE('  Size in KBytes:  '
    ||ROUND((indexsizeestimate*blocksize)/1000,0)||'K');
  DBMS_OUTPUT.PUT_LINE('');
END LOOP;
END estimatetablesize;
```

Create the ESTIMATETABLESIZE procedure in your database and use it to estimate table and index space requirements for applications. Before executing the ESTIMATETABLESIZE procedure using SQL*DBA or SQL*Plus, be sure to set server output on with a buffer of at least 10,000 bytes. When you execute the ESTIMATETABLESIZE procedure, you will see a report something like this:

```
EXECUTE estimatetablesize('ACCOUNTING','SAVINGS',10000)
Size Estimates for Table: ACCOUNTING.SAVINGS
------------------------------------------
Size in KBytes:  172K

Associated Index Size Estimates

  Index Name:        ACCTNUM
  Size in KBytes:  23K

  Index Name:        CUSTOMERNUM
  Size in KBytes:  20K
```

Use the report's size estimates to preallocate all of a table's space in a single extent, such as the following:

```
CREATE TABLE accounts.savings
(ACCTNUM INTEGER
  PRIMARY KEY USING INDEX STORAGE (INITIAL 30K),
 ... other column specifications ... )
STORAGE (INITIAL 180K)
 .
 .
 .
```

NOTE The ESTIMATETABLESIZE procedure generates reasonably accurate size estimates for "average" tables (and their associated indexes). With tables that are miniscule or that have particularly long rows (such that row chaining is unavoidable), the ESTIMATETABLESIZE procedure's results might not be particularly accurate.

Estimating Space for Procedures, Functions, and Packages

Unfortunately, the CREATE commands for procedures, functions, and packages do not allow you to specify a tablespace location; Oracle7 stores all procedures, functions, and packages in the SYSTEM tablespace. Since stored PL/SQL programs can consume significant amounts of space, it is important to plan adequate space in the SYSTEM tablespace for applications that create many procedures, functions, and packages.

To investigate the amount of space PL/SQL programs such as procedures, functions, and packages consume in the SYSTEM tablespace, use the REPORTPROCEDURESIZE stored procedure shown in Listing 10.2 to return the information you need.

Listing 10.2: REPORTPROCEDURESIZE Procedure

```
CREATE PROCEDURE reportproceduresize (objowner IN VARCHAR2) AS
-- This procedure prints a size report of all procedures, functions, package
-- specifications, and package bodies in the specified schema.
```

```
-- cursor to select storage space required by different parts of a procedure
CURSOR objectsize (own IN VARCHAR2) IS
  SELECT owner, name, type, source_size,
    (source_size+parsed_size+code_size+error_size) total_size,
    ROUND((source_size+parsed_size+code_size+error_size) / source_size,1)
    storage_factor
    FROM sys.dba_object_size
    WHERE owner = own
    AND type IN ('PROCEDURE','FUNCTION','PACKAGE','PACKAGE BODY');

BEGIN
-- print report header
DBMS_OUTPUT.PUT_LINE('');
DBMS_OUTPUT.PUT_LINE('Object Size Report '||SYSDATE);
DBMS_OUTPUT.PUT_LINE('---------------------------------------------');
DBMS_OUTPUT.PUT_LINE('');
-- print individual object size reports
FOR dbobjectsize IN objectsize (UPPER(objowner)) LOOP
  DBMS_OUTPUT.PUT_LINE('Object Name:              '||dbobjectsize.name);
  DBMS_OUTPUT.PUT_LINE('Object Type:              '||dbobjectsize.type);
  DBMS_OUTPUT.PUT_LINE('Object Source Size:       '||dbobjectsize.source_size);
  DBMS_OUTPUT.PUT_LINE('Object Total Size:        '||dbobjectsize.total_size);
  DBMS_OUTPUT.PUT_LINE('Source-to-Total Storage Factor:  '
    ||dbobjectsize.storage_factor);
  DBMS_OUTPUT.PUT_LINE('');
END LOOP;
END reportproceduresize;
```

As with the other report-generating procedures in this book, make sure server output is on in SQL*DBA or SQL*Plus with a buffer size of at least 10,000 bytes. Connect to the development test database and execute the REPORTPROCEDURESIZE procedure by specifying the application's schema name. The procedure prints a simple report of all the schema's procedures, functions, packages, and corresponding size information, such as the following:

```
EXECUTE reportproceduresize('SYS')
Object Size Report 21-JUL-96
---------------------------------------------
Object Name:              STANDARD
Object Type:              PACKAGE
Object Source Size:       31225
Object Total Size:        153076
Source-to-Total Storage Factor:  4.9
```

```
Object Name:                     STANDARD
Object Type:                     PACKAGE BODY
Object Source Size:              20986
Object Total Size:               140756
Source-to-Total Storage Factor:  6.7

Object Name:                     DBMS_STANDARD
Object Type:                     PACKAGE
Object Source Size:              1368
Object Total Size:               6027
Source-to-Total Storage Factor:  4.4
.
.
.
```

Perhaps the most interesting field in the report is the Source-to-Total Storage Factor field. As you use this reporting procedure, you may notice trends in the Source-to-Total Storage Factor field, revealing how much total space is required to corresponding bytes of source code. If you discover a trend like this, it can be useful in predicting the amount of disk space required to hold all of an application's PL/SQL programs.

Estimating Space for Database Triggers

As with procedures, functions, and packages, Oracle7 stores all database triggers within the data dictionary and the data files of the SYSTEM tablespace. Therefore, estimating the space requirements for an application's database triggers is also an important step in ensuring that the database's SYSTEM tablespace has adequate space.

Estimating the space for database triggers is even easier than for stored procedures, functions, and packages. That's because Oracle7 does not store database triggers in a compiled form inside the database. Instead, Oracle7 stores only the source code for a database trigger and compiles it the first time a statement fires the trigger. To estimate the space required for an application's database triggers, check the byte count of the script that creates all of an application's triggers.

Monitoring Table and Index Storage Capacities

After you create an application's objects and people work with the application for a while, the tables and indexes of the application normally begin to enter application data that consumes the space preallocated for the objects. As described earlier, if a table or index requires more space than it already has been preallocated, Oracle7 automatically extends the object's storage capacity by allocating one or more new extents for the underlying segment. But as you know, object space extension can continue only up to a limit because the MAXEXTENTS storage parameter controls how many extents an object can ultimately have. When Oracle7 tries to allocate another extent for an object that has reached MAXEXTENTS, Oracle7 returns an error.

The preset limit that MAXEXTENTS imposes often causes the error condition described above. In fact, the "max # extents..." type errors are among the most common problems an administrator must address when managing space in an Oracle7 database. These error conditions are particularly frustrating for application users because they attempt to insert or update application data, but Oracle7 simply refuses to cooperate.

Given that these error conditions can dramatically affect the productivity of an entire team of application users, it is important that you, as an administrator, frequently monitor the current number of extents that each application's objects contain. Specifically, you need to look for any objects with an extent count that is dangerously approaching the limit set by the MAXEXTENTS storage parameter. You can look for these conditions using a very simple query on the DBA_SEGMENTS data dictionary view:

```
SELECT owner, segment_name, segment_type, extents, max_extents
  FROM sys.dba_segments
  WHERE max_extents-extents <= 2
```

This query returns the names of those objects (actually, segments) that can extend only 0, 1, or 2 more times. If you want to be more cautious, simply change the query to ask for those segments that can extend 3 or fewer more times, and so on.

When you find that an object is coming close to its extent limit, you can avoid its reaching the limit using several different approaches:

- Increase the value of the object's MAXEXTENTS storage parameter to allow the object to extend more times.

- Increase the value for the object's NEXT storage parameter so that when the object does extend, its subsequent extents are larger than they were before. This may avoid the object's having to extend again in the future.

- Archive and/or delete data from the object to free space in the current extents of the object.

Checking Row Datatypes for an Application's Tables

When a developer delivers an application's DDL script, don't assume that each table's definition is absolutely correct. Often, the developer hasn't used the best datatypes possible when defining an application's tables but has instead simply used datatypes that work. Specifically, a developer might have an opportunity to choose between two different datatypes that will both work for a particular column but for some reason chooses the datatype that stores the column's data using more database space than the other datatype would have required. Such errors in datatype choice can have significant implications when it comes to the amount of database space necessary to support the application as a whole, especially if the application has very large tables.

The most common datatype choice error arises with the character datatypes, specifically when a developer uses the CHAR datatype when the VARCHAR2 datatype would be more appropriate. Recall that Oracle7 stores data in a VARCHAR2 column very efficiently; it stores only the characters given for the column and nothing more. This contrasts with a CHAR column, where Oracle7 pads all values shorter than the maximum with blanks, and storing blanks requires database space. Consequently, improper use of the CHAR datatype can result in significant amounts of wasted database space. For example, can you figure out how much space would be wasted in a million-row table that has a CHAR(255) column with an average column value length of 5? The answer is 200 million bytes, or 200 megabytes!

Incorrect datatype choices are not always the result of developers being unfamiliar with the space requirements for the different Oracle7 datatypes. For example, older versions of CASE tools that generate application DDL scripts might not support newer Oracle7 datatypes, such as the VARCHAR2 datatype. As a result, the tool uses the older CHAR datatype for tables with character columns, and the developer might miss correcting for this situation before turning in the application's DDL script for installation. In conclusion, know your Oracle7 datatypes and pay close attention to DDL scripts for incorrect datatype usage.

Naming Integrity Constraints to Identify Them Easily

When a developer hands off a new application's DDL script to you for installation, look specifically at the declaration of the integrity constraints in the application schema. In most cases you'll want to take advantage of Oracle7's ability to name integrity constraints so you can easily identify the different constraints in the data dictionary after you create the application's tables.

For example, an application's script might have the following excerpt, which creates a new table:

```
CREATE TABLE item
( id NUMBER(5,0),
  orderid NUMBER(5,0),
  stockid NUMBER(5,0) NOT NULL,
  quantity NUMBER(5,0) NOT NULL,
  total NUMBER(10,2),
  PRIMARY KEY (id, orderid),
  FOREIGN KEY (orderid) REFERENCES orders ON DELETE CASCADE,
  FOREIGN KEY (stockid) REFERENCES stock )
```

Notice that in this CREATE TABLE statement, none of the integrity constraints have names. To name the constraints, simply include the CONSTRAINT clause in each integrity constraint's declaration in the CREATE TABLE statement:

```
CREATE TABLE item
( id NUMBER(5,0),
  orderid NUMBER(5,0),
  stockid NUMBER(5,0) CONSTRAINT itemstockid_nn NOT NULL,
  quantity NUMBER(5,0) CONSTRAINT itemquantity_nn NOT NULL,
  total NUMBER(10,2),
  CONSTRAINT item_pk PRIMARY KEY (id, orderid),
  CONSTRAINT itemorderid_fk FOREIGN KEY (orderid)
    REFERENCES orders ON DELETE CASCADE,
  CONSTRAINT itemstockid_fk FOREIGN KEY (stockid) REFERENCES stock )
```

313

When naming constraints, be sure to set up and follow naming conventions that give all constraints logical and easily identifiable names. If the developer has already named the application's integrity constraints, simply make sure that the constraint names comply with your database system's integrity constraint naming guidelines.

Checking Application Security Settings

When developing an application, the application developer usually takes the first crack at designing the security settings for the application. The application developer must code certain statements within an application (for example, SET ROLE) so the application can take advantage of Oracle7 roles for dynamic privilege management. However, the database security administrator is ultimately responsible for reviewing an application's final DDL script to check that the proposed security settings are satisfactory.

Checking an application's security settings takes several steps. First, look at the proposed roles for the application and ask yourself these questions:

- Does the application's role grant more privileges than are necessary to run the application? For example, if application users only need to insert and retrieve rows from a specific table, the application's role should have only the INSERT and SELECT object privileges for the table, and not have the UPDATE and DELETE privileges.

- Are any of the application role's privileges too powerful? For example, an application's role should never have the SELECT ANY TABLE system privilege but rather the SELECT privilege for the specific tables used by the application.

- Could the application make use of more than one role? For example, some application users should have read-only access to the application's tables to generate reports, while other users should have full access to the application's tables for inserts, updates, and deletes. Such situations justify two different roles for the application.

- Is the application's role protected by authentication? If not, it should be, to prevent unauthorized users from running the application. If so, is the role's authentication method correct for your type of system? As described in Chapter 9, roles should always use password authentication in client/server systems.

Once you've worked out the details of an application's security settings, the next step is fitting the application's security into the grand scheme of things. For example, assume you are installing a new accounting application on a database system for a large company with many users in different divisions. You are probably already using roles to make privilege management easier for the different types of company users—workers in the sales department all have the SALESDEPT role, and workers in the accounting department all have the ACCOUNTINGDEPT role, and so on. Therefore, when you install the new accounting application, you should grant the new application's role(s) to the ACCOUNTINGDEPT role. Figure 10.6 illustrates a hierarchical group of roles that can appear in a corporate database system.

This simple example of role hierarchy can stimulate your creativity for designing a security policy for the big picture—the entire database system, which has many different types of users and several applications.

FIGURE 10.6:
It's likely that you'll want to create a hierarchy of roles in a corporate database's security system.

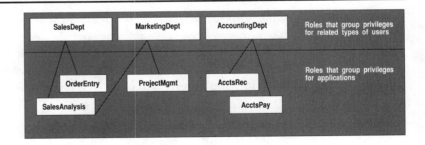

Managing Rollback Segments on Behalf of Applications

As mentioned earlier, as a user's transaction changes data in the database, Oracle7 keeps "undo" information in a rollback segment in case the user decides to roll back rather than commit the transaction. Oracle7 also uses rollback segment data to create read-consistent snapshots of data for queries throughout the system. When you as a database administrator install a new application, it is important to design and create the rollback segments necessary to support the transactions users will generate using the application. The following sections explain how to plan, create, and manage rollback segments on behalf of applications.

Planning Rollback Segments for Applications

Planning rollback segments for an application and, in a larger sense, a database is a tricky job. There are many factors to consider, including

- OLTP applications that issue small update transactions will experience better performance if they use smaller rollback segments. That's because when a rollback segment is small, Oracle7 can probably keep all of the segment in shared memory, thereby reducing or eliminating disk I/O on behalf of transactions that generate rollback information.

- Decision support and reporting applications that issue large or complicated queries can sometimes run across an infamous ORACLE error message: "Snapshot too old." When a query receives this error message, it means that when Oracle7 tried to create a read-consistent snapshot for the query, certain blocks necessary to generate the snapshot had since been overwritten by another transaction and were no longer available. Larger rollback segments tend to reduce the likelihood of such errors because it takes longer for Oracle7 to wrap around and overwrite older rollback segment information.

- Large data loads, all part of a single transaction, can generate large amounts of transaction rollback information. If you do not want to break up a large load into smaller transactions, the database needs a large rollback segment to handle the load.

- Applications can design transactions to use specific rollback segments based on the types of transactions and current application requirements.

With all of these considerations and features to think about, planning rollback segments for an Oracle7 database might seem intimidating. However, Oracle7 provides features that allow you to implement a good rollback segment strategy. The following sections will help you get started with designing rollback segments for applications.

The SYSTEM Rollback Segment

Every Oracle7 database has a rollback segment named SYSTEM. During database creation, the initial database rollback segment is created in the SYSTEM tablespace.

The SYSTEM rollback segment is adequate for initial administrative operations after database creation. However, very soon after database creation, you should begin planning the other rollback segments for the database. For example, to create and use another tablespace (besides the SYSTEM tablespace) in a database, you must create a second rollback segment in the SYSTEM tablespace.

Creating New Rollback Segments

Once you have planned the rollback segments for an application or a database, you can create them using the Create Rollback Segment dialog of SQL*DBA. To access this dialog, from the SQL*DBA menu select Storage ➤ Rollback Segment ➤ Create. Figure 10.7 shows the Create Rollback Segment dialog of SQL*DBA.

FIGURE 10.7:

Use the Create Rollback Segment dialog of SQL*DBA to create a new rollback segment and set its storage parameters

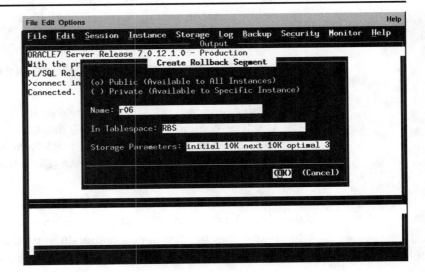

NOTE To use the Create Rollback Segment dialog of SQL*DBA, you need the CREATE ROLLBACK SEGMENT system privilege.

To use this dialog to create a new rollback segment, first specify whether the rollback segment should be public or private. Private rollback segments are much harder to manage than public rollback segments. And unless you have the Oracle7 Parallel Server option, there is no advantage to using private rollback segments. For these reasons, make it easy on yourself and choose the default radio button, Public.

Next, enter a name for the new rollback segment in the Name entry field. Then select a tablespace to store the new rollback segment, as described in the next section. If you want to see a list of available tablespaces, use the [List] key to display a list box of tablespaces. Finally, you can specify the new rollback segment's extent storage parameters in the Storage Parameters entry field. (See the section "Setting Rollback Segment Extent Storage Parameters" a little later in this chapter.) SQL*DBA provides a field list builder if you want help filling in the Storage Parameters field. Once you are satisfied with the settings for the new rollback segment, select the OK button, and Oracle7 creates the new segment.

After creating a new rollback segment, Oracle7 leaves the segment offline. To make the rollback segment available to transactions, you have to bring the rollback segment online. (See the section "Controlling Rollback Segment Availability" later in this chapter.)

Which Tablespace Should Store New Rollback Segments?

As with tables and indexes, you can store rollback segments in any tablespace of a database. It is common for an Oracle7 database to have a "rollback segment tablespace" used exclusively to store rollback segments. For example, the default initial database installed on Oracle7 for UNIX platforms has a tablespace named RBS that stores several rollback segments.

Keeping rollback segments separated in their own tablespace from other types of data makes database administration easier. For example, when you want to take a tablespace offline or drop it, you cannot do so until all of the rollback segments in the tablespace are offline. Once the tablespace is unavailable, the rollback segments within are also unavailable, which is a waste of allocated disk space. You can avoid these problems by creating and using a tablespace specifically for rollback segments.

Setting Rollback Segment Extent Storage Parameters

Just as with tables and indexes, when you create a rollback segment you can set extent storage parameters to control how the extent uses space. However, rollback segments have an additional extent storage parameter, its *optimal size*, that other types of segments do not have. To understand how to set rollback segment storage parameters, it is helpful to know more about how Oracle7 writes data to rollback segments. Figure 10.8 shows how Oracle7 writes undo information to a rollback segment.

FIGURE 10.8:
How Oracle7 circularly writes transaction rollback information to the extents of a rollback segment and allocates additional extents if necessary

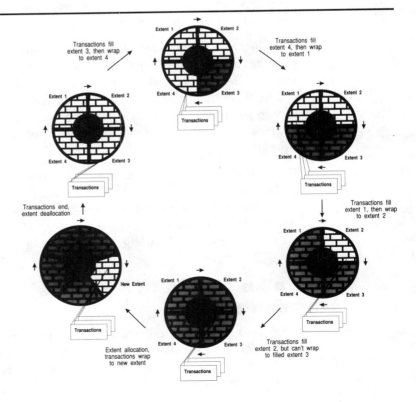

You can think of a rollback segment as a circle because of the method Oracle7 uses to write data to the extents of a rollback segment: Oracle7 assigns transactions on a round-robin basis to available rollback segments. As a new transaction begins, Oracle7 assigns the transaction to an available rollback segment. When a transaction generates rollback data, Oracle7 writes the data to an extent. As the transaction and others assigned to the same rollback segment fill the current extent, they can continue writing by "wrapping" to the next extent in the rollback segment. When transactions happen to fill the last extent of a rollback segment, they can continue writing undo information by wrapping to the first extent in the segment.

Transactions often generate more rollback data than the current extents of a rollback segment can hold. For example, what happens when transactions wrap around to the first rollback segment extent and continue writing until they eventually reach the extent in which they started writing? To allow transactions to be as long as they want and prevent transactions from writing over their own rollback data, Oracle7 extends rollback segments as needed. Therefore, rollback segments can grow and allocate more space to accommodate large transactions.

What happens when a large transaction is over and now an extended rollback segment has all that space? Fortunately, a rollback segment can also shrink in accordance with its "optimal" size. When you create or alter a rollback segment, you can specify its optimal size, in bytes. This determines the number of extents Oracle7 tries to keep for the rollback segment on a regular basis. When Oracle7 needs to wrap extents in an extended rollback segment, it checks to see if it can deallocate any extents to get closer to its optimal size.

The dynamic growth and shrinking capabilities of Oracle7 rollback segments can lead to on-the-fly disk allocations and deallocations that degrade application and system performance. You can avoid this problem by setting rollback segment extent storage parameters carefully. (See the section "Monitoring and Altering Extent Storage Parameters for Rollback Segments" later in this chapter.)

Controlling Rollback Segment Availability

Much like tablespaces, rollback segments can be either online or offline. *Online rollback segments* are available to transactions in the system, while *offline rollback segments* are not. In most cases, rollback segments should be online so transactions can use them. However, when you want to take offline a tablespace that contains an online rollback segment or when you want to drop a rollback segment, you have to take the rollback segment offline first.

To bring an offline rollback segment online, you can use the Set Rollback Segment Online dialog box of SQL*DBA. To access this dialog, from the SQL*DBA menu select Storage ➤ Rollback Segment ➤ Set Online. Figure 10.9 shows the Set Rollback Segment Online dialog of SQL*DBA.

NOTE To use the Set Rollback Segment Online dialog of SQL*DBA, you need the ALTER ROLLBACK SEGMENT system privilege.

To use this dialog to bring an offline rollback segment back online, simply select the rollback segment from the list box and then select the OK button.

To take an online rollback segment offline, you can use the Set Rollback Segment Offline dialog box of SQL*DBA. To access this dialog, from the SQL*DBA menu select Storage ➤ Rollback Segment ➤ Set Offline. Figure 10.10 shows the Set Rollback Segment Offline dialog of SQL*DBA.

FIGURE 10.9:
You can use the Set Rollback Segment Online dialog of SQL*DBA to bring a new rollback segment online.

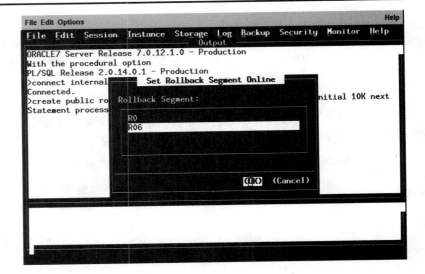

FIGURE 10.10:

You can make a rollback segment unavailable by taking it offline with the Set Rollback Segment Offline dialog of SQL*DBA.

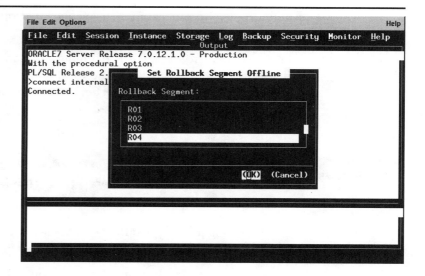

NOTE

To use the Set Rollback Segment Offline dialog of SQL*DBA, you need the ALTER ROLLBACK SEGMENT system privilege.

To use this dialog to take an online rollback segment offline, simply select the rollback segment from the list box and then select the OK button. Oracle7 will take the rollback segment offline after all transactions currently using the rollback segment commit or roll back.

Monitoring and Altering Extent Storage Parameters for Rollback Segments

Once you have created a rollback segment for an application and a database, you should investigate how the settings for the rollback segment's extent storage parameters are working. To monitor rollback segments, you can use the Rollback Segment monitor of SQL*DBA. To access this monitor, from the SQL*DBA menu select Monitor ➤ Rollback. Figure 10.11 shows the Rollback Segment monitor of SQL*DBA.

FIGURE 10.11:

Use the Rollback Segment monitor of SQL*DBA to check whether a rollback segment's optimal size is correct.

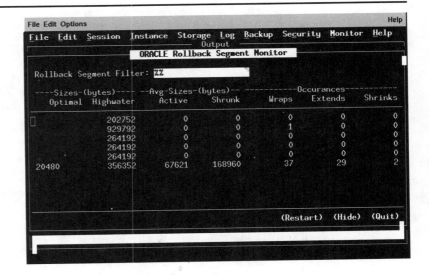

It is important to look at the Shrinks column in the Rollback Segment monitor. This column shows how many times Oracle7 has dynamically shrunk a rollback segment since the current instance started. If the number is high for a rollback segment, Oracle7 is wasting resources by dynamically expanding and shrinking the rollback segment. To remedy the situation, increase the setting for the rollback segment's OPTIMAL extent storage parameter. Then monitor the rollback segment again to see if the number of shrinks holds steady.

NOTE At the expense of consuming additional space for a larger rollback segment, raising a rollback segment's OPTIMAL storage parameter setting serves to reduce the likelihood of users experiencing "Snapshot too old" errors when transactions need to use older transaction undo information in the rollback segment. That's because the rollback segment is larger, so it will take longer for new transactions to overwrite older rollback segment information.

To alter a rollback segment's storage parameter, you can use the Alter Rollback Segment Storage dialog of SQL*DBA. To access this dialog, from the SQL*DBA menu select Storage ➤ Rollback Segment ➤ Alter Storage. Figure 10.12 shows the Alter Rollback Segment Storage dialog of SQL*DBA.

To use this dialog to alter a rollback segment's storage parameters, select the rollback segment from the list box, and then set any of the storage parameters you want to alter.

Dropping Rollback Segments

If you need to drop a rollback segment, you can use the Drop Rollback Segment dialog of SQL*DBA. To access this dialog, from the SQL*DBA menu select Storage ➤ Rollback Segment ➤ Drop. Figure 10.13 shows the Drop Rollback Segment dialog of SQL*DBA.

NOTE To use the Drop Rollback Segment dialog of SQL*DBA, you need the DROP ROLLBACK SEGMENT system privilege.

FIGURE 10.12:
You can alter a rollback segment's storage parameters with the Alter Rollback Segment Storage dialog of SQL*DBA.

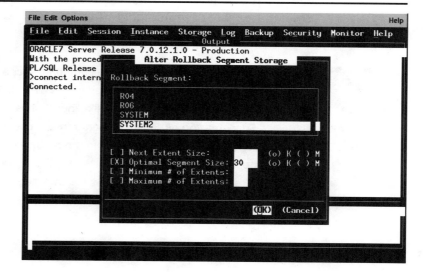

FIGURE 10.13:

The Drop Rollback Segment dialog of SQL*DBA permits you to drop unneeded rollback segments after you take them offline.

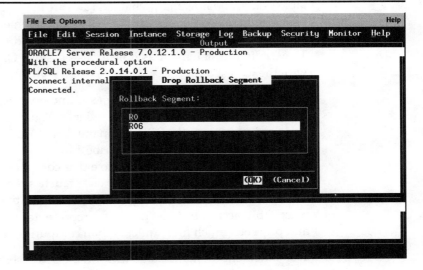

To use this dialog to drop an offline rollback segment, select the segment from the list box and then select OK. Oracle7 will drop the rollback segment as soon as all transactions currently using the rollback segment either commit or roll back.

Generating Optimizer Statistics

When you are planning a long road trip to get to a vacation spot, you usually sit down with some road maps to determine the fastest possible route to the trip's destination. Similarly, when you issue a SQL statement to Oracle7, you want Oracle7 to perform the statement and return the results as quickly as possible so you can be more productive in your work. To make sure SQL statements execute as quickly as possible, all applications rely heavily on the *cost-based optimizer* of Oracle7. For each statement, the optimizer's job is to figure out a good *execution plan*—the best way to execute each SQL statement.

To determine good query execution plans, the Oracle7 optimizer uses statistics about a database's data. For example, Oracle7 can generate statistics that indicate how many rows are in a table, how many data blocks are being used to store the table's data, and how many chained rows are in the table. Oracle7 keeps similar statistics for indexes. When a user issues a SQL statement, Oracle7 reads the pertinent statistics in the data dictionary to determine the *costs* of different execution plans. To execute the statement as quickly as possible, Oracle7 uses the execution plan with the lowest cost.

To avoid affecting performance, Oracle7 updates the statistics for objects only when you as the database administrator tell it to. You can gather statistics for a table, index, or cluster using the SQL command ANALYZE. The ANALYZE command has several options that let you describe how to gather statistics. For example, the ANALYZE command allows you to either compute or estimate statistics for an object. *Computing statistics* gathers exact statistics for the object but can take a long time to complete when the object is large. Alternatively, *estimating statistics* gathers reasonably accurate statistics from a representative sampling of the object's data and proceeds much more quickly than computing statistics.

This statement estimates statistics for the CUSTOMER table using a random 15 percent of the table's data:

```
ANALYZE TABLE customer ESTIMATE STATISTICS SAMPLE 15 PERCENT
```

This statement computes statistics for the CUSTOMER table:

```
ANALYZE TABLE customer COMPUTE STATISTICS
```

To make statistic-gathering easier, Oracle7 also includes a special stored procedure, DBMS_UTILITY.ANALYZE_SCHEMA, that can analyze all of the objects in a schema with a single procedure call. For example, this procedure call (issued in SQL*DBA) gathers statistics for all of the data dictionary tables in an Oracle7 database:

```
EXECUTE dbms_utility.analyze_schema('SYS');
```

This example is important because the information in a database's data dictionary is constantly changing. To make sure Oracle7 performs all internal SQL processing in the most efficient manner, it is important to frequently update the statistics for the SYS schema. Similarly, you should regularly update the statistics for an application schema to keep the corresponding data statistics current.

This chapter has explained many of the key administration tasks necessary on behalf of client database applications, including

- Estimating application object sizes
- Setting application object storage parameters appropriately
- Reviewing a new application's security settings and incorporating them into a database system that supports many applications
- Gathering optimizer statistics for an application's data so the optimizer works the best it can for the application's transactions

At this point, applications are presumably working with your Oracle7 server. Now let's learn how to safeguard important application data from catastrophes with the protective features of Oracle7. The next chapter explains how to back up and recover an Oracle7 database system.

CHAPTER

ELEVEN

Protecting Work and Data

- Configuring a database's transaction log groups and members

- Enabling media recovery and automatic log archiving

- Backing up Oracle7 databases

- Recovering damaged databases offline and online

- Configuring Oracle7 for parallel recovery

Computer systems are not reliable a hundred percent of the time; sometimes things go wrong. After you have spent lots of time creating and configuring a database for client applications, it would be a tragedy to lose all that work if someone tripped over a power cord or, even worse, a disk crashed on the server. Problems like these are the driving force behind the comprehensive and sophisticated data-protection mechanisms built into the Oracle7 database server. This chapter explores Oracle7's protective features, including

- The transaction log—how to configure and manage it to safeguard the work of ongoing transaction processing
- Database backups—the different kinds, how to make them, how to automate the backup process, and how to test a backup strategy to protect data from inevitable disk failures
- Database recovery—the different types of recovery and how to complete database recovery to get a system up and running after a failure

Transaction Logging

A database's transaction log (also called the redo log) is a vital component in Oracle7's protective mechanisms. Its job is to immediately record the changes made by ongoing application transactions in a database so that, in the event of an unforeseen failure, all committed work is protected and fully recoverable. Database recovery operations rely on the data in the transaction log to rebuild, or redo, the committed changes from lost transactions.

Because of its importance in the grand scheme of database protection, you as the database administrator must carefully consider the design of the transaction log to make sure its structure adequately and efficiently safeguards ongoing transaction processing. The following sections explain how to manage the structure of the transaction log and configure the database server to automatically back up the transaction log's data.

Adding Log Groups to a Database's Transaction Log

Each Oracle7 database's transaction log requires at least two fixed-size log groups. While writing to one log group, the server archives the transaction entries in the other group. (See the section "Configuring Transaction Log Archiving" later in this chapter.) Once the current log group fills with new data, a *log switch* occurs and the server continues writing new transaction entries to the other group. The filled group can then be *archived* (backed up), after which it is again available when the next log switch is necessary. The cyclical process of writing to and archiving transaction log groups allows Oracle7 to efficiently use a small amount of static disk space to log the changes made by ongoing transactions.

How many log groups should a database have? The answer is dependent on the demands of a database system. In general, the fewer the number of log groups in the transaction log, the easier it is to manage. However, too few log groups in a transaction log can hamper database performance if log switches have to wait each time for Oracle7 to finish archiving a log group.

Determining the number of log groups for a database is a trial-and-error process. After configuring a transaction log, monitor it closely to see how it is doing. (See the section "Monitoring the Transaction Log" later in this chapter.) If Oracle7 has to wait for a transaction log group to be archived before it can continue transaction logging, add one or more log groups to the database's transaction log; this will help ensure that there are more free log groups in the database's transaction log. Likewise, if Oracle7 archives filled log groups well before they are needed for reuse, the current log configuration might be wasting space. It might be appropriate to drop one or more log groups to obtain a more efficient transaction log configuration.

When you create a new database, you configure the initial transaction log groups in a database. However, you can always add new groups to a database's transaction log using the Add Online Redo Log Group dialog of SQL*DBA. To access this dialog from the SQL*DBA menu, select Log ➤ Add Group. Figure 11.1 shows the Add Online Redo Log Group dialog of SQL*DBA.

FIGURE 11.1:

Use the Add Online Redo Log Group dialog of SQL*DBA to add one or more log groups to a database's transaction log.

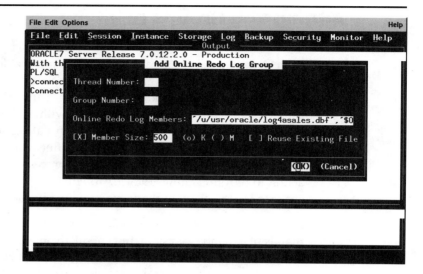

> **NOTE**
>
> To use the Add Online Redo Log Group dialog of SQL*DBA, you must have the ALTER DATABASE system privilege.

This dialog has four simple entry fields that make configuring a new log group easy. In most cases it is best to simply skip entering values in the first two entry fields.

- The Thread Number entry field has relevance only to systems using the Oracle7 Parallel Server option. When a database has multiple instances, each instance has its own set of log groups, or *thread*, within the database's transaction log. The Thread Number entry field simply corresponds to the thread in the log to which the new log group should belong. If you are not using the Oracle7 Parallel Server option, skip entering a number in the field.

- The Group Number entry field permits you to determine the number of the new log group in the database's transaction log. In most cases it is best to not specify a number in this entry field and make Oracle7 pick the next available group number for you.

- In the Online Redo Log Members entry field you indicate the names of all the members in the new log group. As recommended throughout this book, each log group should have at least two members stored at physically different locations. If you need help building a list of file specifications, use the [List] key to display the Specify Online Redo Log Members field builder dialog.

- In the Member Size entry you specify the file size for the members in the new log group. In general, it is best to make the file sizes for all database log groups consistent; there is no advantage to having log groups of different sizes. If you do not want to specify a member size, do not check the box in front of the field. This way, Oracle7 uses the default file size for log members, which is machine dependent. The Reuse Existing File check box applies only when you want Oracle7 to clear the blocks of an existing file and use it for the new member or members in the log group.

The number of log groups you can create is limited by two different factors:

- The MAXLOGFILES parameter of the CREATE DATABASE command used to create a database limits the number of log groups that can be created for the database.
- The LOG_FILES initialization parameter limits the number of log groups that can be opened for the current instance. If LOG_FILES is less than MAXLOGFILES, the limit set by LOG_FILES is in effect; if LOG_FILES is greater than MAXLOGFILES, the limit set by MAXLOGFILES has precedence. It is atypical to set LOG_FILES below MAXLOGFILES.

NOTE Some UNIX file systems limit the possible sizes of raw devices, so you might be forced to make different log groups with different file sizes.

Planning Log Group Member File Placement

Disk drives, like all other types of machinery, are not immune to Murphy's Law, which states that whatever can go wrong will go wrong. They die from old age, they occasionally lose bits of magnetic media, disk arms and controllers fail, and formats go awry. To insulate the Oracle7 transaction log from such potential disk failures, it is important to consider the placement of different log members within the log groups in a database's transaction log.

Using Multiple Members to Mirror Files

Oracle7 permits multiple members in the transaction log's groups so you can mirror the files in the transaction log; this protects the log from isolated disk failures, or single points of failure. For example, assume that a log group has two members, one on disk A and another on disk B. When Oracle7 uses the log group, it writes to both members in parallel. If disk B crashes, Oracle7 can continue logging ongoing transactions without problems because the log member on disk A is still available. Figure 11.2 illustrates this example.

The example illustrates the cardinal rule for configuring the members in a database's log groups: Wisely use the disk drives of the database server so log groups are protected from single points of failure. The more disk drives available to the database server, the more levels of mirroring you can create in a database's transaction log. However, don't get carried away; two to three levels of file mirroring are adequate for most systems.

FIGURE 11.2:
A mirrored transaction log can protect an Oracle7 database system from single points of failure.

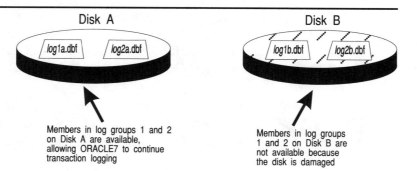

Performance Considerations

While protection of the transaction log is the primary consideration when configuring a database's transaction log groups and members, there are also performance considerations. If your database server has a handful of disk drives, there are file structure designs that can minimize disk I/O contention and eke out more performance for the database server:

- Place data files and log files on different disks whenever possible. This way, transaction logging, log archiving, and database reads and writes do not contend with each other for disk access time.

- If all log members throughout a database's transaction log are on different disks, transaction logging and log archiving never contend for the same files.

The degree to which you spread out different database files depends on the number of disks available to the database server. The more disks you are willing to buy, the greater the number of options available to your configuration and the greater the amount of database protection you can have.

WARNING   Never put a data file on the same disk that stores the archived log files or an unmirrored log group. If you do, you are vulnerable to a single point of failure and, thus, an unrecoverable situation.

Adding Log Members

When you add a new disk drive to a database server, you might want to use the new disk to add another protection layer for the transaction log by mirroring one or more log groups on the new disk with additional members. To add a new member to a database's transaction log group, you can use the Add Online Redo Log Member dialog of SQL*DBA. To access this dialog from the SQL*DBA menu, select Log ➤ Add Member. Figure 11.3 shows the Add Online Redo Log Member dialog of SQL*DBA.

NOTE   To use the Add Online Redo Log Member dialog of SQL*DBA, you must have the ALTER DATABASE system privilege.

FIGURE 11.3:

The Add Online Redo Log Member dialog of SQL*DBA allows you to add members to a log group and thus increase the degree of mirroring in the group.

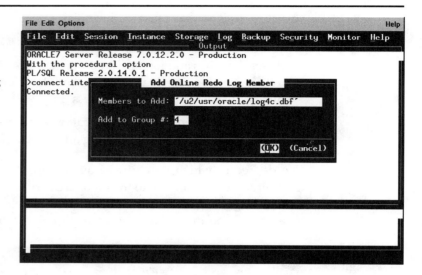

Adding a new member to a group is even easier than adding a new group. In the Add Online Redo Log Member dialog, there are just two entry fields. In the first entry field you specify the filenames for one or more new members to add. (Use the [List] key to display a helpful dialog to build a list of filenames.) In the Add to Group # entry field you specify the group to which you want to add the new log members. (To pick from a list of available log groups, use the [List] key.) If you do not know which group number to specify, see the DATABASEREPORT procedure (Listing 7.1 in Chapter 7) to help you out.

NOTE   The number of log members per group is limited by the setting for the MAXLOGFILES parameter of the CREATE DATABASE command used to create a database. If you try to add more members to a group than this limit allows, Oracle7 returns an error.

Dropping Log Members

Just as there are situations that justify adding new members to a log group, there are opposite situations that call for dropping one or more members from a group. For example, if a disk fails and it will not be replaced, you need to drop the log members on the disk to eliminate the constant error reporting that Oracle7 performs for the damaged file. To drop a log member from a group, you can use the Drop Online Redo Log Member dialog of SQL*DBA. To access this dialog from the SQL*DBA menu, select Log ➤ Drop Member. Figure 11.4 shows the Drop Online Redo Log Member dialog of SQL*DBA.

NOTE To use the Drop Online Redo Log Member dialog of SQL*DBA, you must have the ALTER DATABASE system privilege.

The dialog box displays all the log members in the transaction log, listed by their corresponding groups. Just select one or more members from the list box and then use the OK button to drop the members.

FIGURE 11.4:

Use the Drop Online Redo Log Member dialog to drop unwanted log members from a log group.

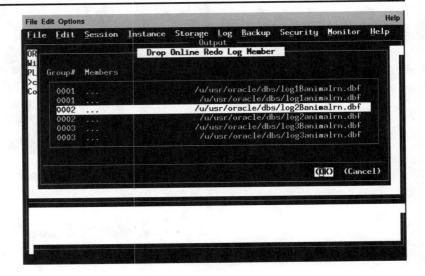

There are several considerations to keep in mind when using the Drop Online Redo Log Member dialog. First, Oracle7 does not allow you to drop the last member of a group; in effect, this would drop the group. Second, Oracle7 will not drop a log member if that member is in the currently active log group or a log group that has not yet been archived.

After you drop a log member from the database, the physical operating system file still exists on disk. To release the space the dropped log member occupies on disk, use your operating system to drop the corresponding file.

Dropping Log Groups

If you find that a database's transaction log has too many log groups and may be wasting space, you can drop one or more log groups to reduce the size of the transaction log. To drop a group from the transaction log, you can use the Drop Online Redo Log Group dialog of SQL*DBA. To access this dialog, from the SQL*DBA menu select Log ➤ Drop Group. Figure 11.5 shows the Drop Online Redo Log Group dialog of SQL*DBA.

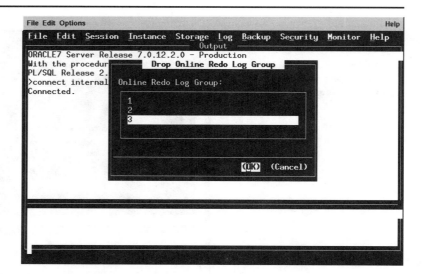

FIGURE 11.5:
Use the Drop Online Redo Log Group dialog to drop an entire group of transaction log members from a database's transaction log.

To use the Drop Online Redo Log Group dialog of SQL*DBA, you must have the ALTER DATABASE system privilege.

Pick the log group(s) to drop by its number, and then select the OK button to drop it. If you do not know the number of the log group you want to drop, use the DATABASEREPORT procedure (Listing 7.1 in Chapter 7) to help you out. Oracle7 will not allow you to drop a log group if it is the current log group, if the log group remains to be archived, or if dropping the log group will leave the transaction log with fewer than two groups.

As when dropping individual transaction log members, after you drop a log group from the database's transaction log, the physical operating system files still exist on disk. To release the space the dropped log members occupy on disk, use your operating system to drop the corresponding files.

Configuring Transaction Log Archiving

As described earlier in this chapter, Oracle7 cyclically writes to the groups in a database's transaction log, allowing it to continuously log transactions in a contained, fixed amount of disk space. The cyclical writing process to transaction log groups causes the information in each log group to be overwritten every time Oracle7 cycles through the log. Therefore, to preserve older transaction entries in a database's transaction log, Oracle7 automatically archives, or backs up, filled log groups after each log switch. Oracle7 notes whether a transaction log group has been archived before allowing itself to overwrite the log group's transaction entries. Archiving log groups as they become filled creates what is called an *archived* or *offline transaction redo log*. A database's archived log consists of a sequence of backup files that correspond to the transaction log groups as they filled during database processing. Figure 11.6 illustrates a database's archived transaction log.

The archived log is the enabling component for complete database recovery from a media failure. For example, when a disk fails and causes the loss of a data file, the

FIGURE 11.6:

The archived log of an Oracle7 database is a sequenced compilation of all the log groups as they filled throughout database processing.

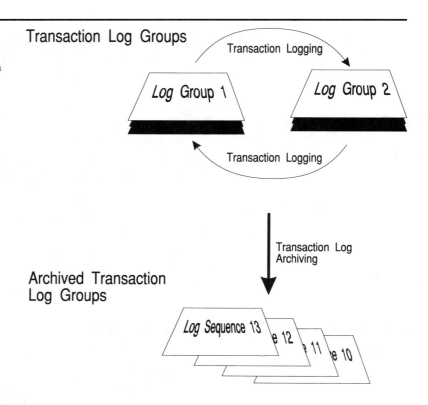

database administrator recovers the database by replacing the disk and then restoring the damaged data file from the most recent backup. However, at this point the restored version of the data file is out of date—it is missing all the changes made since the last backup of the data file. Therefore, the next step in database recovery is application of the transaction log to the restored data file to recover the lost transactions. In most cases, recovery requires transaction entries in both the archived transaction log and the current log groups in the transaction log. (See the section "Database Recovery" later in this chapter.)

The next few sections explain how to configure Oracle7 to archive transaction log groups as they fill.

Enabling and Disabling Media Recovery

When Oracle7 requires log groups to be archived before they can be reused, *media recovery* is enabled because Oracle7 can use backup data files, the archived transaction log, and the current transaction log groups to completely recover all committed transactions from a disk media failure. You also have the option of disabling media recovery. This means that Oracle7 does not archive the transaction log.

However, disabling media recovery is not a recommended mode of operation. No matter how good the configuration of a database's transaction log and backup strategy, the database is vulnerable to any type of disk failure. Therefore, after creating a database, make sure media recovery is enabled and always leave it this way. You can use the DATABASEREPORT procedure (Listing 7.1 in Chapter 7) to determine whether or not media recovery is enabled for a database.

NOTE   When media recovery is enabled for a database, the database is said to be running in ARCHIVELOG mode. When media recovery is disabled, the database is said to be running in NOARCHIVELOG mode. These clumsy terms come from the options of the ALTER DATABASE command that enable and disable media recovery for a database.

After you create a database, media recovery is disabled. For this reason, one of the first post-database creation steps is to enable media recovery. You can do so using the ARCHIVELOG option of the SQL command ALTER DATABASE, as shown here:

```
ALTER DATABASE ARCHIVELOG
```

Although you should almost never use it, the NOARCHIVELOG option of the ALTER DATABASE command disables media recovery:

```
ALTER DATABASE NOARCHIVELOG
```

> **NOTE**
> To enable or disable media recovery using the ALTER DATABASE command, you must have the ALTER DATABASE system privilege, and the database must be mounted but not open. Therefore, this is one particular case where you need to use a different startup procedure—starting up an instance and mounting the database but not opening it.

Before enabling media recovery, you can save yourself a step by configuring the instance for automatic archiving of transaction log groups as they fill. The next section explains how to accomplish this.

Configuring a Database Server for Automatic Log Archiving

After you enable media recovery for a database, Oracle7 does not overwrite a filled transaction log group unless the group has been successfully archived. Consequently, the database server can hit a brick wall if the next group slated for writing in the transaction log has not been archived. In this situation Oracle7 simply suspends all database operations until a log group is freed as a result of being archived.

To make sure a database never hits the brick wall, you can configure an Oracle7 database instance to automatically archive log groups as they fill. The initialization parameters to consider are listed here:

Parameter	Description
LOG_ARCHIVE_ START	Determines whether or not Oracle7 automatically archives transaction log groups as they fill. A setting of TRUE enables automatic archiving, while a setting of FALSE disables automatic archiving. In most cases, set LOG_ARCHIVE_ START to TRUE when media recovery is enabled. Otherwise, you must constantly monitor the transaction log and manually archive log files as they fill

Parameter	Description
LOG_ARCHIVE_ DEST	Determines the location in which Oracle7 creates the archived transaction log. In a few cases, Oracle7 running on some operating systems can archive log groups directly to tape, which means you can specify a tape drive for this parameter. However, most Oracle7 systems do not support direct tape archiving. Therefore, the setting for LOG_ARCHIVE_ DEST should be a directory location on disk. After Oracle7 archives log groups to disk, you can use operating system commands or a special backup utility to compress and move the archived transaction log to offline tape storage, thus freeing up disk space in the archive log location
LOG_ARCHIVE_ FORMAT	Determines the filename format of the files in the archived transaction log. In most cases, it is not necessary to specifically set this parameter; the default value clearly indicates the sequence numbers of the log groups in the filenames. If you want to set this parameter yourself, be sure to decide on a filename format and then stick with it for the life of the data-base. With this kind of foresight you can make a complicated administrative operation, database recovery, a little bit easier

The following example is an excerpt from an initialization parameter file for a database using Oracle7 on a UNIX platform. The example shows how to set two of the three parameters listed above (the LOG_ARCHIVE_FORMAT parameter uses the default value, as recommended):

```
LOG_ARCHIVE_START=TRUE
LOG_ARCHIVE_DEST=/usr/oracle/dbs/arch
```

If your version of Oracle7 does not support direct archiving of log groups to tape, at first you might consider this a problem, another thing to deal with when administering an Oracle7 database system. However, you can also look at this as a positive. That's because you can save offline tape storage space by using operating system commands or a backup utility to compress the archived log before copying it to tape. To make the tape storage of the archived log convenient, integrate the compression and backup commands into the automated backup process you use for the computer that runs Oracle7.

Monitoring the Transaction Log

After configuring a database's transaction log, be sure to monitor it while the database is running in normal operation to see how it is serving database processing. Assuming that the transaction log is mirrored, media recovery is enabled, and automatic archiving is enabled, it's important to monitor that the current structure of the transaction log is not adversely affecting the performance of the database server. For example, if transaction log groups are too small or there are not enough transaction log groups, Oracle7 might have to wait for a transaction log group to be archived before it could continue transaction logging. Consequently, database users would have to wait until Oracle7 caught up with the necessary log archiving.

The easiest way to get some valuable information about a database's transaction log is to query the Oracle7 data dictionary views that pertain to the transaction log. For example, the V$LOG data dictionary view shows information about the groups within the database's transaction log:

```
SELECT group#, sequence#, bytes, members, archived, status
  FROM v$log

GROUP#     SEQUENCE#  BYTES       MEMBERS     ARC STATUS
---------- ---------- ----------- ----------- --- --------
         1      10388     5120000           2 NO  INACTIVE
```

GROUP#	SEQUENCE#	BYTES	MEMBERS	ARC	STATUS
2	10389	5120000	2	NO	INACTIVE
3	10390	5120000	2	NO	CURRENT

Notice that the V$LOG view lists lots of information about the groups in the transaction log. For example, from the preceding query you can quickly see that two log groups, although filled and ready for archiving, remain to be archived. If ongoing transaction logging fills log group 3 before Oracle7 finishes archiving log group 1, users will have to wait until archiving of log group 1 is finished. This situation might warrant a change to the transaction log's structure, such as an additional log group.

The Oracle7 data dictionary also contains other views you can use to monitor the transaction log. For example, you can use the V$LOGFILE to report information about individual members of the database's transaction log.

Database Backup

The same types of disk failures that can damage a database's transaction log can also damage other types of database files, including the database's data files, control file, and initialization parameter files. Oracle7 does not contain file-mirroring (except for control files) and/or automated-backup features for any database files other than the files in the transaction log. Therefore, as a database administrator, it is crucial to develop a sound backup strategy to protect a database's files from disk failures.

Considering Oracle7's configuration options, there are many acceptable ways to back up a database. For example, if a database runs with media recovery enabled, you can back up data files when the database is open or when it is closed; you can back up all of the data files or just some of them; you can back up a database's control file when you back up data files; or you can do it whenever you please. As you can see, planning an Oracle7 database backup strategy can become confusing.

This chapter explains the two basic approaches most administrators use to back up an Oracle7 database system:

- Online database backups
- Offline database backups

Both database backup methods consider backups of a database's data files, control files, and initialization parameter files.

Backing Up a Closed Database: Offline Database Backups

One way to back up a database is to shut down the database before backing up its files. This type of database backup is called an *offline database backup*. Follow these steps to complete an offline database backup:

1. Shut down the current instance of the database, if necessary. When shutting down a database in preparation for an offline database backup, make sure you use the Normal or Immediate option of the SQL*DBA Shut Down menu. Furthermore, make sure the database shutdown completes normally. If you have to abort an instance to complete database shutdown, reopen and shut down the database to make sure the database closes normally before backup.

2. Back up the database's data files, control file, and initialization parameter files using operating system commands or a backup utility.

3. You can also back up a database's transaction log when the database is closed. However, backups of the transaction log files are useful only if media recovery is disabled for the database. Otherwise, skip backing up the database's transaction log.

4. After completing all file backups, start up the database to make it available for application use.

Once you have completed an offline database backup, you are left with a complete set of the files that make up the database with respect to an instant in time (when the database was shut down). Fittingly, some call an offline database backup a *consistent database backup*.

NOTE Offline database backups are the only option available to databases with media recovery disabled. If media recovery is disabled, offline database backups must always include backups of the database's transaction log.

Backing Up an Open Database: Online Database Backups

Many database systems cannot afford to frequently shut down a database to make backups. For example, Oracle7 might support a mission-critical application that needs to run 24 hours a day. In this type of situation, an *online database backup* is necessary—a backup taken while the database is open and in use.

> **NOTE**   Only databases with media recovery enabled can make online database backups.

Online database backups are a bit more involved than offline backups. Here are the necessary steps:

1. Back up the data files of each tablespace, one tablespace at a time.
2. Back up the database's control file.
3. Back up the database's initialization parameter files.

The next few sections explain how to complete each of these steps.

Backing Up Data Files of an Open Database

To back up the data files of an online database, you should back up the data files in each tablespace, one tablespace at a time. To identify each tablespace, its availability status (online or offline), and the corresponding data files, use the DATABASE-REPORT procedure given in Listing 7.1 in Chapter 7.

If there are any offline tablespaces in the online database, back up the corresponding data files first. To back up the data files of an offline tablespace, use operating system commands or a backup utility that compresses and then safely backs up the data files to offline storage.

To back up the data files of an online tablespace, you must first mark the online tablespace for backup using the Begin Online Tablespace Backup dialog of SQL*DBA. To access this dialog, use the hot-key sequence (Esc-T for Oracle7 on

UNIX systems) or, from the SQL*DBA menu, select Backup ➤ Begin Online Tablespace Backup. Figure 11.7 shows the Begin Online Tablespace Backup dialog of SQL*DBA.

The dialog contains a simple list of all online tablespaces in the database. Select the tablespace you intend to back up and select the OK button. Next, use operating system commands or a backup utility to compress and back up the data files in the online tablespace marked for backup. When data file backup is complete, remove the online tablespace from backup mode using the End Online Tablespace Backup dialog of SQL*DBA. To access this dialog, use the hot-key sequence (Esc-E for Oracle7 on UNIX systems) or, from the SQL*DBA menu, select Backup ➤ End Online Tablespace Backup. Figure 11.8 shows the End Online Tablespace Backup dialog of SQL*DBA.

NOTE

To use the Begin and End Online Tablespace Backup dialogs of SQL*DBA, you must have the ALTER TABLESPACE or MANAGE TABLESPACE system privilege.

FIGURE 11.7:

The Begin Online Tablespace Backup dialog of SQL*DBA allows you to put online tablespaces into backup mode.

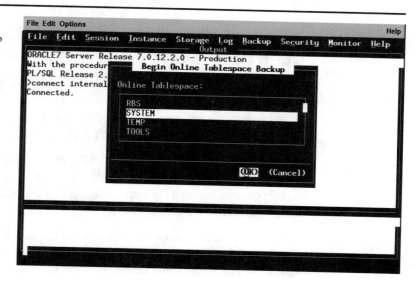

FIGURE 11.8:

The End Online Tablespace Backup
dialog of SQL*DBA allows you to
remove online tablespaces from
backup mode.

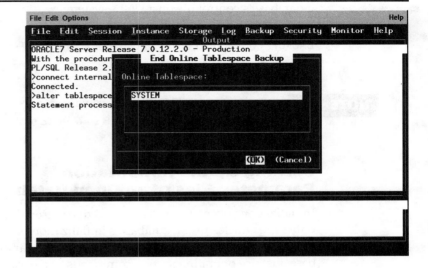

To use the End Online Tablespace Backup dialog, select the online tablespace marked for backup from the list box and select OK. Oracle7 then takes the online tablespace out of backup mode.

WARNING The first and final steps in making an online tablespace backup are extremely important. If an online tablespace is not marked for backup before taking data file backups, the backups are useless. If an online tablespace is not removed from backup mode after data file backup is complete, the database can become damaged if the server runs for several days with this condition, and then the server crashes.

Backing Up the Control File of an Open Database

To back up the control file of an online database, use the BACKUP CONTROLFILE option of the ALTER DATABASE command. For example, this statement backs up a database's control file on a UNIX system:

```
ALTER DATABASE
BACKUP CONTROLFILE TO '/tmp/dbbackup/ctrlsalesbkup.ctl'
```

> **NOTE**
>
> To use the ALTER DATABASE command to back up a database's control file, you must have the ALTER DATABASE system privilege.

Backing Up the Initialization Parameter Files of an Open Database

Initialization parameter files are not actively used during database processing. The only time Oracle7 uses a database's initialization parameter file is during database startup. Therefore, to back up the initialization parameter files of an online database, just use operating system commands or a backup utility.

Other Files to Consider When Backing Up a Database

Even though they are not part of an Oracle7 database, other files on the database server related to Oracle7 are important to back up. For example, consider backing up the following types of files when making a database backup:

- Application-specific files such as executables, source code, configuration files, and so on

- The configuration files for Oracle SQL*Net, including TNSNAMES.ORA, LISTENER.ORA, and so on

- Any special command script files that administrators and other types of users have created

Documenting Database Backups

It is a good idea to keep some type of documentation with each database backup. Simple things like the date of the backup, the database name, and so on can make finding the right backup easier when the pressure is on because of a database failure. Also note the highest log sequence number in the transaction log. You can do this before shutdown using the DATABASEREPORT procedure given in Listing 7.1. If you know the current log sequence number that corresponds to a database backup, you will know which archived transaction log groups to restore if recovery from a disk failure is necessary using the backup.

Automating Database Backups

As the preceding sections demonstrate, performing a database backup includes several steps, some of which are extremely important. Given this and the fact that database backups are one of the most frequently performed database administration operations, most Oracle7 administrators integrate database backup into a system backup procedure or write command scripts to automate the database backup process.

Listing 11.1 shows one command script a database administrator could run from within SQL*DBA to perform an online database backup of a simple database and its supporting files running on Oracle7 for a UNIX system.

Listing 11.1: A Script That Performs an Online Database Backup

```
-- This is a command script to perform an online
-- backup of the SALES database.  Before running
-- this script, use SQL*DBA to connect to the database
-- with an account that has the following system
-- privileges:  ALTER DATABASE, MANAGE TABLESPACE.
-- In addition, the person running the script must
-- have the file permissions for the specified files
-- and directories.

-- clear any old backup files in the backup directory
host rm /tmp/dbbackup/*

-- back up SYSTEM tablespace
ALTER TABLESPACE system BEGIN BACKUP;
host cp $ORACLE_HOME/dbs/systsales.dbf /tmp/dbbackup/systsales.dbf
ALTER TABLESPACE system END BACKUP;

-- back up RBS tablespace
ALTER TABLESPACE rbs BEGIN BACKUP;
host cp $ORACLE_HOME/dbs/rbssales.dbf /tmp/dbbackup/rbssales.dbf
ALTER TABLESPACE rbs END BACKUP;
```

```
-- back up TEMP tablespace
ALTER TABLESPACE temp BEGIN BACKUP;
host cp $ORACLE_HOME/dbs/tempsales.dbf /tmp/dbbackup/tempsales.dbf
TABLESPACE temp END BACKUP;

-- back up TOOLS tablespace
ALTER TABLESPACE tools BEGIN BACKUP;
host cp $ORACLE_HOME/dbs/toolsales.dbf /tmp/dbbackup/toolsales.dbf
ALTER TABLESPACE tools END BACKUP;

-- back up USERS tablespace
ALTER TABLESPACE users BEGIN BACKUP;
host cp $ORACLE_HOME/dbs/usrsales.dbf /tmp/dbbackup/usrsales.dbf
ALTER TABLESPACE users END BACKUP;

-- back up the database's control file
ALTER DATABASE BACKUP CONTROLFILE TO '/tmp/dbbackup/ctrlsales.ctl'

-- back up the database's initialization parameter files
host cp $ORACLE_HOME/dbs/*.ora /tmp/dbbackup
-- back up the SQL*Net V2 configuration files on the server
host cp /etc/*.ora /tmp/dbbackup

-- back up the special admin scripts
host cp $ORACLE_HOME/rdbms/admin/~*.sql /tmp/dbbackup

-- archive and compress the files in the backup directory
host tar -cvf /tmp/dbbackup/dbbackup.tar /tmp/dbbackup/*
host compress /tmp/dbbackup/dbbackup.tar

-- clear all temporary backup files from the backup directory,
-- except the compressed backup file
host rm /tmp/dbbackup/*.dbf
host rm /tmp/dbbackup/*.ctl
host rm /tmp/dbbackup/*.ora
host rm /tmp/dbbackup/*.sql
```

NOTE   As Listing 11.1 shows, the HOST command of SQL*DBA can be useful for executing host operating system commands without exiting SQL*DBA.

Scripts are a simple way of automating the backup process. There are other more complicated but powerful approaches to automating the database backup process as well. For example, you can create a Pro*C program that interactively queries and records the names of all database files and then uses menus to interactively guide and customize a database backup. You can also use operating system facilities, such as UNIX's *cron,* to automatically execute a shell script that performs a database backup at a specified interval. The possibilities for automated database backup are limited only by your imagination. Whatever method you choose, be sure to automate the Oracle7 database backup process somehow to make it easy and more reliable.

Planning a Database Backup Strategy

Now that you understand how to back up an Oracle7 database, the remaining questions are

- When should you make database backups?
- How often should you make database backups?
- How long should you keep older database backups? ·

Like many other administrative operations, database backup strategies vary with each database and installation, depending on things like transaction throughput and database size. However, there are a few standard rules every backup strategy should follow:

- Back up a database frequently. The longer you wait between database backups, the longer it will take to complete a database recovery process. That's because more transaction log groups have to be applied to older versions of data files during the roll forward recovery process.

- Back up a database regularly. No matter whether you back up the database nightly, every other day, or once a week, you are more likely to not forget about or put off database backup if your backup strategy is executed on a regular basis.

- Back up a database after making structural modifications. For example, if you add a new tablespace or data file to the database, alter your backup script to address the new tablespace, and then back up the database that day so the most recent database backup includes the new data files added to the database. It is important to back up a database after database creation, after creating or dropping a tablespace, after adding or renaming data files, and after modifying the configuration of the database's transaction log.

- Hold onto at least the two most recent database backups. This simple rule reduces the likelihood that you will be left empty handed if the most recent database backup has some sort of problem.

Testing Database Backups to Ensure Success

Imagine the horror when you lose a disk and attempt a database recovery, only to find out that for weeks your tape drive has been working incorrectly and your most recent database backups are useless. What do you do now? Situations like this can easily be avoided if you perform regular test database recoveries to guarantee the soundness of a database backup strategy and all of the involved hardware components.

To test a database backup strategy, pick a time when you can shut down the database system for an extended period of time (perhaps on a weekend or overnight). First, copy all of the production database's files (data files, transaction log files, and control file) to a temporary backup location using operating system commands, and verify that the file copies are intact and valid. This step is important to protect the production database in case your database backups have a problem. Next, restore the database from your most recent backup. After restoring the database, perform a database recovery to see if everything works okay. If everything goes well, you can sleep better at night knowing that your database is safe and sound. And you will now be experienced at performing database recovery, so surprises will be less likely when the heat is on during a real database failure. If database recovery does not succeed, it's time to play Sherlock Holmes to determine what is going wrong. After you correct the problem, test a database recovery again and make sure you fixed what you thought you did.

Mirroring Data Files Using Hardware Mirroring

File mirroring is especially important for database systems that require high availability—those that cannot afford to tolerate even a few seconds of down time resulting from hardware-related problems. The mirroring capability of Oracle7's transaction log is an important feature for high-availability systems because the database system can continue to operate without interruption, even when an isolated disk failure damages members in the transaction log.

Unfortunately, Oracle7 does not also support file mirroring for its data files. Does this mean that Oracle7 is not available when a disk crash occurs? Not necessarily. In most cases, when a disk failure causes the loss of a data file, the Oracle7 database system continues to operate. However, the data in the damaged data file is unavailable to users, while the intact data files remain open for use. If Oracle7 supported software file mirroring of a database's data files, the entire set of data files would continue to remain available, even when an isolated disk failure occurs, just as with the transaction log.

NOTE   The only time an Oracle7 database must go offline because of a damaged data file is when the damaged data file is part of the SYSTEM tablespace. That's because the data files of the SYSTEM tablespace store the database's data dictionary information, which is absolutely necessary for Oracle7 to operate.

For sites that require the high level of availability assurance that file mirroring delivers, there is a solution—*hardware disk mirroring*. Disk mirroring can provide the same level of fault tolerance as software file mirroring, but by redundantly writing all files on an entire disk instead of just selected files. And hardware disk mirroring is more efficient than software mirroring because of the way disk arms on mirrored disks move together. You have to buy special hardware and install it, but disk mirroring is well worth the trouble if you need the extra fault tolerance it provides.

Database Recovery

While system and database backup are jobs administrators must perform frequently, with luck an administrator will never have to perform database recovery for real. It is stressful when something goes wrong and the productivity of many workers depends solely on how quickly system and/or database administrators can recover the damaged system.

The following sections explain how Oracle7 can recover from different types of failures.

Database Recovery Basics

Before you can perform a database recovery, it is best to know something about the recovery process so you can understand what is going on and make intelligent decisions when you have to. Figure 11.9 illustrates Oracle7 database recovery.

Figure 11.9 shows the key process in database recovery, which is called *roll forward recovery*. During roll forward recovery, the transaction log is applied to the database's data files to redo all changes that have been lost because of a failure. All types of database recovery include this essential step for restoring lost work.

The next few sections explain the two most basic types of failures and their respective database recovery procedures.

FIGURE 11.9:

The roll forward phase of database recovery applies changes made by transactions to data files.

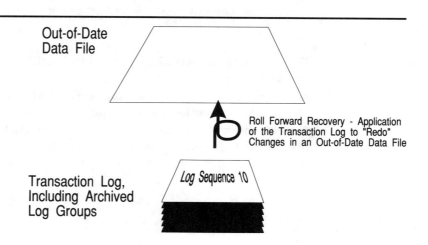

Out-of-Date
Data File

Roll Forward Recovery - Application
of the Transaction Log to "Redo"
Changes in an Out-of-Date Data File

Transaction Log,
Including Archived
Log Groups

Log Sequence 10

Crash Recovery

At any given time, a multi-user Oracle7 database server is processing the transactions of many different application users. But suppose the power unexpectedly goes out. Transactions in process are left in limbo and some committed data in shared memory may not yet have been written to the database's data files. How are you going to recover the database from this mess?

This type of failure is appropriately called a *system crash* or *instance failure*. Building on this terminology, database recovery from a system crash is called *crash recovery*. As bad as it might seem, database recovery from a crash is simple because no one has to do anything; Oracle7 does all the work for you.

After the power is back up and the computer used for the database server is running again, Oracle7 automatically performs crash recovery during the next database startup. That is, Oracle7 applies any necessary changes in the transaction log to the intact data files, thereby rolling them forward and recovering all committed work. Once the database is open, users can employ an application to connect normally and begin working.

Crash recovery transparently happens during the database startup that occurs after any type of abnormal database shutdown, including power failures and aborting a database instance. After an abnormal database shutdown occurs, don't worry if the subsequent database startup operation takes a little longer than normal to complete; it can take a little time for Oracle7 to complete crash recovery before opening the database.

Disk Failure Recovery: Closed Database Recovery

With Oracle7, all the necessary components to complete crash recovery are in place—no data files have been damaged and all of the necessary transaction log groups are still on disk. However, recovery of lost work from a disk failure is not as easy. *Disk failure recovery*, sometimes called *media recovery*, requires help from the database administrator and includes these steps:

1. Repair any hardware problems (for example, replace a damaged disk).
2. Using the most recent database backup, restore any lost or damaged files.

3. Restore any necessary archived transaction log groups on tape to a disk location.

4. Start the database recovery process from SQL*DBA.

5. Clean up when database recovery is successful.

The next few sections explain more about each of these steps.

NOTE The following sections explain how to recover from a disk failure with the database closed. As a result, some refer to the following procedure as *closed database recovery.*

Repairing Hardware Problems

If you need to perform disk failure recovery, the root of the problem is obviously the first thing to fix. If a disk fails, you can fix it, reformat it, or replace it—whatever it takes to get the disk back in operation. After you fix the disk problem, the next step is to regenerate the original file directory structure. One way to do this is by using the most recent system backup.

Restoring Any Damaged Files

If you fix or replace a damaged disk to get up and running, the restoration process is fairly simple: Restore all the database files that were lost because of the disk failure, including data files, transaction log files, copies of the database control file, and any initialization parameter files. What source should you use to restore the different types of files? Depending on the type of file, the answer is different:

- Restore all damaged data files from the most recent database backup. Be sure to restore the files to their original location, if at all possible.

- If you are following the recommendations put forth in this book, the database's transaction log and control file are mirrored. Therefore, you can restore a damaged member in the transaction log or a copy of the database control file by copying an intact version of the file.

- If you lost any other files, such as initialization parameter files or SQL*Net configuration files, restore them from the most recent database backup.

NOTE If you unwisely chose to not mirror a database's transaction log or control file, or even worse, to run a database with media recovery disabled, the database recovery process is the simple restoration of *all* (intact and damaged) database files from the most recent database backup. This means, however, that all work performed since the most recent backup is lost.

Extracting Necessary Archived Log Groups from Tape Archives

If you have good notes with each database backup, you have a good idea which archived transaction log groups the database recovery process will need. If you restore the necessary archived transaction log groups before beginning the database recovery process, database recovery is literally automatic. The only trick is to restore all archived transaction log groups to the location specified by the LOG_ARCHIVE_DEST initialization parameter.

If you do not know which archived transaction log groups will be necessary for the database recovery, don't worry—the Oracle7 recovery procedure will prompt for archived transaction log groups that it cannot find, by log sequence number. Using another operating system session, you can restore necessary archived transaction logs after database recovery begins.

Commencing Database Recovery

After completing all of the preparatory steps, it is time to start the actual database recovery process. As with database backup, there are several options available for database recovery. To avoid confusion, this section sticks to an approach that will work for almost every type of database recovery. (For more advanced recovery operations, see the section "Advanced Types of Database Recovery" later in this chapter.)

If you have restored all damaged files to their original locations and you have already restored all the necessary archived transaction log groups to the location pointed to by LOG_ARCHIVE_DEST, database recovery is easy. The first step is to start SQL*DBA and set automatic recovery on:

```
SET AUTORECOVERY ON
```

This special SQL*DBA statement tells Oracle7 that you expect it can find all of the necessary archived transaction log groups in LOG_ARCHIVE_DEST, so it can suggest and apply the transaction log without prompting for log files.

After connecting to the database as INTERNAL, you can start up, recover, and open the database all in one step using the Startup Instance dialog of SQL*DBA. Just select the Recover Before Open check box and then select OK. During the database startup process, SQL*DBA displays messages in alert boxes that name the data files that will undergo the roll forward recovery process. Simply select the OK button in the alerts, and the recovery process begins.

> **NOTE**
>
> If you did not restore archived transaction log files to the location specified by LOG_ARCHIVE_DEST, Oracle7 prompts for log files, one at a time, by their log sequence number. When prompted, specify the complete filename that indicates the location and name of the requested log file.

Database recovery can take a little time to complete as Oracle7 applies the transaction log to the restored data files. If you suspect that database recovery will take an extraordinary amount of time to complete because there are many archived log groups to apply, you can speed the recovery operation by recovering different data files in parallel. (See the section "Configuring a Database for Parallel Recovery" later in this chapter.)

Once database recovery is complete, the database is left open. The recovered database now contains all committed work that happened before the disk failure. Users can employ applications to connect and start working again.

Cleaning Up after Database Recovery

When database recovery is complete, you will have many archived transaction log groups somewhere on disk that you will not need to use again unless another disk failure occurs in the near future. Therefore, to free some disk space on the database server, use operating system commands to remove the files from disk. However, before doing so, make sure you are not erasing your only copies of these important files—you never know when another disk failure will occur that requires these older log groups to complete database recovery from a disk failure.

Advanced Types of Database Recovery

The preceding sections have offered a simple approach to recovering an Oracle7 database damaged from a disk failure. However, there are other situations where you can benefit from knowing some of the more advanced database recovery operations Oracle7 supports. The following sections briefly explain two different types of advanced Oracle7 database recovery features: parallel recovery and online database recovery.

Configuring a Database for Parallel Recovery

Recovery of a database system can never happen too quickly. When a database system is not available because of a failure, users cannot run applications and be productive workers. Depending on the type of business the database supports, this can translate to lots of lost revenue.

To speed the database recovery process, Oracle7 (release 7.1 and later) allows you to configure an instance for *parallel recovery*. When you start database recovery and an instance is configured for parallel recovery, Oracle7 automatically starts multiple recovery processes at the same time. Multiple data files undergo the roll forward recovery at the same time, which dramatically reduces the time necessary to recover the database. Figure 11.10 illustrates parallel database recovery.

The easiest way to configure an instance for parallel database recovery is to set a couple of special initialization parameter files:

Parameter	Description
PARALLEL_RECOVERY_MAX_THREADS	Determines the number of operating system processes Oracle7 uses when recovering a closed database. Set this parameter to the number of disks the database server uses to store the different data files for the database

FIGURE 11.10:

The database recovery process is quicker with parallel recovery.

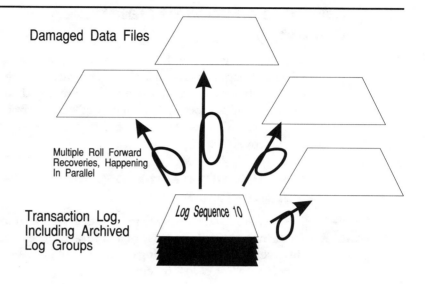

Damaged Data Files

Multiple Roll Forward
Recoveries, Happening
In Parallel

Transaction Log,
Including Archived
Log Groups

Log Sequence 10

Parameter	Description
PARALLEL_RECOVERY_ MIN_THREADS	Determines the number of operating system processes Oracle7 uses when recovering an individual tablespace or data file of the database when the database is online. (See the next section for information about online database recovery.) Determine which tablespace in the database uses the most disks to store its data files, and then set the parameter to the same value

For example, assume that a database server uses five disks to store the different data files of a database and a tablespace in the database uses two disks to store its data files. Here is an excerpt from the database's initialization parameter file:

```
.
.
.
PARALLEL_RECOVERY_MAX_THREADS=5
```

```
PARALLEL_RECOVERY_MIN_THREADS=2
     .
     .
     .
```

When you start database recovery, Oracle7 automatically uses the values for the PARALLEL_... initialization parameters to start multiple recovery processes and make the roll forward recovery process happen more quickly.

Online Database Recovery

Money is time, and down time is lost money. Therefore, Oracle7 supports *online database recovery* to help reduce or eliminate lost productivity caused by localized failures. Online database recovery is the recovery of damaged tablespaces or data files in an online database. For example, assume that only the data files of a single tablespace are damaged in a disk failure. In this case, Oracle7 can continue running uninterrupted while the damaged tablespace is offline and being recovered. Of course, as with all offline tablespaces, the data in the damaged tablespace is not available until the recovery process completes and you bring the tablespace back online. Similarly, you can perform online recovery for individual data files that are damaged.

Two conditions are necessary for online database recovery:

- The database must be running with media recovery enabled.
- All data files of the SYSTEM tablespace must be intact.

NOTE

If you follow the configuration guidelines in this book and place all rollback segments in their own tablespace, the preceding condition list is complete. However, if you have one or more online rollback segments in a damaged, offline tablespace, you should also take the rollback segments offline before attempting online database recovery of the tablespace. This extra step ensures that transactions will not attempt to use the rollback segment(s) in the damaged tablespace during recovery operations.

If your situation meets these conditions, online database recovery is one possibility for solving your problem. Here are the steps for achieving online database recovery from the loss of one or more data files:

1. Identify the damaged tablespaces and take them offline.

2. Repair any hardware problems. (For example, replace a damaged disk.)

3. Using the most recent database backup, restore any lost or damaged files.

4. Restore any necessary archived transaction log groups on tape to a disk location.

5. Start the database recovery process from SQL*DBA.

6. Clean up when database recovery is successful.

Steps 1 through 4 and step 6 in this procedure should be familiar to you by now; they were discussed in earlier sections of this book.

If you have restored all damaged files to their original locations and you have already restored all the necessary archived transaction log groups to the location pointed to by LOG_ARCHIVE_DEST, start SQL*DBA and set automatic recovery on, as you would do with closed database recovery. Then you can begin online database recovery using either the Recover Offline Tablespace or the Recover Offline Data File dialog of SQL*DBA. Figure 11.11 shows the Recover Offline Tablespace dialog of SQL*DBA.

Simply select the offline tablespace to recover, and then select the OK button. Oracle7 automatically applies the transaction log to any damaged data files in the offline tablespace. Additionally, if you configure Oracle7 for parallel recovery, Oracle7 automatically starts a number of multiple recovery processes, as determined by the PARALLEL_RECOVERY_MIN_THREADS initialization parameter, to carry out the online database recovery more quickly. Once recovery is complete, you can bring the offline tablespace back online so it is available for normal application processing.

FIGURE 11.11:

Use the Recover Offline Tablespace dialog of SQL*DBA to perform online database recovery of an offline tablespace.

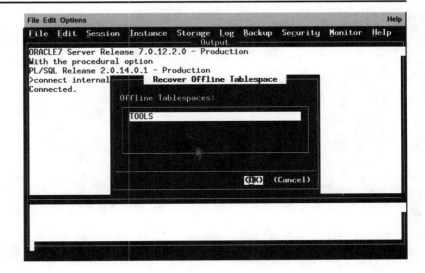

This chapter has described the key features in Oracle7 that permit the database administrator to protect and recover a database from all types of failures that can damage a database. The chapter has shown

- How to configure the structure of an Oracle7 database's transaction log
- How to configure the transaction log for automatic archiving
- How to monitor a database's transaction log for problems
- How to make offline and online backups of an Oracle7 database
- How to increase protection of database availability by mirroring an Oracle7 database's data files with hardware mirroring
- How to recover an Oracle7 database from disk failures using offline and online recovery techniques
- How to configure Oracle7 for quicker parallel recovery operations

CHAPTER

TWELVE

Monitoring and Tuning Database Server Performance

- Tuning an operating system for Oracle7

- Tuning the Oracle7 memory caches

- Eliminating disk I/O contention in an Oracle7 server

- Tuning the size of rollback segments

- Tuning an Oracle7 multithreaded server

- Reducing performance hits caused by checkpoints

After you've driven a car for a while, the car's engine can begin to run poorly. The engine's spark plugs can get old and caked with oil grit and the contacts in the distributor cap can become worn. To keep a car running like new, it is important to regularly tune up the car's engine. The Oracle7 database server is another type of engine that needs an occasional tune-up to keep things running smoothly.

Oracle7 has an intimidating number of knobs and dials that the administrator can adjust to affect the performance of the database server. To make server performance tuning easier to understand, this chapter discusses six tuning tips that noticeably affect the performance of the Oracle7 server:

- Tuning an operating system for the Oracle7 database server
- Reducing disk I/O by adjusting the sizes of the Oracle7 memory caches
- Eliminating disk contention for files and data in an Oracle7 database
- Sizing rollback segments correctly to reduce dynamic space allocations and deallocations
- Tuning the number of processes in the Oracle7 multithreaded server
- Reducing the performance hits that checkpoints can create

As your database system evolves, keep in mind the tuning tips in this chapter and others so that the tuning process is less involved.

Tuning Tip 1: Tune the Operating System for Oracle7

Oracle7 clearly depends heavily on the multi-user operating system used to run the database server. If the database server's operating system does not deliver maximum performance, then no matter how well you tune Oracle7, the database server will not perform as well as it could. Therefore, it makes sense to tune the operating system with the Oracle7 database server in mind.

The following sections discuss three of the most important considerations when tuning an operating system for Oracle7.

Planning System Resources for Oracle7

First, you need to plan how much of the server computer's resources you want to dedicate to the Oracle7 database server. This is an important factor that can significantly affect the performance of Oracle7. For example, if you reserve a lot of memory for Oracle7, it can cache more database data in memory, which reduces disk I/Os to deliver more performance. If you allow Oracle7 to access multiple processors on a multiprocessor computer, Oracle7 can perform work in parallel to reduce wait times for user requests. In summary, first determine what resources are available on the server computer, and then determine how much of the resources you want Oracle7 to use.

In many client/server systems it is reasonable to dedicate all resources of a server computer to run Oracle7. This is especially the case when the server machine is a small, inexpensive microcomputer or workstation, such as a personal computer running SCO UNIX or a Novell NetWare file server. If you decide to dedicate a computer to Oracle7, the primary job is to make sure the server computer has ample resources to run Oracle7.

In contrast, demanding client/server systems can use a large multiprocessor minicomputer at the center of a corporate network. Larger systems such as these are less likely to dedicate all of the server computer's resources to the database system—it is necessary to reserve some system resources for other tasks, such as print queues and electronic mail systems. Determining which resources different applications use and require on larger systems can be a challenge. To make your job easier, consider the use of special system administration utilities that are available to help tune operating system operation. (You can read about some of these utilities in Appendix C.) However, many times tuning the operating system on larger systems is a try-and-see process that takes a significant amount of expertise and time.

Tuning Operating System Virtual Memory Settings

Most operating systems use virtual memory to simulate the presence of more real memory on a computer. *Real memory* is the random-access memory that memory chips in the computer supply for software operation. *Virtual memory* is a reserved area of disk space, often called a *swap space*, that the operating system uses to page information into and out of real memory when there is not enough real memory to handle software requests. Therefore, virtual memory can make it appear as though a computer has more real memory than it really does.

At reasonable levels, paging using virtual memory is beneficial because it provides more memory in which a computer's application programs can work. However, if a computer's memory supply is significantly overloaded, paging can become more of a problem than a benefit. For example, a serious condition known as *thrashing* occurs when a computer's processor spends more time paging information into and out of memory than it does performing useful work on behalf of applications and users. When such a condition occurs, it significantly slows server performance for all applications.

To avoid the performance degradation associated with disadvantageous virtual memory usage, system and Oracle7 administrators should closely monitor swapping activity and aim to reduce or altogether eliminate swapping for the server system. To reduce or eliminate swapping, the only real solution is to purchase and install more memory in the server.

NOTE Most operating systems have utilities or operating system commands you can use to monitor swapping activity on a computer. For example, many UNIX systems support the command "sar", which displays a short report of system swapping activity.

Setting Operating System Process Priorities for Oracle7

Many operating systems allow you to tune their functions by selectively prioritizing the actions of operating system processes. An administrator can give more priority to more important tasks and less priority to less important tasks. The result is that the most demanding tasks complete more quickly than the less demanding tasks, which usually satisfies the majority of system users.

While setting operating system process priorities can be helpful for some applications, it can hurt the performance of the Oracle7 database server. In an Oracle7 database system, all background and foreground database server processes perform equally important actions and need to run with the same priority. Therefore, make sure that when you install Oracle7, all server processes run using the default process priority of the server computer.

Tuning Tip 2: Reduce Disk I/O in Oracle7

Disk access is a very slow operation that can hurt the performance of any computer system. The less disk I/O, the better the performance of the computer. Software applications that use large amounts of data like Oracle7 use memory caches to reduce disk I/O and improve overall performance.

Using Memory Caches

A *memory cache* is a preallocated memory area that Oracle7 specifically reserves to hold frequently requested pages or blocks of information. By holding frequently used data blocks in memory, Oracle7 eliminates the need for costly disk I/Os that would otherwise hurt database server performance for all client applications. Before focusing on ways to tune the sizes of the different memory caches that Oracle7 uses to reduce disk I/Os, let's learn some of the basic terminology related to memory caches:

Term	Meaning
Caching algorithms	Most memory caches are static, preallocated areas in memory. Therefore, there is a limit to how much data a cache can hold. To intelligently decide which data pages to keep in memory caches, software programs use a *caching algorithm* or caching strategy. A common caching algorithm is a *most-recently-used/least-recently-used caching algorithm.* With this strategy, a program keeps a data page in a memory cache according to how long it has been since the last request for the page. Consequently, the most recently requested pages will stay in memory longer, while the least recently requested pages are *aged out* of the cache to make room for new pages not already in the cache

Term	Meaning
Cache hit	When an application requests some information that is already in a memory cache, the program gets the information from memory rather than disk. This is called a *cache hit* or a *cache get*
Cache miss	When an application requests some information that is not in memory, the program gets the information from disk. This is called a *cache miss* or a *cache getmiss*
Cache reload	When an application requests some information that used to be in the memory cache but has since been aged out, the program reloads the information from disk. This is called a *cache reload*

Figure 12.1 illustrates the basic concepts of memory caches.

Now let's see how Oracle7 caches data in memory. Oracle7 has three primary memory caches for different types of data: the library cache, the dictionary cache, and the buffer cache.

FIGURE 12.1:

Caching algorithms, cache hits, misses, and reloads

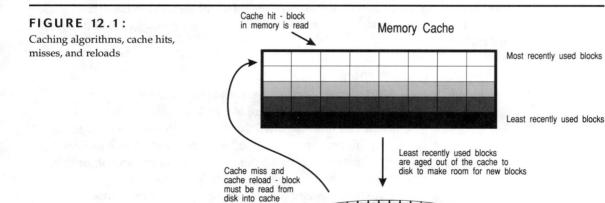

Cache	Description
Library cache	When a user issues a SQL statement, calls a database procedure, or fires a trigger, Oracle7 uses memory to parse and determine execution plans for the statement or procedure. To save memory when many users all execute the same SQL statements and procedures of a compiled application, the *library cache* stores and shares SQL statements and PL/SQL procedures in memory. Shared SQL can also improve application performance because Oracle7 does not have to redetermine a statement's execution plan if it is already in memory
Dictionary cache	During system processing, Oracle7 constantly uses information in a database's data dictionary for almost every operation. To reduce disk I/Os associated with data dictionary tables and indexes, the *dictionary cache* holds dictionary information in memory
Buffer cache	The *buffer cache* reduces disk I/O by storing data that transactions have recently requested. It is also the in-memory work area for transaction processing. For example, when a transaction includes a statement to update a row in a table, Oracle7 finds the data block on disk that contains the requested row. Then Oracle7 reads the block from disk into the buffer cache and updates the row. If another transaction wants to update the same row or another row in the same data block, no disk access is necessary; the row is already in memory

Together, the library and dictionary caches make up the *shared pool*. The shared pool combined with the buffer cache make up the *system global area,* or the *SGA.* Figure 12.2 shows the different memory caches Oracle7 uses.

FIGURE 12.2:

Library, dictionary, and buffer caches in an Oracle7 database server

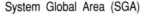

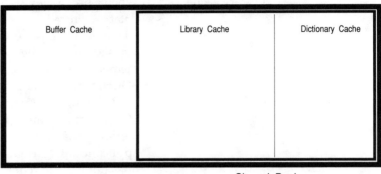

System Global Area (SGA)

To tune an Oracle7 database server's SGA, you must gather some information about the ratio of misses or reloads to hits in the different caches of the SGA. Once you know how the caches are serving application requests, you can tune server performance by increasing or decreasing the sizes of the different caches.

An easy and effective way to monitor the percentage of misses in the library, dictionary, and buffer caches is to use the table and procedure in Listing 12.1.

Listing 12.1: The GATHERSGASTATS Procedure and SGASTATSHISTORY Table

```
CREATE TABLE sgastatshistory (
timepoint DATE,
-- columns for cumulative stats
cumlibraryreloads REAL,
cumlibrarypins REAL,
cumdictionarygetmisses REAL,
cumdictionarygets REAL,
cumsgablockgets REAL,
cumsgaconsistentgets REAL,
cumsgadiskgets REAL,
-- columns for interval percentages
intlibraryreloadpercentage REAL,
intdictionarymisspercentage REAL,
intbuffermisspercentage REAL);
```

```
CREATE PROCEDURE gathersgastats (interval INTEGER, timepoints INTEGER) AS
-- This procedure gathers data points at the specified interval (in minutes)
-- for the given number of timepoints to track the percentage of misses to
-- gets in the library, dictionary, and buffer caches.  Low percentages are
-- good, high percentages mean that the cache sizes need tuning.

counter INTEGER := 0;
-- variables for current cumulative stats
curlibraryreloads REAL;
curlibrarypins REAL;
curdictionarygetmisses REAL;
curdictionarygets REAL;
cursgablockgets REAL;
cursgaconsistentgets REAL;
cursgadiskgets REAL;
-- variables for previous cumulative stats
prevlibraryreloads REAL;
prevlibrarypins REAL;
prevdictionarygetmisses REAL;
prevdictionarygets REAL;
prevsgablockgets REAL;
prevsgaconsistentgets REAL;
prevsgadiskgets REAL;
-- variables for interval stats
intlibraryreloads REAL;
intlibrarypins REAL;
intdictionarygetmisses REAL;
intdictionarygets REAL;
intsgablockgets REAL;
intsgaconsistentgets REAL;
intsgadiskgets REAL;
-- variables for interval percentages
libraryreloadpercentage REAL;
dictionarymisspercentage REAL;
buffermisspercentage REAL;

-- cursor to fetch SGA buffer cache stats
CURSOR bufferdata IS
  SELECT name, value
    FROM v$sysstat
   WHERE name IN ('db block gets','consistent gets','physical reads');

BEGIN

-- set loop for wake/sleep gathering of data points
```

```
WHILE counter < timepoints LOOP

-- query to gather library cache stats
  SELECT SUM(reloads), SUM(pins)
    INTO curlibraryreloads, curlibrarypins
    FROM v$librarycache;
-- query to gather dictionary cache stats
  SELECT SUM(getmisses), SUM(gets)
    INTO curdictionarygetmisses, curdictionarygets
    FROM v$rowcache;
-- open cursor to gather SGA buffer cache stats
  FOR buffercache IN bufferdata LOOP
    IF buffercache.name = 'db block gets' THEN
      cursgablockgets := buffercache.value;
    ELSIF buffercache.name = 'consistent gets' THEN
      cursgaconsistentgets := buffercache.value;
    ELSE
      cursgadiskgets := buffercache.value;
    END IF;
  END LOOP;

-- Calculate libary reload percentage, dictionary miss percentage
-- and buffer cache miss percentage.  Special case first datapoint
-- in a session with NULL percentages.

  IF counter != 0 THEN

-- first, gather previous cumulative stats from SGASTATHISTORY
    SELECT cumlibraryreloads, cumlibrarypins,
       cumdictionarygetmisses, cumdictionarygets,
       cumsgablockgets, cumsgaconsistentgets, cumsgadiskgets
       INTO prevlibraryreloads, prevlibrarypins,
         prevdictionarygetmisses, prevdictionarygets,
         prevsgablockgets, prevsgaconsistentgets, prevsgadiskgets
       FROM sgastatshistory
       WHERE timepoint = (SELECT MAX(timepoint)
                            FROM sgastatshistory);

-- calculate library reload percentage
    intlibraryreloads := curlibraryreloads - prevlibraryreloads;
    intlibrarypins := curlibrarypins - prevlibrarypins;
    libraryreloadpercentage :=
      ROUND((intlibraryreloads/(intlibraryreloads + intlibrarypins))*100,2);

-- calculate dictionary miss percentage
```

```
    intdictionarygetmisses := curdictionarygetmisses - prevdictionarygetmisses;
    intdictionarygets := curdictionarygets - prevdictionarygets;
    dictionarymisspercentage :=
      ROUND((intdictionarygetmisses/(intdictionarygetmisses +
        intdictionarygets))*100,2);

-- calculate buffer cache miss percentage
    intsgablockgets := cursgablockgets - prevsgablockgets;
    intsgaconsistentgets := cursgaconsistentgets - prevsgaconsistentgets;
    intsgadiskgets := cursgadiskgets - prevsgadiskgets;
    buffermisspercentage :=
      ROUND((intsgadiskgets/(intsgablockgets + intsgaconsistentgets))*100,2);
  ELSE
    libraryreloadpercentage := NULL;
    dictionarymisspercentage := NULL;
    buffermisspercentage := NULL;
  END IF;

-- insert datapoint into SGASTATSHISTORY table
  INSERT INTO sgastatshistory
    VALUES (SYSDATE, curlibraryreloads, curlibrarypins, curdictionarygetmisses,
      curdictionarygets, cursgablockgets, cursgaconsistentgets, cursgadiskgets,
      libraryreloadpercentage, dictionarymisspercentage, buffermisspercentage);

  counter := counter + 1;
  dbms_lock.sleep(interval*60);
END LOOP;

END gathersgastats;
```

To gather performance statistics for each of a database server's SGA memory caches, run the GATHERSGASTATS procedure. Notice that this administrative procedure is a wake-and-sleep procedure, like several other procedures given in this book. Therefore, you will have to dedicate the SQL*DBA or SQL*Plus session you use to run this procedure.

The GATHERSGASTATS procedure lets you specify two arguments: the interval (in minutes) to wake up and gather data and the total number of data points to gather. A good strategy is to run the procedure for the duration of a normal day. This way you can see how the SGA cache settings work as the load on the database server fluctuates during a normal day. For example, if you start an instance at the beginning of the day, there will be a high number of misses early on because the caches in the SGA are empty. As applications load data throughout the day, the miss percentages in the different caches should stabilize and give you a good idea of how the instance configuration is working.

After gathering enough data points, you can query the SGASTATSHISTORY table to see the percentages of misses to total gets throughout the statistic-gathering interval. For example, the following statements execute the GATHERSGASTATS procedure every 30 minutes for 8 hours and query the SGASTATSHISTORY table to show how the miss percentages fluctuate in a well-tuned database server's SGA throughout a normal day:

```
SELECT intlibraryreloadpercentage, intdictionarymisspercentage,
  intbuffermisspercentage
  FROM sgastatshistory
```

INTLIBRARYRELOADPERCENTAGE	INTDICTIONARYMISSPERCENTAGE	INTBUFFERMISSPERCENTAGE
1.23	21.61	40.82
.98	17.56	35.91
.77	10.42	28.23
.68	9.97	27.89
.61	8.53	40.13
.55	8.37	36.36
.54	8.32	32.42
.54	10.28	31.51
.54	10.61	30.05
.53	10.21	30.12
.52	11.02	30.87
.54	10.93	29.14
.55	10.54	30.01
.54	9.77	29.88
.54	10.08	29.91

In general, cache misses in the library and dictionary caches are more expensive than misses in the buffer cache. Therefore, you should look to tune the percentage of misses or reloads in the library, dictionary, and buffer caches to less than 1 percent, 15 percent, and 40 percent, respectively.

The next three sections explain the initialization parameters you can use to tune the size of the different caches in an Oracle7 database server's SGA.

Tuning the Library and Data Dictionary Caches

If the average percentage of reloads in the library cache is greater than 1 percent or the average percentage of misses in the dictionary cache is greater than 15 percent, you should increase the amount of memory dedicated to the shared pool. (Try using a query with the AVG SQL function to set these values.) Alternatively, if the miss percentages are lower than the targets, you may be able to maintain good performance and free up some memory for other operating system services by reducing the size of the shared pool.

To adjust the amount of memory allocated to the shared pool, use the SHARED_POOL_SIZE initialization parameter. Set the amount of memory for the shared pool in bytes. This example sets the shared pool size to 4 megabytes:

```
SHARED_POOL_SIZE=4194304
```

After altering the setting for the SHARED_POOL_SIZE parameter in a database's initialization parameter file, you need to shut down and restart the database server for the new setting to take effect.

NOTE Keep in mind that when you increase the size of the shared pool, you can reduce the amount of memory that is available for other uses, such as the SGA's buffer cache, or increase the amount of operating system paging, which is bad. Therefore, be sure you consider the big picture when setting the size of a database server's shared pool.

Tuning the Buffer Cache

If the average percentage of misses in the buffer cache is greater than 40 percent, you should increase the size of the buffer cache. Alternatively, if the average percentage of misses in the buffer cache is less than 40 percent, you may be able to maintain performance and free up memory for other resources by decreasing the size of the buffer cache.

To adjust the amount of memory allocated to the buffer cache, use the DB_BLOCK_BUFFERS initialization parameter. Set DB_BLOCK_BUFFERS to the number of data blocks you want the buffer cache to hold. This example sets the buffer cache size to 500 data blocks:

```
DB_BLOCK_BUFFERS=500
```

The size of a data block buffer corresponds to the setting for the DB_BLOCK_SIZE initialization parameter. To reveal the data block size for a database in bytes, you can query the V$PARAMETER table:

```
SELECT name, value
  FROM v$parameter
  WHERE name = 'db_block_size'
```

NAME	VALUE
db_block_size	2048

Once you know a database's data block size, you can determine the buffer cache's total size in bytes by multiplying the database's data block size by the number of data block buffers allocated to the buffer cache. For example, 500 2K block buffers result in a 1 megabyte buffer cache.

As with other initialization parameters, once you change the value for the DB_BLOCK_BUFFERS parameter in a database's initialization parameter file, you need to shut down and restart the database server for the new setting to take effect.

> **TIP** After database creation, it is impossible to change the database block size. Therefore, changing the value for DB_BLOCK_SIZE after database creation has no effect.

Tuning Tip 3: Reduce Disk Contention

Consider what happens when two different processes make a request to read or write data that resides on the same disk. The disk has only one disk head and, as a result, can serve the disk access request of only one process at a time. This is an example of two processes contending for data on the same disk, or *disk contention*.

Disk contention reduces system performance because some processes must wait while other processes get their disk access requests filled. Disk contention is no stranger to an Oracle7 database system. This tip focuses on ways to reduce disk contention within an Oracle7 database system.

Reducing Disk Contention by Separating Files

When creating new files for an Oracle7 database, whether they are data files for a tablespace or log files for the database's transaction log, carefully consider the disk resources available on the database server. If the server has multiple disks, you can significantly improve database server performance by spreading out files among available disks to reduce contention among a database's data files and transaction log files.

The basic rule for database file separation is to store data files separately from transaction log files. This way, ongoing transaction-processing disk access is not hampered by the disk access necessary for corresponding transaction logging.

If a server has a great many disks, the possibilities for file separation can be more imaginative. For example, suppose that two demanding applications use an Oracle7 database server and each application has a distinct set of data. You can eliminate inter-application disk contention by creating two different tablespaces, one for each application's data. Store the data files for the first application's tablespace on one disk drive and the data files for the second application's tablespace on another disk drive. This strategy physically separates the storage for each application's data, eliminating the possibility of any disk contention between the two applications.

If you have many disks to work with, you can also eliminate a source of disk contention in a database's transaction log. By placing each member of the transaction log on a different disk drive, you can eliminate disk contention when Oracle7 concurrently writes new transaction log records to one log group and reads another filled log group for archiving.

These are just a few of the ways you can improve database server performance if the server computer has many different disks and you use them wisely to spread out file I/O.

Reducing Disk Contention between Tables and Indexes

Almost all tables in an Oracle7 database have indexes to speed the performance of applications by reducing disk I/O for user requests. Internally, Oracle7 stores table data separately from corresponding index data. Therefore, when a user's transaction requests a row in a table, Oracle7 scans the data blocks in the index to find the row and its address, and then the server reads the data block in the table that contains the row.

When many concurrent SQL statements request rows from the same table and index and both the table and index are on the same disk, there is disk contention— Oracle7 can read only table data or only index data at any given time.

To reduce disk contention between table and index data, separate an application's table data from its index data on different physical disks. For example, store an application's table data in a tablespace on one disk and the corresponding index data in a different tablespace on another disk. As a result you eliminate disk contention, and Oracle7 can read table and index data in parallel on behalf of SQL requests.

Tuning Tip 4: Size Rollback Segments Correctly

Rollback segments can dynamically grow and shrink to handle fluctuating transaction sizes. However, the dynamic allocation and deallocation of extents in a rollback segment creates hits of disk I/O that can contribute to poor system performance. The solution to this problem is to tune the storage parameters for each rollback segment so they do not dynamically grow and shrink.

To keep a rollback segment's size relatively static for the average transaction size without wasting database space, it is necessary to set the rollback segment's OPTIMAL storage parameter correctly. Chapter 10 explains when Oracle7 allocates and deallocates extents for a rollback segment, how to monitor the number of growths and shrinks in a rollback segment, and how to adjust the setting of a rollback segment's OPTIMAL extent storage parameter. Use the information in Chapter 10 to reduce the likelihood of a rollback segment changing in size.

Tuning Tip 5: Tune the Oracle7 Multithreaded Server

Most Oracle7 client/server systems use a multithreaded server configuration to reduce the amount of process overhead on the server. If the number of processes in a multithreaded server is not correct for the transaction load, it can degrade system performance. To solve the problem, you can monitor and tune the configuration of the Oracle7 multithreaded server in a client/server database system.

There are two key areas to tune for the multithreaded server configuration: the number of dispatches per network protocol and the number of shared servers.

- If there are many clients for a network protocol and there are too few dispatcher processes for the network protocol, the dispatchers can be a performance bottleneck in accepting and fulfilling the requests of transactions.

- Oracle7 can dynamically start and stop shared server processes based on the load in a database system. If the minimum number of shared server processes is too low, system performance can be hurt because Oracle7 wastes resources to frequently start and stop shared server processes as transaction loads fluctuate. If the maximum number of shared servers is too low, system performance can be hurt because Oracle7 will not allow enough servers to handle heavy loads.

Chapter 8 includes all the information you need to configure, monitor, and tune an Oracle7 multithreaded server configuration. Follow the instructions in Chapter 8 to make sure your multithreaded server is not unnecessarily degrading system performance.

Tuning Tip 6: Reduce the Performance Hits of Checkpoints

Checkpoints are mileposts that regularly occur to write all modified data in memory back to a database's data files. Checkpoints serve several purposes. For one, they make sure that frequently modified data blocks, which Oracle7 will cache in memory for long periods of time, are regularly written back to the database's data files. Checkpoints also indicate to Oracle7 how much of the transaction log to apply to the data files if crash recovery is necessary.

Because a checkpoint writes data to disk, the disk I/Os that correspond to the checkpoint can degrade database server performance. The next two sections explain how to reduce the performance hits associated with checkpoints.

Tuning the Number of Checkpoints

One way to reduce the performance degradation of checkpoints is to make sure checkpoints occur only when necessary.

A database checkpoint always occurs when Oracle7 switches writing from one transaction log group to another. You can also force checkpoints to occur between transaction log group switches by setting the LOG_CHECKPOINT_INTERVAL and LOG_CHECKPOINT_TIMEOUT initialization parameters. However, there are not many situations that justify the performance hits associated with forcing additional checkpoints between log switches. Therefore, you should set the values of these initialization parameters so database checkpoints only occur at log switches.

The LOG_CHECKPOINT_INTERVAL initialization parameter indicates how often Oracle7 should perform checkpoints, based on the number of blocks written to the transaction log. To eliminate additional checkpoints between log switches, set the parameter so that the block threshold is larger than the number of blocks in the members of the database's transaction log.

The LOG_CHECKPOINT_INTERVAL initialization parameter is tricky to set because you specify the threshold as a number of operating system blocks, not data blocks. Therefore, you have to perform a bit of math in order to set the threshold above the size of the transaction log groups.

For example, many UNIX systems use a block size of 512 bytes, and the default log member size for Oracle7 on most UNIX systems is 512K. Therefore, if you use Oracle7 on UNIX and use transaction log members with a size of 512K, there are 1000 operating system blocks for each transaction log member. To eliminate checkpoints between log switches on this type of system, set LOG_CHECKPOINT_INTERVAL to a number greater than 1000:

```
LOG_CHECKPOINT_INTERVAL=1100
```

All members in a database's transaction log should be the same size; there is no advantage to varying the size of log groups. However, if a database's transaction log has members of varying size, set the LOG_CHECKPOINT_INTERVAL parameter higher than the size of the largest transaction log member.

The LOG_CHECKPOINT_TIMEOUT parameter indicates how often Oracle7 should perform checkpoints based on the number of seconds that have passed since the last checkpoint. Simply set this parameter's value to 0 so additional checkpoints do not occur between log switches:

```
LOG_CHECKPOINT_TIMEOUT=0
```

Tuning the Performance of Database Checkpoints

When a checkpoint occurs, three different operations take place. First, the DBWR process writes all modified data blocks in the SGA back to the appropriate data files of the database. Second, the LGWR background process updates the database's control file to indicate when the last checkpoint occurred. Finally, the LGWR background process updates the headers in all the data files to indicate when the last checkpoint occurred. The second and third steps are necessary to allow Oracle7 to determine how much of the transaction log to apply to the data files if crash recovery is necessary.

If you follow the recommendations in this book, you will use a small number of data files in a database. However, as a database grows and you add more and more data files, checkpoints can begin to create noticeable hits on system performance. This is primarily because LGWR must update many data file headers while still performing transaction logging for ongoing transactions. To improve performance, tune the Oracle7 database server to more efficiently complete checkpoints so they do not degrade transaction logging performance.

To relieve the burden on LGWR during checkpoints, you can start the optional CKPT background process. When CKPT is present for an Oracle7 database server, it updates the headers of data files during checkpoints rather than LGWR. Therefore, LGWR can concentrate on its transaction logging duties and serve ongoing transaction processing more effectively.

To use the CKPT background process, modify the database's parameter file to set the CHECKPOINT_PROCESS initialization parameter to TRUE:

```
CHECKPOINT_PROCESS=TRUE
```

Then restart the database server using the updated parameter file.

Once the CKPT background process has started, checkpoints will proceed without negatively affecting ongoing transaction logging. As a result, the Oracle7 database server will perform better during checkpoint operations.

Other Ways to Improve Performance

Suppose you carefully tune an Oracle7 database server using the six performance tuning tips described in this chapter, but application performance is still inadequate. What should do you do next?

There are other areas of the Oracle7 database server you can tweak to tune its performance. However, it is unlikely that these fine-tuning techniques will make a significant difference in improving the performance of the server's applications. It is more productive to shift your tuning efforts to the application itself.

Tuning the Application

There are many things in an application design that can degrade system performance. For example, if a client application always issues SQL statements across a network rather than using stored procedures when possible, the excessive network I/O in the system can be a significant factor for poor application performance. There are many ways to improve application performance. Chapters 16 and 17 concentrate on application-tuning techniques.

Tuning the System's Hardware Configuration

If after tuning the database server and tuning the application, your client/server system still delivers inadequate performance, the next step is to look at your system's hardware configuration. The problem might be that you are trying to make a demanding application perform in a client/server system that is not suited for the job. If this is the case, the next step might be substituting a more powerful server machine for the current server computer to gain additional database server performance. For example, by replacing a uniprocessor server with a multiprocessor computer, you can use the Oracle7 Parallel Query option. By parallelizing server operations across multiple processors, you can dramatically improve the performance of several types of applications, most notably decision-support applications. (For more information about using the Oracle7 Parallel Query option to improve database server performance, see Appendix B.)

Performance-Monitoring Techniques

The only way to know if an Oracle7 database server is performing well is to closely monitor its activities. Monitoring system status and performance is a big job, and the database administrator must pay close attention.

What is the most effective way to monitor an Oracle7 database server? There are two answers to this question, depending on the situation:

- If the database server is running relatively smoothly and you want to make sure it is working as well as it can, it is useful to do general maintenance monitoring that records statistics related to server performance. By studying such statistics, you can make adjustments to fine-tune system performance.

- If there is a critical problem, you need to do emergency monitoring to pinpoint the problem quickly. You will want to make immediate changes in the server to fix the critical problem.

SQL*DBA does not include any features for performing general monitoring for the Oracle7 server. However, an easy way to do so is to use the many different administrative stored procedures given in the listings in this book. For example, the CAPTUREDISPATCHERLOADS procedure given in Listing 8.1 (in Chapter 8) is an effective way to gather performance-related information for tuning a multi-threaded server configuration. Listing 12.1 (earlier in this chapter) is another example of a simple stored procedure and table you can use to gather tuning information for the memory caches in an Oracle7 database server. As long as you know what areas of the database server to focus on, you can create an entire set of administrative stored procedures like the ones in this book to help you tune the server's performance.

If are not sure which areas to monitor or you do not want to create stored procedures to help monitor server performance, another option is to use one of several third-party administrative tools that include built-in monitoring and alerting features. If you are serious about getting the best performance out of your database server, these administrative utilities are well worth the additional cost. (See Appendix C for a list of several third-party administrative utilities.)

If you have a critical problem, the monitors built into SQL*DBA can help reveal the root of the problem. Chapters 8 and 10 discussed how to use several of the different SQL*DBA monitors to firefight problems that need immediate attention.

By no means has this chapter discussed the hundreds of tuning knobs and dials you can adjust for the Oracle7 database server. However, this chapter has focused on the major techniques for making noticeable improvements when tuning an Oracle7 database server:

- Tuning the operating system with the Oracle7 server in mind
- Reducing disk I/O by adjusting the sizes of the Oracle7 memory caches
- Eliminating disk I/O contention for Oracle7 database files and data
- Sizing rollback segments correctly to reduce dynamic space allocations and deallocations
- Tuning the number of processes in an Oracle7 multithreaded server
- Reducing performance hits caused by checkpoints

This chapter concludes Part II of the book, which has covered database administration. The chapters in Part III explain what to consider when developing client applications for an Oracle7 client/server database system.

PART III

Application Development in an Oracle7 Client/Server System

The database server is the central component in a client/server system. However, users can't accomplish any work unless there are client applications that interface with the database server. Chapters 13 through 19 concentrate on the features of Oracle7 that application developers must understand when developing client applications, as well as on other Oracle products developers can use to create client applications.

CHAPTER

THIRTEEN

Application Development for Oracle7

- Defining an application's purpose and logic

- Planning an application's schema

- Determining what goes into a client application

- Using the Oracle7 database server to reduce network I/O

This chapter discusses general topics for application development, including

- The responsibilities of the application developer
- A quick guide to distributing the components in a client/server application: which belong in client-side applications and which belong in the Oracle7 database server

What Does an Application Developer Do?

The person who develops client applications for an Oracle7 database system is the application developer. Like the database administrator, the application developer has a distinct set of responsibilities to consider when developing database applications. The next few sections explain the different types of jobs you need to perform as an application developer.

Defining an Application's Purpose

Before you tackle any type of complicated job, whether it is landscaping a yard, designing a new office building, or developing a client database application, it is important to set clear goals for the project. This makes it easy to determine if you have actually accomplished your purpose.

What are the goals when developing a new client database application? The purpose of an application varies, depending on the needs of the users who will eventually use the application to interact with the database information.

For example, suppose a company wants to use Oracle7 to run its business, including everything from sales orders to inventory management. When you sit down to develop custom applications for the company, the first question to ask is, "What are the needs of the application users?" In a typical business setting you'll find requirements like these:

- Many sales people need a quick way to input a large number of sales orders.
- The marketing folks need to analyze information about sales revenues and product sales.
- The people running the company warehouse need to generate shipping labels and manage product inventory.

This first look at various user needs reveals some early application development goals:

- To provide the sales department with an OLTP application for sales order input
- To provide the marketing department with a decision-support application to permit canned and ad hoc queries for various types of database information
- To provide the shipping department with a set of standard reports for product inventory and shipping labels

From this point you can refine the application development goals into more focused objectives, which will help you make a few more important decisions. For example, members of the sales department are used to filling out paper forms to enter sales information. You might decide to use Oracle Forms to create a client application that mimics the familiar paper form. And executives in the marketing department probably want some standard reports to analyze product sales and sales revenues. You might use Oracle Reports and Oracle Graphics (or other third-party tools) to create some predefined reports and graphs for the marketing department.

As this simple business case demonstrates, you will learn more and more about the application development process as you drill down further into your application goals. You can tell what users really need to be productive in their work, and you can determine which application tools you need to build the enabling client applications.

Defining an Application's Logic

Once you know what you want an application to do, it is time to get on with the job of building the application. Using the application development tool of your choice, you must define the presentation and the internal *logic* of the application.

When defining an application's logic, there are a number of factors to consider. One primary development objective is to present an intuitive user interface that application users can employ to accomplish work with ease. Prudent use of common graphical user interface elements, such as menus, buttons, check boxes, radio button lists, list boxes, and popup menus make working with an application easy to learn, less prone to errors, and consequently very productive.

If you use a 3GL application development approach—for example, with a C compiler and Oracle's Pro*C precompiler—you have to know how to manually create a user interface in the source code of the application. Many language compilers can take advantage of standard windowing libraries to make user interface development somewhat easier, but 3GL user interface development is still a job best suited for experienced programmers.

Putting together a great user interface can be relatively simple when you use a 4GL application development tool, even if you have no programming experience. That's because most 4GL environments have easy-to-use screen painting and visual layout capabilities.

Behind the covers of an application's user interface, the application must have the necessary program code to perform the operations of the application, including any SQL or PL/SQL to interact with the database. When you create an application using a 3GL development tool, not only do you have to write the source code for the user interface, you have to write the source code for the internal application logic and database access calls. The disadvantage of the 3GL approach is that you must be experienced in working with a 3GL to get the job done swiftly. The advantage is that once you know what you are doing, 3GLs offer a great deal of flexibility and power that you can tap into when developing an application.

On the other hand, 4GL tools automatically generate most of the internal application program from the elements you create for a database application. Most 4GLs even have features that will create the necessary SQL to access database information, although they also allow you to write your own SQL. While the 4GL approach to application development can make complicated programming tasks much easier to accomplish, they generally take away some level of the flexibility and power 3GLs can deliver.

As with any application development process, it is important to create the application so it performs well. However, because application processing is distributed across a network in a client/server database system, it is also important to design client database applications so they do not place an excessive burden on either the central database server or the network. For example, a poorly designed client application might not take advantage of database stored procedures to minimize network access. As a result, the application performs an excessive amount of network I/O, which saturates the network and degrades the performance of the entire database system for all users. This simple example shows that developers must have a clear understanding of the application development tool and the Oracle7 database server features that are available to create well-behaved client database applications. (The section "Distributing the Application between the Client and the Server" later in this chapter describes the different features in Oracle7 to consider when developing applications for client/server systems.)

Planning an Application's Schema

Part of developing a client database application is defining the application's schema, or the set of database objects necessary to support the application. For example, every application works with a set of database tables and views that hold information of interest. In addition, other types of database objects may be necessary to support the application, such as table indexes, synonyms, and sequences. Since the developer must create and test the functionality of the application, the developer is the appropriate person to design the application's schema.

There are several ways a developer can design a new application's schema. The easiest approach is using a CASE or database design tool to model the entities and relationships within the application schema. When a design is finished, most CASE tools generate a DDL script the developer can then use to automatically create the new schema. Most CASE tools also store the definition of the schema in a repository, where entity and relationship information is available to other tools for automatic application generation. If a CASE or database design tool is not available to help automate the creation of an application schema, the developer must accomplish the job manually, using SQL commands.

After trying a new database application in a test environment, developers usually hand off the new application to the database administrator for installation into a production database environment. Part of this hand-off is a script that includes the DDL commands for creating the new application's schema.

Distributing the Application between the Client and the Server

Recall that a client/server database application is a fancy term for distributed application processing. In other words, application processing in a client/server environment is distributed between the client application and the database server. To develop sound applications for client/server systems, you need to understand how to distribute the parts of the application between components of the system. The next two sections provide some guidelines for what goes where in a client/server database application.

What's in the Client Application?

The preceding sections have already given you a good idea of what should be in the client application. Client-side applications should focus primarily on presenting and/or analyzing data in a way that is useful for its audience.

Network traffic is one of the most important areas to focus on when developing client applications. Pay close attention to how an application sends information to or receives information from the database server and how much data it sends or receives. In general, network I/O tends to be a bottleneck for application performance in client/server systems. The less network I/O an application generates, the better the application and the entire system will perform.

The key to eliminating unnecessary network traffic from a client application is understanding and taking advantage of Oracle SQL and other features in the Oracle7 database server. For example, consider a reporting application that wants to display total dollars for all of the line items in each sales order. This calculation involves two steps: multiplying the quantity of each line item by the item's unit price and then totaling the amount for all line items for each order. One way the application can accomplish this operation is to request the values for each column, a row at a time, and then perform the calculations inside the application using local variables:

```
SELECT orderid, quantity, unitprice
  FROM item, stock
  WHERE item.stockid=stock.id
  ORDER BY orderid

ORDERID     QUANTITY    UNITPRICE
---------   ----------  -----------
        1           1         6.03
        1           4         21.4
        1           2        87.12
        2           2         8.97
        2           3         21.4
   .
   .
   .
-- other application logic
```

This query sends order ID, quantity, and unit prices for all the line items in the ITEM table. This can be a lot of data if your company is doing a brisk business and the ITEM table has many rows for sales orders.

A more efficient way of performing the same operation with less network I/O would be to have the database server perform the calculations and then ship only the results across the network:

```
SELECT orderid, SUM(quantity*unitprice)
  FROM item, stock
  WHERE item.stockid=stock.id
  GROUP BY orderid
  ORDER BY orderid

ORDERID   SUM(QUANTITY*UNITPRICE)
--------  -----------------------
       1                   265.87
       2                    82.14
   .
   .
   .
```

As you can see, the second query is much more efficient than the first option because it uses a combination of SQL, an Oracle7 SQL function (SUM), and a GROUP BY clause to have the Oracle7 server do the calculations and send less data across the network.

This simple example illustrates how you can use SQL and SQL functions to reduce the amount of network traffic in a client/server environment. It illustrates that developers must be intimately familiar with SQL to create good client database applications. (For more information about SQL and SQL functions, see Chapter 5 and Appendix A.)

What's in the Database Server?

Earlier releases of the Oracle database server supported client connections across a network using SQL*Net. However, Oracle7 is the first release of the Oracle server that has the essential features for client/server work—features to reduce network I/O between client applications and servers. The following sections examine the features of Oracle7 that developers should take advantage of in a client/server system.

Integrity Constraints

All client applications must adhere to a set of predefined data integrity rules and business rules to make sure all of a database's data is valid. (Chapter 2 discussed domain, entity, and referential integrity, and business rules.) There are two ways an application developer can enforce a simple integrity rule:

- Letting the application perform the integrity check
- Using Oracle7 integrity constraints

Letting the Application Perform the Integrity Check   For example, assume you want to make sure all transactions insert new sales orders such that the customer ID in each sales order matches a valid customer ID in the CUSTOMER table. This is simple referential integrity. One way to enforce the referential integrity rule is to have the application perform the integrity check itself. First, an application transaction can query the database to make sure the customer exists in the CUSTOMER table. If the query finds the customer, it must then lock the corresponding row for the duration of the transaction to make sure no one deletes the customer before the transaction inserts the new sales order. Finally, the transaction can safely insert a new row using the validated customer ID and then commit the transaction to release the lock on the CUSTOMER table. Here is an anonymous PL/SQL block that demonstrates client-side application code to enforce referential integrity:

```
DECLARE
  flag INTEGER;
BEGIN
SELECT id INTO flag
  FROM customer
  WHERE id = 3
  FOR UPDATE OF id;

IF SQL%FOUND THEN
  INSERT INTO orders
    VALUES (5, 3, SYSDATE, null, null, 'F');

-- other application logic
COMMIT;

END IF;
END;
```

This process is just one method you can use to enforce the referential integrity rule inside an application. In any event, you can see that the application spends lots of time requesting and sending data across the network just to enforce a simple integrity rule.

Using Oracle7 Integrity Constraints   For several reasons, a better way to enforce simple integrity rules such as referential integrity is to use Oracle7 integrity constraints. For one, you can easily create integrity constraints along with a table definition. Developers can be more productive because they do not have to create, test, and debug complicated data integrity logic to enforce simple integrity rules. Second, an integrity constraint is a centralized method for enforcing an integrity rule. Therefore, Oracle7 forces all applications to adhere to the same integrity rule. (If the application performs the integrity check, developers have to work hard to create, test, and debug the same data integrity logic in each application.) Finally, because Oracle7 enforces integrity constraints without creating any network I/O, client/server systems do not suffer from performance penalties caused by network access. To learn more about data integrity and integrity constraints, see Chapter 2, which introduces integrity constraints, and Chapter 15, which explains how to create integrity constraints for the tables in an Oracle7 database.

Database Triggers

Applications often need to enforce complex business rules that you cannot express using integrity constraints. Rather than revert to enforcing a complex integrity rule inside an application, you can use database triggers to make Oracle7 enforce the rule. By using database triggers to enforce complex business rules, you gain the advantages of ease of creation, centralized rule enforcement, and elimination of unnecessary network I/O that simple integrity rules also provide.

You can use database triggers to centralize and automate other types of application logic too. For example, consider the TOTAL column of the ITEM table. The value in the TOTAL column is the quantity of parts ordered, multiplied by the unit price of the part. The part's unit price is in the STOCK table. How does an application figure out a value for the TOTAL column when inserting a new line item? One way would be to let the application perform the operation using SQL statements:

```
DECLARE
partprice REAL;
BEGIN
SELECT unitprice INTO partprice
  FROM stock
  WHERE id = 4

-- other application logic for calculation

INSERT INTO item VALUES (...)
END;
```

Notice that the application makes a request across the network for the unit price of a part and then inserts the row with a total for the line item. Keep in mind that the application also must include similar logic to account for situations in which users update the quantity of a line item in the ITEM table. Additionally, many users may be placing and updating orders at the same time. In short, this method for calculating the TOTAL column can create lots of network traffic in a client/server system.

Alternatively, you could use a database trigger to derive the TOTAL value for a line item automatically and without any network access when users insert new rows or update the QUANTITY column in the ITEM table. Here is an example:

```
CREATE TRIGGER linetotal
BEFORE INSERT OR UPDATE OF quantity, stockid ON item
FOR EACH ROW
DECLARE
```

```
   itemprice REAL;
BEGIN
   SELECT unitprice INTO itemprice
     FROM stock WHERE id = :new.stockid;
   :new.total := :new.quantity * itemprice;
END linetotal;
```

After creating the LINETOTAL trigger, application developers don't have to consider the problem of keeping the TOTAL column current when programming applications. Furthermore, all clients in the network database system benefit from fewer network I/Os.

This is just one example of how developers can take advantage of database triggers in an Oracle7 system. (Chapter 2 introduced database triggers, and Chapter 18 explains how to create database triggers for an application schema.)

Procedures and Packages

The preceding two sections explained how you can reduce network I/O in an Oracle7 client/server database system: by moving application logic to the database server in the form of integrity constraints and database triggers. You can reduce client/server application network I/O even more by distributing other types of application logic to the database server, using stored procedures. Then, instead of using multiple-network intensive SQL statements to perform database server operations, applications make simple, efficient calls to stored procedures. Packages are a way to encapsulate a number of related procedures inside the database.

Stored Procedures   To illustrate the difference between using SQL and using stored procedures, let's assume you want to insert a new order with some line items. Here's how an application could do this using SQL statements:

```
INSERT INTO orders VALUES (...)
INSERT INTO item VALUES (1, ...)
UPDATE stock SET onhand = ...
INSERT INTO item VALUES (2, ...)
UPDATE stock SET onhand = ...
INSERT INTO item VALUES (3, ...)
UPDATE stock SET onhand = ...
COMMIT;
```

To create a new sales order and insert three line items for the sales order, the application has to issue seven different SQL statements, each of which sends data across the network. To reduce all the network traffic these SQL statements generate in a client/server system, you could create two simple procedures to insert orders and line items:

```
CREATE PROCEDURE placeorder (custid IN INTEGER) AS
BEGIN
  INSERT INTO orders
    VALUES (orderseq.NEXTVAL, custid, SYSDATE, null, null, 'F');
END placeorder;

CREATE PROCEDURE placeitem
  (itemid IN INTEGER, partid IN INTEGER, quan IN INTEGER) AS
BEGIN
  INSERT INTO item (id, orderid, stockid, quantity)
    VALUES (itemid, orderseq.CURRVAL, partid, quan);
  UPDATE stock
    SET onhand = onhand - quan
    WHERE id = partid;
END placeitem;
```

Now, instead of issuing SQL statements to insert a new order and line items, the application can simply call the procedures:

```
placeorder(3)
placeitem(1,3,2);
placeitem(2,8,1);
placeitem(3,9,3);
```

Notice that when an application calls a stored procedure, the only data it sends across the network is the procedure call and the data values for the arguments of the stored procedure.

Packages   Packages are an extension of simple stored procedures, and developers can use them when developing applications. Packages are a way to organize and encapsulate related procedures and functions into a single database program unit on behalf of an application. (To learn more about procedures and packages, see Chapter 18.)

Database Alerts

Database users often need to be alerted when certain things happen in the database so they can take the appropriate actions. For example, if you are an inventory manager, it is important to know when the quantity of any part in stock falls below its reorder point. That way you can order more inventory for the part before it goes out of stock.

Good application designs will include logic to account for alert conditions; this way the application automatically notifies interested application users of alert conditions. For example, when developing an inventory management application, you can program an alert to check for parts that have fallen below their reorder points. One way to accomplish this would be to have the inventory management application regularly issue a SQL query for parts that have fallen below their reorder points:

```
-- every 5 minutes poll for stock problems ...
SELECT id FROM stock
  WHERE onhand < reorder

-- other application code to handle the alert
```

This method of checking for alert conditions has a significant problem in client/server systems: The constant polling to check for alert conditions creates excessive amounts of network I/O, especially when lots of users poll for lots of alert conditions at the same time. A better way to poll for alert conditions is to use Oracle7 *database alerters*. Database alerters automatically signal interested users when a named event occurs. Using simple procedure calls, applications can register and wait for named alert conditions. (To learn more about Oracle7 database alerters, see Chapter 18.)

This chapter has laid the groundwork for understanding the application development process in an Oracle7 client/server database system. You should have a clear understanding of what the application developer does and what types of things go into a client-side database application. The next chapter introduces the Oracle tools and how to use them to develop a simple application.

CHAPTER

FOURTEEN

Overview of Application Development Tools

- Designing, documenting, and validating an Oracle7 application development process

- Using Oracle CASE tools to generate an application schema and all application models

- Porting Oracle applications without modifying application code

- Enhancing an Oracle7 application for client/server systems

This chapter shows you how to develop custom Oracle7 client/server applications from start to finish, using some of the primary tools in the Oracle Cooperative Development Environment (CDE) tool set:

- The Oracle CASE products, including CASE* Dictionary, CASE* Designer, and CASE* Generator

- SQL*Forms 3.0 (character mode)

- Oracle Forms 4.0 for Microsoft Windows

Instead of teaching you how to press buttons and choose menu items, this chapter takes you through a very simple application development process to illustrate some important benefits when using the Oracle CDE tools:

- Using the Oracle CASE tools to design, document, and validate an Oracle7 application development process for better-designed applications the first time

- Using the Oracle CASE tools to automatically generate an application schema and all application modules

- Porting Oracle applications among different operating systems and user interfaces with little or no modification of application code

- Enhancing an Oracle7 application for client/server systems

This chapter focuses on designing and creating simple form applications for the application schema used throughout this book. To begin, let's take a look at the Oracle CASE tools and the fundamentals of the application development process.

Using the Oracle CASE Products to Design and Create Form Applications

This section explains how to use the Oracle CASE tools to design an application schema and generate form applications for Oracle7. But before focusing on the specifics of the Oracle CASE tools, let's learn a little more about the fundamental stages of application system development and maintenance.

Stages of the System Development Life Cycle

The overall goal of computerizing a business's operations with a client/server database system like Oracle7 is to make the business run more efficiently than it otherwise would. For the computer system to successfully meet this high-level objective, the system designers must study and understand the exact needs of the business and its workers and then design and implement a system that adequately addresses these needs. Only then will the business benefit from the computer system that controls the lifeblood of the business, the business's information.

In a nutshell, these are the primary stages of the system development life cycle: strategize, analyze, design, implement, test, and move into production. Let's take a closer look at the distinct stages in the life cycle of a business system.

Strategy   The strategy stage is the initial stage of a business system's life cycle. At this stage you focus on developing an initial, high-level description of the business and the development plan. A good strategy phase always includes initial and follow-up interviews of company personnel to identify and validate key requirements of the system.

Analysis   After strategizing, you can gather specific information, analyze the specific requirements of the business and its workers, and then produce a set of clear-cut functional requirements that the system must address. Like the strategy stage, the analysis stage requires interviews of company personnel to help fill in the details and point out missing information.

Design   Once the analysis stage is successful, you can map identified system requirements to specific application schema and module components to form an initial system design. It is during the design phase that the front-end client applications and the back-end application schema/database start to take shape.

Implementation   Once a system design is available, you can build the actual database and client applications to support the system design. Implementation of new applications typically takes place in a test system so as not to detrimentally affect current production application systems.

Testing   After implementation, you should thoroughly test the system, validating its operations and seeking feedback on user interfaces. If necessary, modify the components of the system to adjust for any problems uncovered during the test stage.

Production   Once you validate a new system, you can move the system from the test environment to the production environment so the business can realize the many benefits of computerizing the associated operations.

What Are CASE Tools?

Computer-aided software engineering (CASE) tools like the Oracle CASE tools are specifically designed to address the different stages of the system life cycle. CASE tools incorporate modeling techniques so system developers can easily represent the processes and data required to make a system work. As a result, CASE tools make system development a logical, documented, and thorough yet reasonably quick process. Better still, CASE tools really pay off because you can develop sound systems from the start. This way, users can be productive with the first version of the application, and developers and administrators don't have to spend lots of time correcting for unforeseen problems or bad application design not considered during development.

The CASE tools have yet other features that can help you save time maintaining a system once it is running. For example, the Oracle CASE tools have impact analysis utilities that allow you to report answers to questions such as, "What application modules are affected when I change the definition of this table?"

Understanding the Roles of the Different Oracle CASE Tools

Let's take a quick look at the different CASE products that Oracle offers so you can understand their role in the system development process.

CASE*Dictionary: The Repository for CASE Application Development Information

CASE*Dictionary is the foundation of the Oracle CASE application development system; it is the repository or dictionary that stores all the information you define throughout the many stages of the system development life cycle. To make things simple, you can consider CASE*Dictionary a back-end database that serves the other Oracle CASE tools. However, as you will see in the following sections, CASE*Dictionary is more than just a set of database tables that hold system development information. CASE*Dictionary itself is a robust form-based application that allows you to completely define all the information necessary for the strategy, analysis, design, and implementation phases of the system development life cycle. In fact, CASE*Dictionary's screens frequently pop up to supplement the functionality of the other Oracle CASE tools.

CASE*Designer: The Graphical Front End for Modeling a System's Life Cycle Stages

If you consider CASE*Dictionary the back-end database or repository that stores all system development information, you can consider CASE*Designer a front-end tool that you use to model the processes and data in a system. CASE*Designer has a set of graphical modeling tools you can use to intuitively define the strategy, analysis, and design phases of the system life cycle. CASE*Designer is fully integrated with CASE*Dictionary, so CASE*Dictionary automatically records system development information as you design process and data models on your screen. And when specific information is necessary that can't be added on a diagram, CASE*Designer automatically pops up the appropriate CASE*Dictionary screens so you can enter all the details about your system designs.

CASE*Generator: The Link to Automatic Application Generation

Once you complete the strategy, analysis, and design stages of system development, it's time to implement the system. CASE*Generator makes this an automatic process by using the information in the CASE*Dictionary repository to generate modules of application code, including menus, forms, and reporting applications—all without your having to type a single line of 3GL, 4GL, or SQL code. CASE*Generator can even generate DDL scripts that create the necessary tables, views, indexes, sequences, and other objects in an application schema.

The Starting Point: Defining a New Application and Granting Application Access in CASE*Dictionary

Now that you have an idea of how to use the different Oracle CASE products, let's begin using these tools to develop a very simple computer system for a fictitious company.

Before you can use any of the Oracle CASE products to develop an application, you must meet several requirements. First, you have to be a valid Oracle7 database user in the database that stores the CASE*Dictionary. Next, the CASE*Dictionary manager has to name a new application in the CASE*Dictionary and then give you access to both the CASE*Dictionary tables and its views, as well as the specific application within CASE*Dictionary. To accomplish this, the CASE*Dictionary manager uses some special management screens of CASE*Dictionary that make creating a new application and granting CASE*Dictionary access a straightforward process. The remaining sections in this chapter assume that the CASE*Dictionary manager has already performed this process.

The next few sections, which focus on the strategy stage of system development, discuss how to use CASE*Designer to put together the high-level process and data models that describe the new system.

An Introduction to the Strategy Stage

The strategy stage is the initial, high-level definition of all system elements. The Oracle CASE products allow you to define the following types of system elements:

- A *business unit* is a part of a company that is treated as an individual unit. Good examples of business units are divisions and departments.

- An *entity* is a unit of information that has significance within the organization. *Attributes* are the details of an entity.

- A *domain* is a business constraint that determines acceptable values for an attribute or a set of attributes.

- A *relationship* indicates how two system elements relate to one another.

- A *function* is a process that the business performs.

- A *data flow* is the movement of data between one function and another.

- A *term* is a special word that has meaning within a business.

As you can see, a business system can have many different types of elements. Although all system elements are important, in the interest of brevity this chapter concentrates on a subset of the most important system elements: functions, data flows, entities, attributes, and relationships.

Strategy: Defining Business Functions with CASE*Designer

The first step in the strategy stage of system development is to define the processes in the system—the overall functions of the business. This way you can get an idea of just what the business is trying to accomplish and how the computer system can help meet those objectives.

Starting CASE*Designer

To begin system development, start CASE*Designer. After CASE*Designer starts, it asks for your database username and password, as well as the name and version of the application system. This chapter looks at the development of the application system named SORD, short for Sales Orders. After you enter the application name SORD and version 1 (since it is new), CASE*Designer presents its main window, as shown in Figure 14.1.

Starting the Function Hierarchy Diagrammer

The options of the CASE*Designer menus allow you access to many tools you can use to develop an application system. Let's start the strategy stage of system development by defining the processes or functions for the business.

FIGURE 14.1:

Main window of CASE*Designer

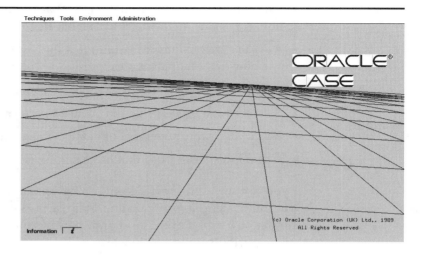

Select Function Diagrammer from the Techniques menu of CASE*Designer to display the Function Hierarchy Diagrammer in a new window. Figure 14.2 shows the Function Hierarchy Diagrammer.

FIGURE 14.2:

CASE*Designer Function Hierarchy Diagrammer

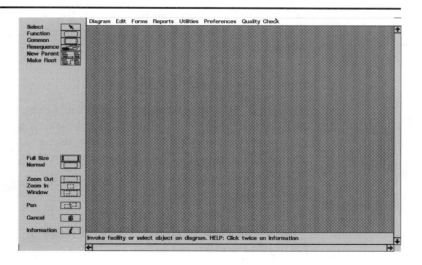

The diagrammer's sidebar has several tools for defining the business functions on a diagram. If you have ever used a graphical tool before, you will probably recognize the functions that the lower set of tools perform—simple window operations such as zoom in, zoom out, full size, and normal magnification of the diagram. Later in this chapter you will see what some of the other, less recognizable tools let you accomplish.

When you start the diagrammer, it automatically gives you a new, untitled diagram to start work on. What you are about to do is create a hierarchical list of all the functions the fictitious business carries out.

Creating a Root Business Function

The first step is to create the *start*, or *root business*, *function*, the function you think is the primary function of the business. In this case the company's root function is to sell widgets to customers. Therefore, begin the business function diagram by selecting the Function tool from the sidebar; then click somewhere in the center of the diagram. CASE*Designer adds a new function and a label to the diagram and waits for you to enter the name of the business function. You can type the label **SORD** to correspond to the application system name and then press the [TTF] key to move to the description field for the business function. Here you can enter the description for the function, **Sell widgets to customers**. When you are finished, press [TTF] again, and CASE*Designer adds the function to the screen, as shown in Figure 14.3.

FIGURE 14.3:

Beginning of a function hierarchy diagram—the root business function

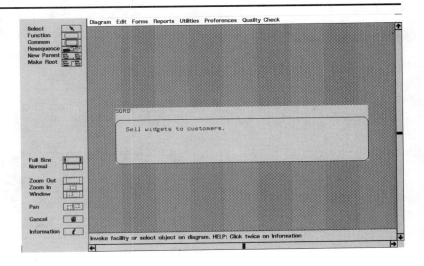

NOTE

Throughout this chapter, different keys are identified by their functions rather than by an exact keyboard name. That's because the Oracle products run on many different types of computers, operating systems, and terminals. As a result, Oracle binds product function keys to different keyboard keys depending on the system you are using. Using the help facility of each Oracle product, you can quickly display the key bindings for the different product functions.

Creating Child Business Functions

The next step is to add *child business functions* (more detailed functions) underneath the root function to flesh out more detail about your business's operations. For example, one child function is to track customers who buy the company's products. To add this new function as a child to the root function, select the Function tool again; then click-and-drag the mouse pointer from inside the root function to a point on the diagram below the root function. CASE*Designer adds a new function label, where you can type the name of the function and its description. When you have finished adding the new child function to track customers, your diagram should look something like the one in Figure 14.4.

FIGURE 14.4:

The root business function and a child business function

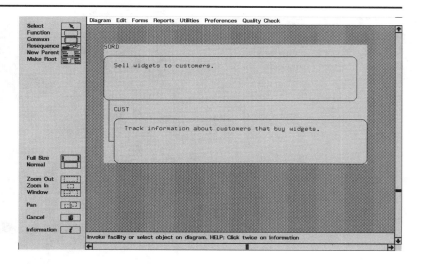

> **TIP**
>
> As you modify a function hierarchy diagram, CASE*Designer automatically records your actions in the CASE*Dictionary repository by performing database transactions. Therefore, you never have to worry about saving your work as you go.

You can continue to develop your business function diagram to any level of detail you want. You can continue adding child functions to the root function or add child functions to child functions to document deeper levels of detail about the company's business processes. At a minimum, add two other child functions to the root function—Inventory, with a description of "Track information about widgets in inventory," and Sales, with a description of "Track information about widget sales." Eventually, you might end up with a complicated function hierarchy diagram similar to the one shown in Figure 14.5.

FIGURE 14.5:

Finished first draft of a business function hierarchy diagram

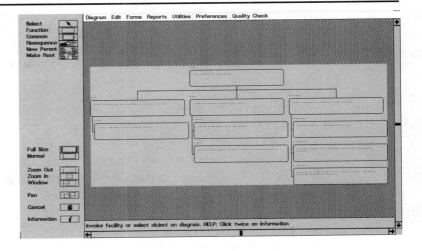

Displaying Information in the Function Hierarchy Diagrammer

As Figure 14.5 shows, you can use the options of the Function Hierarchy Diagrammer's Preferences menu to rearrange the layout of a function hierarchy diagram to show its functions in a format that best suits your needs: horizontal (as in previous figures), vertical, or a hybrid of horizontal and vertical (as in Figure 14.5). And if a diagram contains many different function levels, you can concentrate on specific areas by using the Reopen Up and Reopen Down options on the Diagram menu to open and close lower levels of the child functions throughout a diagram.

TIP

When you open an existing function hierarchy diagram, CASE*Designer lets you specify the start function for the diagram and the number of levels underneath this function that you want to display. That way you can focus on the specific area of the diagram from the start of a new diagramming session.

Fixing Mistakes in a Function Hierarchy Diagram

As you design a function hierarchy diagram, you will no doubt make mistakes, but don't worry about them. You can edit a function label or description simply by selecting it and then choosing Edit ➤ Edit. If you decide that you added a function in error, you can delete it by selecting it and then selecting Edit ➤ Delete. You can also move functions within the hierarchy using the Make Parent and Make Root sidebar tools.

At this point you might be wondering if any more detail is necessary for each business function. During the strategy stage, it is not necessary to include detailed information about each function, as long as you provide each function's name and description. Once you have put together a high-level business function diagram, it's time to print and circulate it for review so you can go back later during the analysis stage and add more details about each function.

Printing a Function Hierarchy Diagram for Review

Once you finish the first draft of a business function hierarchy diagram, you are ready to solicit initial feedback for additional, missing, or inaccurate information. You can print a function hierarchy diagram by selecting Reports ➤ Function Hierarchy in the Function Hierarchy Diagrammer and then filling out the information in the report form.

NOTE

When you select options from some of the CASE*Designer menus, CASE*Designer shows you screens that originate from CASE*Dictionary. For example, when you choose to print a report from CASE*Designer, the CASE*Dictionary Report Parameters screen appears. As mentioned earlier, CASE*Dictionary is the foundation of all the Oracle CASE products and often serves to supplement the functionality of the other CASE products. When you are done using a CASE*Dictionary screen, you can exit the form to return to the calling CASE product. For example, when you finish printing a CASE*Designer report, you can return to CASE*Designer by exiting the Report Parameters screen.

Distribute the printout to different types of workers throughout an organization, asking for feedback to help you make sure you have correctly identified all the functions the business performs. Based on this feedback, you probably will have to modify the diagram to produce a final, working draft of the function hierarchy diagram. During the review process, also ask for specific information about each business function, such as frequency of occurrence, growth rates that are expected, and so on. You'll use this information later on, in the analysis stage, to fill in some more details about your business functions.

Closing the Function Hierarchy Diagrammer

When you have finished using the Function Hierarchy Diagrammer, you can choose to close it to free up space on your display terminal, or you can leave it open so you can work with several CASE*Designer diagrammers in tandem. The latter option is often useful when you want to see related information on the same screen—for example, how business functions appear in a hierarchical diagram and in a data flow diagram (see the next section). However, if you want to free up window space, minimize the window (specific to your GUI environment) or close the Function Hierarchy Diagrammer by choosing Diagram ➤ Quit.

Strategy: Designing a Data Flow Diagram with CASE*Designer

The next step in the strategy stage is to add life to your business functions by putting together a data flow diagram. Data flow diagrams help you better understand how a company's business functions force information to flow throughout the organization. You see where data originates and where it ends up. You see which functions depend on other functions to accomplish work and get an idea of the critical functions in the system. In summary, by understanding the flow of data throughout a company, you can develop better supporting systems.

Starting the Dataflow Diagrammer

To diagram the data flow in a system, you use the CASE*Designer Dataflow Diagrammer. To start this diagrammer, select Techniques ➤ Dataflow Diagrammer in the main CASE*Designer window. Figure 14.6 shows the Dataflow Diagrammer.

FIGURE 14.6:

Dataflow Diagrammer of CASE*Designer

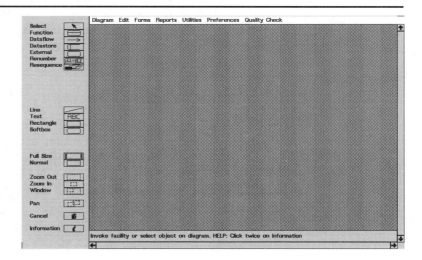

The Dataflow Diagrammer has its own special set of sidebar tools that allow you to define data flow diagram objects, such as functions, data flows, data stores, and external objects. It also has the standard set of tools to manage the view in the window, as well as some special drawing tools you can use to illustrate a diagram with background objects for emphasis. (For example, you might draw a map to point out where certain business functions take place.)

Creating a New Data Flow Diagram

Once the Dataflow Diagrammer is started, you can create a new data flow diagram by selecting Diagram ➤ New. CASE*Designer presents you with a dialog where you enter the name of the function label for the diagram. Enter the name of the business function for which you would like to show the data flow. For this first diagram, let's show the data flow around the root business function, SORD. After you type **SORD** and accept the dialog, CASE*Designer asks you to specify a page size for the diagram and locate the page in the diagrammer. Then it places the root business function in the diagram, as shown in Figure 14.7.

FIGURE 14.7:

Root business function SORD in the Dataflow Diagrammer

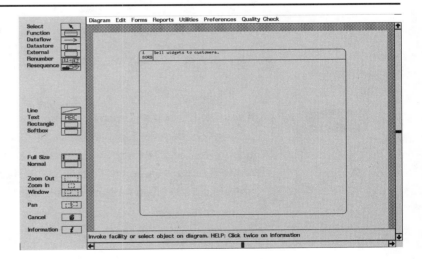

Loading Child Functions into the Diagram

Now it is time to bring in the child functions that are internal to the root business function to show how data flows throughout this part of the system. The Dataflow Diagrammer of CASE*Designer allows you to easily load previously defined business functions. When you select Edit ➤ Copy In Function, a dialog appears with the child functions of the diagram's root function. From this dialog, select a child and place it on the diagram. Repeat this process with each child until you have a data flow diagram similar to the one shown in Figure 14.8.

FIGURE 14.8:

Root business function and its children in the Dataflow Diagrammer

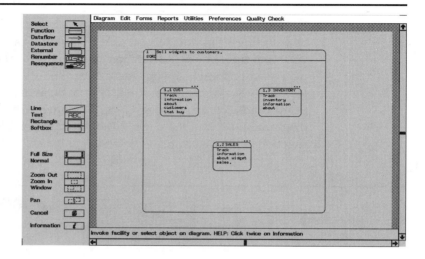

<table>
<tr><td>**NOTE**</td><td>If you want to add a new child function that you did not think of when putting together the function hierarchy diagram, select the Function sidebar tool and add it to the diagram. Like the Function sidebar tool of the Function Hierarchy Diagrammer, this tool lets you name and provide a description for the new functions you add.</td></tr>
</table>

Notice in Figure 14.8 that each child function has an ellipsis (…) along its top-right edge. The ellipses indicate that each of the functions has child functions of its own. However, you cannot add a child function's children to the diagram because the Dataflow Diagrammer allows only two levels of depth in a data flow diagram. Instead you can create separate data flow diagrams for each node in each level of a business function hierarchy.

Adding Data Flows to the Diagram

Unlike function hierarchy diagrams, data flow diagrams show the movement of data among the different processes in a business. Once the functions appear in a data flow diagram, you can easily add data flows among them using the Dataflow sidebar tool of the Dataflow Diagrammer: Select the Dataflow tool; then click-and-drag the mouse pointer from inside the function that creates the data flow to the function the data flow acts upon. CASE*Designer adds an arrow from one function to the other and then gives you a label for entering a description to indicate what type of data is moving between the functions. For example, since inventory supplies the products for sales, it's logical to have a data flow named "products" that flows from the Inventory function to the Sales function, as shown in Figure 14.9.

FIGURE 14.9:

Products data flow between the Inventory and Sales functions

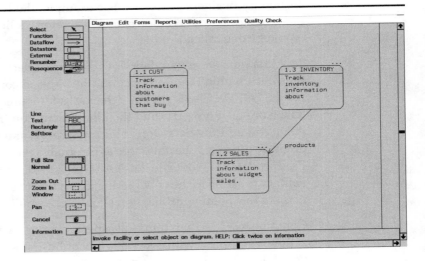

You can continue to flesh out the data flows in a system by repeating the steps just given.

NOTE As you continue to develop data flow diagrams, you will probably need to adjust the placement or size of different diagram objects. To size an object, select it to reveal sizing handles. To move an object, select it and then click-and-drag the object to the desired location. As with the Function Hierarchy Diagrammer, you can edit the text of labels and descriptions using Edit ➤ Edit and delete objects using Edit ➤ Delete.

Adding Data Stores to the Diagram

Unlike function hierarchy diagrams, with data flow diagrams you can link functions to data by adding data stores. A *data store* is a storage area for the data used or created by business processes. For example, the Inventory function must have a place to store product information. Therefore, a likely data store in this diagram would be one called Product.

To add a data store to a data flow diagram, select the Datastore sidebar tool and then click within the root function (the large, encompassing function, in this case named SORD). CASE*Designer then asks for a unique identifying number for the data store (just type **D1**) and then the description (**PRODUCT**) for the data store. After you add the data store, you can select it and move it anywhere on the diagram. To represent the data store as external to the root business function, move the Product data store outside the SORD function. Finally, add a data flow from the Inventory function to the new Product data store to show that Inventory tracks products. At this point your diagram should look similar to the one in Figure 14.10.

Continue to add to and refine all aspects of your data flow diagram. If your organization is complex, with several levels of business functions, you can create additional data flow diagrams to reveal data movement through each child function of the system. When you have completed the data flow diagrams for the company's business functions, circulate reports of these diagrams for feedback that can enhance the completeness and accuracy of system development.

FIGURE 14.10:

Data flow diagram with the new Product data store

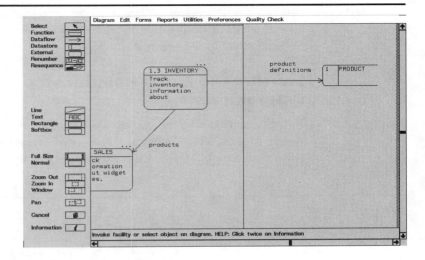

Saving a Data Flow Diagram

As you add work with the Dataflow Diagrammer, it automatically saves system information about functions and data flows in the CASE*Dictionary. However, you must also save the layout of your data flow diagrams. To save your diagram, simply select Diagram ➤ Save.

Closing the Dataflow Diagrammer

As with any diagrammer of CASE*Designer, you can leave the Dataflow Diagrammer open while you work with other diagrammers. If you want to close the Dataflow Diagrammer, select Diagram ➤ Quit.

Strategy: Creating an Entity-Relationship Diagram with CASE*Designer

Once you have completed business function diagrams and data flow diagrams for a system, you should have a solid understanding of the processes in the system. Now it's time to define the data that supports the business processes.

You can model a system's data with *entity-relationship (ER) diagrams*. An entity is a related set of attributes that represent system data. The entities of a system often have specifically defined relationships.

Starting the Entity Relationship Diagrammer

To define a system's data, you use the Entity Relationship Diagrammer of CASE*Designer. To start, select Techniques ➤ Entity Diagrammer in the main CASE*Designer window. Figure 14.11 shows the Entity Relationship Diagrammer.

FIGURE 14.11:
CASE*Designer Entity Relationship Diagrammer

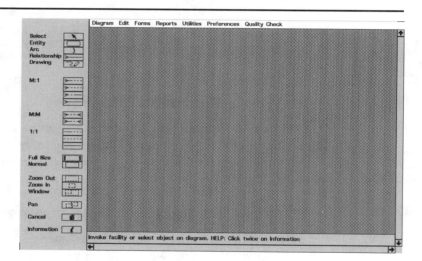

Notice that the Entity Relationship Diagrammer has its own set of sidebar tools that you can use to put together ER diagrams. Let's learn how to use them by creating a new ER diagram for the SORD application.

Creating a New ER Diagram

Begin a new diagram by selecting Diagram ➤ New. CASE*Designer asks you to enter a name for the new diagram. Since this simple application system, with just a few bits of information, will require only one ER diagram to document all the data, you can name the new diagram SORD and select OK. Then select a page size for the new diagram and position it in the diagrammer. Now you are ready to begin developing the ER diagram for the system.

NOTE   If your application system is large and complex, you will probably have many different entities. For this reason it is best to create a number of ER diagrams, each focusing on a specific area of the business. Since CASE*Designer allows you to place the same entity on any number of ER diagrams, you can easily show the relationships among many detailed ER diagrams.

Representing System Data: Creating Entities in an ER Diagram

After studying the processes of a business, you should have a pretty good idea of the data the system will generate. With this information you can define the entities that represent how the system should store its data. For example, it's apparent from the earlier process diagrams that entities are needed to store information about the company's products, the sales orders for these products, and the customers who order the company's products.

To create a new entity, select the Entity sidebar tool and then click anywhere in the diagrammer. CASE*Designer presents you with a new entity and asks for the name of the entity. Type name for the first entity—in this case, **CUSTOMER**—which will store details about customers who order the company's products. Repeat these steps to add the ORDER, ITEM (for order line items), and STOCK entities, which keep track of sales orders and product inventory. When you have added the new entities, your diagram should look like the one in Figure 14.12.

FIGURE 14.12:

ER diagram with the CUSTOMER, ORDER, ITEM, and STOCK entities

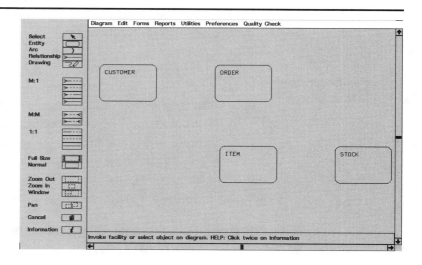

TIP

The Entity Relationship Diagrammer allows you to move, edit, and delete diagram objects just as you can with the other diagrammers of CASE*Designer.

Creating the Relationships That Link Entities in an ER Diagram

Once you have the entities on your diagram, the next task is to indicate how these entities relate to one another. You can draw relationships using the different sidebar tools of the Entity Relationship Diagrammer. The diagram in Figure 14.13 is a key that defines the different relationship tools.

The following relationships exist in the example ER diagram:

- A customer may be the source of one or more sales orders.

- A sales order must be placed by one and only one customer.

- A sales order may be made up of one or more line items.

- A line item must be on one and only one sales order.
- A stock item may be on one or more line items.
- A line item must be for one and only one stock item.

Given these relationships, let's add them graphically to the ER diagram, using the appropriate sidebar tools of the Entity Relationship Diagrammer. For example, to add the relationship between the CUSTOMER and ORDER entities, select the first M:1 tool; then click-and-drag inside the ORDER entity to inside the CUSTOMER entity. When you release the mouse button, CASE*Designer presents you with a label box for each side of the relationship (starting on the side of the first entity in which you clicked) so you can clearly represent the relationship on the diagram. Use similar steps to add the other relationships between the other entities, and you will end up with a diagram similar to the one in Figure 14.14.

FIGURE 14.13:

Key to the different relationship sidebar tools of the Entity Relationship Diagrammer

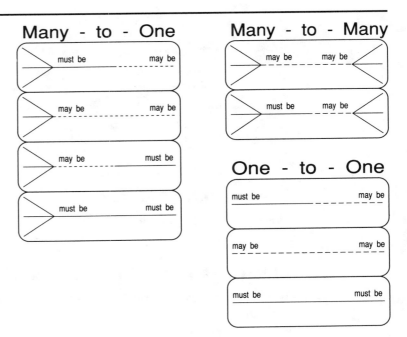

FIGURE 14.14:

ER diagram with relationships

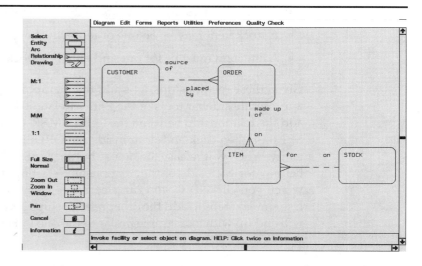

> **NOTE**
>
> As with process diagrams like function hierarchy and data flow diagrams, it is not necessary to fill out the details of entities in an ER diagram during the strategy stage of system development. Instead, concentrate on a high level of information, distribute your diagrams for review, and gather detailed information in preparation for the analysis stage.

Saving an ER Diagram

Once you complete an ER diagram, be sure to save it so you don't lose any of your work. To save an ER diagram, select Diagram ➤ Save.

Closing the Dataflow Diagrammer

You can choose to leave the Entity Relationship Diagrammer open while you work with other diagrammers. If you want to close the Entity Relationship Diagrammer, select Diagram ➤ Quit.

Strategy: Defining a Matrix Diagram with CASE*Designer

The first steps in the strategy stage are to identify and diagram different system elements, primarily the processes and data in a business system. To complete the strategy stage and validate the system at this point, you associate the different elements in the system that depend on one another. This section focuses on linking the system processes with the system data or the functions with the entities so you can later validate the entire system. You can do this graphically with CASE*Designer's Matrix Diagrammer.

Starting the Matrix Diagrammer

To start the Matrix Diagrammer, select Matrix Techniques ➤ Diagrammer in the main CASE*Designer window to display the Matrix Diagrammer shown in Figure 14.15.

FIGURE 14.15:
CASE*Designer Matrix Diagrammer

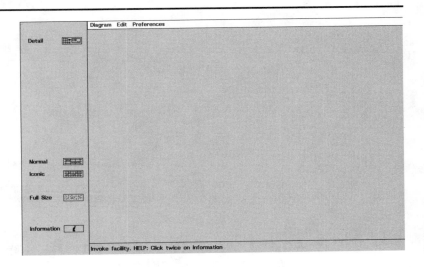

The following sections explain how to use some of the sidebar tools and menus available with the Matrix Diagrammer.

Opening a New Matrix Diagram

The Matrix Diagrammer displays the associations of different system elements as intersections in a standard table (column-and-row) format. You can display matrix diagrams that show the associations between any two types of system objects. Now that you know how to create business functions and entities, let's open the matrix diagram for these objects: Select Diagram ➤ Open. CASE*Designer presents you with a dialog asking you to pick the type of system element to display as columns in the matrix diagram. Select Business Function and then dismiss the dialog. When you do, a dialog appears prompting you to pick the type of system element to display as rows in the matrix diagram. Pick Entity and dismiss the dialog to display a matrix diagram similar to the one in Figure 14.16.

FIGURE 14.16:

Matrix diagram for system business functions and entities

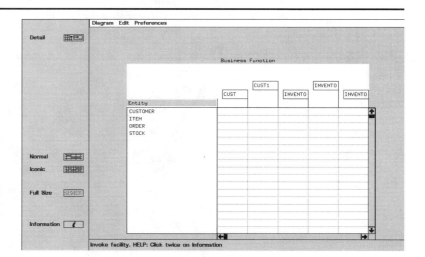

Adjusting Matrix Diagram Display Properties and Widths

As you can see, the information shown in Figure 14.16 is a bit hard to understand— the function labels don't reveal the descriptions of the functions, the labels are too small, and you can't see all of them at the same time. Let's make some adjustments.

First, select the Preferences ➤ Properties to Be Displayed… option. A dialog appears asking which axis you want to adjust the properties for. Select Column from the dialog, dismiss the dialog, and then select Short Definition as the new property for the column headings. Next, adjust the display lengths of column and row elements using the Display Length option of the Preferences menu. In the dialog that appears, enter new display lengths for columns and/or rows and then dismiss the dialog. Finally, select Diagram ➤ Re-open to reopen the matrix diagram with the new display lengths. Figure 14.17 shows a much more readable matrix diagram than the original version.

FIGURE 14.17:
Matrix diagram with adjusted display settings

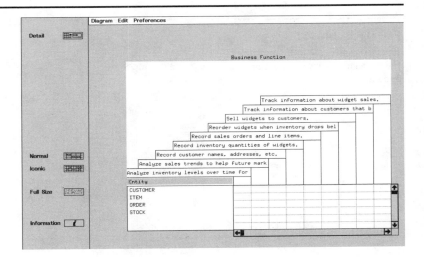

At this point the matrix diagram for system business functions and entities looks great, but there is really no information in the diagram because you haven't indicated any associations yet. The next section discusses how to associate processes and data.

Adding Associations to the Matrix Diagram

As you might imagine, creating an association between a function and an entity is as easy as selecting the respective intersecting cell in the diagram. For example, add a new association by selecting (double-clicking) the cell that intersects the **CUSTOMER** entity and the **Record customer names, addresses, etc.** business function.

A dialog appears that allows you to enter specific information about the association, such as a comment, and indicate what actions the function performs on the entity. In this case you can type **Y** for the Create, Retrieve, Update, and Delete options and then close the dialog. When you return to the matrix diagram, CASE*Designer indicates the new association with an ellipsis.

You can continue adding new associations to the matrix diagram until you feel you have identified all of them. When you are finished, the matrix diagram might resemble the one shown in Figure 14.18.

FIGURE 14.18:
Finished matrix diagram, indicating the associations among functions and entities

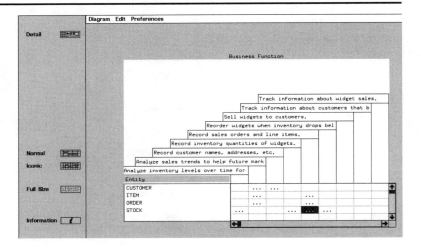

This completes the discussion of the strategy stage in this chapter. Circulate all the initial information you have created and get feedback for the next stage, analysis.

An Introduction to the Analysis Stage

Let's assume that the reviews from the strategy stage produced good feedback and you can move right on with the next stage of system development, analysis. This stage focuses largely on filling in the details for the system elements created in the strategy stage. Let's begin by entering some details about the functions and data flows in the system.

Analysis: Entering Details about Business Functions

You can enter the details about business functions using CASE*Designer from the function hierarchy diagrams or data flow diagrams in which they appear. For the example, select Diagram ➤ Open to open the Dataflow Diagrammer and then open a specific diagram. To enter details about a business function, simply select the function on the diagram and then select Forms ➤ Function Definition. CASE*Designer opens a new window that displays the Function Definition screen of CASE*Dictionary, as shown in Figure 14.19.

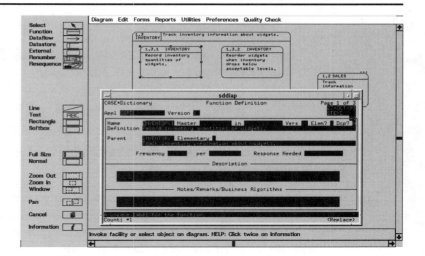

Using the pages of the Function Definition screen, you can enter detailed information about the selected function. For example, from the first page of the screen you can enter an occurrence frequency for the function, responses necessary, and additional notes and comments, and from subsequent pages you can add details about the entities and attributes associated with the function.

NOTE If you completed a matrix diagram for functions and entities, the second page of the Function Definition automatically shows you the entities associated with the selected function.

Use the data gathered from the strategy stage to fill in details about the many business functions in the system.

Analysis: Entering Details about Data Flows

Just as you enter details about functions, you can use the Dataflow Diagrammer to do the same for the data flows in the system. Select a data flow and then select Forms ➤ Dataflow Content Definition. CASE*Designer shows you the Dataflow Content Definition screen of CASE*Dictionary, which you can use to enter details about the selected data flow. As with business functions, be sure to enter the details about every data flow in the system, using the feedback from the strategy stage.

Analysis: Entering Attributes for Entities

Once you have entered the details about the processes in the system, the next step in the analysis phase is to enter the details about the entities in the system—that is, the attributes for each entity. You can enter details for entities from ER diagrams in the Entity Relationship Diagrammer of CASE*Designer. After you open the diagrammer and open an ER diagram, you select an entity and then select Forms ➤ Attribute Definition. CASE*Designer creates a new window to display the Attribute Definition screen of CASE*Dictionary, as shown in Figure 14.20.

Using the pages of this screen, you can create the attributes for the selected entity. For example, the first page, shown in Figure 14.20, creates an attribute called COMPANYNAME for the CUSTOMER entity. Figure 14.21 shows the second page of the Attribute Definition screen, which allows you to enter additional information about each entity attribute. In this case there is information about the STATUS attribute for the ORDER entity.

FIGURE 14.20:

First page of the Attribute
Definition screen of
CASE*Dictionary, as accessed
from CASE*Designer

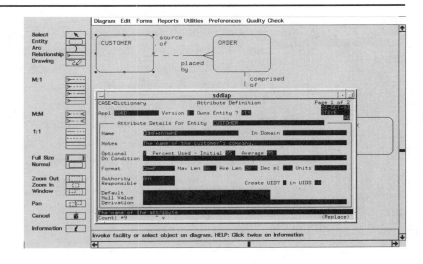

FIGURE 14.21:

Second page of the Attribute
Definition screen

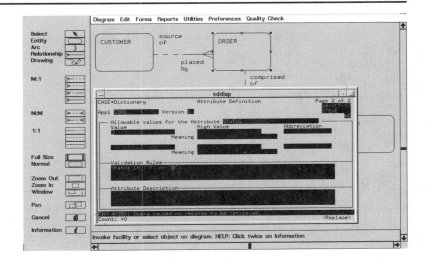

> **WARNING**
>
> As you create attributes, be sure *not* to include columns that specifically serve to relate different entities in the system. (For example, an attribute such as CUSTOMERID should not be created in the ORDER entity to specifically relate each order to a customer.) CASE*Generator automatically creates foreign keys when you generate an application schema using the relationships you define in CASE*Dictionary.

Use the pages of the Attribute Definition screen along with the information in Table 14.1 to create the attributes for the CUSTOMER entity.

TABLE 14.1: CUSTOMER Entity Attributes

Attribute	Format	Max Len	Ave Len	Dec Pl
Id*	INTEGER	–	–	–
Companyname	CHAR	50	20	–
Lastname*	CHAR	50	10	–
Firstname*	CHAR	50	10	–
Address	CHAR	100	30	–
City	CHAR	50	10	–
State	CHAR	2	2	–
Zipcode	CHAR	10	5	–
Phone	CHAR	20	12	–
Fax	CHAR	20	12	–

*For the Id attribute, also set the Optional field to N and the Create UID? field to Y. For the Lastname and Firstname attributes, set the Optional field to N.

Use the pages of the Attribute Definition screen along with the information in Table 14.2 to create the attributes for the ORDER entity.

TABLE 14.2: ORDER Entity Attributes

Attribute	Format	Max Len	Ave Len	Dec Pl
Id*	INTEGER	–	–	–
Orderdate	DATE	–	–	–
Shipdate	DATE	–	–	–
Paiddate	DATE	–	–	–
Status	CHAR	1	1	–

*For the Id attribute, also set the Optional field to N and the Create UID? field to Y.

Use the pages of the Attribute Definition screen along with the information in Table 14.3 to create the attributes for the ITEM entity.

TABLE 14.3: ITEM Entity Attributes

Attribute	Format	Max Len	Ave Len	Dec Pl
Id*	INTEGER	–	–	–
Quantity	INTEGER	–	–	–
Total	MONEY	20	10	2

*For the Id attribute, also set the Optional field to N and the Create UID? field to Y.

Use the pages of the Attribute Definition screen along with the information in Table 14.4 to create the attributes for the STOCK entity.

Analysis: Indicating Other Details about Entities

Creating attributes is just one form of detail you can enter for an entity during the analysis stage. There are other menu options on the Forms menu that permit you to enter more detailed information about an entity in general (use the Entity/attribute Definition option), the unique identifiers of an entity (use the Unique Identifier Definition option), and so on.

TABLE 14.4: STOCK Entity Attributes

Attribute	Format	Max Len	Ave Len	Dec Pl
Id*	INTEGER	–	–	–
Unitprice	MONEY	20	5	2
Onhand	INTEGER	–	–	–
Reorder	INTEGER	–	–	–
Description	CHAR	250	20	–

*For the Id attribute, also set the Optional field to N and the Create UID? field to Y.

Circulating New Information for Review

Just as with the strategy stage, it is very important to now distribute the detailed analysis stage information for review. This way you can identify problems and make any necessary modifications before putting a lot of work into the design stage of system development.

An Introduction to the Design Stage

Once you have defined and refined the business model for a system with the strategy and analysis stages, you are ready to begin the design stage of system development. The design stage is when you put together the designs for the system data model (the application schema) and the system process model (the application's modules). During the design stage, CASE*Dictionary has utilities that allow you to quickly design many different types of system data structures, including tables, columns, views, indexes, sequences, and clusters. The DBA can also use CASE*Dictionary to design things for a new application system such as a new database, tablespace and data files, rollback segments, and users. Although all of these components are important, this chapter concentrates on the application modules and the tables that are necessary to support them. First, let's focus on designing the system's tables.

Starting CASE*Dictionary

During the design stage you use the screens of CASE*Dictionary. After you start CASE*Dictionary (system dependent), it prompts for a username and password and then displays the main menu. To proceed with the design stage, select the Design Menu option from the CASE*Dictionary main menu.

Design: Creating Schema Tables from Entities

CASE*Dictionary has some design-stage utilities that permit you to move quickly from the analysis stage to the design stage. One such utility is the Fastpath Table Mapping screen. To access this utility, select Design ➤ Data Design Utilities Menu ➤ Fastpath Table Mapping Screen. Figure 14.22 shows a filled-in version of this screen.

FIGURE 14.22:

Fastpath Table Mapping screen of CASE*Dictionary

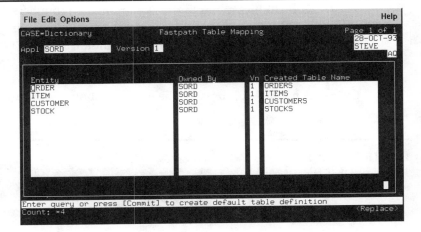

When you enter the screen, it prompts you to enter the name of the application (if not already present). In this case type **SORD**. At this point the records in the Entity field should be empty. To insert all of the entities defined in the system, press the [Execute Query] key. You can create table names that correspond to the listed entities simply by moving the cursor to each entity name and then pressing the [Commit] key for each one. When you are finished, the screen should look like the one in Figure 14.22. You can then exit the screen to return to the Data Design Utilities menu of CASE*Dictionary.

Design: Creating Columns for Tables

Once you create tables from the entities in the system, you can proceed with creating the columns for the tables. CASE*Dictionary uses the system information in the repository about entity attributes and relationships to create a candidate set of columns that you can later modify if necessary. To create table columns automatically, select Data Design Utilities ➤ Default Database Design. Answer the prompts for action (choose R for Replace), the application system name (SORD), the system version (1), and table names (CUSTOMERS, ORDERS, ITEMS, STOCKS); CASE*Dictionary then creates the columns for the tables you specify. When you are finished viewing the report that follows, you can return to the Data Design Utilities menu.

To get a look at the new columns for the system tables, step back from the Data Design Utilities menu to the Design menu. From here, select Database Design Menu ➤ Table Columns and Keys Menu ➤ Column Definition Screen. CASE*Dictionary presents you with the Column Definition screen. At this point the screen should be empty. Enter a table name—for example, **CUSTOMERS**—and press the [Next Field] key. CASE*Dictionary then fills in columns with information about the newly generated columns for the entity, as shown in Figure 14.23.

FIGURE 14.23:

First page of the Column Definition screen of CASE*Dictionary

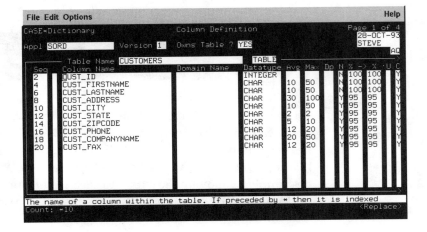

Because the table and column definitions you see now are merely designs in CASE*Dictionary, not real tables in a database, you can edit the column names, datatypes, default column values, and so on if you want to make modifications. You can also move to other system tables and do the same. Exit the screen when you are finished.

Design: Creating Table Constraints

As you know from Chapter 2, constraints are an important feature that Oracle7 can use to make sure the data in your system tables adheres to a set of integrity rules. PRIMARY KEY, UNIQUE, and FOREIGN KEY integrity constraints are all examples of Oracle7 constraints you can use to help validate system data integrity. Therefore, when you design your system tables, it's important to use integrity constraints whenever possible.

The Oracle CASE products are designed to work with the Oracle database server. To take advantage of Oracle7 integrity constraints, the CASE products can automatically set up different integrity constraints from the information you provide about your system design. For example, recall the earlier section in this chapter, "Analysis: Entering Attributes for Entities," where you use the Attribute Definition screen of CASE*Dictionary to specify attributes for the entities in the system. When you specify Y in the Create UID? field for an attribute, this action tells CASE*Dictionary that the attribute is (or is part of) the entity's primary key. And later on, when you generate tables and their columns from the entities and their attributes, CASE*Dictionary knows to create PRIMARY KEY constraints along with the columns that correspond to primary key attributes. Similarly, the CASE products configure FOREIGN KEY integrity constraints for related columns that establish referential integrity.

To examine the key constraints that CASE*Dictionary creates for you, select Table Columns and Keys ➤ Table Key Constraints Definition Screen. From this screen enter a table name in the system, and then use the [Next Field] and [Next Block] keys to see the primary key, alternate keys, and foreign keys for the table. While moving throughout the pages of the screen, you can supplement the information about the keys that is already present. For example, for each key definition, enter an error message that you want applications to display when someone incorrectly enters a key value.

While CASE*Dictionary works hard to automatically configure the different keys in your system tables, sometimes it cannot identify all the keys that are necessary from the given information. In such cases use the Table Key Constraints Definition screen to modify or add new keys to a table. For example, enter the CUSTOMERS table in the Table Name field, move the cursor to the Unique Key block with the [Next Block] key, and then add a new composite alternate key (unique key) that includes the LASTNAME and FIRSTNAME columns (using the [List] and [Next Field] keys). Similarly, for the ITEMS table, add the ORDER_ID column to the table's primary key. When you finish updating all keys in your system tables, be sure to commit your changes.

Design: Creating Sequences for Table ID Columns

The Sequences feature of Oracle7 allows applications to automatically generate unique primary key integers without contention in a multi-user application. Chapter 16 discusses the benefits of sequences in detail. For now, let's see how CASE*Dictionary can automatically create sequences for the tables in your system.

First, step back to the Database Design menu and select Sequence Definition Screen. CASE*Dictionary reveals the Sequence Definition screen, which you can use to define new sequences. For example, the screen in Figure 14.24 shows how to define a sequence named CUST_SEQ.

FIGURE 14.24:

Sequence Definition screen of CASE*Dictionary

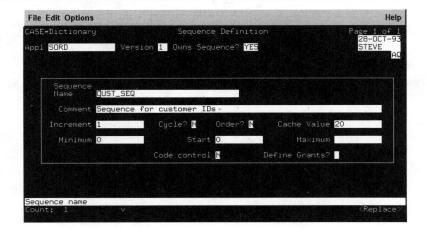

Notice that the Sequence Definition screen allows you to specify several settings for a sequence of numbers, including

- The sequence's name

- A comment to describe the sequence's purpose in the system

- How to increment the sequence (A positive integer creates an ascending sequence, while a negative integer creates a descending sequence.)

- Minimum, maximum, and starting values for the sequence

- Whether or not you want the sequence to cycle when it reaches its maximum value (or minimum value, in the case of a descending sequence)

- The number of values you want to pregenerate and cache in the memory of the database server to reduce disk I/O and improve application performance

For complete information about these and other settings for sequences, see Chapter 16. In the meantime, use the information in Figure 14.24 and the Sequence Definition screen to create the CUST_SEQ. Similarly, use the defaults of the Sequence Definition screen to create two other sequences: ORD_SEQ (for sales order IDs in the ORDERS table) and STOCK_SEQ (for stock item IDs in the STOCKS table).

Design: Tying Sequences to Table Columns

Once you have created a sequence, you need to tell CASE*Dictionary what column(s) will use the sequence. To link a sequence with a specific column, you need to return to the Column Definition screen, move to the second page, and specify the sequence for the column in the Sequence field. The screen in Figure 14.25 shows how to specify the CUST_SEQ sequence for the CUST_ID column of the CUSTOMERS table.

Repeat the preceding operations as necessary for the ORDERS.ORD_ID, ITEMS.ITEM_ORD_ID, and STOCKS.STOC_ID columns in their corresponding system tables. Exit the screen when you are finished.

FIGURE 14.25:

Specifying a sequence for a table column

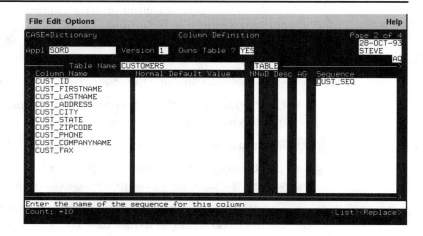

TIP

In the ITEMS.ITEM_ORD_ID column you want all of an order's line items to use the same order number. You can accomplish this two different ways. One way is to name the same sequence, ORD_SEQ, for both the ORDERS.ORD_ID and ITEMS.ITEM_ORD_ID columns. Alternatively, you can name the ORD_SEQ for the ORDERS.ORD_ID column and enter SP (short for "sequence of parent") in the AG (automatic generation) column of the Column Definition screen.

Design: Designing Form Application Modules

The previous sections have shown you how to design the data for the application system using CASE*Dictionary. Now it's time to focus on designing the front-end form applications for the new application system. The following sections describe how to design a simple one-block form for maintenance of customer records and a more complicated, two-block master-detail form for maintenance of sales orders and line items.

Defining Application Module Names in CASE*Dictionary

Before you can design a new application module, you have to register its name in the CASE*Dictionary repository. To do this, select Design ➤ Module Design Menu ➤ Module Definition Screen. CASE*Dictionary presents the Module Definition screen. In this form you can enter lots of information for the module, including the long and short names for a new module, as well as the type, format, and complexity of the module. Figure 14.26 shows the Module Definition screen and the settings for the Customer Maintenance module.

FIGURE 14.26:

Module Definition screen for the Customer Maintenance module

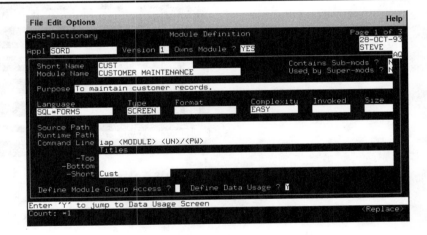

Complete the Module Definition screen for the Customer Maintenance module. Be sure to type a **Y** in the Define Data Usage field before you commit the screen. This ensures that you can move to the Module Data Usage screen next, which allows you to define detailed information about the data that supports the module.

Defining the Data for the Customer Maintenance Application Module

After naming a new module, you must specify the data that supports the module before you can implement the module. If you follow the directions in the previous section, you can press the Enter key, and CASE*Dictionary automatically moves you to the Module Data Usage screen after defining a new module name. Here you can enter the tables and corresponding columns that the module uses. You can even specify which columns to display, which operations the module allows on each column, column display formats, labels for each column, and much more. The screen in Figure 14.27 shows how the Customer Maintenance module uses the CUSTOMERS table and shows the sequence of CUSTOMERS table columns that the module uses.

FIGURE 14.27:

Defining the data usage of an application module

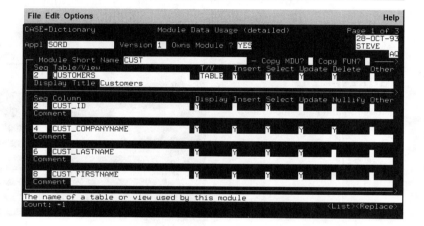

Use the information in Figure 14.27 and Table 14.5 to define the data usage of the CUSTOMERS table in the Customer Maintenance module.

When you are finished entering the settings for the Customer Maintenance module, commit your work and exit the screen. You are done designing this module!

Defining the Data for the Sales Orders Application Module

When you have completed the design of the Customer Maintenance module, return to the Module Definition screen to design the Sales Orders module. Here, you can enter information similar to that for the Customer Maintenance module, but make sure you enter its short name as SALES and its module name as Sales Orders.

After you define the Sales Orders module using the Module Definition screen, as described earlier in this chapter, you need to define its data usage with the Module

TABLE 14.5: Column Settings for the CUSTOMERS Tables in the Customer Maintenance Module

Column	Display?	Insert?	Select?	Update?	Nullify?	Length	Prompt
CUST_ID	y	N	y	N	N	5	Customer ID
CUST_COMPANYNAME	y	y	y	y	y	20	Company Name
CUST_LASTNAME	y	y	y	y	N	20	Last Name
CUST_FIRSTNAME	y	y	y	y	y	20	First Name
CUST_ADDRESS	y	y	y	y	y	20	Address
CUST_CITY	y	y	y	y	y	10	City
CUST_STATE	y	y	y	y	y	2	State
CUST_ZIPCODE	y	y	y	y	y	10	Zip Code
CUST_PHONE	y	y	y	y	y	20	Phone
CUST_FAX	y	y	y	y	y	20	Fax

Data Usage screen. This time, though, the module uses several different tables. OR-DERS and ITEMS are the primary tables for the form, but CUSTOMERS and STOCKS are also necessary for lookup lists. Tables 14.6 through 14.10 explain the settings for the tables and columns used by the Sales Orders module.

Once you have set the table and column settings, you are finished defining the Sales Orders module. Finally, it's time to move to the implementation stage!

TABLE 14.6: Table Settings for the Sales Order Module

Column	Insert?	Select?	Update?	Delete?
ORDERS	y	y	y	y
ITEMS	y	y	y	y
CUSTOMERS	N	y	N	N
STOCKS	N	y	N	N

TABLE 14.7: Column Settings for the ORDERS Table in the Sales Order Module

Column	Display?	Insert?	Select?	Update?	Nullify?	Length	Prompt
ORD_ID	y	N	y	N	N	5	Customer ID
ORD_CUST_ID	N	–	–	–	–	–	–
ORD_ORDERDATE*	y	N	y	y	N	8	Order Date
ORD_PAIDDATE*	y	y	y	y	y	8	Paid Date
ORD_SHIPDATE*	y	y	y	y	y	8	Ship Date
ORD_STATUS	y	y	y	y	N	1	Status

*Also, set the display format for all date columns to MM/DD/YY.

TABLE 14.8: Column Settings for the ITEMS Table in the Sales Order Module

Column	Display?	Insert?	Select?	Update?	Nullify?	Length	Prompt
ITEM_ID	y	y	y	N	N	7	Line ID
ITEM_ORD_ID	N	–	–	–	–	–	–
ITEM_STOCK_ID	N	–	–	–	–	–	–
ITEM_QUANTITY	y	y	y	y	N	8	Quantity
ITEM_TOTAL	y	N	N	N	y	10	Line Total

TABLE 14.9: Column Settings for the CUSTOMERS Table in the Sales Order Module

Column	Display?	Insert?	Select?	Update?	Nullify?	Length	Prompt
CUST_ID	N	–	–	–	–	–	–
CUST_LASTNAME	y	N	y	N	N	20	Last Name
CUST_FIRSTNAME	y	N	y	N	N	10	First Name

TABLE 14.10: Column Settings for the STOCKS Table in the Sales Order Module

Column	Display?	Insert?	Select?	Update?	Nullify?	Length	Prompt
STOC_ID	N	–	–	–	–	–	–
STOC_DESCRIPTION	y	N	y	N	N	20	Stock Item
STOC_UNITPRICE	y	N	y	N	N	10	Unit Price

An Introduction to the Implementation Stage

The implementation stage takes the system design and turns it into a real system—an application schema and corresponding application modules that users can use to get work done. The following sections show you how to use CASE*Generator to automatically generate the DDL script for the application system schema and the corresponding SQL*Forms applications for customer maintenance and sales order entry.

Starting CASE*Generator and Setting User Preferences

In the implementation stage of system development, you use CASE*Generator to accomplish work. Once you have started CASE*Generator (system dependent), enter your username and password and then select the CASE*Generator option from the main CASE*Generator menu. In this example you create SQL*Forms applications, so select the CASE*Generator for SQL*Forms Menu option next.

Before you begin implementing your new system, you have to set some user preferences so CASE*Generator understands which application system you want to work with, what types of applications you want to generate, and so on. To do so, select User Preferences Screen option to display the User Preferences screen. Enter the application system name (**SORD**) and the application system version number. Notice that CASE*Generator automatically fills in your username and description. Next, from the menu in the center of the screen, select U so you can edit your user preferences. In the lower portion of the screen, CASE*Generator shows you the products for which you can generate applications. In this case make sure you position the cursor on CASE*Generator for SQL*Forms, version 3; then move to the second page of the screen using the [Next Block] key so you can enter specific user preferences for this product.

Once you are on the second page of the User Preferences screen, you need to specify only one preference—TEMFRM, which indicates a template form for SQL*Forms application generation. When you attempt to move into the preferences block of the screen (using [Next Block]), CASE*Generator displays a dialog where you can type the preference name. Type **TEMFRM** and then press the [Next Field] key. CASE*Generator returns you to the screen, which now contains some more information. Simply clear the "CFGTA3" (a name of a template form) from the Value field and commit the changes with the [Commit] key. Now you are ready to begin implementing your system. Return to the CASE*Generator for SQL*Forms menu.

Implementation: Generating the Application Schema DDL Script

The first step in the implementation stage is to create the underlying data structures necessary for the application modules. CASE*Generator has all the utilities necessary to accomplish this step quickly and easily. Select CASE*Generator for SQL*Forms ➤ CASE*Generator Utilities Menu ➤ DDL Command Generator. CASE*Generator then displays the command-line utility that prompts you for some simple information, such as the application system name, its version number, the type of database (CASE*Generator can generate DDL commands for IBM DB2 databases as well as Oracle databases), the type of objects to generate ("user" will generate tables, views, indexes, sequences, and clusters; "dba" will generate databases, tablespaces, rollback segments, users, and grants), and the name of the output file for the DDL script. Respond to the prompts as shown in Figure 14.28.

After generating the DDL script, CASE*Generator indicates that it is finished and allows you to return to the CASE*Generator Utilities menu.

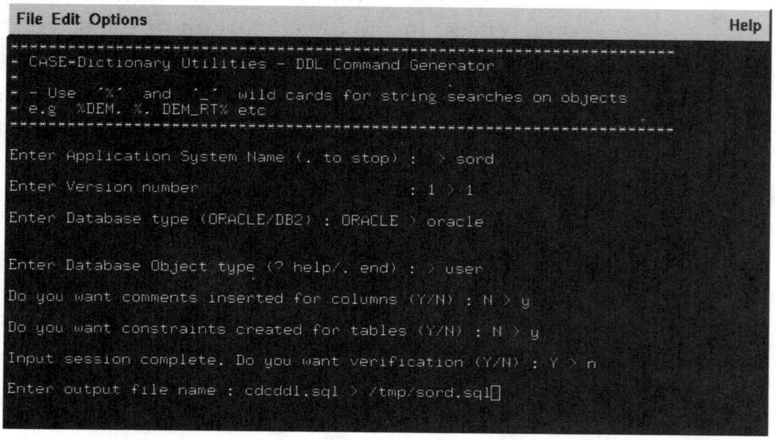

FIGURE 14.28:
Prompts of the CASE*Generator
DDL Command Generator utility

Viewing and Modifying the Application Schema DDL Script

After you have used CASE*Generator to create the application schema DDL script, open it in your favorite text editor to get a look at it. The screen in Figure 14.29 shows a portion of the generated script in the ScoEdit text editor.

After reviewing the DDL script, you'll probably want to fix some simple details. For example, if you plan to run the script using SQL*DBA instead of SQL*Plus, you need to remove all the PROMPT commands because SQL*DBA does not support the PROMPT command.

FIGURE 14.29:

Portion of the generated application schema DDL script for the SORD system

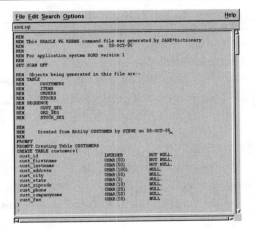

WARNING

In general, don't edit object definitions in a generated DDL script, because you don't want to change any important facts that would conflict with definitions in CASE*Dictionary. For example, don't change the name of a table, column, or other object; if you do, CASE*Generator can't create applications to match the implemented application schema. Instead, when you need to make important changes, always go back to CASE*Dictionary, make the changes using the appropriate screens, and then generate a new DDL script using CASE*Generator.

Implementation: Executing the DDL Script to Create the Application Schema

Once you are satisfied with the application schema DDL script, create the corresponding schema in an Oracle7 database by running the script from SQL*Plus or SQL*DBA. When you execute an application's DDL script, make sure you connect to Oracle7 using the username you employ when working with the Oracle CASE products. This way you can access the application tables when generating the application modules in the next section. Once you run the application DDL script, you are halfway home—you have implemented the data for the new application system.

WARNING
If you use older versions of the Oracle CASE products, note that they create DDL scripts for syntaxes supported by an older version of the Oracle RDBMS. If you use older CASE products with Oracle7, use SQL* Plus and be sure to issue the SET COMPATIBILITY V6 command before running your generated DDL script.

TIP
It is a good idea to create the first version of an application in a test environment rather than a product environment. This way you can test new applications without affecting the productivity of users in live systems.

The Implementation Stage: Generating Application Modules

When the necessary data structures are in place, you can continue the implementation stage by generating the application modules. To begin this process, select CASE*Generator for SQL*Forms ➤ CASE*Generator for SQL*Forms—Generate. Next, enter the short name of one of the modules that you previously defined (CUST or SALES) and then press the [Commit] key.

CASE*Generator then presents a screen with a couple of simple prompts. It asks for the number of rows you want to display for each block on a form. For the CUSTOMER block of the Customer Maintenance module, enter **1** to display a single customer record at a time. For the ORDER and ITEM blocks of the Sales Orders module, enter **1** and **5**, respectively.

For the Sales Orders module, CASE*Generator asks if you want it to automatically link the different blocks of the form using the foreign keys that exist among the tables used by the form. Answer Yes to all prompts of this nature.

NOTE   Depending on your CASE user environment settings, CASE*Generator also asks if you want to create a help system for your forms as you generate them.

When it has finished prompting you for information, CASE*Generator automatically creates the application.

After generation is complete, CASE*Generator even asks if you want to run the application right away. Select Yes to get a look at the new application. The screens in Figures 14.30 and 14.31 show the Customer Maintenance and Sales Order SQL*Forms applications with some data.

FIGURE 14.30:

The SQL*Forms character-mode version of the Customer Maintenance application

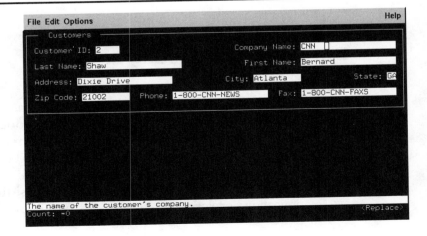

FIGURE 14.31:

The SQL*Forms character-mode version of the Sales Order application

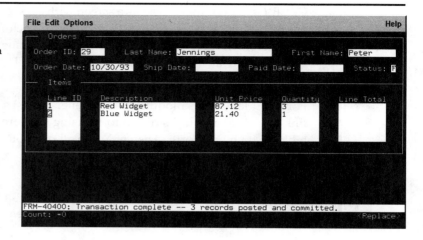

As you use the applications, you begin to see the real power of the Oracle CASE development method. Without your having to type a single line of 3GL code or play around with a 4GL screen development tool, the layout of the forms is quite presentable, list boxes are available where appropriate to help fill in foreign key values, sequences automatically generate primary keys, default column values automatically appear in the form, and so on. And this example shows only a little of the power of the Oracle CASE development environment. You can continue system development by automatically developing other form applications (for example, one for maintaining inventory), reporting applications, and menu applications to tie together all related applications—and all without complicated programming.

The Remaining Stages of System Development: Testing and Production

Once you develop the first cut of some applications in a test environment, you are responsible for validating the behavior and performance of each application. You should also solicit feedback from users on the user interface and possible enhancements you can incorporate before creating the first production version of the application. In many cases you might be able to make all modifications within the Oracle CASE environment. In others you may have to use the actual design module of the application development tool itself (for example, Oracle Forms or Oracle Reports) to make finer adjustments. Later in this chapter you see examples of such adjustments. But in the next section, learn how to port (move) the generated Sales Order form application to another operating system and user interface.

Porting Oracle CDE Applications among Different Operating Systems

One of the great advantages of the Oracle CDE tool set is that once you generate an application, it is automatically *portable* among all operating systems and user interfaces, no matter what type of system you use to develop it. This is especially important for client/server systems because they are often heterogeneous in nature—they have a mix of different types of client workstations (UNIX workstations, PCs, Macintoshes), operating systems (UNIX, DOS, Macintosh, OS), and user interfaces (character mode, Motif, Windows, Macintosh). Without application portability, you would have to develop the same application multiple times for each target client environment, which obviously means a lot of extra work for you.

To give you an idea of the power of portability, let's port the Sales Order application created in the previous sections of this chapter. In these sections application development was performed using Oracle CASE tools that run on the SCO UNIX operating system and generated applications that run in character-mode SQL*Forms version 3.0 for SCO UNIX. In the next few sections you port the very same application to a PC running DOS and Microsoft Windows.

Copying the Source File for the Application

When the Oracle CDE tools create a new application, they create different files. One file is the portable source code for the application. For example, in the previous sections you created SQL*Forms 3.0 applications; the portable files in this case are the files with the .inp extension. The first step in porting an Oracle application among different operating systems is to copy the portable source file from one system to another.

To copy the portable source file for an Oracle application, you can use many different methods. For example, you could copy the source file from the server to a floppy disk or tape and then use this removable medium to move the file to the target computer. Even easier, if the source computer and target computer are attached by a network, you can copy the file using a network file copy command. For example, if a PC running DOS is connected across a TCP/IP network to a UNIX server, you could use the TCP/IP command FTP (file transfer protocol) to copy the file. Choose an appropriate method for your system to complete this first step of application porting. To port the Sales Order application, copy the Sales.inp file from the UNIX server to the DOS PC.

Generating the Application on the Target System

Once you have copied the application source file to the target system, you complete the porting process by generating the application on the new system. For example, if you are using Oracle Forms for Microsoft Windows, you perform this step using Oracle Forms 4.0 Generator. The next section introduces Oracle Forms and shows you how to generate, modify, and run the generated Sales Order application.

Using Oracle Forms for Windows to Generate, Modify, and Run Form Applications

Like its predecessor SQL*Forms version 3.0, Oracle Forms version 4.0 is Oracle's form application development tool, with which you create, compile, and run form applications. However, unlike SQL*Forms, Oracle Forms supports applications in bitmapped graphical user interfaces, such as Microsoft Windows, Motif, and Macintosh. In the following sections you'll see how Oracle Forms for Windows works.

Oracle Forms has three different modules: Designer, Generator, and Runform. Developers use all three modules to design, generate, and test the functionality of an

Oracle Forms application. End users use only the Runform module, to run production form applications. In the sections that follow you will see how to use all three modules of Oracle Forms.

Starting Oracle Forms and Connecting to the Oracle7 Database Server

The way you start an Oracle Forms module is system dependent. For example, to start the Oracle Forms Designer on Microsoft Windows, just double-click the Oracle Forms Designer icon in the Oracle Program Group of Program Manager. To start Oracle Forms on other systems, you might have to enter an operating system command.

After starting an Oracle Forms module, you must connect to the database server to get any work done. For example, if you use the Oracle Forms Runform module to run a form, it automatically displays a dialog after startup to ask which form to run and to which database to connect. On the other hand, when you use the Oracle Forms Designer to modify the layout of a form, you connect to the database using the Connect option in the File menu.

Whichever way you connect, you must enter a database username, password, and connect string. When connecting from a client workstation in a client/server environment, enter a SQL*Net alias to indicate the database to which you want to connect. If you are not familiar with SQL*Net aliases, review Chapter 8.

Generating a Form with the Oracle Forms Generator

Before you can run an Oracle Forms application, you have to generate (compile) it. To generate an Oracle Forms application, start the Oracle Forms Generator. It then displays a dialog that asks for the source file to generate, your database username and password, and several other options. Figure 14.32 shows the startup dialog of the Oracle Forms Generator.

After completing the dialog, select the OK button, and Generator goes to work. After compiling a form, Generator displays a message indicating the name of the new executable form application.

FIGURE 14.32:

Startup dialog of the Oracle Forms Generator

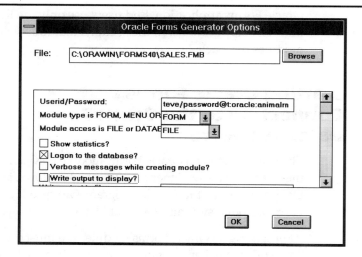

You can try out the Oracle Forms Generator by continuing where you left off with porting the Sales Order application—compile the source file for the SALES application. Be sure to select the Upgrade... check box since we are upgrading a SQL* Forms 3.0 application to an Oracle Forms 4.0 application. Once you have generated the SALES application, you can run it.

Running a Form with the Oracle Forms Runform Module

To run a generated form, you can use the Oracle Forms Runform module. When you start this module, it displays a dialog asking for a form to run, your username and password, and so on. Fill in the appropriate information and select OK. Oracle Forms then executes the form application. For example, the screen in Figure 14.33 shows the SALES form created from CASE*Generator and compiled by Oracle Forms Generator.

Notice that the SALES form has two different areas: one for entering the master record information for a sales order, and one for entering child record information for a sale order's line items. These different areas on the form are called *blocks*. The information in the Orders block and the Items block are related by the master detail relationship of the corresponding tables.

FIGURE 14.33:

SALES application in the Oracle
Forms Runform module

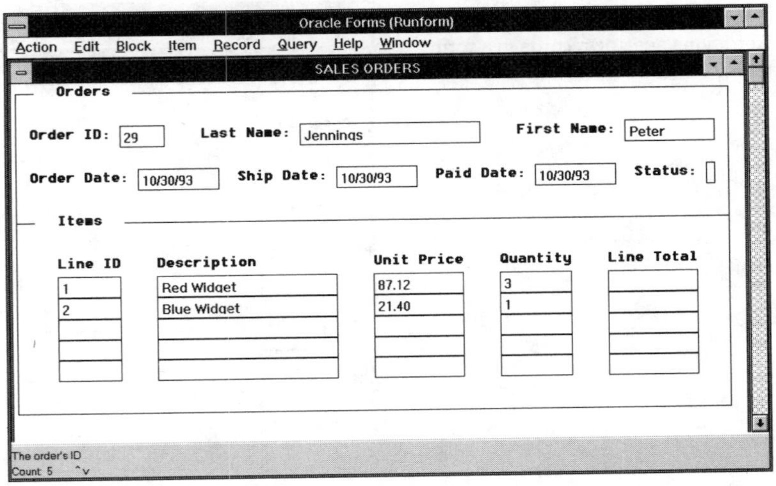

You can navigate through the form's fields using the mouse or the [Next Field], [Previous Field], [Next Block], and [Previous Block] keys. When you move around, you might find that Oracle Forms will not let you move because of some form triggers tied to a particular field.

You can go ahead and use the form to query and enter sales orders in the simple example database. For example, to query all of the sales orders, press the [Enter Query] key. The status line at the bottom of the form instructs you to enter any query criteria and then press the [Execute Query] key. To retrieve all sales orders, simply press the [Execute Query] key. Or you could retrieve specific orders by entering query criteria in the fields of the form. For instance, you can have the form retrieve all the orders placed after a specific date by entering a date expression in the Order Date entry field, as shown in Figure 14.34.

As you might guess, Oracle Forms automatically converts the information on the screen into a SQL query that it sends to the Oracle7 database server. Oracle7 then sends the query results back to Oracle Forms, which takes care of displaying the information in the appropriate fields on the form.

After using the SALES form, you will likely think of ways to improve it. For example, after the porting process, the form still has a character-mode look and feel. The following sections explain how to use the Oracle Forms Designer to modify the SALES form in several ways.

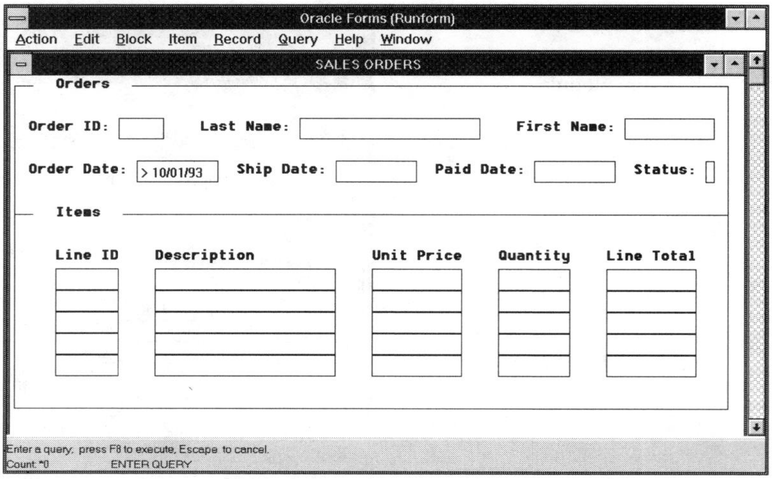

FIGURE 14.34:
Retrieving specific records in a form
using a query expression

Opening a Form for Modification in the Oracle Forms Designer

Once you have connected to an Oracle7 database server, you can open a source file for a form in the Oracle Forms Designer using the File ➤ Open command. When you attempt to open a form's source file, Oracle Forms presents a dialog to ask you where the form is stored: in your computer's file system or within the Oracle database. Pick the correct option and press OK. You are then presented with a list of available form files. Once you pick a form from the list, Oracle Forms displays the form in a window. The screen in Figure 14.35 shows the SALES form that CASE*Generator created in the earlier section "The Implementation Stage: Generating Application Modules."

Improving the Visual Appearance of a Form with the Oracle Forms Designer

One way to improve a form is to adjust the layout and appearance of the form, giving it a better look and feel. For example, you can change the fonts of form items and labels, add color backgrounds or boxes to organize form areas, move form

FIGURE 14.35:

SALES form application in the
Oracle Forms Designer

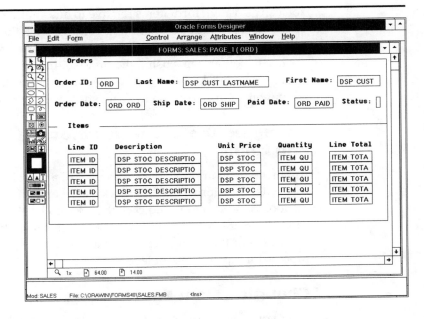

items to a better area, and so on. The following sections explain several ways you
can modify the SALES form to make it more visually appealing.

Moving Items on a Form

To move a form item, first change the current tool to a selection arrow using the Oracle Forms tool palette. Next, select the item to move with the mouse, drag the item
to the new location, and release it. If you want to move several items at once, select
the first item, and then hold down the Shift key and select other items. Now you
can drag several items with one operation.

You can more exactly move form items using the Oracle Forms Designer's grid and
ruler. To set up the Designer's grid and ruler spacings, select Arrange ➤ Ruler Settings. A dialog appears showing you the current ruler and grid settings; change
them as you like. After dismissing the dialog, select Arrange ➤ Grid Snap to make
sure the grid snap feature is on. Now when you move a form item, it snaps to the
grid points you have specified.

You can also align form items relative to one another. First, select the items to align. Then select Arrange ➤ Alignment Settings. Pick the alignment options you desire and then dismiss the dialog to have Oracle Forms align the items. If you want to align some other items using the same settings as before, use the Arrange ➤ Align option or its hot-key shortcut (Ctrl+L in Windows). Otherwise, be sure to use the Alignment Settings option to again specify the correct alignment settings.

Changing the Labels for Blocks and Items

Another way to improve the appearance of a form is to change some of the labels on the fields of the form. To edit a block's label or an item's label, select the label, change the tool to the Text tool, and click the selected label. The label changes appearance to show a cursor bar you can use to edit the label text. When you are finished, click another area of the form to change the tool to the selection tool. You can repeat this process for any number of labels.

Changing Item Fonts

After you have set the text of a form's labels, you might want to change the font Oracle Forms uses to display the labels. To change the font for a form's labels, select all of the related labels together (use Shift+click, as the previous section describes); then select Attributes ➤ Font. Use the Font dialog to select the font you want (you get a preview in the preview window), and then dismiss the dialog with the OK button. You can use the same operation to change the fonts of any items, too.

NOTE When adjusting the fonts on a form, don't get carried away—a form with too many different fonts can be distracting. However, you might want to make the font for the block labels slightly different from the font for the item labels, to distinguish them from each other.

Figure 14.36 shows what the SALES form looks like after changes to the text and font of the form's labels.

FIGURE 14.36:
SALES form with some edited labels and new fonts

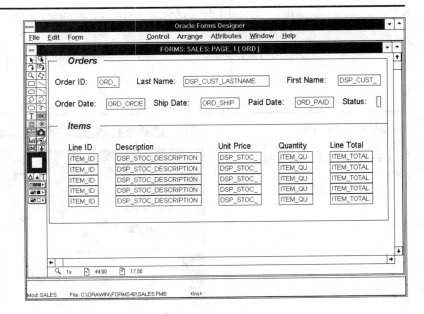

Adding Objects and Color to a Form

Another way to improve the appearance of a form is to add different form objects to organize and add color. The Oracle Forms Designer tool palette has several tools you can use to add objects and color to a form. For example, you can add lines using the line tool, rectangles using the rectangle tool, and ellipses using the ellipse tool. You can then select and arrange the layers of different objects using Arrange ➤ Bring to Front and Arrange ➤ Send to Back.

> **NOTE** You can add squares and circles with the rectangle and ellipse tools, respectively, by constraining your drawing freedom when drawing an object. To do so, simply hold down the Shift key when you draw.

The tools at the bottom of the Oracle Forms Designer tool palette allow you to change the pattern and color of an object's outline and fill. Play with these tools when you add new objects to the form surface and get just the color and patterns that you want.

Figure 14.37 shows how adding several objects to a form's layout can improve the appearance of the SALES form.

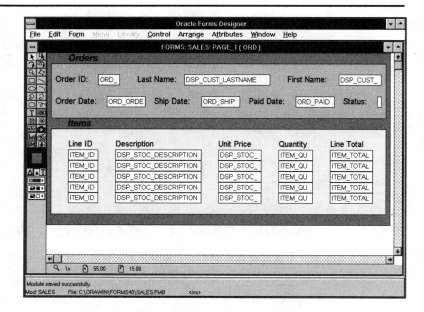

Applying Changes and Saving a Form Layout

When you load a form into the Designer, Oracle Forms keeps the information about the form in a memory area called the *object layer*. As you modify a form's layout, changes are not made directly to the object layer; they only appear on the screen. When you are happy with the layout changes in the Oracle Forms Designer, you save your work by applying the layout changes on screen to the object layer and then saving the object layer to disk.

To apply screen changes to the object layer, select Control ➤ Apply. This option writes the temporary layout changes from the Designer's screen to the object layer.

Then you can save the object layer to disk by selecting File ➤ Save.

If you do not like the changes on screen and want to revert to the form currently in the object layer, select Control ➤ Revert.

Once you have improved the layout of your form, you can add more functionality using some other options of the Oracle Forms Designer, as described in the following sections.

Improving the Functionality of the Form with the Oracle Forms Designer

Adding functionality to a form makes it easier to use. For example, custom hints on the status line for each field would help a new user figure out what to enter in the fields of the form, and lists that pop up for certain fields make it unnecessary for a user to remember appropriate field values. The following sections explain how to add functionality to the SALES form.

Adding Hints for Items

As a user navigates through the items on a form, the status line at the bottom of the Oracle Forms window displays hints. When you entered a description for each entity's attributes, CASE*Generator used the description to create default hints for each field on the form. However, you might want to change the item hints to be more descriptive.

To change an item's status line hint, use the mouse to double-click the item. Oracle Forms displays a dialog that allows you to adjust several attributes for the item:

- The table's name
- The table column to which the item corresponds
- The item's position in the navigation sequence
- The item's position on the form
- The item's default value
- The item's hint

The Hint entry field is where you can enter a specific text string as a hint that you want to display when a user enters the form item.

Changing an Item's Type

While you are changing an item's hint, you can also change other item attributes. One item attribute is the item's type. For example, it would be easier to use the SALES form if the Status item is a check box rather than an entry field. This way the user can simply check the box if the order is filled and uncheck it when an item is backlogged.

To change an item's type, double-click it and choose its type from the Type dropdown list; for example, change the Status item's type to a check box. When you change an item to a check box, the dialog changes to show attribute information for an item that is a check box. Figure 14.38 shows this dialog.

FIGURE 14.38:
Oracle Forms dialog that allows you to set an item's attributes

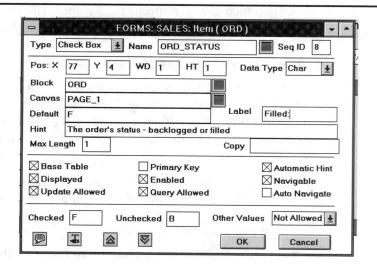

Two of the more important entry fields that appear are the Checked and Unchecked entry fields. These are the fields in which you can enter the values that Oracle Forms supplies when a user checks or unchecks the check box in the form. After setting all of the item's attributes the way you want, dismiss the dialog with the OK button. The form now shows the Status item as a check box.

Changing the Allowed Operations for Blocks

Sometimes you want to design a form for specific database operations only. For example, you might want the SALES form to allow insert and query operations but not update or delete operations. The original settings come from the table settings in the CASE*Dictionary Module Data Usage screen that you set earlier in this chapter. If you want to change these, change the attributes for the blocks in the form.

To change a block's attributes, select Form ➤ Blocks. A dialog appears that lists the blocks in the form. Select the block you want to edit and then click the Edit button. Next, a dialog appears that reveals several attributes for the block. Figure 14.39 shows the dialog.

FIGURE 14.39:

Oracle Forms dialog that allows you to set a block's attributes

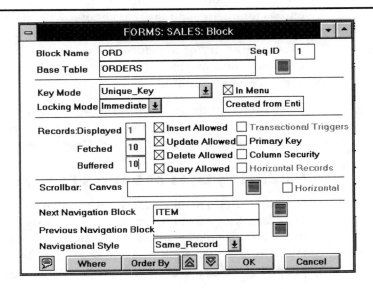

In the middle of the dialog are four check boxes that allow you to determine which DML operations Oracle Forms allows within the block. Check or uncheck these boxes as you see fit. For example, to allow only insert and query operations in the block, check the Insert Allowed and Query Allowed check boxes and uncheck the Update Allowed and Delete Allowed check boxes. If you want other blocks in the same form to have the same attributes, make sure you select and modify the same attributes for those blocks as well.

> **NOTE** You can allow or disallow certain DML operations on specific items by changing settings in an item's attribute dialog. For example, you might not want to permit anyone to update the primary key for a master record, such as a sales order.

Buffering and Fetching Rows for Client/Server Performance

Two other important attributes for blocks are the number of rows that Oracle Forms fetches for queries and the number of rows that Oracle Forms buffers for input to the database. These are especially important for client/server environments in which you are trying to reduce network traffic. By fetching (inserting) a number of rows all at the same time, you can dramatically reduce the number of network I/Os to reduce network traffic.

Enter values for the Fetched and Buffered fields (see Figure 14.39 for an example) to tune the performance of network I/O for the form application. When you are finished changing a block's attributes, dismiss the dialog with the OK button.

Modifying Lists of Values for Items

Sometimes fields require values that are not readily apparent to an application user. For example, the SALES form has a field for the ID of the customer who made an order. You are unlikely to remember the names of all customers in the CUSTOMER table. To make the form easier to use, it would be nice if a list of values (LOV) popped up when a user entered the Last Name field on the SALES form.

Conveniently, CASE*Generator automatically creates LOVs for all foreign keys on form applications during application generation. However, as you may have noticed when you used the SALES application immediately after porting, the LOVs are much wider than necessary. You can edit the LOVs to change their display width.

FIGURE 14.40:

Oracle Forms dialog to edit a list of values for a form item

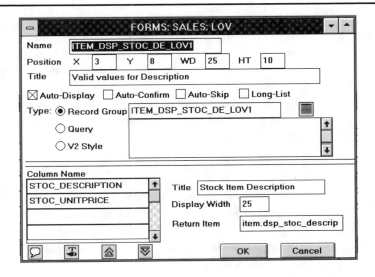

To edit a LOV, select Form ➤ LOVs. A dialog appears that lists all the LOVs in the form. To edit a LOV, select it from the list and then click the Edit button at the bottom of the dialog. A second dialog appears that you can use to edit any LOV. Figure 14.40 shows this dialog.

When editing a list of values for an item, you can set several characteristics. First, you can specify the position and size of the list box using the coordinate entry fields at the top of the dialog. Use trial-and-error until you get a feel for the coordinate settings for Oracle Forms. Next, specify the title of the list box in the Title field (the first one). The line of check boxes under the Title field lets you control several functions for the list box:

- When Auto-Display is checked, the list box automatically appears when a user enters the field that corresponds to the list of values.

- When Auto-Confirm is checked, Forms automatically returns a value to the corresponding item when the list has only a single item.

- When Auto-Skip is checked, Forms moves the cursor to the next field after a user makes a choice from the list of values.

- When Long List is checked, Forms lets a user enter an optional constraint before displaying the list.

The Type option for the list of values determines how to generate the values for the list box. When you create a new list of values, select Query and enter a query in the adjacent entry field. Then click the Apply button (not shown in the figure) to generate information about the query in the lower portion of the dialog, which is originally blank. In the example in this chapter, the LOV is already set, so there is no need to edit the settings.

The information in the lower portion of the dialog shows the list of columns in the list box's query. Move through each column in the query and determine its settings using the field on the right. For example, set each column's title and width. If you do not want to display a column in the list box, make its width 0. Pick one item in the list of columns to fill in a value as a return item on the form. Once you are finished with the layout and functionality of the new list of values, dismiss the dialog with the OK button.

TIP

> If a list of values does not correspond to a dynamic set of values, such as values that change in a database table, you can reduce network traffic in a client/server system by using a static list of values. A static list of values does not require a query to generate the list box. To create a static list of values for an item, modify the item's attributes and change its type to List. Then you can set the possible values for the item's static list and corresponding values.

Applying Changes and Saving a Form Layout

As described in the section "Applying Changes and Saving a Form Layout" earlier in this chapter, anytime you make some changes to a form in the Oracle Forms Designer, be sure to apply the changes made on screen to the object layer and save the modified object layer to disk.

Generating and Running the Modified Form

Once you have saved your new form, generate the form and run it to see how it works. Figure 14.41 shows the new layout of the SALES form in the Oracle Forms Runform module.

FIGURE 14.41:
New layout of the SALES form in the Oracle Forms Runform module

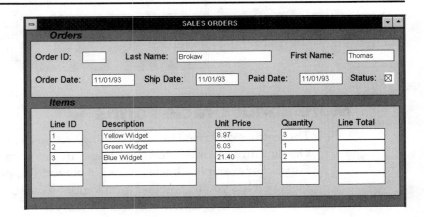

> **TIP**
>
> You can generate (and run) a form that is currently open in the Oracle Forms Designer straight from the Oracle Forms Designer. To do so, select File ➤ Generate. When Oracle Forms finishes generating the form application, you can run the form application by selecting File ➤ Run.

The first thing you might use the new version of the form for is placing a new order. Only this time, the form will work differently. Figure 14.42 shows the list of values that appears when you move the cursor to the Description field.

Continue to test the form. For example, after you enter an order, you might query all the orders in the database using the form. Then you might decide to try to update a value in one of the orders. Once you validate the functionality of your new form, you can put it to use in a production database system.

FIGURE 14.42:

A list of values for stock items in the SALES form

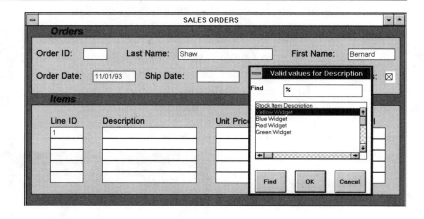

More about Oracle Forms

The features described in the preceding sections have given you a good idea of how Oracle Forms works. However, there are many, many more features in Oracle Forms. For example, Oracle Forms is a powerful application development environment that lets you tie together form logic and database stored procedures to reduce network traffic even more in a client/server environment. You can also display graphics images within a form and run an Oracle Graphics application to display information graphically.

This chapter has given you a head start in developing good applications quickly with the Oracle CDE tools. The next chapter takes a step back to look at the process of planning an application's schema and also explains how to manually create an application schema if you do not use CASE tools.

CHAPTER

FIFTEEN

Designing an Application's Schema

- Planning the tables and integrity constraints for an application schema

- Using views and synonyms in application schemas

- Managing tables, views, and synonyms for an application

A building is only as good as the foundation upon which it is built. Likewise, you can develop a quality database application only if the application uses well-designed data structures. This chapter describes how to create an application schema—the collection of database objects an application uses—including

- Planning the database tables in an application schema
- Setting integrity rules and defining table relationships in an application schema
- Using views effectively for an application
- Creating and managing tables and views

Designing an Application Schema

For the database administrator, planning the physical structure of a database is crucial before creating a new Oracle7 database. Similarly, the application developer must carefully plan and create an application's database objects before diving into application development. This approach ensures a sound application development foundation from the start, one that can save lots of application development work in the long run.

The concept of normalization and database design techniques is a complicated one. The following sections discuss the key topics to consider when planning the tables, integrity constraints, and views in an application's schema and present a few examples to give you an idea of the possibilities.

Designing Tables and Normalization

The theory of *normalization* is a key element of database design when putting together an application schema. In simple terms, normalization is the process of decomposing and arranging the attributes in a schema, which results in a set of tables with very simple structures. The purpose of normalization is to make tables as simple as possible.

You can quickly understand one aspect of the normalization process by studying a simple example involving the CUSTOMER table. Figure 15.1 shows two ways you could create the CUSTOMER table. Notice that the first version has the attribute NAME, which holds concatenated values of a customer's first and last name. You can normalize the CUSTOMER table to a degree, as shown in the second version, by splitting the NAME column, which contains a relation in itself, into a simpler structure—one with a column for the LAST and FIRST name of each customer.

FIGURE 15.1:

Denormalized and more normalized versions of the CUSTOMER table

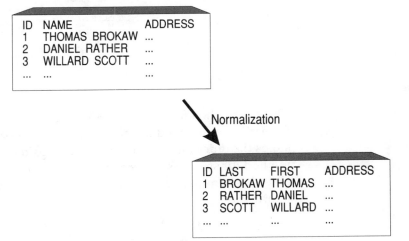

Clearly, normalization can directly affect the functionality and performance of an application. For example, using the denormalized version of the CUSTOMER table, it is difficult to develop a reporting application that prints customer records in order of the last names of customers. The more normalized version of the CUSTOMER table makes this common reporting requirement a trivial task using this query:

```
SELECT ... FROM customer
  ORDER BY last
```

A key focus of normalization is reducing the redundancy of information within a database. For example, consider the two options for storing sales order information shown in Figure 15.2.

FIGURE 15.2:

Two options for storing sales data, showing how to reduce redundancy of information

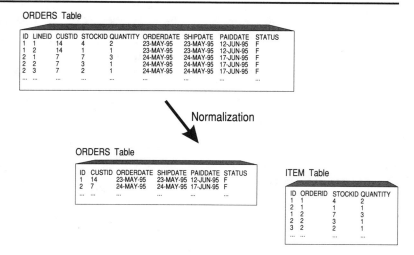

The first method for storing sales orders is inefficient because of the redundant information represented in each order; for each order line item, the ORDERS table stores the order number, order, ship and paid dates, and order status. The second method for storing sales orders is much more efficient; the ORDERS table stores all order information just once and the ITEM table stores related order line item information.

TIP

In most situations you should strive to eliminate data redundancy within a database design. However, in some situations you can improve the performance of applications noticeably by creating data redundancy on purpose. That's because by lumping attributes together in the same table (as in the first version of the ORDERS table in Figure 15.2), the database design eliminates the need for applications to perform join operations across related but separately stored tables. While this can improve application performance, the drawback is wasted storage space. When designing a schema, carefully consider the trade-offs between data redundancy and normalized tables.

Another focus of normalization is determining the relationships that exist between different attributes in a schema. For example, the ORDERS and ITEM tables in Figure 15.3 are related by the ID of each order. Furthermore, the relationship is a one-to-many relationship because there can be more than one line item for each order. The process of clearly identifying table relationships is the basis for determining the primary keys and referential integrity rules in a database.

FIGURE 15.3:

An entity-relation diagram graphically represents the data and relationships in an application schema.

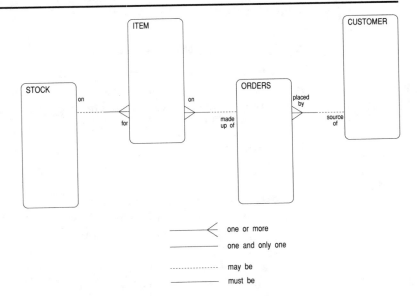

Relationship determination in a schema can be represented using simple diagrams. Figure 15.3 shows an *entity-relation diagram* of the database used in this book.

Diagrams like the one in Figure 15.3 are the foundation for CASE and database design methodologies used by tools such as Oracle's CASE tools. The different shapes in the diagram indicate different parts of the schema (tables are rectangles, relationships are lines, and so on). (For more information about entity-relation diagramming and CASE tools, see Chapter 14.)

Choosing Keys and Determining Integrity Rules

As you design the tables in an application schema, it is important to determine the keys in the tables and the relationships you want between tables. You can then enforce the integrity rules identified by your analysis using such Oracle7 integrity constraints as PRIMARY KEY, UNIQUE, and FOREIGN KEY. Let's take a quick look at some important issues to consider when planning the integrity rules for a schema.

Choosing Primary Keys

Every table in a database should have a primary key—a column or set of columns whose values uniquely identify each row in the table. When you create a new table, it is important to correctly set the table's primary key; otherwise, applications that use the table might not work as planned.

Primary keys for tables have three qualities: They are unique, they remain static, and they are concise.

Uniqueness   By definition, a table's primary key cannot contain any duplicate values; if it did, you would not be able to use it to uniquely identify each row in the table. Implicit in the quality of uniqueness is the fact that a primary key cannot contain any NULLs, because it is impossible to distinguish between two NULLs. Schema designs commonly have tables with ID columns that serve as primary keys to uniquely identify each row in the database. However, in certain tables this may not be necessary; for example, an employee table might use each employee's social security number as the primary key for employee records.

A Static State   Primary keys are columns that do not undergo frequent changes. Once you assign a row's primary key, the primary key should be static for the life of the row; otherwise, the primary key has no meaning. For example, a person's social security number is the same throughout that person's life.

Conciseness   In terms of primary keys, the shorter they are, the better, especially since most applications look for rows using primary key values. The best type of primary key is a single column that contains integers, such as the ID type of primary key seen throughout the example tables in this book. (Keep this recommendation in mind as you read Chapter 16. This chapter shows how to tune application performance using another Oracle7 feature, sequences, which an application can use to automatically generate unique integer values for primary keys.)

Follow the preceding guidelines when selecting primary keys for the tables in a new application schema. But keep in mind that in some situations you cannot follow all of the recommendations. For example, it is appropriate for the ITEM table to use a *composite primary key*—one made up of more than one column. Although Oracle7 supports composite primary key specifications, avoid them whenever possible to make application development an easier process in the long run.

Once you determine the primary keys in an application schema, you can enforce the associated integrity rule of guaranteed uniqueness using Oracle7 PRIMARY KEY integrity constraints. (See the section "Managing Tables and Security Constraints" later in this chapter for more information about specifying integrity constraints when creating tables.)

Identifying Alternate Keys and Columns to Index

When determining the primary keys for the tables in a schema, you should also look for any alternate keys in a table. In fact, you might have to choose a table's primary key from two or more candidate keys. Alternate keys contain unique values that applications commonly use to find rows in a database. For example, the CUSTOMER table shown in earlier examples in this book has an alternate key—applications might commonly query customer records by customer name instead of customer ID.

To find the alternate keys in a schema, simply identify those columns an application will commonly use to query rows. Once you find the alternate keys, you can use the analysis to identify the columns in unique keys when creating tables for the new schema.

When looking for alternate keys, you might also find columns that applications commonly query but that do not necessarily contain unique values. These columns, although not primary or alternate keys, are important to flag for later work when tuning application performance with indexes. (Chapter 16 explains how you can create indexes on columns of a table to improve application performance.)

Identifying and Enforcing Relationships in a Schema

As you normalize tables in a schema, you break apart large, complicated tables into smaller, simple tables that have relationships. During this process, you must clearly map out the table relationships so you can enforce associated data integrity rules using referential integrity constraints. Let's take a look at some of the issues to consider when identifying relationships in an application schema.

You can classify a relationship in a schema as one of three varieties: one-to-one, one-to-many, and many-to-many. Understanding a relationship's type helps you determine the different types of integrity constraints that are necessary to enforce necessary integrity rules.

One-to-many relationships are common in most application schemas. For example, review the entity-relation diagram in Figure 15.3. The ORDERS and ITEM tables relate by the IDs for each sales order. In this relationship, there should be unique order numbers, but there can be many different line items for an individual order. Therefore, a one-to-many relationship exists between an order and its line items. To enforce the one-to-many relationship rule, make the ID column of the ORDERS table a primary key with a PRIMARY KEY integrity constraint and the ORDERID column of the ITEM table a foreign key with a referential integrity constraint.

Similarly, you can use Oracle7 integrity constraints to enforce one-to-one relationships. For example, one-to-one relationships occur when you partition a table into vertical sections. You can make sure there is a one-to-one relationship between vertical table partitions by simply making the primary key in the secondary partition a foreign key to the primary partition of the table. Figure 15.4 illustrates how to enforce a one-to-one relationship between partitions of a modified version of the CUSTOMER table.

After identifying different relationships in a schema, flush out the referential integrity rules even further to understand the referential actions you want to enforce. Referential actions tell Oracle7 how to maintain referential integrity when users want to modify or delete parent key values that have dependent foreign key values. For example, how do you want Oracle7 to maintain referential integrity when a user tries to delete a sales order in the ORDERS table but the order has dependent line items in the ITEM table?

FIGURE 15.4:

Modified version of the CUSTOMER table, showing how to vertically partition row data and establish a one-to-one relationship between the partitions

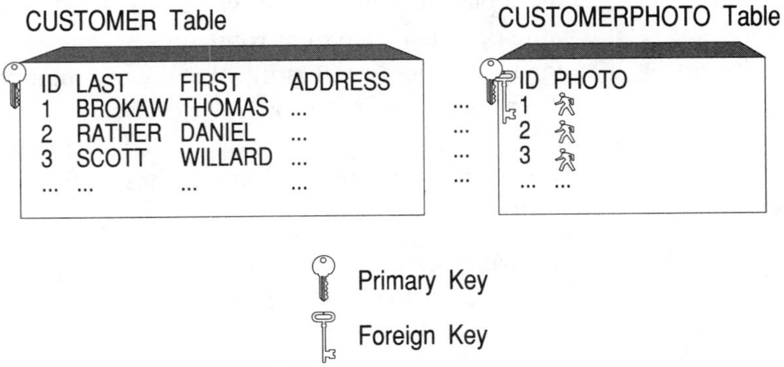

CUSTOMER Table

CUSTOMERPHOTO Table

ID	LAST	FIRST	ADDRESS
1	BROKAW	THOMAS	...
2	RATHER	DANIEL	...
3	SCOTT	WILLARD	...
...	...	...	...

ID	PHOTO
1	
2	
3	
...	...

Primary Key

Foreign Key

Oracle7 referential integrity constraints support two different types of referential actions:

- The update/delete restrict action restricts anyone from updating a parent key value or deleting a parent table row when the parent key value has at least one dependent foreign key value.

- The delete cascade action cascades the delete of a parent table row to all child rows that depend on the parent key in the deleted parent table row. (Note that Oracle7 enforces update restrict when you specify delete cascade.)

The referential integrity constraints in the ITEM table clearly demonstrate both types of referential actions. One foreign key references the ORDERS table with the delete cascade referential action (as shown in the section "Using Integrity Constraints to Enforce Standard Data Integrity Rules" in Chapter 2). Therefore, when someone deletes a sales order from the ORDERS table, Oracle7 automatically cascades the delete by removing all corresponding order line items in the ITEM table. The other foreign key in the ITEM table uses the update/delete restrict referential action, which restricts all operations on a parent key that has dependent child rows. Therefore, Oracle7 prohibits a user from updating a part number or deleting a part from the STOCK table if the part has dependent order line items.

The relational model includes other types of referential actions not enforced by Oracle7 integrity constraints, including update cascade (cascade the update of a parent key value to any dependent foreign key values), update/delete set null (set dependent foreign key values to NULL when someone updates a parent key value or deletes a parent row), and update/delete set default (set dependent foreign key values to a default value when someone updates a parent key value or deletes a parent row). Although Oracle7 cannot enforce these other referential actions automatically using simple referential integrity constraints, it is possible to use database triggers to enforce many of these rules. (See Chapter 18 for more information about using database triggers in an application schema.)

To learn more about creating and managing tables and integrity constraints in an application schema, see the section "Managing Tables and Integrity Constraints" later in this chapter.

Using Views Effectively in a Schema Design

Chapter 2 introduced the use of views for several purposes: to add more levels of security, to show table data with a different perspective, and to hide complex queries. This section delves more deeply into the subject of how and when to use views within an application schema design.

Isolating Application Logic

One of the best reasons to use views in an application schema is to isolate application logic from direct dependence on table structure. For example, assume that an application directly references a database table by name using SQL commands. It is not hard to predict what would happen to the application if at some point you changed the name of the table—you would need to modify the source code of the application to adjust all SQL references to the old table name and then recompile the application. Alternatively, if you use a view on top of the table, you can hide the rename of the table from the application by simply replacing the definition of the view. The application still references the view, but everything continues to work fine because the view now refers to the new table name. Figure 15.5 represents this advantage of using views.

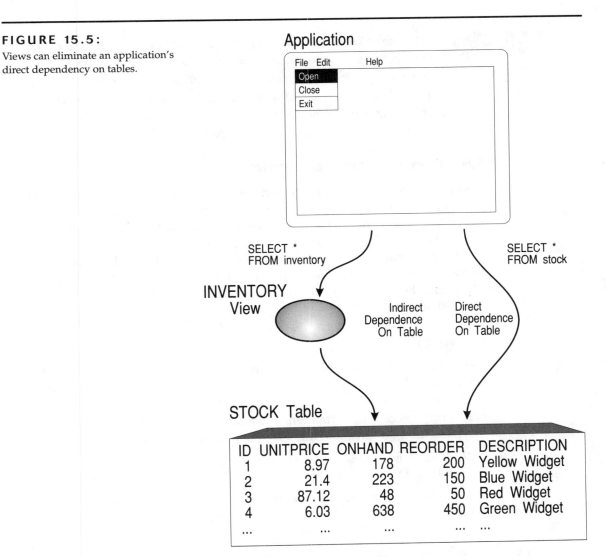

Views can eliminate an application's
direct dependency on tables.

> **NOTE**
>
> Using views is just one way you can isolate applications from directly referencing tables; you can use synonyms or stored procedures as well. See the section "Using Synonyms Effectively in a Schema Design" later in this chapter for information about synonyms, and see Chapter 18 for more information about stored procedures.

Eliminating SQL Commands

Another reason to use views is to eliminate complicated SQL commands from application code, which improves the productivity of application development. For example, applications can use complicated SQL queries that join data from multiple tables or use simple queries on views that perform the same joins. In the latter case you have to code and test a complicated join query only once when creating a view, as opposed to the former case, where you have to work with complicated queries every time the application needs to join table data. Figure 15.6 illustrates this benefit of using views.

Security

Security is another reason you might use views in an application schema. For example, if a client/server system supports ad hoc query tools for end users, you might want those end users to query table information indirectly through views to hide certain pieces of information. The following view allows a user to query employment information about himself or herself but not about other users:

```
CREATE VIEW myinformation AS
  SELECT * FROM emp WHERE ename = USER
```

To learn more about creating and managing views in an application schema, refer to the section "Managing Views" later in this chapter.

Using Synonyms Effectively in a Schema Design

In the previous section you learned how it can be beneficial to use views to isolate application logic from direct dependence on tables; specifically, if an application references a view and the name of the view's base table changes, the application can continue to work without modification by simply redefining the view to address

FIGURE 15.6:

Use views to hide complicated
queries and improve application
development productivity.

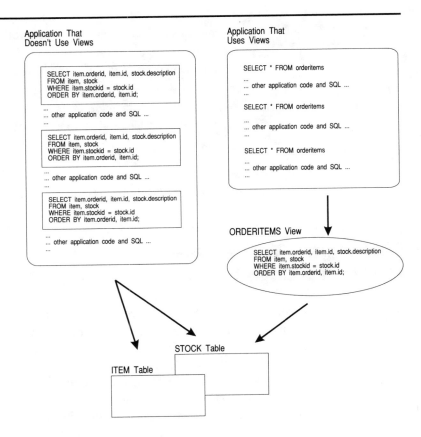

the new table name. Similarly, you can use another Oracle7 feature, synonyms, to
accomplish the same goal, but on a broader scale. A *synonym* is simply an alias (an
alternative name) for an Oracle7 table, view, sequence, stored procedure, function,
package, or another synonym. Use synonyms when you want to remove an application's direct dependence on these types of objects. For example, the following
statements show how the INVENTORY synonym functions to hide the real name
of the STOCK table from application code:

```
CREATE SYNONYM inventory FOR stock

INSERT INTO inventory VALUES (...)

DELETE FROM inventory WHERE id = 5
```

> **NOTE**
>
> Synonyms play an important role in distributed database systems, where applications can reference both local and remote database objects to accomplish work. In a distributed database, you can make application code simpler and more flexible to changes by using synonyms to hide the location of data structures from applications and create what is called location transparency.

To learn more about how to create and manage synonyms for an application schema, see the section "Managing Synonyms" later in this chapter.

Managing Tables and Integrity Constraints

If you do not have the luxury of using a CASE or database design tool to help create an application's schema, you have to manually plan out and diagram the schema on paper and then create an application's tables and views using SQL commands. Even when you use a CASE tool for schema design and creation, it is nice to know how to use the DDL commands of SQL that create, alter, and drop tables and views in case you ever have to use them. The following sections describe how to use several DDL commands of SQL to create and manage tables and their integrity constraints. (Later sections in this chapter describe the same operations for views. Also see Chapter 16, which discusses other schema objects, such as indexes and sequences, you can use to improve an application's performance.)

Creating Tables

When you want to create a new table for an application, use the SQL command CREATE TABLE. Here's a statement that creates a new table to store sales order information:

```
CREATE TABLE sales.orders
( id INTEGER PRIMARY KEY,
  customerid INTEGER NOT NULL REFERENCES customer,
  orderdate DATE DEFAULT SYSDATE NOT NULL,
```

```
shipdate DATE DEFAULT SYSDATE,
paiddate DATE DEFAULT SYSDATE,
status CHAR(1) DEFAULT 'F' CHECK (status IN ('F','B'))  )
```

When you name a table, you can specify the schema that will contain the new table. Simply precede the table name with the schema name and a dot. The preceding example creates the ORDERS table in the schema SALES. If you omit a schema name, Oracle7 assumes you want to create the table in your schema.

NOTE   To use the CREATE TABLE command, you must have the CREATE TABLE system privilege to create tables in your schema and the CREATE ANY TABLE system privilege to create tables in another schema.

A table's name can be any literal up to 30 characters (or bytes) in length. However, the table's name must begin with an alphabetic character, and it cannot conflict with an Oracle reserved word. For example, most of the table names in this book are singular (such as ITEM rather than ITEMS). However, the table in the preceding example is the plural ORDERS because ORDER is an *Oracle reserved word*—Oracle7 uses the word ORDER in the ORDER BY clause of SQL.

If you really want to, you can name a table (or any other database object) using an Oracle reserved word by delimiting the table name with double quotation marks in the CREATE TABLE statement:

```
CREATE TABLE "order"
.
.
.
```

However, most programmers avoid using Oracle reserved words for object names because it makes work difficult when using SQL; all references to a table named with an Oracle7 reserved word must also include quotation marks:

```
SELECT * FROM "order"
INSERT INTO "order" ...
```

You can save yourself some headaches by not using Oracle reserved words for table and other object names.

Finally, make sure a table's name is a unique object name within the target schema. For example, there cannot be two ORDERS tables in the SALES schema.

As the preceding example shows, the CREATE TABLE command offers several options for customizing the structure of a new table. The options of concern to an application developer include those for specifying columns and establishing integrity constraints. The next few sections explain more about these two important options for the CREATE TABLE command.

Specifying Columns and Datatypes

The first thing to consider when creating a new table is the table's columns. These columns define the structure for the rows of data that the table can hold. The example CREATE TABLE statement in the preceding section showed how to specify the different parts of a column specification.

To specify a table's columns in the CREATE TABLE command, you include a comma-separated list of *column specifications*. Each column specification can consist of several parts. At the very least, a column specification requires a column name and a column datatype. A column's name can be any literal up to 30 characters (or bytes) in length that begins with an alphabetic character and does not conflict with any Oracle reserved words. A column's datatype can be any Oracle datatype, including CHAR, VARCHAR2, NUMBER, DATE, LONG, RAW, LONG RAW, and ROWID. (See Table 2.1 in Chapter 2 for more information about Oracle datatypes.)

TIP

For convenience you can also specify a column's datatype using most ANSI, IBM DB2, or IBM SQL/DS datatypes. The CREATE TABLE example earlier in this chapter uses the INTEGER datatype for the ID and CUSTOMERID columns. If you choose to specify a column's datatype using a non-Oracle datatype, Oracle7 automatically converts the non-Oracle datatype specification to an equivalent Oracle datatype specification. In the example, Oracle7 automatically converts the ANSI INTEGER datatype specification to the ORACLE NUMBER(38) datatype.

Optionally, a column specification in a CREATE TABLE statement can include a default column expression and integrity constraints for the column. (See the next section for information about integrity constraints inside a column specification). A column's *default expression* is a convenient SQL feature that indicates the value to supply for an INSERT statement that does not specify a value for the column. You can specify any default column expression that does not include reference to another column or a sequence. A default column expression can also be an Oracle7 SQL function, such as SYSDATE or USER; the date columns in the ORDERS table of the previous example all use the SQL function SYSDATE to fill in a date if INSERT statements do not specify order, ship, and paid dates. If you do not specify a default column expression for a column, Oracle7 supplies NULL for missing column values in INSERT statements (assuming that the column permits NULLs).

Specifying Integrity Constraints

Chapters 2 and 18 explain the significant advantages that integrity constraints can provide in a client/server database system. When you plan a new table, be sure to also plan its integrity constraints. Then, when you create a new table, you can create its integrity constraints at the same time.

SQL lets you create a new table's integrity constraints both inside and outside column specifications. The CREATE TABLE example earlier in this chapter demonstrates several integrity constraints within column specifications.

If Oracle7 allows you to specify integrity constraints both inside and outside column specifications of the CREATE TABLE statement, how do you decide which option to use? In most cases the choice is yours because it is no more than a syntactic option of SQL. There are only two situations that call for a specific method of integrity constraint specification:

- You must specify NOT NULL integrity constraints inside the respective column specification.

- When an integrity constraint involves more than one column, you have to specify the integrity constraint outside any one column specification. For example, you might want to create a composite primary or unique key on multiple columns.

To demonstrate these considerations, the following CREATE TABLE statement shows how to create several NOT NULL constraints within column specifications and a composite PRIMARY KEY constraint outside any one column specification:

```
CREATE TABLE item
( id INTEGER,
  orderid INTEGER REFERENCES orders ON DELETE CASCADE,
  stockid INTEGER NOT NULL REFERENCES stock,
  quantity INTEGER NOT NULL,
  total DECIMAL(10,2),
  PRIMARY KEY (id, orderid) )
```

Notice that including integrity constraint specifications inside a column specification when possible clearly shows the integrity rules that apply to each column.

TIP   **Don't spend a lot of time debating which syntactic option to use. Get the job done and move on to more important issues.**

Other Options

If you look at a complete syntax diagram of the Oracle7 CREATE TABLE command, you will see that there are many other options. (For example, Chapter 10 explains how to specify various storage parameters for a new table with the TABLESPACE and STORAGE clauses of the CREATE TABLE command.) If you are an application developer working in a test environment, the other options of the CREATE TABLE command will rarely be of interest to you because your tables are just prototypes that contain very little data. However, if you are creating tables for a production database, these other options are important. Usually the administrator addresses the complicated storage considerations for a new table when installing a new application to ensure that the correct amount of space is allocated for each table. (For more information about setting storage options for tables, see Chapter 10.)

Modifying Tables

How many times have you created a masterpiece only to find that later on you need to change something about it? When you are involved in the complicated process of creating new tables for an application, you will often discover something new and want to modify the structure of a table. Oracle7 includes the SQL command ALTER TABLE so you can change a table without having to drop the old version and start again.

The ALTER TABLE command is also convenient when you need to alter a table while an application is using the table in a production database. Instead of suspending or shutting down the application for maintenance operations, Oracle7's ALTER TABLE command lets you modify the table without affecting the availability of the application.

NOTE To alter a table with the ALTER TABLE command, you must own the table, have the ALTER object privilege for the table, or have the ALTER ANY TABLE system privilege.

Adding and Modifying Columns

One way to alter a table is to modify an existing column or add another column that you originally forgot to include. The ADD and MODIFY clauses of the ALTER TABLE command let you change the structure of an existing table easily. Here are some examples that show how to use the ALTER TABLE command to add and change the definition of columns:

```
ALTER TABLE customer ADD (fax VARCHAR2(10))

ALTER TABLE customer MODIFY (fax VARCHAR2(20))

ALTER TABLE sales.orders MODIFY (status CHAR(1) DEFAULT null)
```

The first statement adds a new column to the CUSTOMER table for the customer's fax number. The second statement modifies the new FAX column to expand its maximum length. The third statement changes the default column expression for the STATUS column in the ORDERS table.

NOTE You can also use the MODIFY clause to decrease a column's size or change its datatype. However, Oracle7 allows you to perform these operations only when all column values are NULL.

Adding and Modifying Integrity Constraints

Rules are rules, but rules can change. If you decide you need to change the integrity rules tied to a table, you can use the ADD, MODIFY, and DROP clauses of the ALTER TABLE command. To add and drop integrity constraints using the ALTER TABLE command, you must learn a few keywords in the Oracle SQL syntax:

- To add a new integrity constraint separately from a new column definition in the ADD clause, you can use the PRIMARY KEY, UNIQUE, FOREIGN KEY, and CHECK clauses, just as with the CREATE TABLE command.

- To drop an integrity constraint in the DROP clause, you can use the keywords PRIMARY KEY and UNIQUE to drop a primary or unique key and use CONSTRAINT to drop FOREIGN KEY and CHECK constraints by their constraint names.

The following statements show how you can use these different clauses to modify a table's integrity constraints:

```
ALTER TABLE customer ADD (fax VARCHAR2(20) NOT NULL)

ALTER TABLE customer MODIFY (fax VARCHAR2(20) NULL)

ALTER TABLE customer ADD (PRIMARY KEY (id))

ALTER TABLE customer DROP UNIQUE (lastname, firstname)

ALTER TABLE customer DROP PRIMARY KEY CASCADE

ALTER TABLE customer DROP CONSTRAINT sysc0991
```

The first statement is somewhat of a repeat of a previous example; however, this example shows that you can add a new column to a table simultaneously with a new integrity constraint in a column definition. The second example shows how to remove a NOT NULL integrity constraint from a column definition. The third example demonstrates how to add a PRIMARY KEY integrity constraint, and the remaining examples show how to remove specific integrity constraints. Notice the statement that drops the primary key in the CUSTOMER table; it also includes the keyword CASCADE, which cascades the drop of the primary key to all dependent foreign keys.

Determining Names for Integrity Constraints

To determine the names for the different integrity constraints in a database, you can query the DBA_CONSTRAINTS or USER_CONSTRAINTS data dictionary view. For example, the following query returns the names of all constraints on the ITEM table:

```
SELECT constraint_name, constraint_type, search_condition
  FROM sys.dba_constraints
  WHERE owner = 'SALES'
  AND table_name = 'ITEM';
```

```
CONSTRAINT_NAME        C SEARCH_CONDITION
-------------------    ----------------------
SYS_C00436             C STOCKID IS NOT NULL
SYS_C00437             C QUANTITY IS NOT NULL
SYS_C00438             P
SYS_C00439             R
SYS_C00440             R
```

Notice that the CONSTRAINT_TYPE column (shown in the printout with the heading "C") reveals the different types of constraints: "P" stands for PRIMARY KEY constraint, "U" stands for UNIQUE constraint, "R" stands for referential constraint, and "C" stands for CHECK constraint as well as NOT NULL constraints. You can distinguish between CHECK constraints and NOT NULL constraints by looking at the SEARCH_CONDITION column.

Dropping Columns

Because Oracle7's ALTER TABLE command does not include an option to drop a column of a table, all the benefits the ALTER TABLE command provides (such as availability) are not there when you want to drop a column in a table. Consider the side effects (loss of data availability and a lot of extra work), and if you still want to drop a column in a table, follow these steps:

1. If you are working in a production database that is currently available to application users, shut down the applications that need to access the table.

2. Create a new copy of the table, making sure not to include the columns you want to drop. Use a temporary name for the new version of the table.

3. Use an INSERT statement with a subquery to copy the data from the old table to the new table:

```
INSERT INTO newtable SELECT col1, col2, col3 FROM oldtable
```

4. Rename the old and new versions of the table:

```
RENAME oldtable TO oldtabletemporary
RENAME newtable TO oldtable
```

5. Grant the same access privileges for the new version of the table that exist for the old version of the table.

6. Re-create any views and procedures that depended on the dropped column. If views and procedures did not explicitly refer to the dropped column, they will use the new version of the table without problems.

You can eventually drop the old version of the table to reclaim its disk space once you verify that the applications using the new version of the table still function correctly and that you did not complete the process in error.

Dropping Tables

If you want to completely remove a table from an application's schema, you can drop the table using the SQL command DROP TABLE. The following statements demonstrate how to use this command:

```
DROP TABLE item
```

```
DROP TABLE orders CASCADE CONSTRAINTS
```

The first statement shows how to drop a table that does not contain a primary or unique key to which other tables refer. The second statement shows how to drop a table that has a primary or unique key to which other tables refer. By using the CASCADE CONSTRAINTS option, Oracle7 automatically drops the foreign keys that depend on the primary key in the table being dropped.

NOTE To drop a table with the DROP TABLE command, you must own the table or have the DROP ANY TABLE system privilege.

Managing Views

Once you have finished crafting the tables in an application's schema, the next thing you might do is create different views on top of the application's tables. You can use views for many reasons in an application schema. (See the section "Using Views Effectively in a Schema Design" earlier in this chapter.) The following sections explain the procedural details of creating and managing views for an application schema.

Creating Views

To create a new view for an application, you use the SQL command CREATE VIEW. The rules for naming a view are identical to those for naming tables. (See the section "Creating Tables" earlier in this chapter for more information about naming rules for tables.)

You can specify many options in the CREATE VIEW command to create a new view, including

- The defining query of a view
- Column aliases for the column names in a view
- Integrity constraints for a view

The next few sections explain each of these options.

> **NOTE** To create a view, you must have the CREATE VIEW or CREATE ANY VIEW system privilege.

Specifying a View's Query

The primary consideration when creating a new view is the view's defining query. A view's query describes exactly what table data the view will represent. A view's query can be simple, such as this one, which creates the view to mask the name of a table:

```
CREATE VIEW inventory AS
  SELECT * FROM stock
```

When users use the INVENTORY view, it will look exactly the same as when they work with the STOCK table. The following examples show how SELECT and INSERT statements work identically for both the INVENTORY view and STOCK table:

```
SELECT * FROM inventory
```

ID	UNITPRICE	ONHAND	REORDER	DESCRIPTION
1	8.97	178	200	Yellow Widget
2	21.4	223	150	Blue Widget
3	87.12	48	50	Red Widget
4	6.03	638	450	Green Widget
.				
.				
.				

```
SELECT * FROM stock
```

ID	UNITPRICE	ONHAND	REORDER	DESCRIPTION
1	8.97	178	200	Yellow Widget
2	21.4	223	150	Blue Widget
3	87.12	48	50	Red Widget
4	6.03	638	450	Green Widget
.				
.				
.				

```
INSERT INTO inventory VALUES (5, 7.93, 600, 250, 'Orange Widget')

INSERT INTO stock VALUES (6, 23.52, 300, 150, 'Black Widget')
```

A more restrictive view query creates a view that corresponds only to selected table columns and/or rows:

```
CREATE VIEW reorder AS
  SELECT id, onhand, reorder FROM stock
  WHERE onhand < reorder
```

The REORDER view is an example of a view that corresponds to very specific table data based on particular columns and row values in the STOCK table:

```
SELECT * FROM reorder

ID         ONHAND     REORDER
---------- ---------- ----------
         1        178        200
         3         48         50
.
.
.
```

Another example of a view that targets specific data is one that includes a join query:

```
CREATE VIEW orderreport AS
  SELECT orders.id "ORDER ID", orders.orderdate,
    item.id "LINE ID", stockid
  FROM orders, item
  WHERE item.orderid=orders.id
```

When users query the ORDERREPORT view, Oracle7 joins the related row data from the ORDERS and ITEM tables:

```
SELECT * FROM orderreport

ORDER ID   ORDERDATE LINE ID     STOCKID
---------- --------- ----------- ----------
         1 23-MAY-95           1          4
         1 23-MAY-95           2          2
         1 23-MAY-95           3          3
         2 23-MAY-95           1          1
         2 23-MAY-95           2          2
.
.
.
```

The query you use for a view directly affects the functionality of the resulting view. For example, users can use simple views like the INVENTORY view—ones that reference only a single base table in their defining query—for all DML operations, including SELECT, INSERT, UPDATE, and DELETE operations. However, users cannot use complex views like the REORDER view for INSERT, UPDATE, and DE-LETE statements since it is unclear how Oracle7 should map such statements to the base tables. You can consider complex views those views that include a join operation, set or DISTINCT operators, group functions, and GROUP BY, CONNECT BY, or START WITH clauses.

View Functionality

View functionality can be tricky to understand if you create a view in one schema that is based upon tables or views from another schema. In this case, the view owner's object privileges for the base tables determine the functionality of a view. This way Oracle7 prevents a simple view definition from bypassing the internal security controls for object access.

For example, assume that you create the INVENTORY view (shown earlier in this chapter) for the STOCK table, which is in another user's schema, and that you have only the SELECT privilege for the STOCK table. Consequently, you can use the IN-VENTORY view for SELECT statements only, not for INSERT, UPDATE, or DE-LETE statements. Additionally, you cannot use any object privileges obtained from roles (as opposed to being granted the object privileges directly) to create a view.

These caveats should not concern you when you are creating an application schema that contains all the objects necessary for an application. That's because the owner of (or schema that contains) all application objects, including views and underlying base tables, is one and the same—you will never need to consider these tricky privilege requirements.

Using Column Aliases to Name the Columns in a View

In many cases you might want to use alternate names for a view's columns instead of those that correspond to the underlying table column names. For example, when creating a view that joins two different tables, it is important to clearly distinguish columns with identical names that originate from different tables. The ORDERRE-PORT view shown earlier in this chapter illustrates one way of specifying view column aliases: by indicating individual column aliases just as you do in a SELECT statement. CREATE VIEW, as shown in the next example, also allows you to specify a comma-separated list of column aliases before a view's defining query. If you use this method, the number of column aliases must match the number of columns in the defining query.

```
CREATE VIEW orderreport (order_id, order_date, line_item_id, stock_id) AS
  SELECT orders.id, orders.orderdate, item.id, stockid
    FROM orders, item
    WHERE item.orderid = orders.id
```

Creating Integrity Constraints for Views

A table's integrity constraints enforce integrity rules from all points of access, including any work done on the table through a view of the table. Oracle7 does not permit anyone to bypass a table's integrity rules by creating and using a view.

If you create a view for an application that users will employ to insert or update table data, consider using a special integrity constraint that you can create for the view. If you specify the CHECK option of the CREATE VIEW command when creating a view, Oracle7 permits users to insert and update through the view only those rows that the view in turn can select. For example, this statement defines a view to show only those customers in the state of California:

```
CREATE VIEW california AS
  SELECT companyname, lastname, firstname, city FROM customer
  WHERE state = 'CA'
  WITH CHECK OPTION
```

Now, see if you can predict which of the following two UPDATE statements Oracle7 disallows because of the CALIFORNIA view's integrity constraint:

```
UPDATE california
  SET city = 'SOUTH LAKE TAHOE'
  WHERE id = 7593

UPDATE california
  SET state = 'WA'
  WHERE id = 7593
```

If you picked the second statement, you're right. Oracle7 does not permit the second statement because it would result in a row that the CALIFORNIA view could not select—a record for a customer located in the state of Washington.

Replacing Views

Sometimes it is necessary to replace the current version of a view with a new definition. For example, if you add a new column to a table, you might want to change the definition of an associated view to show the new column in the table.

One way to replace a view with a new version is by dropping the current view and then re-creating the view with the new definition. However, when you replace a view by dropping it and then re-creating it, you also remove all privilege grants made for the view. You would then have to regrant the necessary privileges for the new version of the view to get an application back in business. To avoid this problem, Oracle7 provides an option to replace the current version of a view with a newer version—the REPLACE option of the CREATE VIEW command:

```
CREATE OR REPLACE VIEW ...
```

TIP
Like the ALTER TABLE command, the REPLACE option of the CREATE VIEW command is convenient when you need to replace the definition of a view while an application is online in a production database environment. Instead of suspending or shutting down the application for maintenance operations, you can simply replace the view without affecting the availability of the application.

Dropping Views

If you find that a view is no longer needed, it is best to drop the view to clean up the application's schema and the database's data dictionary. To drop a view, you use the SQL command DROP VIEW:

```
DROP VIEW reorder
```

You can always drop a view that you own. To drop a view in another schema with the DROP VIEW command, you must have the DROP ANY VIEW system privilege.

Managing Synonyms

When you are finished creating the tables and views for an application schema, the next step might be to consider creating synonyms for the database objects that the application will reference to accomplish work. This way you eliminate any direct dependence the application would otherwise have on database objects (see the discussions about this topic earlier in this chapter). The following sections explain how to create and manage the synonyms in an application schema.

Creating Public and Private Synonyms

Before creating a synonym you must consider whether or not you want the synonym to be publicly accessible or private to the containing schema. A public synonym is available to all users in the database. When you create a public synonym, you provide a name that all users can reference (although users still need privileges for the underlying database object). A private synonym is available only to the user who creates the private synonym and the users who have access to the private synonym's base object. (For more information about the considerations of security privileges for both public and private synonyms, see Chapter 19.)

Once you decide which type of synonym is appropriate, you can create a synonym for a table, view, sequence, stored procedure, function, package, or another synonym with the SQL command CREATE SYNONYM. The following examples illustrate the creation of both public and private synonyms.

```
CREATE SYNONYM sales.inventory FOR sales.stock;

CREATE PUBLIC SYNONYM parts FOR sales.stock;
```

> **NOTE**
>
> To create a public synonym, you must have the CREATE PUBLIC SYNONYM system privilege; to create a private synonym in your schema, you must have the CREATE SYNONYM system privilege; and to create a private synonym in another user's schema, you must have the CREATE ANY SYNONYM system privilege.

Using Synonyms

Once you create a public or private synonym, application developers can reference the synonym in application code to accomplish work. For example, application code could equivalently reference either the STOCK table or its private synonym INVENTORY.

```
INSERT INTO stock VALUES (...)
UPDATE stock ...
DELETE FROM stock WHERE ...

INSERT INTO inventory VALUES (...)
UPDATE inventory ...
DELETE FROM inventory WHERE ...
```

As when referencing database objects directly, the application user must have the appropriate privileges for a synonym's base object to successfully complete the request performed by a SQL statement.

Dropping Synonyms

If you drop a synonym's base object for good or decide that you no longer need a synonym, it's best to drop the synonym to clean up the database's data dictionary. You can drop a synonym using the DROP SYNONYM command. When dropping a public synonym, be sure to include the PUBLIC keyword.

```
DROP SYNONYM sales.inventory

DROP PUBLIC SYNONYM parts
```

NOTE

To drop a private synonym, you must own the synonym or have the DROP ANY SYNONYM system privilege. To drop a public synonym, you must have the DROP PUBLIC SYNONYM system privilege.

This chapter has discussed the essential database objects of an application's schema, including

- Planning tables with regard to normalization and choosing keys

- Identifying and enforcing domain, entity, and referential integrity rules using Oracle7 integrity constraints

- Using views to eliminate application code from directly depending on schema tables, improve application security, and make complicated SQL coding much easier

- Using synonyms to eliminate application code from having to depend directly on schema tables

- Creating, altering, and dropping tables, views, and synonyms

The next chapter builds on the information in this chapter by beginning a discussion of how to tune client/server application performance using a variety of other Oracle7 schema objects, including indexes, data clusters, and sequences.

CHAPTER

SIXTEEN

Tuning Applications with Database Structures

- Using indexes and data clusters to limit disk I/O and speed up data retrieval times

- Using sequences to automatically generate primary keys without contention in a multi-user database system

Once you have an application schema's tables and views in place, you can develop and run the application. However, soon after you begin using it, you might find that the application does not perform as well as you might like. Now begins the tuning phase of the application development process.

This chapter explains the first phase in the application tuning process: creating and using supplementary database objects to tune the use of an application's tables and views, including

- Using indexes and data clusters to speed the retrieval of specific rows in a table
- Using sequences to automatically create unique primary keys for tables without contention among concurrent users who are inserting new rows

Using Indexes to Speed Applications

To find the pages in a book that discuss a very specific subject, you would use the book's index. But assume that the book is terrible and that there is no index. Now it is a bit tougher to find the pages you want. Your next step might be to use the table of contents, but it is unlikely that this very specific subject will appear there. Your only remaining option is to read every word on every page. And if the book is large, it will take you a lot of time to find what you are looking for.

Database management systems such as Oracle7 also use indexes to find specific pieces of table data without having to do complete table scans. Furthermore, an Oracle7 table's index works the same way as the index in a book. Figure 16.1 shows what an index looks like in an Oracle7 database and how it speeds the retrieval of certain rows.

Notice in Figure 16.1 that an Oracle7 index is an ordered tree of data blocks or nodes. When Oracle7 uses an index to find an index value, it descends from the root node to the branch nodes and then to the leaf nodes, searching for the requested index value. Each read of a node results in a disk I/O unless the corresponding data block is currently cached in the database server's buffer cache. In each leaf node of an index, there are index values along with their corresponding physical addresses. When Oracle7 finds the requested index value, it reads the physical address of the corresponding table's row so it can immediately access the row.

FIGURE 16.1:

An index for a table allows Oracle7 to quickly find rows by their index values with minimal disk I/O.

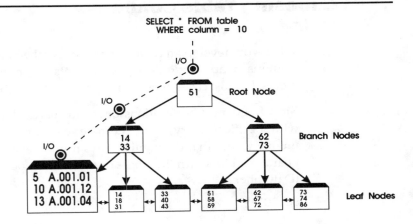

Indexes are supplementary, optional database structures that you can add to an application's tables to make access to the table much faster. When you do not have an index on a table, Oracle7 can still find the rows an application user requests, but it takes longer because the server has to scan all of the rows in the table. If the user requests only a handful of rows in a large table, the database server ends up performing a lot of unnecessary disk I/Os to find the requested rows. Alternatively, if the server can use an index to find rows in a table, the server can access only the specifically requested rows without very much disk access.

When an index is present on a table, Oracle7 automatically uses the index if it finds that using it will improve the performance of a statement. Oracle7 transparently uses indexes for all types of SQL statements, including SELECT statements with WHERE clauses and subqueries for UPDATE and DELETE statements (WHERE clauses). If a statement updates an indexed value in a row, Oracle7 automatically updates the value in the index along with the value in the table's row.

While indexes can speed the performance of applications, they are not appropriate for every column in a table. The following section explains how to choose the correct columns to index in a table.

Choosing Table Columns to Index

When you develop an application and its schema, it is important to note all of the columns an application's SQL statements use in the WHERE clauses of SQL statements. In most cases, these are the columns that should have an index.

Most frequently, applications query for particular table rows by asking for rows with specific primary key or alternate key values. That's because a table's keys hold unique values that distinguish rows from one another. For example, this query is guaranteed to return the single row that corresponds to the customer identified by ID number 3:

```
SELECT *
  FROM customer
  WHERE id = 3
```

There is no need for you to create an index on a primary key or an alternate key that is already declared for the table; Oracle7 automatically creates unique indexes behind the PRIMARY KEY and UNIQUE integrity constraints for a table.

Table columns without PRIMARY KEY or UNIQUE integrity constraints are not guaranteed to have unique column values. However, applications often use some of these columns to find specific table rows. For example, the ORDERS form application in Chapter 14 can issue this query to find the IDs of the backlogged sales orders:

```
SELECT id
  FROM orders
  WHERE status = 'B'
```

In this case it might improve the performance of the ORDERS form application if you created an index on the STATUS column of the ORDERS table. That way Oracle7 could find all of the rows in the index with a backlog status.

When you identify a non-key column as a candidate for indexing, consider these factors to determine if an index will actually improve application performance:

- The table you want to index should not be too small. If Oracle7 can store all of a table's rows in a just a few data blocks, there is no point in creating an index; it will not reduce the amount of disk I/O to access rows in the table.

- Index the columns that statements use to join related tables. Most often, statements join tables by their primary key/foreign key relationships. Since a table's primary key already has an index, all you have to do is index the foreign key. While following this suggestion can improve the performance of retrieval operations involving related tables, it also slows down the performance of update operations on the columns of the foreign key. Carefully consider the number of retrieval operations versus the number of update operations to determine whether or not it is appropriate to index the foreign key.

- Queries and subqueries for UPDATE and DELETE statements should regularly search for less than 20 percent of the table's rows. Statements that search for more than 20 percent will probably receive no performance gain from using an index because Oracle7 performs an equivalent or larger amount of disk I/O to access both the index's data blocks and the table's data blocks.

- Queries and subqueries that point to indexes with NOT NULL searches do not use indexes. That's because Oracle7 does not store NULLs in an index.

- The only limiting factor that determines the number of possible indexes for a table is the number of column combinations possible for an index. Otherwise there is no limit to the number of indexes per table. However, also consider that the more indexes you add to a table, the more indexes Oracle7 has to maintain when users modify index values in the table. If a table is in a decision support database where DML activity is rare, then more indexes per table are reasonable to improve the performance of different types of queries. However, when a table is in an OLTP database where DML activity is high, many indexes per table will no doubt slow down application response time.

- If an application requests many table lookups on a set of columns and none of the individual columns are themselves highly specific, but the entire set of columns together is, consider building a composite index of multiple columns. Composite indexes can contain up to 16 columns in the same table, assuming that the amount of data for each index entry is less than the database's data block size (minus some overhead).

- You cannot index LONG and LONG RAW columns.

For example, do you think that indexing the CUSTOMER table's STATE column is justifiable? If applications frequently query rows in the CUSTOMER table by a customer's state, the table has quite a few customer records, and customers are spread out among many different states, the STATE column would be a prime candidate for an index. However, if most customers are all in the same state, creating an index for the STATE column might be a waste.

What about indexing the QUANTITY column of the ITEM table? Considering that most sales order line items are for one, two, or three parts, an index on the QUANTITY column probably will not make much of a difference for queries that select line items by the quantity ordered.

Creating Table Columns for Indexes

Now that you have some understanding of which columns to index, it is time to learn how to create an index for a table. To do so you use the SQL command CREATE INDEX. For example, this statement creates a new index for the STATE column of the CUSTOMER table:

```
CREATE INDEX sales.stateindex ON customer (state)
```

NOTE To use the CREATE INDEX command, you must own the table you are trying to index, or you must have the CREATE ANY INDEX system privilege or have been granted the INDEX object privilege for the table.

The preceding index is for a single column in a table. You can also create *composite indexes* to index the concatenated values of more than one table column. This statement creates a composite index:

```
CREATE INDEX index ON table (column1, column2, ...)
```

When you create a composite index, it is critical that you order the columns in the index with some thought; if you don't, some queries might not be able to use the index at all. The leading columns in a composite index's column list should be the columns that most queries use to find table rows.

Rebuilding Indexes

If a table experiences a good deal of update and delete activity, the table's indexes can get out of balance, uncondensed, and as a result, somewhat ineffective in maximizing lookup performance. The telltale sign is when users notice that operations involving the index gradually slow down over time.

If your client/server application modifies a table's index values frequently and application performance with respect to that index gradually slows down over time, a problem index might be the reason. The first thing you can do is use the ANALYZE command to make sure the statistics corresponding to the index are current in the data dictionary. If statistics are not current with the data in the index, the optimizer might not be making intelligent decisions. If you are not familiar with analyzing tables and indexes, see Chapter 10.

If reanalyzing application data fails to improve application performance with respect to a specific index, the next step is to assume that the index has become unbalanced and uncondensed. In this case the only solution is to rebuild the index. Rebuilding an index means that you have to drop and re-create the index. The best time to rebuild an index is when the corresponding application(s) is offline or under a light load.

How often should you rebuild indexes that applications frequently modify? As you might expect, the answer is specific to your particular situation. For example, you might find it necessary to rebuild an index every few months or just once a year. Be sure to consider how quickly an index becomes unbalanced as a result of user activity and how much performance gain user operations experience from rebuilding the index.

> **TIP**
>
> To drop and re-create the indexes behind PRIMARY KEY and UNIQUE integrity constraints, simply disable and enable the constraints. Oracle7 automatically drops a constraint's index when you disable the constraint and re-creates the index when you enable the constraint. (See Chapter 6 for more information on disabling and enabling integrity constraints.)

Dropping Indexes

If after you create an index you find that the index does not improve performance or if you are in the process of rebuilding an index, you need to know how to drop an index. To drop a table's index, you use the SQL command DROP INDEX. This statement drops the STATEINDEX index of the CUSTOMER table:

```
DROP INDEX sales.stateindex
```

> **NOTE**
> To use the DROP INDEX command, you must own the index or have the DROP ANY INDEX system privilege.

After you drop an index, Oracle7 frees the space used by the index for other objects. Applications can still access the table as before, but the index is no longer available to help process statements.

> **TIP**
> When you drop a table, Oracle7 automatically drops any associated indexes, so you do not have to waste time dropping a table's indexes before dropping the table.

Using Data Clusters

When you go to the registration area at a big trade conference, there are usually several registration booths that correspond to several ranges of attendees' last names. For example, there might be one booth for attendees with last names that begin with the letters "A" through "E," another booth for "F" through "K," and so on. The idea is to improve the efficiency of registering many attendees by organizing different booths to separate and clump together premade conference badges, conference materials, and so on for each range of attendees by last name.

Using the same idea as the conference registration booths, Oracle7's *data clusters* can physically store related rows together to improve the performance of certain operations. For example, if a reporting application regularly generates reports of customer information according to the state in which a customer lives, it might be beneficial to the reporting application if you cluster all of the rows in the CUSTOMER table by the STATE column. This way, when you generate a report of customers from the state of New York, Oracle7 has to read only the one data block (or a small number of blocks) that contains all of the customer records from New York.

To contrast this with an unclustered table, Oracle7 stores a new row in whatever data block can hold the row. Therefore, if a statement wants to retrieve all of the rows that have a specific column value, it is likely that Oracle7 will have to read many data blocks to retrieve all of the rows. For example, if you want to retrieve all of the records from an unclustered CUSTOMER table for customers who live in the state of New York, Oracle7 will probably have to read several data blocks. Figure 16.2 illustrates the difference between a clustered and an unclustered table.

Oracle7 supports two different types of data clusters: indexed data clusters and hash data clusters. In an *indexed data cluster,* Oracle7 physically stores rows by the key values in the data cluster's index. In a *hash data cluster,* Oracle7 physically stores rows by the result of a hash function that is applied to each row's key value. The next section explains more about the different types of data clusters and when to use them to improve the performance of an application's SQL statements.

Deciding When to Use Data Clusters

If your application is working more slowly than you think it should, when do you consider using data clusters to help performance?

Indexed Data Clusters

As the example in the preceding section illustrates, the idea of using an indexed data cluster to physically locate and cluster rows by their key values seems like a promising approach to improve the performance of certain operations. Oracle7 even allows you to have *multi-table data clusters* in which related rows of master and detail tables are physically prejoined on disk in the same data blocks. It would seem that prejoining tables on disk would improve the performance of join queries. However, indexed data clusters have been available in several versions of Oracle

FIGURE 16.2:

Clustered and unclustered versions
of the CUSTOMER table

Rows placed in specific data
blocks according to STATE
column values.

CUSTOMER Table (Clustered Version)

ID	LASTNAME	FIRSTNAME	ADDRESS	CITY	STATE	PHONE	FAX	
...	...	...	...	...	CA	...	...	
...	...	...	...	...	CA	...	...	Data Block 0
...	...	...	...	...	CA	...	...	
...	...	...	...	...	CA	...	...	
...	...	...	...	...	CT	...	...	
...	...	...	...	...	CT	...	...	Data Block 1
...	...	...	...	...	CT	...	...	
...	...	...	...	...	CT	...	...	
...	...	...	...	...	NY	...	...	
...	...	...	...	...	NY	...	...	Data Block 2
...	...	...	...	...	NY	...	...	
...	...	...	...	...	NY	...	...	

CUSTOMER Table (Unclustered Version)

ID	LASTNAME	FIRSTNAME	ADDRESS	CITY	STATE	PHONE	FAX	
...	...	...	...	...	CA	...	...	
...	...	...	...	...	WA	...	...	Data Block 0
...	...	...	...	...	CT	...	...	
...	...	...	...	...	NY	...	...	
...	...	...	...	...	WA	...	...	
...	...	...	...	...	CT	...	...	Data Block 1
...	...	...	...	...	NY	...	...	
...	...	...	...	...	CA	...	...	
...	...	...	...	...	CA	...	...	
...	...	...	...	...	NY	...	...	Data Block 2
...	...	...	...	...	CT	...	...	
...	...	...	...	...	WA	...	...	

Rows placed in any data blocks
without any consideration of
STATE column values.

leading up to Oracle7, and in that time Oracle users consistently report minimal gains, if any, from using indexed data clusters. In certain situations, Oracle7's indexed data clusters can improve the performance of limited read operations, but they degrade the performance of insert, update, and delete operations. Without a doubt, there are some cases where the use of an indexed data cluster can make a noticeable improvement. In general, though, you should avoid using indexed data clusters and use tables with indexes, hash data clusters, or both.

Hash Data Clusters

Hash data clusters can significantly improve application performance when an application continuously issues exact-match queries on a lookup table. (This type of operation is common in most relational database schemas.) *Exact-match queries* are those that ask for a row by a specific value:

```
SELECT description
  FROM stock
  WHERE id = 4
```

Hash data clusters are a good idea for exact-match queries because Oracle7 can find the data block that holds the requested row with a single disk I/O. Oracle7 applies a hash function to the value in the WHERE clause of the query, which automatically tells Oracle7 which data block stores the requested row. The idea of using hash clusters is not so much to physically clump together many related rows (as with indexed data clusters), but to physically locate rows so Oracle7 can find them with only one disk I/O.

> **TIP**
>
> Like indexed data clusters, Oracle7 allows you to physically store multiple tables in a single hash data cluster. But since the primary benefit of hash clusters is not the clustering of related rows, it is best in most cases to consider hash data clusters for a single table.

Right now you are probably thinking of many Oracle7 tables that you might want to store in a hash data cluster to tune application performance. But before you get to work, also consider that a table in a hash cluster should also be relatively static. In other words, applications should use a table in a hash cluster primarily for queries, not for INSERT, UPDATE, and DELETE statements. Oracle7 physically preallocates space when creating a hash cluster so it can locate the rows within. Consequently, a volatile table can quickly unorganize the physical layout of the hash cluster, taking with it the performance benefits.

Unclustered Tables with Indexes versus Hash Clusters

When should you use hash data clusters and when should you use unclustered tables with indexes to improve the performance of your application? To make your decision, answer two simple questions:

- Is the table static or volatile?

- Do applications use equality or range searches on the table's key?

Figure 16.3 shows a flow diagram that illustrates the decision-making process.

Notice that the flow diagram in Figure 16.3 can lead to three different results. First, if a table is volatile rather than static, you should always use an unclustered table with indexes, as explained in the preceding section.

FIGURE 16.3:

How to decide between unclustered tables with indexes and hash data clusters

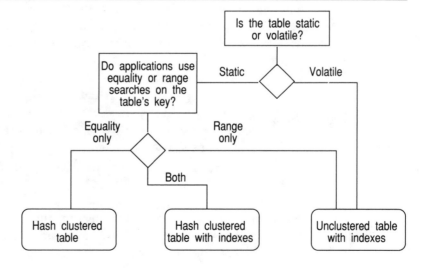

The second question attempts to determine the types of queries an application issues on a static table. In general, you cannot go wrong with an unclustered table with indexes; they are very good at improving the performance of all queries because they reduce the disk I/O necessary to complete both range and equality queries.

If you want the very best performance for equality queries on a static table, hash clusters are the way to go; they require only one disk I/O to find the rows requested by an equality search. However, hash clusters are very bad for range searches; Oracle7 has to perform a full table scan to find the rows requested by a range query when only a hash cluster is present.

A third possibility arises when applications issue both range and equality searches on a static table. In this case it is appropriate to both cluster the table and have supplementary indexes on the keys of the table. Oracle7 automatically takes care of this for you when you declare the primary key and alternate keys for a table, whether or not you create the table in a hash cluster. When an application issues a query, the Oracle7 optimizer will choose the hash approach to find rows requested by equality searches and choose the index approach to find rows requested by range searches. Therefore, you have both cases covered if you combine the two approaches.

Creating and Using Data Clusters

NOTE This section focuses on creating and using hash data clusters only, for reasons stated in the section "Indexed Data Clusters" earlier in this chapter.

To create a hash data cluster, you use the SQL command CREATE CLUSTER. For example, this statement creates a hash cluster in preparation for the STOCK table:

```
CREATE CLUSTER stockcluster (id INTEGER)
   SIZE 40
   HASH IS id
   HASHKEYS 1000
```

To place a table in a hash cluster, you specify the cluster when you create the table:

```
CREATE TABLE stock
( id INTEGER PRIMARY KEY,
  ... other columns ... )
CLUSTER stockcluster (id)
```

> **NOTE**
>
> To create a cluster, you must have the CREATE CLUSTER or CREATE ANY CLUSTER system privilege. To create a table in a hash cluster, you must own the cluster and have the CREATE TABLE system privilege or the CREATE ANY TABLE system privilege.

Notice that when you create a hash cluster, you must specify the key for the cluster. In most cases you will want the key for a clustered table to be one of the table's keys: primary, alternate, or foreign; after all, most queries will attempt to identify rows by a key value.

Also notice that the CREATE CLUSTER command has a few special clauses that allow you to determine the physical layout of a hash cluster's storage. Since the developer knows the application behavior, it is up to the developer to set these parameters correctly:

- The optional SIZE clause allows you to specify the size of the rows in the hash cluster. SIZE is specified in bytes. For example, the SIZE specification for the STOCKCLUSTER is 40, meaning that the average size of a row in the STOCK table is approximately 40 bytes. Oracle7 uses this parameter to determine how many unique hash values it can map to each data block. If you omit the SIZE clause, Oracle7 stores only one hash key value in each data block, which can lead to a tremendous amount of wasted space. Therefore, use the techniques shown in Chapter 10 to determine the average table row size, and use this value to set a hash cluster's SIZE parameter correctly.

- The HASH IS clause is optional. Use this clause of the CREATE CLUSTER command only when the cluster's key is a single, numeric column and the key contains uniformly distributed values. For example, the key for the

STOCKCLUSTER is the ID column of the STOCK table. Since the ID column is the primary key of the STOCK table (all values must be unique), the values in the cluster key are uniformly distributed.

- The HASHKEYS clause is required. It specifies the number of unique keys you think will ever be in the table in the cluster. For example, the setting shown earlier in this section means that the STOCK table will contain, at most, 1000 unique parts.

Dropping Clusters

If you try a cluster and decide that it is not helping application performance or if you want to drop the table in the cluster for another reason, you can drop the cluster and any tables within by using the SQL command DROP CLUSTER. This statement drops the STOCKCLUSTER cluster:

```
DROP CLUSTER stockcluster
```

If you want to drop a cluster that currently contains one or more tables, you can drop the cluster and the tables all in one operation by using the INCLUDING TABLES option of the DROP CLUSTER command:

```
DROP CLUSTER stockcluster
  INCLUDING TABLES
    CASCADE CONSTRAINTS
```

If you want to keep the table data but remove it from a cluster, you have to create a new version of the table and copy the old table's data to the new version before dropping the cluster:

```
CREATE TABLE newstock
(id INTEGER PRIMARY KEY,
 ... other columns and constraints ... )

INSERT INTO newstock SELECT * FROM stock

DROP CLUSTER stockcluster
```

After creating the new, unclustered version of the table and dropping the old version, rename the new table and then grant the same privileges that existed for the clustered version of the table.

The CASCADE CONSTRAINTS option is just like the same option of the DROP TABLE command. Specify this option only if you are dropping a table that contains a primary key referenced by a foreign key in another table. Otherwise, you must manually drop the dependent foreign keys before dropping the clustered table with the primary key.

Using Sequences

OLTP applications are characterized by many small insert and update transactions. OLTP environments usually demand high performance because the productivity of many workers hinges on the database server's ability to quickly complete a high number of transactions.

Most OLTP applications are specifically insert intensive. For example, a sales order application that services many different sales representatives can bombard the database server with new sales orders, especially when business is good. Inherent in inserting new records into a table is the requirement that each row have a unique primary key value. Imagine the logic a developer would have to code into a multiuser client/server sales order application to make sure every new sales order had a unique ID, much less to make it efficient enough that it does not saturate the network with database requests and slow down the productivity of sales representatives. Fortunately, application developers do not have to consider such problems when working with Oracle7 because of an OLTP feature called the sequence generator.

The Oracle7 *sequence generator* generates sequences of unique integers that applications can use as primary key values for insert-intensive applications. The following sections explain how to create and use sequences for the tables in an application schema to improve the performance of the application.

Creating Sequences

To create a new sequence of numbers, you use the SQL command CREATE SEQUENCE. For example, these statements create sequences for a couple of tables in an application schema:

```
CREATE SEQUENCE sales.customersequence
  START WITH 1
  INCREMENT BY 1
  NOMINVALUE
```

```
      NOMAXVALUE
      NOCYCLE
      NOCACHE

CREATE SEQUENCE sales.ordersequence
      START WITH 1
      INCREMENT BY 1
      NOMAXVALUE
      NOCYCLE
      CACHE 5
```

NOTE To create a sequence you must have the CREATE SEQUENCE or CREATE ANY SEQUENCE system privilege.

There are several parameters you can set when creating a new sequence of integers. For example, you can determine the starting integer for the sequence and how to increment the sequence (negative integers indicate descending-sequence integer generation), as well as minimum and maximum sequence integers. You can also indicate whether or not you want the sequence to cycle. (An ascending sequence cycles upon reaching its maximum value and a descending sequence cycles upon reaching its minimum value.) Finally, the CACHE parameter lets you pregenerate and cache a number of integers all at one time to reduce the disk I/O when applications use the sequence. (Disk I/O is necessary because Oracle7 needs to keep track of a sequence's current number in the data dictionary.)

NOTE If you cache sequence numbers, some sequence numbers may be lost, for example, when the database server shuts down. However, primary keys should have no particular meaning other than to uniquely identify rows in a table. Therefore, if you lose some sequence numbers, this should have no effect on the readability of a table.

Using Sequences in Applications

Now that you know how to create a sequence of numbers, this section shows how you can use sequences to improve the performance of an application.

Typically, INSERT statements use a sequence to generate a unique primary key for the new row. To reference a sequence and generate a new sequence number, reference the sequence with the pseudo-column NEXTVAL:

```
INSERT INTO customer
  VALUES (customersequence.NEXTVAL, ... )
```

NOTE   To use a sequence, you must have the SELECT object privilege for the sequence or the SELECT ANY SEQUENCE system privilege.

The preceding INSERT statement generates the next unique sequence integer for the CUSTOMERSEQUENCE and assigns this value to the user session that generated the value; once an application user generates a sequence number, no other sessions can use the same value.

After generating a new sequence number, the same session can reuse the current sequence number by referencing the sequence with the CURRVAL pseudo-column. This is primarily useful when inserting detail records along with a master record. For example, this transaction inserts a new sales order and three line items for the same order, using the ORDERSEQUENCE to generate and reuse a unique sales order ID:

```
INSERT INTO orders
  VALUES (ordersequence.NEXTVAL, ... )
INSERT INTO item
  VALUES (1, ordersequence.CURRVAL, ...)
INSERT INTO item
  VALUES (2, ordersequence.CURRVAL, ...)
INSERT INTO item
  VALUES (3, ordersequence.CURRVAL, ...)
COMMIT
.
.
.
```

This example uses the ORDERSEQUENCE for both the ORDERS and ITEM tables, revealing that sequences are not tied in any way to specific database tables in the Oracle7 data dictionary; users can use any sequence to generate unique numbers for any table.

Altering Sequences

If you find that you would like to adjust one of the parameters for a sequence in an application schema, you can alter the sequence using the SQL command ALTER SEQUENCE. For example, suppose that sales orders are entered more quickly than you thought. To reduce disk I/O on behalf of the sequence, you decide to increase the number of sequence numbers to cache for the ORDERSEQUENCE:

```
ALTER SEQUENCE ordersequence
  CACHE 50
```

NOTE   To alter a sequence you must own the sequence, or you must have the ALTER object privilege for the sequence or the ALTER ANY SEQUENCE system privilege.

Dropping Sequences

Although a sequence is not directly linked by Oracle7 to specific database tables, applications do associate a sequence for use with specific tables. Therefore, if you drop a table, you should determine whether or not sequences related to the table have any more use in the database. If not, then you should also drop the sequences to clean up the data dictionary.

To drop a sequence, you use the SQL command DROP SEQUENCE. For example, the following statement drops the CUSTOMERSEQUENCE:

```
DROP SEQUENCE sales.customersequence
```

This chapter has shown you the most basic ways you can tune an ORACLE7 application's performance—by using supplementary database structures like indexes, clusters, and sequences. You have learned

- How indexes, indexed data clusters, and hash data clusters can reduce disk I/O for SQL operations and thus improve performance for corresponding applications

- How to decide when indexes or data clusters can indeed help application performance

- How to decide which columns to index

- How to create and manage indexes and data clusters

- How the Oracle7 sequence generator can improve the performance of OLTP applications by automatically generating unique primary keys without contention in a multi-user database system

- How to create, use, and manage sequences

The next chapter continues the discussion of Oracle7 application tuning but focuses on tuning an application's logic, including SQL statement tuning, transaction design, and manual locking strategies.

CHAPTER
SEVENTEEN

Tuning Application Logic

- Using **EXPLAIN PLAN** and hints to tune SQL statements

- Designing transactions for maximum performance

- Overriding default locking mechanisms and using **SET TRANSACTION**

- Pinning an application's code in server memory

- Using array processing to reduce network traffic

Once you have done all you can to tune an application with indexes, clusters, and sequences, you still might find that it is not delivering the performance you expect or require. This leads you to the next phase of application tuning: tuning the logic within the application itself. This chapter explains several areas to focus on when trying to tune the logic of an Oracle7 client application, including

- Designing SQL statements to take advantage of available indexes and hash clusters
- Examining and tuning SQL statement execution
- Tuning transaction behavior for maximum performance
- Using all available Oracle7 client/server features to reduce network traffic between clients and the database server

Tuning SQL Statements

One of the first places to look when tuning an application's logic is the SQL statements the application issues to the database server. If your statements are not well designed or if the server is not executing them efficiently, you need to make some changes. The following sections explain

- How to design SQL statements intelligently
- How to display the Oracle7 server's execution plan for a SQL statement
- What to look for when tuning SQL statements for a client/server environment
- How to influence SQL execution with Oracle7 hints

Designing Statements for Optimal Performance

Chapter 16 focused on using supplemental Oracle7 features, such as indexes and hash clusters, to improve the performance of SQL statements. But the mere fact that a table has an index or is in a hash cluster does not mean Oracle7 can improve the performance of every statement that uses the table. Only by designing SQL statements intelligently to take advantage of indexes and clusters can you produce significant performance gains.

For example, consider this query:

```
SELECT * FROM item
  WHERE orderid = 3
```

Recall that the ITEM table has a composite primary key of the ID and ORDERID columns. Since the ITEM.ORDERID column is indexed, you might expect Oracle7 to use the index to complete the query. However, Oracle7 cannot use the index behind the primary key because the query does not make reference to the leading portion of the concatenated index values—the ID of the line items.

To get the query to return the same results but use the available index, you need to reference the leading portion of the index. This rewrite of the query shows one way to do it:

```
SELECT * FROM item
  WHERE id < 1000
  AND orderid = 3
```

The second query includes a reference to all line items with an ID of less than 1000 (there should not be any orders with more than a few line items, so 1000 is a safe bet) and an ORDERID of 3. With this simple rewrite of the original query, Oracle7 now uses the index that includes the ORDERID column.

This example is just one of many possible situations in which poor SQL statement design leads to nonoptimal behavior. The next section explains the EXPLAIN PLAN feature of Oracle7, a tool you can use to reveal the execution plans for SQL statements.

Explaining Statement Execution to Diagnose Tuning Problems

Once an application's SQL statements are designed to use all available indexes, hash clusters, and sequences, you can turn your attention to tuning the execution of the SQL statements within the application. In most cases you do not have to worry about the internals of statement execution. That's because Oracle7's cost-based optimizer can make intelligent decisions in order to execute all SQL statements the fastest way possible. However, there are situations when the optimizer can be doing the wrong thing. Before exploring these situations, let's learn a little about diagnosing problem statements.

The first trick is identifying statements you suspect might need some tuning. You might be able to identify those statements by reviewing an application's code. For example, a simple INSERT statement is less likely to need tuning than a query that joins and sorts information from three different tables. This simple type of code analysis can target some initial statements to analyze for tuning improvements.

Examining the application's code helps you identify the easy cases. But in many other cases it may not be apparent that a statement is executing more slowly than it should. To help you pinpoint problematic SQL statements that might benefit from analysis and tuning, rely on the feedback from application users.

Once you have targeted a SQL statement to analyze for tuning, you can use the SQL command EXPLAIN PLAN to find out how Oracle7 is executing it. But before you attempt to use this command, you must create a table to store its output. To create an EXPLAIN PLAN table, run the UTLXPLAN.SQL script that comes with Oracle7. This script creates a table called PLAN_TABLE that can receive the output of an EXPLAIN PLAN statement. The UTLXPLAN.SQL script's location is system dependent; for example, on UNIX systems the UTLXPLAN.SQL script is in the $ORACLE_HOME/rdbms/admin directory, and on Novell NetWare the script is in the ORACLE_HOME\rdbms\admin directory.

Once you have created the PLAN_TABLE table, you can run EXPLAIN PLAN statements to diagnose tuning problems for SQL statements. For example, the following statement checks how the Oracle7 server executes a statement and places this information in the PLAN_TABLE table:

```
EXPLAIN PLAN
  SET STATEMENT_ID 'NY Customers1'
  INTO plan_table
  FOR
    SELECT lastname, firstname
    FROM customer
    WHERE state = 'NY'
```

To check the statement execution output from this EXPLAIN PLAN statement, issue a simple query on PLAN_TABLE:

```
SELECT statement_id, operation, options, position cost
  FROM plan_table
```

STATEMENT_ID	OPERATION	OPTIONS	COST
NY Customers1	SELECT STATEMENT		25
NY Customers1	TABLE ACCESS	FULL ACCESS	0

Notice that the EXPLAIN PLAN statement shows that Oracle7 found the customers in New York by doing a full table scan (in the OPTIONS column). The cost of the statement's execution is revealed by the POSITION column in the first row for a statement in the PLAN_TABLE table (renamed in the example using the column alias COST).

TIP

The numeric value of a statement's cost is an arbitrary measurement—it does not correspond to anything real (for example, milliseconds or logical I/Os). Therefore, analyze the costs that you gather with the EXPLAIN PLAN command using a comparative method rather than a quantitative method.

Remember that the CUSTOMER table has an index on the STATE column. But then why didn't Oracle7 use this index? In this case there might be a very simple answer—that the administrator has not analyzed the STATEINDEX index recently created for the CUSTOMER table.

NOTE

The EXPLAIN PLAN command of Oracle7 uses the current statistics in the data dictionary to do its best to return an accurate execution plan and corresponding cost of executing a statement. However, if statistics are not up to date, then, of course, the EXPLAIN PLAN command might not return an accurate execution plan and cost.

After you analyze the CUSTOMER table (or just the STATEINDEX index), the same EXPLAIN PLAN statement produces the expected results:

```
ANALYZE TABLE customer COMPUTE STATISTICS

EXPLAIN PLAN
  SET STATEMENT_ID 'NY Customers2'
  INTO plan_table
  FOR
    SELECT lastname, firstname
    FROM customer
    WHERE state = 'NY'

SELECT statement_id, operation, options, position cost
  FROM plan_table
```

STATEMENT_ID	OPERATION	OPTIONS	COST
NY Customers1	SELECT STATEMENT		25
NY Customers1	TABLE ACCESS	FULL ACCESS	0
NY Customers2	SELECT STATEMENT		4
NY Customers2	TABLE ACCESS	BY ROWID	0
NY Customers2	INDEX	RANGE SCAN	1

The next section examines some of the more common situations to look for when troubleshooting unexpected statement executions revealed by the EXPLAIN PLAN feature of Oracle7.

Troubleshooting Unexpected Statement Execution Plans

Neglecting to analyze a table or its indexes can cause the Oracle7 optimizer to pick less-than-optimal SQL statement execution plans. Here is a list of other common problems to check for when the EXPLAIN PLAN reveals what you feel are incorrect statement execution plans made by the Oracle7 optimizer:

- Oracle7 makes all of its decisions based on the statistics for objects in the data dictionary. If an object experiences a lot of DML activity, older statistics may no longer represent the object's actual data. Therefore, Oracle7 is making the correct choice based on the object's statistics; but this turns out to be the wrong choice because the statistics are incorrect. To remedy the situation, the database administrator should frequently and regularly analyze an application schema to keep all statistics current.

- If Oracle7 is not using an index you believe it should be using and the index's statistics are current, the index might be unbalanced and undercompressed because of a lot of DML activity. To remedy this situation, rebuild the index (as described in Chapter 16).

- If Oracle7 is not using a hash cluster for a table search, it could be that the table has experienced enough DML activity that the hash cluster layout is no longer effective. In this case the Oracle7 optimizer is making the right decision because the hash cluster is in such bad shape. This problem is hard to fix because it appears that you have made a bad choice by putting a volatile table in a cluster.

Dynamically Controlling Oracle7's Optimizer for Interactive and Batch Mode Applications

Client applications can vary the types of SQL statements they issue. For example, consider two different types of queries an application might issue. The first is a batch mode operation, a query with an aggregate function, such as this:

```
SELECT SUM(total)
  FROM item
  WHERE orderid < 1000
```

In this situation it's best to have Oracle7 execute the entire query for maximum throughput because the query returns only one row as an answer—the total amount of income from all sales orders with an ID of less than 1000.

Now consider an interactive mode operation, a query for a cursor in a PL/SQL block:

```
DECLARE
  CURSOR ordercursor IS
    SELECT orderid, SUM(total)
      FROM item
      WHERE orderid < 1000
      GROUP BY orderid
      ORDER BY orderid;
  ordernumber INTEGER;
```

```
   ordertotal REAL;
BEGIN
   OPEN ordercursor;
   LOOP
     FETCH ordercursor INTO ordernumber, ordertotal;
     ... other application-processing logic ...
     EXIT WHEN ordercursor%NOTFOUND;
   END LOOP;
   CLOSE ordercursor;
END;
```

In this example the PL/SQL block is interactive because it does something with each row returned by the cursor's query, one row at a time. Because there is the potential for Oracle7 to total all of the line items for up to 1000 sales orders, it might take Oracle7 a long time to completely identify the return data for the cursor's query before even returning control for the first row. Consequently, the application or user waits and wastes valuable time.

In interactive mode applications, it's best if Oracle7 optimizes the query for fastest response time rather than for maximum throughput. This way Oracle7 quickly finds the first set of rows that satisfy the query and returns those rows to the application, which can then immediately begin other processing using the rows. Meanwhile, Oracle7 can find the remainder of the rows for the cursor. When Oracle7 optimizes statements like this for better response time, applications or users can be more productive.

An Oracle7 client application can dynamically tune when Oracle7 optimizes application statements for a goal of maximum throughput or faster response time. An application session can set the optimization goal after application startup (or at any time) by issuing an ALTER SESSION command with the SET OPTIMIZATION clause and one of the following options:

```
ALTER SESSION
   SET OPTIMIZER_GOAL = FIRST_ROWS

ALTER SESSION
   SET OPTIMIZER_GOAL = ALL_ROWS
```

The FIRST_ROWS option tunes the optimizer's goal for faster response times, while the ALL_ROWS option tunes the optimizer's goal for maximum throughput. After issuing an ALTER SESSION statement, Oracle7 optimizes application statements according to the setting unless a statement specifically overrides the setting.

(The next section explains how individual statements can override the current optimizer setting for an application session.)

Note that as a database administrator you determine the Oracle7 optimizer's default tuning goal for all applications, using the OPTIMIZER_MODE initialization parameter:

```
OPTIMIZER_MODE = FIRST_ROWS
```

NOTE   An application can change the optimizer's goal for specific application sessions by issuing an ALTER SESSION statement.

Influencing Statement Execution with Hints

In most situations Oracle7 executes an application's statements in the way that delivers the best performance possible for the application. However, if after diagnosing a statement's execution plan you find that the server executes an application statement in a way you feel is less than optimal, you can influence or force Oracle7 to execute an application statement the way you want by including hints in SQL statements. A *hint* is a directive enclosed within a comment of a SQL statement that instructs Oracle7 to execute the statement using a particular approach.

The following sections explain how to specify hints in SQL statements and describe the hints that are available in Oracle7.

Expressing Hints within SQL Statements

To specify an Oracle7 hint, you include the hint within a comment of a SQL statement. Unlike SQL comments that do not contain hints, Oracle7 requires that you code a comment with a hint in a specific location within a statement. Also, the comment must include a plus sign (+) to tell Oracle7 that the comment contains a hint. The following examples illustrate the correct locations and syntax for SQL comments that contain hints within SELECT, UPDATE, and DELETE statements:

```
SELECT /*+ INDEX(customer stateindex) */
  lastname, firstname
  FROM customer
  WHERE state = 'WA'

UPDATE --+ INDEX(customer stateindex)
  customer
  SET ...

DELETE --+ INDEX(customer stateindex)
  FROM customer
  WHERE state = 'WA'
```

All of the preceding statements include a hint to force Oracle7 to use the STATE-INDEX index of the CUSTOMER table.

Notice that SQL comments can either begin with the "--" characters or begin with the "/*" characters and end with "*/". In either case the beginning comment delimiter must be immediately followed by the +. Also, a comment with a hint must immediately follow the SELECT, UPDATE, or DELETE command keyword.

TIP   You can indicate multiple hints in the same SQL comment by separating the different hints with one or more blank spaces.

Now that you know how to specify a hint in an application's statement, let's learn what the different hints are that you can use with Oracle7.

Controlling the Optimizer's Goal with Hints

The section "Dynamically Controlling Oracle7's Optimizer for Different Applications" earlier in this chapter discusses how an application can determine when Oracle7 optimizes SQL statements for maximum throughput or faster response times. To override an application session's optimizer goal setting for individual SQL statements, you can use the FIRST_ROWS and ALL_ROWS hints. Like the options for the ALTER SESSION command, the FIRST_ROWS hint forces the optimizer to execute a statement for a faster response time, while the ALL_ROWS hint forces the optimizer to execute a statement for maximum throughput.

```
SELECT /*+ ALL_ROWS */ SUM(total)
  FROM item
  WHERE orderid < 1000

DECLARE
  CURSOR ordercursor IS
    SELECT --+ FIRST_ROWS
      orderid, SUM(total)
      FROM item
      WHERE orderid < 1000
      GROUP BY orderid
      ORDER BY orderid;
... remainder of the PL/SQL block ...
```

When a SQL statement does not contain either the FIRST_ROWS or ALL_ROWS hint, Oracle7 executes the statement according to the current session setting optimizer behavior.

NOTE The second example shows that hints can be included within PL/SQL blocks, including anonymous blocks, stored procedures, database triggers, and so on. However, hints are identified and used only with those Oracle products that support PL/SQL version 2.0 or greater (for example, Oracle7) and not those that support PL/SQL 1.x (for example, SQL*Forms 3.0).

Controlling Table Access Methods Using Hints

Depending on the situation, Oracle7 can execute a SQL statement by accessing a table using a full table scan or using an index, indexed cluster, or hash cluster. Oracle7 has several hints that allow you to suggest a table access method for a statement. If the suggested table access method is available, Oracle7 will use it.

Here are some of the hints you can use to suggest table access methods:

Hint	When You Use It
FULL(table)	When you want Oracle7 to perform a full table scan on a table rather than use an index or a cluster
CLUSTER(table)	When you want Oracle7 to use the cluster index associated with a table in an indexed cluster rather than a full table scan or a separate table index
HASH(table)	When you want Oracle7 to use a hash scan rather than an index or a full table scan for a table in a hash cluster
INDEX (table index(es))	When you want Oracle7 to use an index scan for a table rather than a full table scan, an index scan using a different index, or a hash scan. If you include a list of indexes, Oracle7 considers the listed indexes and picks the one that delivers the lowest execution cost. If you specify no indexes, Oracle7 considers all indexes and picks the one that delivers the lowest execution cost
INDEX_ASC(table index(es))	When you want Oracle7 to use an index scan for a table, scanning the index in ascending order of index values, rather than other types of table access methods (similar to the INDEX hint)

Hint	When You Use It
INDEX_DESC (table index(es))	When you want to scan an index in descending order (similar to INDEX_DESC)
AND_EQUAL (table index(es))	When you want Oracle7 to merge index scans from several single-column indexes

Now that you know the different hints that can control table access methods for a SQL statement, let's take a look at how and when you might use them.

Considering the CUSTOMER table and the STATEINDEX index described earlier in this book, what do you think would be the best way for Oracle7 to execute the following statement?

```
SELECT lastname, firstname
  FROM customer
  WHERE state = 'NY'
```

If customers are uniformly distributed across many states and there are many customers in the table, the best method might be for Oracle7 to perform an index scan using the STATEINDEX to find the ROWIDs of all customers in the state of New York and then access those rows using their ROWIDs. However, if the customer table contains clients located mostly in New York, a full table scan would deliver a lower cost than using the STATEINDEX.

Let's consider the former case. You would expect Oracle7 to use the STATEINDEX index for the query. However, when you use the EXPLAIN PLAN command, you find that Oracle7 is using a full table scan to get the New York customers:

```
EXPLAIN PLAN
  INTO plan_table
  FOR
  SELECT lastname
  FROM customer
  WHERE state = 'NY';

SELECT position cost, operation, options
  FROM plan_table;
```

```
COST OPERATION                 OPTIONS
---- --------------------- -----------
   4 SELECT STATEMENT
   0 TABLE ACCESS           FULL
```

To reveal the cost of executing the same query when using the STATEINDEX index, include a hint in the EXPLAIN PLAN statement:

```
EXPLAIN PLAN
  INTO plan_table
  FOR
  SELECT --+ INDEX(customer stateindex)
  lastname
  FROM customer
  WHERE state = 'NY';

SELECT position cost, operation, options
  FROM plan_table;

COST OPERATION                 OPTIONS
---- --------------------- -----------
   4 SELECT STATEMENT
   0 TABLE ACCESS           FULL
  18 SELECT STATEMENT
   0 TABLE ACCESS           BY ROWID
   1 INDEX                  RANGE SCAN
```

Aha! Maybe your customers are not as equally distributed as you thought they were. The cost of using the STATEINDEX index to find the New York customers is more than four times greater than the cost of performing a full table scan. In this case using the hint to force the SQL statement to execute using an index is not the correct choice.

Controlling Joins with Hints

Joins are among the more complicated statements that SQL supports. Oracle7 includes three hints that allow you to affect the execution of queries that join information:

Hint	When You Use It
USE_NL(table[s])	To make Oracle7 join tables using a nested-loops join strategy. A *nested-loops join* means that Oracle7 picks the first row from the *inner* or *driving* table. Then it finds the rows in the outer table to join, returns the results, finds the second row in the driving table, finds the rows in the outer table to join, returns the results, and so on. A nested-loops join has the advantage of returning the first results early and the disadvantage of requiring more overall work to complete the join
USE_MERGE (table[s])	To make Oracle7 join tables using a sort-merge join strategy for an *equality-join query* (that is, table1.column1 = table2.column2). A *sort-merge join* means that Oracle7 first sorts data from both tables (in the order of the joining attributes) and then merges the sorted results to perform the join. A sort-merge join has the advantage of reduced overhead to complete the join but the disadvantage that the first set of results cannot be returned until much of the sorting work is complete
ORDERED	To make Oracle7 join tables according to the order in which a query lists them. In other words, the ORDERED hint lets you pick the driving table in a join

When should you use the different hints to influence the nature of joins? As always, it's best to let the Oracle7 optimizer pick the right join strategy for you. However, if you feel that for some reason Oracle7 is not executing a join query as it should be, check its execution with the EXPLAIN PLAN feature. Then suggest a new approach with any of the three preceding hints.

In particular, the USE_NL or USE_MERGE hint can come in handy when applications want to optimize statement execution for faster response time or optimal throughput, respectively (similar to the FIRST_ROWS and ALL_ROWS hints). Note that nested-loops joins return the first set of results more quickly that do sort-merge joins, but sort-merge joins deliver better overall throughput than do nested-loops joins.

Tuning Transaction Behavior

A key to good application performance is not only good SQL statement design but good transaction design. Especially in an OLTP environment where many users are modifying a single database at the same time, poorly implemented OLTP transactions can dramatically slow down overall application performance. This section addresses some issues to think about when designing transactions for your applications.

Designing Transactions Correctly

Remember that a database transaction is a logical unit of work that completes or fails as a unit. When you sit down to design a client application, not only must you consider how you program the application's SQL statements, you must also consider the transactions that encompass them, for two key reasons:

- The locks a transaction's SQL statements acquire are held for the duration of the transaction.

- The rollback segment space that a transaction's SQL statements consume is held for the duration of the transaction.

With these two points in mind, let's consider how a client/server database system would perform when an application uses either short or long transactions. If an application uses short transactions, data locks and rollback segment space are released shortly after they are acquired by each transaction. Therefore, application users are less likely to contend for the same data and rollback segment space. However, if a client application uses long transactions, data locks and rollback segment space are held for longer periods of time, increasing the likelihood that users will bump into each other when trying to accomplish work. In other words, the longer an application's transactions, the better the chances that users will have to wait for one another to complete work. A key goal of transaction design is to make sure each transaction is in fact a "unit" of work, not "units" of work. This in turn will keep database transactions as short as possible, reduce resource contention in the system, and deliver maximum performance.

Overriding Oracle7 Default Locking Mechanisms to Improve Application Performance

Chapter 2 described how Oracle7's automatic row-level locking and multi-versioning mechanism works to create data concurrency in a multi-user database system. Although most applications will perform well with Oracle7's default locking mechanisms, there are situations in which manual locking strategies can improve application performance. This section describes when and how transactions can manually lock data in an Oracle7 database to improve application performance.

Explicitly Locking Tables to Improve Application Performance

If a single statement or transaction is going to update many or all of the rows in a table, Oracle7's row-level locking mechanism can result in extra server overhead and force application users to sit idle.

Here's the scenario: Assume that an application is about to issue an UPDATE statement to update all of the rows in a table. When the application starts the update of the table, Oracle7 acquires exclusive row locks on each of the rows in the table, one at a time. Since the statement is eventually going to exclusively lock all of the rows in the table, Oracle7 ends up taking many exclusive row locks when a single exclusive table lock would do the trick much more efficiently and with much less overhead. Furthermore, if Oracle7 encounters a row that is currently locked, it waits indefinitely until the transaction that has the row locked completes and releases the lock; an application user might sit around unproductively while waiting for one lock out of a thousand.

To avoid these problems, when an application transaction is going to issue one or more statements that modify a large majority or all of the rows in a table, the transaction should attempt to acquire a lock on the table instead of on individual rows, one at a time. Acquiring a table lock accomplishes two goals:

- Applications can specify that they do not want to wait if an attempt to acquire a table lock does not immediately complete. In this case, when an application attempts to acquire a table lock but other locks prohibit the table lock, the application can attempt to acquire the lock again or move on to another operation instead of sitting idle.

- The application acquires a single table lock instead of many row locks to accomplish the same thing. One table lock is much more efficient than many row locks, and this leads to reduced server overhead and better overall system performance.

To explicitly acquire table locks, an application can use the SQL command LOCK TABLE:

```
LOCK TABLE orders IN EXCLUSIVE MODE

LOCK TABLE orders IN EXCLUSIVE MODE NOWAIT

LOCK TABLE orders, item IN EXCLUSIVE MODE NOWAIT
```

The first two examples show how an application can exclusively lock the ORDERS table. The first example statement will wait when Oracle7 cannot immediately acquire the table lock because of other table or row locks on the ORDERS table. The second example returns control to the application if Oracle7 cannot immediately acquire the table lock on the ORDERS table. The third example shows how you can lock more than one table at a time if a transaction needs to acquire table locks on related tables.

These examples show one of the most common types of table locks Oracle7 can acquire using the LOCK TABLE command: an exclusive table lock. However, Oracle7 allows you to acquire several types of table locks using the LOCK TABLE command, including exclusive, share row exclusive, share, row exclusive, and row share table locks. Let's focus on the two types of table locks that most applications explicitly acquire to improve application performance: exclusive and row exclusive table locks.

Exclusive Table Locks An *exclusive table lock* prohibits other transactions from performing DML operations on the locked object, including other types of table- and row-level locks. To improve performance, an application might acquire an exclusive table lock before updating or deleting all (or many) of the rows in a table, as explained earlier in this section. Oracle7 takes an exclusive table lock only when an application specifically requests one.

Row Exclusive Table Locks A *row exclusive table lock* is a sort of counterbalance to the exclusive table lock because it ensures that no other transaction can exclusively lock the table for its own purpose. Oracle7 automatically acquires a row exclusive table lock when a transaction updates or deletes one of the rows in the table, explicitly acquires a row exclusive lock on a row in the table (see the next section), or when a user explicitly requests a row exclusive table lock using the LOCK TABLE command:

```
LOCK TABLE orders ROW EXCLUSIVE MODE
```

The only time an application can improve its performance by acquiring a row exclusive table lock is when the same or other applications are acquiring exclusive table locks. Performance gains can be seen for transactions that want to modify tables but don't want to wait behind transactions that acquire exclusive table locks.

Explicitly Locking Rows to Improve Application Performance

The preceding section explained how the acquisition of table locks can help application performance. Likewise, there are application situations in which explicitly acquiring row-level locks can improve application performance.

Here's a common scenario in which this type of locking can help performance: Assume that an application opens a cursor and then selectively updates some or all of the rows in the return set of the cursor. Unless the application locks all of the rows in the cursor's return set when opening the cursor, there is a chance that another transaction will lock one of the rows in the cursor's return set while the application processes other rows in the cursor. Then, when the application tries to update the row in the cursor's return set that is locked by the other transaction, the application must wait until the other transaction completes and releases the lock on the desired row. As a result, application users can sit idle, waiting for other users to finish their work.

To avoid this type of situation in your applications, an application transaction can explicitly lock the rows in the return set of a cursor (or a query) using the FOR UPDATE OF clause of the SELECT command, thereby guaranteeing that the transaction has exclusive rights to update the row before all other transactions:

```
DECLARE
CURSOR ordercursor (orderid INTEGER) IS
SELECT orderdate, shipdate, paiddate
  FROM orders
  WHERE id = orderid
  FOR UPDATE OF orderdate, shipdate, paiddate;
... remainder of the PL/SQL block ...
```

In this example, the PL/SQL block acquires an exclusive row-level lock for the specified sales order to make sure no other transaction can intervene to update the order while the program finishes processing the row. As with other row locks, the transaction holds the lock on the sales order until the transaction commits.

Explicitly Locking Other System Resources to Improve Application Performance

Rows and tables are database resources that applications rely on to accomplish work done on behalf of system users. However, applications sometimes rely on other types of resources to get work done. For example, reporting applications make extensive use of a shared system printer. If several users want to print out several reports at the same time, then they can contend for a resource—in this case, a printer.

If you have Oracle7 with the Procedural option, you can use the procedures in a utility package called DBMS_LOCK to help you manage other types of resources that applications might use. For example, users of one or more applications can use the following package to coordinate the use of up to five shared peripherals (printers, modems, and so on):

```
CREATE PACKAGE sharedperipherals AS
  FUNCTION lockperipheral (peripheral IN VARCHAR2, handlenum IN OUT VARCHAR2)
    RETURN VARCHAR2;
  FUNCTION releaseperipheral (handlenum IN VARCHAR2)
    RETURN VARCHAR2;
```

```
  peripheralhandle1 VARCHAR2(50);
  peripheralhandle2 VARCHAR2(50);
  peripheralhandle3 VARCHAR2(50);
  peripheralhandle4 VARCHAR2(50);
  peripheralhandle5 VARCHAR2(50);
END sharedperipherals;

CREATE PACKAGE BODY sharedperipherals AS

-- This function attempts to acquire an exclusive lock on the specified
-- peripheral.  Success or failure is indicated by the function's return value.
FUNCTION lockperipheral (peripheral IN VARCHAR2, handlenum IN OUT VARCHAR2)
  RETURN VARCHAR2 IS
  resourceflag INTEGER := 9;
  returnvalue VARCHAR2(50) := 'Peripheral '||peripheral||' could not be locked';
BEGIN
  dbms_lock.allocate_unique(peripheral, handlenum);
  resourceflag := dbms_lock.request(handlenum);
  IF resourceflag = 0 THEN
    returnvalue := 'Peripheral '||peripheral||' successfully locked';
  END IF;
  RETURN returnvalue;
END lockperipheral;

-- This function attempts to release a lock on the specified
-- peripheral. Success or failure is indicated by the function's return value.
FUNCTION releaseperipheral (handlenum IN VARCHAR2)
  RETURN VARCHAR2 IS
  resourceflag INTEGER := 9;
  returnvalue VARCHAR2(50) := 'Lock on peripheral could not be released';
BEGIN
  resourceflag := dbms_lock.release (handlenum);
  IF resourceflag = 0 THEN
    returnvalue := 'Lock on peripheral successfully released';
  END IF;
  RETURN returnvalue;
END releaseperipheral;

END sharedperipherals;
```

For example, a reporting application can call the LOCKPERIPHERAL function before it prints a report to make sure it has exclusive access to a printer:

```
x := sharedperipherals.lockperipheral
  ('PRINTER1', sharedperipherals.peripheralhandle1);
```

The return value of the function tells the application if the requested printer is available so the application can provide feedback to the user. Once the application is finished with the printer, it can use the RELEASEPERIPHERAL function to release the lock on the printer so other applications can use it:

```
x := sharedperipherals.releaseperipheral
  (sharedperipherals.peripheralhandle1);
```

These examples illustrate just a few of the procedures and functions in the DBMS_LOCK utility package that you can use to manage resources in a client/server application environment.

However, the programs in the DBMS_LOCK utility package do not actually lock any real resources. For instance, in the preceding example, if one application acquires a lock on a printer, another application can still send a report to the printer without checking for locks on the printer. If the printer is not busy, the application without the lock might very well be able to use the printer ahead of the application that has the lock. That's because the locks acquired by the DBMS_LOCK utility package are just a way of managing locks for external system resources within the database server. Therefore, locking of arbitrary system resources external to the database can work only when all applications acquire a named set of resource locks using the DBMS_LOCK utility package.

Using the SET TRANSACTION Command to Control Transaction Behavior

Oracle7 offers another feature that application developers should consider to help the performance and behavior of application transactions: the SQL command SET TRANSACTION. This command allows you to set several transaction characteristics when you begin a new database transaction. The following sections explain some of these options of the SET TRANSACTION command, but keep in mind that you must always make sure the SET TRANSACTION statement is the first one in a new transaction; otherwise, Oracle7 will return an error.

```
... statements of transaction ...
COMMIT                              -- end of transaction
SET TRANSACTION ...                 -- beginning of new transaction
... statements of new transaction ...
.
.
.
```

Now let's learn about some of the most important transaction characteristics that the SET TRANSACTION command allows you to control: read consistency and rollback segment usage.

Using SET TRANSACTION to Control Read Consistency

In Chapter 2 you learned how Oracle7 uses multi-versioning instead of read locks to guarantee read consistency—a consistent, accurate set of results for every query. To deliver read consistency, Oracle7 uses rollback segments and multi-versioning to hide the work that other transactions might concurrently be performing on the data you query. By default, Oracle7's multi-versioning mechanism guarantees statement-level read consistency because every row in a single query's result set is consistent with respect to a specific timepoint—in Oracle7, the time that the query begins.

In most application situations, Oracle7's default of statement-level read consistency is acceptable. However, some applications might require a higher degree of read consistency: transaction-level read consistency. Transaction-level read consistency means that for the duration of a transaction, no matter how many queries you issue and no matter how many tables are involved, all query results are consistent with respect to the same point in time (the beginning of the transaction). Transaction-level read consistency is often important for decision support/reporting applications that issue many long, complicated queries that must return consistent, accurate results.

One way to establish transaction-level read consistency is to exclusively lock tables of interest using the LOCK TABLE command. After a transaction exclusively locks tables, other transactions cannot modify the tables until the locking transaction ends and releases the locks.

```
-- exclusively lock tables to prevent other transactions from using
-- the same tables and ensure transaction-level read consistency
LOCK TABLE orders, item EXCLUSIVE

-- return initial query results for locked tables
SELECT ... FROM orders, item ...

... other transaction statements ...

-- subsequent query results see same data as the first query
-- because other transactions cannot modify the tables
SELECT ... FROM orders, item ...
    .
    .
    .
COMMIT
```

While exclusive table locks allow you to create transaction-level read consistency, this method has one primary disadvantage: It eliminates data concurrency with respect to the locked tables because no other users can modify the locked tables. If you want transaction-level read consistency without the penalty of lost data concurrency, consider a read-only transaction. Using the READ ONLY option of the SET TRANSACTION command, a transaction can issue any number of queries against any number of tables and see read-consistent results without locking any data, thus preserving complete data concurrency in a multi-user/multi-transaction environment.

```
COMMIT                          -- end of transaction
SET TRANSACTION READ ONLY       -- begin new read-only transaction
SELECT ... FROM orders, item    -- return initial query results
    .
    .
    .
SELECT ... FROM orders, item    -- return same query results
    .
    .
    .
```

To guarantee transaction-level read consistency, Oracle7 extends its multi-versioning model for all queries in the transaction. The only limitation of read-only transactions is that they are just what their name indicates—read-only transactions. If you attempt to issue anything other than a SELECT statement, Oracle7 returns an error.

Using SET TRANSACTION to Target Specific Rollback Segments

In Chapter 10 you learned a lot about rollback segments: how the administrator must plan, create, and manage them to support client applications, and how different-size rollback segments can have different performance and behavioral results when applications use them. Normally, Oracle7 assigns a transaction to a rollback segment according to availability and on a round-robin basis to make sure that all rollback segments carry a similar transaction load. However, Oracle7 allows you, as the application developer, to target specific rollback segments for transaction use with the USE ROLLBACK SEGMENT clause of the SET TRANSACTION command:

```
COMMIT                                      -- end transaction
SET TRANSACTION USE ROLLBACK SEGMENT rs2    -- begin new transaction
... other transaction statements ...
.
.
.
COMMIT
```

When you design your application, you can use the SET TRANSACTION...USE ROLLBACK SEGMENT command to improve the performance of the application in several ways. For example, OLTP applications might decide to target transactions for small rollback segments cached in memory so that Oracle7 never has to write rollback segment information to disk. Alternatively, batch operations like bulk data loads that contain long transactions might target extremely large rollback segments to reduce the likelihood of dynamic extent allocation/deallocation for rollback segments.

Pinning Application Code in Database Server Memory

In Chapter 12 you learned about the memory caches of the Oracle7 database server and how the administrator can tune them to minimize processing and the amount of disk I/O that is necessary for client/server applications to function. One such memory area is the shared pool, a buffer cache that holds shared, parsed, optimized application code (SQL statements and stored procedures) in memory so that repeated executions work much more quickly. But no matter how well the administrator tunes the size of the shared pool, if application code is somewhat large and not regularly used, Oracle7 will likely flush it out of the shared pool when it is necessary to make room for other code not in memory. Therefore, if an application executes a SQL statement or procedure that is no longer in the shared pool, extra processing (optimization and so on) and possibly disk I/O are necessary to complete the request, which can slow application performance.

If you develop applications and have the Oracle7 Procedural option, Oracle7 has a utility package, DBMS_SHARED_POOL, with several procedures to allow you to control which pieces of application code can and cannot be flushed from the shared pool. Therefore, you can pin important pieces of application code in server memory to maximize application performance. The following list describes the different procedures available in the DBMS_SHARED_POOL package:

Procedure	Description
sizes (minsize NUMBER)	Prints a report of all objects in the shared pool larger than minsize. The report lists the name and size of each object, as well as whether or not the object is to be pinned in the shared pool. Execute this procedure in SQL*DBA or SQL*Plus after enabling server output
keep (name VARCHAR2)	Pin the named object in the shared pool
unkeep (name VARCHAR2)	Release the pin on the named object in the shared pool

To illustrate the use of the DBMS_SHARED_POOL package, let's look at one way that applications commonly use the utility. Most client/server applications typically use individual stored procedures, or packages of stored procedures, to reduce network I/O and improve application performance. Therefore, it's reasonable to pin an application's package in the shared pool. For example, upon application startup, a developer might include the following procedure calls to pin an application's packages in the shared pool:

```
dbms_shared_pool.keep('sales.customermanager')
dbms_shared_pool.keep('sales.partmanager')
.
.
.
```

Likewise, when terminating an application, it's best to unpin an application's packages to free unused space in the shared pool:

```
dbms_shared_pool.unkeep('sales.customermanager')
dbms_shared_pool.unkeep('sales.partmanager')
.
.
.
```

Array Processing: Another Way of Reducing Network Traffic

Reducing network I/O between clients and a database server has been a primary focus throughout this book. That's because network traffic in a heavily loaded client/server system can quickly saturate the network to slow application performance. We have already seen that SQL functions, integrity constraints, triggers, stored procedures, and database alerts are key Oracle7 features that all client applications should take advantage of to minimize network traffic in a client/server system. However, one Oracle7 client/server feature not yet discussed in detail is the ORACLE array-processing interface.

Figure 17.1 illustrates how array processing can improve client/server application performance. Instead of sending network packets with single rows when a client application inserts a row or requests a row from the server with a query, *array processing* allows applications to reduce network traffic by buffering rows for insert or retrieval into arrays and then send the arrays in very few network packets across the network. The end result is less network traffic and improved database system performance for all applications.

FIGURE 17.1:

Oracle7's array-processing interface can dramatically reduce network traffic for INSERT and SELECT statements in a client/server system.

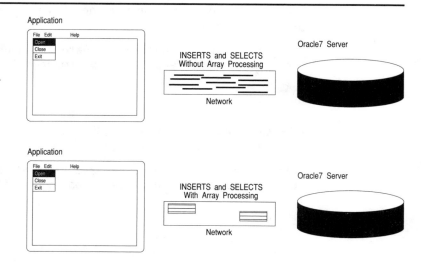

Array processing is built in to many Oracle CDE tools, including Oracle Forms and SQL*Plus. For example, Chapter 14 showed how simple it is to use array processing in an Oracle Forms application; by just setting a couple of options in a dialog, the blocks in a form can take advantage of array processing to improve application performance. The Oracle precompilers and OCI 3GL development environments also contain commands you can include in an application to take advantage of array processing.

This chapter has discussed several issues to focus on when tuning the logic of an Oracle7 client application for better performance, including:

- SQL statement design tips
- Hints to influence statement execution
- Transaction design to reduce contention among transactions for data and rollback segment space
- Manual locking options to optimize application locking strategies
- How to pin pieces of application code in the shared pool

- The Oracle7 array-processing interface to reduce network traffic for INSERT and SELECT statements in a client/server system

The next chapter discusses how to use the programmatic constructs of Oracle7 in a client/server database system, including stored procedures and packages, database triggers, and database alerts.

CHAPTER

EIGHTEEN

Centralizing Application Logic in the Database Server

- Using database stored PL/SQL programs in Oracle7 client/server systems

- Creating and managing database stored procedures, functions, packages, and triggers

- Using the Oracle7 programmer utility packages to enhance client/server applications

Chapter 15 showed you how to plan, create, and manage the foundation of an application's schema—the tables, integrity constraints, and views the application uses to work with a database system. This chapter explains other types of application schema objects you can use to enhance the performance and functionality of a client/server system by centralizing selected bits of application logic in the database with the features available from Oracle7's Procedural option. This chapter discusses

- Procedures
- Functions
- Packages
- Triggers
- Programmer utilities, including database alerts and database pipes

(If you are not familiar with the concepts of procedures, functions, packages, and triggers, see the beginning of Chapter 2.)

Using Database Procedures and Triggers Effectively

As you already know, planning is an important part of any complicated project, especially client/server application development and database design. When designing a client database application and its underlying schema, you must consider the opportunities where you can store application logic inside the database using procedures, functions, packages, and triggers. The following sections explain some of the most common situations in which you can use procedures, functions, packages, and triggers to encapsulate application logic inside an Oracle7 database.

Using Procedures and Triggers to Reduce Client/Server Network Traffic

Throughout this book, one of the recurring themes for client/server application development has been the focus on reducing network I/O between clients and the database server to eliminate the network as a bottleneck to application performance. Procedures and triggers can be significant players in accomplishing this goal because applications that use them rather than SQL statements generate much less network traffic. (Chapter 13 showed a good example of how procedures and triggers generate much less network traffic than equivalent SQL statements.)

Using Procedures and Triggers to Enforce Data Integrity

Procedures and triggers are also useful for enforcing complex data integrity rules. A procedure is a compiled method of data access that users cannot dynamically change. Therefore, if a procedure includes both an operation and an integrity rule, you force all applications that use the procedure to also abide by the integrity rule. For example, the DELETECUSTOMER procedure makes sure to log a customer's ID and name into a customer history table before deleting the customer record from the CUSTOMER table:

```
CREATE PROCEDURE deletecustomer (custid IN INTEGER) AS
-- This procedure deletes the specified customer from the CUSTOMER table.
-- Before deleting the customer, the procedure inserts the customer's ID and
-- name into a history table.
  last VARCHAR2(50);
  first VARCHAR2(50);
BEGIN
  SELECT lastname, firstname INTO last, first
    FROM customer WHERE id = custid;
  INSERT INTO customerhistory VALUES (custid, last, first);
  DELETE FROM customer WHERE id = custid;
EXCEPTION
  WHEN NO_DATA_FOUND THEN
    raise_application_error (-20100, 'Invalid Customer ID');
END deletecustomer;
```

You can also use triggers to enforce complex integrity rules. The next example shows how to enforce the integrity rule in the DELETECUSTOMER procedure using a database trigger:

```
CREATE TRIGGER deletecustomer
BEFORE DELETE ON customer
FOR EACH ROW
```

```
BEGIN
  INSERT INTO customerhistory
    VALUES (:old.id, :old.lastname, :old.firstname);
END deletecustomer;
```

Using Procedures to Increase Object Security

Procedures are a great way to add an additional level of security to a database system. That's because users never require the object privileges to access database objects directly (for example, SELECT, INSERT, UPDATE, and DELETE object privileges); they require only the privilege to execute procedures that access the database objects (EXECUTE). And because a procedure is a compiled method of data access, you can be sure that users access an object only by using a method included in the procedure.

Using Procedures and Triggers for Complex Security Checks

Procedures and triggers are also useful for enforcing complex security checks. For example, consider the following trigger, which does not permit users to update or delete customer records before 7 A.M. or after 7 P.M.:

```
CREATE TRIGGER timecheck
BEFORE UPDATE OR DELETE ON customer
BEGIN
  IF TO_CHAR(SYSDATE, 'HH24') NOT BETWEEN 7 AND 18 THEN
    raise_application_error(-20108, 'Customer changes not allowed at this time');
  END IF;
END timecheck;
```

Using Procedures and Triggers for Enhanced Functionality

You can use procedures and triggers to enhance the functionality of an application. Part II of this book includes several listings with stored procedures that the administrator can use to generate and print out reports about a database and its configuration.

Procedures versus Triggers

If you can use both procedures and triggers to enforce complex integrity rules and security checks, how do you decide which approach to use? In general, if you need to apply a rule or check across all applications that might access the database, including ad hoc query environments, use a database trigger to centralize and automate the process in the database. This way you are sure that Oracle7 always enforces the check no matter how someone gets to the data, whether through the use of a procedure or by issuing a SQL statement. On the other hand, if you only need to enforce an integrity rule or security check for one or just some applications, create a procedure and make the interested applications call the procedure. This way other applications can access the database without being subject to the integrity rule or check.

NOTE Also consider that you can call database stored procedures from within triggers.

Individual Procedures and Functions versus Packages

When creating procedures and functions, you can create them as stand-alone, individual stored procedures and functions or as procedures and functions that are encapsulated inside a package. How do you decide which approach to use? If you are creating an application that will use several different database procedures and functions to consistently perform work, it's best to code the PL/SQL programs as part of a package that corresponds to the application. The many benefits include

- Organization: Encapsulation of related application procedures and functions inside a package makes the PL/SQL development process easy to manage.

- Additional functionality: Using packages permits database server–managed global variables that have a persistent state for the life of an application user's database session.

- Enhanced performance: Calling an object in a package loads the entire package into the shared pool of the server, thereby eliminating individual disk I/Os for each first call to a procedure or function.

Creating, Managing, and Using Procedures, Functions, and Packages

Now that you have a good idea of when to use PL/SQL programs for storing application logic within an Oracle7 database, the following sections explain the details of creating, managing, and using database stored procedures, functions, and packages and provide a number of examples to show you how to enhance an application by using database stored PL/SQL programs.

Using a Text Editor for Programming Productivity

When programming in 3GL language development environments such as C, you typically use an editor to create the source file for an application. After you save the source file, you can try compiling it with the 3GL compiler. Unless you code a program absolutely correctly on the first try, the compiler returns messages to indicate all of the compile errors it finds in the source file. Next, you fix the problems the compiler identified by editing the source file in your editor and then try to compile the application's source file again. You repeat this process until you eliminate all syntax and logic errors and get everything working just the way you want.

PL/SQL is a 3GL that adds procedural functionality to Oracle SQL. Therefore, when developing an application's PL/SQL programs like procedures and triggers, you can use the same development approach as for a 3GL language compiler: Use an editor to write and save the source code for procedures, functions, packages, and triggers, and then run the source files as command scripts from an Oracle tool such as SQL*Plus. If you ever need to change the functionality of an application's PL/SQL programs, you can retrieve the source files in an editor, modify them, and then recompile the new source code in the Oracle7 database server.

> **NOTE**
>
> Several independent companies offer development tools for database 3GL environments such as Oracle PL/SQL. Such tools offer debugging environments, code versioning and control systems, and so on. If you do a lot of PL/SQL coding, the use of such programming utilities can greatly improve the productivity of application development.

Creating Procedures, Functions, and Packages

To create procedures, functions, and packages, you use the SQL commands CREATE PROCEDURE, CREATE FUNCTION, and CREATE PACKAGE, respectively. The following statements show how to create a procedure and a function:

```
CREATE PROCEDURE sales.newcustomer (company IN VARCHAR2 DEFAULT null,
  last IN VARCHAR2, first IN VARCHAR2, street IN VARCHAR2 DEFAULT null,
  city IN VARCHAR2 DEFAULT null, state IN CHAR DEFAULT 'F',
  zipcode IN VARCHAR2 DEFAULT null, phone IN VARCHAR2 DEFAULT null,
  fax IN VARCHAR2 DEFAULT null) IS
-- This procedure adds a new customer to the CUSTOMER table.  At a
-- minimum, the caller must provide the new customer's last and first
-- name.  The procedure uses a sequence to generate a new customer ID.
BEGIN
INSERT INTO sales.customer
  VALUES (customersequence.NEXTVAL, UPPER(company), UPPER(last), UPPER(first),
    INITCAP(street), INITCAP(city), INITCAP(state), zipcode, phone, fax);
END newcustomer;

CREATE FUNCTION findcustomerid (last IN VARCHAR2, first IN VARCHAR2)
  RETURN INTEGER AS
-- This function returns a customer's ID given the customer's last
-- and first names.
custid INTEGER;
BEGIN
  SELECT id INTO custid FROM customer
    WHERE lastname = UPPER(last) AND firstname = UPPER(first);
  RETURN custid;
EXCEPTION
  WHEN NO_DATA_FOUND THEN
    raise_application_error (-20101,'Invalid Customer Name');
END findcustomerid;
```

> **NOTE**
>
> To create a procedure, function, or package in an application schema, you must have the CREATE PROCEDURE system privilege. To create a procedure, function, or package in another schema, you must have the CREATE ANY PROCEDURE system privilege.

If you create a PL/SQL program in one schema that references objects in another schema, privilege requirements can become a bit complicated. In this case the owner of the PL/SQL program must have the necessary privileges to access the objects in the other schema. This way Oracle7 prevents a simple procedure definition from bypassing the internal security controls for object access.

For example, assume that you create the SALES.NEWCUSTOMER procedure shown earlier in this chapter to access the CUSTOMER table, which is in another user's schema. Oracle7 will not compile the SALES.NEWCUSTOMER procedure unless SALES has the INSERT object privilege for the CUSTOMER table.

These caveats should not concern you when you are creating an application schema that contains all the objects necessary for an application. Because the owner of all application objects, including procedures and underlying base tables and views, is one and the same, you will never need to consider these tricky privilege requirements.

Specifying Procedure and Function Parameters

After you specify a new procedure's or function's name, you must specify the procedure's or function's parameters—the values you want to pass into the body of the program. A parameter specification includes a name and a datatype. For each parameter you should indicate whether the parameter is an IN, OUT, or IN OUT parameter. See the section "Defining Procedure and Function Parameters" in Chapter 5 if you need a review of parameter types.

Notice that the package specification for the CUSTOMERMANAGER package shows that you can also assign default parameter values for the parameters of procedures or functions. If an application calls a procedure or function and does not supply a value for a parameter that has a default value, Oracle7 automatically substitutes the parameter's default value to complete the program call.

Specifying a Function's Return Value

Unlike a procedure definition, a function definition must indicate the datatype of the function's single return value and use the PL/SQL command RETURN to relay the function's return value. For example, the preceding statement defines the return value for the FINDCUSTOMERID function as an integer. The body of the function returns the value of the CUSTID variable, using the RETURN statement.

Separating a Package's Specification and Body

Creating packages of procedures and functions is similar to creating and managing stand-alone procedures and functions. However, there are some differences because each package has two parts: a specification and a body. A package's specification is a simple declaration of all the package components that the outside world can access. Procedures, functions, variables, cursors, and constants that you declare in a package's specification are public because applications can reference them to accomplish work.

To create a package specification, you use the SQL command CREATE PACKAGE. For example, this statement creates the specification for the CUSTOMERMANAGER package:

```
CREATE PACKAGE sales.customermanager IS
PROCEDURE newcustomer (company IN VARCHAR2 DEFAULT null,
   last IN VARCHAR2, first IN VARCHAR2, street IN VARCHAR2 DEFAULT null,
   city IN VARCHAR2 DEFAULT null, state IN CHAR DEFAULT 'F',
   zipcode IN VARCHAR2 DEFAULT null, phone IN VARCHAR2 DEFAULT null,
   fax IN VARCHAR2 DEFAULT null);
FUNCTION findcustomerid (last IN VARCHAR2, first IN VARCHAR2) RETURN integer;
PROCEDURE updatecustomer (custid IN INTEGER, fieldtype IN CHAR,
   newvalue IN VARCHAR2);
PROCEDURE deletecustomer (custid IN INTEGER);
PROCEDURE deletecustomer (last IN VARCHAR2, first IN VARCHAR2);
END customermanager;
```

The specification of the CUSTOMERMANAGER package declares four public procedures and one public function. Notice that the package specification includes only the arguments for each public procedure and function, not the logic of each. When you code public procedures and functions in the body of a package, the arguments must match those in the package specification.

> **NOTE**
>
> Notice that you can *overload* the procedure or function names in a package. For example, the CUSTOMERMANAGER package contains two public procedures named DELETECUSTOMER. One version of the procedure deletes a customer when you supply the customer's ID; the other version deletes a customer when you supply the customer's name. When an application calls the DELETECUSTOMER procedure, Oracle7 automatically determines which version of the procedure to execute, based upon the types and number of arguments the call supplies.

The body of a package specifies the logic of all the procedures and functions within the package. A package body must define all public procedures and functions—those included in the package specification. A package body can also define other procedures, functions, variables, constants, and cursors that the package specification does not declare. Objects that the package body defines but that the package specification does not declare are private, not available to the outside world. However, procedures and functions in the package itself can make use of all private package objects.

To create a package body you use the SQL command CREATE PACKAGE BODY. For example, this statement creates the body for the CUSTOMERMANAGER package:

```
CREATE PACKAGE BODY sales.customermanager AS
errnum INTEGER := -20000;
errmess VARCHAR2(2000) := 'Standard Error';
---------------------RETURNERROR procedure ---------------------------
PROCEDURE returnerror (errorstring IN VARCHAR2) IS
-- This private procedure sets the error number and message for the error
-- asked for by a package procedure or function.
BEGIN
  SELECT errornumber, errormessage
    INTO customermanager.errnum, customermanager.errmess
    FROM usererrors
    WHERE errormessage LIKE errorstring||'%';
  raise_application_error(customermanager.errnum, customermanager.errmess);
EXCEPTION
  WHEN NO_DATA_FOUND THEN -- if no matching error message, use standard error
  raise_application_error(-20000, 'Standard error');
END returnerror;
```

```
-----------------------NEWCUSTOMER procedure ----------------------------
PROCEDURE newcustomer (company IN VARCHAR2 DEFAULT null, last IN VARCHAR2,
-- This procedure adds a new customer to the CUSTOMER table.  At a
-- minimum, the caller must provide the new customer's last and first
-- name.  The procedure uses a sequence to generate a new customer ID.
  first IN VARCHAR2, street IN VARCHAR2 DEFAULT null,
  city IN VARCHAR2 DEFAULT null, state IN CHAR DEFAULT null,
  zipcode IN VARCHAR2 DEFAULT null, phone IN VARCHAR2 DEFAULT null,
  fax IN VARCHAR2 DEFAULT null) IS
BEGIN
INSERT INTO customer
  VALUES (customersequence.NEXTVAL, company, last, first,
    street, city, state, zipcode, phone, fax);
END newcustomer;
-----------------------FINDCUSTOMER function -------------------------
FUNCTION findcustomerid (last IN VARCHAR2, first IN VARCHAR2)
  RETURN INTEGER IS
-- This function returns a customer's ID given the customer's last
-- and first names.
custid INTEGER;
BEGIN
  SELECT id INTO custid FROM customer
    WHERE lastname = last AND firstname = first;
  RETURN custid;
EXCEPTION
  WHEN NO_DATA_FOUND THEN
    customermanager.returnerror ('Invalid Customer Name');
END findcustomerid;
-----------------------UPDATECUSTOMER procedure ----------------------
PROCEDURE updatecustomer (custid IN INTEGER, fieldtype IN CHAR,
  newvalue VARCHAR2) IS
-- This procedure updates a customer record given the customer's ID,
-- field to update, and a new field value.
BEGIN
  IF UPPER(fieldtype) = 'C' THEN -- update the customer's company name
    UPDATE customer
      SET companyname = newvalue
      WHERE id = custid;
  ELSIF UPPER(fieldtype) = 'L' THEN -- update the customer's last name
    UPDATE customer
      SET lastname = newvalue
      WHERE id = custid;
  ELSIF UPPER(fieldtype) = 'F' THEN -- update the customer's first name
    UPDATE customer
      SET firstname = newvalue
```

```
      WHERE id = custid;
  ELSIF UPPER(fieldtype) = 'A' THEN -- update the customer's address
    UPDATE customer
      SET address = newvalue
      WHERE id = custid;
  ELSIF UPPER(fieldtype) = 'T' THEN -- update the customer's city
    UPDATE customer
      SET city = newvalue
      WHERE id = custid;
  ELSIF UPPER(fieldtype) = 'S' THEN -- update the customer's state
    UPDATE customer
      SET state = newvalue
      WHERE id = custid;
  ELSIF UPPER(fieldtype) = 'Z' THEN -- update the customer's zip code
    UPDATE customer
      SET zipcode = newvalue
      WHERE id = custid;
  ELSIF UPPER(fieldtype) = 'P' THEN -- update the customer's phone number
    UPDATE customer
      SET phone = newvalue
      WHERE id = custid;
  ELSIF UPPER(fieldtype) = 'X' THEN -- update the customer's fax number
    UPDATE customer
      SET fax = newvalue
      WHERE id = custid;
  ELSE
    customermanager.returnerror ('Invalid Field Type');
  END IF;
  IF SQL%NOTFOUND THEN
    customermanager.returnerror ('Invalid Customer ID');
  END IF;

END updatecustomer;
---------------------DELETECUSTOMER procedure ----------------------
PROCEDURE deletecustomer (custid IN INTEGER) IS
BEGIN
  DELETE FROM customer
    WHERE id = custid;
  IF SQL%NOTFOUND THEN
    customermanager.returnerror ('Invalid Customer ID');
  END IF;
END deletecustomer;
```

```
---------------------DELETECUSTOMER procedure ----------------------
PROCEDURE deletecustomer (last IN VARCHAR2, first IN VARCHAR2) IS
BEGIN
            DELETE FROM customer
              WHERE lastname = last AND firstname = first;
            IF SQL%NOTFOUND THEN
              customermanager.returnerror ('Invalid Customer Name');
            END IF;
          END deletecustomer;

          END customermanager;
```

The CUSTOMERMANAGER package body defines all of the public procedures and functions in the package specification, as well as the private procedure RE-TURNERROR. The CUSTOMERMANAGER package body also declares two private global variables, ERRNUM and ERRMESS, that work with the private RETURNERROR procedure.

Logic Restrictions within PL/SQL Programs

Oracle7 places relatively few significant restrictions on the types of logic you can include in PL/SQL programs. For example, a database PL/SQL program can include any PL/SQL statement and any DML SQL statement, including SELECT, INSERT, UPDATE, and DELETE. A PL/SQL program can also include the SQL transaction control statements, such as COMMIT, ROLLBACK, and SAVEPOINT. However, a PL/SQL program cannot include any DDL statements (for example, CREATE, ALTER, and DROP) or DCL statements (for example, GRANT and REVOKE).

Calling Procedures and Functions

Once you have created a procedure, function, or package, you need to know how to call it from an application to make use of its logic. The following sections explain several methods applications can use to call database procedures and functions.

Directly Calling Database Procedures and Functions Inside an Application

One way an application can call a database procedure or function is to directly call the procedure. For example, to call the SALES.NEWCUSTOMER procedure an Oracle Forms application might issue this call from inside a procedure or trigger in a forms application:

```
sales.newcustomer('NBC','Gumble','Bryant')
```

Since the call to the NEWCUSTOMER procedure does not include all of the procedure's parameters, Oracle7 substitutes the default parameter values for those that are absent and executes the procedure.

Calling a public procedure or function that is part of a package is no different than calling a stand-alone procedure or function, except that you must include the program's package name as a prefix to the program name. For example, an application can call the CUSTOMERMANAGER.NEWCUSTOMER package procedure using this call:

```
sales.customermanager.newcustomer('NBC','Gumble','Bryant')
```

Applications can also access a package's public package variables to get a value or assign a variable a new value.

NOTE To execute a procedure or function, you must own the procedure, function, or package that encapsulates the program or have the EXECUTE object privilege for the PL/SQL program. By requiring a user to have only the EXECUTE privilege for a PL/SQL program, Oracle7 lets you create an additional level of security in your system. Application users do not need the object privileges to any objects; they need only the privilege to execute application procedures.

Referencing PL/SQL Functions in SQL Expressions

Another way of calling database functions is to reference them inside a SQL statement. Consider this query, which uses a subquery to determine the ID of Thomas Brokaw and then return the ID of all the sales orders placed by him:

```
SELECT id
  FROM orders
  WHERE customerid =
    (SELECT id FROM customer
       WHERE lastname = 'Brokaw'
       AND firstname = 'Thomas')
```

Instead of using the subquery, the SQL statement can call the CUSTOMERMAN-AGER.FINDCUSTOMERID function to return the value needed in the SQL statement's WHERE clause:

```
SELECT id
  FROM orders
  WHERE customerid =
      sales.customermanager.findcustomerid('Brokaw','Thomas')
```

Package State

Package variables are different from their stand-alone procedure and function counterparts because the *state* of package variables (current values) persists for the life of a database session that uses the encompassing package. For example, in the CUSTOMERMANAGER package, Oracle7 initializes the ERRNUM and ERRMESS private package variables the first time a user's session makes a call to the package. Oracle7 retains the error number and error message values on behalf of the session until the session closes. Each database session that uses a package has its own state values for all package variables.

Replacing Procedures, Functions, and Packages

During the life of an application, the application's procedures, functions, or packages might become out of date as a result of changes in the underlying application schema or the application logic. It is common to have to replace the current version of a procedure, function, or package with a new version to account for such changes.

If you need to replace a procedure, function, or package with a new version, you can do so without dropping the current program version, using the OR REPLACE option of the CREATE PROCEDURE, CREATE FUNCTION, or CREATE PACKAGE command:

```
CREATE OR REPLACE PROCEDURE newcustomer ...

CREATE OR REPLACE FUNCTION findcustomerid ...

CREATE OR REPLACE PACKAGE customermanager ...

CREATE OR REPLACE PACKAGE BODY customermanager ...
```

Dropping Procedures, Functions, and Packages

In certain situations a procedure, function, or package will become obsolete. For example, if you remove an application from an Oracle7 database system, the application's package is no longer needed. In such cases you should drop procedures, functions, and packages to clean up the corresponding database's data dictionary and release some space in its SYSTEM tablespace.

To drop a procedure, function, or package, you use the SQL command DROP PROCEDURE, DROP FUNCTION, or DROP PACKAGE:

```
DROP PROCEDURE newcustomer

DROP FUNCTION findcustomerid

DROP PACKAGE customermanager
```

NOTE To drop both the specification and body of a procedure, function, or package, you must own the program or have the DROP ANY PROCEDURE system privilege.

If you want to drop only a package's body, not its specification, use the DROP PACKAGE BODY command:

```
DROP PACKAGE BODY customermanager
```

Before dropping a database procedure, function, or package, consider the problems that might result if other procedures, packages, or applications depend on the program to be dropped. For example, if an Oracle Forms application relies on a database procedure to do some work and you drop the procedure, the application cannot function correctly; you must modify the application to account for the drop of the procedure.

Within the database itself Oracle7 has a sophisticated mechanism that tracks the dependencies of all objects within the database. For example, if procedure A calls procedure B and you drop procedure B, Oracle7 immediately marks procedure A as "invalid." The next time an application calls procedure A, Oracle7 automatically tries to recompile the invalid procedure and finds that procedure B is no longer available. In this case Oracle7 returns the error message to the application, which alerts the administrator that the application logic is no longer valid and requires modification.

Creating and Managing Triggers

The following sections explain the details of how to create, manage, and use database triggers.

Creating Triggers

To create a database trigger you use the SQL command CREATE TRIGGER:

```
CREATE TRIGGER updatestockquantity
-- This trigger makes sure that when users insert, update,
-- or delete line items for sales orders, an appropriate
-- change is made to the on-hand quantity of the line item's part.
--------------------- TRIGGERING STATEMENTS ---------------------
AFTER INSERT OR UPDATE OF quantity OR DELETE ON item
--------------------- ROW TRIGGER -------------------------------
FOR EACH ROW
--------------------- TRIGGER RESTRICTION -----------------------
--------------------- TRIGGER BODY ------------------------------
BEGIN
  IF INSERTING THEN
```

```
      UPDATE stock
        SET onhand = onhand - :new.quantity
        WHERE id = :new.stockid;
    ELSIF UPDATING THEN
      IF :new.quantity > :old.quantity THEN
        UPDATE stock
          SET onhand = onhand - (:new.quantity - :old.quantity)
          WHERE id = :new.stockid;
      ELSE
        UPDATE stock
          SET onhand = onhand + (:old.quantity - :new.quantity)
          WHERE id = :new.stockid;
      END IF;
    ELSE
      UPDATE stock
        SET onhand = onhand + :old.quantity
        WHERE id = :new.id;
    END IF;
END updatestockquantity;
```

The comments in the trigger example show the different parts of a trigger definition. The following sections explain the different parts of a trigger.

TIP

Oracle7 does not store a trigger's body as a compiled PL/SQL code block as it does with procedures, functions, and packages. Instead, the first time an operation fires a trigger, Oracle7 reads the trigger's source code from the data dictionary, compiles the trigger, and stores the compiled version in the shared pool. Therefore, it might take a bit longer to complete an operation when it is the first time a specific trigger is fired. To avoid such performance hits when triggers are particularly large (for example, more than 60 lines of code), developers can improve performance by putting all trigger logic inside a stored procedure and have the trigger body simply call the stored procedure.

Specifying a Trigger's Triggering Statement

A trigger's *triggering statement* indicates which statement automatically fires (executes) a trigger. A trigger's triggering statement can be an INSERT, UPDATE, or DELETE statement for a specific table. One trigger can have multiple triggering statements, as the example of the UPDATESTOCKQUANTITY trigger earlier in this chapter shows. To minimize the complexity of how multiple triggers fire, it's best to include the logic for a number of triggering statements all together in one trigger, if possible. (See the section "Specifying a Trigger's Execution Time" later in this chapter, which discusses how to execute different blocks of logic in a trigger body based on the type of triggering statement that fires a trigger.)

If you indicate that a trigger's triggering statement includes UPDATE statements, you can optionally indicate specific columns to fire on. That way the trigger does not unnecessarily fire when a statement updates the target table but not a column of interest. If you omit the "OF column-list" clause after UPDATE, the trigger fires when a user updates any column in the target table.

Specifying a Trigger's Execution Time

A trigger can fire its body either before or after the triggering statement executes. Decide which type of trigger to use based upon when you want to perform the trigger's logic in relation to the triggering statement. For example, if you use a trigger to perform a security check before allowing an UPDATE to occur, it makes sense to use a BEFORE trigger. If you use a trigger to check the integrity of a table after inserting a new row, it might make more sense to use an AFTER trigger.

If you specify the BEFORE keyword at the start of the triggering statement specification, Oracle7 fires the trigger body before executing a triggering statement. If you specify the AFTER keyword at the start of the triggering statement specification, Oracle7 fires the trigger body after the triggering statement completes.

Specifying Row and Statement Triggers

Oracle7 supports two types of triggers: row triggers and statement triggers. A *row trigger* fires its body once for every row that the triggering statement touches. A *statement trigger* fires its body only once, no matter how many rows the triggering statement affects. Which type of trigger should you use? That depends on the logic you include in a trigger's body. For example, if you use a trigger to perform a security check before allowing a user to insert, update, or delete rows in a table, the security check needs to occur only once, not for every row the triggering statement touches.

To specify a row trigger, include the FOR EACH ROW clause after specifying the triggering statement in the CREATE TRIGGER statement. To specify a statement trigger, simply omit the FOR EACH ROW clause. (See the TIMECHECK trigger in the section "Using Procedures and Triggers for Complex Security Checks" earlier in this chapter for an example of a statement trigger.)

Specifying a Trigger Restriction for a Row Trigger

If you have a row trigger that should fire only in select situations based upon the values in a row, you can improve application performance by eliminating otherwise unnecessary trigger firings with a trigger restriction. A *trigger restriction* is a simple Boolean condition that Oracle7 checks before actually firing the body of a trigger.

You specify a trigger's restriction right after the FOR EACH ROW clause. For example, the REORDER trigger presented in the section "The DBMS_ALERT Package" later in this chapter shows a restriction that compares two field values in the target table. In the next example, if the value of a row's ONHAND column is less than that of the REORDER column, the condition evaluates to TRUE and Oracle7 fires the trigger:

```
WHEN (new.onhand < new.reorder)
```

Special PL/SQL Extensions for Trigger Bodies

To enhance the capabilities of triggers, there are some special PL/SQL extensions you can use in a trigger body: conditional predicates and correlation values.

The *conditional predicates* INSERTING, UPDATING, and DELETING allow you to conditionally execute different blocks of statements, depending on the type of triggering statement that fires a trigger. You need to use conditional predicates only when a trigger's condition includes two or all three types of triggering statements.

The previous example of the UPDATESTOCKQUANTITY trigger demonstrates the use of all the conditional predicates.

Correlation values allow statements in the body of a row trigger to use the old and new column values of the row on which the trigger is currently positioned when the trigger is firing. For example, the UPDATESTOCKQUANTITY trigger uses the new and old QUANTITY values of the ITEM table to adjust corresponding stock on hand quantity values in the STOCK table when someone inserts, updates, or deletes line items in the ITEM table.

NOTE When the triggering statement is an INSERT statement, the old correlation values are NULL (there is no old row from which to obtain values); when the triggering statement is a DELETE statement, the new correlation values are NULL (there is no new version of the row from which to obtain values); and when the triggering statement is an UPDATE statement, both old and new correlation values are available.

Logic Restrictions within Trigger Bodies

Oracle7 restricts the logic within the body of a trigger more than that of a procedure or function: A trigger body can contain any DML SQL statement, including SELECT, INSERT, UPDATE, and DELETE statements, but cannot include any transaction control SQL statements (for example, COMMIT, ROLLBACK), DDL SQL statements (for example, CREATE, ALTER, DROP) or DCL SQL statements (for example, GRANT, REVOKE). Also, Oracle7 returns an error when a trigger calls a procedure that includes a transaction control statement such as COMMIT or ROLLBACK.

Mutating and Constraining Tables Triggers have specific logic restrictions to correctly handle complicated situations in which one session tries to perform many operations at the same time as a result of triggers being fired and/or integrity constraints being enforced. To avoid run-time application errors, you must consider these restrictions when designing triggers. The following list explains some new terms and these special restrictions:

- Oracle7 considers a table as *mutating* when a session is currently modifying the table in some way—for example, with an UPDATE, DELETE, or INSERT statement, or as the result of delete cascade referential integrity constraint action. For example, when your session updates one or more rows in a table with an UPDATE statement and the same statement also fires a row trigger, the table is mutating with respect to the trigger. To prevent row triggers from seeing an inconsistent set of data, Oracle7 prohibits the statements in a trigger body to read or modify a mutating table. See the section "Debugging Oracle7 PL/SQL Programs" a little later in this chapter for an example of a mutating table error condition.

- Oracle7 considers a table as *constraining* when a session issues a SQL statement that fires a trigger and the trigger needs to read the table on behalf of a statement in the trigger's body or on behalf of an integrity constraint. For example, when your session issues a SQL statement that fires a trigger and the trigger includes a query of the STOCK table, the STOCK table is a constraining table. To prevent order- and index-dependent success and failure of SQL statements, Oracle7 prevents the statements of a row trigger from changing the values in any key (primary, unique, or foreign) of a constraining table.

Replacing Triggers

Much like replacing procedures and packages, you can use the OR REPLACE option of the CREATE TRIGGER command to replace the current version of a trigger with a new one:

```
CREATE OR REPLACE TRIGGER updatestockquantity ...
```

Dropping Triggers

If you want to remove the operation performed by a database trigger, you can drop the trigger using the DROP TRIGGER command:

```
DROP TRIGGER updatestockquantity ...
```

If you drop a table that has triggers, Oracle7 automatically drops all of the triggers associated with the table.

Debugging Oracle7 PL/SQL Programs

If you've programmed in a third-generation programming language before, you know that code without bugs is an oxymoron, even with the smallest of programs. One of the most time-consuming and important jobs that face the application developer is the process of debugging a program so it works as intended. Programming with Oracle's PL/SQL is no different. Unfortunately, Oracle7 doesn't come out of the box with a true PL/SQL development environment (for example, like debuggers that come with 3GL compilers) that would make PL/SQL programming more productive. Consequently, you have to learn some debugging tricks to be productive at PL/SQL development. This section explains some basic ways to get started in debugging PL/SQL programs.

Types of Errors and Oracle7 PL/SQL Error Messages

Unless you are a programming wizard, the first time you try to compile a PL/SQL program like a procedure, function, package, or trigger using an interactive database access tool such as SQL*Plus or SQL*DBA, it's likely that Oracle7 will spit out error messages galore to tell you all that is wrong with your program. The error messages serve as the starting point from which you must debug your program.

Parse Errors

Oracle7 can return two rounds of PL/SQL error messages when you try to compile a PL/SQL program. The first wave of error messages will be the parse errors that Oracle7 finds in the program. *Parse errors* are those that result from incorrect use of command syntax—both PL/SQL commands and SQL commands. For example, see if you can find the parse error in the following code example for the CUSTOMERID function:

```
CREATE FUNCTION customerid (last IN VARCHAR2, first IN VARCHAR2)
RETURN INTEGER AS
  customerid  INTEGER;
BEGIN
  SELECT id INTOO customerid FROM customers
    WHERE lastname = last AND firstname = first;
```

```
    RETURN customerid;
END customerid;
```

If you can't find the parse error, take a close look at the SELECT command in the function. Notice that the INTO keyword has an extra "O" at the end. Such a syntax error results in a parse error. If you tried to compile the previous version of the CUSTOMERID function from within SQL*DBA, you would receive the following error message:

```
DBA-00072: Warning: FUNCTION CUSTOMERID created with compilation errors.
```

To reveal PL/SQL errors when using SQL*Plus or SQL*DBA, you can use the special SHOW ERRORS command. Use this command to reveal the errors that result from any CREATE PROCEDURE, CREATE FUNCTION, CREATE PACKAGE, CREATE PACKAGE BODY, CREATE TRIGGER, or CREATE VIEW statement. For example, the following command reveals the parse error identified in the previous example:

```
SHOW ERRORS FUNCTION customerid

Errors for FUNCTION CUSTOMERID:
LINE/COL ERROR
---------------------------------------------------------------------------
5/19     PLS-00103: Encountered the symbol "CUSTOMERID" when expecting one
of the following: , into
```

TIP

If you use the SHOW ERRORS command of SQL*Plus or SQL*DBA without specifying an object, the command returns the errors present for the most recently created procedure, function, package, package body, trigger, or view.

Notice from the preceding example that Oracle7 typically is not outstanding at telling you exactly what you did wrong, even with simple parse errors. Often, you'll have to interpret what the error message reveals to identify a problem. In this case, Oracle7 didn't expect the CUSTOMERID variable reference because it didn't interpret the INTO keyword correctly. After you work with Oracle7 PL/SQL for a while, your experience will help interpret Oracle7 PL/SQL error messages so you can identify problems more readily.

Using SHOW ERRORS, find and fix all of the parse errors in the source file for your PL/SQL program. Then resubmit the code and see if it works. Remember to first drop the older version of the code that has the errors, or simply use the OR RE-PLACE option of the respective CREATE command to replace the older, bug-ridden version of the program, as the following example shows:

```
CREATE OR REPLACE FUNCTION customerid (last IN VARCHAR2, first IN VARCHAR2)
RETURN INTEGER AS
   customerid  INTEGER;
BEGIN
   SELECT id INTO customerid FROM customers
     WHERE lastname = last AND firstname = first;
   RETURN customerid;
END customerid;
```

Compile-Time Errors

The next round of errors that Oracle7 identifies is compile-time errors. Compile-time errors happen when Oracle7 tries to compile the object but encounters some type of error. Common compile-time errors include things like incorrect object references or trying to reference an object for which you have no privileges. If you read the earlier chapters in this book and have a good memory and an outstanding eye for detail, you'll be able to identify the compile-time error in the preceding code example. When trying to create this CUSTOMERID function with SQL*DBA, you'll find the following error is returned:

```
DBA-00072: Warning: FUNCTION CUSTOMERID created with compilation errors.

SHOW ERRORS

Errors for FUNCTION CUSTOMERID:
LINE/COL ERROR
----------------------------------------------------------------------
5/34     PLS-00201: identifier 'CUSTOMERS' must be declared
5/3      PL/SQL: SQL Statement ignored
```

Now do you remember? The table name is CUSTOMER, not CUSTOMERS. Another quick fix, and the procedure will finally compile correctly:

```
CREATE OR REPLACE FUNCTION customerid (last IN VARCHAR2, first IN VARCHAR2)
RETURN INTEGER AS
  customerid   INTEGER;
BEGIN
  SELECT id INTO customerid FROM customer
    WHERE lastname = last AND firstname = first;
  RETURN customerid;
END customerid;
```

Run-Time Errors

Run-time errors occur when your program compiles successfully but then returns errors when someone uses it. Oracle7 cannot identify and tell you about run-time errors until you actually run the program. To learn more about run-time errors, let's take a close look at a perfect example of a run-time error condition: a mutating table situation. Consider the following procedure and trigger definitions:

```
CREATE PROCEDURE restockpart (partid IN INTEGER) AS
  reorderstatus    INTEGER := 0;
  quantity         INTEGER := 0;
  reorderpt        INTEGER := 0;
BEGIN
-- First, check to see if part hasn't already been reordered.
  SELECT count(*) INTO reorderstatus FROM reorder WHERE id = partid;
-- If the part hasn't already been reordered, then reorder it now.
  IF reorderstatus = 0 THEN
    SELECT onhand, reorder INTO quantity, reorderpt
      FROM stock WHERE id = partid;
    INSERT INTO reorder VALUES (partid, quantity, reorderpt);
  END IF;
END restockpart;


CREATE TRIGGER reorder
AFTER UPDATE OF onhand ON stock
FOR EACH ROW
WHEN (new.onhand <= new.reorder)
BEGIN
  restockpart(:new.id);
END;
```

Now consider what happens when someone updates the STOCK table to update a part's onhand quantity to be less than the part's reorder point:

1. The REORDER trigger fires. At this point the STOCK table is mutating with respect to the user session that fired the trigger.

2. The REORDER trigger calls the RESTOCKPART procedure. The RESTOCK-PART procedure attempts to query the STOCK table, which, as previously stated, is mutating.

When Oracle7 identifies that the STOCK table is mutating, it returns the following run-time error messages:

```
ORA-04091: table SALES.STOCK is mutating, trigger may not read or modify it
ORA-06512: at "SALES.REORDERPART", line 10
ORA-06512: at line 2
ORA-04088: error during execution of trigger 'SALES.REORDER'
```

Logic Errors

Logic errors occur when the program compiles successfully but doesn't work as you intended it to. This might be anything from an unhandled exception to the program's not working under certain conditions that you didn't foresee. For example, consider the previous version of the CUSTOMERID function and how it works with the CUSTOMER table. If all customers' last and first names are stored in uppercase letters in the CUSTOMER table, what do you think would happen when an application (in the following case, an anonymous PL/SQL block) calls the CUS-TOMERID function as follows:

```
DECLARE
    x INTEGER;
BEGIN
    x := customerid('Brokaw', 'Thomas');
    dbms_output.put_line(x);
END;
```

The answer: The CUSTOMERID function will not find any customer records with the requested name, Thomas Brokaw, even though there is a customer named THOMAS BROKAW. The previous situation describes a simple logic error—the CUSTOMERID function doesn't account for variances in the case of function parameters. The addition of a SQL function or two can quickly fix this error condition:

```
CREATE OR REPLACE FUNCTION customerid (last IN VARCHAR2, first IN VARCHAR2)
RETURN INTEGER AS
  customerid  INTEGER;
BEGIN
  SELECT id INTO customerid FROM customer
    WHERE lastname = UPPER(last) AND firstname = UPPER(first);
  RETURN customerid;
END customerid;
```

The previous examples of a mutating table error condition and a logic error are just two of many possible types of errors you might encounter after successfully compiling a PL/SQL program. As with any programming project, one of the most important steps is to thoroughly test and validate the system to make sure the program works as intended.

Using the DBMS_OUTPUT Utility Package to Debug PL/SQL Programs

If you debug a 3GL program without the use of a nice debugger, it's hard to tell what is going on when the program is running. Therefore, it's hard to debug the program and get it working correctly. To get around the limitations of your compiler, you can include statements that produce output and tell you what is going on. For example, when using C, you might include some PRINTF statements to reveal the values of several program variables as they change during program execution. You can then look at the output and figure out what is happening.

As described earlier, Oracle7 doesn't include a debugger to help you program with PL/SQL. Therefore, you might consider using the previous method of program output to reveal what is happening as a PL/SQL program executes. To produce output from a PL/SQL program, use the functions of the DBMS_OUTPUT utility package. If you are not familiar with the DBMS_OUTPUT package, see the section "Providing Terminal Output from PL/SQL" later in this chapter.

Using the Oracle7 Programmer Utilities

The Procedural option of Oracle7 ships with several scripts that create useful programmer utilities in the form of PL/SQL packages. These packages contain a number of procedures and functions you can call to increase the functionality of an application's stored procedures, functions, and database triggers. The following sections describe each of these programmer utilities.

Supplementing SQL Functionality Inside PL/SQL

Oracle7 includes several utility packages for increasing the functionality of SQL inside PL/SQL programs. The following sections explain the packages you can use to add specific SQL functionality to your PL/SQL programs.

The DBMS_SESSION Package

The DBMS_SESSION package contains several procedures and functions applications can use to control an application user's session. Two useful utilities are the SET_ROLE procedure, which allows a PL/SQL program to change an application user's current database role, and the IS_ROLE_ENABLED function, which allows an application to determine whether or not a specified role is enabled. (Chapter 19 includes a discussion of how to use the SET_ROLE and IS_ROLE_ENABLED programs in the DBMS_SESSION package.)

The DBMS_SESSION package also includes the RESET_PACKAGE procedure, which allows an application to reinitialize the state of all a session's current packages. For example, an application can use the RESET_PACKAGE procedure to reinitialize the current values for all global package variables in an application session:

```
dbms_session.reset_package
```

Another useful function in the DBMS_SESSION package is UNIQUE_SESSION_ID, which assigns a unique session ID to an application session. The UNIQUE_SESSION_ID function is useful for applications that open multiple connections to the server and must coordinate processing among the open sessions.

Applications can keep track of each connection with variables that receive the unique session ID assigned by Oracle7:

```
session1 := dbms_session.unique_session_id;
```

NOTE   The UNIQUE_SESSION_ID function merely assigns unique ID values among currently connected sessions; the function doesn't guarantee to create different session IDs each time someone calls it. For example, you might connect, get a session ID, disconnect, reconnect, and then get the same session ID as the first time.

The DBMS_TRANSACTION Package

The DBMS_TRANSACTION package permits a PL/SQL program to perform restricted transaction control. Here are some of the more useful ones:

Procedure	Description
COMMIT	Commits a transaction
ROLLBACK	Rolls back a transaction
SAVEPOINT	Declares a transaction savepoint
ROLLBACK_SAVEPOINT	Rolls back a transaction to a declared savepoint
USE_ROLLBACK_SEGMENT	Specifies a specific rollback segment for a new transaction

However, many of these procedures have limited usefulness because of usage restrictions. For example, you cannot use any of these procedures inside database triggers, and you can use only one, the USE_ROLLBACK_SEGMENT procedure, in procedures called by Oracle Forms.

The DBMS_DDL and DBMS_UTILITY Packages

The DBMS_DDL and DBMS_UTILITY packages also contain procedures and functions that extend the functionality of PL/SQL with a limited number of DDL operations and other internal server operations. Several of the procedures in these packages will be of more interest to database administrators than to application developers. For example, Chapter 10 discusses the DBMS_UTILITY.ANALYZE_SCHEMA procedure, which the administrator can use to update the statistics for all objects in a specified application schema.

Providing Terminal Output from PL/SQL

Oracle7 includes several utility packages to provide output from within PL/SQL programs. The following sections explain the utility packages you can use to generate application output from within PL/SQL programs.

The DBMS_STANDARD Package

For the most part, the procedures and functions in the DBMS_STANDARD utility package are used by other utility packages. However, applications can directly call one procedure, RAISE_APPLICATION_ERROR, to raise user-defined errors and error messages. (Chapter 5 discusses how to use the RAISE_APPLICATION_ERROR procedure, and several code listings throughout this book demonstrate the use of the procedure.)

The DBMS_OUTPUT Package

The DBMS_OUTPUT utility package contains several procedures and functions applications can use to produce terminal output from database procedures and triggers. For example, the ENABLE procedure creates a buffer to enable output from other DBMS_OUTPUT procedures, the PUT_LINE procedure puts a specified text string as a new line in the output buffer, the GET_LINE procedure retrieves a single line from the output buffer, and the GET_LINES procedure retrieves an array of lines from the output buffer.

SQL*DBA and SQL*Plus make the management of the output buffer transparent with the SERVEROUTPUT option of the SET command. Several examples of stored procedures throughout this book demonstrate how to use cursors and the PUT_LINE procedure to return multiple rows of output from a stored procedure.

Passing Information among Database Sessions

Oracle7 includes several utility packages to allow communication among different database sessions. The following sections explain the different utility packages you can use to allow database sessions to communicate.

The DBMS_LOCK Package

The DBMS_LOCK utility package allows applications to coordinate access to shared resources that are external to the database server. Chapter 17 includes examples that show how to use several of the procedures and functions in the DBMS_LOCK utility package to coordinate application access to a number of shared system peripherals, such as printers and modems.

The DBMS_ALERT Package

Most types of client applications require user interaction to get work done with a database system. For example, a forms-based application might provide entry fields, where users can enter new records of information, as well as a button that, when pressed, notifies the application to send the new data records to the database server. In this case the application user drives the communication between the client and the server to get work done. But intelligent applications include two-way communication logic so the database server can alert an application user when certain conditions exist in the database. For example, a powerful inventory management application might alert an inventory manager that the stock on a particular product has dropped below its reorder point, or even worse, to nothing. If the inventory management application did not include such alerting logic, the inventory manager would not discover an inventory crisis unless the inventory manager frequently and consistently remembered to query the database for problem situations.

One way an Oracle7 client application can identify an alert condition is to regularly poll the database server for an alert situation using a SQL query. For example, an inventory management application might issue this query every five minutes to check for parts below their reorder point:

```
SELECT id, description
  FROM stock
  WHERE onhand < = reorder;
```

The primary drawback of such polling is that it can significantly degrade system performance, especially when many client applications all poll for many alert conditions. If this happens, the database server is subject to an extraordinary burden just in checking for alert conditions that might never exist, not to mention a significant amount of extra network traffic.

A much more efficient way to identify and signal alert conditions in an Oracle7 database is by using database alerts. As Chapter 13 discusses, database alerts allow applications to create, register for, and signal when alert conditions arise in an Oracle7 database without polling. Because database alerts do not perform any polling to identify alert conditions, database alerts can keep application users abreast of any alert situations while placing no extra burden on the Oracle7 database server and keep network traffic to a minimum. Figure 18.1 contrasts the different methods of identifying and signaling database alert conditions.

Applications can create, register for, and signal database alerts using the procedures and functions in the DBMS_ALERT utility package. Here is a list of the primary procedures:

Procedure	Description
REGISTER	Used by an application to register interest in a named database alert
WAITONE and WAITANY	Used by an application to wait for a signal that a specific database alert or any database alert has occurred for which the application has registered
SIGNAL	Included by the developer in an application procedure or database trigger to identify when an alert condition happens

FIGURE 18.1:

Database alerts place much less burden on the database server and the network than does polling to alert applications of specific conditions.

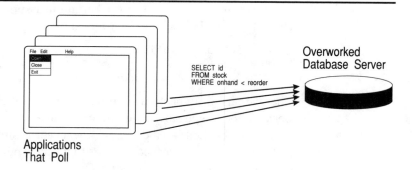

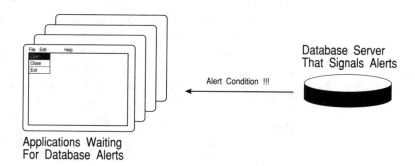

One of the best ways to learn how to use database alerts is to look at a sample application that uses the procedures and functions of the DBMS_ALERT package. The following examples show how to include database alert logic in an inventory management application to notify an inventory manager when the stock is low on a part in inventory.

To be signaled when an alert condition happens, the first thing an application needs to do is register for the alert using the DBMS_ALERT.REGISTER procedure. For example, the inventory management application can register for the alert named STOCKLOW by making this procedure call after application startup or when a menu item is selected:

```
dbms_alert.register('STOCKLOW');
```

Oracle7 keeps track of sessions that register for an alert and makes a note to signal these sessions when something triggers the alert condition. However, registering for named alerts is not enough for an application to be signaled when the alerts happen. Because the Oracle7 server does not support *synchronous communication* (communication independent of user directives), Oracle7 can notify an application of an alert condition only when the application is waiting for an alert signal. To wait for one or more alert conditions, an application should create a dedicated connection to the database apart from the primary focus of the application.

For example, the inventory application might create a second database session when opening a separate window that has some indicators to show the current status of several alert situations. The session tied to the alert window simply waits for alert conditions to happen. When there are no alert conditions, the window might show an array of green lights to indicate that all systems are in good shape. When an alert condition arises, the application can beep and change a light to a flashing red to indicate that the corresponding alert condition has occurred.

To wait for an alert signal for a registered alert, an application can use the DBMS_ALERT.WAITONE procedure or the DBMS_ALERT.WAITANY procedure. The WAITONE procedure waits for a signal from a specific registered alert, while the WAITANY procedure waits for a signal from any registered alert. For example, this PL/SQL block shows how a database session in an inventory management application might use an endless loop to wait for a signal that the STOCKLOW alert condition has occurred:

```
DECLARE
message VARCHAR2(256);
status INTEGER;
BEGIN
LOOP
  dbms_alert.waitone('STOCKLOW', message, status, 5);
  IF status = 0 THEN
    dbms_output.put_line(message);
  END IF;
END LOOP;
END;
```

Notice that the return status of the WAITONE (and WAITANY) procedure indicates whether or not an alert condition is positive; 0 indicates that an alert occurred, and 1 indicates that a time-out occurred. When calling the WAITONE (and WAITANY) procedure, you can indicate the time to wait, in seconds. In the previous example, the WAITONE procedure waits for five seconds.

NOTE If a session waiting for alert signals uses a lengthy time-out period, the session should connect to the database server using a dedicated server connection rather than a multithreaded, shared server connection. That's because while a session is waiting for an alert to occur, Oracle7 binds a shared server to the waiting session and prevents all other sessions from using the shared server.

The previous examples show what is necessary from the perspective of client-side application logic. However, one last thing is necessary to make a database alert work: a procedure or trigger that actually signals an alert condition. This is the trick that makes polling unnecessary and saves all of the overhead on the server.

For example, consider the following rewrite of the REORDER trigger shown in Chapter 5. Recall that the REORDER trigger inserts a new row into a table called REORDER that keeps track of all the parts in inventory where the part's stock has fallen below its reorder point. The only modification we will make in this version of the REORDER trigger is to add a line to signal that a STOCKLOW alert condition exists:

```
CREATE or replace TRIGGER reorder
AFTER UPDATE OF onhand ON stock
FOR EACH ROW
WHEN (new.onhand <= new.reorder)
BEGIN
  INSERT INTO reorder VALUES (:new.id, :new.onhand, :new.reorder);
  dbms_alert.signal('STOCKLOW','Part '||:new.id||' reordered; low on stock');
END;
```

When an application transaction updates the STOCK table to lower a part's inventory supply, the preceding version of the REORDER trigger checks to see if the part's new inventory supply is lower than its reorder point. If so, the trigger automatically reorders the part and signals an alert condition, which might appear as a flashing red beacon on the inventory manager's terminal:

```
UPDATE stock
  SET onhand = onhand - 100
  WHERE id = 7
```

> **NOTE**
>
> Alert signals wisely depend on the outcome of transactions. Therefore, Oracle7 does not immediately signal registered sessions when a procedure or trigger signals the alert. Instead, Oracle7 signals registered sessions only if the transaction that signals the alert commits. This logic can be very important. For instance, consider what happens if an application user's transaction updates the STOCK table to lower a part's inventory quantity below its reorder point, but then the user rolls back the transaction. Since the transaction never really happened, Oracle7 does not signal the alert condition, so the inventory manager does not see an alert that didn't really happen.

The inventory management alert example is just one way you can use database alerts to enhance the functionality and power of your Oracle7 database applications. As you plan an application, discuss with users the different types of alerts that would make the application better for their job. If you use database alerts wisely in an application, you can positively affect the productivity of application users.

The DBMS_PIPE Package

The DBMS_PIPE utility package allows different database sessions connected to the same database instance to communicate with one another using *database pipes*—channels for intersession communication. For example, an application might open multiple sessions to a database server as in the database alert example shown in the preceding section. To allow communication among the different application sessions, you can use database pipes.

The more important procedures and functions in the DBMS_PIPE package include

Procedure	Description
PACK_MESSAGE	Places a specified message text string, number, or date into the message buffer
UNPACK_MESSAGE	Extracts a message from the message buffer into a specified local variable

Procedure	Description
SEND_MESSAGE	Sends a message in the message buffer to a named pipe
RECEIVE_MESSAGE	Receives a message sent to a named pipe

To send and receive intersession messages, client applications must execute the different procedures and functions in the DBMS_PIPE package in specific orders. For example, to send a message to a pipe, client applications should first place the message in the message buffer using the PACK_MESSAGE procedure and then assign the message to a named pipe using the SEND_MESSAGE function. This PL/SQL block illustrates the importance of the order of DBMS_PIPE calls:

```
DECLARE
x integer;
BEGIN
dbms_pipe.pack_message('Here is an example of a message');
x := dbms_pipe.send_message('PIPE1'); -- send message to PIPE1
IF x = 0 then
  dbms_output.put_line('Success');
ELSE
  dbms_output.put_line('Failure');
END IF;
END;
```

Similarly, to receive messages on a pipe, client applications need to check for a message on a named pipe using the RECEIVE_MESSAGE function and, if present, extract the message into a local application variable using the UNPACK_MESSAGE procedure. This PL/SQL block demonstrates these operations:

```
DECLARE
x INTEGER;
message VARCHAR2(256);
BEGIN
LOOP
  x:= dbms_pipe.receive_message('PIPE1',60); -- wait 60 secs for PIPE1 messages
  IF x = 0 then
    dbms_pipe.unpack_message(message); -- extract message into variable MESSAGE
    dbms_output.put_line(message);
  END IF;
END LOOP;
END;
```

The explanations and examples in this chapter have given you an understanding of the powerful features available for application development in the Oracle7 Procedural option, including

- How and when to use database stored procedures, functions, packages, and triggers effectively in an application design

- How to create, manage, and use database stored procedures, functions, packages, and triggers

- How to use special utility packages included with the Oracle7 Procedural option (for example, DBMS_OUTPUT, DBMS_STANDARD, DBMS_ALERT, and DBMS_PIPE packages) to enhance the functionality of Oracle7 client/server applications

CHAPTER

NINETEEN

Securing Applications

- Granting and revoking access to database objects

- Using roles to manage privileges for applications

- Enabling and disabling roles for applications

After reading all of the chapters in Part II of this book, you must feel like there is an endless array of things to consider when developing a client application for an Oracle7 database system. After application interface design, defining the application's schema and application logic, and then tuning the application's performance, what else could there possibly be? Add to the list application security issues. To finish this book's discussion of Oracle7 client/server application development, this chapter explains how to control access to the data in an application schema using roles and database object privileges.

The ABCs of Application Security

Once you develop, test, and install an application in an Oracle7 client/server database system, it's ready to be put into action—into the hands of the real workers, the application users. However, not just any database user can run an application to accomplish work. There are many security controls that prevent unauthorized users from executing an application.

In many environments the operating system presents the first security hurdle to an application user: a user must have the appropriate file system privileges to run the application's executable. For example, if a user intends to use a UNIX workstation to run a client application, the user must have the necessary file permissions on the application executable. Most multi-user operating systems have similar security checks.

> **NOTE** If a client application executes on a single-user operating system like DOS, Microsoft Windows, or Apple, there is probably no way to control who can execute the application on a PC.

After getting past the operating system, an application user must be able to connect to the Oracle7 database server. This requires the application user to have a valid database username and password and to be able to create a database session. (See Chapter 9 for a discussion of how the database administrator creates database usernames and passwords for application users, as well as an introduction of system privilege management for application users.)

Even after an application user has the necessary operating system file permissions and can connect to an Oracle7 database, there are other controls that prevent unauthorized use of an application's data: database object privileges. *Database object privileges,* such as SELECT, INSERT, UPDATE, DELETE, and EXECUTE allow you to explicitly authorize which database users can manipulate an application's table data and execute an application's stored procedures. It is the Oracle7 database object privileges that the application developer needs to consider when putting together a security policy for an application. The following section explains the different object privileges that control access to the data in an Oracle7 database.

Understanding Database Object Privileges

An application schema can contain many different types of database objects, including tables, indexes, views, sequences, procedures, functions, and packages. To execute and use a client database application, an application user must have the necessary object privileges to many of the objects that the application uses. The following table lists the Oracle7 object privileges that are available for the different types of database objects:

Object	Privileges Available
Tables	SELECT, INSERT, UPDATE, DELETE, ALTER, INDEX, REFERENCES
Views	SELECT, INSERT, UPDATE, DELETE
Sequences	SELECT, ALTER
Procedures, functions, and packages	EXECUTE

In many cases the access that each database object privilege protects will be obvious. For example, the SELECT privilege for a table authorizes a user to issue SELECT statements against the table. However, in some cases it is not apparent what each object privilege corresponds to. The following list of the commonly misunderstood object privileges should help shed some light:

Privilege	Description
INDEX (table privilege)	Permits a user who does not own the table to create an index for the table
REFERENCES (table privilege)	Permits a user who does not own a table to reference the table in the declaration of a referential integrity constraint
SELECT (sequence privilege)	Permits a user who does not own the sequence to reference the sequence with the NEXTVAL and CURRVAL pseudo-columns

You should also check with a database's administrator to see if the server enforces privileges for searched updates. A *searched update* is an UPDATE or DELETE statement that includes a subquery to find the target rows. For example, the following UPDATE and DELETE statements qualify as searched updates because of the subqueries present as WHERE clauses:

```
UPDATE stock SET onhand = onhand - 100 WHERE id = 3

DELETE FROM stock WHERE id = 7
```

If an Oracle7 server enforces privileges for searched updates, a user needs the SELECT privilege to update a table with a searched update. For example, to execute the first of the two preceding example statements, an application user needs both the UPDATE and SELECT object privileges for the STOCK table, not just the UPDATE privilege.

NOTE The administrator can determine whether or not a server enforces privileges for searched updates using the SEARCHED_UPDATE initialization parameter. The possible values are TRUE and FALSE.

Database Object Privileges and Synonyms

Chapter 15 discussed how you can use synonyms to remove an application's direct dependence on tables, views, procedures, and other database objects. In terms of security for an application's objects, there are no special privileges to consider when referencing an object's synonym instead of the object itself; just as a user must have the privileges to reference an object by its name, the user must have the privileges to reference an object by a synonym. For example, to query data from the STOCK table, you must have the SELECT privilege for the STOCK table. To query data from the STOCK table using its INVENTORY synonym, you must still have the SELECT privilege for the STOCK table.

You can also grant (or revoke) an object's database object privileges to a user or role by referencing a synonym of the object. For example, the following two statements are equivalent, considering that the STOCK table has a synonym, INVENTORY:

```
GRANT SELECT ON stock TO tjefferson
```

```
GRANT SELECT ON inventory TO tjefferson
```

As you can see, there are many different object privileges to consider for an application, particularly for the most common types of objects that an application uses (tables and views). To make it easier to manage the privileges necessary to run an application for many different users, it is wise to take advantage of roles to manage an application's privileges. The following section explains how to use roles for application privilege management.

Using Roles for Application Privilege Management

A role is a collection of related privileges. Chapter 9 showed how the security administrator for a system can create and use roles to greatly simplify privilege management for the different types of database system users. In the same manner, an application developer can create roles to manage and group together the related object privileges necessary to run an application. Then, as part of application installation, the database security administrator grants the application's role to the users who need to run the application. If the privilege requirements for the application change at some time, it's no problem—all that is necessary is a quick change to the privileges in the application role, not to the privileges of many application users.

Use of roles in an Oracle7 client/server database system provides another important benefit: dynamic privilege management for application users. As a user moves from one application to another, each application's role ensures that the user has only the privileges necessary to run the current application and does not carry over privileges from another application.

When planning the security for an application, you might identify different types of application users. For example, it is common that some users will be responsible for creating reports only, not for changing data. Therefore, you should create an application role for these users so they can only read data using the application. Other users might need to use the application to insert new data. Likewise, you need another application role that has the privileges to insert new data using the application. A third application role is necessary if still other users need to have both read and write access to data using the application. And instead of granting an application's roles directly to users, the administrator might decide to grant application roles to other roles that define distinct sets of users in the database. Figure 19.1 shows how a hierarchy of roles can grow from the simple goal of managing application privileges.

Now that you have an idea of the issues to consider when managing an application's security, the following sections explain how to create roles for an application and manage its privilege domain.

Creating Roles to Manage Application Privileges and Application Users

Chapter 9 explained how you can use the CREATE ROLE dialog of SQL*DBA to create a role and set its authentication method. However, as an application developer, you will probably want to include the definition of an application's roles in it's DDL script. Therefore, you will most likely want to create application roles with the equivalent SQL command CREATE ROLE. For example, these statements

FIGURE 19.1:

Example of a hierarchy of roles used to manage application privileges

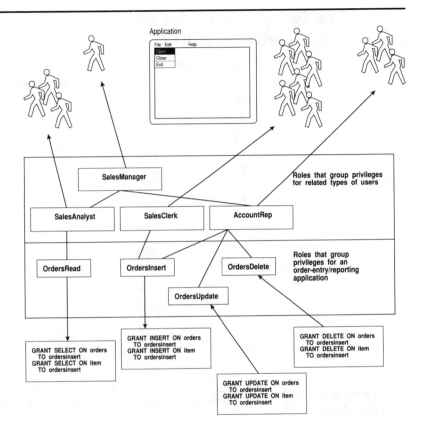

demonstrate the different options available in the CREATE ROLE command:

```
CREATE ROLE ordersread

CREATE ROLE orderswrite
  IDENTIFIED BY gomitgomat

CREATE ROLE ordersreadwrite
  IDENTIFIED BY phloristigoo
```

Follow the guidelines for client/server systems presented in Chapter 9 concerning role authorization. For example, do not use operating system authentication; instead, use passwords that have no real meaning.

Granting Privileges to an Application's Roles

Once you have created a role to manage an application's privileges, the next task is to establish the role's *privilege domain*, or set of privileges for the role. You manage a role's privilege domain using the SQL commands GRANT and REVOKE, along with the different object privileges for the application objects. For example, this set of statements creates a role for insert-only access using an order entry application:

```
CREATE ROLE ordersinsert
  IDENTIFIED BY wiffopnertu

GRANT INSERT ON orders TO ordersinsert

GRANT INSERT ON item TO ordersinsert
```

The next statements show how you can grant several object privileges for a single table all in one GRANT statement:

```
CREATE ROLE ordersreadwrite
  IDENTIFIED BY phloristigoo

GRANT SELECT, INSERT, UPDATE, DELETE ON orders TO ordersreadwrite
```

NOTE   As Chapter 9 showed, you can also grant system privileges to any database role. However, most application users should not have the access that powerful system privileges supply. Use extreme caution when considering the grant of a system privilege to an application role.

Column-Specific Object Privileges

The examples of the GRANT command in the preceding section show how to grant object privilege access for all columns in a table or view. As an alternative, you may want to grant object privilege access for specific columns in a table or view. Oracle7 supports object privilege access for specific columns with the INSERT, UPDATE, and REFERENCES privileges only.

```
GRANT UPDATE (shipdate, paiddate) ON orders TO ordersupdate
```

Although Oracle7 does not support granting the SELECT privilege for specific columns of a table, it's easy to work around this limitation by using views. For example, if you want some users to be able to see only the ID, LASTNAME, and FIRSTNAME columns of the CUSTOMER table, create a view that selects these columns, and then grant the SELECT privilege on the view to the users:

```
CREATE VIEW customernames AS
  SELECT id, lastname, firstname
  FROM customer

GRANT SELECT ON customernames TO ...
```

Revoking Object Privileges from an Application's Roles

If an application's privilege requirements change, you might need to revoke a previously granted object privilege from the application's role. Revoking an object privilege is just as easy as granting it; you use the SQL command REVOKE:

```
REVOKE SELECT ON reorder FROM inventorymanager
```

If a grant exists for a table or view and you want to revoke access to only specific columns, you must first revoke access altogether and then regrant column-selective access:

```
REVOKE UPDATE ON orders FROM ordersupdate

GRANT UPDATE (shipdate) ON orders TO ordersupdate
```

Enabling Application Roles on Application Startup

Once you have created an application's roles and defined the privilege domains for each role, you need to create a mechanism in the application to enable the application's role. This ensures that an application user has the correct privileges to successfully run the application. Enabling a specific role for an application also disables a user's other roles, including the user's default roles. (See Chapter 9 for a discussion of default roles.) Most commonly, an application enables its roles at application startup. The following sections explain how an application can enable specific roles for application privilege management.

TIP

A user can enable an application role only after the database administrator has granted the role to the user. When you hand over an application to an administrator for installation, make sure the administrator knows to grant the application roles to the application users directly, or indirectly through other database roles that group related users. (See Chapter 9 for more information about granting roles to users.)

Using the SET ROLE Command

To enable a role, an application can use the SQL command SET ROLE:

```
SET ROLE ordersread
```

```
SET ROLE orderswrite
  IDENTIFIED BY gomitgomat
```

Notice that if the role is protected by a password, a SET ROLE statement must also include an IDENTIFIED BY clause to specify the role's password.

The SET ROLE command also allows an application to enable multiple roles:

```
SET ROLE
  ordersread
  orderswrite IDENTIFIED BY gomitgomat
```

```
SET ROLE
  orderswrite IDENTIFIED BY gomitgomat,
  ordersreadwrite IDENTIFIED BY phloristigoo
```

In the first example, one role requires a password while the other does not. The second example shows how to enable multiple roles that all have passwords.

When an application uses the SET ROLE command to explicitly enable one or more roles, Oracle7 implicitly disables all other roles that the user currently has enabled.

Using the DBMS_SESSION Package to Work around Development Environment Limitations

Many application development environments do not support the use of the SQL command SET ROLE. This can make life difficult when trying to use roles for application security. However, if an application development environment permits calls to database stored procedures and you have Oracle7 with the Procedural option, an application can work around this problem by calling the SET_ROLE procedure in the DBMS_SESSION utility package.

The DBMS_SESSION.SET_ROLE procedure allows access to the SET ROLE command through a procedural interface. For example, an Oracle Forms application can use the SET_ROLE procedure in a pre-form trigger to enable a specific role for the form application:

```
dbms_session.set_role('orderswrite IDENTIFIED BY gomitgomat');
```

Notice in this example that you have to specify a role's password in the SET_ROLE procedure. If you code a role's password into an application, as the previous example shows, you can open up a potential security hole—a malicious user could look at the application's source code or reverse-engineer the application's code to discover a role's password. To work around this potential security hole, create a dialog at application startup that prompts the user for the application's role and password, and then feed the entered values as variables in a call to the SET_ROLE procedure:

```
dbms_session.set_role(:rolename||' IDENTIFIED BY '||:rolepassword);
```

If a role does not have a password, call the SET_ROLE procedure without the IDENTIFIED BY part of the parameter:

```
dbms_session.set_role('ordersread')
```

This chapter has described how to approach security for individual Oracle7 applications, including the following topics:

- What database object privileges are, as well as how to grant them to and revoke them from users and roles

- How to use roles to manage the group of related object privileges necessary for users to run a database application

- How an application can enable and disable application roles using the SET ROLE command and the procedures in the DMMS_SESSION utility package

APPENDIX

A

Quick Reference Tables
for Oracle7

This appendix includes a number of lists to use as references when working with Oracle7, including

- SQL commands (Table A.1)
- PL/SQL commands (Table A.2)
- SQL functions (Tables A.3 through A.8)
- The SQL*DBA menu structure (Figure A.1)
- Data dictionary views (Tables A.9 through A.11)
- Datatypes (Table A.12)
- System privileges (Table A.13)
- Object privileges (Table A.14)

Oracle7 SQL Commands

Table A.1 includes quick descriptions for all the Oracle7 SQL commands (not including embedded SQL commands). In the table, † means the command is available only with the Oracle7 Procedural option, and †† means the command is available only with the Oracle7 Distributed Database option.

TABLE A.1: Oracle7 SQL Commands

SQL Command	Description
ALTER CLUSTER	Modifies the structure of an indexed or a hash cluster
ALTER DATABASE	Modifies the structure and/or operational mode of an Oracle7 database; allows database recovery
ALTER FUNCTION †	Manually forces a function to recompile
ALTER INDEX	Modifies the storage parameters for an index
ALTER PACKAGE †	Manually forces a package to recompile
ALTER PROCEDURE †	Manually forces a procedure to recompile
ALTER PROFILE	Modifies the resource limits of a profile

† Available only with the Oracle7 Procedural option
†† Available only with the Oracle7 Distributed Database option

TABLE A.1: Oracle7 SQL Commands (continued)

SQL Command	Description
ALTER RESOURCE COST	Modifies the weighting costs for the composite resource limits
ALTER ROLE	Modifies a role's password or authentication method
ALTER ROLLBACK SEGMENT	Modifies the availability or storage parameters of a rollback segment
ALTER SEQUENCE	Modifies the characteristics of a sequence
ALTER SESSION	Modifies database session settings
ALTER SNAPSHOT † ††	Modifies a snapshot's refresh mode and/or time, or storage characteristics
ALTER SNAPSHOT LOG † ††	Modifies a snapshot log's storage characteristics
ALTER SYSTEM	Dynamically modifies several current database server system settings
ALTER TABLE	Modifies a table's physical structure, storage parameters, and/or integrity constraints
ALTER TABLESPACE	Modifies a tablespace's availability, backup mode, or storage parameters, or adds data files to increase tablespace capacity
ALTER TRIGGER †	Enables or disables a trigger
ALTER USER	Modifies a user's account settings, password, or authentication method
ALTER VIEW	Manually recompiles a view
ANALYZE	Generates optimizer statistics or lists chained rows for a table, an index, or a cluster. Can also validate the structure of an index
AUDIT	Sets audit options for the system and database objects
COMMENT	Creates in the data dictionary a comment for a table, view, snapshot, or column
COMMIT	Commits a transaction to make transaction changes permanent in the database
CREATE CLUSTER	Creates an indexed or a hash cluster

† Available only with the Oracle7 Procedural option
†† Available only with the Oracle7 Distributed Database option

TABLE A.1: Oracle7 SQL Commands (continued)

SQL Command	Description
CREATE CONTROLFILE	Creates a new database control file to replace a damaged or badly sized control file
CREATE DATABASE	Creates a database
CREATE DATABASE LINK††	Defines a named path to a remote database. Database links are available without the Distributed Database option, but for read operations only
CREATE FUNCTION †	Creates a stored function
CREATE INDEX	Creates an index for a table
CREATE PACKAGE †	Creates a stored package specification
CREATE PACKAGE BODY †	Creates a stored package body
CREATE PROCEDURE †	Creates a stored procedure
CREATE PROFILE	Creates a named profile of resource limits
CREATE ROLE	Creates a role to group related privileges
CREATE ROLLBACK SEGMENT	Creates a rollback segment
CREATE SCHEMA	Creates a number of tables and views, all in one statement, in a current database account
CREATE SEQUENCE	Creates a named sequence of numbers
CREATE SNAPSHOT † ††	Creates a snapshot of a remote table
CREATE SNAPSHOT LOG † ††	Creates a refresh log for a snapshot
CREATE SYNONYM	Creates a synonym for a database object
CREATE TABLE	Creates a new database table
CREATE TABLESPACE	Creates a new tablespace
CREATE TRIGGER †	Creates a database trigger for a table
CREATE USER	Creates a new database username and password
CREATE VIEW	Creates a view of a table or other views
DELETE	Deletes one or more rows from a database table
DROP CLUSTER	Drops an indexed or a hash cluster
DROP DATABASE LINK††	Drops a named path to a remote database
DROP FUNCTION †	Drops a stored function

† Available only with the Oracle7 Procedural option
†† Available only with the Oracle7 Distributed Database option

TABLE A.1: Oracle7 SQL Commands (continued)

SQL Command	Description
DROP INDEX	Drops an index on a table
DROP PACKAGE †	Drops a stored package specification and body
DROP PACKAGE BODY †	Drops a stored package body
DROP PROCEDURE †	Drops a stored procedure
DROP PROFILE	Drops a named profile of resource limits
DROP ROLE	Drops a role of related privileges
DROP ROLLBACK SEGMENT	Drops a rollback segment
DROP SEQUENCE	Drops a named sequence of numbers
DROP SNAPSHOT † ††	Drops a snapshot of a remote table
DROP SNAPSHOT LOG † ††	Drops a log for a snapshot
DROP SYNONYM	Drops a synonym for a table or view
DROP TABLE	Drops a database table
DROP TABLESPACE	Drops a tablespace
DROP TRIGGER †	Drops a trigger on a table
DROP USER	Drops a database username, as well as the user's objects
DROP VIEW	Drops a view
EXPLAIN PLAN	Puts into a database table the optimization strategy for a SQL statement
GRANT	Grants roles, system privileges, and/or object privileges to users and/or roles
INSERT	Inserts one or more new rows into a database table
LOCK TABLE	Manually locks a table
NOAUDIT	Disables audit options for the system and database objects
RENAME	Renames a table, view, sequence, or synonym
REVOKE	Revokes roles, system privileges, and/or object privileges from users or roles
ROLLBACK	Rolls back the changes made by the current transaction
SAVEPOINT	Identifies an intermediate transaction savepoint

† Available only with the Oracle7 Procedural option
†† Available only with the Oracle7 Distributed Database option

TABLE A.1: Oracle7 SQL Commands (continued)

SQL Command	Description
SELECT	Retrieves all or specific column and row information from one or more tables or views
SET ROLE	Enables one or more specific roles of related privileges and disables all others
SET TRANSACTION	Specifies transaction characteristics
TRUNCATE	Deletes all rows from a table and optionally releases all space allocated to the table
UPDATE	Updates all or specific rows in a table

† Available only with the Oracle7 Procedural option
†† Available only with the Oracle7 Distributed Database option

PL/SQL Commands

Table A.2 provides a quick reference to the Oracle7 PL/SQL commands.

TABLE A.2: Oracle7 PL/SQL Commands

PL/SQL Command	Description
CLOSE	Closes a cursor
EXCEPTION_INIT	Associates a declared exception name with an Oracle error number to trap and handle an Oracle error with a PL/SQL exception handler
EXIT	Exits a loop
FETCH	Fetches the next row from a cursor
GOTO	Goes to a named block of PL/SQL code
IF	Conditional statement to execute a PL/SQL block
LOOP	Creates a loop to execute one or more statements a number of times
NULL	Performs no action
OPEN	Opens a declared cursor
RAISE	Raises a declared exception

TABLE A.2: Oracle7 PL/SQL Commands (continued)

PL/SQL Command	Description
RETURN	Completes the execution of a PL/SQL program and, if in a function, returns a value to the calling environment
SELECT INTO	Retrieves one or more column values from a single row in a table into specified PL/SQL variables

NOTE

PL/SQL also supports the DML SQL commands, such as INSERT, UPDATE, DELETE, and LOCK TABLE, as well as transaction control SQL commands, such as COMMIT, ROLLBACK, and SAVEPOINT. Also, Table A.2 does not include other PL/SQL functionality, such as variable declarations and assignment statements (assigning values to variables), because they are not commands.

Oracle7 SQL Functions

Tables A.3 through A.8 are quick references to the various Oracle7 SQL functions. The tables organize the SQL functions by type.

TABLE A.3: Oracle7 Numeric SQL Functions

SQL Function	Description
ABS(x)	Returns the absolute value of x
CEIL(x)	Returns the smallest integer greater than or equal to x
COS(x)	Returns the cosine of x
COSH(x)	Returns the hyperbolic cosine of x
EXP(x)	Returns e raised to the xth power
FLOOR(x)	Returns the largest integer less than or equal to x

TABLE A.3 : Oracle7 Numeric SQL Functions (continued)

SQL Function	Description
LN(x)	Returns the natural logarithm of x
LOG(x,y)	Returns the base x logarithm of y
MOD(x,y)	Returns the remainder of x divided by y
POWER(x,y)	Returns x raised to the y power
ROUND(x[,y])	Returns x rounded y places to the right of the decimal place. Default y is 0. If y is negative, x is rounded to the left of the decimal place
SIGN(x)	Returns the sign of x as -1 if negative, 0 if 0, and 1 if positive
SIN(x)	Returns the sine of x
SINH(x)	Returns the hyperbolic sine of x
SQRT(x)	Returns the square root of x
TAN(x)	Returns the tangent of x
TANH(x)	Returns the hyperbolic tangent of x
TRUNC(x[,y])	Returns x truncated to y decimal places. Default y is 0. If y is negative, x is truncated to the left of the decimal place

TABLE A.4 : Oracle7 Character SQL Functions

SQL Function	Description
ASCII(x)	Returns the decimal representation of the character x
CHR(x)	Returns the character in the database character set that corresponds to integer x
CONCAT(x,y)	Returns x concatenated with y
INITCAP(x)	Returns the string x, with the first letter in each word in uppercase and the remaining letters in each word in lowercase
INSTR(w,x[,y[,z]])	Returns the starting character position of string x in string w, if present. Returns 0 if string x is not present in string w. If you specify y, search starts at character position y in string w. If you specify z, search looks for the zth occurrence of string x in string w, starting at character position y
INSTRB(w,x[,y[,z]])	Same as INSTR, except that y and the return value are expressed in bytes instead of character position. Useful only when using multi-byte character strings for w and x

TABLE A.4: Oracle7 Character SQL Functions (continued)

SQL Function	Description
LENGTH(x)	Returns the string length of x
LENGTHB(x)	Returns the byte length of x
LOWER(x)	Returns x with all letters in lowercase
LPAD(x,y[,z])	Returns x left-padded with spaces with length y. Use the optional argument z to specify a padding string
LTRIM(x[,y])	Trims characters from the left of string x and returns the resulting string. Use z to specify a set of characters to be trimmed. Default y is a blank space to remove left blank padding from strings
NLS_INITCAP (x[,y])	Same as INITCAP, except optional argument y allows you to specify a language for consideration in the function
NLS_LOWER(x[,y])	Same as LOWER, except optional argument y allows you to specify a language for consideration in the function
NLSSORT(x[,y])	Returns the string of bytes used to sort x based on the language specified by y. Useful for comparing strings in different languages
NLS_UPPER (x,[y])	Same as UPPER (see below), except optional argument y allows you to specify a language for consideration in the function
REPLACE(x,y[,z])	Returns x with all occurrences of y replaced by z. If z is omitted, all occurrences at y are simply removed
RPAD(x,y,z)	Returns x right-padded with spaces to length y. Use the optional argument z to specify a padding string
RTRIM(x[,y])	Trims characters from the right of string x and returns the resulting string. Use y to specify a set of characters to be trimmed. Default y is a blank space to remove right blank padding from strings
SOUNDEX(x)	Returns the phonetic representation of x (a four-character representation of how the first part of x sounds)
SUBSTR(x,y[,z])	Returns the portion of x beginning with the character y. If you specify z, returns the portion that is z characters long. If y is negative, Oracle7 counts backwards from the end of x
SUBSTRB(x,y[,z])	Same as SUBSTR, except that arguments y and z are expressed in bytes rather than characters. Useful only when using multi-byte character strings
TRANSLATE(x,y,z)	Translates the values of x as seen in set y to the corresponding values in set z and returns the result
UPPER(x)	Returns x with all letters in uppercase

TABLE A.5: Oracle7 Date SQL Functions

SQL Function	Description
ADD_MONTHS(x,y)	Returns the date of x plus y months
LAST_DAY(x)	Returns the last day in the month specified by the date x
MONTHS_BETWEEN(x,y)	Returns the number of months between the dates x and y
NEW_TIME(x,y,z)	Returns the corresponding time in time zone z of the time of x in time zone y
NEXT_DAY(x,y)	Returns the date of the first day of the week named y after the date x
ROUND(x[,y])	Returns x rounded to the nearest day to the format model specified by y (for example, month or year)
SYSDATE	Returns the current date and time
TRUNC(x[,y])	Returns x with the time portion of the day truncated to the specification of the format model y

TABLE A.6: Oracle7 Conversion SQL Functions

SQL Function	Description
CHARTOROWID(x)	Converts a character string x to an Oracle7 ROWID
CONVERT(x,y[,z])	Converts the character string x using the character set y. Use the optional argument z to specify the source character set
HEXTORAW(x)	Converts the character string of hex digits x to raw (binary) data
RAWTOHEX(x)	Converts raw data x to a hexadecimal character string
ROWIDTOCHAR(x)	Converts the Oracle7 ROWID value x to a hexadecimal character string
TO_CHAR(x,[y])	Converts a date or number to a character string. When x is a date, y is a format model; when x is a number, y is a format model for varying character strings
TO_DATE(x[,y])	Converts the character string x to a date using the format model y
TO_LABEL(x[,y])	Converts a character string to a value for the MLSLABEL datatype using the format model y. Useful only with Trusted Oracle7
TO_MULTI_BYTE(x)	Converts the character string x with single-byte characters to multi-byte characters
TO_NUMBER(x[,y])	Converts the character string x to a number using the format model y
TO_SINGLE_BYTE(x)	Converts the character string x with multi-byte characters to single-byte characters

TABLE A.7: Oracle7 Miscellaneous SQL Functions

SQL Function	Description
DUMP(w[,x[,y[,z]]])	Returns a character string containing the datatype code, length in bytes, and internal representation of w. Specify the optional argument x to indicate the return value notation (8=octal, 10=decimal, 16=hexadecimal, and 17=single characters). The optional argument y indicates the start position in w and the optional argument z indicates the length of w starting at y to dump
GREATEST(x[,y][, ...])	Returns the greatest of x, y,... values. Type comparisons are based on the datatype of the first value or expression x
GREATEST_LB(x[,y][, ...])	Returns the greatest lower bound of the list of labels x, y,.... Useful only with Trusted Oracle7
LEAST(x[,y][, ...])	Returns the least of x, y,... values. Comparisons are based on the first value or expression x
LEAST_UB(x[y],[, ...])	Returns the least upper bound of the list of labels x, y,.... Useful only with Trusted Oracle7
NVL(x,y)	Returns y if x is NULL; otherwise, returns x. Useful for representing NULLs in queries
UID	Returns the integer that uniquely identifies the current user
USER	Returns the database username of the current user
USERENV(x)	Returns environment information about the current database session. For example, when x is LANGUAGE, Oracle returns the language in use by the session. Possible values for x include ENTRYID, LABEL, LANGUAGE, SESSIONID, and TERMINAL
VSIZE(x)	Returns the number of bytes in the internal representation of x

TABLE A.8: Oracle7 Group SQL Functions

SQL Function	Description
AVG([DISTINCT|ALL] x)	Returns the average expression value for x. When you specify DISTINCT, Oracle considers only distinct column values in x; when you specify ALL, Oracle considers all column values in x. ALL is the default
COUNT(* | [DISTINCT|ALL] x)	Returns the number of rows returned by the query. If you specify *, the count includes all duplicate and NULL values found. If you specify the column argument x rather than *, the count is the number of rows where column x is NOT NULL. The optional DISTINCT and ALL work as with AVG
GLB([DISTINCT|ALL] x)	Returns the greatest lower bound of label x. DISTINCT and ALL work as with AVG
LUB([DISTINCT|ALL] x)	Returns the least upper bound of x. DISTINCT and ALL work as with AVG
MAX([DISTINCT|ALL] x)	Returns the maximum column value for column x. DISTINCT and ALL work as with AVG
MIN([DISTINCT|ALL] x)	Returns the minimum column value for column x. DISTINCT and ALL work as with AVG
STDDEV([DISTINCT|ALL] x)	Returns the standard deviation of the number column x. DISTINCT and ALL work as with AVG
SUM([DISTINCT|ALL] x)	Returns the sum of the number column x. DISTINCT and ALL work as with AVG
VARIANCE([DISTINCT|ALL] x)	Returns the variance of the number column x. DISTINCT and ALL work as with AVG

The SQL*DBA Menus

Figure A.1 provides a quick reference to the SQL*DBA menus. The figure shows each option of the main menu bar, as well as the menu that appears for each main menu option.

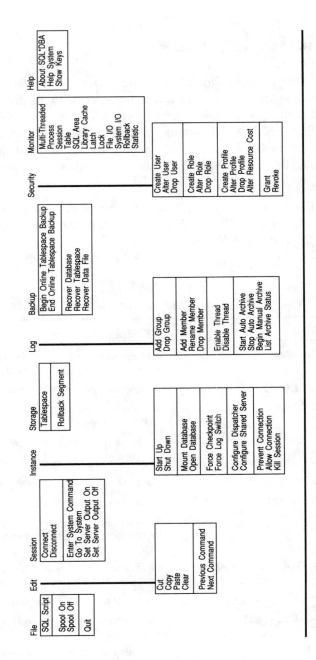

FIGURE A.1:

SQL*DBA menus

Oracle7 Data Dictionary Views

Table A.9 lists the prefixed Oracle7 data dictionary views. Views prefixed with ALL_ are available to all users and show things specific to the privilege domain of the user issuing the query. Views prefixed with DBA_ are available only to users with the SELECT ANY TABLE system privilege and show everything in the database. Views with the USER_ prefix are available to all users and show things specific to the user issuing the query. Words in parentheses are synonyms for the preceding view.

For example, the following entry for Table A.9 means that there are ALL_CATALOG, DBA_CATALOG, and USER_CATALOG dictionary views, along with the CAT synonym for the USER_CATALOG view:

```
CATALOG (ALL_, DBA_, USER_ (CAT))
```

TABLE A.9: Oracle7 Prefixed Data Dictionary Views

View Name	Description
2PC_NEIGHBORS (DBA_)	Information about incoming and outgoing connections for pending distributed transactions
2PC_PENDING (DBA_)	Information about pending distributed transactions
AUDIT_EXISTS (DBA_)	Audit trail entries made on behalf of the AUDIT EXISTS command
AUDIT_OBJECT (DBA_, USER_)	Audit trail entries for audited database objects
AUDIT_SESSION (DBA_, USER_)	Audit trail entries concerning database sessions
AUDIT_STATEMENT (DBA_, USER_)	Audit trail entries for audited statements
AUDIT_TRAIL (DBA_, USER_)	Collection of all audit trail entries
BLOCKERS (DBA_)	Sessions whose locks are blocking other transactions from performing work. See related view DBA_WAITERS
CATALOG (ALL_, DBA_, USER_ (CAT))	Information about database tables, views, synonyms, and sequences
CLU_COLUMNS (DBA_, USER_)	Relation of table columns to cluster keys
CLUSTERS (DBA_, USER_ (CLU))	Information about indexed and hash clusters in the database
COL_COMMENTS (ALL_, DBA_, USER_)	Comments for table and view columns

TABLE A.9: Oracle7 Prefixed Data Dictionary Views (continued)

View Name	Description
COL_PRIVS, (ALL_, DBA_, USER_)	Information about grants on specific columns
COL_PRIVS_MADE (ALL_, USER_)	Information about grants made on specific columns
COL_PRIVS_RECD (ALL_, USER_)	Information about grants received on specific columns
CONS_COLUMNS (ALL_, DBA_, USER_)	Information about columns involved in integrity constraints
CONSTRAINTS (ALL_, DBA_, USER_)	Information about integrity constraints in the database
DATA_FILES (DBA_)	Information about the database's data files
DB_LINKS (ALL_, DBA_, USER_)	Information about database links in the database
DDL_LOCKS (DBA_)	Information about locks taken on behalf of DDL operations
DEF_AUDIT_OPTS (ALL_)	Information about default object auditing options
DEPENDENCIES (ALL_, DBA_, USER_)	Information about object dependencies in the database
DML_LOCKS (DBA_)	Information about DML locks in the server
ERRORS (ALL_, DBA_, USER_)	Information about compile errors detected for procedures, functions, package specifications, and package bodies in the database
EXP_FILES (DBA_)	Description of export files
EXP_OBJECTS (DBA_)	Information about objects that have been incrementally exported with the Export utility
EXP_VERSION (DBA_)	Version number of the last Export utility session
EXTENTS (DBA_, USER_)	Information about the extents for objects in the database
FREE_SPACE (DBA_, USER_)	Information about the free extents in the tablespaces of a database
IND_COLUMNS (ALL_, DBA_, USER_)	Information about the columns that correspond to table indexes
INDEXES (ALL_, DBA_, USER_ (IND))	Information about indexes in the database
LABELS (ALL_)	Information about system labels. Useful only with Trusted Oracle7
LOCKS (DBA_)	Information about all DDL and DML locks in the database server

TABLE A.9: Oracle7 Prefixed Data Dictionary Views (continued)

View Name	Description
MOUNTED_DBS (ALL_)	Information about all mounted databases. Useful only with Trusted Oracle7
OBJ_AUDIT_OPTS (DBA_, USER_)	Information about auditing options set for database objects
OBJECT_SIZE (DBA_, USER_)	Size information for all procedures, functions, package specifications, and package bodies in the database
OBJECTS (ALL_, DBA_, USER_ (OBJ))	Information about database objects in the database
PRIV_AUDIT_OPTS (DBA_)	Information about auditing options set for privileges
PROFILES (DBA_)	Information about resource limit profiles in a database
RESOURCE_LIMITS (USER_)	Information about resource limits for the current user session
ROLE_PRIVS (DBA_, USER_)	Information about roles granted to a user
ROLES (DBA_)	Information about roles in the database
ROLLBACK_SEGS (DBA_)	Information about rollback segments in the database
SEGMENTS (DBA_, USER_)	Information about segments in the database
SEQUENCES (ALL_, DBA_, USER_ (SEQ))	Information about sequences in the database
SNAPSHOT_LOGS (DBA_, USER_)	Information about snapshot logs in the database
SNAPSHOTS (ALL_, DBA_, USER_)	Information about snapshots in the database
SOURCE (ALL_, DBA_, USER_)	Source code of procedures, functions, package specifications, and package bodies in the database
STMT_AUDIT_OPTS (DBA_)	Information about auditing options set for statements
SYNONYMS (ALL_, DBA_, USER_ (SYN))	Information about synonyms in the database
SYS_PRIVS (DBA_, USER_)	System privileges granted to a user
TAB_COLUMNS (ALL_, DBA_, USER_ (COLS))	Information about the columns of tables and views in the database
TAB_COMMENTS (ALL_, DBA_, USER_)	Comments for tables and views in the database
TAB_PRIVS (ALL_, DBA_, USER_)	Information about object privilege grants

TABLE A.9: Oracle7 Prefixed Data Dictionary Views (continued)

View Name	Description
TAB_PRIVS_MADE (ALL_, USER_)	Information about object privileges that were granted
TAB_PRIVS_RECD (ALL_, USER_)	Information about object privileges that were received
TABLES (ALL_, DBA_, USER_ (TABS))	Information about tables in the database
TABLESPACES (DBA_, USER_)	Information about tablespaces in the database
TRIGGER_COLS (ALL_, DBA_, USER_)	Information about the columns that database triggers use
TRIGGERS (ALL_, DBA_, USER_)	Information about triggers in the database
TS_QUOTAS (DBA_, USER_)	Information about user tablespace quotas
USERS (ALL_, DBA_, USER_)	Information about users in the database
VIEWS (ALL_, DBA_, USER_)	Information about views in the database
WAITERS (DBA_)	Information about sessions waiting on a lock held by another session

Table A.10 provides a list of miscellaneous Oracle7 data dictionary views, and Table A.11 gives you the virtual Oracle7 data dictionary views.

TABLE A.10: Oracle7 Miscellaneous Data Dictionary Views

View Name	Description
AUDIT_ACTIONS	Mapping of audit trail action numbers to descriptions
CHAINED_ROWS	Output information about chained rows from the ANALYZE command. Created by the UTLCHAIN.SQL administrative script
COLUMN_PRIVILEGES	Information about column grants
DBMS_ALERT_INFO	Information about registered alerts created by the DBMS_ALERT utility package
DBMS_LOCK_ALLOCATED	Information about user-defined locks created by the DBMS_LOCK utility package
DEPTREE	Information about object dependencies. Created by the UTLDTREE.SQL administrative script

TABLE A.10: Oracle7 Miscellaneous Data Dictionary Views (continued)

View Name	Description
DICT_COLUMNS	Information about data dictionary columns
DICTIONARY (DICT)	Information about data dictionary tables and views
EXCEPTIONS	Output information for integrity constraint exceptions. Created by the UTLEXCPT.SQL administrative script
GLOBAL_NAME	Information about the global name of the database
IDEPTREE	Information about object dependencies. Created by the UTLDTREE.SQL administrative script
INDEX_HISTOGRAM	Statistical information about indexes generated from the ANALYZE INDEX…VALIDATE INDEX command
INDEX_STATS	Statistical information about indexes generated from the ANALYZE INDEX…VALIDATE INDEX command
LOADER_COL_INFO	Information for SQL*Loader regarding columns
LOADER_CONSTRAINT_INFO	Information for SQL*Loader regarding integrity constraints
LOADER_INDCOL_INFO	Information for SQL*Loader regarding indexed columns
LOADER_IND_INFO	Information for SQL*Loader regarding indexes
LOADER_PARAM_INFO	Information for SQL*Loader regarding parameters
LOADER_TAB_INFO	Information for SQL*Loader regarding tables
LOADER_TRIGGER_INFO	Information for SQL*Loader regarding triggers
NLS_DATABASE_PARAMETERS	Information about database NLS settings. Useful only if the server uses National Language Support (NLS)
NLS_INSTANCE_PARAMETERS	Information about database server NLS settings. Useful only if the server uses National Language Support (NLS)
NLS_SESSION_PARAMETERS	Information about session NLS settings. Useful only if the server uses National Language Support (NLS)
PLAN_TABLE	Output information about optimizer execution plans from the EXPLAIN PLAN command. Created by the UTLXPLAN.SQL administrative script
PUBLIC_DEPENDENCY	Information about object dependencies
RESOURCE_COST	Information about the costs of system resources
ROLE_ROLE_PRIVS	Information about roles granted to other roles
ROLE_SYS_PRIVS	Information about system privileges granted to roles
ROLE_TAB_PRIVS	Information about object privileges granted to roles

TABLE A.10: Oracle7 Miscellaneous Data Dictionary Views (continued)

View Name	Description
SESSION_PRIVS	Information about privileges available to a session
SESSION_ROLES	Information about roles available to a session
STMT_AUDIT_OPTION_MAP	Mapping of audit trail action numbers to descriptions
SYSTEM_PRIVILEGE_MAP	Mapping of system privilege numbers to descriptions
TABLE_PRIVILEGES	Information about object privilege grants
TABLE_PRIVILEGE_MAP	Mapping of object privilege numbers to descriptions

TABLE A.11: Oracle7 Virtual Data Dictionary Views

View Name	Description
V$ACCESS	Information about objects currently in use
V$ARCHIVE	Information about the archived transaction log of the database
V$BACKUP	Information about the backup status of all online tablespaces in the database
V$BGPROCESS	Information about all background server processes of the database server
V$CIRCUIT	Information about all circuits (user connections) in a multithreaded server configuration
V$DATABASE	Information about a database from the database's control file
V$DATAFILE	Information about the database's data files
V$DBFILE	Information about the database's data files
V$DB_OBJECT_CACHE	Information about objects in the database server's object cache, including tables, views, indexes, and procedures
V$DISPATCHER	Information about dispatcher background server processes currently up in a multithreaded database server
V$ENABLEDPRIVS	Information about enabled privileges
V$FILESTAT	Statistical I/O information about database files
V$FIXED_TABLE	Information about all fixed tables in the database
V$INSTANCE	Information about the current state of the database server (instance)

TABLE A.11: Oracle7 Virtual Data Dictionary Views (continued)

View Name	Description
V$LATCH	Information about the internal locks (latches) in the database server
V$LATCHHOLDER	Information about sessions that currently hold internal locks (latches)
V$LATCHNAME	Information about internal locks (latches) in the database server
V$LIBRARYCACHE	Statistical information about library cache management
V$LICENSE	Information about Oracle software license limits
V$LOADCSTAT	Information about SQL*Loader statistics compiled during a direct path load
V$LOADTSTAT	Information about SQL*Loader statistics compiled during a direct path load
V$LOCK	Information about DML locks in the database server
V$LOG	Information about a database's transaction log
V$LOGFILE	Information about a database's transaction log files
V$LOGHIST	Information about a database's transaction log sequence history
V$LOG_HISTORY	Information about a database's transaction log
V$MTS	Tuning information for the multithreaded server configuration
V$NLS_PARAMETERS	Information about current National Language Support parameter values
V$OPEN_CURSOR	Information about each database session's open cursors
V$PARAMETER	Information about each database server initialization parameter
V$PROCESS	Information about currently active processes
V$QUEUE	Information about the multithreaded server queues
V$RECOVERY_LOG	Information about the archived transaction log groups needed to perform database recovery
V$RECOVER_FILE	Status information about data files needing recovery
V$REQDIST	Statistical information about request times
V$RESOURCE	Information about system resources
V$ROLLNAME	Information about all online rollback segments
V$ROLLSTAT	Statistical information about all online rollback segments
V$ROWCACHE	Statistical information about data dictionary activity
V$SECONDARY	Information about secondary mounted databases. Useful only with Trusted Oracle7

TABLE A.11: Oracle7 Virtual Data Dictionary Views (continued)

View Name	Description
V$SESSION	Information about database sessions
V$SESSION_EVENTS	Wait statistic information for each session and each event
V$SESSION_WAIT	Information about resources that sessions are waiting for
V$SESSTAT	Statistics information about database sessions
V$SESS_IO	Information about each session's I/O usage
V$SGA	Information about the database server's SGA memory area
V$SGASTAT	Statistical information about the database server's SGA memory area
V$SHARED_SERVER	Information about shared foreground servers of a multithreaded database server
V$SQLAREA	Information about shared cursors
V$SQLTEXT	Information about statements corresponding to shared cursors
V$STATNAME	Descriptions for session statistic codes shown in V$SESSTAT
V$SYSLABEL	Information about system labels. Useful only with Trusted Oracle7
V$SYSSTAT	Information about system-wide statistics for each statistic in V$SESSTAT
V$SYSTEM_EVENTS	System information of all per-session event statistics
V$THREAD	Information about threads of the database's transaction log
V$TIMER	The current system time in hundredths of a second
V$TRANSACTION	Information about current database transactions
V$TYPE_SIZE	Information about low-level data components to aid in the prediction of space usage estimates
V$VERSION	Information about versions of core software libraries of the Oracle7 server
V$WAITSTAT	Statistical information about data block contention among transactions

Oracle7 Datatypes

Table A.12 lists the Oracle7 datatypes. The equivalent ANSI and/or IBM DB2 or SQL/DS datatypes you can use are shown in parentheses.

TABLE A.12: Oracle7 Datatypes

Datatype	Description
CHAR(size) (CHARACTER, CHAR)	Stores fixed-length character strings
DATE (DATE)	Stores time-related information, including dates and times
LONG (LONG VARCHAR)	Stores large, variable-length character strings, up to 2 gigabytes
NUMBER(precision, scale) (FLOAT, NUMERIC, DECIMAL, DEC, INTEGER, INT, SMALLINT, REAL, DOUBLE PRECISION)	Stores numbers of all types, including integer, floating point, and so on
LONG RAW	Stores long binary strings, up to 2 gigabytes
MLSLABEL	Stores the binary format of an operating system label. Useful only with Trusted Oracle7
RAW(size)	Stores small binary strings, less than 2000 bytes
ROWID	Stores hexadecimal ROWID values that correspond to Oracle table ROWIDs. Note that columns declared with the ROWID datatype should not be confused with the pseudo-column of a table, ROWID, which stores the ROWIDs for all rows in a table
VARCHAR2(size) (VARCHAR, CHARACTER VARYING)	Stores variable-length character strings

Oracle7 System Privileges

Table A.13 lists the Oracle7 system privileges. Prefixed system privileges have the available prefixes in parentheses. For example, the following system privilege table entry:

```
CLUSTER (CREATE, CREATE ANY, ALTER ANY, DROP ANY)
```

translates to these system privileges:

```
CREATE CLUSTER
CREATE ANY CLUSTER
ALTER ANY CLUSTER
DROP ANY CLUSTER
```

TABLE A.13: Oracle7 System Privileges

System Privilege	Description
ANALYZE ANY	Analyzes any table, index, or cluster in the database using the ANALYZE command
AUDIT ANY	Sets audit options for any database object
AUDIT SYSTEM	Permits auditing of system operations
CLUSTER (CREATE, CREATE ANY, ALTER ANY, DROP ANY)	Creates, alters, and drops clusters
DATABASE (ALTER)	Modifies the database using the ALTER DATABASE command
DATABASE LINK (CREATE, CREATE PUBLIC, DROP PUBLIC)	Creates and drops database links
INDEX (CREATE ANY, ALTER ANY, DROP ANY)	Creates, alters, and drops indexes
PRIVILEGE (GRANT ANY)	Grants any system privilege
PROCEDURE (CREATE, CREATE ANY, ALTER ANY, DROP ANY, EXECUTE ANY)	Creates, recompiles, drops, and executes procedures
PROFILE (CREATE, ALTER, DROP)	Creates, alters, and drops resource limit profiles
RESOURCE COST (ALTER)	Sets costs for session resources
ROLE (CREATE, ALTER ANY, DROP ANY, GRANT ANY)	Creates, alters, drops, and grants roles
ROLLBACK SEGMENT (CREATE, ALTER, DROP)	Creates, alters, and drops rollback segments
SESSION (CREATE, ALTER, RESTRICTED)	Creates and alters database sessions. RESTRICTED corresponds to creating restricted database sessions
SEQUENCE (CREATE, CREATE ANY, ALTER ANY, DROP ANY, SELECT ANY)	Creates, alters, drops, and uses sequences
SNAPSHOT (CREATE, CREATE ANY, ALTER ANY, DROP ANY)	Creates, alters, and drops snapshots
SYNONYM (CREATE, CREATE ANY, CREATE PUBLIC, DROP ANY, DROP PUBLIC)	Creates and drops synonyms
SYSTEM (ALTER)	Alters the database server settings using the ALTER SYSTEM command

TABLE A.13: Oracle7 System Privileges (continued)

System Privilege	Description
TABLE (CREATE, CREATE ANY, ALTER ANY, BACKUP ANY, DROP ANY, LOCK ANY, COMMENT ANY, SELECT ANY, INSERT ANY, UPDATE ANY, DELETE ANY)	Creates, alters, backs up, drops, locks, comments, or manipulates tables
TABLESPACE (CREATE, ALTER, MAN-AGE, DROP, UNLIMITED)	Creates, alters (extends), manages (backup, availability), drops, or uses space in tablespaces
TRANSACTION (FORCE, FORCE ANY)	Manages the outcome of pending distributed transactions
TRIGGER (CREATE, CREATE ANY, ALTER ANY, DROP ANY)	Creates, alters, or drops triggers
USER (CREATE, BECOME, ALTER, DROP)	Creates, alters, or drops users. BECOME is required for performing full database exports using the Export utility
VIEW (CREATE, CREATE ANY, DROP ANY)	Creates or drops views

Object Privileges

Table A.14 provides a quick reference to the Oracle7 object privileges.

TABLE A.14: Oracle7 Database Object Privileges

Object	Privileges Available
Tables	SELECT, INSERT, UPDATE, DELETE, ALTER, INDEX, REFERENCES
Views and Snapshots	SELECT, INSERT, UPDATE, DELETE
Sequences	SELECT, ALTER
Procedures, functions, and packages	EXECUTE

APPENDIX

B

Configuring and Using the Oracle7 Parallel Query Option for Parallel Processing

Release 7.1 of the Oracle7 database server includes the Parallel Query option, which can dramatically enhance the performance of Oracle7 database systems that use multiprocessor computers. The Parallel Query option permits Oracle7 to take full advantage of the combined power in a multiprocessor computer to speed up complicated, time-consuming database operations. In this appendix you will learn about parallel query processing and the Oracle7 Parallel Query option.

What Is Parallel Processing?

Whether or not you realize it, parallel processing is all around us. For example, you've probably never considered how a publisher might produce a book like this one. Let's examine the steps in this type of job to learn what parallel processing is. One way to produce a book would be as follows:

1. The author writes the entire manuscript and then sends it to the publisher. Meanwhile, the editors sit idle waiting for the author to finish the book manuscript.

2. The editors review the entire manuscript, make comments, and then send it back to the author for final review. Meanwhile, the author sits idle waiting for the editors to finish editing the manuscript.

3. The author incorporates the changes suggested by the editors and then sends the entire edited manuscript back to them. Meanwhile, the editors sit idle waiting for the author to finish reviewing the edits.

4. The editors finalize the manuscript from the edits and produce the book.

In this situation only one activity (writing, editing, and so on) is occurring at any one time. Additionally, valuable resources often sit idle instead of doing productive work. Consequently, the time to complete the overall process is the sum of the times necessary to complete each subtask. This situation is an example of *serial processing*—only one task in the book production process is carried out at a time.

Now let's study parallel processing. *Parallel processing* is just what it sounds like—multiple processes work in parallel (at the same time) to finish a job more quickly than it would otherwise take. For example, consider how parallel processing can speed up the job of producing a book. After writing a chapter, the author immediately sends it to the publisher. Then the author can continue writing subsequent chapters. Meanwhile, the publisher's editors can be busy editing finished chapters. Consequently, the parallel processing situation utilizes all resources at the same time to produce the book much more quickly.

The objective of parallel computer processing is literally the same as that of the book production process: to split up one large, complex job into many smaller jobs and then have multiple workers complete each smaller job in parallel to complete the entire operation quickly. In the case of parallel database query processing, the "workers" are multiple computer processors, and the "complicated operations" are relational database server operations, such as relational queries and index builds.

First, let's take a look at a fundamental issue for parallel processing—multiprocessor computers and how they work.

The Foundation of Parallel Processing—Multiprocessor Computers

An implicit requirement for parallel processing is a *multiprocessor computer*. Computers that have multiple processors come in several varieties. Figure B.1 shows some different types.

Perhaps the most common type of multiprocessor computer is the *symmetric multiprocessor (SMP)* computer. An SMP computer usually has between 2 and 16 processors, all of which share the computer's single memory source and storage devices. Because of their design regarding memory usage, SMPs are commonly referred to as *tightly coupled multiprocessor systems*.

Another type of multiprocessor computer shown in Figure B.1 is a *clustered multiprocessor system*. In clustered systems, each processor has its own, private memory area, but all processors can share the same storage devices. Because of their design regarding memory usage, clustered systems are commonly referred to as *loosely coupled multiprocessor systems*.

An extension of the loosely coupled architecture is the *massively parallel processing system*, or *MPP*. An MPP is characterized by many loosely coupled processors—perhaps 50 or even hundreds of processors—all of which can share the same storage devices or work with their own private storage devices.

FIGURE B.1:

Multiprocessor computer
architectures

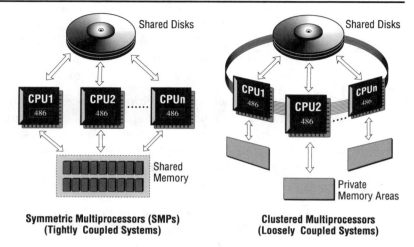

Symmetric Multiprocessors (SMPs)
(Tightly Coupled Systems)

Clustered Multiprocessors
(Loosely Coupled Systems)

Massively Parallel
Processing Systems (MPPs)

NOTE   Hybrid multiprocessor architectures are also common—that is, systems
that have loosely coupled clusters of tightly coupled systems.

Choosing a Multiprocessor Computer for an Oracle7 Database System

Now that you know a little about the different types of multiprocessor systems, you are probably asking yourself about the advantages and disadvantages among the different varieties when considering the design of a database management system like Oracle7. First, let's take a look at SMPs.

SMPs of up to 16 processors are a popular choice for database management systems for several reasons. First of all, SMPs are very cost effective, considering the price-to-performance gains they can deliver. This, coupled with the fact that SMPs are the most mature multiprocessor architecture and have lots of available software, makes SMP machines a good choice for many application environments. However, because of their tightly coupled processor/memory design, SMPs tend to top out on performance as a result of disk I/O or memory contention problems after reaching a certain number of processors.

If a database system tops out on performance of an SMP, the next move up is usually to an MPP system. Because MPPs have a loosely coupled processor architecture and, perhaps, a non-shared disk design, they do not suffer from the performance limitations inherent in SMPs. If the database software can take advantage of the many processors in an MPP computer, you can use literally thousands of processors to complete complicated database operations at lightning-fast speeds. Naturally, because MPPs have more processing power than smaller SMPs, their cost is greater—but you get what you pay for. The only real disadvantage of MPPs is that they are a relatively new and complicated hardware model for which to develop software, which means that there is limited software available that takes advantage of their tremendous processing power. For example, MPPs have traditionally been used for scientific applications that are extremely computing intensive. However, as more and more software companies learn how to take advantage of the power of MPPs, they will no doubt become more popular in all types of computing environments, including database processing systems.

Understanding Linear Performance—Speedup and Scaleup

One of your most important goals when using any type of multiprocessor computer should be to notice *linear scaling* or *speedup* as you add more and more processors to attack a single computing task. Linear speedup occurs when a doubling of resources (in this case, processors) halves response time. Linear speedup is important—if response time does not decrease by a factor of 1 each time you add a new processor to the operation, you are not getting your money's worth of work from each processor on the system. Figure B.2 shows some graphs that represent linear and nonlinear speedup for multiprocessor systems.

To make multiprocessor computing systems deliver linear speedup, special versions of computer operating systems are available. For example, many UNIX vendors offer multiprocessor versions of the UNIX operating system to explicitly take advantage of SMP, clustered, and MPP systems. Microsoft Windows NT is another operating system that supports multiprocessor systems.

FIGURE B.2:
Linear speedup occurs when the multiprocessor computer reduces an operation's response time by a factor of 1 for every processor you use to handle the operation.

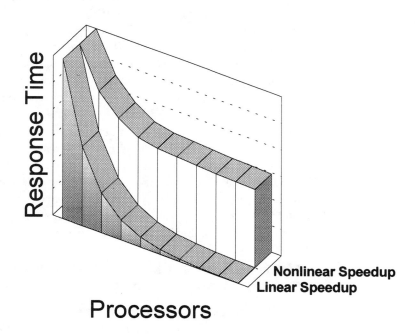

Linear and Nonlinear Parallel Processing

Response Time

Nonlinear Speedup
Linear Speedup

Processors

Much like an operating system, relational database management software must have special features to take advantage of multiprocessor computers and deliver linear speedup. In fact, that's what the remainder of this appendix focuses on—the features of the Oracle7 Parallel Query option that allow you to tap into the power of all types of multiprocessor computers.

Parallelizing Database Operations for Maximum Performance

To review, the objective of parallel processing is to take a single and perhaps complicated database operation, intelligently break it down into logical subtasks, and then feed the subtasks to multiple computer processors that can work in parallel to reduce the overall time necessary to complete the database operation. Without parallel processing features, a database server executing on a multiprocessor computer is really not much better than a database server using a single processor computer. The illustration in Figure B.3 contrasts parallel and nonparallel database query processing models using a multiprocessor computer.

FIGURE B.3:
Without parallel query processing, a single processor of a multiprocessor computer completes all parts of a query while other processors sit idle. Parallel query processing takes advantage of all available processors to speed up response time.

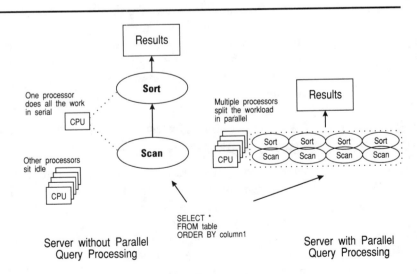

Figure B.3 compares how a full table scan and sort are performed by serial and parallel processing models. Notice that with serial processing, the time it takes to complete one large operation is the sum of the times necessary to complete each subtask (scan, sort) in the larger operation. A parallel processing database server identifies each relational operator (scan, sort), breaks down each operator into subtasks, and then assigns the subtasks to individual processes for processing. In Figure B.3 scans and sorts can happen simultaneously to decrease the overall time necessary to complete the SQL query.

Relational database management systems such as Oracle7 are perfect candidates for parallel processing. That's because they already hide the complexities of data access from the developer. Developers can design client database applications without ever considering what type of computer will be used to run the application or the database server. Also, existing applications automatically benefit from parallel processing enhancements added to the server. For example, a SELECT statement issued to a database server has the same syntax whether the server uses a single processor or multiprocessor computer. If the database server happens to use a multiprocessor computer, the internal mechanisms of the server automatically take advantage of parallel processing capabilities to deliver maximum performance for all applications.

As you might guess, parallel database processing makes its biggest impact on demanding database operations rather than simple ones. For example, decision-support applications that regularly issue complicated join queries or queries that access a lot of data will see greater performance improvements from parallel processing than will online transaction-processing applications that issue simple INSERT statements.

Capabilities of the Oracle7 Parallel Query Option

Oracle7 with the Parallel Query option automatically parallelizes almost every type of relational database operation, including all types of SQL operations, such as joins, scans, sorts, aggregates, groupings, and any mix of these. Users and developers don't have to ever consider the complexities of parallel processing because Oracle7 transparently parallelizes these operations for all SELECT statements, as well as for subqueries in INSERT, UPDATE, DELETE, and CREATE TABLE statements. Oracle7 also uses parallel processing to build indexes much more quickly.

This is particularly useful when a database has particularly large tables and the corresponding indexes take a very long time to create.

The Oracle7 Parallel Query Process Architecture

To parallelize database operations, Oracle7 with the Parallel Query option uses a special operating system process architecture, as shown in Figure B.4.

FIGURE B.4:

Process architecture of Oracle7 with the Parallel Query option

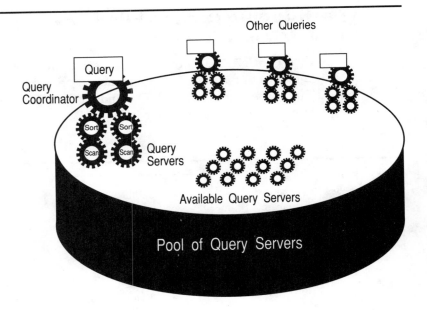

Notice that the Oracle7 parallel query process architecture contains some special processes—a query coordinator and query servers. A *query coordinator* is similar to a typical shared foreground server process of a nonparallel Oracle7 system—it is the process that receives a database request from the dispatcher. However, a query coordinator is a foreground server process that has special capabilities, making it the focal point of a parallelized operation. A query coordinator's job is to read a query (or any other type of statement), intelligently break it down into smaller requests that will execute efficiently, coordinate sending out the requests to available query servers, and merging request results.

A *query server* simply performs the request that a query coordinator asks of it. As Figure B.4 shows, Oracle7 keeps a pool of shared query servers available for use by any query coordinator that needs work done. As parallel processing loads fluctuate in the database system, Oracle7 automatically tunes its parallel processing architecture by starting and stopping more query servers as necessary to vary the size of the query server pool according to current demands. Therefore, the database administrator does not have to constantly monitor the parallel processing architecture to make sure things are running smoothly.

Partitioning Data to Eliminate Disk I/O Bottlenecks

The Oracle7 Parallel Query option solves the problem of processing database operations in parallel. However, another critical bottleneck that can limit performance speedup is disk I/O bandwidths. For example, consider the parallel processing examples shown in Figure B.5.

FIGURE B.5:
No matter how well a database server can parallelize database operations, data that is not partitioned can be a significant bottleneck in performance speedup.

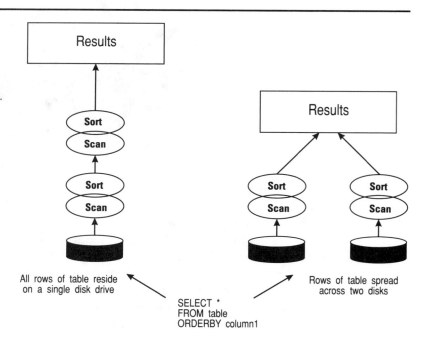

Figure B.5 shows what happens when an Oracle7 server with the Parallel Query option executes the same SQL query (a full table scan with a sort) using nonpartitioned and partitioned table data. In both cases, Oracle7 parallelizes the query into two degrees of parallelism (it breaks the scan and sort operators into two scans and two sorts). However, when all the table's data resides on a single disk, the disk head can serve the request of only one scan operation at any given time. Consequently, even though the server did a great job of parallelizing the query, the single disk forces the server to execute the two scan operations serially, thus limiting the response time for the query. Alternatively, when the table data is partitioned on two disks, two scan operations can happen in parallel, and the response time for the query is much better.

The second part of Figure B.5 shows a system with database partitioning. *Database partitioning* means that the data in a single database is physically spread out across multiple disk drives to reduce the limiting effects of disk I/O bandwidths. In the example, because the table to scan is spread out across different disk drives, the database server can complete two table scans in parallel to reduce the overall time needed to scan the table, taking perhaps half the time it would to perform them with a nonpartitioned database.

Several database partitioning strategies are possible. Chapter 12 discusses one strategy you should be using to some degree—schema partitioning, or the separation of different objects within a single application schema across different disks—and mentions one form of schema partitioning—storing a table's indexes on a different disk drive from the drive that stores the table, thus permitting Oracle7 to read index data and table data in parallel.

> **TIP**
>
> Schema partitioning provides no advantage for Oracle7 with the Parallel Query option. Instead, focus on the other types of partitioning mentioned in this section.

Adequately eliminating disk I/O limitations in parallel processing database systems for almost every type of database operation requires granular partitioning strategies, such as *horizontal table partitioning,* or separating the rows of a single data table across multiple disks. You can partition the rows of a single table using several different strategies. For example, *key partitioning* separates a table's rows into different partitions according to the key value in each row. Another horizontal partitioning strategy is *round-robin partitioning,* where the system randomly scatters the rows of a table in available table partitions.

Each horizontal partitioning strategy has its own calling, depending on application characteristics. For example, if an application frequently processes rows in groups according to key values, then key partitioning is not the appropriate partitioning solution—all the rows in a group are on the same disk. In this case, round-robin partitioning is a better approach because it is more likely to spread rows with similar key values across multiple disk drives. Round-robin partitioning is essential for temporary work areas (used for sorting, joins, and so on) where the characteristics of temporary data might not necessarily be known beforehand. In fact, in most cases round-robin partitioning is the best approach because it can adequately separate the rows that any type of application might request or work with.

An alternative to internal database partitioning that can yield the same results for parallel processing is external operating-system disk striping. Many multiprocessor operating systems support utilities that can perform *disk striping*—randomly distributing the pages of files across many different disks. Since striping is done at the operating-system level, all types of files, including those related to the database, can be spread out on different disks for better performance in a parallel processing environment. Many system administrators prefer to use external disk striping because it allows a multiprocessor to reduce disk I/O bottlenecks associated with database files as well as other types of application files, and because it centralizes administration at the operating-system level.

Now that you have a solid understanding of parallel database processing and data partitioning, the following sections explain how to configure and use the Oracle7 Parallel Query option and set up your data partitioning strategy.

Configuring and Tuning the Parallel Query Option

Configuring the Oracle7 Parallel Query option is not too complicated—the database administrator need only set a few initialization parameters and consider some unique options when creating tables and indexes. Once you accomplish this, you are ready to begin exploiting the full power of a multiprocessor Oracle7 database server. First, let's learn how to configure the size of the query server pool.

Setting Thresholds to Limit the Size of the Query Server Pool

Oracle7 automatically tunes its parallel processing architecture by starting and stopping query servers to vary the size of the query server pool according to current processing demands. Therefore, you never have to spend lots of time monitoring and tuning Oracle7's Parallel Query option. However, you must pay attention to the minimum and maximum number of query servers allowed by Oracle7's dynamic architecture. If you allow too many query servers, the process overhead on the server can become excessive and actually degrade system performance, and if you permit too few query servers, there won't be enough processes to adequately parallelize concurrent user requests.

To set the thresholds for the minimum and maximum number of query servers in the query server pool, you use the two initialization parameters PARALLEL_MIN_SERVERS and PARALLEL_MAX_SERVERS. The following excerpt from an initialization parameter file shows how easy it is to set these parameters:

```
PARALLEL_MIN_SERVERS=10
PARALLEL_MAX_SERVERS=100
```

As with other parameters, configuring the thresholds for the query server pool takes a bit of trial and error at first. When setting the initial thresholds for the query server pool, consider the characteristics of both the hardware and the database system. For example, the maximum number of processes your multiprocessor computer can adequately support might serve as an upper limit for the query server pool. Likewise, the average number of users who concurrently access the database system at any given time might serve as the lower bound for the query server pool.

Once Oracle7 with the Parallel Query option is up and running, it is useful to monitor how Oracle7 varies the pool of query servers according to normal system demands. Throughout a normal day, you might query the Oracle7 data dictionary to get a quick idea of how many query servers are up at any given time. However, just as when tuning the thresholds for shared servers in a multithreaded Oracle7 server, it is useful to record the fluctuation of query servers in a parallel processing environment over a time period. You can do this by creating a table and a stored procedure similar to the ones shown in Chapter 8 (Listing 8.2). You can even create a single stored procedure to gather dispatcher, shared server, and query server information at the same interval for the same amount of time. This way you will have to dedicate only one session to monitoring the multithreaded server and query server pool at the same time.

Once you have gathered fluctuation information for the query server pool, use the information along with the current settings for the initialization parameters PARALLEL_MIN_SERVERS and PARALLEL_MAX_SERVERS to tune the threshold settings. For example, if any of the query counts touch the current thresholds, consider lowering the lower threshold or raising the upper threshold to allow more fluctuation in query server counts. Continue to monitor the fluctuation of the query server pool until you feel you have correctly tuned the system.

Another initialization parameter to consider for query servers is the PARALLEL_SERVER_IDLE_TIME parameter. This parameter determines how long Oracle7 will let a query server sit idle before removing the process from the query server pool. Setting this time interval correctly avoids the processing overhead associated with constantly starting and stopping query servers. The PARALLEL_SERVER_IDLE_TIME parameter is set as a number of minutes. For example, this setting instructs Oracle7 to terminate a query server process only after it has been idle for at least 10 minutes:

```
PARALLEL_SERVER_IDLE_TIME=10
```

Controlling Runaway Parallelism

As the old saying goes, it's possible to have too much of a good thing. The parallelism of database operations is no different. For example, if one statement unnecessarily hoards too many available query servers to parallelize its work, other queries will suffer in performance because they end up having to execute using serial processing.

Parallelism can get out of control, particularly for table scan operations. Theoretically, you could have one scan process for every row requested by a statement. To prevent such situations, Oracle7 includes several mechanisms to control the *degree of parallelism*, or the number of query servers used to process a single statement. The following sections discuss the controls for the degree of parallelism in an Oracle7 database server.

System-Wide Control of Parallelism

As an administrator, you can set a default degree of parallelism for all database tables using the PARALLEL_DEFAULT_SCANSIZE initialization parameter. Oracle7 uses this setting only when table- or statement-level controls for parallelism are not in use (see the next two sections).

To set the system-wide default for parallelism correctly, it's important to understand how Oracle7 calculates the degree of parallelism using the PARALLEL_DEFAULT_SCANSIZE initialization parameter. When a user requests data from a table, Oracle7 calculates the degree of parallelism using this formula:

```
degree of parallelism = # blocks in the table × PARALLEL_DEFAULT_SCANSIZE
```

Consequently, Oracle7 gives greater degrees of parallelism for larger tables. But how do you correctly set PARALLEL_DEFAULT_SCANSIZE? One way might be to determine the average table size in the database and how many disks hold rows for the average table. Set the PARALLEL_DEFAULT_SCANSIZE parameter such that the degree of parallelism equals the average number of disks that contain blocks for the average table.

The PARALLEL_DEFAULT_MAX_SCANS parameter determines the maximum degree of parallelism for any operation in the system. No matter what control you use to determine the degree of parallelism, nothing can exceed the setting for PARALLEL_DEFAULT_MAX_SCANS.

Controlling the Degree of Parallelism on a per-Table Basis

To set the default degree of parallelism for all parallel database operations concerning a specific table, you can create the table with the PARALLEL option. For example, this statement creates the ITEM table, setting the default degree of parallelism for the table to 10:

```
CREATE TABLE item
(... column specifications ...)
PARALLEL 10
```

If you partition a table across multiple disks, an appropriate setting for the PARALLEL option of a CREATE TABLE statement is the number of disks you use to store the table. Be sure not to set PARALLEL higher than the current system-wide maximum degree of parallelism—the setting of the PARALLEL_DEFAULT_MAX_SCANS initialization parameter—since nothing can override this system setting.

Alternatively, if by default you do not want Oracle7 to parallelize operations on a table, you can specify the NOPARALLEL option. This option is appropriate for small lookup tables where parallelism is not likely to improve performance of scan operations.

```
CREATE TABLE stock
( ... column specifications ...)
NOPARALLEL
```

NOTE   If you create a table without specifying a default degree of parallelism, Oracle7 automatically uses the system-wide default degree of parallelism when parallelizing an operation.

Controlling the Degree of Parallelism on a Per-Statement Basis Using Hints

If you are an application developer, you have the power to explicitly control the degree of parallelism for each table referenced in an individual statement using the PARALLEL and NOPARALLEL hints. These hints are the tuning knobs you can use to maximize application performance by making wise use of available database server resources. You can increase parallelism for demanding statements and reduce or eliminate parallelism for less-demanding statements.

```
SELECT --+ PARALLEL(sales.item, 10)
  MAX(SUM(linetotal)), MIN(SUM(linetotal)), AVG(SUM(linetotal))
  FROM sales.item
  GROUP BY orderid

SELECT --+ NOPARALLEL(sales.stock)
  description
  FROM sales.stock
  WHERE id = 5
```

In the first example above, a reasonable degree of parallelism is warranted because the query has to perform a complete table scan of a large table to get the necessary values for the aggregate functions (SUM). The statement also has to perform grouping. Alternatively, it is unlikely that parallelism will increase the response time of the second statement, because the query accesses a small table using an index to find a single row.

> **NOTE**
>
> If you issue a statement and do not use hints to control the degree of parallelism, Oracle7 first uses the degree of parallelism specified for the tables in the statement. If a referenced table does not have a specific degree of parallelism, Oracle7 then uses the system-wide default degree of parallelism.

Controlling the Degree of Parallelism when Building Indexes

Building and rebuilding indexes is a common undertaking for database administrators because an index can get out of balance as a result of frequent DML operations on the corresponding table. To reduce the time it takes to build an index for a large table, Oracle7 with the Parallel Query option automatically builds indexes using parallel processing.

By default, Oracle7 builds each index using the degree of parallelism specified for the corresponding table. If you wish, you can override this setting and indicate a specific degree of parallelism to use when building an index. For example, you can use the PARALLEL option of the CONSTRAINT clause of the CREATE TABLE command or the PARALLEL option of the CREATE INDEX command. The following set of statements rebuilds the index behind the PRIMARY KEY for the ITEM table:

```
-- drop the primary key index by disabling the primary key constraint
ALTER TABLE item
  DISABLE PRIMARY KEY

-- rebuild the primary key index by enabling the primary key, using a degree of
-- parallelism equal to 10
ALTER TABLE item
  ENABLE PRIMARY KEY
    USING INDEX PARALLEL 10
```

The PARALLEL option for an index allows you to explicitly specify the degree of parallelism to use when building the index. In the preceding example, the degree of parallelism for the index build is 10.

Alternatively, the NOPARALLEL option of the CONSTRAINT clause of the CREATE TABLE command or the NOPARALLEL option of the CREATE INDEX command permits you to create an index without any parallel processing at all. Use the NOPARALLEL option to avoid unnecessary parallelism on small tables that might otherwise hurt overall system performance.

Relieving Disk I/O Limitations to Maximize the Performance of Parallel Processing

As mentioned earlier, disk I/O can significantly limit the performance speedup of parallel database processing. The following sections explain ways you can remove disk I/O as a bottleneck and realize the maximum performance speedup possible from parallelizing database operations with the Oracle7 Parallel Query option.

Caching Tables in Memory to Avoid Disk I/O

One way to remove disk access as a performance bottleneck is to avoid disk I/O altogether with data caching. That's just what the data buffer in an Oracle7 database server does for the most frequently requested blocks of database data (see Chapter 12). Building on this capability, the Oracle7 Parallel Query option offers special options of the CREATE TABLE and ALTER TABLE commands that allow you to specifically control the caching of a table's data in memory: the CACHE and NOCACHE options.

```
CREATE TABLE stock
  (... column specifications ...)
  CACHE
  NOPARALLEL
```

```
CREATE TABLE item
   (... column specifications ...)
   NOCACHE
   PARALLEL 10
```

When you specify the CACHE option of the CREATE TABLE or ALTER TABLE command, Oracle7 caches the entire table in the SGA of the Oracle7 database server. Unless you have an incredibly large amount of memory available to the database server, the CACHE option is appropriate only for small lookup tables in an application schema. That's because caching large tables in memory can quickly consume the available shared memory of the database server and hurt overall system performance. With large tables it is more appropriate to use the NOCACHE option of the CREATE TABLE or ALTER TABLE command.

Notice the relationship of the PARALLEL and NOPARALLEL options of the CREATE TABLE and ALTER TABLE commands with the CACHE and NOCACHE options. If you decide to cache an entire table in memory with the CACHE option, the PARALLEL option is not appropriate because all table data is in memory, thereby making it unnecessary to consider the number of physical parallel table scans. Likewise, if you specify NOCACHE, you should take time to appropriately set the PARALLEL option, as described in the preceding section.

TIP

If you use the Oracle7 Parallel Query option as well as the Oracle7 Parallel Server option for loosely coupled multiprocessor systems, you can also use the CACHE PARTITIONS option of the CREATE TABLE or ALTER TABLE command. This option allows you to cache the table in all instances of a parallel server configuration.

Schema Partitioning

Partitioning database data is another way to minimize disk I/O bottlenecks in a parallel database processing system. The easiest way to physically partition data in an Oracle7 database is by schema partitioning. Unfortunately, schema partitioning does not offer any significant benefits for the Oracle7 Parallel Query option. Therefore, we will instead focus on other ways of partitioning data in an Oracle database.

Horizontal Table Partitioning

The Oracle7 Parallel Query option offers no built-in mechanism to make sure Oracle7 horizontally partitions the rows of a single table across multiple disks as users insert new rows into tables. However, if your database is primarily a decision-support database (that is, a static, read-only database), you can be clever and use SQL*Loader to load a single table's rows in different data files throughout the same tablespace. Therefore, if you place the data files of a single tablespace on multiple disks, you can, in effect, use SQL*Loader to partition the rows of a table across multiple disks. Following are the steps necessary to accomplish horizontal table partitioning in a decision-support database:

1. Use the Create Tablespace dialog of SQL*DBA to create a tablespace with multiple data files. Each data file should be on a different disk drive. The number of data files you choose for the tablespace can be no more than the number of disks that are available and should correspond to the degree of data partitioning you want to create for any table that resides in the tablespace. For example, the SALES tablespace might have ten different data files, all of which reside on different disks.

2. Create the table you want to partition in the previously created tablespace.

3. Use a text editor or a custom-written program to partition the table's rows among several different SQL*Loader input files. For example, the rows for the ORDERS table might end up in the SQL*Loader input files named ORDERS1.DAT, ORDERS2.DAT,...ORDERS10.DAT. The number of SQL*Loader input files you create determines the degree of data partitioning for the table and should be no greater than the number of data files in the table's corresponding tablespace. You can partition the table's rows using any of the previously described horizontal partitioning strategies, such as key partitioning or round-robin partitioning.

4. Use SQL*Loader to load each input file into the table. Be sure to use the SQL*Loader control file option FILE to specifically target the data file that should store the new table rows being loaded. For example, here are excerpts

from two different SQL*Loader control files that correspond to the ORDERS table:

```
LOAD DATA
INFILE 'orders1.dat'
FILE = '/disk1/dbs/sales1.dbf'
INSERT INTO TABLE orders

LOAD DATA
INFILE 'orders2.dat'
FILE = '/disk2/dbs/sales2.dbf'
INSERT INTO TABLE orders
.
.
.
```

When you have completed all the data loads for the same table, repeat the operation for the other tables in the database that you want to horizontally partition.

Database Partitioning Using the Operating System Disk Striping

Disk striping is the easiest way to horizontally partition an Oracle7 table's data across multiple disks. Furthermore, it is the only way to horizontally partition an Oracle7 table if users continue to update its data. Many multiprocessor operating systems have utilities that allow you to physically scatter the pages of one or more files across a number of available disks. For example, the Pyramid DC/OSx operating system has the vdisk utility, and the Sequent DYNEX/ptx operating system has the Sequent Volume Manager (ptx/SVM). If your multiprocessor operating system has such a utility, you should consider using it to partition the data in your database.

Using the Parallel Query Option

Once you have configured a system for the Oracle7 Parallel Query option and have partitioned the database's data, applications automatically start benefiting from parallel database processing. That's because Oracle7 automatically parallelizes most database operations, including SELECT statements; the subqueries of IN-SERT, UPDATE, DELETE; and CREATE TABLE statements. Therefore, users transparently see performance enhancement from the Oracle7 Parallel Query option. On the other hand, developers should consider explicit use of the PARALLEL and NOPARALLEL hints to control and maximize parallel processing performance, as described earlier in this appendix.

APPENDIX

C

Guide to Independent Oracle7 Client/Server Solutions

Oracle7 was designed with an open architecture to allow other software companies to develop administrative utilities, CASE tools, application development tools, and ad hoc query and reporting tools, not to mention out-of-the-box vertical applications that complement the offerings from Oracle Corporation. Since Oracle7 is one of the most popular relational database management systems, there are literally hundreds of independent software components you can buy to help you build your Oracle7 client/server database system or that become part of it. To help you sift through all of the confusion, this appendix takes a look at several of the most popular independent Oracle7 client/server solutions.

Administrative Utilities

This section describes the following independent database administration utilities:

- Data Junction, a data-loading utility
- Desktop DBA, a simple, easy-to-use database administration utility for Microsoft Windows
- EcoTOOLs and Patrol, two administrative utilities that allow you to perform total client/server system management from a single administrative terminal

Data Junction (Tools & Techniques, Inc.)

General Description

As your company works with an Oracle7 client/server system, you will often need to convert data from one file format to another. For example, DOS PC systems might contain valuable information in the form of single-user dBASE databases or Microsoft Excel spreadsheets that you would like to add to an Oracle7 database. Such situations are a perfect job for Data Junction, a powerful data conversion and loading utility for DOS and UNIX systems. It converts data files of one type to data files of other types.

> **TIP**
>
> Data Junction is a useful companion product for Oracle's SQL*Loader because SQL*Loader does not support many file formats. You can use Data Junction to convert data from almost any source into a format that SQL*Loader supports. Then you can use SQL*Loader to load large amounts of data into a database quickly with its direct path load option and parallel load capability (if you have the Oracle7 Parallel Query option).

Usage Brief

To use Data Junction, first you convert a source file into a Data Junction file. Once you have a Data Junction file, you can manipulate your data in many ways before moving the data to a target file. For example, you can view data, enter new data, add new fields, search for and replace data, and even merge or split fields. When you are finished manipulating your data as a Data Junction file, you can select all data or specific data in the Data Junction file, in any order, and convert it to any type of file the Data Junction conversion utilities support, including

- Accounting packages, such as Dac Easy, SBT, CYMA, and PeachTree
- Spreadsheets, such as Lotus 1-2-3, Quattro Pro, and Excel
- Record managers, such as Btrieve, c-tree, and C-ISAM
- Databases, such as Oracle, DB2, SQL/DS, SQL Server, Informix, Paradox, dBASE, and Clipper
- Flat files, such as ASCII formats and EBCDIC files
- Mail-merge data, such as WordPerfect and Microsoft Word

Unique Features

The file formats Data Junction supports are available in three levels: Standard, Professional, and Advanced. The Standard level supports the fewest file formats and the Advanced level the most. The price varies according to the number of file formats each level supports. If you want Oracle support, you'll need the Advanced level of Data Junction.

Available Platforms

Data Junction is available for both DOS and UNIX systems.

Desktop DBA (Datura Corporation)

General Description

Desktop DBA lets you manage remote Oracle7 databases from a Microsoft Windows client. The three main features of Desktop DBA are

- A complete tool set to manage all sorts of database objects
- The ability to open multiple, concurrent database sessions to different databases and perform related operations among the databases (such as a table copy from one database to another)
- A SQL script window for editing and executing SQL command scripts

Usage Brief

Desktop DBA's tool set has all you need to manage Oracle7 databases. For example, the Tables window displays lots of information and tools for managing the tables in a database. A list box shows the names of all the tables in a database, and after you select a specific table, the window displays the name of the tablespace that contains the table and the indexes associated with the table. The Tables window also has buttons that bring up other dialogs for creating, altering, renaming, and dropping tables, as well as for locking and granting privileges for tables. Desktop DBA includes similar tools for other types of database objects, such as tablespaces, indexes, clusters, views, sequences, users, roles, privileges, procedures, packages, triggers, synonyms, and snapshots.

Unique Features

If you have multiple databases to manage, you'll like the fact that Desktop DBA allows you to connect to and manage multiple databases at the same time. Desktop DBA even includes features that make operations involving multiple databases very easy. For example, if you want to copy a table, view, or other object from one database to another, you can simply drag-and-drop the object from the source database to the target database. Desktop DBA prompts for a few tidbits of information (for example, the new object's name) and then does the rest for you.

The SQL Scripts window of Desktop DBA allows you to edit and execute SQL command scripts for your database. This window has a couple of toolbar buttons that make script editing a little bit easier. For example, after selecting a table name from the Object list box in the toolbar, you can click the toolbar's Paste button to automatically paste in the CREATE TABLE statement necessary for re-creating the selected table.

Available Platforms

Desktop DBA is available only for the Microsoft Windows environment. It supports Oracle7 as well as other database servers, including Sybase SQL Server. To have Desktop DBA work with Oracle7, you need an Oracle SQL*Net driver for Windows.

EcoTOOLS (EcoSystems Business Group, Compuware Corporation)

General Description

EcoSystems' EcoTOOLS is one example of a new breed of administrative utility built just for client/server system administration. It is a total system management utility an administrator can use to address all important management aspects in the UNIX client/server database environment, including the network, the operating system, and the database server. All this functionality is presented on one terminal that uses an intuitive graphical user interface to make the presentation and interaction with the utility as easy as possible.

Usage Brief

One key strength of EcoTOOLS is the extensive set of agents that ships with the out-of-the-box product. An agent is a requester of information that corresponds to a specific administrative function. The EcoTOOLS agents use an event-action mechanism that enables them to alert administrators to potential problems and take proactive, corrective actions at the database, system, or network level.

EcoTOOLS features two types of agents: event agents and data agents. Data agents gather the operating system, network, and database information using an efficient polling mechanism to avoid bogging down the network. In addition, the event agents use an exception-based reporting method. They monitor for specific thresholds (or warning signs) in your databases, systems, or networks. Only after one of these thresholds has been crossed will the agent trigger any network traffic by reporting back to a remote management station.

EcoSystems obviously spent a lot of time determining what system and database administrators need to know about their client/server database systems because the EcoTOOLS agents target most of the important system activities. To give you an idea of the variety of EcoTOOLS agents that ship with the product, here is a partial list of what they can do:

- Discover client/server system information, such as the status of clients, users, databases, applications, and servers

- Track system software information, such as database and tools software versions

- Examine database configuration information, such as data files and transaction log setup

- Monitor disk and database space allocation by the operating system and database users

- Automatically detect changes in the status of computers, databases, and peripherals in the client/server system and then take action by running a selected program or alerting administrative personnel, using alarms, electronic mail, pagers, or screen icons that indicate situations worth noting

- Monitor important operating system processing information, such as CPU utilization, context switching, and interrupts

- Detect excessive paging at the operating system and determine if swap space is low

- Detect important network information, such as lost connections and excessive network traffic

- View transactions per second for any application

- Detect critical database server problems, such as database corruptions and core dumps

- Determine if database objects are near maximum extension
- Automatically coalesce free space to minimize fragmentation
- Free archive space to avoid transaction log archiving errors
- Check for permission holes in system directories and files

Figure C.1 shows how ECOTools graphically displays the information gathered by several of the agents mentioned above.

FIGURE C.1:

ECOTools graphically displays information about all parts of a client/server system, using icons to represent different computers and databases.

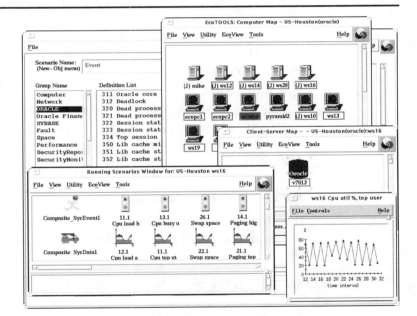

Unique Features

Keep in mind that the preceding list describes only a few of the many EcoTOOLS agents. EcoTOOLS allows you to add your own custom agents to the mix to customize the utility even more. For example, you might have an administrative script or procedure that you use to help manage your system. You can design your own custom EcoTOOLS agent to take advantage of your script or procedure and make it work within the framework of EcoTOOLS. And to help administrators who are new to the job, you can automate complicated management tasks using an Eco-TOOLS feature called scenarios, which is a way to group agents for different administrative functions.

To make the system efficient with so many possible agents, when you configure your EcoTOOLS workstation you can choose only the agents you are interested in. Next, you can set a custom polling interval for each agent if you like, and then Eco-TOOLS does the rest.

Another unique strength of EcoTOOLS is its reporting capabilities. EcoTOOLS comes with many different reports that allow you to graphically display important system information, such as resource utilization, performance data, or application statistics. You can use reports to view data in real time or gather and study historical data for trend analysis. You can even output report data in popular formats, such as spreadsheets.

To complement your EcoTOOLS environment, EcoSystems offers the companion products EcoCHARGEBACK and EcoSCHEDULER. EcoCHARGEBACK is a UNIX/RDBMS resource accounting product. EcoSCHEDULER is a tool for scheduling jobs based on a calendar, job dependencies, and the availability of UNIX and RDBMS resources.

Available Platforms

EcoTOOLS supports many popular UNIX server platforms, as well as popular client platforms, such as PCs and UNIX workstations.

Patrol (Patrol Software, Inc.)

General Description

Patrol is a total system management utility, similar to EcoTOOLS, that lets you manage all parts of a UNIX Oracle7 client/server system from one terminal, using a friendly graphical user interface.

Usage Brief

The main map of Patrol displays each component in the system as an icon on a graphical desktop. You can relate machines in a system using machine groups, which makes it easier to manage many computers in a large system. The attributes of the icons tell you something about the status of each component. For example, if a computer in the system is currently experiencing what you determine is a serious problem (for example, the computer is unavailable because of a system crash), the computer's icon on the Patrol main map might flash to indicate a problem. Patrol's alerting capability allows you to handle specific conditions in certain ways. For example, if a computer is down, Patrol can run a script to automatically restart the computer or notify an administrator with an electronic mail message or beeper.

Patrol ships with a number of Knowledge Modules, a set of prebuilt parameters you can apply to specific components in the system. Patrol has Knowledge Modules for Oracle Server, Sybase SQL Server, Ingres, Informix-Online, and the UNIX operating system. For example, the ORACLE Knowledge Module supports parameters to monitor important database server statistics, such as active transactions, buffer cache hits, DBWR checkpoints, DDL and DML locks, free and used database space, the extents for database tables and indexes, system processes, transaction log information, and rollback segment usage. Patrol can display each parameter just as you want it—in graphs, gauges, or reports. In addition, for each parameter you can specify thresholds for different alert conditions and corresponding recovery actions to execute (for example, run a UNIX shell script, execute a SQL command or SQL script, send a mail message, or notify an electronic pager/beeper), thereby allowing system administration to be relatively automatic if you so choose.

To eliminate unnecessary network traffic, server-side Patrol agent software issues all database requests on behalf of Patrol parameters. Network traffic is necessary only when Patrol needs to notify client-side Patrol terminals of display information or alert conditions.

Unique Features

Menu options of the Patrol Oracle Knowledge module also support Oracle7 database startup and shutdown, the startup of SQL*DBA or SQL*Plus sessions, and the ability to enter ad hoc SQL statements. Additionally, if you have special requirements you can extend the capability of Patrol by adding your own agents, which might be in the form of UNIX shell scripts or SQL command scripts.

Available Platforms

Patrol is available for many popular UNIX platforms and is slated for availability on other platforms, including VAX VMS, Windows NT, and DOS.

CASE Tools

Chapter 14 gave you a good idea of how the Oracle CASE tools work to increase system development productivity. The following sections describe several independent CASE tools you can use instead of or with the Oracle tools to help you build your client/server system:

- Application Development Workbench, a full-featured set of CASE tools that allows for total system development on many different platforms

- Easy CASE System Designer, a modeling tool for Microsoft Windows that lets you design your application schema

- ERwin/ERX, a database design tool for Microsoft Windows and Sun workstations that you can use to design or reverse engineer database schemas

Application Development Workbench (KnowledgeWare, Inc.)

General Description

KnowledgeWare's Application Development Workbench (ADW) is an integrated set of CASE tools you can use to analyze, plan, and model a business's process and data requirements and then use those requirements to automatically generate client/server applications. The ADW tools work together to address all phases of application development.

Usage Brief

The first step in systems development is perhaps the most critical—understanding the needs and priorities of a company so that systems development focuses on the correct objectives in the appropriate order. The Planning Workstation (ADW/PWS) addresses this first phase of systems development. Using the ADW/PWS association matrix designer, you can quickly and easily establish the framework for system development throughout a corporation. You use ADW/PWS to build an enterprise model for all systems in your company, defining its organizational structure, business functions, goals, critical success factors, and the information needs of each organization unit in the company. Then ADW/PWS can help determine candidate projects, prioritize them according to your company's critical success factors, and suggest project scopes. ADW/PWS stores all gathered information in the ADW encyclopedia, to which all other components of the system have access.

The Analysis Workstation (ADW/AWS) is a modeling tool that further refines the information gathered with ADW/PWS. ADW/AWS includes several graphical diagrammers to facilitate refinement of the system: a decomposition diagrammer, a data flow diagrammer, an entity-relationship diagrammer, and an information type diagrammer. These tools allow you to define a given business area for an organization. Again, ADW/AWS stores all its information in the central ADW encyclopedia so that other components in the system have access to it.

The RAD Workstation (ADW/RAC) is a prototyping tool for previewing the initial designs of end-user applications. You can save lots of time and avoid headaches later in the application development process because ADW/RAD allows you to quickly generate a prototype application and then gather feedback on how the application prototype addresses user requirements. Therefore, when you begin the development process for the functional application, you will save time because you will have already found and eliminated a lot of initial problems in the prototyping phase.

The Design Workstation (ADW/DWS) and Construction Workstation (ADW/CWS) generators allow you to create generic physical designs of client/server applications and relational and hierarchical databases using information gathered by the previously described ADW products. The CWS generators can then use the generic physical designs to create client/server applications targeted to UNIX/Motif, OS/2 Presentation Manager, DOS/Windows 3.x, AS/400, and MVS. The generators support many database technologies, including Oracle7, Sybase SQL Server, DB2, DB2/2, IMS, VSAM, and ANSI-compliant relational databases.

The Documentation Workstation (ADW/DOC) is an extensive reporting component of the ADW family of products that allows you to fully document your company's entire system development process.

Unique Features

ADW includes some redevelopment products to help maintain the investment that companies might have in legacy applications that were not developed with a sophisticated system development approach. ADW/Inspector analyzes COBOL applications for conformance with structured programming principles. ADW/Pinpoint identifies potential problems in a COBOL program and can reveal just what a program is doing. And ADW/Recorder can recode an existing application into a simpler format by generating structured code equivalent to the original application code.

If your company has a large team of developers, you'll be interested in using the ADW/Workgroup Coordinator and ADW/Workgroup Manager products. The ADW/Workgroup Coordinator is a multi-user encyclopedia manager that safely manages concurrent access to an ADW project encyclopedia among a team of developers who work together in a LAN. The ADW/Workgroup Manager extends the functionality of the ADW/Workgroup Coordinator by providing specific controls for project encyclopedia management, including project checkout, project ownership, and other security and integrity features.

As previously mentioned, ADW components centrally store all their information in the ADW encyclopedia. To extend the access of your work in ADW, this product set also supports the ROCHADE client/server repository, a nonproprietary CASE repository architecture.

Available Platforms

KnowledgeWare supports the ADW family of products for the DOS/Windows, OS/2, UNIX, MVS, and VM operating systems and the Oracle7, Sybase SQL Server, and IBM DB2 relational database servers.

Easy CASE System Designer (Evergreen CASE Tools, Inc.)

General Description

Easy CASE System Designer is a graphically oriented system design tool for the Microsoft Windows environment.

Using System Designer's extensive feature set, you can model all parts of the analysis and design phases of Oracle7 application schema development. And when you're done building and testing your design, you can generate the schema for any one of a number of database systems, including Oracle7, using the System Designer's schema generator feature. Figure C.2 shows an IDEF1X entity-relationship diagram of an order/inventory application schema, along with the schema System Designer generates from the diagram.

FIGURE C.2:

Easy CASE System Designer's diagrammers make it easy to model the processes and data in an application schema. Then, using System Designer's Schema Generator, you can quickly generate the DDL script necessary to create your application's schema.

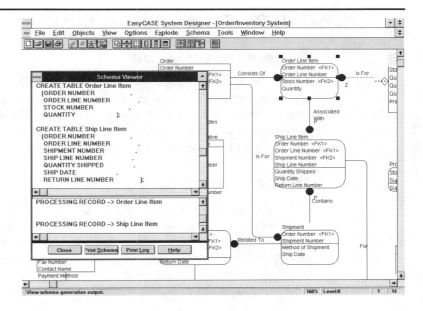

Unique Features

System Designer supports just about every design methodology you might want to take advantage of when analyzing and designing a new application schema. For example, to define the processes in your system, you can create data flow diagrams using Yourdon/DeMarco, Gane & Sarson, and SSADM methodologies; and to define the data in your system, you can create entity relationship diagrams using Chen, Martin, Bachman, IDEF1X, Shlaer & Mellor, or Merise methodologies. Each diagram and methodology has a rule checker that allows you to validate your designs. If you don't understand the uses, differences, and advantages of all the diagramming options and methodologies, don't worry; System Designer comes with tutorials, online help, and a good documentation set.

Available Platforms

System Designer supports schema generation for many popular database servers, including Oracle7, DB2, RdB, both Sybase and Microsoft SQL Server, Informix, Ingres, SQLBase, and Progress, as well as PC database managers, such as FoxPro, Paradox, dBASE, and Clipper. It is available solely for the Microsoft Windows environment.

ERwin/ERX (Logic Works, Inc.)

General Description

ERwin/ERX is a graphically oriented database design tool that supports both forward and reverse engineering of database systems for many database servers, including Oracle7. These features, coupled with ERwin/ERX's full support for each database server's unique DDL extensions and capabilities, make ERwin/ERX a powerful tool for complete client/server system design.

Usage Brief

ERwin/ERX's forward engineering capability is based on an IDEF1X graphical entity-relationship diagrammer you can use to quickly design and generate a new application schema. Once you are done designing a system, you can use ERwin/ERX's complete schema generation facility to create a DDL script with which you can then create an entire application schema or database. The product also has extensive reporting capabilities to help document each part of your system design.

Unique Features

ERwin/ERX's reverse-engineering capability is a key feature for situations in which you want to document or build upon existing database systems that were not designed using a modeling tool like ERwin/ERX. ERwin/ERX's reverse-engineering capability allows it to read the system catalogs of an existing database and then automatically create a design of the system in the form of an IDEF1X entity-relationship diagram. From this point you can document the existing design or, with the click of a mouse button, transform the schema design in the diagrammer to a new database in another format by generating a new schema for that database server. ERwin/ERX can read from and write to many database server formats, including Oracle7, DB2, both Sybase and Microsoft SQL Server, Rdb, Informix-Online and Informix-SE, SQLBase, Ingres, and NetWare SQL.

Another unique feature of ERwin/ERX is its full support for the unique extensions and capabilities of each supported database server. For example, ERwin/ERX can create all integrity constraints supported by the Oracle7 database server, such as PRIMARY KEY, UNIQUE, NOT NULL, and CHECK, and referential integrity constraints, including those with the DELETE CASCADE option. To address the importance of server-enforced integrity even further, ERwin/ERX's schema generator can create database triggers so that the database server can enforce referential integrity actions that are not supported using declarative referential integrity constraints. For example, ERwin/ERX can create database triggers to enforce the UPDATE/DELETE SET NULL referential integrity action. To help you out in many situations, you can use ERwin/ERX's trigger toolbox, which contains an extensive suite of built-in trigger templates.

Available Platforms

ERwin/ERX is available for both Microsoft Windows and Sun SPARC client workstations.

Application Development Tools

When you start to look at independent application development tools, you'll be amazed at how many different tools are available to help you build your Oracle7 client/server system. This section takes a look at just a few of them, including

- DataEase, PowerBuilder, and SQLWindows, application development tools for developing client form and reporting applications for Microsoft Windows clients
- TUXEDO System, a transaction manager for enhancing any client/server application environment with transaction-management facilities

DataEase (DataEase International, Inc.)

General Description

If you have a significant application development backlog that you want to eliminate quickly, a good choice for your development tool might be DataEase from DataEase International. DataEase allows you to create application startup menus, customer user menus, entry forms for data input and modification, and reports for displaying, manipulating, and printing information in text format.

Usage Brief

DataEase's ease of use is good when you need to rapidly develop many new applications. When developing a new application, you can use DataEase in one of two different modes. If an application schema already exists in the database server, DataEase can read in table definitions to automatically aid in the creation of forms and reports. Alternatively, DataEase allows you to create an application from scratch, defining form field attributes and relationships as you go. Then, based upon the application definitions, DataEase creates the corresponding application schema for you in the database server. The former approach is useful for those who use a CASE tool to model and test an application schema; the latter approach is useful for those who do not have access to a CASE tool and do not want to deal with creating an application schema from scratch.

The DataEase Quick Reports feature allows you to quickly develop standard reports using a query-by-example (QBE) approach. You can pick the tables and fields for a report from lists on the Quick Reports screen and then use the report editor's visual layout capabilities to set up the look and feel of the report.

For situations in which DataEase's QBE capabilities do not meet your objectives, you can use DataEase's native programming language, DataEase Query Language (DQL). DQL allows you to manipulate database data and supports many language constructs to extend the power of DataEase, including common 3GL constructs, such as conditional processing (for example, IF…THEN, WHILE…DO). You put together DQL statements to form queries (DQL blocks that query database data) and procedures (DQL blocks that manipulate database data). For new users, DataEase makes programming in DQL simple because the product has an interactive editor with menus that help you put DQL commands into queries and procedures. DataEase applications can then use DQL queries and procedures to perform work.

Unique Features

DataEase is good at adapting to a changing business environment because the product lets you change applications quickly. Because the product maintains relationships between application screens and database tables, DataEase can automatically adjust one or the other, depending on what you do to change your environment. For example, when you change a field length in an Oracle7 database table, DataEase provides an automated way to resynchronize a form with the new version of the table.

While DQL is adequate for extending application functionality in most situations, it is not as strong as the programming languages supported by other environments. If you need to extend an application's functionality even further than DataEase DQL supports, you can write custom-designed functions in C, assembler, or any other supported programming language and then have DataEase call them through its Custom Designed Functions (CDF) feature. In addition to writing custom-designed functions, you can make use of many CDF libraries and functions available from DataEase's third-party community.

Available Platforms

DataEase is available for several operating systems. The full-blown product, DataEase, is available for character-mode DOS, OS/2, and bitmapped Microsoft Windows. DataEase Express for Windows is a graphical version of the DataEase product that allows for quick and easy development of query and reporting applications under Microsoft Windows. Also, to connect to an Oracle7 database server with any of the DataEase products, you'll need the DataEase companion product called SQL Connect for Oracle7.

PowerBuilder, Enterprise Edition (Powersoft, Inc.)

General Description

Powersoft's PowerBuilder and associated products of the Enterprise Edition work together to deliver a powerful client/server application development system for Microsoft Windows. And don't let the continued presence of the word "power" intimidate you; PowerBuilder's interface presents all of the product's power in a way that makes it easy to create form and reporting applications.

Usage Brief

PowerBuilder is easy to work with because the interface is based on using intuitive 4GL painters to create different components of an application, such as windows, menus, and so on. PowerBuilder has several different painters to help with all areas of application development, including

- Application Painter
- Window Painter

- Menu Painter
- DataWindow Painter
- Database Painter
- Query Painter
- Report Painter

Once you have created application components using a PowerBuilder Painter, you bind scripts (sets of commands) to the different application components so they perform the desired application functionality. You can use the PowerBuilder development process to create sound client/server applications quickly and easily. And when you finish developing a new application, you can create a stand-alone executable that is ready for distribution to users of the system.

Let's take a quick look at how you might use PowerBuilder to accomplish a typical development operation—adding a new application window and a button. First, you can create a new window for an application using PowerBuilder's Window Painter. Simply click the Window Painter icon button in PowerBar to start the Window Painter and create a new window. PowerBuilder's PowerBar contains a number of icon buttons for accessing the PowerBuilder painters, no matter where you are in PowerBuilder. Once you add the new window, you can use your mouse to size it, change its title or background color, and so on. Next you might add a control to the window, such as a button. You can do this by selecting a button tool from the Window Painter PainterBar (another set of icon buttons specific to the painter you are using) and clicking the window to add a button. Then you can use your mouse to select the button, size it, change its colors, and so on. To add functionality to the new window or its button, you can double-click the object and then create a script for the object. With PowerBuilder's extensive BASIC-like scripting language, PowerScript, you can use over 400 commands and functions to do just about anything within an object's script. An integrated debugger makes it easy to find and fix the inevitable mistakes you make while coding scripts. Figure C.3 shows the PowerBuilder Window Painter with a window and several controls, including data fields, check boxes, and buttons. The figure also shows how easy it is to change the selected picture button's attributes and access its script.

FIGURE C.3:

PowerBuilder's Window Painter makes it easy to create new application windows, add controls to them, and attach scripts to the objects to establish application functionality.

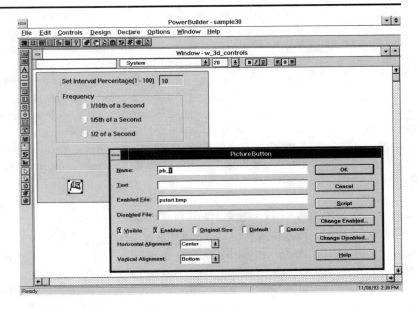

Similarly, you can use the other PowerBuilder painters to quickly develop the many parts of a PowerBuilder application. For example, with the Query Painter you build new queries using a visual, nonprogrammatic system that includes query-by-example. You can then use the DataWindow Painter to make use of and control the presentation layout of your queries in a data window that might be present in an application window.

Unique Features

The PowerBuilder Enterprise Edition comes with two other products that allow end users to supplement a client/server system's professionally developed Power-Builder applications with personal applications: PowerMaker and PowerViewer. With these application development tools end users can easily create their own custom queries, forms, reports, and graphs without programming.

As you use PowerBuilder, you'll notice that the product supports many object-oriented programming features to help you develop better applications more quickly. In a sense, the PowerBuilder painters are class generators that allow you to create window classes, menu classes, and so on. And after you have created a Power-Builder application object, you can use the object to create subclasses that inherit the attributes and function of the parent. For example, you might create a generic application window that has a specific background color, OK and Cancel buttons, and other objects. You can then reuse the generic application window to create many other more specialized windows that derive common attributes and functionality from the generic application window. Developers save time because it is easier to create subsequent application windows, and the application has a consistent look and feel for all of its windows. And if a generic change is necessary for all windows based on the parent, a simple change to the parent automatically changes all descendant windows.

Available Platforms

PowerBuilder is available for the Microsoft Windows environment. PowerBuilder supports many different data sources, including relational database systems like Oracle7, both Sybase and Microsoft SQL Server, Informix, and others. PowerBuilder's Enterprise Edition even comes with the WATCOM SQL database system for Windows so you can develop part of an Oracle7 application on the client computer before actually having to connect to Oracle7 for later stages of development. This way you can offload all the processing requirements for application development from the centralized Oracle7 database server.

SQLWindows, Corporate Edition (Gupta Corporation, Inc.)

General Description

The Corporate Edition of SQLWindows is a group of products that form a powerful application development environment for Microsoft Windows. Using SQLWindows and its companion products, you can create forms and report applications for your Oracle7 client/server database system.

Usage Brief

The most striking difference between SQLWindows and any other development tool is its user interface. It mixes 3GL and 4GL capabilities so you can easily see both the code and the appearance of an application as you develop it. As you work with application objects either in a form window or in the Outliner, SQLWindows synchronizes any changes to keep the different application views consistent with each other. In this example, a button is selected in a form window, and its corresponding code in the application is selected in the Outliner (the window titled Main). Figure C.4 shows an example of the SQLWindows application development interface.

FIGURE C.4:

The SQLWindows interface mixes both 3GL and 4GL capabilities.

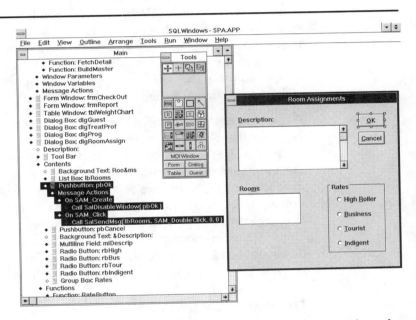

Notice that the SQLWindows interface consists of three areas: a form window, the Tools palette, and the Outliner. The form window is the 4GL that shows the user's view of an application as you develop it. With the tools on the Tools palette, you can add form objects, such as data fields, buttons, and text fields. The SQLWindows Tool palette also supports Multiple Document Interface (MDI) windows, which allows a parent window to contain child windows, each of which you can move, resize, tile, minimize, or maximize.

The Outliner is the 3GL part of the SQLWindows interface; it shows the textual description of the application as you develop it. Application logic is arranged in sections, which appear in a hierarchical format that one might expect in an outline. One advantage of the Outliner is that it allows you to readily look at the logic in your application without having to click objects or use menus to present additional information about application objects. And don't worry about large applications; as its name indicates, the Outliner allows you to collapse and expand different sections of the application so you can see just the areas of application code in which you are currently interested.

The Outliner and the form window are tightly integrated tools in the SQLWindows development interface. For example, if you select an application object in the form window, SQLWindows selects the corresponding logic in the Outliner so you can quickly see what the object does. The reverse holds true if you select some text in the Outliner. And SQLWindows lets you work the way that is best for you—you can develop an application from either the form window or the Outliner at any time. When you make changes to an application from one area, SQLWindows immediately synchronizes the changes in the other area.

As you use the SQLWindows Outliner, you'll notice the underlying programming language that SQLWindows uses to perform actions: the SQLWindows Access Language (SAL). SAL is a thorough 3GL programming language that can satisfy even the most demanding programming requirements—there are hundreds of SAL functions and SQLWindows SQL functions in the Outliner to accomplish application work. To help the novice become familiar with the SQLWindows programming language or the expert with typing keystrokes, the Outliner Options dialog displays all the functionality of the SQLWindows SAL and SQL functions. SQLWindows also has an integrated debugger with the standard features for finding and correcting the problems that arise during application development.

Unique Features

To help non-SQL programmers with application development, SQLWindows allows you to incorporate features of Quest, another Gupta product found in the SQLWindows Corporate Edition. Quest is a graphical, ad hoc query-by-example tool that allows you to get information from tables without using SQL.

If you or your development team plans to build lots of related applications, your productivity can benefit from SQLWindows' object-oriented programming features. SQLWindows supports the definition of window (graphics) and function classes within the application system. For example, you might create a dialog box that you can then reuse throughout the same application or a number of different applications. You can also take advantage of inheritance by declaring subclasses of a base class. SQLWindows even supports multiple inheritance, so a single class can be derived from one or more base classes. Finally, SQLWindows supports polymorphism such that a message, when sent to different object classes, causes different but appropriate actions. For example, you might have a base class PERSON and subclasses EMPLOYEE and CUSTOMER. When sent the CHANGE_ADDRESS message, objects of class PERSON, EMPLOYEE, and CUSTOMER all react appropriately.

The Corporate Edition of SQLWindows includes a companion product, TeamWindows, designed to support development teams. TeamWindows is an integrated set of tools that includes features such as project management, source code control (check-in and check-out), error logging, modification tracking, and management of template libraries and screens. Templates are an object-oriented feature. You create the visual layout and methods of an application screen object once as a template and store it in the TeamWindows central repository. Then all developers can use the template to avoid duplicate work and quickly build a set of applications with similar functionality and characteristics. TeamWindows also performs impact analysis, which determines and reports which applications will be affected if you change a template or the underlying database of an application.

Available Platforms

SQLWindows supports the development of Microsoft Windows applications for many database servers, including Oracle7, both Microsoft and Sybase SQL Server, Informix, Ingres, Gupta's own SQLBase, DB2, AS/400, Supra, Netware SQL, HP AllBase, and HP Turbo Image. The SQLWindows Corporate Edition also comes with SQLBase to facilitate stand-alone application development. In order to connect to Oracle7 with SQLWindows, you'll also need Gupta's networking product, SQLRouter/Oracle.

TUXEDO System (Information Management Company)

General Description

TUXEDO System from Information Management Company is a transaction manager for UNIX database server systems. Transaction managers, also called transaction processing monitors (TP monitors), play an important role in many client/server systems. They are a type of middleware you can use to enhance the capabilities of a client/server database system.

Transaction managers such as TUXEDO offer the following capabilities:

- Application transaction coordination and prioritization: Using a transaction manager, you can coordinate and prioritize the execution of application transactions so more important transactions execute before less important transactions. Additionally, transaction managers often support asynchronous communication—that is, applications can request information from a server, and while the server is processing the request, the application can focus on other areas of work instead of waiting for the server to respond to the request. When the server finishes processing the request, the transaction manager notifies the application of the response. In short, transaction managers that support asynchronous communication allow applications to be programmed so that users realize maximum productivity.

- Reduced server overhead: Similar to Oracle7's multithreaded server configuration, transaction managers allow large numbers of clients to perform work using only a few foreground server processes, thereby minimizing server overhead and maximizing the use of resources on the database server.

- A highly productive application development interface: Client applications perform transactions by calling "canned" procedures stored in the application server, which then forwards requests to the appropriate database server. Because of a transaction manager's modular programming application interface, applications can be developed quickly on any platform without regard to special operating system, GUI, network, or database system considerations.

Because of a transaction manager's ability to coordinate and prioritize transactions using a minimal amount of server resources, a transaction manager is a common component in demanding OLTP application environments where performance is very important.

Additionally, transaction managers have other benefits for distributed environments, especially heterogeneous distributed database systems. For example, transaction managers can coordinate distributed transactions across different database servers, such as an Oracle7 server and an Informix database server.

Usage Brief

TUXEDO supports all the features mentioned in the preceding section and more, using several system components:

- TUXEDO System/T is the transaction monitor component that sits between the client and data servers to support coordinated transaction management facilities.
- TUXEDO System/WS is the client-side component used for client workstations. This component allows client applications written in C or COBOL to interface with TUXEDO System/T using its procedural application-transaction monitor interface.
- TUXEDO System/Q is an extension of the TUXEDO System that permits applications to queue messages and requests on stable storage for later processing.
- TUXEDO System/Host is an extension of the TUXEDO System product line that allows open UNIX servers to access proprietary CICS systems. CICS is another transaction manager that interfaces specifically with IBM MVS mainframe systems.
- TUXEDO Open Transport is an extension of the TUXEDO System that allows open UNIX servers to access proprietary IMS/DC and MVS/CICS systems using TCP/IP communications. IMS and CICS are other transaction managers that operate in IBM mainframe environments.

In conclusion, if you are developing a demanding commercial application for a UNIX Oracle7 client/server environment, you would be wise to investigate the possible enhancements that are possible through the use of a transaction manager such as the TUXEDO System.

Available Platforms

Which platforms are available depends on which component of TUXEDO you use:

- Applications access TUXEDO System/T resources using a standard 3GL programming language, including C and COBOL.
- TUXEDO System/WS is available for DOS, Microsoft Windows, OS/2, and UNIX workstations.

- TUXEDO System/Q may be combined with TUXEDO System/WS in either the COBOL or C programming language.

- TUXEDO System/Host is available for UNIX servers.

- TUXEDO Open Transport is available for UNIX servers.

Query and Reporting Tools

Getting information out of a database system is just as important as putting the information in. There are several independent query and reporting tools you can use to quickly access your Oracle7 database information in order to analyze it and make good business decisions. The following sections preview some independent query and reporting tools.

BusinessObjects (Business Objects, Inc.)

General Description

BusinessObjects from Business Objects, Inc., is a query and reporting tool that allows nontechnical users to easily get to information in an Oracle7 database without any knowledge of SQL or relational database concepts, such as tables, views, and relationships.

Usage Brief

When using BusinessObjects, users ask about database information using a *universe,* which is a layer of data representation between the user and the database that hides the technical details of SQL database access. A universe consists of several components created by the application developer:

- Business objects: Correspond to the everyday business terminology of end users. For example, marketing executives need information about customers, sales revenues, and advertising budgets, while financial analysts need information about working capital, net margins, and internal rates of return. Each object corresponds to a selection, calculation, or function of data in a database. You can define an object by its relationship to other objects. For example, you can define an object called sales-revenues.

- Classes of Objects: A way to organize related objects in a universe. For example, you might put all the objects related to employees in a class.

- Joins: BusinessObjects stores join conditions that link different database tables so you can define relationships once and have them be transparent to end users.

- Contexts: Describe sets of paths in a complex relational database to resolve the problem of loops. A loop occurs when two or more paths join different tables. BusinessObjects uses contexts in such cases to resolve a query and return accurate results.

A database administrator or application developer uses the Manager Module of BusinessObjects to create and define universes. The Manager Module has a click-and-point graphical user interface that makes it easy to create BusinessObjects universes. For example, the following listing describes the data representations of several business objects and joins in a typical Sales universe:

```
Business Object          SQL Equivalent
---------------          --------------
Customer                 customer.first_name,
                         customer.last_name,
                         customer.phone

Address                  customer.address
City                     customer.city

First Name               customer.first_name
Last Name                customer.last_name

Reference ID             orders.id

Date of Order            orders.orderdate

Sales Revenue            sum(items.price*order_lines.quantity)

Quantity Sold            sum(order_lines.quantity)
```

```
Joins
-----
items.item_id=order_lines.item_id
customer.id=orders.cust_id
orders.id=order_lines.orders_id
```

Once the developer uses the Manager Module to define a universe, users can query the universe with the User Module. The User Module also has a graphical user interface that the end user uses to select business objects and to set conditions and sorts to create database queries using a nontechnical approach. The User Module also contains tools for saving commonly used queries and creating reports and graphs of the data they query.

Because a user selects data using everyday business terminology, the BusinessObjects approach is intuitive. The definition of the universe also controls what data end users see and how they see it, which the developer can easily change using the Manager Module.

Available Platforms

BusinessObjects supports several database servers, including Oracle7, using the Microsoft Windows environment.

Forest & Trees (Trinzic Corporation, formerly Channel Computing, Inc.)

General Description

Forest & Trees is a tool for collecting, combining, and presenting information from different data sources to monitor and analyze business. It's a query and reporting tool that can help you be more informed about the data around you so you can make better business decisions.

Usage Brief

Using Forest & Trees, you can build decision-support applications to display the information using all the graphical features of the Microsoft Windows environment.

Forest & Trees application views can display database information in several ways. For example, if you choose to display information as a table of text, the view can have buttons that permit the user to quickly change the view's perspective. If you want to use graphs to show data trends more easily, you can pick from several formats, including bar, line, scatter, and pie graphs. The application in Figure C.5 illustrates the flexibility with which Forest & Trees can display database information.

FIGURE C.5:

With Forest & Trees, with just the touch of a button you can immediately change the perspective from which you view your database data.

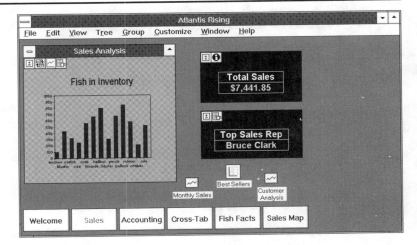

Unique Features

Data presentation is just one part of Forest & Trees' power. The product has some unique features that make it extremely useful for decision support and data monitoring, including a schedule tool, control functions, and alarms. For example, once you present database information in an application view just the way you want, you can use Forest & Trees' schedule tool to automatically refresh the view's data at regular intervals—every minute, hour, day, week, or month. When the server ships the requested data back to the Forest & Trees application, you can use special control functions to filter out facts about the new information and automatically perform related actions, such as triggering a visual or an audible alarm or sending an electronic mail message. Forest & Trees can even create a history log of the information your application requests so you can analyze long-term information trends.

Available Platforms

Forest & Trees is available for Microsoft Windows only. It can gather data from many different data sources, including database servers such as Oracle7 (using Oracle's SQL*Net networking product), Rdb, both Sybase and Microsoft SQL Server (and Sybase Net Gateway), Ingres, SQLBase (and Gupta Gateway for DB2), and Netware SQL, as well as PC data sources like Windows Dynamic Data Exchange, 1-2-3, Excel, dBASE, Paradox, EDA-SQL Gateway, and Lotus Notes.

Natural Language (Natural Language, Inc.)

General Description

Natural Language is an ad hoc query and reporting tool that permits nontechnical users to get at the database information they need while insulating them from the complexities of SQL and relational databases. However, unlike other tools that perform similar feats, Natural Language is unique in the way that it allows a user to interact with a database—using English.

Usage Brief

Here is an example of how you might use Natural Language. Instead of entering a SQL statement or manipulating graphical screen objects to find out which customers live in New York City, a user can find the answer by entering the following simple question:

```
what customers live in New York City
```

Other human-language products have been introduced in the past to interface with other types of software (for example, HAL for Lotus 1-2-3), and it is clear that to be effective and useful, such products must have a keen understanding of human language. Natural Language has a substantial understanding of the English language, based on the knowledge of over 100,000 concepts and words, as well as an understanding of verb tenses and time.

The first step in using Natural Language is to "teach" it about the database. No matter how much understanding a human-language software product has, there will be special terms and concepts that you need to introduce for specific applications.

Therefore, you start with Natural Language by explaining certain pieces of database information (table and view names, aliases, primary and foreign keys, join paths, and so on) to enhance Natural Language's comprehension with the knowledge of your particular database. Most likely, this is a job for an application developer. Once you teach Natural Language about your system, end users can use Natural Language to access your database without any knowledge of SQL or database concepts.

Natural Language includes a reporting feature that lets users generate both graphical and text reports of the data they query. For example, to graph the number of customers in each state, you might issue the following English question:

```
pie chart how many customers are in each state
```

Unique Features

To supplement the power of Natural Language, the program also allows you to transfer data seen in Natural Language to other types of files, such as spreadsheets, electronic mail, word processors, and so on. For example, you might transfer some data you gather with Natural Language to a spreadsheet file so you can use Lotus 1-2-3 to perform sophisticated calculations on the information.

Available Platforms

Natural Language supports Oracle7 on the DOS/Windows, VMS, Sun OS, Solaris, HPUX, SCO UNIX, Ultrix, and AIX operating systems, supporting Motif, OPEN LOOK, DECWindows, and character-based terminals.

Independents, Unite!

One of the primary advantages Oracle's CDE tool set has over the independent solutions is that it is a complete, integrated set of tools that you can use to develop all types of applications for your entire business. More important, the integration of Oracle's CDE tools allows you to develop an entire business system, from start to finish, with Oracle tools. As Chapter 14 demonstrates, the tight integration of the Oracle tools lets you use the Oracle CASE tools to design the business system and then automatically generate associated Oracle Forms applications, Oracle Reports applications, and so on, as well as the underlying Oracle7 application schema. The end result is that developers can produce well-designed business systems very quickly.

Most independent software companies do not have the resources necessary to offer every type of software for users in a client/server system. Therefore, the independents are at something of a competitive disadvantage when matched with Oracle. Consequently, many independent software companies are creating other products or establishing technical agreements with one another so that products from different companies can be integrated into a single client/server development environment. This is great news for you the customer because now you can choose the tools you want to use and still gain the benefits of an integrated tool set. For example, Logic Works' ERwin EXchange will allow the ERwin tools to work with Oracle's CASE*Dictionary as the CASE repository. Therefore, if you would rather work with the ERwin data modeler than with Oracle's CASE*Designer, you can do so. Additionally, Powersoft and Gupta Corporation have made agreements with Logic Works so you can integrate the power of ERwin/ERX with either PowerBuilder or SQLWindows to develop client/server applications much more quickly.

The previous examples are just a few of the many ways in which independent tool vendors are beginning to band together so that their tools fit in as part of more integrated sets of tools for client/server application development. If you want to experience the benefits that an integrated client/server application development environment offers, be sure to research the cooperative agreements in which your favorite independent software vendors participate.

INDEX

Note to the Reader: **Boldfaced** numbers indicate pages where you will find the principal discussion of a topic or the definition of a term. *Italic* numbers indicate pages where a topic is illustrated in a figure.

Special characters

3GL and 4GL development tools, 80–83
… (ellipsis), in data flow diagrams, 420

A

access privileges. *See* privileges; security
accessing
  SQL*DBA Dispatcher monitor, *251*
  SQL*DBA Shared Server monitor, 255–256, *256*
adapter cards, network, 100
ADD clause, ALTER TABLE command, 493–494
Add Data File to Tablespace dialog box, SQL*DBA, 212–213, *212*
Add Online Redo Log Group dialog box, SQL*DBA, 331–332, *332*
Add Online Redo Log Member dialog box, SQL*DBA, 335–336, *336*
adding
  associations to matrix diagrams, 431–432, *432*

child functions to data flow diagrams, 419–420, *420*
data files to tablespaces, 212–213
data flows to data flow diagrams, 421–422, *421*
data stores to data flow diagrams, 422, *423*
integrity constraints, 494
log groups, 331–333
log members, 335–336
addresses, port addresses for listener process, 247
administrative utilities, **85–88**. *See also* client applications; SQL*DBA; SQL*Loader
  Oracle Import and Export utilities, 86
  third party applications, 88
alert conditions, 402–403, 588–593, *589*
aliases. *See also* synonyms
  naming view columns with, 500–501
Alter Profile dialog box, SQL*DBA, *284*
Alter Rollback Segment Storage dialog box, SQL*DBA, *324*
ALTER SEQUENCE command, 525
ALTER TABLE command, **492–495**
  ADD, MODIFY, and DROP clauses, 493–494
Alter User dialog box, SQL*DBA, 268, *269*, *280*
altering. *See* changing; modifying
alternate keys, 36, 481

analysis stage of application development, **407**, **432–438**. *See also* CASE*Dictionary
  circulating new information for review, 438
  entering attributes for entities, 434–438
  entering details about business functions, 433–434
  entering details about data flows, 434
ANALYZE command, 513
anonymous PL/SQL blocks, **139–140**
ANSI/ISO SQL standard, 113
APIs (application programming interface), 103–105
APPEND option, SQL*Loader control files, 180
application DDL scripts. *See* DDL scripts
application development, **394–403**. *See also* application schemas; CASE tools; database administration for applications; form applications; Oracle Forms application; PL/SQL; utilities
  analysis stage, **407**, **432–438**. *See also* CASE*Dictionary
  circulating new information for review, 438
  entering attributes for entities, 434–438
  entering details about business functions, 433–434

P

listed, **632**
overview of, 599–600
revoking for roles, 605
setting for roles, 604–605
synonyms and, 601
extending and restricting, 53–54
overview of, **53**
system privileges, **54**, 54, 281, **630–632**
Procedural option, 66. *See also* PL/SQL; programmer utilities
procedures
in database servers, **401–403**
estimating space requirements for, **308–310**
in PL/SQL, **558–573**
calling, **569–571**
creating, **563–569**
versus database triggers, 561
defining parameters, 141, 564
deleting, **572–573**
enforcing data integrity with, 559–560
enforcing security checks with, 560
enhancing application functionality with, 560
executing, 142
executing package procedures, 146
increasing object security with, 560
overview of, 140–141
packages versus individual procedures, 561
reducing network traffic with, 558–559
replacing, **571–572**
stored procedures
in database servers, **401–402**
defined, **43**
enforcing custom integrity rules with, 43–46, *45*
process monitor (PMON), 109
production stage of application development, **408**, **456–457**

productivity
client/server systems and, 15
object-oriented programming and, 94
programmer utilities, **585–595**
DBMS_ALERT package, 588–593, *589*
DBMS_DDL package, 587
DBMS_LOCK package, 546–548, 588
DBMS_OUTPUT package, 584, 587–588
DBMS_PIPE package, 593–594
DBMS_SESSION package, 585–586, 607
DBMS_SHARED_POOL package, 552–553
DBMS_STANDARD package, 587
DBMS_TRANSACTION package, 586
DBMS_UTILITY package, 587
project relational operator, 24
protecting, database availability, 272–273
public synonyms, 503–504

Q

queries
cursors and, 129–130
defined, **25**
defining for views, 497–500
exact-match queries, data clusters and, 517
views for complex queries, 33–34
query coordinators, 641
query and reporting tools, **77–80**, **680–685**. *See also* client applications
BusinessObjects, 680–682
Forest & Trees, 682–684, *683*
Natural Language, 684–685
Oracle Data Browser, 80, *81*

Oracle Graphics application, 79, *80*
Oracle Reports application, 78, *79*
overview of, 77–78
SQL*Plus query tool, 79
quick reference tables. *See* reference tables

R

RAISE_APPLICATION_ERROR PL/SQL procedure, 138–139
read consistency
controlling, 549–551
queries, multi-versioning and, 49, *50*
real memory, **369**
rebuilding indexes, 513
RECORD PL/SQL datatype, 126–128
records, defined, **22**
Recover Offline Tablespace dialog box, SQL*DBA, 364–365, *365*
recovering databases, 64, *65*, **161**, **356–365**. *See also* backups; transaction logs
closed database recovery, 64, *65*, **357–360**
cleaning up after, 360
extracting archived log groups, 359
overview of, 357–358
performing, 359–360
repairing hardware problems, 358
restoring damaged files, 358–359
roll forward recovery, *356*
crash recovery, **357**
online database recovery, **363–365**
overview of, 64, *65*, *356*
parallel recovery, **361–363**, *362*
redo logs. *See* transaction logs
reducing. *See also* performance
checkpoint performance hits, **383–386**
tuning checkpoint performance, 385–386

u

MAKE A GOOD COMPUTER EVEN BETTER.

350pp. ISBN: 1301-X.

The *PC Upgrade Guide for Everybody* is the no-hassle, do-it-yourself PC upgrade guide for everyone. If you know the difference between a screwdriver and a pair of pliers, this book is for you.

Inside you'll find step-by-step instructions for installing hardware to make your computer even more fun and productive. Add memory chips, CD-ROM drives and more to your PC.

You'll also learn how to diagnose minor PC problems and decide whether to repair or replace faulty components —without schlepping your PC to the shop and paying big bucks.

SYBEX. Help Yourself.

2021 Challenger Drive
Alameda, CA 94501
1-800-227-2346

SYBEX

POCKET-SIZED PC EXPERTISE.

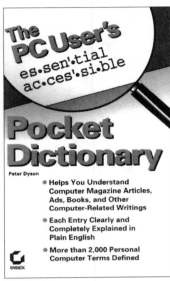

Maximize Your Investment in Client/Server

with Training from

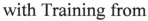

ANiMATEd LEARNiNG

Multimedia Courseware For The Client/Server Revolution

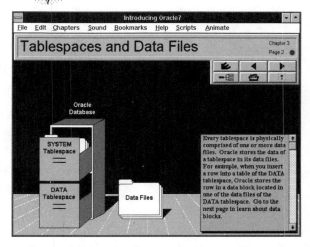

- Each course includes several modules that address different client/server issues, and each module includes several chapters with pages and pages of training information.
- Animated graphics represent complex client/server concepts with ease.
- Sound emphasizes screen actions to make learning fun and long-term retention outstanding.
- Supporting text helps to explain difficult client/server issues.
- A table of contents and index make it easy to find just the right information.
- Bookmarks permit users to conduct training over several sessions.
- Quizzes test user knowledge.
- A centralized logging system allows training administrators to track the progress of many users.

Animated Learning's revolutionary line of multimedia courseware quickly teaches any user the complex concepts of today's most popular client/server database systems (Oracle7, Sybase, Informix, and others) using animated graphics, sound, and text. Consequently, learning is fun and retention is outstanding. We're so sure you'll like our courseware, we're prepared to make you an offer you can't pass up.

FREE Introductory Module with This Page – Save $99!

Call us right now to get a free, no-obligation look at what you are missing. Simply mention that you own *Mastering Oracle7 & Client/Server Computing*, and we'll send you a free copy of the introductory module for our Oracle7 courseware, *Introducing Oracle7*. That's a $99 value, yours absolutely free!

Call us today!
1-800-235-3030

Mastering Oracle7 & Client/Server Computing

GET A FREE CATALOG JUST FOR EXPRESSING YOUR OPINION.

Help us improve our books and get a *FREE* full-color catalog in the bargain. Please complete this form, pull out this page and send it in today. The address is on the reverse side.

Name _____   Company _____

Address _____   City _____ State ____ Zip _____

Phone ( ) _____

1. How would you rate the overall quality of this book?

❏ Excellent
❏ Very Good
❏ Good
❏ Fair
❏ Below Average
❏ Poor

2. What were the things you liked most about the book? (Check all that apply)

❏ Pace
❏ Format
❏ Writing Style
❏ Examples
❏ Table of Contents
❏ Index
❏ Price
❏ Illustrations
❏ Type Style
❏ Cover
❏ Depth of Coverage
❏ Fast Track Notes

3. What were the things you liked *least* about the book? (Check all that apply)

❏ Pace
❏ Format
❏ Writing Style
❏ Examples
❏ Table of Contents
❏ Index
❏ Price
❏ Illustrations
❏ Type Style
❏ Cover
❏ Depth of Coverage
❏ Fast Track Notes

4. Where did you buy this book?

❏ Bookstore chain
❏ Small independent bookstore
❏ Computer store
❏ Wholesale club
❏ College bookstore
❏ Technical bookstore
❏ Other _____

5. How did you decide to buy this particular book?

❏ Recommended by friend
❏ Recommended by store personnel
❏ Author's reputation
❏ SYBEX'S reputation
❏ Read book review in _____
❏ Other _____

6. How did you pay for this book?

❏ Used own funds
❏ Reimbursed by company
❏ Received book as a gift

7. What is your level of experience with the subject covered in this book?

❏ Beginner
❏ Intermediate
❏ Advanced

8. How long have you been using a computer?

years _____
months _____

9. Where do you most often use your computer?

❏ Home
❏ Work

❏ Both
❏ Other _____

10. What kind of computer equipment do you have? (Check all that apply)

❏ PC Compatible Desktop Computer
❏ PC Compatible Laptop Computer
❏ Apple/Mac Computer
❏ Apple/Mac Laptop Computer
❏ CD ROM
❏ Fax Modem
❏ Data Modem
❏ Scanner
❏ Sound Card
❏ Other _____

11. What other kinds of software packages do you ordinarily use?

❏ Accounting
❏ Databases
❏ Networks
❏ Apple/Mac
❏ Desktop Publishing
❏ Spreadsheets
❏ CAD
❏ Games
❏ Word Processing
❏ Communications
❏ Money Management
❏ Other _____

12. What operating systems do you ordinarily use?

❏ DOS
❏ OS/2
❏ Windows
❏ Apple/Mac
❏ Windows NT
❏ Other _____

13. On what computer-related subject(s) would you like to see more books?

_____

_____

_____

_____

14. Do you have any other comments about this book? (Please feel free to use a separate piece of paper if you need more room)

_____

_____

_____

_____

- - - - - - - - - - - PLEASE FOLD, SEAL, AND MAIL TO SYBEX - - - - - - - - - - - -

SYBEX INC.
Department M
2021 Challenger Drive
Alameda, CA
94501

Oracle7 SQL Commands (continued from inside front cover)

SQL Command	Description
CREATE SNAPSHOT†‡	Creates a snapshot of a remote table
CREATE SNAPSHOT LOG†‡	Creates a refresh log for a snapshot
CREATE SYNONYM	Creates a synonym for a database object
CREATE TABLE	Creates a new database table
CREATE TABLESPACE	Creates a new tablespace
CREATE TRIGGER†	Creates a database trigger for a table
CREATE USER	Creates a new database username and password
CREATE VIEW	Creates a view of a table or other views
DELETE	Deletes one or more rows from a database table
DROP CLUSTER	Drops an indexed or a hash cluster
DROP DATABASE LINK‡	Drops a named path to a remote database
DROP FUNCTION†	Drops a stored function
DROP INDEX	Drops an index on a table
DROP PACKAGE†	Drops a stored package specification and body
DROP PACKAGE BODY†	Drops a stored package body
DROP PROCEDURE†	Drops a stored procedure
DROP PROFILE	Drops a named profile of resource limits
DROP ROLE	Drops a role of related privileges
DROP ROLLBACK SEGMENT	Drops a rollback segment
DROP SEQUENCE	Drops a named sequence of numbers
DROP SNAPSHOT†‡	Drops a snapshot of a remote table
DROP SNAPSHOT LOG†‡	Drops a log for a snapshot

†Available only with the Oracle7 Procedural option

‡Available only with the Oracle7 Distributed Database option